The Jewish Anarchist Movement in America
A Historical Review and Personal Reminiscences

By Joseph Cohen

Praise for *The Jewish Anarchist Movement in America*:

"A landmark publication in the history of Jewish anarchism in the US. The big, lively volume—so long awaited—brings together the original history by Joseph Cohen, the translation skills of the anarchist stalwart Esther Dolgoff, and the apt annotation of Kenyon Zimmer. Cohen writes as historian and participant. He defends anarchism while navigating its internal divisions and bringing its characters, many lost in existing accounts, to life."

> —**David Roediger**, professor of American Studies and History at the University of Kansas, author of *The Wages of Whiteness* and coeditor of *Haymarket Scrapbook*

"This monumental yet humble book offers the best of history-from-below. Better yet, it does so through a series of charming, page-turning reminiscences by a participant who lived and helped make this history, allowing us, in Cohen's words, to 'look back to the future' as inspiration for our pursuit of the 'grand ideal [of] complete liberation' in the present. Thanks to Kenyon Zimmer's meticulous edits and annotations, Cohen's stories, at once so engagingly anarchist and so Jewish, come to life, along with the names, lives, and actions of hundreds of otherwise-forgotten Jewish rebels. A true labor of love, *The Jewish Anarchist Movement in America* fills an enormous missing chapter of anarchist history and is a kaddish to honor the beautiful legacy of (our) Jewish anarchist ancestors."

> —**Cindy Barukh Milstein**, editor of *There Is Nothing So Whole as a Broken Heart*

"This long-overdue translation of Cohen's landmark memoir opens a unique window to the vibrant world of agitators, educators, and organizers who animated the American anarchist movement in the early twentieth century. Fluently transmitted and thoroughly annotated, it deserves attention from contemporary activists, who are increasingly turning to their movements' rich heritage for insight and inspiration."

> —**Uri Gordon**, cofounder of the Anarchist Studies Network and coauthor of *Anarchists Against the Wall: Direct Action and Solidarity with the Palestinian Popular Struggle*

The Jewish Anarchist Movement in America
A Historical Review and Personal Reminiscences

By Joseph Cohen

Translated by Esther Dolgoff

Edited and annotated by Kenyon Zimmer

with a Biographical Sketch of Esther Dolgoff, by Anatole Dolgoff

The Jewish Anarchist Movement in America:
A Historical Review and Personal Reminiscences
© 2024 Kenyon Zimmer
This edition © 2024 AK Press (Chico / Edinburgh)

ISBN 978-1-84935-548-3
E-ISBN 978-1-84935-549-0
Library of Congress Control Number: 2023948350

AK Press   AK Press
370 Ryan Avenue #100   33 Tower Street
Chico, CA 95973   Edinburgh, EH6, 7BN
USA   Scotland
www.akpress.org   www.akuk.com
akpress@akpress.org   akuk@akpress.org

The addresses above would be delighted to provide you with the latest AK Press catalog, featuring several thousand books, pamphlets, audio and video products, and stylish apparel published and distributed by AK Press. Alternatively, visit our websites for the complete catalog, latest news and updates, events, and secure ordering.

The publisher would like to acknowledge the Sam & Esther Dolgoff Institute for their support of this project. Visit them at: https://www.dolgoffinstitute.com

Originally published in Yiddish in 1945 as *Di yidish-anarkhistishe bavegung in Amerike: Historisher iberblik un perzenlekhe iberlebungen* by the Radical Library, Branch 273 of the Workmen's Circle, Philadelphia

Cover design by John Yates | www.stealworks.com
Cover photograph of Chicago anarchist group, courtesy of Elijah Baron

Printed in the United States of America on acid-free paper

Dedicated to the memory of Sophie Cohen

Contents

Part One: Historical Overview

Part Two: In Philadelphia, 1903–1913

Part Four: The Great Depression and the Second World War

Editor's Preface

Kenyon Zimmer

This translation of Joseph Cohen's history of the Jewish anarchist movement, first published in Yiddish in 1945, is literally generations in the making. The book's long-delayed publication in English fills an enormous gap in the available material on what was, at its height in the first two decades of the twentieth century, the largest segment of North America's anarchist movement.

In the late 1970s Esther Dolgoff, a veteran anarchist fluent in both Yiddish and English, undertook the monumental task of translating the text. Esther and her husband Sam had been leading personalities in the anarchist Vanguard Group (1932–1939), the Why? Group (1942–1947), the Libertarian Book Club (1945–c. 2014), and the Libertarian League (1954–1965), as well as the Industrial Workers of the World, and they were instrumental in bridging the largely immigrant anarchist movement of the early twentieth century with the radicalism of the New Left and the revival of anarchism that followed. Esther and Sam had also known Joseph Cohen in the 1930s and 1940s—for a few years the Dolgoffs and Cohen had even lived in the same anarchist intentional community, or "colony," in Stelton, New Jersey—and they respected his judgement and integrity. Esther completed her translation, which consisted of more than eight hundred handwritten pages, around 1980, but all attempts to find a publisher were unsuccessful.

When I first began to research and write about anarchist history in the late 1990s, I read a duplicate of Dolgoff's handwritten translation—a faded photocopy of a photocopy—held by the Kate Sharpley Library in California. Shortly thereafter, when discussing possible future projects with

1

Charles Weigl and other members of the AK Press collective, an annotated version of Dolgoff's translation topped my list. And for two decades that is where things stood, with this project perpetually remaining something that I intended to get around to someday.

Then, in December 2017, Eric A. Gordon contacted me after reading an article I had written about American anarchists in the Spanish Civil War that also mentioned my book on Jewish and Italian anarchists. He wished to talk with me, he wrote, "about a project involving a translation from Yiddish to English of a book about the anarchist movement." Immediately I knew he could only mean the Dolgoff manuscript. Gordon, it turns out, was an erstwhile anarchist who had written a PhD dissertation about Brazilian anarchism and had been a friend of Esther and Sam Dolgoff back in the 1970s and 1980s. Shortly before her death in 1989, Gordon told me, Esther had entrusted the manuscript to him for possible publication. He and historian Paul Avrich saw to it that the text was transcribed into a word-processing file, but there the project stalled, again for lack of a publisher. Now Gordon, himself advanced in age and fearing that he would not be able to see the project through to completion, passed the torch to me.

My own progress began slowly, in spare moments between other commitments, and was interrupted by the outbreak of the COVID-19 pandemic. But two major breakthroughs made this project feasible: the development of OCR (Optical Character Recognition) technology for Yiddish texts, and the digitization of the *Fraye arbeter shtime* (Free Voice of Labor) and other Yiddish-language anarchist newspapers.[1] Suddenly I had the ability to instantaneously search both Cohen's original Yiddish manuscript and nearly a century of the Yiddish radical press, and to use machine translation software to aid my research.[2]

---

1. *Fraye arbeter shtime* is the modern YIVO transliteration of the newspaper's Yiddish title. However, until 1941 the paper used the more Germanic spelling *arbayter* rather than *arbeter*, and throughout its publication it included the heavily Germanized transliteration "Freie Arbeiter Stimme" on its masthead.

2. The digital holdings of the National Library of Israel's Newspaper Collection (a source that Cohen, a lifelong anti-Zionist, would surely find ironic) includes the full run of the *Fraye arbeter shtime* and other Yiddish anarchist newspapers: https://www.nli.org .il/en/newspapers/titles. Cohen's original Yiddish text is available digitally through the Stephen Spielberg Digital Yiddish Library at the Yiddish Book Center at https://ocr .yiddishbookcenter.org.

As editor my goal has been to make Cohen's text as readable and as useful to twenty-first-century readers as possible, be they specialists in Jewish radical history or newcomers, Yiddish speakers or Anglophones. At the same time, I have sought to retain as much of the author's original perspective and voice as possible. This first meant comparing Esther Dolgoff's translation against the original Yiddish.[3] In general, Dolgoff masterfully conveyed Cohen's words, though her translation is rather loose at times and occasionally awkward. This edition restores as much of Cohen's original sentence structure and terminology as possible, without, I hope, doing any disservice to Dolgoff's colossal work. This includes reinserting Cohen's occasional religious allusions and quotations, and adding his original Yiddish terms in parentheses where I felt the specific use of Yiddishisms or Hebraisms may be of interest to some readers.

I have also edited and slightly abridged Cohen's text. Factual errors have been silently corrected; first or last names of individuals have been added wherever these could be identified; and a few chapter titles have been altered to indicate their content more clearly. All quotations were checked against the original sources and corrected if necessary. Because the original book sometimes repeated information or circled back to topics, I have consolidated or moved some sections and slightly changed the chapter order. In addition, I have removed some passages that do not directly touch on the Jewish anarchist movement—in large part because the further Cohen strayed from this topic, the less reliable or relevant his chronicle became. These include his cursory survey of anarchistic ideas from prehistory to the nineteenth century; overviews of the American and German-American labor movements up to the 1880s (drawn almost completely from John R. Commons's *History of Labor in the United States*);[4] a chapter summarizing the 1907 International Anarchist Congress in Amsterdam that relies entirely on Emma Goldman's report in her magazine *Mother Earth*;[5] others on the

---

3. I also consulted a separate translation of chapter 14 of this volume published as Joseph Cohen, "The Jewish Anarchist Movement in America," trans. Emil Kerenji, *In geveb*, September 29, 2015, https://ingeveb.org/texts-and-translations/the-jewish-anarchist-movement-in-america-my-first-years-in-philadelphia.

4. John R. Commons et al., *History of Labor in the United States*, 4 vols. (New York: Macmillan, 1918–19).

5. Emma Goldman, "The International Anarchist Congress," *Mother Earth*, October 1907, 307–19. By Cohen's own assessment, "The congress had no constructive effect on the

Lawrence strike of 1913 and the Sacco-Vanzetti trial that do not connect these events to the activities of the Jewish anarchist movement; and so on. In every case these abridgements were undertaken to enhance the book's readability and usefulness, and no information was removed that cannot be easily found—usually in better and more reliable form—elsewhere.

The bulk of my labor on this book, however, involved adding citations and annotations to the text. Cohen inconsistently cited his own sources, and his original citations are indicated as such with bracketed notes. Wherever possible, I have added citations to the other sources he mentions or quotes from.[6] This book was also originally written for an audience of aging Yiddish-speaking anarchists who had lived through most of the events it describes and were familiar, directly or by reputation, with the hundreds of individuals named throughout. Today even most experts in anarchist history would be at a loss to identify most of the people Cohen references. The majority were not famous or infamous and never appeared in English-language newspapers or the accounts of later historians. In many cases the surviving information about them comes from just two sources: census records, and obituaries printed in the *Fraye arbeter shtime*.[7] Sometimes even these were lacking. Nevertheless, I have been able to identify and provide biographical annotations for more than seven hundred individuals Cohen names.[8] These biographical annotations offer vital

---

movement." A much more detailed account of the congress in English can now be found in *The International Anarchist Congress: Amsterdam (1907)*, ed. Maurizio Antonioli, trans. Nestor McNab (Edmonton: Black Cat Press, 2009).

6. To save space, full publication information is only provided for works directly cited in the text or notes.

7. Census and related records were accessed through Ancestry.com. Other sources consulted are too numerous to list, but some that proved especially valuable were John Patten, *Yiddish Anarchist Bibliography* (London: Kate Sharpley Library; Cambridge, MA: Anarchist Archives Project, 1998); Paul Avrich, *Anarchist Voices: An Oral History of Anarchism in America* (Princeton: Princeton University Press, 1995); Paul Avrich, *The Modern School Movement: Anarchism and Education in the United States* (Princeton: Princeton University Press, 1980); Victor Sacharoff, ed., *Recollections from the Modern School Ferrer Colony* (Altamont, NY: Friends of the Modern School, 2007); Chaim Weinberg, *Forty Years in the Struggle: The Memoirs of a Jewish Anarchist*, ed. Robert P. Helms, trans. Naomi Cohen (Duluth: Litwin Books, 2008); and Samuel Niger and Jacob Shatzky, eds., *Leksikon fun der nayer yidisher literatur*, 8 vols. (New York: Alveltlekhn Yidishn Kultur-Kongres, 1956). This last source has been translated by Joshua Fogel at http://yleksikon.blogspot.com.

8. Due to the limitations of most census records, my annotations describe all those born

context to Cohen's chronicle and I hope may provide starting points for future researchers.

I have also updated the transliteration of Yiddish words to conform to the modified YIVO system outlined by Isaac L. Bleaman.[9] In the titles of Yiddish publications like the *Fraye arbeter shtime*, therefore, only the first word is capitalized. Jewish personal names, where applicable, are spelled according to how they were transliterated into English at the time in either published works or government records, but the proper YIVO transliteration is also provided parenthetically in the notes.[10] All Yiddish words and titles are transliterated as they are spelled in the original text and documents, which in some cases differ from standardized modern spellings.

Several individuals have aided me in the preparation of this work. Julie Herrada at the University of Michigan's Joseph A. Labadie Collection tracked down obscure sources referenced by Cohen, and the Interlibrary Loan Department at the University of Texas at Arlington fulfilled dozens of odd requests associated with my research for this volume. Tom Goyens, Tony Michels, Jenny Schwartzberg, and Inna Shtakser answered obscure queries, and Maria Chomard helpfully corrected some of my annotations regarding Jewish anarchists in Canada. Barry Pateman read through the entire manuscript and notes, and Bob Helms provided voluminous and invaluable information on members of Philadelphia's anarchist movement. Anna Elena Torres aided me with Yiddish transliterations. Anatole Dolgoff and the members of the Sam and Esther Dolgoff Institute (https://www.dolgoffinstitute.com) have given both moral and material support to this project. Finally, my thanks to Charles Weigl and Zach Blue at AK Press for shepherding this project to completion, and Chris Dodge for copyediting it.

---

within the Russian Empire as "Russian-born," rather than distinguishing between those who originated in territories that are today part of Belarus, Latvia, Lithuania, Poland, Ukraine, et cetera. For less-well-known individuals, I also include citations for published obituaries when possible.

9. Isaac L. Bleaman, "Guidelines for Yiddish in Bibliographies: A Supplement to YIVO Transliteration," *In geveb*, July 2, 2019. This includes using YIVO's preferred spelling of *frayheyt* (freedom or liberty) rather than the more common *frayhayt*. I deviate slightly from Bleaman's guidelines by capitalizing place-names and other proper nouns in titles.

10. Following common practice, when a *yud* comes at the end of a Yiddish name I have transliterated it as a *y* rather than an *i* (for example, Yanosvky), except in instances where the Anglicized version of the name ends in an *i* (for example, Almi).

I approached my work on this book with a deep sense of respect for, and responsibility to, those who came before me—to Joseph Cohen, who first assumed the monumental task of recording these people and events; to the hundreds of individual activists and revolutionaries he memorializes in the book's pages; and to those, especially Esther Dolgoff, who played a role in preparing this text for eventual publication in English. May their memories change the world.

List of Acronyms

For the sake of readability, acronyms in the text have been kept to a minimum. The following abbreviations, however, appear in the notes and annotations.

ACWA   Amalgamated Clothing Workers of America

AFL   American Federation of Labor

CIO   Congress of Industrial Organizations

FAS   *Fraye arbeter shtime*

ILGWU   International Ladies' Garment Workers' Union

IWW   Industrial Workers of the World

SLP   Socialist Labor Party

Joseph Jacob Cohen (1878–1953) and the Jewish Anarchist Movement

Kenyon Zimmer

"Cohen was a builder."

—*Boris Yelensky (in Paul Avrich's* Anarchist Voices*)*

Although today he is all but forgotten, Joseph Jacob Cohen—"J. J." to his friends—was a central figure of twentieth-century American anarchism. Born Joseph Jacob Kantorowitz (Yoysef Yakov Kantorovitsh in Yiddish) in what is today Belarus, he was the third of ten children. His father, Leib Kantorowitz, was a forester, horse-dealer, and "learned, religiously orthodox Jew," and his mother Sarah was likewise deeply religious.[1] In 1881, before he had turned three, Cohen survived a pogrom in his home village—part of a wave of anti-Jewish riots that erupted in the wake of the assassination of Tsar Alexander II. "My very first recollections," he later wrote, "are those which impressed upon me that I was born a Jew, a scion of a persecuted race suffering oppression, misery and injustice all through the ages."[2]

Cohen's parents soon sent him to *cheder* (Jewish religious primary school) "to study the Torah and in time become a rabbi—the innermost wish of every Jewish mother for at least one of her sons."[3] This kind of religious education was shared by nearly every eastern European Jewish boy of

---

1. Joseph J. Cohen, *The House Stood Forlorn: Legacy of Remembrance of a Boyhood in the Russia of the Late Nineteenth Century* (Paris: [Editions Polyglottes], 1954), 137.

2. Ibid., 17.

3. Ibid., 37.

Cohen's generation, including the tens of thousands who, like him, eventually rejected religion in favor of radicalism. The vocabulary and metaphors of Judaism, however, remained a common touchstone of even secular Jewish radical writing, as can been glimpsed throughout this volume.

Young Joseph immediately took to his studies. "I was henceforth to be forever enrolled in the army of the book-worms," he later mused, "to spend my life on the written and printed word."[4] Cohen's daughter Emma similarly observed, "Father never cared about possessions, about things. Only books—and even that was not to possess them but to use them, to learn from them."[5] He was hailed as a prodigy and at age thirteen entered the Mir Yeshiva to train as a rabbi, though he had to lie to school administrators about his age. Soon, however, the cerebral young man harbored grave doubts. "It did not stand to reason that out of all the human beings on earth, God was interested in the behavior and well-being of a handful of Jewish males," he concluded. "It did not make sense, the contention that God Almighty, the Creator of all, took a personal interest in the prayers of single individuals and derived satisfaction from their exaggerated homilies."[6] The stress of such heretical thoughts took a physical toll, and Cohen was hospitalized following a nervous collapse. Never again would he place blind faith in anything or anyone. Six decades later, in his last major Yiddish publication, Cohen still condemned any "belief" (*gloybn*)—be it in God, an ideology, or science—that was not based on "careful observation, experimentation and factual evidence."[7]

Adrift and periodically homeless, Cohen scraped by as a private tutor in Minsk. Newly exposed to revolutionary ideas through Hebrew and Russian writings, he also joined an underground socialist circle and commenced what he would spend much of the rest of his life doing: organizing. Cohen helped workers in different trades form mutual aid organizations and strike funds. These activities, however, were cut short when a police interrogation prompted Cohen's parents to demand that he return home. There he

---

4. Ibid.

5. Paul Avrich, *Anarchist Voices: An Oral History of Anarchism in America* (Oakland: AK Press, 2005), 225.

6. Cohen, *The House Stood Forlorn*, 87–88.

7. Joseph Cohen, *Der urshprung fun gloybn* (The Origin of Belief) (Tel Aviv: E. Hirshauge, 1950), 30. All translations in this essay are by the editor.

Figure 1: Sophie Kaplan (Kolpenitzky), c. 1903
Courtesy of Jenny Schwartzberg

worked as a lumberman for a few years but also found ray of light: Sophie Kolpenitzky (who later Americanized the name to Kaplan), "a reserved young woman, with thick, russet-brown braids wound round her head, and a walk imbued with such animal grace that it was a lovely thing to behold."[8] The two met in 1898 when Cohen's older sister married Sophie's half-brother. But their budding romance was interrupted when Cohen was inducted into four years of mandatory military service.

Stationed at the Grodno garrison, Cohen found comfort in a familiar source. "There was a good library in Grodno," he recalled. "In my off-hours

8. Cohen, *The House Stood Forlorn*, 173.

I would haunt the place, utilizing its facilities to the utmost, often smuggling books into the garrison."[9] He also formed a secret radical reading circle for other soldiers in the garrison, which formulated plans to seize the artillery in the event of an insurrection.

In 1903, after his service expired, Joseph married Sophie, and the couple emigrated to the United States, where his older brother already lived. The couple settled in Philadelphia, and Joseph took up cigarmaking. Both he and Sophie were quickly swept up in the Yiddish-speaking anarchist movement, where Joseph distinguished himself through his organizational pragmatism. Jewish labor unions, worker-run cooperatives, Philadelphia's Radical Library, New York's Francisco Ferrer Center, the Stelton Colony and the Sunrise Colony, and the Yiddish anarchist press—all were shaped by his tireless activity, as recounted in the pages that follow.

Cohen is less forthcoming in the text about his personal life and family. He does not discuss his own period of doubt in anarchism's prospects following the Russian Revolution.[10] He says little of his experiences as a cigarmaker and member of the Cigar Makers' International Union, and he neglects to mention that he had to abandon the trade in the 1920s due to worsening asthma.[11] He then worked full-time as editor of the main Yiddish anarchist newspaper, the *Fraye arbeter shtime* (Free Voice of Labor), for twelve years and he notes of this time, "Only thanks to the hard work of my wife Sophie was it possible for us to endure," but he omits the fact that she suffered from severe rheumatism since at least as early as 1911.[12] Nevertheless, according to longtime Philadelphia anarchist Benjamin Axler, Sophie Cohen played a large role behind the scenes and "was the practical and de facto leader in [the anarchist movement's] organized institutions."[13] The couple also had two children: Emma (b. 1904), named after Emma Goldman, and Emanuel Voltaire (b. 1912), whose middle name was in honor of anarchist Voltairine de Cleyre, a close friend who had taught English to both Joseph and Sophie.

9. Ibid., 174.

10. See Paul Avrich, *The Modern School Movement: Anarchism and Education in the United States* (Princeton: Princeton University Press, 1980), 347–48.

11. Avrich, *Anarchist Voices*, 212.

12. Voltairine de Cleyre to Joseph J. Cohen, April 12, 1911, File 4, Box 1, Papers of Voltairine de Cleyre and Joseph Cohen, Record Group 1485, YIVO Institute of Jewish Studies, New York (hereafter De Cleyre and Cohen Papers).

13. *FAS*, December 8, 1944.

Figure 2: Joseph Cohen, 1946
Photo by Senya Flechine; courtesy of Tamiment Library, New York
University

In one curious episode when Emanuel was nineteen years old, Joseph filed
a petition on his son's behalf to legally change his last name to Conason,
because Emanuel hoped to attend Harvard University, which at the time
limited the number of Jewish applicants it admitted. The petition garnered
national attention when the Jewish judge, Aaron J. Levy, demanded it be
revised to remove a sentence in which Joseph had bitterly noted that the
surname Cohen was regarded as "un-American."[14]

14. See, for example, *Evening News* (Wilkes-Barre, PA), February 26, 1932.

Joseph Cohen cut an imposing figure. Five ten and wiry, he "looked like an old bird of prey: hawk nose, hunched shoulders, glasses, tall, owlish look. You could almost feel the wings."[15] Despite the many prominent roles that he played in the anarchist movement, he was also a divisive personality. Nearly all his comrades agreed that he was a strong, capable, intelligent, pragmatic, and tenacious individual, with a talent for practical organizing. But even his closest friends also noted his aloofness and hard-headedness.[16]

Voltairine de Cleyre once told Cohen that he was "undaunted, indefatigable, and—yes, inscrutable."[17] Dovid Zaltsberg, one of Cohen's collaborators in Paris in the early 1950s, remarked: "With his extraordinary intellectual ability he was always able to approach the core of a problem. With a rare gift for clarity, he was able to answer the most complex questions in a simple way. [But] outwardly he made an impression of cold marble with an Olympic indifference."[18] According to Philip Trupin, who lived alongside the Cohens at the Sunrise Colony in Michigan in the 1930s, "He was a very able administrator but not tolerant enough of other people's view and mistakes. . . . He was too aloof, abrupt, cold. 'If you put a glass of tea by him, it would freeze,' said his *Fraye arbeter shtime* associates."[19] Cohen was not unaware of this aspect of his personality. As he writes in this book, "Born and raised in Lithuania, in a cold, skeptical atmosphere, I did not have the kind of fiery enthusiasm that flares up and ignites others. I am by nature cautious, skeptical, and cool-blooded—I always see both sides of the coin, the good as well as the bad, and I seldom get hung up on one thing." Elsewhere he casually noted, "The thought occurs to me that all during my adult life I have been known as one who has never shed a tear, no matter what the occasion."[20] Cohen, in short, was not a people person.

---

15. Johanna Boetz in Avrich, *Anarchist Voices*, 386.

16. Voltairine de Cleyre to Joseph J. Cohen, November 23, 1910, File 3, Box 1, De Cleyre and Cohen Papers; Harry Kelly to Max Nettlau, March 29, 1921, Folder 700, Max Nettlau Papers, International Institute of Social History, Amsterdam (hereafter IISH); *FAS*, October 9, 1953; Avrich, *The Modern School Movement*, 181; Avrich, *Anarchist Voices*, 75, 233, 240, 305, 307, 336, 352, 376, 389.

17. Voltairine de Cleyre to Joseph J. Cohen, October 30, 1911, File 4, Box 1, De Cleyre and Cohen Papers.

18. *Der frayer gedank*, November 1953.

19. Avrich, *Anarchist Voices*, 297.

20. Cohen, *The House Stood Forlorn*, 79.

Nor was he inclined to compromise. Once he had studied a problem and arrived at a conclusion, Cohen had little patience for differing views. Another member of the Sunrise Colony recalled, "He was a capable man, but he was dogmatic and didn't like to be criticized. If he thought something was good, it was good!"[21] Boris Yelensky described Cohen as "a great man, a man who did very big work . . . to bring out a generation of workers for our movement" but also "a man who like[d] to swim against mobs."[22] Philadelphia anarchist Alexander Brown framed this tendency more diplomatically, observing that "Joseph Cohen had the courage to say things that his colleagues at times did not agree with."[23] This included questioning certain anarchist taboos, such as abstention from voting in elections. Others in the anarchist movement interpreted Cohen's bull-headed certainty as authoritarianism and his criticisms of others as jealousy. According to critics, he was "a Jesuit" with a "dictatorial attitude," an "autocrat" who was "cold and inflexible," or, worse, he was "devious and a self-seeker."[24] Yet Cohen himself insisted, "I am not of a quarrelsome disposition," and he appears to have been genuinely befuddled and hurt by the negative reactions he often provoked.[25]

In 1939 Cohen went into semi-retirement as a chicken farmer at the Stelton Colony in New Jersey. But in 1943 Sophie's declining health forced the couple to relocate to Washington, DC, and her death the following year "wrought the great crisis in, and turning point of, his life."[26] Sophie's illness and passing coincided with an invitation from the Radical Library: to write an account of that organization's forty-year history. Cohen was a logical choice—not only had he cofounded the Radical Library in 1905 and overseen its first decade of activity, in 1925 he had also completed a similar assignment, writing a short history and analysis of the Stelton Modern

---

21. Aaron Rockoff in Avrich, *Anarchist Voices*, 303.

22. Boris Yelensky to Dora Cohen, September 29, 1953, Folder 34, Boris Yelensky Papers, IISH.

23. *FAS*, October 23, 1953.

24. "A Jesuit" and "dictatorial attitude": Michael Cohn to Rudolf Rocker, December 10, 1930, Folder 78, Rudolf Rocker Papers, IISH; "autocrat" and "cold and inflexible" : Hilda Adel in Avrich, *Anarchist Voices*, 61; "devious and a self-seeker": Madga Schowenwetter in Avrich, *Anarchist Voices*, 230.

25. Joseph J. Cohen to Alexander Berkman and Emma Goldman, October 8, 1930, Folder 10, Alexander Berkman Papers, IISH.

26. Dora Fox Cohen, preface to Cohen, *The House Stood Forlorn*, 13.

School for its tenth anniversary.[27] He threw himself into the new task with abandon and quickly expanded the project's scope to encompass the entire history of America's Yiddish-speaking anarchist movement. Perhaps he found some measure of escape or comfort by burying himself in this work. When Cohen completed the manuscript in November 1945, he dedicated it to Sophie's memory.

❀ ❀ ❀

"Cohen's book tells so many things that you wouldn't get anywhere [else]."
—*Esther Dolgoff*
(*Oral History of the American Left Collection, New York University*)

Joseph Cohen's *Di yidish-anarkhistishe bavegung in Amerike: Historisher iberblik un perzenlekhe iberlebungen* was a hefty 557-page tome that sold for $2.50. Almost immediately, however, it became, like its author, a source of conflict.

Surprisingly, the *Fraye arbeter shtime* savaged the book. It ran a front-page critique by historian Jacob Shatzky—who was not an anarchist and in his review scoffed at the very notion of either a "Jewish anarchist" or an "anarchist movement," and the paper's manager, Sol Linder, penned no fewer than seven articles criticizing Cohen's work for all manner of faults: imprecise dates, missing citations, minor factual errors, lack of objectivity, and what Linder considered its defamation of prominent anarchists like Saul Yanovsky and Michael A. Cohn.[28] But Linder was no neutral reviewer; he and Cohen had bad blood dating back to Cohen's criticisms of Linder's friend and mentor Rudolf Rocker during Cohen's editorship of the *Fraye arbeter shtime*.

---

27. Joseph J. Cohen and Alexis C. Ferm, *The Modern School of Stelton: A Sketch* (Stelton, NJ: Modern School Association of North America, 1925).

28. *FAS*, July 26, September 27–October 18, November 1, November 8, and December 6, 1946.

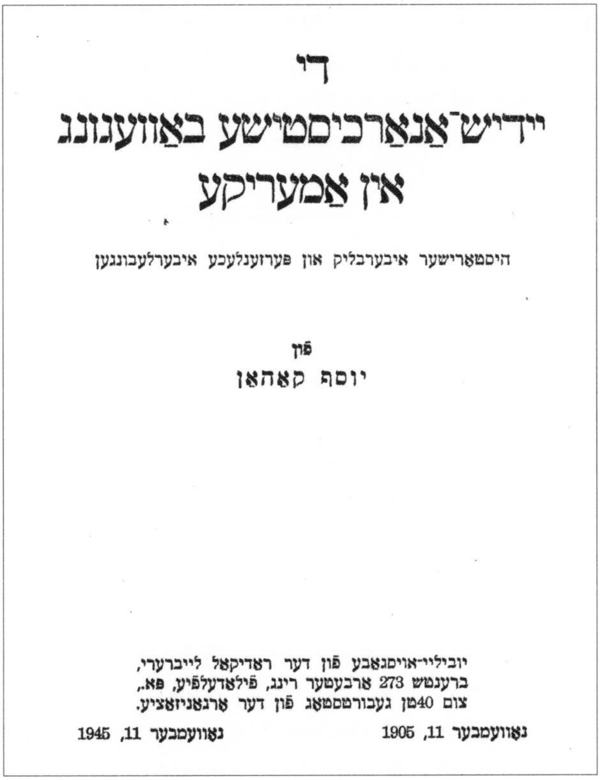

די

יידיש אנארכיסטישע באװעגונג
אין אמעריקע

היסטאָרישער איבערבליק און פֿערזענלעכע איבערלעבונגען

פֿון
יוסף קאהאן

יוביליי-אויסגאַבע פֿון דער ראַדיקאַל לייברערי,
ברענטש 273 אַרבעטער רינג, פֿילאַדעלפֿיע, פּאַ.,
צום 40סטן געבוירטסטאָג פֿון דער אָרגאַניזאַציע.
נאָװעמבער 11, 1945   נאָװעמבער 11, 1905

Figure 3: Original edition of *The Jewish Anarchist Movement in America*
Title page of the 1945 Yiddish edition

Many other veteran anarchists, however, rose to the defense of Cohen and his book.[29] Benjamin Axler condemned what he described as the "lynching party" against Cohen in the *Fraye arbeter shtime*, and the Radical Library organized an entire symposium to discuss "the pros and cons of the book."[30] Isidore Wisotsky, who would himself go on to edit the *Fraye arbeter shtime* in the 1960s, maintained, "This book is a useful book, an important book, full of information about our movement, which until now has never been collected in book form."[31]

---

29. See, for example, *FAS*, November 15 and December 20, 1946.
30. *FAS*, November 8, 1946, and June 20, 1947.
31. *FAS*, December 13, 1946.

Outside of anarchist circles, *Der tog* (The Day), a major Yiddish daily newspaper, ran a generally positive review by literary critic Moyshe Shtarkman, while Hillel Rogoff in the socialist *Forverts* (Forward) belittled the book as a work of gossip and rumor and used the opportunity to heap scorn upon anarchism in general.[32] In the only review to appear in an academic journal, historian B. Weinryb likewise dismissed it as "an unfortunate book" that was composed of "a hodgepodge of partly unrelated and mostly unimportant facts" and engaged in "name calling."[33]

It is not difficult to imagine Cohen's disappointment at this reception. But today, far removed from the personal quarrels of the past and aspirations to "scientific" history, the book's critics appear petty, at best. Cohen made no claim to being a professional historian or to providing an objective account. The book's subtitle, as its defenders repeatedly noted, emphasized that the work was a combination of historical research and the author's own personal experiences and views. In other words, it is both a primary and a secondary source, and it holds up remarkably well as either.

Although several other Jewish anarchists and former anarchists published memoirs in English—most famously, Emma Goldman's *Living My Life*—few of these discuss the Yiddish-speaking movement in any depth.[34] Several additional memoirs appeared in Yiddish, but nearly all, aside from Cohen's, were written by members of the founding generation of Jewish anarchists and do not extend their coverage past the 1890s.[35] Cohen's eye-

---

32. *Der tog*, June 24, 1946; *Forverts*, July 7, 1946.

33. B. Weinryb, review of *The Jewish Anarchist Movement in the United States* [sic] by Joseph Cohan [sic], *Jewish Social Studies* 9, no. 2 (1947): 184–85.

34. Irving Abrams, *Haymarket Heritage: The Memoirs of Irving S. Abrams*, ed. Dave Roediger and Phyllis Boanes (Chicago: Charles H. Kerr, 1989); Alexander Berkman, *Prison Memoirs of an Anarchist* (New York: Mother Earth, 1912); Thomas B. Eyges, *Beyond the Horizon: The Story of a Radical Emigrant* (Boston: Group Free Society, 1944); Sam Dolgoff, *Fragments: A Memoir* (Cambridge, England: Refract Publications, 1986); Marie Ganz, *Rebels: Into Anarchy—and Out Again* (New York: Dodd, Mead, 1919); Emma Goldman, *Living My Life*, 2 vols. (New York: Alfred A. Knopf, 1931); Lucy Robins Lang, *Tomorrow Is Beautiful* (New York: Macmillan Company, 1948); Rose Pesotta, *Bread upon the Waters* (New York: Dodd, Mead, 1945); Rose Pesotta, *Days of Our Lives* (Boston: Excelsior Publishers, 1958).

35. I. A. Benequit, *Durkhgelebt un durkhgetrakht* (Lived Through and Thought Through), vol. 2 (New York: Farlag "Kultur Federatsie," 1934); A. Frumkin, *In friling fun idishn sotsializm: zikhroynes fun a zshurnalist* (In the Springtime of Jewish Socialism: Memoirs of a Journalist) (New York: A. Frumkin Yubiley Komitet, 1940); I. Kopeloff, *Amol in Amerike: zikhroynes fun dem yidishn lebn in Amerike in di yorn 1883–1904* (Once upon a Time in America: Memories of

witness accounts of people and events in the first decades of the twentieth century are therefore irreplaceable. This study is also, more than seventy years later, still the *only* book-length history of the Yiddish-speaking anarchist movement in the United States—in Yiddish, English, or any other language. This alone makes it indispensable to anyone researching American anarchism or the Jewish radical and labor movements between the Gilded Age and the Cold War.

❋ ❋ ❋

"[This book] is not a story about 'generals' and 'leaders,' but about activists, participants, organizers, collaborators, and those who have taken part in the anarchist movement; it's the story of us all, of everyone who has been involved in our movement over the last forty years or more—all receive some mention, appreciation, and recognition."
—*The Radical Library Group*
(from the preface to the original Yiddish edition)

One of the most significant and challenging aspects of this book is Cohen's desire to pay tribute to and acknowledge as many members and allies of the anarchist movement as possible—he references several hundred by name. Some passages are little more than lists of "active comrades" in various cities

---

Jewish Life in America in the Years 1883–1904) (Warsaw: Kh. Bzshoza, 1928); Sh. Yanovsky, *Ershte yorn fun yidishn frayheytlekhn sotsializm: oytobiografishe zikhroynes fun a pioner un boyer fun der yidisher anarkhistisher bavegung in England un Amerike* (First Years of Jewish Libertarian Socialism: Autobiographical Reminiscences of a Pioneer and Builder of the Jewish Anarchist Movement in England and America) (New York: Fraye Arbeter Shtime, 1948). An exception is Chaim Weinberg, *Fertsik yor in kamf far sotsyaler bafrayung: zikhroynes fun a frayheytlekhn agitator oyf der yidish-amerikanisher gas*, ed. Herman Frank (Philadelphia: C. L. Weinberg Book Publishing Committee, Radical Library Group, 1952), which was published in English as *Forty Years in the Struggle: The Memoirs of a Jewish Anarchist*, ed. Robert P. Helms, trans. Naomi Cohen (Duluth: Litwin Books, 2008) and discusses some of the same events as Cohen's book.

across the United States and Canada. Why this compulsion to name-check? As Anna Elena Torres and I have noted elsewhere, this kind of biographically focused approach was not unique to Cohen. "For historians . . . who identify and sympathize with their anarchist subjects, biography is a way to recover and ennoble these lives, to bear witness and to honor them—to eulogize or say kaddish for them, if you will."[36] Cohen set out to write a history of anarchism from the bottom up and to honor the fundamental role of rank-and-file activists and supporters. This translation's addition of biographical notes about these individuals is carried out in the same spirit.

Despite his prominent role in so many areas of the movement, Cohen himself did not aspire to leadership. As he explained in a letter to Alexander Berkman and Emma Goldman, "I am . . . not over-ambitious. I took on the editorship [of the *Fraye arbeter shtime*] as a duty, not as a pleasure, honor, or *position*."[37] But he was deeply distrustful of those who, in his estimation, did seek such distinction. His account of Jewish anarchism is therefore unsparing in its criticisms of many prominent figures of the movement. Saul Yanovsky, Emma Goldman, Rudolf Rocker—none are above reproach. Yet this is not, as some of Cohen's critics saw it, a symptom of jealousy, for there are others of equal stature about whom Cohen has not a negative word, including Johann Most, Alexander Berkman, and Voltairine de Cleyre. He is unrestrained in his critiques but not indiscriminate. In Cohen's own relentlessly analytical fashion, he simply expresses his conclusions regardless of their potential to offend. Moreover, he also highlights the positive qualities and contributions of people like Yanovsky, whom Cohen deeply respected but by whom he was also deeply disappointed. Although many of his comrades found Cohen's treatment of beloved figures scandalous, it makes his study a more balanced and self-reflective radical history than most written by participants. This book is not a hagiography but rather an earnest and unflinching evaluation of the movement to which the author dedicated fifty years of his life. It is, however, perhaps less measured in its criticisms of social democrats like *Forverts* editor Abe Cahan, who is portrayed extremely unflatteringly throughout.

---

36. Anna Elena Torres and Kenyon Zimmer, "Conclusion: The Past and Futures of Jewish Anarchist History," in *With Freedom in Our Ears: Histories of Jewish Anarchism*, ed. Anna Elena Torres and Kenyon Zimmer (Urbana: University of Illinois Press, 2023), 241.

37. Joseph J. Cohen to Alexander Berkman and Emma Goldman, October 8, 1930, Folder 10, Alexander Berkman Papers, IISH. Emphasis in original.

Cohen's writing is, of course, not without its flaws. It is a product of the time and circumstances in which it was written. The author was not a trained historian, and he researched and wrote the book in great haste, completing most of the work in under two years and with limited access to materials. He also shared many of the blind spots of the cultures in which he grew up and lived. His book tends to focus on male activists, often omitting women who were active in the movement, or mentioning them only as the wives of comrades. At one point it even lists "women's rights" (*froyen-rekht*) among "things which had no direct connection to the fundamental problems of social coexistence" and proved a distraction of the anarchist movement. To his credit, however, in several other places Cohen does specifically call attention to the role and contributions of women.

The book also displays no analysis of racism, colonialism, or imperialism, even in its critiques of the Zionist movement.[38] Nor does it mention Indigenous peoples or reflect on anarchists' use of the word "colony" to describe their intentional communities, even when, like the Mohegan Colony, these bore the name of the land's original occupants. Some twenty-first-century readers may be justifiably disappointed by such shortcomings, but they should not be surprised to find them in a book written in the 1940s.

❋ ❋ ❋

---

38. There is also the question of Cohen's racial terminology. The four times he mentions Black people, Cohen uses the Yiddish words *neger* or *niger* (twice each). In the late nineteenth and early twentieth centuries both were common and neutral Yiddish terms for people of African descent. However, by the 1940s *niger* was rarely still employed except as a Yiddish transliteration of the English-language racial slur, and today both words have fallen out of favor. I have opted to translate both as "Negro" rather than "Black" to signal their anachronistic and potentially offensive connotations, without necessarily attributing racist intent. On the history and usage of these terms, see Erika Davis, "No More Yiddish N-Word," *Forward*, July 25, 2012, https://forward.com/life/159773/no-more-jewish-n-word; Jonah S. Boyarin, Ri J. Turner, and Arun Viswanath, "'Black Lives Matter' and Talking about Blackness in Yiddish: Stakes, Considerations, and Open Questions," *In geveb*, October 2020, https://ingeveb.org/blog/black-lives-matter-in-yiddish; Eli Bromberg, "We Need to Talk about Shmuel Charney," *In geveb*, October 2019, https://ingeveb.org/articles/we-need -to-talk-about-shmuel-charney.

"Our comrades did not *write* history; they *made* history. . . . The
work of systematically recording events they left to other, often
hostile elements, who ignored our contribution, often maliciously
misrepresenting it, trying to give the impression that we simply
disrupted others' work, tilting at windmills and contributing nothing constructive ourselves."
—*Joseph Cohen*

Whatever its flaws, *The Jewish Anarchist Movement in America* is the most
comprehensive survey of the topic that exists. Nowhere else can you find
a detailed overview of the different Jewish anarchist groups across North
America, of the activities of Jewish anarchists within American labor
unions, and of the vast constellation of individuals whose support allowed
the movement's institutions to persist for nearly a century. The book also
documents the involvement of a number of well-known figures who were
onetime anarchists or allies but whose anarchist ties have been almost completely overlooked by later historians: union leaders Israel Feinberg, Morris
Feinstone, Louis Levy, Bernard Shane, Morris Sigman, and Ossip Walinsky;
economist Isaac Hourwich; engineer Leon Moissieff; Russian revolutionaries I. N. Steinberg and Alexander Krasnoshchekov; historian Louis Levine/
Lewis Lorwin; anti-Zionist journalist William Zuckerman; Canadian newspaper publisher Feivel Simkin; Communist Party leaders William Z. Foster
and Robert Minor; Works Progress Administration official Jacob Baker;
and more. Cohen's chronicle illustrates how anarchists' influence and ties
extended far beyond their own circles.

Nearly all other Yiddish-language studies of Jewish radicalism, by
contrast, were written by social democrats and Communists who mini-
mized the role of the anarchist movement or ignored it completely. Later
English-language research that built on these faulty foundations com-
pounded its errors. The result was that over the course of the twentieth
century and into the twenty-first, as the writing of histories about Jewish radicalism shifted from Yiddish to English, Yiddish-language sources by or about
anarchists suffered particular neglect. As Yiddish faded from use, the avail-
ability of translations of Yiddish sources became particularly consequential,

but up until the 2010s virtually no Yiddish anarchist documents had been published in English.[39] With each iteration of scholarship—from Yiddish works based on Yiddish sources, to English works based on Yiddish sources, to English works based on other English sources—anarchism receded further from view.[40] The Jewish anarchist past was literally lost in translation.

This erasure and the inaccessibility of Yiddish sources also shaped the historiography of anarchism. Most general studies of the anarchist movement neglect its Yiddish-speaking component almost entirely, aside from Emma Goldman (who wrote primarily in English).[41] And even many of those that do touch on this history have had to rely on limited, non-Yiddish sources.[42] Paul Avrich was one of the first modern historians of American anarchism

---

39. Since 2008, however, the following translations have appeared: Weinberg, *Forty Years in the Struggle*; Helene Minkin, *Storm in My Heart: Memories from the Widow of Johann Most*, ed. Tom Goyens, trans. Alisa Braun (Oakland: AK Press, 2015); Brian Moen, ed., *The J. Abrams Book: The Life and Work of an Exceptional Personality*, trans. Ruth Murphy (Mexico City: Rebecca Nestle, 2016). See also the online teaching supplement to Torres and Zimmer, *With Freedom in Our Ears*, at https://www.press.uillinois.edu/books/?id=p087141.

40. Compare, for example, Hertz Burgin, *Di geshikhte fun der idisher arbayter bevegung in Amerike, Rusland un England* (The History of the Jewish Labor Movement in America, Russia, and England) (New York: Fareynigte Idishe Geverkshaften, 1915) and Bernard Weinstein, *Di idishe yunyons in Amerike: bleter geshikhte un erinerungen* (The Jewish Unions in America: Pages of History and Memories) (New York: Feraynigte Idishe Geverkshaften, 1929) to Moses Rischin, *The Promised City: New York's Jews, 1870–1914* (Cambridge, MA: Harvard University Press, 1962); Irving Howe, *World of Our Fathers* (New York: Simon and Schuster, 1976); Arthur Liebman, *Jews and the Left* (New York: John Wiley & Sons, 1979); and Gerald Sorin, *The Prophetic Minority: American Jewish Immigrant Radicals, 1880–1920* (Bloomington: Indiana University Press, 1985). An important but neglected exception is Melech Epstein, *Jewish Labor in U.S.A.: An Industrial, Political and Cultural History of the Jewish Labor Movement*, new ed., 2 vols. ([New York]: Ktav Publishing House, 1969).

41. See, for example, Max Nettlau, *A Short History of Anarchism*, ed. Heiner Becker (London: Freedom Press, 1996); George Woodcock, *Anarchism: A History of Libertarian Ideas and Movements* (New York: Meridian, 1962); James Joll, *The Anarchists*, 2nd ed. (Cambridge, MA.: Harvard University Press, 1979); Peter Marshall, *Demanding the Impossible: A History of Anarchism*, rev. ed. (Oakland: PM Press, 2010); Michael Schmidt and Lucien van der Walt, *Black Flame: The Revolutionary Class Politics of Anarchism and Syndicalism* (Oakland: AK Press, 2009); Mike Finn, *Debating Anarchism: A History of Action, Ideas and Movements* (New York: Bloomsbury, 2021).

42. Such works include William O. Reichert, *Partisans of Freedom: A Study in American Anarchism* (Bowling Green: Bowling Green University Popular Press, 1976); Elaine J. Leeder, *The Gentle General: Rose Pesotta, Anarchist and Labor Organizer* (Albany: State University of New York Press, 1993); Andrew Cornell, *Unruly Equality: U.S. Anarchism in the Twentieth Century* (Berkeley: University of California Press, 2016).

who could read Yiddish, but over the more than fifty years of his academic career he published only a single essay focused on the Yiddish-speaking movement, though many of his other works touch on certain of its members, including Joseph Cohen.[43] Only in the twenty-first century, which has seen a revival of interest in the Yiddish language, have researchers begun to return to Yiddish sources to recover this long-neglected story.[44] The publication of this translation, however, makes Cohen's work accessible to a vastly larger audience of researchers, students, and activists.

❋ ❋ ❋

"In so many phases of the anarchist movement, he was either a prime mover or a very active person."
—*Esther Dolgoff*
(Oral History of the American Left Collection, New York University)

A new restlessness overtook Cohen after he completed this book, perhaps spurred by the disappointing response it received. In 1946 he moved to Mexico City, a haven for Russian Jewish exiles, accompanied by his new wife, a widow named Dora Fox (née Convissor). In 1948 the couple moved to Home, Washington, the site of an anarchist community founded in 1898,

---

43. Paul Avrich, "Jewish Anarchism in the United States," in *Anarchist Portraits* (Princeton: Princeton University Press, 1988), 176–99; Paul Avrich, *The Russian Anarchists* (Princeton: Princeton University Press, 1967); Paul Avrich, *An American Anarchist: The Life of Voltairine de Cleyre* (Princeton: Princeton University Press, 1978); Avrich, *Modern School*; Avrich, *Anarchist Voices*; Paul Avrich and Karen Avrich, *Sasha and Emma: The Anarchist Odyssey of Alexander Berkman and Emma Goldman* (Cambridge: Harvard University Press, 2012).

44. Tony Michels, *A Fire in Their Hearts: Yiddish Socialists in New York* (Cambridge, MA: Harvard University Press, 2005); Kenyon Zimmer, *Immigrants against the State: Yiddish and Italian Anarchism in America* (Urbana: University of Illinois Press, 2015); Kenyon Zimmer, "Saul Yanovsky and Yiddish Anarchism on the Lower East Side," in *Radical Gotham: Anarchism in New York City from Schwab's Saloon to Occupy Wall Street*, ed. Tom Goyens (Urbana: University of Illinois Press, 2017), 33–53; Anna Elena Torres, *Horizons Blossom, Borders Vanish: Anarchism and Yiddish Literature* (New Haven: Yale University Press, forthcoming); Torres and Zimmer, eds., *With Freedom in Our Ears*.

and in December of that year they expatriated to Paris, where Cohen learned French, revitalized that city's small Jewish anarchist group, and launched a new Yiddish anarchist journal, *Der frayer gedank* (Free Thought). The couple also traveled extensively, visiting England, Spain, Italy, Czechoslovakia, and Israel, where in the summer of 1949 Cohen helped organize an anarchist center and library in Tel Aviv, to which he personally donated three hundred books. (Comrades in the United States subsequently sent another five thousand volumes in Yiddish, Hebrew, and English.)[45]

The couple returned to New York from February to November 1950, then permanently in June 1952. Joseph delivered talks on what he had observed abroad and continued to edit and contribute monthly articles to *Der frayer gedank*. He remained an anarchist, atheist, and fierce critic of the state of Israel—although he felt an obligation to support the Jewish refugees living there and believed there was much potential in the libertarian socialism of the kibbutz movement.[46] Cohen also criticized the *Fraye arbeter shtime* and other anarchists who reluctantly backed the United States in the emerging Cold War. "American capitalism," he argued, "has the advantage: it is more humane, politically more free-spirited, and economically incomparably richer, satisfying a much larger part of its population," and therefore communism presented no real threat to it. "The difficulty, of course," he dryly commented, "lies in the fact that the capitalist order is based on a shattered foundation of injustice, fraud, exploitation and insecurity."[47] Although the anarchist had himself voted for Franklin D. Roosevelt's reelection in 1936 and supported liberal Democratic presidential nominee Adlai Stevenson in 1952, these were calculated, pragmatic decisions, not a sign that he had renounced his radicalism or embraced the Democratic Party.[48] As Cohen writes in the final chapter of this book, "Anarchism is fundamentally a revolutionary worldview—an approach to social questions that calls for fundamental change and demands that this change be carried out by the people, through

---

45. *FAS*, October 27, 1950, and November 1, 1966.

46. *FAS*, October 27, 1950. For Cohen's commentary on Israel see, for example, *Der frayer gedank*, June and July-August, 1949 and January 1950; *FAS*, February 3, 1950.

47. *Der frayer gedank*, September 1949.

48. Joe Conason, email to the author, July 13, 2022; Laurence Veysey, *The Communal Experience: Anarchist and Mystical Counter-Cultures in Twentieth Century America* (New York: Harper & Row, 1973), 173.

unwavering action. . . . Either we are anarchists and believe in the possibility of free, peaceful communal life without any government or coercion, and do everything we can to bring such a social organization about; or we no longer wholeheartedly believe in such a possibility and do nothing practical for its realization other than spouting and repeating anarchist slogans—in which case we are no longer anarchists and must have the courage to say so. No middle ground is possible."

Joseph Cohen died on September 28, 1953, at the age of seventy-five. Throughout his final years he continued to chronicle his own life experiences, leaving behind two unfinished manuscripts that were published after his death: *The House Stood Forlorn* (1954), a memoir of his childhood and life prior to emigrating to the United States, and *In Quest of Heaven: The Story of the Sunrise Co-operative Farm Community* (1957), a detailed account and analysis of his most ambitious attempt to create a functioning libertarian communist community. But his history of the Jewish anarchist movement, arguably his greatest gift to posterity, languished in obscurity—until now.

Esther Dolgoff (1905–1989): A Biographical Sketch

Anatole Dolgoff

"Embracing me, Esther greeted me as her 'young comrade.'
The eighty-three-year-old white-haired anarchist was wearing a
brightly colored housedress and the black and red badge of the CNT
(Confederación Nacional del Trabajo), the Spanish anarchist union
on her collar. Her spontaneous friendliness, unconventional appear-
ance, and profound humanity made all the elegant old ladies of
the Upper East Side, whose appearance had fascinated me, pale in
comparison."

We have the German journalist Ulrike Heider to thank for that accurate, loving description of my mother, Esther Judith Miller Dolgoff, in her old age.[1] "Profound humanity" is the key quality. It extended beyond humanity to all living things, plant and animal, down to the tiny mouse that flitted across the kitchen linoleum to the trash can. "Poor thing," she would say, "all it is trying to do is survive in this world."

The roots of Mother's compassion were sunk in the rich cultural soil of the Pale of Settlement: the region within which the Jews of the eighteenth- and nineteenth-century Russian Empire were confined. Religious orthodoxy, revolutionary socialism, anarchism, entrepreneurial capitalism,

---

1. Ulrike Heider, *Anarchism: Left, Right, and Green,* trans. Danny Lewis and Ulrike Bode (San Francisco: City Lights Books, 1994), 9.

Figure 4: Esther and Sam Dolgoff, 1978
Courtesy of Mimi Rivera

art, literature—these strains mixed within that confined space, often in the same large families, often in the same individuals!

Mother traced her radical family history back to that region and to her much older cousin whom she never met. An interview conducted by Doug Richardson in the 1970s is most revealing:

> Esther: My father's nephew was an anarchist and he was in that move-
> ment where the students went to the people to teach them how to
> read. . . . And even before he came to America, my mother would tell
> me how he didn't care about himself, how she would get a hold of him
> and make him mend his clothes, and feed him up because he looked
> like he forgot to eat. And he and his wife staged a strike, and his wife

became very ill, she caught the flu, and he was arrested and was going to be sent to Siberia. And during all this trouble his wife died of the flu, and according to Jewish law they have to bury the body before sundown, but his mother-in-law at a time like that was arranging to get him out to London through the sort of underground railroad that they had then. The people threw stones into the house [because] she hadn't buried the body of her daughter.

Doug: So you had sort of a radical family history. . .

Esther: *Yes, these were some of the sources.*[2]

Her father, Abraham Miller, my grandfather, was another source. He was a veteran of the tsar's army and a socialist with strong anarchistic leanings who was influenced by the writings of the anarchist-pacifist Gustav Landauer— and this twenty years prior to Landauer's martyrdom. Abraham, his wife Ida, and six-month-old Esther settled in Cleveland, Ohio, in 1906. There Abraham and Ida raised six children, of whom Esther was the oldest. He was a well-paid bricklayer, a builder of restaurant ovens and exhaust chimneys, and a staunch union man.

It is fair to describe the Millers as a typical, striving immigrant family. All six children attended college, no small achievement even today for a working-class family, and more than that in the 1920s. Esther graduated from Western Reserve University with a degree in English literature; her diploma, which I cherish, is written on genuine sheepskin. She was also admitted to medical school—a very difficult thing for a woman—but was forced to withdraw for financial reasons as the Great Depression closed in. Conventional stuff you might say, but Mother remained unconventional and became an active member of the Anarchist Forum and similar organizations in the Cleveland area.

My father, who preferred to be called by his first name, Sam, often joked to Mother's mock chagrin, "This proper young lady chased me up and down Cleveland in a taxi!" He said that she fell in love with him, this itinerant Wobbly hobo, after he had hopped an all-night freight train from Detroit to speak at the Forum. Jokes aside, he was well aware that meeting Mother

---

2. Doug Richardson, "Interview with Esther and Sam Dolgoff," *Black Rose* (Somerville, MA), Spring 1975, 66.

was the best thing that ever happened to him. It is an understatement to say that Mother's family was not uniformly delighted by her choice. "He'll give you syphilis," sister Sarah hissed upon first sight of my roughly dressed, roughly mannered, bluntly spoken future father. Certainly Mother could have sought a more "suitable" mate; an attractive, educated young woman, she had many such opportunities. But she would have none of it and chose to live a principled life in partnership with my housepainter father instead. They remained together for nearly sixty years, until Mother's death in 1989 (Father died in 1990). Their lives were inseparable. Mother stayed home with my brother Abraham and me rather than pursuing a career of her own—not because she felt compelled to do so by the customs of the day; rather, she felt that the care and nurturing of her children was more important than any job that paid her.

Abraham and I frequently reminisced after our parents were gone that Mother's devotion to her family and to anarchism came at a cost: the suppression of her ego and her creativity. She wrote promising short stories as a young woman, including one that impressed Paul Goodman, a literary comrade, to the extent that he tried to help her get it published. And she had an offbeat way of cutting to the bone on cultural matters. I remember her caustic comment regarding Philip Roth's Portnoy's Complaint, which, to be fair, conflates the author with the central character of the novel: "Let's see if I got this right. He's a grown man and can't get an erection. That he blames on his mother. But he did grow up to become a world-famous writer, didn't he? That's a bit of credit he saves for himself!"

Unfortunately, Mother's personal creative efforts were sporadic, and she did not find the time to follow them up. Instead, her sentences are woven into my father's articles and books, into unsigned pieces in various publications, in notices and speeches, et cetera. But there was one aspect of her creativity that never varied: her love of Yiddish, the rich day-to-day language of the European Jews before Hebrew became the language of the emergent Israel. She loved the stories of Sholem Aleichem, Sholem Asch, Isaac Bashevis Singer, and so many others.

Her Yiddish was impeccable, and this is confirmed by the best source: her devoutly religious European neighbors from the co-op my parents lived in. They'd stop me in the hall and make a kissing gesture with the fingertips from their lips. "Your mother speaks a beautiful Yiddish," they'd exclaim.

She made several attempts to put her love of Yiddish to use. In the late 1940s or early 1950s she was so impressed with the Yiddish version of the autobiography of Louise Michel that she translated it into English, but the project fell through.[3] The same fate awaited her translation of the present book by Joseph Cohen—the work of a man she deeply admired—until Kenyon Zimmer took on the herculean task of preparing it for publication.

I know this: It is too bad Mother did not live to see her work, with her name on it, in print! To hold it in her hands! The satisfaction, the *nakhes* it would have brought her. Thank you, Kenyon, for this tribute to her memory.

---

3. First published in French in 1886, Michel's memoir appeared in Yiddish as *Luize Mishel's lebensbeshaybung: geshriben fun ir aleyn,* trans. A. Frumkin (London: Arbeter Fraynd, 1906). It was eventually published in an English translation as *Red Virgin: Memoirs of Louise Michel,* trans. Bullitt Lowry and Elizabeth Gunter (Tuscaloosa: University of Alabama Press, 1981).

Author's Preface to the 1945 Yiddish Edition

I owe my gratitude to my comrades of the Radical Library in Philadelphia for the opportunity to describe the course pursued by our Jewish anarchist movement in this country for the last sixty years and the important events in the general labor movement, which at the time greatly influenced our lives and activities.

The undertaking is very large and important, and to an extent beyond my powers and capacities to carry out correctly. Our movement played a preeminent role in the development of the Jewish labor movement in this country, as well as in the cultural life and spiritual development of the entire community of Jewish immigrants. And not only in this country but also in the wider world, in the most remote places where Jewish wanderers had been cast, our words reached them through our newspapers, journals, books, and pamphlets that we published here and distributed all over. There is not a corner of the globe that has not heard David Edelstadt's inspiring battle hymns, Joseph Bovshover's songs, or where the crystal-clear thoughts of Peter Kropotkin translated into our Yiddish mother tongue has not reached. Here in this country, especially, the activities of our comrades have influenced the development of the broad Jewish immigrant masses, both those who worked and struggled for their existence—who filled the ranks of the powerful labor unions, of the grand Workmen's Circle and hundreds of other cultural organizations—and even those few who did not belong to the ranks of the proletariat and seemed to succumb to the plight of the middle class—professionals and the fully Americanized petite bourgeoisie. In their youth, in their first years here in this country, few of them missed the opportunity to come into contact with our movement, to fall under the influence of its activities: the giant mass meetings, the big entertainments, the antireligious agitation, and the general educational efforts carried out by our comrades. More than one generation of Yiddish writers and poets first appeared in our publications. Our literature educated thousands of Jews, acquainting them for the first time with the social and cultural problems of our time. And, most importantly, they learned to think independently, to look critically at the printed and spoken word. Every social phenomenon in our Jewish world in the last sixty years received expression and illumination in the activities of our comrades. The unique American Jewish way of life has been shaped to a large degree by the wide-ranging activity of our movement all these years.

In the hustle and bustle of life, in the momentum of activities, the historical side of our movement has been completely neglected. Our comrades did not *write* history; they *made* history. Few of our comrades even found it necessary to pen personal memoirs. The work of systematically recording events they left to other, often hostile elements, who ignored our contribution, often maliciously misrepresenting it, trying to give the impression that we simply disrupted others' work, tilting at windmills and contributing nothing constructive ourselves.

A few years ago comrades Morris Beresin and Charles Saltz of Philadelphia came up with the excellent idea of celebrating the fortieth anniversary of the Radical Library by publishing a historical overview of the work of that organization during the forty years of its existence. They offered me the honor of taking up the responsibility of editing such a volume, with material from many other contributors.

As soon as I got to work, it became clear to me that to begin with the founding of the library in 1905 would be impossible, because it would be incomprehensible to the reader. Where did we come from, how did we get the idea to build a library, and on what foundation did we start building? The work required a detailed description of those times, an explanation of how the anarchist movement spread among the Jewish immigrants, and the development it underwent up until 1905, when we first stepped on stage.

I began to gather material for a concise account of our movement in the 1880s, in its early childhood, and writing down the events and encounters in which I had participated during my ten years in the movement in

Philadelphia, up to the end of 1913. The work began to take on a definite form in 1944, a much broader one than was originally conceived.

In addition, it turned out that collaborating with a number of other people would mean delaying this project indefinitely. Most of our elderly comrades are either very busy people or are not avid writers and find it beyond their power to jot their memories down on paper. We began to see that if we truly wanted to publish the history of the Radical Library in time for the fortieth anniversary, a single individual would have to assume the task of completing it on time.

At a conference with some of the older comrades at the end of that year, we decided to take the latter path. Comrade Benjamin Axler, one of the founders of the Radical Library, suggested that the scope of the book should be broadened to include as much of a historical overview of the whole movement as is possible for one individual to create. Comrade Morris Beresin, for his part, emphasized the need to give an overview of the evolution of the anarchist idea in addition to describing events over time. Comrades Axler and Beresin are personally responsible for the scope and form of the book as it is here presented to the reader.

Their responsibility is, of course, only for the form and not the content or the way in which the task was performed. I and only I alone am responsible for the content. The comrades gave me a free hand, even in the selection of material that I have collected and subsequently what I have excluded. My opinions and conclusions, such as they appear, are solely my personal ones and do not always express the view of the comrades who have undertaken the publishing of this book.

This work was, as I have said, to a certain extent beyond my capacities. I am not a historian. I have no experience in such work, and I have unfortunately, in addition, not had access to all the primary sources required for such an undertaking. I always felt that such a large and important undertaking needed a better prepared person, a professional, to carry it out correctly. But the awareness that no one else was available to take on the job led me to accept the offer in the hope that the mistakes which I will most likely make will be corrected over time by other, more experienced historians.

There was a second consideration at work: our movement has a both a written testament (*toyre simkhes*) and a spoken testament (*toyre shebalpe*). In addition to those events written about and published, there are details and explanations that have not been recorded anywhere. They live in the memory of those who participated in them. And as our generation, and especially the generation which preceded us, is now quickly moving off the stage, I felt that we could no longer wait to record what had happened in the past.

❀ ❀ ❀

The work, as the reader will note, was not easy. It required reviewing decades of the *Fraye arbeter shtime*, *Mother Earth*, and other periodicals produced by us and others. It was necessary to become acquainted with the memoirs and historical events of the entire period, as well as with the most important events in the labor movement, which required consulting dozens of larger works, each illuminating events from a different viewpoint.

There were two ways in which I could proceed: I could record the events as they occurred, bringing together all the details and data that could be fully researched, and leave it to the reader or the future historian to interpret their meaning and significance—the way that a professional historian would probably choose—or I could select and highlight certain events, explain them in accordance with my understanding of the goals of our movement in my young years, and how I understand them now in the light of a lifetime of activism.

I preferred the second way, the nonprofessional approach, and I describe my work as "a Historical Review *and Personal Reminiscences*." I do not make any claims to historical perfection or objectivity in my relationship to the events that I relate. For the same reason, I did not worry too much about the exact chronological order in which events are presented and did not break the flow of the story in order to place every incident in its proper sequence, only to relay how they later resolved many pages later, which breaks up events and confuses the reader. I have in most cases chosen to describe a single event in one chapter, even those that unfolded over several years. This largely destroys the chronological flow of the history—leading me in my writing to jump back and forth between dates and years—but it provides, in my view, a better opportunity for the reader to understand and comprehend exactly what happened in each case. And this, after all, I considered to be the most important task of the entire enterprise.

It remains for others to judge the extent to which I have correctly carried out my work. The facts that I have gathered here will serve as material for the future historian of our movement, who will in time take up this work with better preparation and under more favorable circumstances. Readers, and especially my comrades, will, I hope, find in this work a reflection and reminder of their youth, of a time when they lived, believed, and worked toward the realization of our great ideal. That time was glorious, hopeful, and gratifying for those who strived with all their heart and soul for a better future.

This was a labor of love and sincere devotion, undertaken voluntarily without any material considerations. I want to thank the comrades of the Radical Library for giving me the honor and the pleasure of having an opportunity to occupy myself with such a worthy undertaking in my old age, as well as for taking on the difficult task of raising the material means to publish this work. In particular, the Anniversary Committee of the Radical Library, comrades Saltz, Beresin, Harry Melman, Alexander Brown, Max Grishkan, Sarah Greenburg, and others, greatly deserve recognition for their tireless work throughout.

I owe a special thanks to my friend and comrade Benjamin Axler, who aided me greatly with advice and deeds in planning out the work and also recalling the correct sequence of events in which he and I had participated in our younger years.

I also received much help from Isidore Wisotsky, a man with a phenomenal memory for details that has no equal; comrade Melman, who also excels in that field; and comrades David Isakovitz, Sol Linder, Isaac Radinowsky, and Morris Michael, who assisted with instructions and significant technical advice. Thanks as also due to Mrs. Agnes Inglis, librarian at the University of Michigan Library in Ann Arbor, for her tireless work in providing ancient documents and historical data of the utmost importance. Without the help of all these people, it would not have been possible for me to carry out my task.

Joseph Cohen
November 1945
Washington, DC

PART ONE

Historical Overview

CHAPTER 1

The Preliminary Period

The first blossoms of the Jewish anarchist movement here in America are buried in the dark past. Just as a plant whose seed must first develop and spread roots in the earth in order to gather strength with which to break through the soil above, so every new movement develops in the subconscious minds of the people before it breaks through to the public.

The first prominent signs of anarchist tendencies among the Jewish immigrant masses occurred in the 1880s when the whole country was greatly agitated by the unrest in the labor movement. About the period before this—the seeding time—we have absolutely no knowledge. But we do know that, around 1882, Jews came in great numbers after the first pogroms in Russia.[1] They left their homeland after the passage of draconian, restrictive laws which drove the Jews from the Russian provinces into the Pale of Settlement,[2] into the ghettoes of the hungry Jewish cities. Then began the desperate wandering, starting with the loosely and superficially organized migrations of cooperative groups to Palestine and the United States. The terrorized and frightened Jewish people fled to wherever they could find entrance. They fled to London, to Africa, to Palestine, to South America, and especially to the United States. Here they found long-established Jewish

---

1. Between 1881 and 1884, following the assassination of Tsar Alexander II, more than two hundred anti-Jewish riots, or **pogroms**, took place in Russia. Attackers killed dozens of victims, injured and raped hundreds more, and burned and looted Jewish homes and businesses.

2. **The Pale of Settlement** was a western region of the Russian Empire (including present-day Belarus, Lithuania, and Moldova, as well as parts of Latvia, Poland, and Ukraine), outside of which most Russian Jews were forbidden from residing.

communities. These were Jews who had come many years earlier and were very sympathetic to the newcomers. But the older communities were different. The German Jews were Reformed.[3] Their synagogues looked like churches. The Polish and Hungarian Jewish people carried out an Orthodox Jewish life, with religious schools, rabbis, cantors, and other religious functionaries, but it did not have the same atmosphere; it did not evoke the same feelings in the new arrivals as their synagogues in Russia and Lithuania. They felt alienated, lost, and depressed.

Their first experiences with trying to earn a living were very disappointing to those who had dreamed so long and had had such hopes about free America. There were only two ways open to those for whom all other doors were closed for earning a living. One, the degrading business of peddling, looked to them like begging. The other was to work long hours in a sweatshop owned by a Jewish contractor who paid them just enough to keep body and soul together.

I will attempt to give an idea of the origin and the development of social and political views among the immigrant Jews of that period. We must critically examine the human element that came here, the physical, moral, spiritual, and social baggage that they carried with them from the old country, the atmosphere into which they were catapulted, the circumstances—economic, political, and social—under which they lived the first years after their arrival, and also the influence that their surrounding neighbors had on them—all this I will attempt to do in short, general strokes.

❀ ❀ ❀

Who were these Jews who emigrated from Russia? There are records of memoirs by individuals, intellectuals, and semi-intellectuals who at the time of emigration dreamed and dedicated themselves to vague nationalistic ambitions. They sought to rehabilitate the entire life of the Jewish people on a new

---

3. **Reform Judaism** is a more liberal denomination of the Jewish religion, influenced by the Enlightenment and founded in Germany in the early nineteenth century. Although it had relatively few followers in Europe, it became and remains the largest denomination of Judaism in the United States.

foundation of productive work. Those who came to America belonged to the organization Am Olam,[4] and those who went to Palestine were known as the Biluim.[5] However, it is clear that these dreamers were but a minority of the Jews emigrating. The great wave of immigrants was composed of ordinary people without any pretensions, without any dreams—little storekeepers, impoverished merchants, a few artisans and workers, and not a few young people looking for the wherewithal to earn a living that the impoverished Jewish communities of Europe no longer provided.

The intellectuals left records behind, as observed above. They wrote about their impressions and experiences of their first years in America. But they wrote these in their old age, when they looked back at their own pasts with the eyes of Americanized, worldly people with a completely different perspective than that of their youth. Their interpretations must, therefore, be taken with a considerable grain of salt, as the Americans say, in order to get the real taste of the food they would serve us.

One thing is clear: among the emigrants there were quite a number of university students, many *"eksternikes"* [self-taught students], and a greater number of yeshiva students, *maskilim,* and those who loved learning for its own sake.[6] Still others had had contact with the Russian Revolutionary movement and were imbued with generally socialistic tendencies. Some brought with them Narodnik attitudes—they wished to "go to the people," to live with the hardworking masses and lift them to a higher consciousness.[7] Some were under the influence of Nikolay Chernyshevsky's teachings on cooperative labor and cooperative living.[8] They came to America with the

---

4. **Am Olam** (Hebrew for The Eternal People), founded in 1881, was a movement of Russian Jews who sought to establish cooperative farms in the United States. Many figures of the early Jewish anarchism first arrived as members of Am Olam groups.

5. **Biluim** (Hebrew for Pioneers) were Russian Jewish emigrants belonging to the *Bilu* (Pioneer) movement who, beginning in 1882, formed agricultural settlements in Palestine.

6. *Maskilim* refers to largely secular European Jews influenced by the *Haskalah,* or "Jewish Enlightenment," of the eighteenth and nineteenth centuries.

7. The **Narodniks**, or Populists, were early Russian socialists who in the 1870s pursued a strategy of "going to the people" to prepare the peasantry for revolution against the tsar and capitalism.

8. **Nikolay Chernyshevsky** (1828–1889) was a Russian novelist and revolutionary who helped found the Narodnik movement. His novel *What Is to be Done?* (1863) influenced generations of Russian radicals, including Emma Goldman, Alexander Berkman, and Vladimir Lenin.

idea of trying to apply these teachings and views practically—to establish cooperative colonies and to live together as one big family.

The Narodnik outlook and the great tragedy that had befallen the Jewish people in Russia caused these intellectuals to think and feel not only about themselves, about their own little circle, but about the entire Jewish people. They dedicated themselves to being an example for the others. Jews needed to return to productive work founded on a cooperative socialistic ethos—that is the most noble task that people can face.

It is very doubtful they knew anything, even after they had been here for quite a few years, about the numerous attempts to found colonies that had been made in this country by Robert Owen and the followers of Charles Fourier, Étienne Cabet, and other social reformers some fifty years before they came.[9] Regardless, they tried to carry out both of their goals—to live from productive work and to form cooperative colonies—as best as they could. But they were not successful. The spirit was willing, but physically it was impossible for them to contend with the difficult conditions of life. All their colonies in Louisiana, in Kansas, in Oregon, and in North Dakota were disbanded in a short span of time. The cooperative homes in the large cities also did not see many days and fell apart. Even efforts to live by productive work did not last long. The idealistic intelligentsia shook off their dreams—and again buried themselves in their books and went for professional careers which at that time in this country made no great demands on learning and knowledge, or they became salesmen for new gadgets or household wares, shopkeepers, contractors, or simply intellectuals (*luftmentshn*). In short, almost without exception, they reverted to their typical Jewish lifestyle using their wits rather than hard physical work. Only for a short time did they taste the bitter life of the laboring man in the sweatshops and the frightening poverty of the Jewish ghetto.

What was left were the recollections of the spiritual baggage they

---

9. **Robert Owen** (1771–1858) was a Welsh manufacturer, philanthropist, and pre-Marxian socialist. From 1824 to 1828 he lived in the United States, where he attempted to put his ideas into practice in the utopian colony of New Harmony, Indiana. **François Marie Charles Fourier** (1772–1837) was a French philosopher and pre-Marxian socialist who promoted the formation of socialist communes he called phalanxes. His ideas gained a strong international following in the mid-nineteenth century, including in the United States. **Étienne Cabet** (1788–1856) was a French philosopher and pre-Marxian socialist and founder of the Icarian movement, which established socialist communes in several US states.

brought with them from home in the old country, a longing for the "good old days" when they dreamed of living like good and noble people (*mentshn*). Living years later on aristocratic Riverside Drive, Morris Hillquit recalled with nostalgia the long discussions about Karl Marx and Mikhail Bakunin that he had with friends many years earlier on hot summer nights "on the roofs of Cherry Street."[10] But the dreams of youth are never to be forgotten.

The immigrant masses continued to ceaselessly slave away and suffer in the sweatshops and in the frightfully cramped tenement houses. Life lacked all enjoyment—there were not deep bonds between people. Prayers, synagogues, and temples no longer aroused the ordinary people. Religion lost meaning to these unfortunate immigrants who had to work so hard for a bit of bread. The gathering place for these Jewish workers on a free day or evening was the *khazer mark* ("pig market"), the employment agency of the time, with the "market" often being raided by the police just like in Russia. The ignorance of the masses was very terrible; they were incapable of coming together in unions or organizations. The intelligentsia were only sporadically interested in the fate of the workers. They were on the threshold of leaving the working class and so did not develop an influence on its path or development.

There were no enduring unions of Jewish workers until the great wave of immigration years later brought a new type of Jewish youth without nationalistic dreams, without grand ambitions. These youths were instead willing

---

10. Morris Hillquit, *Loose Leaves from a Busy Life* (New York: MacMillan, 1934), 1–11. **Hillquit** (Moris Hilkvit, 1869–1933), born Hilkovitsh, was a Russian-born Jewish attorney and socialist. He immigrated to New York in 1886 and soon became a leading figure in the SLP and then the Socialist Party and was a staunch opponent of anarchism and syndicalism. Hillquit was also the longtime legal counsel for the ILGWU. **Karl Marx** (1818–1883) was a German philosopher and political theorist, coauthor of *The Communist Manifesto* (1848), and a leader of the International Workingmen's Association (the First International). In the second half of the eighteenth century, he became the most influential socialist thinker in the world. **Mikhail Bakunin** (1814–1876) was a Russian intellectual and anarchist. Born into the aristocracy, he became a revolutionary and was confined to life imprisonment for taking part in a revolutionary uprising in Dresden in 1848. Bakunin escaped in 1861 and traveled to Europe via Japan and the United States. He joined the First International in 1864 and became Marx's chief rival and head of the organization's "anti-authoritarian," or anarchist, wing, resulting in his expulsion in 1872. Bakunin is considered by many to be the founder of the modern anarchist movement, and despite his occasional antisemitic remarks he was held in high esteem by Jewish anarchists.

to work for their living and to fight for improvements. From these kinds of struggles, the Jewish labor movement began to develop in this country. The role and contribution of the intellectuals at this time consisted of speaking to the masses, encouraging them in their struggles, and playing the role of their spokespeople, to present the workers' point of view.

During the first few years, when the intellectuals had a taste of the life of a toiler in the sweatshops, when Abe Cahan cut roots from tobacco leaves for three dollars a week, and Morris Hillquit sewed shirts for the same payment, the first attempts were made to "enlighten" the Jewish workers and to interest them in social problems.[11] The intellectuals regarded themselves as socialists, revolutionaries, world-changers, and reformers, without being entirely clear as to what could and should be done. Their political views were influenced in this country mostly by the German labor movement, through the socialist publication *Nyu-Yorker yidishe folkstsaytung* (New York Jewish People's Newspaper).[12] Especially helpful was one of the editors, the Russian Sergius Schewitsch.[13]

The movement, as much as there was a movement in these years among the immigrant Jews, was social-revolutionary.[14] It mostly consisted of talks, lectures, discussions, and social events, conducted in Russian, German, and lastly in Yiddish. The German language, the German form of organization and understanding, long dominated and influenced the Jewish immigrants.

The terrible need of the Jewish workers often drove them to fight against their oppressors. The pattern in those years was to go on strike first and then to organize a union. In most of the Jewish trades, people had to strike every season, when the work began. At the point in the season when there

---

11. **Abraham Cahan** (1860–1951) was a Russian-born Jewish editor and socialist, best known as the longtime editor of New York's influential Yiddish daily socialist newspaper *Forverts* (Forward). Before becoming a socialist he had in the 1880s briefly belonged to the anarchist movement.

12. **Di Nyu-Yorker yidishe folkstsaytung** (1886–1889), edited by Abba Braslavsky (1864–?) and Moses Mintz (Moyshe Mints, 1860–1930), was one of the first Yiddish socialist newspapers in the United States.

13. **Sergius Schewitsch**, or Sergei Shevitch (1835–1912), was a Russian-born editor and socialist. From a noble Latvian family but educated in Germany, he was a prominent figure in America's Socialist Labor Party and edited New York's German-language socialist newspaper *New Yorker Volkszeitung*, but in 1891 he returned to Europe.

14. **"Social-revolutionary"** was a term used in the 1870s and 1880s to refer to both anarchists and anti-parliamentary revolutionary socialists.

was enough work in the shops, the workers calmly let their newly formed "unions" extinguish like a candle, and at the start of the following season they would have to begin all over once more.

The Jews knew very little about the American labor movement. The Jewish *inteligentn* viewed the native labor movement a bit like a monstrosity; it was seemingly a labor movement yet not a labor movement, as it obstructed what was necessary. Nearer to their hearts was the German American labor movement, with which they had come into contact. The German socialists were the ones who helped to organize the United Hebrew Trades in New York before there were enough unions to put together such a central body.[15] But this came much later, near the end of the 1880s when the split between the socialists and the anarchists was already sharply defined.

❀ ❀ ❀

In 1881 an anarchist gathering was held in London at which the leading spirits of the movement of that time were present.[16] The convention adopted a declaration of extreme revolutionary principles, urging comrades to fight with all means against the institutions of existing government.

At the convention there were two delegates who represented the German social-revolutionary clubs of America. They brought back the resolutions of the convention and organized anarchist groups among the German workers here.[17]

A year later, at the end of 1882, Johann Most came to the United States and brought his publication *Freiheit* (Freedom) with him.[18] He had spent

---

15. The **United Hebrew Trades** (Fareynikte Yidishe Geverkshaftn, or UHT) was a federation of predominantly Jewish labor unions founded in New York in 1888. By 1910 it included more than a hundred unions and 150,000 members.

16. The **International Revolutionary Socialist Congress** of London convened July 14–20, 1881. More than forty delegates from at least fourteen countries voted to reestablish an international anarchist federation, reject parliamentary methods, and endorse "propaganda of the deed" as a revolutionary tactic.

17. These delegates were German-born anarchists Carl Seelig and Johann Neve (1844–1896). Neve, however, was a proxy delegate who never traveled to the United States.

18. **Johann Most** (1846–1906) was a German-born editor, socialist, then anarchist. Repeatedly arrested for incendiary writing and speeches, he sat as a deputy of the Social Democratic Party of Germany in the Reichstag from 1873 until 1878, when he fled to France and

some time in prison in "free" England for praising the *attentat* that did away with Alexander II. [19] On his arrival he found a ready-made environment in the social-revolutionary clubs. At a convention in Pittsburgh in 1883, a declaration of revolutionary anarchist principles was adopted that was very similar to the one adopted in London two years before. [20]

Most was an outspoken revolutionary, a fiery agitator whose words lit hearts aflame and awakened the spirit of revolt. He described revolution as an event that must inevitably come and demanded that everyone do everything possible to hasten its arrival. He taught his listeners to use arms, dynamite, and poison—all means were kosher for this great goal.

He carried out his agitation among workers, but he did not put much importance on unions and their parochial demands. He declared that employers will concede nothing out of the goodness of their hearts. For every little improvement, people must struggle and give up many martyrs. What sense does it make to demand a few pennies more or a few hours less? If we have to struggle, let it be for the complete emancipation of the worker!

It seems that Johann Most lectured more at Jewish meetings in New York than he did at German ones. Besides all the other lectures, he addressed a meeting on Friday nights on the Lower East Side regularly for years. His influence among the Jewish immigrants was enormous. Philip Krantz, a convinced social democrat for all his years, later testified that Johann Most was

---

then England to escape Germany's Anti-Socialist Law and gravitated toward anarchism. After relocating to New York, he remained the leading figure in the German American anarchist movement. Most founded *Freiheit* (1879–1910) in London and transplanted it in 1882 to New York, where it became one of the most important anarchist newspapers in the United States.

19. *Attentat* (French for "attack" or "attempt") was the common term used for assassinations and other attacks on the ruling order carried out by revolutionaries. **Alexander II** (1818–1881), though a comparatively liberal tsar of the Russian Empire, was assassinated in Saint Petersburg by members of the revolutionary socialist movement Narodnaya Volya (The People's Will).

20. "The Pittsburgh Manifesto" was the declaration of principles adopted by the Pittsburgh Congress of 1883, a gathering of anarchists and social-revolutionaries who formed the International Working People's Association (IWPA), intended to be the American branch of the ephemeral Anarchist International founded in London in 1881. Coauthored by Johann Most, the document called for "destruction of the existing class rule by all means—i.e., by energetic, relentless, revolutionary, and international action"—and "establishment of a free society based upon co-operative organization of production." At its height the IWPA counted at least five thousand members, but it collapsed following the Haymarket bombing of 1886 and was defunct by the turn of the twentieth century.

Figure 5: Johann Most's *Freiheit*
Freiheit, October 20, 1883

by nature best suited to spread the first seeds of socialism among the Jewish workers, in London and then in New York.[21] Abe Cahan, writing many years later, adds that in his own first years in this country he was himself anarchistically inclined. He fondly recalls this youthful phase of his life.[22]

---

21. Philip Krantz, "Mit 25 yohr tsurik," *Fraye gezelshaft*, August 1910, 679–80. **Krantz** (1858–1922), real name Jacob (Yankev) Rombro, was a Russian-born Jewish journalist and socialist. He briefly edited the *Arbeter fraynd* in London before coming to the United States in 1890 to become editor of the *Di arbeter tsaytung* and subsequently edited and wrote for many other Yiddish publications.

22. Abe Cahan, *The Education of Abraham Cahan*, trans. Leon Stein, Abraham Conan, and Lynn Davison (Philadelphia: Jewish Publication Society of America, 1969), 254–58.

Most's followers, Germans as well as Jews, did not follow him the whole way. The revolution was indeed on its way, it appeared, but the immediate demands of the workers' struggle should not therefore be neglected. Such a faction most clearly developed in Chicago, where the revolutionary wing of the German socialist movement was strongly represented. They had a number of their own publications— the *Arbeiter-Zeitung* (Workers' Newspaper), a German daily; *Verbote* (Harbinger)—adding to *The Alarm*, an English weekly paper, and a Bohemian [Czech] weekly.[23] They also had a large number of good speakers and organizers and with all of their might devoted themselves to building and strengthening the organized workers' movement.

When the Jewish immigrants arrived on the scene in the 1880s in great numbers, they learned from the Germans the doctrines of social action and participation in the socialist movement. The movement was divided between adherents of political tactics, adherents of immediate forcible revolution, practical activity in the unions, and those who combined more than one type of tactic. The Jewish worker inherited these doctrines in all their particulars; their movement reflected them in its splintering and ideological diversity.

---

23. The **Chicagoer Arbeiter-Zeitung** (1877–1931) was edited from 1883 to 1886 by German anarchist August Spies; it remained an anarchist newspaper until 1910, when it became a socialist publication. **Verbote** (1873–1924) was for many years the weekly edition of the *Chicagoer Arbeiter-Zeitung* and included future Haymarket trial defendants August Spies and Michael Schwab among its editors. **The Alarm** (1884–1889) was founded by Albert Parsons and served as the main English-language newspaper of the IWPA. **Budoucnost** (The Future, 1883–1886) was the main Czech-language newspaper of the IWPA.

CHAPTER 2

Years of Hope and Disillusionment

In 1884 the then very young American Federation of Labor (AFL) at its annual convention decided to inaugurate the eight-hour workday on the first of May 1886 and to agitate vigorously for that purpose.[1] The federation was still young, small, and weak. It didn't have more than a handful of members throughout the country. Its decision had little practical significance. It was considered as a means of agitation more than something that it would actually be implemented.

The Knights of Labor were immediately skeptical of the entire undertaking.[2] Terrence Powderly, the Grand Master Workman of the order, declared openly that the number of organized workers was far too small to be able to carry out such a step.[3] But among the workers such a resolution found

---

1. **The American Federation of Labor** (AFL) was a national federation of labor unions founded in 1881. For the first five decades of its existence, it generally eschewed politics and focused on securing better conditions for the members of the craft unions that comprised most of its constituents. By the twentieth century the AFL was the largest labor organization in the United States, and in 1955 it merged with the Congress of Industrial Organizations to form the AFL-CIO.

2. **The Knights of Labor**, founded in 1869, was the first major federation of labor organizations in the United States. It was generally inclusive across lines of skill, gender, and race (often excepting Chinese workers) and vaguely socialistic in orientation. By 1886 it had a membership of over seven hundred thousand, including many anarchists, but the Knights collapsed in the second half of the decade.

3. **Terence V. Powderly** (1849–1924) was an American-born labor organizer and politician. He was the former mayor of Scranton, Pennsylvania, and head of the Knights of Labor from 1879 to 1893. Powderly supported Henry George's single-tax movement, and later became a lawyer and Commissioner General of Immigration from 1897 to 1902.

great sympathy. The only city in which eight-hour agitation was done on a large scale and with great resolve was Chicago. There our comrades, who openly declared themselves anarchists, carried on a mighty propaganda campaign for the shorter workday and especially for the strike on the first of May. They made speeches, wrote, formed unions, and organized massive demonstrations in the streets, in which thousands of workers participated. In the spring of 1886, there was the widespread impression in Chicago that on the first of May industry in the whole country would come to a standstill by way of a general strike for the eight-hour workday. The mood was so prevalent that some employers instituted the eight-hour day before May 1 to prevent a strike.

The awaited day finally came, but the disappointment was just as great as the anticipation, if not greater. In Chicago, an estimated eighty thousand workers went out on strike, but in other cities throughout the country the total number of strikers barely reached two hundred thousand—not more than a drop in the bucket! The movement was a failure from the start.

A few days later an incident occurred that no one had foreseen or expected. At a meeting of strikers near the McCormick Reaper Works in a neighborhood of Chicago, where there was already an ongoing struggle that had no connection to the first of May, a confrontation between strikers and scabs took place. The police attacked the strikers and killed several of them. August Spies, who happened to be present and witnessed the brutality of the police, became so enraged that he hurried to the office of the *Arbeiter-Zeitung*, of which he was editor, and wrote a hotheaded leaflet calling workers to a protest meeting the following evening.[4] The leaflets were only printed and distributed on the day that the meeting was held. The result was a not well-attended protest with no more than twelve hundred people present.

The police were prepared to make a bloodbath of the gathering. Two hundred well-armed reserves waited in a nearby police precinct to assault the assembled people. But the mayor of Chicago, Carter Harrison, fearing trouble, came to the meeting alone to listen to what the speakers said, and

---

4. **August Spies** (1855–1887) was a German-born labor activist, editor, and anarchist. He belonged to the SLP until 1880, then cofounded the anarchist IWPA in 1883 and edited the *Arbeiter-Zeitung* from 1884 until 1886. He was executed in 1887 for alleged conspiracy in connection with the Haymarket bombing.

he did not permit the police to take action.[5] The meeting was addressed by August Spies, Albert Parsons, and Samuel Fielden.[6] It began to rain just as the last speaker commenced, and most of the people started to leave. The mayor too headed home but stopped in at the police precinct and told Captain John Bonfield that, as everything was in good order, he could disband the reserves and get some sleep.[7]

But Bonfield only waited for the mayor to leave and stop interfering with his work. He led his two hundred police to assault those attending the meeting, just as it was ending. When the armed men approached the gathering with their clubs and revolvers in hand, a bomb tore through their ranks. A number of police were torn to bits, and about sixty others were wounded.[8]

It is impossible to describe what happened next. The next morning, after no more bombs exploded, the police became heroically brave and went after all the radicals, labor leaders, and well-known anarchists; they arrested them and looted their newspaper offices. I will not take up space relating the

---

5. **Carter Harrison Sr.** (1825–1893) was an American-born lawyer and former Democratic congressman who served as mayor of Chicago from 1879 to 1887 and was sympathetic to organized labor. He was reelected mayor in 1893 but assassinated just a few months later by a disgruntled former supporter.

6. **Albert Parsons** (1848–1887) was an Alabama-born former Confederate soldier turned Radical Republican, labor editor, and eventual anarchist. In 1873 he and his mixed-race wife and fellow radical Lucy Parsons moved to Chicago where Albert became an organizer for the Knights of Labor and joined the SLP. He withdrew from the SLP in 1879 and cofounded the anarchist IWPA in 1883, editing its newspaper, *The Alarm*. In 1886 Parsons was one of the main organizers of the eight-hour-day movement in Chicago, and he was executed in 1887 for alleged conspiracy in connection with the Haymarket bombing. **Samuel Fielden** (1847–1922) was an English-born laborer and anarchist. The son of a Chartist, he immigrated to the United States in 1868 and settled in Chicago, where he was active in the Chicago Teamsters Union and became a lay Methodist preacher. By 1883 he was active in the Freethought movement, and in 1884 he joined the American Group of the anarchist IWPA. He was finishing his speech at the Haymarket Square meeting when the bomb was thrown. Sentenced to death at the ensuing trial, Fielden's punishment was reduced to life imprisonment, and he was pardoned by Illinois governor John P. Altgeld in 1893.

7. **John A. Bonfield** (1836–1898) was a Chicago police inspector known as "Black Jack" Bonfield due to his rough handling of striking workers. He was forced to resign in 1889 after being accused of selling prisoners' property and then formed a short-lived private detective agency.

8. One police officer was killed immediately, and six others were fatally wounded; another died two years later from complications related to his injuries. Some police were shot by panicked fellow officers.

reign of terror, the home invasions, the poisonous hate of the capitalist press throughout the land, and above all the shameful trial that the eight accused anarchists received. It would take us too far afield from our subject.

Seven innocent men were condemned to death and one to many years of imprisonment for a crime that, as in the course of the trial it became clear, not one of them had committed. The labor movements of every country, from across the civilized world, became deeply aroused. They undertook appeals to the highest courts, petitions, protests, and massive demonstrations, and the affair held the public's anxious attention for over a year. Socialists, liberals, and others of all shades of opinion protested against the death sentence and demanded a new trial. There were two exceptions: Powderly, from the Knights of Labor, and Henry George, founder of the single-tax movement.[9]

The first forbade the assemblies of his organization to gather money for the defense, under the excuse that it would ruin the reputation of the Knights. He declared: "It were better that seven times seven men hang than to hang the millstone of odium around the standard of this order in affiliating in any way with this element of destruction."[10] The second, Henry George, simply declared: "If a jury of twelve men and a judge found the accused guilty, I have nothing to say. Perhaps they are guilty and must suffer the punishment."[11] It was precisely during these two years, when the shadow of the gallows hung over the heads of the condemned men, that George was running for political office, and he did not intend to lose even one vote from the frightened electorate.[12]

---

9. **Henry George** (1839–1897) was an American-born economist and journalist. His proposed "single tax" sought to abolish rent and achieve greater economic equality through a land value tax, and his book *Progress and Poverty* (1879) was translated into many languages and sold millions of copies worldwide.

10. T. V. Powderly, *Thirty Years of Labor: 1859 to 1889* (Columbus, Ohio: Excelsior, 1889), 552.

11. Cohen appears to have loosely paraphrased the following statement from George's newspaper the *Standard*, October 8, 1887: "Seven men were tried on the charge of being accessory to the crime, and after a long trial were convicted. . . . That seven judges of the highest court of Illinois, men accustomed to weigh evidence and to pass upon judicial rulings, should, after a full examination of the testimony and the record, and with the responsibility of life and death resting upon them, unanimously sustain the verdict and the sentence, is inconsistent with the idea that the Chicago anarchists were condemned on insufficient evidence."

12. In 1886 George ran for mayor of New York as a member of the short-lived United Labor Party, with support from many socialists and even some anarchists. In 1887 he unsuccessfully ran for secretary of state of New York.

On the other hand, many people became so intensely interested in the trial and its gruesome verdict that they earnestly studied the topic and became converts to the teachings of the condemned. Foremost among them were Voltairine de Cleyre and Emma Goldman, who subsequently dedicated their entire lives to spreading anarchist ideals.[13] But they were not the only ones. Hugh O. Pentecost, John Turner, George Pettibone, William Haywood, George Brown, Saul Yanovsky, and scores of others took up the torch that had been so cruelly snatched from the hands of the martyrs.[14]

---

13. **Voltairine de Cleyre** (1866–1912) was an American-born writer, poet, and anarchist. Born to a poor family in Michigan, she attended a Catholic convent school in Ontario before embracing atheism and becoming active in the Freethought movement. After moving to Philadelphia in 1889, she became one of the most prominent anarchist women of her day. As a result of her contacts with Philadelphia's Jewish anarchist movement, de Cleyre learned Yiddish and taught English to many Jewish immigrants, including Joseph Cohen. **Emma Goldman** (1869–1940) was a Russian-born Jewish writer, speaker, and anarchist. Radicalized after immigrating to the United States in 1885, Goldman initially honed her public speaking skills under the tutelage of Johann Most and went on to become the foremost anarchist lecturer in the America. She championed birth control, free love, antimilitarism, and syndicalism and was arrested at least sixteen times. Although Goldman could read and speak Yiddish, she was not fluent and preferred to express herself in Russian, German, and English. In 1919 she was deported to Russia, which she left, disillusioned, in 1921. She lived the rest of her life in exile but continued to write for anarchist publications in the United States and elsewhere up until her death.

14. **Hugh O. Pentecost** (1848–1907) was an American-born Protestant minister-turned-freethinker, editor, attorney, and radical. He condemned poverty and supported the single tax, socialism, nonviolent resistance, and, for a time, anarchism, advocating these causes first as a minister and then as editor of the Freethought magazine *Twentieth Century* (1888–1898) until 1892. Pentecost publicly renounced his past politics in 1893 during an unsuccessful bid for a post as an assistant district attorney, severely damaging his reputation in radical circles, though he continued to espouse radical views until his death. **John Turner** (1865–1934) was an English-born labor organizer and anarchist. He was a member of London's Freedom Group, general secretary of the Shop Assistants' Union, and an advocate of revolutionary syndicalism. Turner toured the United States in 1896, but when he returned again in 1903 he was arrested and became the first person deported under the Anarchist Exclusion Act. **George Pettibone** (1862–1908) was an American-born miner and radical labor leader who belonged to the Western Federation of Miners. He was arrested in 1905 for alleged involvement in the assassination of former Idaho governor Frank Steunenberg and later acquitted. **William ("Big Bill") Haywood** (1869–1928) was an American-born miner and radical labor leader who counted many anarchists among his friends. He belonged to the Western Federation of Miners and Socialist Party of America and cofounded the syndicalist IWW in 1905. That same year he was also arrested for alleged involvement in the assassination of former Idaho governor Frank Steunenberg and acquitted. He was arrested again in 1917 as part of the mass federal trial of IWW leaders for allegedly conspiring to interfere

The impression made on the revolutionaries among the Jewish workers and intellectuals was immense. To whom other than Jewish and Russian revolutionaries could the martyrdom of innocent men have appealed so strongly? Anarchism in America received its baptism in the blood of the Chicago martyrs. The innocent victims left their idealism, motivation, and teachings as a legacy to the workers here, among whom it was taken up with great resolve by the Jews in the ghettoes of Chicago, New York, and other big cities. A distinct anarchist movement began to emerge among the Jewish immigrants of this country.

❄ ❄ ❄

Many comrades wonder to this very day why during the whole period of the Haymarket martys' imprisonment and after their execution, there came no act of vengeance against the legal murder of the innocent victims. The explanation is simple: during the time of the trial and up until the last day before their executions, it was still hoped that the state would not dare to carry out this horrible crime in the face of the great protests taking place in all corners of the world. When hope was beginning to vanish, there were brave individuals here and there who were willing to sacrifice themselves in an act of revenge. An older comrade related to me that one man left from Philadelphia with enough ammunition on him to blow up half of a city. But nothing happened. Why? Nobody knows except that the city of Chicago was well-guarded with police. Chicago was impossible for such an act. But we could never accept this explanation. A determined person could always find

---

with the war effort and sentenced to twenty years in prison. In 1921, while out on appeal, he fled to Soviet Russia, where he remained until his death. **George Brown** (1858–1915) was an English-born shoemaker and anarchist. After immigrating to Chicago in 1886 he joined the Knights of Labor and was present at the Haymarket bombing, in the aftermath of which he became an anarchist. In the early 1890s Brown moved to Philadelphia, where he participated in the Ladies' Liberal League and the Radical Library Group and contributed to anarchist newspapers like *Free Society* and *Lucifer, the Light Bearer*. **Saul Yanovsky** (Shoel-Yosef Yanovsky, 1864–1939) was a Russian-born Jewish editor and anarchist. He immigrated to the United States in 1885 and was soon a leading figure in New York's Yiddish-speaking anarchist movement. He briefly edited the anarchist newspaper *Di varhayt* (1889) and then moved to London, where he edited the *Arbeter fraynd* from 1891 to 1894. After returning to the United States, Yanovsky became editor of the *FAS* from 1899 to 1919.

Figure 6: The Haymarket Martyrs
Fraye arbeter shtime, November 7, 1890

a way. The Russian tsar could not hide forever from an assailant no matter how well guarded he was by an army of spies and soldiers.

In 1912, in a twenty-fifth anniversary account of the bloody tragedy put out by the magazine *Mother Earth*, we find the true explanation.[15] William Holmes, an intimate friend of Parsons, Spies, and Adolph Fischer,[16] in whose home Parsons hid during the first days after the explosion of the bomb, wrote: "I am growing old. I am in poor health and quite weary of life as it is to me. Of necessity I cannot last much longer. . . . I know that certain comrades were summoned to the County jail by Fischer and others, and cautioned to stop any and all movements with revenge as their object."[17] They saw that it would be more in accordance with our ideas if their martyrdom was unstained by human blood.

In the face of death, for the diffusion of our ideal and the betterment of the labor movement, they would die as martyrs, unblemished by human blood. Adolph Fischer, Holmes writes, personally communicated that he summoned to prison those comrades who were ready to do something, and he argued with them, convinced them, and forbade them to take steps in that direction. No one, you understand, would dare to do anything against the wishes of the martyrs.

---

15. **Mother Earth** (1906–1917) was an influential anarchist magazine published by Emma Goldman and edited by Alexander Berkman and Max Baginski. It was suppressed by the US government due to its opposition to the First World War.

16. **William T. Holmes** (1851–1928) was an English-born worker, teacher, labor organizer, and anarchist. He immigrated to the United States with his father at age six and in Chicago joined the SLP and then the American Branch of the IWPA. William and his wife, anarchist Lizzie M. Holmes, helped produce *The Alarm* and contributed to several other American anarchist newspapers well into the twentieth century. **Adolph Fischer** (1858–1887) was a German-born anarchist and editor. He immigrated to the United States in 1873 and in 1883 settled in Chicago, where he became a printer for the *Chicagoer Arbeiter-Zeitung* and joined the IWPA. Fischer coedited the short-lived newspaper *Der Anarchist* (The Anarchist, 1886) with fellow Haymarket defendants Georg Engel and Louis Lingg. He attended the Haymarket Square meeting but left before the bombing occurred. Fischer was one of the four defendants executed by hanging.

17. William Holmes, "Reminiscences," *Mother Earth*, November 1912, 287–91.

CHAPTER 3

The Flourishing of the Jewish Socialist Movement in America

The years 1886–87 marked the beginning of a new era in the development of the socialist movement in this country among the Jewish immigrant masses. The period of being schooled (*geyn in kheyder*) by the Germans and of imitating them in every detail had now ended. From then on, the Jewish movement went along on its own path and wrote its own history.

From their former teachers, the Germans, the Jewish workers inherited their forms of organization, terminology and political slogans, and the range of viewpoints and squabbles that divided the movement into enemy camps. The political socialists organized themselves into assembly districts and devoted themselves to electoral activities during campaign time. The revolutionary socialists—the anarchists, as they now began to call themselves—organized themselves into groups and occupied themselves mostly with education and union organizing.

The first Jewish anarchist organization took the high-sounding Germanic name Pionire der Frayheyt (Pioneers of Liberty), and it was composed of a number of intelligent Jewish workers who energetically carried on activity for a number of years.[1]

The Jewish workers brought to the movement a world of enthusiasm and a hopeful outlook. They honestly and completely believed every word of their new Torah, which they had only recently adopted, and at any moment they were ready to sacrifice everything in order to bring about the

---

1. The modern Yiddish rendering of this name would be "Pionirn di Frayheyt." The choice of a Germanized spelling reflected the influence of the German anarchist movement on the group. Its name is also sometimes translated as "Pioneers of Freedom."

Figure 7: "A Hebrew Anarchist Meeting at Military Hall in the Bowery"
Harper's Weekly, August 20, 1892

millennium (*geulah*), which according to the prophecies was just around
the corner. The workers' oppressive lives in their sweatshops and narrow,
pest-ridden tenement houses drove them to seek solace in the movement, in
the frequent gatherings for lectures, meetings, and assemblies. New York's
Lower East Side was full of life and activity. Not far behind were the Jewish
ghettoes of the country's other large cities. Everywhere, the socialist word
rang out and encouraged the downtrodden to fight for a better life.

All tendencies of the socialist movement stood together in this respect.
The anarchists displayed more devotion, more enthusiasm in their public
appearances—their activity for a time was more effective and successful. In
the words of observer Bernard Weinstein, a stubborn social democrat all his
years, the anarchist lectures at 56 Orchard Street were regularly attended by

hundreds of workers.[2] The social democrats, however, were not far behind in their activity. The rivalry between the two movements was over principles and consistency. Each side represented its standpoint with unwavering conviction and deep belief. The effect on the listeners was positive.

This, however, did not last long. The first local split came in 1888, in the "Russian Progressive Union," the members of which were Jewish workers.[3] The socialists confiscated the library and the few dollars in the organization's treasury, which they handed over to the Eighth Assembly District of the Socialist Labor Party (SLP).[4] When the anarchists brought the case before the central committee of the Eighth Assembly District, the committee decided in favor of the socialists. This was a foretaste of the struggle for hegemony that the social democrats would continue against the anarchists, and of the methods that they would resort to in this struggle.

A year later, in 1889, the anarchists made the first attempt to publish a weekly of their own, *Di varhayt* (The Truth). They brought over Joseph Jaffa from London, England, to be editor.[5] They also bought their own printing

---

2. **Bernard Weinstein** (1866–1946) was a Russian-born Jewish cigarmaker, union organizer, and socialist. He came to New York in 1881 as a member of Am Olam and soon became a prominent Jewish member of the SLP and later the Socialist Party of America, as well as secretary of the United Hebrew Trades. In his memoir, first published in Yiddish in 1929, Weinstein recalled: "The rallies of the Pioneers of Liberty were held in a hall at 56 Orchard Street every Friday night, and they drew between two to three hundred men and women. That was a lot in those days." *The Jewish Unions in America: Pages of History and Memories*, trans. Maurice Wolfthal (Cambridge: Open Book Publishers, 2018), 60.

3. **The Russian Progressive Union** was a short-lived organization founded by Russian-speaking Jewish immigrants in New York in 1886. It included both socialist and anarchist members.

4. **The Socialist Labor Party** (SLP), founded in 1876 as the Workingmen's Party of the United States, was the country's first socialist party. In 1881 social-revolutionary members split off to form the Revolutionary Socialist Labor Party, which in 1883 was absorbed into the anarchist International Working People's Association, and by the mid-1880s the membership of the IWPA surpassed that of the SLP. Another split in 1899 led to the formation of the competing Socialist Party of America, which quickly overtook the SLP, though the SLP maintained a nominal existence into the twenty-first century.

5. **Joseph Jaffa** (Yosef Yaffa, 1853–1915) was a Russian-born Jewish housepainter, writer, and anarchist. He was involved in the Jewish socialist movement in Germany and France before settling in London in 1887 and becoming editor of the *Arbeter fraynd*. After coming to the United States in 1887 he edited and contributed to many radical Yiddish periodicals, and he translated many works into Yiddish, including Johann Most's *The God Pestilence* (*Di gottes pest*, 1888), Alexandre Dumas's *The Count of Monte Cristo* (*Graf Monte Kristo*, 1899),

press and for several months' time, with hardship, published the newspaper but without success. They simply were not able to manage to sustain it. However, the desire to publish a paper was very great, and they already had the technical means for this purpose, a printing press, in their hands.

During this time the social democrats decided to organize the United Hebrew Trades, which was to play a considerable role in the conflict between the socialists and anarchists. It was not made up of Jewish unions already in existence—there were no such organizations at its founding. A few individuals representing the various socialist bodies gathered, which attracted a few people from the German-language socialist paper *New Yorker Volkszeitung* (New York People's Paper) and a representative from the United German Trades (Deutsche Vereignte Gewerkshaften) who came to show them how to establish such a union.[6] The Jewish labor organizations represented were two half-dead bodies, the typesetters and the choristers. Both unions combined numbered forty-five members.[7] With a donation of ten dollars sent by the German trade unions, the new central body began to function. This happened in 1888. The newly created United Hebrew Trades was entirely under the control of the social democrats. By the end of 1889, they had succeeded in organizing several small unions, the entire existence of which depended on the federation.

After the demise of the anarchist *Varhayt* the Pioneers of Liberty group continued with its broad array of educational activities. With the arrival of the High Holidays (*Yamim Noraim*), the group published thousands of copies of the first *Tefila zaka* (Pure Prayers), which made a strong impression in the Jewish quarter;[8] and they endeavored to put on a Yom Kippur gathering and ball, on the evening of Kol Nidre, in Clarendon Hall, where the Jewish

---

and Harriet Beecher Stowe's *Uncle Tom's Cabin* (*Onkl Toms kebin, oder di schvartse shklaven in Amerika,* 1911).

6. The *New Yorker Volkszeitung* (1878–1932) was the longest-running daily German-language socialist newspaper in the United States. Its editors included Sergei Shevitch and Ludwig Lore.

7. Other sources give their combined membership as either forty or seventy-five; see Morris U. Schappes, "The Political Origins of the United Hebrew Trades, 1888," *Journal of Ethnic Studies* 5, no. 1 (1977): 20.

8. *Tefila zaka la-yamim ha-nora'im, le-shabatot, le-mo'adim, u-lekhol yemot ha-shana* (A Pure Prayer for the Days of Awe, for Sabbaths, Holidays and for All Days of the Year) was a satirical antireligious publication produced annually on Yom Kippur by the Pioneers of Liberty from 1890 to 1894.

Figure 8: Satirical anarchist "prayers" for the Jewish High Holidays
*Tefila zaka la-yamim ha-nora'im, le-shabatot, le-mo'adim, u-lekhol
yemot ha-shana*, 1892

workers held all their assemblies and dances. The pious Jews, through the
medium of the police, appealed to the owner of Clarendon Hall to break his
contract and not open the hall that evening.

Thousands of people filled the streets around the hall. Thousands
more gathered to behold the evil wonder. Pious Jews leaving the synagogues after their prayers stopped to argue with the heretics. Fights broke
out, and the police moved in and dispersed the crowd. Reporters from the
English-language newspapers picked up on the story and spread it in their

publications. Certainly, from an agitational standpoint, the comrades gained more than they could ever hope to expect from a successful gathering.

Because of this publicity, the Pioneers were able to hold a huge protest meeting at the Cooper Union against the police and religious zealots, who had violated their rights to free assembly and free speech. The owner of Clarendon Hall, fearing that working people now would boycott his venue, compensated the Pioneers for their troubles with a considerable amount of money. Isidore Kopeloff, in his memoir *Amol in Amerike* (Once upon a Time in America), states that they received $500, which seems a bit exaggerated.[9]

In the autumn of 1889, the Pioneers of Liberty group possessed its own printing press and a considerable sum of money. But it did not wish to again publish its own partisan newspaper. The majority of members thought that a sectarian paper would not find enough support to exist. They had the examples of Abe Cahan's *Naye tsayt* (New Times) and of Dr. Charles Raevsky's attempt to publish the *Naye velt* (New World), as well as their own attempt with *Di varhayt*.[10] These papers were only able to exist for a few months.

They came to the conclusion that they should endeavor to interest the entire socialist movement in a communal newspaper, with a general socialist orientation of service and acceptable to all. With these forces united behind it, such a paper had some chance for survival.

They sent out a call to all the various socialist organizations throughout the country to attend a convention in New York City to be held the last week in December. The United Hebrew Trades answered with a demand that each of its unions be represented individually. Some members of the Pioneers

---

9. I. Kopeloff, *Amol in Amerike: zikhroynes fun dem yidishn lebn in Amerike in di yorn 1883–1904* (Warsaw: H. Bzshoza, 1928), 180. **Isidore Kopeloff** (Yisroel-Yekhiel Kopelof, 1858–1933), sometimes referred to as Israel Kopeloff, was a Russian-born Jewish anarchist and businessman. He arrived in New York in 1882 and, after joining the Pioneers of Liberty, wrote for several radical newspapers, including the *FAS* and the *Forverts*. In 1905 he became a supporter of Chaim Zhitlowlsky and socialist territorialism. After retiring from the Zimmerman Meat Company in 1917, he published three volumes of memoirs in Yiddish.

10. **Di naye tsayt** (1886), the first Yiddish-language socialist newspaper in the United States, folded after just four issues for lack of funds. **Charles Raevsky** (Tsharls Rayevsky, 1861–1930), real name Ezra Shamraevsky, was a Russian-born Jewish doctor and socialist. Active in revolutionary politics in his native Ukraine, he arrived in the United States around 1882 as a member of Am Olam and soon collaborated with Abe Cahan in publishing *Di naye tsayt*. Raevsky later became a contributor to the *Forverts*. **Naye velt** (1888) was a socialist newspaper that lasted just five issues.

were immediately suspicious that there was an ulterior motive behind this demand, but the group decided to comply and proceed with the preparations for the event.

The convention gathered on December 25, 1889, and thirty-one organizations were represented. Delegates came from New York, Philadelphia, Baltimore, Boston, Chicago, New Haven, Hartford, and several smaller cities. Around fifty delegates were present. The meetings took place at the Pioneers' premises in the Essex Market Hall on the corner of Essex and Grand Streets—a building that was city property.

The first order of business was the need for a working-class paper, which was quickly taken up. All delegates agreed that such a paper was necessary. But when the question of the orientation of the newspaper was raised the next day, the delegates engaged in debates that lasted from early morning until after midnight, every day for a week. The Pioneers proposed a general socialist paper in which every socialist tendency should be able to freely represent its position. In order to carry out this platform they suggested that the paper have two editors, one socialist and one anarchist. The social democrats under the leadership of Louis Miller opposed the proposal;[11] they laughed at it and called its defenders neither fish nor fowl (*pareve lokshn*). They insisted that the newspaper should be a social democratic publication—having come up with this idea at a meeting convened by the anarchists. Miller was helped in this noble work by his close friend Abe Cahan, who was not even a delegate and who kept his distance from the Jewish labor movement at that time. But Cahan came to every meeting of the convention to argue with all his might with visitors and delegates alike. When, even after all these heated debates, the delegates were evenly divided, the socialists demonstratively left the convention as a body and went off to do their own thing (*makhn shabes far zikh*).

One convention became two. Instead of one movement that would work more or less harmoniously in a single direction, there were now two hostile

---

11. **Louis E. Miller** (1866–1927), real name Efim Bandes, was a Russian-born Jewish union organizer, editor, and socialist. Active in the revolutionary movement in Vilna (present-day Vilnius), he emigrated to New York in 1884 and joined the SLP in 1888. Miller cofounded the socialist papers *Di arbeter tsaytung* and *Forverts* with Abe Cahan, but in 1905 he split with Cahan over Zionism, which Miller supported, and founded the rival *Di varhayt* (The Truth, 1905–1918), though he was removed as editor of that paper in 1915 for supporting the Allied war effort.

camps which from then on gave more time and energy to fighting each other than fighting their common enemy. The Jewish movement was embroiled in a fratricidal war, which had dire consequences for the weak unions and small educational groups. At the same time, however, it provoked a high level of passionate activity, fierce competition, and a strong will among those on each side to do everything possible for the success of their faction.

Here I must point out two historical facts in connection with this historical split. First, the anarchists never approved of factionalism. This was not the only occasion on which they stood up for united activity within the broad socialist movement. In every case of such splits, they always opposed such treacherous steps and demanded unity within the broader framework of socialism, in which each local organization should be free to conduct its activities in its own manner. Such was the case in the First International in the 1870s as well as in the Second International at the end of the 1880s and in the mid-1890s.[12] In each case it was the socialists who isolated themselves and clamored for a centralized, narrow, barracks-like discipline for all affiliated groups.

The second fact is that each split, made in the name of unity and longevity, led to the opposite—more fragmentation, more disintegration—especially in the case of the split in the Jewish labor movement with which we are dealing here. It was the beginning of a series of splits that continued for fifty years, erupting with great bitterness every four or five years. The split between the socialists and anarchists was followed a few years later by an even more bitter split in the socialists' own ranks: the fights between the De Leonites and the

---

12. **The First International** (officially named the International Workingmen's Association, 1864–1876) was a global coalition of socialist and labor organizations founded in London. In 1872 Mikhail Bakunin and his anarchist supporters were expelled and reconstituted their own Anti-Authoritarian International that continued to function until 1877, with some local sections continuing into the 1880s. The original organization, left under the control of the Marxists, relocated its headquarters to New York City in 1872 but dissolved soon after. **The Second International** (1880–1920) was a global coalition of socialist political parties founded in Paris in 1889 as the successor of the First International. Although many anarchist organizations attempted to join the organization—Saul Yanovsky, for example, was a delegate for London's Berner Street Club to its 1891 congress in Brussels—they were officially excluded at its 1893 Zurich congress. The Second International was irrevocably split by the First World War, when many member parties supported their countries' war efforts and others, including the Socialist Party of America and the Bolshevik faction of the Russian Social Democratic Labor Party, took a firm antimilitarist stance.

"kangaroos" and "skunks," as they nobly designated each other,[13] and the fights between Abe Cahan and Joseph Barondess, Abe Cahan and Louis Miller, Abe Cahan and Jacob Gordin, between the "old ones" (*alte*) and the "young ones" (*yunge*), between the *Forverts* and the Jewish Socialist Federation, between the *Forverts* and the *Tsukunft*, and dozens of other wars that kept the Jewish community in a state of disarray and reached its climax in the split between the "Rights" and the "Lefts," and those affiliated with the "Lovestoneites" and "Trotskyists," as they were afterward called.[14] With a clear conscience we can

13. **Daniel De Leon** (1852–1914) was a Dutch West Indies–born attorney and socialist. After graduating from Columbia University Law School, he became a supporter of Henry George and then in 1890 joined the SLP. In 1892 De Leon became editor of the SLP newspaper *The People* (1891–2008) and was soon the intellectual leader of the party. His rigid adherence to Marxist orthodoxy (as he understood it) led to numerous political rivalries and organizational splits.

14. **Joseph Barondess** (Yosef Barondes, 1867–1928) was a Russian-born Jewish garment worker, labor organizer, and radical. The son of a Hassidic rabbi, in 1885 he immigrated to London, where he was active in the Jewish labor movement. After moving to New York in 1888, he became an organizer for the Cloakmakers' Union and the United Hebrew Trades. Barondess was sympathetic to anarchism and contributed to the *FAS*, but after 1895 he aligned himself with the SLP and then the Socialist Party of America, and he later became a Zionist. In 1900 he helped create the ILGWU, and in 1919 he cofounded the American Jewish Congress. **Jacob Gordin** (Yankev Gordin, 1853–1909) was a Russian-born Jewish writer and socialist. After immigrating to the United States in 1891 he contributed to Russian and Yiddish socialist papers, including the *Arbeter tsaytung* and *Forverts*, and joined the SLP and then the Socialist Party of America. However, Gordin is best known as the preeminent playwright of the American Yiddish theater and author of such plays as *Der idisher kenig Lir* (The Yiddish King Lear, 1892) and *Got, mentsh un tayvl* (God, Man, and the Devil, 1900). **Forverts** (1897–2019), often referred to in English as *The Jewish Daily Forward*, was a socialist newspaper founded by a group of dissident SLP members, including Louis Miller and Abe Cahan, who resented Daniel De Leon's dogmatic control of the party and instead aligned themselves with the Social Democratic Party of America, which in 1901 became the Socialist Party. The *Forverts* soon became the most popular Yiddish newspaper in the United States, peaking at a circulation of more than two hundred thousand copies per issue in 1917. It ceased its print edition in 2019 but as of 2024 still exists as an online news source. **The Jewish Socialist Federation** (1912–1921) was founded at a convention in Paterson, New Jersey, as the Yiddish-language federation of the Socialist Party of America. Cahan and the *Forverts* opposed its formation on the grounds that it fostered "separatism" in the socialist movement. By 1915 the federation claimed five thousand members. The organization split at its 1921 convention between a majority that voted to disaffiliate from the Socialist Party and join the Communist International, and a minority that walked out and formed the Jewish Socialist Verband of the Socialist Party, which lasted into the 1980s. **Di tsukunft** (The Future, 1892–1897, 1902–2013) was founded as a monthly theoretical journal of the SLP under the editorship of Philip Krantz and then Abe Cahan, but it suspended publication in 1897 because of the split in the

say that the history of the Jewish socialist movement in America has been, since 1889, the history of insurmountable divisions, strife, and bitter internal struggles in the movement itself.

Returning to the story of the convention, we now had two factions, each with the dedicated purpose of putting out a newspaper for the enlightenment of the Jewish working masses. For reasons that are now completely incomprehensible, the socialists were able to quickly finish the preparatory work of raising funds, buy a printing press, import Philip Krantz from London as editor, and begin publishing their *Arbeter tsaytung* (The Workers' Newspaper).[15] The first issue appeared on March 7, just two months after the convention.

The anarchists had a more difficult time even though they had their own printing press, an inheritance from the defunct *Varhayt*, as well as the funds received from the landlord for the canceled Yom Kippur ball. The only plausible explanation I can find is that, for some time after the split, the anarchists still believed that reconciliation could be reached. For this

---

party's Jewish membership. In was revived in 1902 by the Workmen's Circle and exchanged bitter recriminations with the *Forverts*, which the journal accused of watering down socialism and practicing yellow journalism to increase sales. In 1913, however, the *Tsukunft* was itself purchased by the Forverts Association and became a major forum for Yiddish literature and criticism, publishing many socialist as well as anarchist writers. The Communist Party (Opposition) (1929–1940), popularly known as **Lovestoneites**, emerged under the leadership of former general secretary of the Communist Party USA Jay Lovestone (1897–1990). Lovestone and other supporters of Soviet leader Nikolai Bukharin, known internationally as the "Right Opposition," were expelled from their respective Communist Parties following Stalin's consolidation of power. Though the Lovestoneites never counted more than fifteen hundred members, several were influential members of the ILGWU and the International Fur and Leather Workers Union, and in the 1930s they allied with anarchist members to form "Progressive" factions within both organizations. American **Trotskyism** emerged in 1928 following the expulsion of members of the "Left Opposition," which supported Leon Trotsky's critiques of the Communist International's leadership, from the Worker's Party of America (as the Communist Party was known at the time). The expelled members formed the Communist League of America (1928–1934) and Workers Party of the United States (1934–1936), before entering the Socialist Party of America en masse but were expelled in 1937 and went on to form the Socialist Workers Party (1938–present)—which has never exceeded fifteen hundred members—and various smaller splinter groups.

15. **Di arbeter tsaytung** (1890–1902) appeared as a weekly organ of the SLP and the United Hebrew Trades, edited by Philip Krantz and then Abe Cahan. It quickly rose from a circulation of around six thousand copies to eleven thousand in 1894. In 1897 Cahan and most of the *Arbeter tsaytung*'s publishing committee broke away to found the *Forverts*.

purpose, they sent speakers across the country, distributed thousands of leaflets explaining the damage that fraternal strife in the movement would cause, and demanded unity within socialist ranks. As a matter of fact, from all sides protests against the decision to publish an exclusively partisan newspaper began to spread. The Wendell Phillips Club from Providence, Rhode Island, the Chicago Workers' Educational Club (Arbeter Forbildungs Fareyn), and other social-democratic groups, not to mention anarchist organizations from all over the country, all protested vigorously. Cahan, Miller, and company paid no attention to the protests and continued their work.

Finally, having no choice, the anarchists came out with the first issue of their own newspaper, the *Fraye arbeter shtime* (The Free Voice of Labor), on July 4, 1890.[16] The editor, Roman Lewis, was an energetic young man, very capable, but he was not a successful editor.[17] The paper had to compete with the socialist *Arbeter tsaytung* which was already established and better composed. The *Fraye arbeter shtime* rotated through a series of editors. From Roman Lewis, the editorship passed into the hands of Dr. Jacob A. Maryson— one of the most sincere activists in our movement, an original thinker and clear theorist, but by nature he was not suited to the rigorous work of putting out a weekly paper.[18] He was only editor until the annual convention at

---

16. The ***Fraye arbeter shtime*** (1890–93, 1899–1977) was the second-longest running anarchist publication in the world (after London's *Freedom*) and, with a peak circulation of thirty thousand copies in 1914, one the largest and most influential anarchist newspapers in American history.

17. **Roman Lewis** (Roman Louis or Luis, 1864–1918) was a Russian-born Jewish garment worker and anarchist. He immigrated to the United States in the mid-1880s and joined the Russian Progressive Union and the Pioneers of Liberty and was also an organizer for the Cloakmakers' Union. As Cohen later narrates, Lewis left the anarchist movement in 1892, and he later took his own life.

18. **Jacob Abraham Maryson** (Yankev-Avrom Merison, 1866–1941), born Yankev-Avrom Yerukhimovitsh, was a Russian-born Jewish medical doctor, writer, translator, and anarchist. A well-educated and gifted linguist by the time he immigrated to the United States in 1887, he worked in a garment sweatshop while earning his medical degree at Columbia University, which he completed in 1892. Maryson also became one of the Yiddish anarchist movement's most respected writers and intellectuals—earning the moniker "the Kropotkin of the Jewish anarchist movement"—and married fellow anarchist doctor and intellectual Katherina (Katerina) Yevzerov (1870–1928). In 1913 Maryson founded the Kropotkin Literary Society, which published his translations of works by Henry David Thoreau, Herbert Spencer, Karl Marx, Errico Malatesta, and Peter Kropotkin, among others. He continued to write for the anarchist press up until his death.

Figure 9: David Edelstadt
Courtesy of the Joseph A. Labadie Collection, University
of Michigan

the end of 1890, when he resigned. The burden was then taken up by David
Edelstadt, who had arrived the previous year as a delegate from Cincinnati.[19]

---

19. **David Edelstadt** or Edelshtat (Dovid Edelshtadt, 1866–1892) was a Russian-born
Jewish garment worker, poet, editor, and anarchist. Raised in a Russified Jewish family, he
came to the United States in 1882 as a member of Am Olam. While living in Cincinnati,
Edelstadt became influenced by the anarchism of the IWPA and was fully radicalized by the
Haymarket executions. He moved to New York in 1889 and began contributing poems to *Varhayt* and other anarchist newspapers. Edelstadt contracted tuberculosis and in 1891 moved
to Denver, where he died the following year at age twenty-six. His "proletarian" poetry was
immensely popular and influential, and many of his works were later put to music and sung
by Jewish workers and radicals around the world.

Edelstadt infused the *Fraye arbeter shtime* with his poetic soul and the lifeblood of his noble, suffering heart. Much later, when I had the honor and privilege to be at the helm of the paper, I always kept Edelstadt's photograph on my desk to remind me of the warmth of his wonderful personality, and to remind me of the legacy he left us. Edelstadt's diseased lungs could not cope with the rigors of the hard work and appallingly poor living conditions in the editorial office of the paper. We were forced to send him to a sanatorium in Denver, where he died on October 17, 1892.

Moyshe Katz was next chosen as editor.[20] A prolific journalist in later years, he wrote a column for the *Forverts* from shortly after its founding and also became editor of the *Yidishe velt* (Jewish World) in Philadelphia,[21] but he could not make a go of it with the *Fraye arbeter shtime*. The paper struggled for its existence, and it was only through the superhuman efforts of our poor comrades that issue after issue of their beloved newspaper was able to appear. Isidore Kopeloff tells of a comrade named Morris Diamond who gave his last few dollars of rent money for his tenement apartment to the newspaper and was evicted with his family.[22] So great was the devotion of the comrades to their publication. But despite all the sacrifices, at the beginning of the summer of 1892, the *Fraye arbeter shtime* was forced to suspend publication. In the spring of 1893 a new attempt at publication was made; for all the hard work, this also failed. After new hardships, the *Fraye arbeter shtime* had to shut down again, this time for many years.

---

20. **Moyshe Katz** (Moyshe Kats or Katts, 1864–1941) was a Russian-born Jewish journalist, playwright, and anarchist. In Russia he moved from the Narodnik movement to the Socialist-Revolutionary Party to Zionism. After fleeing to the United States in 1888 to avoid arrest and joining the anarchist movement in New York, Katz quickly became one of its foremost speakers and writers. Following a series of pogroms in Russia in 1905, he became a supporter of the Labor Zionist movement Poale Zion but continued to consider himself an anarchist. Katz also wrote plays, contributed to many Yiddish newspapers, and was literary editor of the *Forverts* from 1900 to 1905. In 1912 he moved to Philadelphia, where he continued to financially support anarchist causes but was no longer active in the movement.

21. **Di yidishe velt** (1913–1942) was a daily newspaper edited by Moyshe Katz, and the most popular Yiddish paper in Philadelphia. It had no fixed political orientation but leaned toward a "progressive-national" stance and published writings by anarchists such as Abraham Frumkin.

22. Kopeloff, *Amol in Amerike*, 340–41. **Morris Diamond** (Moris Daymond, 1856–1926) was a Russian-born Jewish furrier and anarchist. In the 1880s he immigrated to London, where he first joined the Yiddish anarchist movement, then came to New York in 1888 and was a dedicated supporter of the *FAS*. Obituary: *FAS*, December 31, 1926.

This failure was caused in part by the socialists and the associated United Hebrew Trades, organized some two years before the launch of the paper. The printing shop of the *Fraye arbeter shtime* employed a number of typesetters—union men, of course. At that time there were no linotype machines, and the type was set by hand, which meant that a weekly newspaper had to employ many workers, as well as a foreman, also a union man, who had to finish the galley by early Wednesday morning in order for the issue to be ready for the press in the afternoon.

One fine morning the foreman, a man by the name of Y. Milkhiker, arrived at work as usual. But after a short while he suddenly took off his work apron and left. Two hours went by, a whole day passed, and still no foreman. The paper was not ready for the press. The next morning, the foreman came back to work and acted as if nothing had happened. When the comrades asked for an explanation, he began to shout, "What kind of anarchists are you? Does a worker have to account for where he has been? I went where I wanted! To a see a broad or to go to a saloon—it's none of your business!"

Such insolence was more than the comrades could bear. They strongly suspected it was a trick on the part of their rivals at the *Arbeter tsaytung* so that the *Fraye arbeter shtime* should not appear on schedule. They dismissed the man, and a committee, composed of Kopeloff and Dr. Hillel Solotaroff, was sent to the typesetters' union to tell them what had happened and ask for the foreman's replacement.[23] To the astonishment of the committee, the president of the union insisted that Milkhiker should continue as foreman in the print shop. When the committee refused to accept this verdict, the typesetters called a strike against the *Fraye arbeter shtime*.

It was not hard to get Jewish typesetters at the time. Only a small fraction of them, as in all other trades, were unionized. And, as in other trades, the typesetters' union stood on shaky legs—one day there was a union, and the next day it was no more. But in the case of the strike against the *Fraye*

---

23. **Hillel Solotaroff** (Hilel Zolotarov, 1865–1921) was a Russian-born Jewish doctor, writer, and anarchist. He immigrated to the United States with his parents in 1882 as part of the Am Olam movement, and soon joined the Jewish anarchist movement, becoming one of its foremost speakers and writers. Solotaroff worked in his father's tailor shop while earning his medical degree at New York University and contributed to a wide range of Yiddish anarchist newspapers. Although he later supported socialist territorialism and Labor Zionism, he remained an anarchist until his death. His collected writings were posthumously published in Yiddish in three volumes.

ישראל קאָפּעלאװ   מיכאל קאהן

משה קאַטץ   הלל זאָלאָטאַראָװ

Figure 10: Four prominent Jewish anarchists

Clockwise from top left: Isidore Kopeloff, Michael A. Cohn, Hillel Solotaroff, and Moyshe Katz; from Elias Tcherikower, ed., *Geshikhte fun der yidisher arbeter-bavegung in di Fareynikte Shtatn*, 1945, courtesy of the YIVO Institute for Jewish Research

arbeter shtime, the typesetters' union showed remarkable strength. Moreover, all the other trade unions in United Hebrew Trades immediately came to its aid and imposed a boycott of the *Fraye arbeter shtime*. A committee took to the streets to confiscate the *Fraye arbeter shtime* from the newsstands, carrying on a vigorous campaign against the paper.

The anarchists answered in kind. They encouraged the typesetters in their shop to join the "Big 6" local of the International Typographical Union—the largest union local in the country. In the name of unionism, the anarchists fought the United Hebrew Trades and its unions and publications. It was a lively struggle that did neither side any good, neither the *Fraye arbeter shtime* nor certainly the unions either. Everywhere, people were at each other's throats, fighting, defaming, and spitting upon one another. The socialists were masters at this sort of thing, better than the anarchists. Louis Miller, for example, was beyond compare.

Benjamin Feigenbaum—a devoted social democrat all his life—wrote much later about the methods his comrades used against the anarchists: "I refused the invitation to become a contributor to the *Arbeter tsaytung* because it led the criminally exaggerated and absolutely immoral attacks on the anarchists."[24]

In their general educational activities, socialist historians (Bernard Weinstein, Hertz Burgin, etc.) admit that the anarchists were more successful than the socialists in this era.[25] They had more enthusiasm and sincere

---

24. *Yubileum-shrift tzu Ab. Cahans 50stn geburtstog* (New York: Jubilee Committee, 1910), 67 [Cohen's note]. **Benjamin Feigenbaum** (Benyomen Feygenboym, 1860–1932) was a Russian-born Jewish writer, editor, and socialist. Born into a Hassidic family and educated in a Yeshivah in Warsaw, he became an ardent atheist at a young age. In 1884 Feigenbaum moved to Belgium, where he quickly joined the socialist movement and began writing for radical Yiddish publications. In 1888 he accepted an invitation to edit the *Arbeter fraynd* in London, where that same year he organized the first antireligious Yom Kippur Ball—an institution that would later become associated with Jewish anarchists. Feigenbaum immigrated to New York in 1891, was later a regular contributor to the *Forverts* and *Tsukunft*, and from 1900 to 1903 served as the first secretary of the Workmen's Circle. Feigenbaum was best known for his atheist and anti-Zionist writings.

25. **Hertz Burgin** (Herts Burgin Shmuel, 1870–1949) was a Russian-born Jewish teacher, writer, and socialist. In 1903 he was exiled to Siberia for radical activities but escaped and came to the United States, where he contributed to the *Forverts* and *Tsukunft* as well other Yiddish and Russian publications and became a national officer in the Workmen's Circle. In 1915 Burgin was commissioned by the United Hebrew Trades to write a history of the Jewish labor movement, and the resulting book, *Di geshikhte fun der yidisher arbayter-bavegung in*

devotion to the work. But in building and maintaining labor unions, these same historians claim that the socialists were more successful, although they do not give facts to substantiate these claims. Their activity in the unions consisted of introducing politics, influencing the unions to support their socialist publications and to support their candidates during campaigns, which was very divisive to the membership. For example, when the socialists were instrumental in the founding of the United Garment Workers, they pushed through a resolution in support of the *Arbeter tsaytung, The People*, and the *Folkstsaytung* as labor organs.[26] This provoked a sharp protest from the United Tailors' Union local in Philadelphia and other groups. This brought about a sharp conflict in the needle trades until the United Garment Workers joined the AFL and became the most reactionary organization among the local workers. This was the fruit of the socialist education that Abe Cahan and Louis Miller gave to them.

At that time, the Cloakmakers' Union had an even worse experience. In the summer of 1890 a big cloakmakers' strike that had lasted for several months ended in victory for the strikers. Their leader was Joseph Barondess, a socialist very much influenced by the anarchists, who were among the most active members of the militant union. His socialist comrades never forgave him for this crime. Bernard Weinstein makes this terrible accusation against Barondess: "He invited his new comrades, the anarchist speakers, to his meetings!" A little later, Weinstein writes:

> The Jewish anarchists of the day thought that with the help of Barondess, they would be able to convert all cloakmakers to anarchism. During the elections for officials and executive board members, there were continual struggles between social democrats and anarchists. But

---

Amerike, Rusland un England (The History of the Jewish Labor Movement in America, Russia, and England), remains an essential work on the topic. He later became a leading figure of the left wing of the Socialist Party and then joined the Communist Party.

26. **The United Garment Workers of America** (1891–1994) was a union of menswear workers founded in 1891. It immediately absorbed the existing United Tailors' Union, one of the first unions organized by the United Hebrew Trades, but affiliated with the AFL and became increasingly hostile to radicalism, leading several socialist-dominated locals to break away in 1910 to form the Amalgamated Clothing Workers of America. **The People** (1891–2008) was the official English-language newspaper of the SLP and the longest-running radical periodical in the United States. From 1892 to 1914 it was edited by Daniel De Leon.

the great majority of the cloakmakers knew very little about anarchism, despite the fact that they often elected anarchists to office. They voted for anarchists just to please Barondess, which ultimately weakened the influence of the socialist unions' central bodies, the Central Labor Federation and the United Hebrew Trades. The result was that all the active delegates of the German- and English-speaking unions helped to build the, at the time, mighty Cloakmakers' Union, consisting of 7,000 dues-paying members.[27]

Weinstein would like to give credit for building the Cloakmakers' Union to the delegates of the English and German unions, who at best could not contribute much in this area, rather than to Barondess and his anarchist collaborators, who had actually built the union and brought it to a position that would not be matched during twenty years of subsequent socialist leadership.

A year later the employers tried break free from the union, but they were not successful. By this point the union was large and strong and well-known in the city. There was a whole wave of strikes in New York that ended in complete victory for the workers. Only one scab-ridden shop hidden away on Long Island remained because it was too difficult to reach. Finally a committee of brave workers traveled to Long Island to give the scabs a lesson in loyalty to their fellow workers, and in the tumult a little heating stove was overturned and burned the child of the scabs' contractor. The committee was able to get away except for one member, Frank Reingold, who was detained by police during the ferry ride to New York. The next morning, the boss had Barondess and the whole executive committee arrested. The capitalist press made a fuss, claiming that the workers used acid and scorched little children. The arrested men were put under $10,000 bail each.

The union was able to put up bail for Barondess, but as soon as he was released he was arrested on another charge: he was accused of extorting money from a manufacturer. The union again raised the money for his bail.

---

27. Bernard Weinstein, *Fertsik yor in der idisher arbeter bavegung* (New York: Der Veker, 1924), 142 [Cohen's note]. **The Central Labor Federation of New York** was founded in June 1890 by eighty-five delegates representing thirty-nine socialist-leaning unions, under the auspices of the SLP. The organization applied for membership in the AFL in 1890 and 1893 but was rejected both times. In 1895 it was absorbed into the SLP's new Socialist Trade and Labor Alliance, but it withdrew from that body in 1898.

The Long Island court freed all the men except for Reingold, who was given a sentence of five years in prison. An appeal to the governor, backed by all the unions, was able to get him freed after six months.

At the second trial of Barondess, on the false charge of extortion—he had once made a point of forcing a boss to make out a check of $200 to him personally for a fine that the union had imposed against him as punishment—he was sentenced to one year and nine months in prison. Again the union raised bail money. Again Barondess acted foolishly. During the appeal he fled to Canada. The bondsman had to travel to Canada to convince Barondess to return to New York. In the meantime, the appeal was dismissed by the court and Barondess was put in jail. A movement for an appeal to the governor to release Barondess began immediately. It soon collected over half a million names. The American unions supported the appeal, and the governor saw fit to pardon him.

However, the socialists were unable to forgive Barondess for his collaboration with the anarchists and perhaps for his energetic and militant methods in his union struggles. Louis Miller chastised Barondess in the June 10 issue of the *Arbeter tsaytung*, as only he knew how to, for accepting the governor's pardon.[28] This precipitated a bitter struggle by the socialists against the influence of Barondess in the union. During Barondess's trouble with the law, Cahan took Barondess's place in the union and, with the help of Miller, reduced the organization to a small number of members who continued to quarrel and split each other's heads open.

We could continue to give many such examples of what terrible effect that the split between the socialists and the anarchists wrought upon the labor movement of that time, but that would be redundant. These two are sufficient to establish the facts and to prove what methods the socialists used in their holy struggle.

Eventually there was fighting in their own socialist ranks. Morris Winchevsky, editor of the paper *Der emes* (The Truth), wrote on August 9, 1895, asking the question of his own party: "Is it rotten or putrefied?"[29] In

---

28. Hertz Burgin, *Di geshikhte fun der yidisher arbayter-bavegung in Amerike, Rusland un England* (New York: Fareynigte Idishe Geverkshaften, 1915), 768 [Cohen's note].

29. **Morris Winchevsky** (Moris Vintshevsky, 1856–1932), real name Lipe Bentsien Novakhovits, was a Russian-born Jewish writer, poet, editor, and socialist. In 1879, to avoid arrest, he fled to London, where he adopted the name Morris Winchevsky, befriended

return, Abe Cahan, editor of the *Arbeter tsaytung,* named the other paper
"The House of Lords." Daniel De Leon meanwhile had organized the Socialist Trade and Labor Alliance in opposition to the existing unions, whose
members he called "skunks" and "kangaroos."[30] There were all kinds of
name-calling between the various splinters. Each agitated the Jewish workers in the name of socialism and set them one against the other as if they had
no other care in the world. Hertz Burgin, in his history of the Jewish labor
movement, writes about the harsh language of this era:

> De Leon blamed Miller and Hourwich; Hourwich attacked De Leon;
> the *Abend blat* accused Hourwich; Miller ridiculed the *Abend blat;*
> Krantz called Miller a "scoundrel" (*kanalie*); Miller sued the *Abend blat*
> for $5,000; the *Abend blat* countered by stating that the *Forverts* was
> falsifying the facts; Meyer London printed a leaflet that was widely dis-
> tributed accusing the SLP of dishonesty; the *Abend blat* made charges
> against Cahan, who made counter-charges and denials, etc. It was a
> ridiculous symphony (*khad gadya*) of accusations and demoralizing
> insinuations.[31]

Johann Most, and participated in German socialist organizations. In 1884 he began publishing *Der poylisher yidl* (The Little Polish Jew), one of the first radical Yiddish newspapers
in the world, which in 1885 he replaced with the *Arbeter fraynd,* and became well-known
for his radical satires and poems. Winchevsky immigrated to New York in 1894 and joined
the SLP but sided with Louis Miller and Abe Cahan in the 1897 split, helping to launch the
Forverts and eventually joining the Socialist Party of America. However, he soon broke with
Cahan and the *Forverts* and after 1919 became a supporter of the Communist Party. *Der emes*
(1895–1896) was a short-lived newspaper published by the Jewish Section of Boston's SLP
in an attempt to transcend factionalism in the SLP. Morris Winchevsky, however, published
editorials criticizing the party's editorial control of its newspapers, leading to his dismissal
and the closure of the paper.

30. **The Socialist Trade and Labor Alliance** was a labor union federation formed in
1895 by former members of the Knights of Labor who belonged to the SLP. By 1898 it had
chartered 228 locals and claimed thirty thousand members, but it never functioned as an
effective labor organization and was soon reduced to a few thousand members. In 1905 it was
absorbed into the new IWW. Its members included anarchist and future ILGWU president
Morris Sigman.

31. Burgin, *Di geshikhte fun der yidisher arbayter-bavegung,* 436 [Cohen's note]. **Isaac
Aronovich Hourwich** (Yitskhok-Ayzik Halevi Hurvitsh, 1860–1924) was a Russian-born
Jewish lawyer, economist, and radical. In 1890 he fled to the United States to avoid arrest and
remained an independent radical who at various points supported the anarchists, Edward
Bellamy's "nationalist" movement, the SLP, the Progressive Party, the Socialist Party of

In their fights with the socialists, the anarchists did not emerge with entirely clean hands. The mudslinging left each side splattered. It was impossible for either side to avoid falling into the position of the adversary. But in comparison with the socialists, the anarchists were innocence personified. Our comrades never allowed themselves to be dragged down into the swamp of calumny where Louis Miller, Abe Cahan, and his associates had dragged Jewish socialism.

Despite all the evils that have been pointed out, for the movement of that time, both the socialists and the anarchists, this was a flourishing period. The enthusiasm and eagerness were great. Most of the participants acted in these struggles from the highest motives, and they fought for what they believed in. All historians and memoirists speak with warmth and longing for the good old days, when socialism was young and vibrant in the Jewish community.

America, and Zionism. He wrote for variety of radical publications, including the *FAS*, and briefly served on that paper's editorial board in 1891. Hourwich earned a PhD in economics from Columbia University in 1893 and in 1919 he became a legal advisor to the Russian Soviet Government Bureau in New York.He briefly visited Soviet Russia in 1922, which led him to become a critic of communism—though his son, Nicholas Hourwich (1882–1934), was a founding member of the Communist Party of America and later immigrated to the Soviet Union. Hourwich's unfinished autobiography, "Zikhroynes fun an apikoyres" (Memoirs of a Heretic), was serialized in the *FAS* from November 11, 1921 through December 28, 1923.

 Dos abend blat (The Evening Sheet, 1894–1902) was established by the SLP as the first Yiddish socialist daily newspaper in the world. Its first editor was Philip Krantz, and disagreements between Krantz his supporters, on the one hand, and Abe Cahan and his supporters, on the other, precipitated the 1897 split within the SLP that led to the founding of the *Forverts*. **Meyer London** (1871–1926) was a Russian-born Jewish attorney, politician, and socialist. His father, Ephraim London (1850–1911), was a former Talmudic scholar turned anarchist printer who published a short-lived radical paper, *Der morgenshtern* (The Morningstar, 1890), in New York. Meyer joined his father in the United States in 1891 and earned his law degree at New York University. He also belonged to the SLP until the 1897 split, then joined the Socialist Party of America. London was elected to the House of Representatives on the Socialist Party ticket from 1914 to 1918 and again from 1920 to 1922.

CHAPTER 4

Anarchists' Activities in the 1880s and 1890s

Among the other educational activities that occupied our comrades in the late 1880s and for a long time afterward, antireligious agitation was the field on which the Jewish anarchists largely concentrated. Their efforts were centered mostly on the holy days of the New Year, Rosh Hashana and Yom Kippur. For several years, beginning in 1889, the anarchists would print their own "new" version of the Yom Kippur prayer (*Tefila zaka*), which would be distributed by the thousands. On Yom Kippur, the holiest of days, they arranged meetings and entertainment—Yom Kippur balls, the main feature of which were speeches on religion—to which large crowds would come, which brought the anarchists into serious confrontations with observant religious Jews.

I have told of the Yom Kippur ball in 1889, which was to have taken place at Clarendon Hall and was prevented from occurring by the machinations of the Orthodox Jews with the police, forcing the owner of the hall to pay a sizable sum of money for damages. In 1890, the Pioneers were able to rent the Labor Lyceum in Brooklyn, owned by German socialists whom the police could not intimidate. Here the comrades thought that they could spend the evening undisturbed and with great success. They announced that Johann Most would be the featured speaker, and this alone they thought would certainly draw a big audience. But these calculations underestimated of the viciousness of the opposition. It was true that the police could not intimidate the executive board of the Labor Lyceum, but this was not the only method by which the police could disrupt a meeting. This time they simply captured the hall, filling it with their own people in civilian clothes, and declared that there was little room left for visitors. They would allow only a small number of people to enter. And, of course, no speakers could lecture. Under these circumstances the undertaking had to be abandoned. The German Reform Jews and the Orthodox Jews had united for this maneuver with the police. Rabbi Marcus Friedlander had translated the leaflet announcing the ball from Yiddish into English and smuggled in a few words about dynamite and bombs that were not in the original text.[1] This translation was provided to the police, who were, of course, shocked and took strong measures to prevent the dissemination of such dangerous material to the public.[2] The *Fraye arbeter shtime* of September 26, 1890, reports that five thousand people sought admission to the Yom Kippur ball and were turned away by the brutal obstruction of the police.

In Philadelphia our comrades had an even worse experience with a Yom Kippur meeting the following year. At that time our movement was very successful in that city. In 1915 Hertz Burgin, writing the official *History of the Jewish Labor Movement*, declared in the chapter on the United Hebrew Trades: "The anarchist propaganda found a good foothold, mostly in Philadelphia, which became a stronghold of the Jewish anarchists. Even today Philadelphia has plenty of anarchist elements."[3]

He states further that, in 1890, anarchists in Philadelphia had two active groups, the Riter der Frayheyt (Knights of Liberty) and the Pioneers of Liberty.[4] Both groups were active in the labor movement as well as in the general educational work. The comrades decided in 1891 to celebrate Yom

---

1. **Marcus Friedlander** (1862–1944) was a German-born Jewish Reform rabbi who headed the Ninth Street Temple in Brooklyn from 1888 to 1893. On his translation of the leaflet, see *Brooklyn Daily Eagle*, September 25, 1890.

2. N. Goldberg, "Di antireligyeze bavegung," in *Geshikhte fun der yidisher arbeter-bavegung in di Fareynikte Shtatn*, ed. Elias Tcherikower, vol. 2 (New York: YIVO, 1945), 466 [Cohen's note].

3. Hertz Burgin, *Di geshikhte fun der yidisher arbayter-bavegung in Amerike, Rusland un England* (New York: Fareynigte Idishe Geverkshaften, 1915), 340 [Cohen's note].

4. **The Knights of Liberty** (sometimes translated as Knights of Freedom) was established in Philadelphia in 1889 by Jewish immigrants who had been active in a group of the same name formed in London in 1887. Similarly named counterparts soon appeared in New York and Boston. The Philadelphia group lasted until 1900 and grew, according to member Chaim Weinberg, to a membership of 120. Chaim Leib Weinberg, *Forty Years in the Struggle: The Memoirs of a Jewish Anarchist*, ed. Robert P. Helms, trans. Naomi Cohen (Duluth: Litwin Books, 2008), 24.

Kippur with a meeting on the evening of Kol Nidre and a picnic the following day of Yom Kippur in Camden, New Jersey. The Orthodox Jews, having gotten wind of the coming Yom Kippur affair, informed the police that a Mr. Moscowitz, while handing out leaflets to the public announcing the ball, had made incendiary, subversive speeches advocating assassination of all high-ranking government officials.

The Orthodox Jews had great hatred for Julius Moscowitz.[5] Unwittingly, he had played a prank on them a year or two before that they could not forget or forgive. He was owner of a little stand in a market on Bainbridge Street, between Third and Fifth Streets, where he sold rice, beans, barley, and other cereals. Across the market opposite the stand was a big synagogue. One bright Yom Kippur day, Mr. Moscowitz decided to show his contempt and defiance against religion by opening his stand as usual. Peacefully, he sat reading his *Tefila zaka* (the version put out by his anarchist group). He expected no customers. This was his personal demonstration. When the Jews in their yarmulkes and prayer shawls came out of the synagogue after the reading of the Torah to get a bit of fresh air, they were shocked and dismayed to see this godless man. They began to gather around the stand and to admonish him for his blasphemy. He ignored them. The uproar among the pious crowd grew, and it looked like they would soon lynch him.

An Irish policeman came along, looked the scene over from a distance, and decided that Moscowitz was an innocent man minding his own business who was being victimized by these clamoring madmen who looked ready to commit the worst crime. The Irish policeman responded in the usual manner by calling the police station and asking for two patrol wagons and police reinforcements. The Orthodox Jews, attired in their religious paraphernalia, were pushed into the patrol wagons and taken off to jail, where they were kept for a whole day.

We can easily imagine the attitude that this episode engendered among the Jewish religious community. Moscowitz became the symbol of all that is wicked. Now the Orthodox Jews had an opportunity to get even with

---

5. The only **Julius Moscowitz** (Moskovits) residing in Philadelphia in 1900, according to census records, was a Romanian Jew born in 1864 who immigrated around 1886. He moved between many occupations over the years, including tailor, watchman, deputy sheriff, and salesman, and died in 1936.

Moscowitz. One fellow swore to the police that Moscowitz and his companion, Louis Jacobson, had made subversive speeches as they handed out the leaflets.[6]

The police were only too glad to accept this at face value. They frightened the owner of the hall where the anarchists' Kol Nidre was to be held. The comrades instead held their meeting in a small room belonging to the social democrats. There, Isidore Prenner, Chaim Weinberg, and Jacob Appel delivered their speeches to a small audience.[7]

Everything went off smoothly, except, when the meeting was over, as the people were leaving the hall, the police arrested Moscowitz, Jacobson, and speakers Prenner and Appel. They also made a mistake: instead of Weinberg they arrested Meyer Gillis, who, like Weinberg, walked with a limp, was a cigarmaker, and was a bit of a speechmaker. A socialist, he also looked a bit like Weinberg.[8]

A Jewish policeman by the name of Henry Caspar, a red-baiter and a rat, testified against the speakers, and a religious Jew, Tsadik Levy, testified against the anarchists who had distributed the leaflets.[9] Both swore falsely

---

6. **Louis Jacobson** (Luis Jakobson, 1864–?) was a Russian-born Jewish shoemaker and fruit retailer who immigrated to the United States around 1887.

7. **Isidore Prenner** (Izidor Prener, c. 1872–1934) was a Russian-born Jewish cigarmaker and anarchist. He immigrated to New York in 1885 and joined the Pioneers of Liberty around 1887, quickly distinguishing himself as a powerful speaker. Around 1889 Prenner moved to Philadelphia and joined the Knights of Liberty, and in 1890 he helped lead a failed strike of cloakmakers there. He withdrew from the anarchist movement following the events narrated here and later became a lawyer and engineer. **Chaim Leib Weinberg** (Khayim-Leyb Vaynberg, 1861–1939) was a Russian-born Jewish cigarmaker, labor organizer, and anarchist. Born to a landowning family in Grodno, he briefly attended a yeshiva in Bialystok and first came to the United States briefly in 1882 to work as a peddler, then returned permanently in 1884. He joined the anarchist movement in New York after reading pamphlets by Johann Most and Morris Winchevsky and was recruited by Joseph Barondess as an organizer for the Cloakmakers' Union. Weinberg subsequently settled in Philadelphia, where he joined the Knights of Liberty and was one of that city's foremost anarchist speakers up until his death. His memoir, *Forty Years in the Struggle*, was posthumously published in Yiddish in 1952 and in English in 2008. **Jacob Appel** (Y. Apel) is listed as the head of the *FAS* "branch office" in Philadelphia for the years 1891 and 1892.

8. **Meyer Gillis** (Gilis, 1865–1940) was a Russian-born Jewish cigarmaker and socialist. He was a founding member of the *Forverts* and worked for that paper from 1902 until 1939.

9. **Henry Caspar** (c. 1845–?) was an Austrian-born Jewish policeman. He immigrated to the United States in 1875 and, as Philadelphia's only Yiddish-speaking police officer, was frequently dispatched to surveil and break up meetings of Jewish radicals. In 1893 Caspar

that the accused had incited the audience to commit acts of violence against senior government officials. Gillis's protests that he was not an anarchist and did not speak at the meeting were to no avail. They all were sentenced to prison for a year, and after eight months and a few days they were freed, with the stipulation that they would never again engage in such propaganda.

These martyrs brought no gain to the anarchist movement. Isidore Prenner, a talented young man and a fine speaker who had done very good work for the movement, left for Chicago to study. When he came back to Philadelphia after many years, he was a nationalist, a Zionist, and what-have-you but no longer an anarchist. Gillis, of course, was no anarchist. He went to New York and became one of the most important members of the Forverts Publishing Association and engaged in the *Forverts'* politics. Julius Moscowitz remained in Philadelphia. After being a prisoner, he became respectable Jew and eventually worked his way up to become treasurer of a Jewish burial society. Jacob Appel and Louis Jacobson remained with the comrades for some time, but they did not make a significant contribution to the movement.

❀ ❀ ❀

Antireligious agitation did not diminish, even though there was great harassment and intimidation. The campaign continued year in and year out for nearly twenty-five years. Even in our time, it played an important role in our activities, as we shall see later. The sustainability and great success of the movement are in fact the best evidence that these activities were necessary and fruitful. Yet lately, among ex-radicals, it has become the fashion to ridicule this activity.

They did not refrain from making pogroms in this era, in 1906, on private homes in Boston and a number of other cities, as well as on the "private premises" of the Bundists and the Socialist-Revolutionaries in New York, where they met peacefully to spend the day on Yom Kippur.[10] But all this is

---

arrested Abe Cahan during one of the editor's visits to the city. See *Philadelphia Inquirer*, March 26 and August 28, 1893.

10. **The General Jewish Labor Bund in Lithuania, Poland and Russia** ("the Bund" for short) was a Jewish socialist organization founded in 1897 to pursue both social democracy and legal status and cultural autonomy for Jews in the Russian Empire. The Bund was

of minor importance. The underlying question is, was it necessary to carry out antireligious agitation in the early years of the movement, and is there not even now a need for such propaganda?

I have mentioned in a previous chapter that the great majority of the Jewish immigrants coming to America did not have strong ties to religion. On one hand were the students, *externikes*, ex-yeshiva students, and ordinary *maskilim* who had already in the old country shaken off the dust of religion and tradition. On the other hand, there were the mass of young artisans, who had been apprenticed at a very early age to a master to learn a trade and spent their wretched youth under his heavy hand and did not receive enough religious education to fit on the point of a fork. One could not expect them to have strong religious ties here in America. For many, the life of empty promiscuity, drunkenness, playing cards, and visiting cheap vaudeville houses held more attraction than the American synagogue, which had become a caricature of its former self. During the year the prayer houses stood empty and desolate. One could not bring together a *minyan*, not even for Kaddish.[11]

But in the weeks before the Jewish High Holidays, the religious hypocrites became busy in a genuinely American style. Not only the synagogues but also stables and abandoned buildings were hastily outfitted to become houses of God, with rabbis, cantors, and carnival barkers attracting a crowd to sell tickets for the great wonder. It looked more like a circus than a place

---

a founding section of the Russian Social Democratic Labor Party (RSDLP) in 1898, but in 1903 it withdrew from that body due to the Bolshevik faction's opposition to its autonomy. Bundists played a leading role in the 1905 Russian Revolution, and the organization rejoined the RSDLP in 1906, siding with the Menshevik faction in the party's 1912 split. The Bund collapsed within Russia following the 1917 revolution, but small Bundist groups and factions continued to exist abroad into the twenty-first century. **The Socialist-Revolutionary Party** was founded in Russia in 1902 as a successor to the Narodnik movement. It had a non-Marxist socialist program centered on land reform, and the left wing of the party was ideologically quite close to the anarchists. The Socialist-Revolutionaries undertook several successful and attempted assassinations of tsarist officials as a means of inspiring the masses and extracting political concessions. Following the February Revolution of 1917, they enjoyed the most popular support of any party in Russia, but the Bolshevik seizure of power in the October Revolution and the trial of the party's leaders in 1922 for assassinating a German ambassador and leading an uprising against Bolshevik rule effectively destroyed the organization.

11. A *minyan* is the quorum of at least ten adults required in Judaism to carry out public prayer and other functions. **Kaddish** is the chant recited during Jewish rituals of mourning.

of worship. It could hardly appeal to the intelligentsia or the ordinary workingman.

The hustle and bustle generated by the religious hypocrites before the High Holidays, however, did have a small effect upon the masses, who were destitute, in a strange land, living in poverty and hardship, and who had no repose or quiet in a comfortable home. When even the most blood-sucking bosses closed down their shops, factories, and stores for Rosh Hashanah and Yom Kippur, the Jewish worker simply had no place to spend his days unless he went to the synagogue to participate in religious ceremonies in which he no longer believed. What better time to educate him about the true nature of religion and to provide entertainment than on those holy days?

The Jewish intelligentsia faced a choice. Either leave the ignorant masses to the monkey business of the religious zealots, who had turned religion into a good business for themselves; or bring the masses out of the stables of religious study and take advantage of the free time and good opportunities to fulfill everyone's daily desire to go somewhere, to be with other like-minded people, for the purpose of enlightening themselves and elevating their thinking, learning and seeing the world and the people around them in their true light. To the credit of the intellectuals, and of our comrades in particular, it must be noted that they chose the correct path and have for many years conducted extremely important and fruitful work in this field. We have the testimony of hundreds of people that antireligious agitation opened their eyes for the first time and revealed a whole new world. The agitation drew many young people away from empty extravagance and brought them into a milieu where they studied, discussed, and became acquainted with serious social issues and problems. This achievement made a difference and was very important.

In the early years the Jewish socialists were just as devoted to this agitational work as the anarchists. Some of them, like Benjamin Feigenbaum, Leo Rosenzweig, and others devoted themselves to this work all their lives.[12] But the official leaders of the Jewish socialists in the 1890s took up the supposed position of the Social Democratic Party of Germany that religion is a

---

12. **Leo Rosenzweig** (Rozentsvayg, 1869–1916) was a Romanian-born Jewish lawyer and socialist. He immigrated to the United States in 1891 and served as one of the first general secretaries of the Workmen's Circle, from 1903 to 1904. Rosenzweig was a contributor to the *Forverts* and *Tsukunft* and published many antireligious writings.

private affair, and they interpreted that position in a very simplistic way. Abe Cahan began to preach that it was now allowed. Freethinkers, that is, could now not only eat matzo balls, but also say the *hagadah*—the German social democrats had so decided!

But the truth is something very different. The exact language of Point 5 of the historical "Erfurt Program" of 1891 reads: "Declaration that religion is a private matter. Abolition of all expenditures from public funds for ecclesiastical and religious purposes. Ecclesiastical and religious communities are to be regarded as private associations that regulate their affairs entirely autonomously."[13] It is obvious that this meant taking away the privileges of the church, separating it from the state and the community—not about putting religion in a privileged position so that it should not be violated. To this day, we do not know whether the vulgar interpretation of Point 5 was due to ignorance or evil intent. To accept the first sentence in the paragraph and ignore what follows makes the matter very suspicious.

In addition, the term "religion" is very broad, encompassing various and often contradictory concepts. Religion in its purely abstract sense, as the striving of people to understand and connect with the world around them, is certainly a private matter for every single person. In this sense, atheists and agnostics are generally more religious than the fanatical zealots—insofar as they take the issue more seriously and approach it in a rational way, according to their own understanding and conception. But, of course, when religion is mentioned one thinks of established dogmas, of thousands of different sects competing with each other, each claiming the only true revelation of a personal God who has given his representatives a certain amount of knowledge, prescribing what to do and what not to do. No reasonable person—if thinking seriously about the question—could ever submit to such a conception of religion.

There is another conception of religion as a church, as an institution, which holds an immensely strong influence on society and on the behavior of the individual. On this aspect we have the historical record, which shows that the church served the rich and the powerful everywhere and at all times

---

13. **The Erfurt Program** was the influential platform adopted by the Social Democratic Party of Germany in 1891. The English translation here is from the Marxists Internet Archive: https://www.marxists.org/history/international/social-democracy/1891/erfurt-program.htm.

and helped to keep the people enslaved and in ignorance, poverty, and need. Religion in this sense is really the opium of the people—the worst and most harmful infestation, from which we must try with all our might to free ourselves before we can begin to think about changing the political and economic structure of society.

To preach, then, that religion in this sense is a private affair is the work of irresponsible adventurers who seek to pander to the prejudices of the ignorant mass, in order to gain something for themselves—readers for their newspapers, votes at election time, and the like, which has nothing to do with the serious question of religion and society.

Our cynical critics and doubters have a seemingly substantial argument. They say, "You will see for yourselves as you grow older, more settled; you will shake off all of your former childish folly." This is nothing more than a half-truth: the facts are correct, but the statement is false. Antireligious agitation goes hand in hand with revolutionary fervor always and everywhere. At the time of the Great French Revolution, antireligious feeling was so great that it tore everything religious out by its roots. Again, during the great Russian Revolution the same phenomenon occurred in every detail. The cessation of antireligious agitation is always a sign of spiritual decline in the social sphere. This same phenomenon occurred in this country during the time of the American Revolution. The most active revolutionists and leaders were atheists or agnostics. In the two principal historical documents of that period, the Declaration of Independence and the Constitution, the word "God" does not appear. The founders of the republic sought to ensure that religion should have no influence on the social conditions of the country. Thomas Paine, the great heretic, was the most prominent spiritual leader among the young republicans. It was not until years later, when the people began to worship the golden calf—the almighty dollar—that this new religion gained power, placing on silver and gold coins the slogan "In God We Trust."[14]

The same thing occurred in the Jewish socialist movement. When the movement was young and full of vitality and energy, antireligious agitation was an important aspect of its educational work of enlightenment. After the

---

14. This slogan was first stamped on US two-cent pieces in 1909. It would not be adopted as the official motto of the United States until 1956.

failure of the first Russian Revolution, when "Saninism" took the place of real revolutionary activity,[15] despair and pessimism gradually took hold of even our own circles. A kind of pseudo-nationalist progressivism began to float about, which the *Forverts* defended with never-ending philosophical expositions. It stopped not only the antireligious agitation but also the whole spirit of social development of the local Jewish working class. The entire spiritual catastrophe of the Jewish working class, this turning back of the clock to *tallit* and *tzitzit*,[16] is the result of this reaction that has entered our spiritual life.

15. **Saninism** refers to the influence of the 1907 erotic novel *Sanin* by Mikhail Artsybashev (1878–1927), which scandalized Russian society with its celebration of nihilistic hedonism.

16. A **tallit** is a fringed prayer shawl worn by religious Jewish men (and sometimes women); it is adorned with ritual knotted tassels called **tzitzit**.

CHAPTER 5

Alexander Berkman's *Attentat*

In the summer of 1892 our movement was in a deplorable condition. The *Fraye arbeter shtime* was no longer being published. This paper had kept up the spirit of the comrades and demanded immediate effort on their part each week. In the middle of July, however, the movement was shaken as if from a thunderbolt: Alexander Berkman had attempted to assassinate Henry Clay Frick at his office in Pittsburgh.[1] The newspapers all over the country were full of the story. Among the Jewish working class, Berkman's deed created great enthusiasm and admiration. He became the hero of the day, and in the anarchist movement he and his deed aroused great interest.

True, not everyone was enthusiastic. Johann Most, the eternal rebel, the agitator for "propaganda of the deed" and personal initiative, made little of Berkman's deed. He declared publicly that given the circumstances and conditions of the country's labor movement, Berkman's deed would not have agitational value. This declaration struck up a storm of controversy among the comrades. The Jewish anarchists were never blind followers of a preacher, and Most's statement had no effect on most comrades. They stood on their

---

1. **Alexander Berkman** (1870–1936) was a Russian-born Jewish typesetter, editor, and anarchist. After migrating to New York in 1888, he took part in the German and Yiddish anarchist movements. Following fourteen years in prison for attempting to assassinate Henry Clay Frick, Berkman became editor of Emma Goldman's magazine *Mother Earth* and then moved to San Francisco and founded *The Blast* (1916–1917). Following his deportation in 1919 and expulsion from Russia in 1922, he lived in European exile and continued to write for anarchist publications and work on behalf of imprisoned anarchists and revolutionists up until his death by suicide. **Henry Clay Frick** (1849–1919) was an American-born industrialist, opponent of organized labor, and chairman of the Carnegie Steel Company.

own, insisting that Berkman's act was justified, timely, and desirable. They only regretted that they had no publication of their own in which to illuminate, explain, and popularize the deed.

Emma Goldman was wounded by Johann Most's attitude. She and Berkman had long been under the direct influence of Most. It is fair to say that Most had introduced Emma to a speaker's career. He had seriously devoted himself to her cultural development and had an intimate relationship with her.

In those years, Berkman dreamed of returning to Russia, where he felt he could participate in real revolutionary work. In America he felt frustrated. He decided to learn the typesetters' trade so that when he returned to Russia he could establish an underground printing press. Most helped by employing him in the printing shop of *Freiheit* to study the profession. He also sent out an appeal for funds to pay for Berkman's trip back to Russia.

Around 1890, antagonism developed between Most and Berkman, which grew more and more acrimonious. It would take us too far afield to go into details of the causes. There were differences of opinion regarding one's personal relationship to the movement—Berkman was a fanatical revolutionist. For him it was unthinkable that a revolutionary could forget himself for even a moment and enjoy life. It may have also had its roots in a bit of suppressed jealousy over Emma Goldman. At any rate, at the annual convention of the Jewish anarchists in 1890–91, Berkman brought charges against Johann Most, demanding an investigation into Most's mistreatment of another comrade, Josef Peukert, whom Most had accused of committing a serious crime against the movement.[2]

Most could never tolerate any opposition. He seemed to think, "If you are not with me, you are against me." He persecuted such people with all the sharpness of his biting pen.

---

2. **Josef Peukert** (1855–1910) was an Austrian Bohemian-born editor and anarchist. At age sixteen he migrated to Germany, where he became involved in socialist and then anarchist groups. In 1881 Peukert was a delegate to the International Social Revolutionary Congress in London, then returned to Austria and became editor of the anarchist-leaning newspaper *Die Zukunft* (The Future, 1879–1884). In 1890 he migrated to New York, where he edited the papers *Die Autonomie* (Autonomy, 1886–1893) and *Der Anarchist* (The Anarchist, 1889–1895). Johann Most blamed Peukert for the 1887 arrest of anarchist Johann Neve, who was apprehended by German police based on information supplied by an informant and friend of Peukert named Theodor Reuss. Peukert later belonged to the Chicago Debaters' Club and attended the 1905 founding of the IWW as a delegate from that organization.

When Most allowed himself to condemn Berkman's *attentat*, Emma Goldman suspected that he had done so because of his old hatred of Berkman. She could find no other motive, for she knew very well that it had nothing to do with cowardice. His stance before and during Chicago tragedy, which led to him being sentenced twice to Blackwell's Island, made it clear that Most feared nothing. Only bitter hatred, she concluded, could blind him to Berkman's great deed.

She came to one of Most's lectures and attacked him with a whip. This caused a great scandal in and around the movement.

Berkman, also, spent a long time in prison wracking his brain to understand Most's behavior. It was not until ten years later, after Leon Czolgosz shot President McKinley, that Berkman, not noticing the irony of the situation, expressed in a letter to Emma Goldman virtually the same opinion about Czolgosz's deed that Most had expressed about Berkman's deed years before.[3] He wrote:

> To prove of value they must be motivated by social rather than individual necessity and be aimed against a direct and immediate enemy of the people. The significance of such a deed is understood by the popular mind, and in that alone lies the propagandistic, educational import of an *Attentat*, except if it is exclusively an act of terrorism.
>
> Now, I do not believe that this deed was terroristic; and I doubt whether it was educational, because the social necessity for its performance was not manifest. That you may not misunderstand, I repeat: as an expression of personal revolt it was inevitable, and in itself an indictment of existing conditions. But the background of social necessity was lacking, and therefore the value of the act was to a great extent nullified.[4]

---

3. **Leon Czolgosz** (1873–1901) was an American-born laborer and anarchist. One of eight children of Polish immigrant parents, he took up factory jobs as a teenager and soon began reading radical literature and attending socialist and anarchist meetings. However, Czolgosz was met with suspicion in these circles. He shot William McKinley on September 6, 1901, and the president died eight days later. Czogolsz was quickly convicted and executed by electric chair, after proclaiming: "I killed the president because he was the enemy of the good people—the good working people."

4. Alexander Berkman, *Prison Memoirs of an Anarchist* (New York: Mother Earth, 1912), 416.

Both Berkman and Emma began to understand the position which Most had taken on this question nine years before. The truth is that both Most and Berkman were justified in their skeptical attitude toward these two deeds. This does not, however, detract from Berkman's generosity and sincerity— he had, after all, been willing to sacrifice his young life to help the striking workers in their struggle and to avenge their slain brothers' spilled blood— and it does not diminish the value of his act to point out, as many did, that he did not evaluate the situation correctly and therefore did not achieve his goal.

The story was as follows:

In the summer of 1892, in Andrew Carnegie's big steel mills in Homestead, Pennsylvania, near Pittsburgh, the contract that the company had with the Amalgamated Association of Iron and Steel Workers expired.[5] Carnegie did not wish to renew the contract since he was planning to cut the wages of the workers. He was embarrassed to do this piece of dirty work all by himself, so he left the execution of his plan in the hands of his new partner Henry Clay Frick, a notorious union breaker, and took a trip to Scotland, which he had left many years before as a poor emigrant.

The new administrator prepared for battle. He had a high, strong fence miles long built around the steel mills and brought food and ammunition into the factories as if to prepare for a siege. The workers watched and understood what this meant. But they kept cool and calm, convinced of their power. They were organized, firmly established in their town, where the whole government was in their hands—even the mayor was a worker, one of their own. He refused to allow scabs to be brought in and sworn in as deputies, as had been done in similar situations.

Finally things came to a head. The company, being unable to break the strike using open methods, resorted to undercover means. It collected three hundred strikebreakers, Pinkertons, from Ohio, armed them, put them aboard two barges, and had a tugboat pull them up the river at night to Homestead.[6]

---

5. **Andrew Carnegie** (1835–1919) was a Scottish-born industrialist and philanthropist. After immigrating to the United States with his working-class family in 1848, he went on to become one of the richest men in the country and owner of the Carnegie Steel Company, based in Pittsburgh.

6. **The Pinkerton National Detective Agency** is a private security and detective agency founded in 1855. It long specialized in infiltrating labor and radical organizations and supplying armed agents to help break strikes.

Figure 11: Alexander Berkman, 1892
Courtesy of the Library of Congress

This was on the night of July 5–6, 1892. The workers had surmised that something of this nature might take place, so they kept pickets at the shore day and night. About four o'clock in the morning, the pickets sighted the barges and sounded the alarm. All the bells in the city were rung. The whole population ran to the edge of the river.

The walls of the barges were protected inside by thick iron, so no bullet could penetrate them. The Pinkertons, feeling confident and rowdy, began to shoot at the strikers from behind the iron-clad walls. One of the strikers was hit by a bullet. Then the battle broke loose. The workers answered with a hail of bullets from the shore. But the Pinkertons were in a much better position than the strikers. They were better-protected in the barges.

The captain of the tugboat steamer, sizing up the situation that he was in the middle of and getting hit from both sides, untied the ropes that held the two barges, left them to God's will, and fled the scene of battle. The shooting continued for some time, with the workers getting the worst of it until the strikers brought an old cannon, which stood in the center of the town as a trophy from the Civil War, and began firing on the barges. But the big cannon balls were not effective either. The workers then brought barrels of oil which they spilled upon the waters and then ignited. The flames engulfed the barges in the river and forced the Pinkertons to put down their guns and surrender. It was early in the morning. The battle had raged for eight hours.

The Pinkertons were escorted with catcalls, derision, and blows to City Hall, where they were interrogated about where they had come from. Then in the evening each and every one of them was shipped home by train.

There were casualties on both sides—more among the workers than the Pinkertons, of course. But the workers had spoken. Right was on their side. According to Pennsylvania law, the company had no jurisdiction to import armed men from another state. The workers could not even be blamed for engaging in armed battle.

That summer Emma Goldman and Alexander Berkman lived in Worcester, Massachusetts, where they had a little lunchroom that sold sandwiches and ice cream. There Emma saw the story of the battle in the newspapers and believed that innocent, helpless, working-class blood had been spilled in Homestead. She passed on this news to Berkman, who immediately decided that this was the moment for him to sacrifice his life and show the capitalist beast that it could not shed workers' blood with impunity. That same day, they abandoned their business to the four winds and left for New York to make the necessary preparations for the deed. This took just two weeks.

On July 2, Berkman entered Frick's office and tried to shoot him. Of the three bullets fired, one hit Frick's neck and wounded him seriously.[7] A carpenter, who happened to be in the office repairing something, felled Berkman from behind with a blow on the head from his hammer. A number of people then ran in, beat him up, and then had him arrested.

Berkman lived and breathed by the principles of the Russian revolutionists. They never had a lawyer defend them at their trials. Berkman was kept for weeks on death row, a section of the penitentiary kept only for those sentenced to execution, although after a time the doctors were sure that Frick would not die. Since Berkman could not be tried for murder, he was finally put in a different section of the jail. Then one bright morning, without warning, he was brought to court. He was charged with six separate crimes in connection with the one act. This was too much even for the judge. He reduced the number to three counts. Under Pennsylvania law, Berkman was to be sentenced to seven years imprisonment for attempted murder. But the judge sentenced him to three consecutive seven-year sentences and another year in the workhouse for "carrying concealed weapons." Twenty-two years of imprisonment—the same number of years as Berkman's age at the time!

After Berkman's arrest Emma arranged for a big meeting in New York to explain Berkman's *attentat*. Joseph Barondess volunteered his help to Emma because he himself had been imprisoned for a short while a year earlier. The speakers at the meeting were Dyer D. Lum, Francesco Saverio Merlino, and Barondess.[8] Emma was chair. Among the comrades in New

---

7. In fact, two of Berkman's bullets hit Frick in the neck, and Berkman also managed to stab Frick four times in the leg before being subdued.

8. **Dyer D. Lum** (1839–1893) was an American-born bookbinder, labor organizer, writer, and anarchist. After serving in the Union Army in the US Civil War, he became active in the Knights of Labor and then the AFL and worked for a time as secretary to AFL president Samuel Gompers. By 1885 Lum had become an anarchist and joined the IWPA, though he also incorporated elements of mutualist and individualist anarchism into his thought. As a close friend of many of the Haymarket defendants, he was active in their defense campaign and edited a revived version of Albert Parsons's paper *The Alarm* from 1887 to 1889. Lum also served as a mentor to Voltairine de Cleyre. **Francesco Saverio Merlino** (1856–1930) was an Italian lawyer, anarchist, and later socialist. Merlino became involved in anarchist circles while a student in Naples and in 1884 went into exile. In 1892–93 he lived in New York, where he founded the anarchist newspapers *Solidarity* and *Il Grido degli oppressi* (The Cry of the Oppressed, 1892–1894). After returning to Italy, Merlino began to publicly question anarchist doctrines, particularly abstention from electoral politics, and in 1899 he joined the Italian Socialist Party. In 1900 he was defense attorney for anarchist regicide Gaetano Bresci, discussed in chapter 10.

York, the deed was received with great admiration. After the terrible sentence, a committee to appeal for a new trial was formed. Among the most active comrades who made up the committee were a number of well-known socialists. Isaac Hourwich, Louis Miller, Michael Zametkin, and Sergius Schewitsch, editor-in-chief of the German paper *Volkszeitung*, which had a great influence on the East Side, strongly defended Berkman's act from day one.[9] All our comrades were inspired by Berkman's heroism, with the exception of Roman Lewis, the first editor of the *Fraye arbater shtime*, who suddenly disagreed with such anarchist tactics. He declared himself a social democrat, and the socialists received him with open arms. But their joy with the big win did not last long. For Lewis descended further down the mountain and a short time later in Chicago was elected on the Democratic ticket as assistant district attorney.

Berkman's deed, however, did not meet with the approval of the Homestead strikers. They suspected that Berkman's assassination attempt was something Frick himself had concocted to win public sympathy for his side. When Berkman arrived in Pittsburgh, the city was besieged by soldiers. The company had accused the leaders of the strike of conspiracy that led to murder, and they were each held under $10,000 bail. The workers accused the company's officials of the same crime, and they also had to put up $10,000 bail. All the trials came to naught. The jury had cleared the accused workers. Berkman's intervention at this juncture was incomprehensible to the strikers.

Among the soldiers was a young fellow by the name of W. L. Iams who, standing at attention with his company, shouted "Hurrah for Berkman!"[10] For this crime, he was hanged for several hours by his thumbs, then half of his head was shaved, and he was expelled from the militia.

Every attempt to obtain a new trial failed. Because Berkman had been his own lawyer, he made no objections at the trial, and without such technical tricks there was no basis for an appeal. His hope of being able to explain

---

9. **Michael Zametkin** (Mikhl Zametkin, 1859–1935) was a Russian-born Jewish garment worker, labor organizer, and socialist. Having been involved in revolutionary circles from a young age, he immigrated to New York in 1882 as a leader of the Am Olam movement. Zametkin became an organizer for the Shirt Makers' Union and briefly belonged to the anarchist Pioneers of Liberty before cofounding the Jewish section of the SLP. He was a talented speaker and prolific writer and cofounded both *Di arbeter tsaytung* and the *Forverts*.

10. According to numerous sources, Iams actually shouted, "Three cheers for the man who shot Frick!"

his deed to the court had also come to nothing. He had written his speech to the court in German and immediately noticed that the court translator was twisting his meaning in the most shameful way. When he protested, the judge refused to let him give his speech at all, and the fiasco ended.

For many years Berkman was incarcerated in a hellish purgatory called the Western Penitentiary, in Pittsburgh. But he served our movement as a living symbol of heroism and self-sacrifice. They did not forget his deed and his martyrdom for one moment until he was finally freed in 1906.

CHAPTER 6

The Great Crisis of 1893

In 1893 a terrible crisis developed in the United States. There was a run on the banks for money by the depositors. The banks were forced to close their doors, and thousands of people were financially ruined. Hundreds of people committed suicide. The entire country was in a panic that it seemed unable to shake off. Factories closed, and there were throngs of unemployed. Hungry people filled the cities. The devastation was massive. Concerned people opened soup kitchens for the hungry, and breadlines formed. The unemployed stood in lines for hours until they were doled out a piece of dry bread and a cup of coffee. Organized labor sent committees to Albany, New York, to appeal to the governor and the legislature to do something to alleviate the situation, but to no avail.

On Saturday, August 19, 1893, a big demonstration in Union Square was organized for the unemployed. Emma Goldman, carrying a red flag, led the demonstration and delivered a fiery speech. She condemned the lawmakers and ridiculed all those who hoped for the state to come to their aid. Then she quoted Cardinal Manning's words that "necessity has no law, and a starving man has a natural right to his neighbor's bread."[1] She ended her speech with a call, "Do you not see the stupidity of asking relief from Albany with immense wealth within a stone's throw from here? Fifth Avenue is laid in gold, every mansion is a citadel of money and power."[2]

---

1. **Henry Edward Manning** (1808–1892) was the archbishop of Westminster, known for his advocacy of social justice and mediation of the successful London dock strike of 1889. The quotation is from a letter Manning published in the *Fortnightly Review*, January 1, 1888.

2. Cohen took the text of this speech from Emma Goldman, *Living My Life*, 2 vols. (New York: Alfred A. Knopf, 1931): 1:122–23. However, according to Goldman's full account

Emma's speech was applauded, but nothing was done. The meeting ended without incident. The same day, Emma left for Philadelphia, where the comrades were also planning activity to help the unemployed. A meeting was planned for Monday, August 21. Emma spent Sunday with comrades at the apartment of Natasha Notkin.[3] On Monday, the morning papers carried an article declaring that the New York police were coming to Philadelphia to arrest Emma Goldman for her provocative speech in Union Square. Emma wanted to avoid arrest until after the meeting. She was almost successful. As she quietly slipped in by herself through the doorway to the meeting, a comrade called out in excitement, "Here is Emma!" Immediately, a heavy hand was placed on her shoulder, and a rough voice bellowed, "Miss Goldman, you are under arrest!" There was a small commotion, but the police surrounded her with revolvers in their hands and delivered her to City Hall.

But the meeting was not disrupted. Voltairine de Cleyre was the main speaker, and she vented all her bitterness against the exploiters and oppressors of the people.

This was the fine welcome that Emma received on her first visit to Philadelphia. Over the following years, the same scenario was repeated more than once.

At City Hall, Goldman was detained overnight and asked if she would voluntarily leave for New York in the company of detectives. She refused. She was then taken to Moyamensing Prison to await extradition papers. This took some time. Finally the papers came and she was taken back to New

---

her address did not end here but with the more militant words: "They will go on robbing you, your children, and your children's children, unless you wake up, unless you become daring enough to demand your rights. Well, then, demonstrate before the palaces of the rich; demand work. If they do not give you work, demand bread. If they deny you both, take bread. It is your sacred right!"

3. **Natasha Notkin** (1870–1920) was a Russian-born pharmacist and anarchist. She was involved in the Narodnik movement in Russia before immigrating to the United States in 1885 and soon became a prominent member of Philadelphia's anarchist movement as well as a friend of both Voltairine de Cleyre and Emma Goldman. In 1890 Notkin cofounded the Daughters of Israel, an aid organization for Jewish immigrants (strongly suggesting Jewish heritage of her own), and in 1905 she raised funds and recruited volunteers for the revolution in Russia. She also served as Philadelphia's agent for the anarchist publications *Free Society* and *Mother Earth* and opened a drug store there in 1905. In 1918 Notkin married fellow anarchist pharmacist William Eidelson, and the couple moved to Los Angeles, where they opened a pharmacy in Boyle Heights. She died two years later in the influenza pandemic.

York, where she was put under $5,000 bail. The bail was arranged in advance by Dr. Julius Hoffman, who put up the required amount.[4] Emma, accompanied by a group of comrades, then went off to the famous anarchist beer hall of Justus Schwab to celebrate.[5]

Berkman had advised her not to make the same mistake as he had made in his defense. Emma agreed to get a very famous lawyer, a certain A. Oakey Hall, who had been mayor of New York City and took her case without fee.[6] The trial began on September 28 and lasted for ten days. The prosecutor seemed little concerned with what she did or did not say in Union Square. He kept prodding her on her views of religion, family, government, and the like, in order to show what a dangerous woman she was.

One of the witnesses for the defense, a reporter from the *World*, made a very good impression on the jury. He verified that Emma's speech had not incited the audience to any direct criminal acts. The prosecutor then produced an article from the *World*—which the editors had embellished quite a bit—which portrayed the whole incident in a different light. The jury was out for a long time and came back once to ask the judge for clarification about the law; finally they brought a verdict of guilty. The judge set October 16 for sentencing.

Emma prepared a long speech which she planned to make to the court before the verdict was announced. The editors of the *World* offered a huge sum of money for her speech if she would let them print it beforehand, so the paper would have it as soon as she was the sentenced. They guaranteed that they would not change one word. Emma agreed and let them have a copy.

The streets around the court were filled with armed police on October 16. The newspapers had spread a rumor that the anarchists would seek to free Emma by force. At the sentencing, her lawyer was not present. He

---

4. **Julius L. P. Hoffman** (1841–?) was a German-born doctor and anarchist. He immigrated to the United States in 1865 and opened a medical practice in New York's Lower East Side, where he became a close friend of anarchists Justus Schwab, Johann Most (whose bail he paid on at least one occasion), and Emma Goldman, whom he employed as a nurse in his practice for a time. Hoffman had a special interest in East Asian culture and corresponded with the Japanese anarchist Kotoku Shusui (1871–1911).

5. **Justus Schwab** (1847–1900) was a German-born saloonkeeper and anarchist. He immigrated to the United States in 1869 and opened a saloon in New York's Lower East Side that became a hub for radicalism. Schwab joined the SLP but in 1880 split away to form a social-revolutionary group that later became part of the anarchist IWPA.

6. **Abraham Oakey Hall** (1826–1898) was an American-born lawyer, journalist, and Democratic politician who was New York City's mayor from 1869 to 1872.

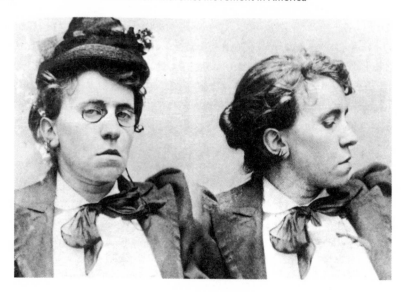

Figure 12: Emma Goldman, 1893
Courtesy of the Department of Records, City of Philadelphia

insisted on appealing the case to a higher court, but Emma had absolutely refused. She knew from the experiences of Johann Most that this would be a wasted effort. Besides, she was willing to share, in a way, the experiences of Alexander Berkman and other revolutionaries. When the judge asked if she had anything to say, she replied that she had plenty to say. The judge insisted that he wanted no long speeches. The only thing Emma was able to say under the circumstances was: "I had expected no justice from a capitalist court. The Court might do its worst, but it was powerless to change my views."[7]

7. Cohen quotes here from Goldman, *Living My Life*, 1:131. According to the New York *World*, Goldman's actual words were: "Your Honor, in view of the fact that the police have done everything they could to incite my friends the Anarchists, to some demonstration, so that they could put them in jail also, I shall refrain from delivering any speech here."

The judge then sentenced her to one year on Blackwell's Island. On the way to the island, she had the satisfaction of hearing the newsboys shouting, "Extra! Extra! Emma Goldman's speech in court!" The speech, which she would have given before a small audience in a small courtroom, was now publicized before the whole wide world.[8]

---

8. The text of Goldman's undelivered speech was printed in the New York *World*, October 17, 1893.

CHAPTER 7

The Revival of the *Fraye arbeter shtime*

The lack of a publication of our own was strongly felt in our movement, especially after Berkman's *attentat*. It needed a paper to explain what had happened, campaign for a new trial, and also help in the general work of the movement. The comrades launched a new effort to revive the *Fraye arbeter shtime* on March 17, 1893, and the newspaper happily began publication again.

But the paper was not very successful this time around either. The socialists and the trade unions renewed their boycott against it, and the embers of old disagreements and disputes burst into flames again. The paper did not even please many of the comrades. A movement began among them to bring Saul Yanovsky from London, where he had successfully edited the anarchist newspaper *Arbeter fraynd* (Worker's Friend) for several years, and make him the editor of the *Fraye arbeter shtime*.[1] Some comrades were confident that, under his editorship, the paper would quickly win new readers and exert a great influence.

It took much correspondence and time to convince Yanovsky to make the trip. He arrived by ship accompanied by Louis Finkelstein, who was a very young man at the time.[2] Onboard the ship the idea came to both of

---

1. The ***Arbeter fraynd*** (1885–1915, 1920–1923) was a radical Yiddish newspaper founded in London in 1885 by Morris Winchevsky. From 1891 to 1894 it was edited by Saul Yanovsky, under whom it became an explicitly anarchist paper, and Rudolf Rocker became its editor in 1898. The publication was suppressed by the British government during the First World War but revived in 1920.

2. **Louis Finkelstein** (Finkelshteyn, 1874–1953) was a Russian-born Jewish writer, editor, and anarchist. He migrated to London around 1892, then in 1894 to New York, where he wrote for the *Arbeter fraynd*, the *FAS*, and other radical papers. Finkelstein briefly served as

them that, since Yanovsky had been in the United States before for several years and was well known as an anarchist and a revolutionist, there was some danger that he might have some difficulty entering. There was no anti-anarchist law yet, but nevertheless you may always expect the worst from a capitalist government. They exchanged travel documents: Yanovsky became Finkelstein and Finkelstein was transformed into Yanovsky. If Finkelstein was to be detained on Ellis Island, the trouble would not be so great. Yanovsky would meanwhile disembark from the ship, and it would not be difficult to prove that Finkelstein was too young, had never been here before, and could not be legally detained.

But all these precautions were unnecessary. The doors to America were still wide open at that time. Due to its rapid industrialization, capitalism needed more and more hands. The immigrants left the ship without incident. No questions were asked.

Meanwhile the conditions in the movement had changed again for the worse. The *Fraye arbeter shtime* again gave up the ghost even before the new editor arrived and could take over. Among the more intellectual comrades the epicurean idea developed that a weekly newspaper would not be such a great a blessing to the movement. First, a weekly publication would drain energy, time, and resources from other activities. Secondly, and this is the most important thing, it is in the nature of weeklies to be agitational and superficial and to pander to the tastes of the ignorant masses; meanwhile the publishers themselves, the comrades, needed a thorough education and had to seriously study the social question before they undertook the education of other people. They thought that the publication of a serious scientific journal would be more appropriate. This discussion caused conflict and confusion among the comrades.

The welcome meeting for Yanovsky that his followers had prepared at the Thalia Theater did not come off as successfully as expected. The intellectuals of the movement did not come to greet him, and the crowed was not very large or very enthusiastic either. Yanovsky was not a new face. He had come to America in 1885 and had been drawn to the anarchist movement under the influence of the Chicago tragedy. He had taken part in the movement

---

manager of the *FAS* under Saul Yanovsky and later became Yanovsky's associate editor of the ILGWU paper *Gerekhtigkeyt*. From 1921 to 1924 he coedited the *FAS*, and from 1927 until his death he was the labor editor for the daily *Der tog*.

Figure 13: Saul Yanovsky
From *Ershte yorn fun yidishn frayheytlekhn sotsializm: oytobiografishe
zikhroynes fun a pioner un boyer fun der yidisher anarkhistisher bavegung in
England un Amerike*, 1948

for several years and gained many supporters but still more enemies. His
biting sarcasm and his poisonous epithets did not allow for the fostering of
many friendships. Upon his return from London, he was very disappointed
by the entire movement, and he withdrew and found a job as an agent for an
insurance agency, keeping distant from everything and everyone.

I shall relate an incident of that period in his life that he once told to me.
He had a bit of an occupational rivalry with Isidore Kopeloff. Yanovsky had
worked for some time to sell a substantial policy to one of the movement's
better-established doctors, Max Girsdansky or some such person.[3] There

---

3. **Max Girsdansky** (Maks Girzhdansky, 1864–1932) was a Russian-born Jewish doctor,
anarchist, and later socialist. He immigrated to the United States in 1879 and earned his medical degree from New York University. Girsdansky was a prominent member of the anarchist

was light at the end of the tunnel—soon, soon he would have the necessary funds. Yanovsky happened to mention this in the presence of Kopeloff, and to his great surprise a few days later he found out that Kopeloff had run off and clinched the sale himself, taking the bread from Yanovsky's mouth. One can easily imagine his bitterness and chagrin. But what is not so easy to understand is the motivation that caused Kopeloff to become Yanovsky's enemy for the rest his life and to describe him so vulgarly and untruthfully in his memoirs.[4] This treatment is simply scandalous, and can only be interpreted as evidence of a guilty conscience that made Kopeloff try to justify his own bad behavior.

Yanovsky was no saint (*tzadik*), nor was he always careful in his words and actions. But he was in no way inferior to the other important Jews of his generation, and he was far from the black devil that Kopeloff described with such zeal. Yanovsky's contributions to our anarchist movement in particular, and to the Jewish labor movement in general, to Yiddish literature, and to the generation of writers he helped educate, cannot be diminished by such vicious attacks. Despite all his shortcomings—and few people have suffered as much from them as the writer of these lines—Yanovsky was a significant figure with considerable accomplishments to his credit.

In October 1895, the *Fraye gezelshaft* (Free Society) appeared—"a monthly magazine of the most advanced ideas, edited by M. Leontieff and Moyshe Katz."[5] Its stapled pages were filled with a world of good anarchist and literary analyses. A whole series of articles was translated, mostly from the French, from Peter Kropotkin, Élie and Élisée Reclus, Bernard Lazare,

---

Pioneers of Liberty, but in the 1890s he became a socialist and in 1901 was a founding member of the Socialist Party of America. By 1913 he was no longer involved in radical politics.

4. I. Kopeloff, *Amol in Amerike: zikhroynes fun dem yidishn lebn in Amerike in di yorn 1883–1904* (Warsaw: H. Bzshoza, 1928), 387–94 [Cohen's note]. Kopeloff described Yanovsky as self-promoting and "the sole boss of the *FAS*," accused him of embezzling money intended for Alexander Berkman's legal appeal, and claimed that he had abandoned his idealism to become someone for whom anarchism was merely "a kind of 'sport'-talk."

5. M. Leontieff (or Leontiev) was the pseudonym of **Leon Moissieff** (Moiseyev, 1872–1943), a Russian-born Jewish engineer and anarchist. Already involved in socialist politics as a teenager, he immigrated to the United States in 1891 and became active in the anarchist movement, writing for Johann Most's *Freiheit*, the *FAS*, and other radical papers. He later helped to produce the daily *Der tog*. Moissieff meanwhile earned an engineering degree from Columbia University in 1895 and became one of the country's premier suspension bridge engineers, designing the Manhattan Bridge and consulting on the Golden Gate Bridge.

Warlaam Tcherkesoff, Augustin Hamon, Sebastien Faure, and others.[6] Some extremely interesting original articles were written by Dr. Jacob A. Maryson, Dr. Hillel Solotaroff, and Dr. Iser Ginzburg.[7] Under the heading "Literature

---

6. **Peter Kropotkin** (1842–1921) was a Russian-born naturalist and anarchist. Born into nobility and a prominent geographer and evolutionary scientist, he was moved by the plight of the Russian peasantry and in the 1870s joined the Narodnik movement and the First International, leading to his imprisonment, escape, and exile in western Europe. In London he was a founding member of the anarchist Freedom Group and its newspaper *Freedom*. An editor of numerous anarchist newspapers and author of both radical and scientific tracts, Kropotkin was best known for his advocacy of anarchist communism and the theory that mutual aid plays as large a role as competition in the evolution of species. **Élie Reclus** (1827–1904) was a French-born anthropologist and anarchist. He participated in the Paris Commune of 1871, during which he was head of the Bibliotheque National. Afterward he went into exile in England and the United States until he was amnestied in 1879. **Élisée Reclus** (1830–1905) was a French-born geographer, writer, and anarchist, and a younger brother of Élie Reclus. He traveled extensively, including an 1853 trip to the United States, and participated in the defense of the Paris Commune, for which he was banished from France. Living in Switzerland and then Belgium, he continued to publish influential geographical and anarchist writings, including his twenty-volume *La Nouvelle Géographie universelle* (New Universal Geography, 1876–1894) and *L'Homme et la Terre* (Man and the Earth, 1905–1908). **Bernard Lazare** (1865–1903), real name Lazare Marcus Manassé Bernard, was a French-born Jewish writer, critic, and anarchist. He is best known for his central role in the defense of Jewish army officer Captain Alfred Dreyfus against antisemitic accusations of treason. The Dreyfus Affair aroused in Lazare a concern for Jewish emancipation, and he attended the First Zionist Congress in Basel in 1897 but rejected the goal of creating a Jewish nation-state. **Warlaam Tcherkesoff** (Varlam Cherkezishvili, 1846–1925) was a Russian-born journalist and anarchist. Born into Georgian royalty, he joined the Russian socialist movement in the 1860s and was exiled to Siberia in 1869. In 1876 Tcherkesoff escaped to London, where he joined the Freedom Group and contributed to the international anarchist press. After briefly returning to Russia during the 1905 Revolution, he cofounded the London Anarchist Red Cross. During World War I Tcherkesoff joined Peter Kropotkin in supporting the Allies, and in 1917 he again returned to Russia, where he was elected to the short-lived Constituent Assembly of the Democratic Republic of Georgia until driven into exile by the Bolsheviks in 1921. **Augustin Hamon** (1862–1945) was a French writer, social psychologist, anarchist, and later socialist. He wrote for many anarchist newspapers and founded and edited the anarchist magazine *L'Humanité nouvelle* (The New Humanity, 1897–1907). Hamon, however, frequently used antisemitism as a vehicle to promote anticapitalism. During the Second World War he participated in the French Resistance and joined the French Communist Party shortly before his death. **Sébastien Faure** (1858–1942) was a French writer, editor, and anarchist. He was the longtime editor of the Parisian anarchist newspaper *Le Libertaire* (1895–1914, 1917, 1919–1939), a defender of Alfred Dreyfuss, and founder of the anarchist school La Ruche in 1904.

7. **Iser Ginzburg** (1872–1947) was a Russian-born Jewish doctor, journalist, and socialist. He immigrated to the United States in 1893 and earned his medical degree at Cornell

and Life," Leontieff (Moissieff) wrote in every issue of the journal, in which he sought to acquaint readers with the works of the best European authors of the time. Katz, it seems, spent most time with the editing and translations. Only two or three articles during the life of the magazine bear his name.

The journal was put together extraordinarily well. Many of the articles were later printed as pamphlets and widely distributed, and the rest should still be made into pamphlets and distributed. This very fine journal had one great failing, however: it had nothing to do with the living of life at the time. Throughout the year and a half of its existence, not a single current event was touched upon. The journal could have just as well appeared in 1875 as in 1895, or in 1945—it had no connection to the contemporary world.

As a journal of anarchist enlightenment and education, the *Fraye gezelshaft* fulfilled its goal and gained a certain following among the radical intelligentsia. When it quit publication in 1897, it left a sizeable readership that longed for such a journal. But, on the other hand, there were those comrades who saw the need for a weekly anarchist newspaper to inspire and agitate for anarchism. The movement was divided into these two factions, and for two years the comrades were unable to gather enough support to publish either a newspaper or a magazine. However, the movement continued with its other activities. Classes, debates, and discussions were intermittently held. Some comrades even gathered substantial funds for written propaganda—that is, for a journal or a newspaper—but no real activity in this area came about until the middle of 1899, when the two groups again began to work together in earnest.

Peter Kropotkin's visit to North America in the winter of 1897–98 was, to a large extent, responsible for bringing this about. Britain's Royal Geographical Society had sent him as a delegate to a congress of geographers in Canada. He took this opportunity to visit the largest cities in the continent and held lectures on anarchism arranged by various local groups. His visits helped unify the comrades and even attracted many who had long ago left the ranks to the movement. The lectures everywhere brought together large crowds and made a lasting impression. It is without doubt that his visit gave the first boost to our dormant movement toward new activity.

University. Ginzburg wrote for many radical Yiddish newspapers, including the *Fraye gezelshaft*, the *FAS*, *Tsukunft*, and the *Forverts*, and he authored numerous books on topics such as religion and Jewish history.

CHAPTER 8

The Anarchist Movement in Philadelphia in the 1880s and 1890s

Our Philadelphia comrades have left no exact record of their activities. They never attempted to publish a newspaper of their own. This work was left to the comrades in New York, who always involved the Philadelphia comrades in partnership in these enterprises. The *Fraye arbeter shtime* carried on its masthead the designation "New York and Philadelphia," as a reminder of the period when the opinions of the comrades from Philadelphia were taken seriously. All that remains are beautiful legends of a glorious past when Philadelphia was a fortress of anarchism and social democratic speakers were not listened to.

These legends are not without basis in fact. We have the words of socialists like Hertz Burgin (whom I have quoted above), Bernard Weinstein, and others. I personally heard Louis Miller tell me from the platform about a time when socialist speakers had to work especially hard to hold the attention of a Philadelphia audience. This is no figment of the imagination, but the exact period of anarchist dominance is difficult to ascertain. Comrade Benny Moore, who came to Philadelphia in 1891, recounts that even at that time the comrades were nostalgic for the good old days.[1] That means this

---

1. **Joseph Ben-Zion (Benjamin Joseph or "Benny") Moore** (Yosef Ben-Tsion "Beni" Mur, 1873–1949) was Russian-born Jewish tailor, manufacturer, and anarchist. He was raised in a religious family but joined the anarchist movement after immigrating to the United States in 1899. Moore was the longtime secretary of Philadelphia's Radical Library, and by 1910 he owned his own skirt-making factory. His wife, Sarah Moore, was also an active anarchist. Around 1944 the couple moved to Los Angeles, where they were active in the Kropotkin Literary Society, Branch 413 of the Workmen's Circle. Obituaries: *FAS*, May 27 and June 10, 1949.

era was between 1887, when anarchism crystallized into a distinct movement, and late 1891, when Prenner and others were arrested on Yom Kippur
and sentenced to a year in prison. Hardly long enough, in truth, to create
such legends that persisted for decades. The fact remains, however, that
Philadelphia always had a large number of powerful speakers, writers, and
poets, whereas the socialists had not a single speaker or lecturer in their
ranks. They always had to import people from New York to represent their
position in public. With the exception of a few years when B. Charney
Vladeck lived in Philadelphia, the Jewish socialists never had a prominent
figure among them.[2]

The anarchists, on the other hand, had always been blessed with speak-
ers, lecturers, and writers. In the early 1890s the active speakers and lecturers
in our movement were Robert Wilson, Isidore Prenner, Dr. Max Staller,
Dr. Samuel Gordon, Dr. Leo Gartman, Dr. Max Barbour, Dr. Julius Segal,
Bernard Pockras, George Seldes, Jacob L. Joffe, Natasha Notkin, Bertha
Lieb, Gretch, and Moses Levene.[3] These last two comrades were great

---

2. **Baruch Charney Vladeck** (Borekh-Nakhmen Vladek-Tsharni 1886–1938), real
name Baruch Nachman Charney, was a Russian-born Jewish politician and socialist.
Although raised in a Hassidic family, as a teenager he joined the Bund and was arrested
multiple times for his activism, leading him to emigrate to the United States in 1908. Vladeck
joined the Socialist Party and became manager of the *Forverts* Philadelphia offices in 1912
before moving to New York and assuming management of the paper until his death. In 1917
he was elected to New York City Board of Aldermen as a Socialist, and in 1937 he was elected
to the New York City Council on the American Labor Party ticket. The Yiddish writers
Shmuel Niger and Daniel Charney were his brothers.

3. **Robert Wilson** (Vilson, 1869–1905) was a Russian-born Jewish cigarmaker and anarchist. He immigrated to the United States in 1884 and contributed articles to the *FAS* beginning in 1899 but committed suicide in 1905. Obituary: *FAS*, February 11, 1905. **Max Staller**
(Maks Staler, c. 1868–1919) was an Austrian Galician-born Jewish cigarmaker, surgeon, and
anarchist. He immigrated to the United States in 1881 and later joined Philadelphia's Knights
of Liberty. Staller became a well-known anarchist speaker and helped lead a Philadelphia
cloakmakers' strike in 1890. He wife, Jennie Magul Staller (1872–1957), was also active in the
anarchist movement. In 1895 Staller moved to Chicago to earn his medical degree at the University of Illinois, and after returning to Philadelphia he gradually withdrew from anarchist
circles. In 1900 he cofounded Mount Sinai Dispensary, which later became Philadelphia's
Mount Sinai Hospital. **Samuel H. Gordon** (1871–1906) was a Russian-born Jewish cigarmaker, labor organizer, doctor, and anarchist. He immigrated to Philadelphia in 1890, became
a well-known anarchist speaker and labor organizer, and had a tumultuous six-year romantic
relationship with Voltairine de Cleyre. In 1898 Gordon graduated with a medical degree from
the Medico-Chirurgical College of Philadelphia, and he soon withdrew from the movement.

Talmudists and good debaters on matters of religion. Throughout those years, and for the first three decades of the twentieth century, our movement had at its service the incomparable public speaker and union organizer Chaim Weinberg, who was much beloved by the people. Among the writers

---

After de Cleyre was shot in 1902 he refused requests to aid her, earning him the enmity of many anarchists. Obituary: *FAS*, November 17, 1906. **Leo N. Gartman** (c. 1865–1930) was a Russian-born Jewish cigarmaker, doctor, and anarchist. The son of German Jewish immigrants to Ukraine, he accompanied his entire family to the United States in 1882 as members of Am Olam. In 1889 Gartman and two of his brothers opened a cigar factory in Philadelphia, and he was soon active in anarchist circles. He subsequently earned a medical degree from Jefferson Medical College in 1894 and oversaw Voltairine de Cleyre's recovery after she was shot. **Max Barbour** (Maks Barber, 1877–1963) was a Russian-born Jewish garment worker, doctor, and anarchist. He immigrated to Philadelphia in 1890 with his parents and was soon involved in anarchist circles, serving as president of an anarchist cooperative. Barbour graduated from the Medico-Chirurgical College of Philadelphia in 1898 and soon drifted away from the movement. He later joined the Zionist Organization of America. **Julius Segal** (c. 1868–1952) was a Russian-born Jewish physician and anarchist. Around 1890 he immigrated to Philadelphia, where he earned a medical degree and opened a private practice while also becoming a prominent anarchist speaker. In 1913 Segal was arrested for performing "an illegal operation" on a woman—almost certainly an abortion (*Philadelphia Inquirer*, March 27, 1913). He supported the *FAS* for decades but began contributing articles on anarchism and scientific topics to it only in 1944, when he was in his mid-seventies. Obituary: *FAS*, November 7, 1952. **Bernard Pockrass** (Pokras, 1863–1942) was a Russian-born Jewish attorney and anarchist who immigrated to the United States in 1897. He later had a bitter falling out with fellow Philadelphia anarchists over outstanding legal fees and left the movement; see Chaim Leib Weinberg, *Forty Years in the Struggle: The Memoirs of a Jewish Anarchist*, ed. Robert P. Helms, trans. Naomi Cohen (Duluth: Litwin Books, 2008), 37–40. **George S. Seldes** (Georg S. Zeldes, 1864–1931) was a Russian-born Jewish pharmacist, intellectual, and anarchist. He immigrated to United States in 1882 as a member of Am Olam then moved to Philadelphia in the late 1890s. Seldes corresponded extensively with Leo Tolstoy and Peter Kropotkin and was a supporter of the single tax movement. In 1907 he left Philadelphia for New York and then Pittsburgh and remained active in the anarchist movement until his death. His son George H. Seldes (1890–1995) became a famous muckraking journalist. Obituary: *FAS*, February 13, 1931. **Jacob L. Joffe** (Yankov L. Yafe, 1871–1946) was a Russian-born Jewish garment worker, pharmacist, and anarchist. After immigrating to the United States in 1886, he was active in Philadelphia's anarchist movement and the Knee-Pants Makers' Union. He soon became a pharmacist and opened his own drugstore, where he apprenticed Natasha Notkin and other anarchists in the trade and hosted anarchist meetings after hours. **Bertha Lieb** (Lib) was a Jewish writer and anarchist. Fluent in both English and Yiddish, she offered English-language instruction to fellow immigrants and contributed to both the *FAS* and *Free Society*. Lieb was a member of Philadelphia's Frayheyt Group and wrote and spoke on "the woman question" and women's role in the anarchist movement. **Gretch** or Gratz (Gratsh) was a Jewish peddler and anarchist. He spoke in support of an 1891 tailors' strike in

and poets our movement possessed were Ozer Smolenskin, J. S. Prenowitz, Ephraim-Leib Wolfson, and David Apotheker.[4] The latter was an interesting fellow; a short little Jew with an intelligent face, he was always elegantly dressed in a nice, professional suit with a top hat on his head. The comrades regarded him coldly—a man with strange manners and a strange appearance, as though from another world—yet they never succeeded in driving him from the movement. He was a diligent writer with an old-fashioned, intellectual (*maskilish*) humor. His short stories, signed "Der Hinkediker Shlimazl" (The Lame Good for Nothing), had a certain charm and pleased his readers.

During my time in Philadelphia, around 1905–1906, David Apotheker lived on Fifth Street near South Street. He had what was supposedly an office for insurance, real estate, and other such enterprises, and in addition he was a notary. From all these he made a very poor living. However,

---

Philadelphia, during which the *Philadelphia Inquirer* (June 20, 1891) identified him as "Professor E. Gratz," apparently based on his previous rabbinical education. He died sometime before 1904. **Moses Levene** (Moyshe Levin, 1849–1917), also known as "Old Man Levene" (*de alter Levin*), was a Russian-born Jewish restaurant owner and anarchist. He immigrated to the United States in 1882 and operated a restaurant on Philadelphia's South Fifth Street, and later at 61 Marshall Street, which often hosted anarchist meetings. Levene was also a prominent advocate of Esperanto and contributed to the journal *Amerika Esperantisto* (1907–1963). Obituary: *FAS*, June 30, 1917.

4. **Ozer (Oyzer) Smolenskin** (1862–1934) was a Russian-born Jewish salesman, poet, and anarchist. He immigrated to the United States with his wife and children in 1893 and settled in Philadelphia, where he began contributing poems to the *FAS*, *Di fraye gezelshaft*, the *Arbeter fraynd*, and many other publications, becoming a well-known Yiddish writer. **Joseph Solomon Prenowitz** (Yoysef-Shloyme Prenovits, 1871–1938) was a Russian-born Jewish writer, poet, anarchist, and later socialist. He immigrated to the United States in 1891 and moved to Philadelphia in 1895. Prenowitz contributed poetry and articles to the *Arbeter fraynd*, *FAS*, *Arbeter tsaytung*, *Tsukunft*, *Forverts*, *Gerekhtigkeyt*, and other newspapers. He later joined the Socialist Party of America and worked for the *Forverts*. Obituary: *FAS*, December 23, 1938. **Ephraim-Leib Wolfson** (Efrayim-Leyb Volfson, 1867–1946) was a Russian-born Jewish poet, anarchist, and later socialist. In 1888 he immigrated to the United States and in 1896 began to contribute radical and humorous poetry to the *Arbeter fraynd* and other newspapers. In 1911 Wolfson moved to New York where he was associated with the *Forverts*. **David Apotheker** (1855–1911) was a Russian-born Jewish poet, playwright, and anarchist. Arrested as a student in Kiev in 1879 for revolutionary activity, he escaped and began to write satirical, radical poetry in Hebrew, German, and Yiddish. In 1888 Apotheker migrated to the United States, where he founded a cooperative women's clothing factory in New York, then opened a small publishing house. In 1895 he moved to Philadelphia, where he was active in the Jewish labor and anarchist movements and continued to write humorous poems and plays.

his office was a good place for comrades to meet and take care of movement business.

Our movement in Philadelphia, as in other big cities, was occupied with three kinds of activities: anarchist propaganda and agitation among the Jewish masses; the distribution of pamphlets which were published in London; and work for the revolutionary movement in Russia. We had a special group dedicated to this cause in Philadelphia for many years. Natasha Notkin, an intelligent woman, a pharmacist, was a typical Nihilist, devoted body and soul to that movement and steeped through and through with Russian revolutionary traditions. In Philadelphia in 1893 she organized the "Russian Tea Party," which became for several decades the big social event of the winter season. Natasha never missed an opportunity to do something on behalf of the Russian revolutionary movement. In this work she had the help of her friends William Eidelson, Jacob L. Joffe, and George Seldes, who were also pharmacists.[5] At the same time, they were also active in every other endeavor in our movement.

At that time in Philadelphia there was also a separate, English-speaking anarchist group composed of native-born Americans, made up of some very learned and talented people. Outstanding in this group was Voltairine de Cleyre, a fine speaker, a poet, and a significant writer. In her youth she received a good education in a Catholic convent, but there she lost her belief in God and emerged a lecturer on free thought. A lecture by Clarence Darrow on the social question, which she happened to hear, impressed her deeply and started her thinking about many problems.[6] She became an anarchist and thereafter dedicated her whole life and her many talents to spreading our ideal. In Philadelphia she began to teach English to foreigners, especially Jewish immigrants, and prepared many of them for entrance exams into institutions of higher learning. Most of the Jewish intelligentsia,

---

5. **William Eidelson** (Volf Etelson, 1877–1956) was a Russian-born Jewish pharmacist and anarchist. He immigrated to the United States in 1891 became active in the Philadelphia's anarchist movement, marrying Natasha Notkin in 1918. The couple relocated to Los Angeles and opened a pharmacy in Boyle Heights.

6. **Clarence Darrow** (1857–1938) was a prominent American-born lawyer, socialist, and freethinker. A former railroad attorney, he defended Eugene V. Debs during the 1894 Pullman Strike and subsequently launched a high-profile career as a labor lawyer and defense attorney for progressives and radicals, including many anarchists. He was a proponent of the single tax, an opponent of the death penalty, and a member of the American Civil Liberties Union.

Figure 14: Voltairine de Cleyre
Courtesy of Wikimedia Commons

including all the doctors, lawyers, and pharmacists, were her pupils and under her influence adopted anarchist doctrines.

A second very active member of this movement was George Brown. He was an Englishman by birth, a shoemaker by trade but a highly educated man and a powerful speaker. On the platform he looked and acted like a professor, with great erudition and a fine sense of humor. He had a weakness for alcohol, but never, as far as I know, did he drink to excess. He acted as chairman at all important English-speaking anarchist meetings. His imposing figure always made a fine impression on the audience.

In his youth, an English capitalist company had sent him to India to run a shoe factory there. He was to engage Hindus to work and make them into good industrial slaves. The Hindus, however, had no wish or need for such civilization. True, they were poor and often hungry, but the prospect of working day after day in a factory for a loaf of bread held no attraction for them. The English capitalists tried to civilize and educate them, by creating in them a desire for material things, such as jewelry, clothing, furniture, and the like, which they were offered on credit and then forced to pay off by working. But even this did not succeed. The Hindus did not allow themselves to be caught in the trap of civilization. They would come to the factory but only on the condition that they get paid each day after work. As soon as the worker made enough to buy a sack of rice, he would disappear and not return until he had eaten all the rice—a few weeks. They refused to work for unnecessary luxury items.

This made a deep impression on the young George Brown, who began to think deeply about the so-called capitalist civilization that enslaved the vast majority of the population through all kinds of childish trinkets. He began to study the subject seriously, reading everything that came his way, and eventually gave up his good job, came to America, and went to work in a shoe factory as a simple worker who devoted his free time to studying and working for our movement.

A third person, the extreme opposite of George Brown, was Thomas Earle White, the son of an aristocratic, wealthy family of Philadelphia.[7] He was a famous lawyer and a fine speaker. He became involved in our circles and for many years did valuable work for our movement.

---

7. **Thomas Earle White** (1857–1916) was an American-born lawyer and anarchist from a prominent Philadelphia family with roots in the abolitionist and anti-vivisection movements. He belonged to an anarchist study group formed by Voltairine de Cleyre, donated money to anarchist publications and defense funds, lectured on anarchism, and authored the pamphlet *The Individual and the State* (1891). As Cohen later relates, White withdrew from the movement following the 1901 assassination of William McKinley.

There were also active and intelligent women in that circle: Mary Hansen, Perle McLeod, and others who helped a great deal in the work.[8] Their main activity was to hold open-air anarchist meetings in front of City Hall every Sunday. This lasted for many years, until the assassination of President McKinley, when the wild hysteria across the country put an end to all public anarchist gatherings. Beyond and in addition to the City Hall meetings, the English group used to conduct lectures and discussions at permanent locations. For a long time, the anarchist women maintained an organization of their own called the Ladies' Liberal League. They had their own premises where they kept a large library that they called the Radical Library. At the same time, they published *A Catechism of Anarchy*, a kind of primer that consisted of short, clear questions and answers about anarchist ideas, theory, and practice.[9]

The Jewish anarchist movement was a world unto itself. Its headquarters were for a long time in the Jewish ghetto, in a room over a bank on Pine Street, at the corner of Second Street. Public meetings were usually held in big halls in different parts of the densely populated ghetto. In the early 1890s the Jewish anarchist groups in Philadelphia often carried out propaganda work in two or three different locations simultaneously, all of them well attended. The lecturers were warm and friendly, beloved by the public, and really contributed to the education of the masses.

Our comrades were also active in organizing workers, helping them in their frequent struggles. They organized most of the Jewish unions in Philadelphia, which in those years had to be reconstituted at the beginning

---

8. **Mary Hansen** (1874–1952) was a London-born domestic servant, teacher, poet, and anarchist. The child of a Danish father and English mother, she was brought to Philadelphia with her family in 1875. Hansen was a founding member of the Ladies' Liberal League and the anarchist Social Science Club, and wrote for *Free Society, Lucifer, the Light Bearer*, and *Mother Earth*. She was a close friend of Voltairine de Cleyre and the companion of anarchist George Brown and taught at the Radical Library's Sunday School and later the Ferrer Modern School in Stelton, New Jersey, both of which her and Brown's daughter Heloise Hansen Brown attended. In her old age she lived at the single-tax colony at Arden, Delaware. **Margaret Perle McLeod** (1861–1915) was a Scottish-born hatmaker and anarchist. Her family immigrated to the United States when she was a child, and she cofounded Philadelphia's Ladies' Liberal League and the Social Science Club. McLeod moved to New York 1897 and was active in anarchist and progressive organizations there until her death from cancer.

9. [Mary Hansen et al.,] *A Catechism of Anarchy* (Philadelphia: Social Science Club, 1902).

of each work season. In 1890 our comrades organized a Jewish Federation of Labor—a kind of united Jewish trade union, which did not admit delegates from the weak social democratic "sections." That same year, a strike of the cloakmakers broke out. The leaders of the strike were Max Staller and Isidore Prenner. (It is quite possible that this strike was the reason that the established German Jews later incited the police to arrest and prosecute these comrades on Yom Kippur, in retaliation for their leadership of the strike.) After eighteen weeks of struggle, the workers were forced to surrender.

Chaim Weinberg relates in his memoirs that one fine day he visited Dr. Staller in his office and found him giving information to a strange young man about the recent strike. When the young man left, Weinberg asked Staller, "Do you know who that young man is?" "No," answered Dr. Staller, "I don't know; I only know that he came from New York!" Weinberg then told him, "That is Louis Miller (who was already known as a terrible devourer of anarchists), he'll certainly 'fix' your report properly."[10] And so he did. Louis Miller came out in the socialist *Arbeter tsaytung* with a sensational headline: "Deceived"—saying, that is, that the anarchists had deceived the strikers in Philadelphia, causing thousands of families to suffer in vain. "Reading this report," Benjamin Feigenbaum wrote years later, "It was easy to see that this was nothing more than blasphemy!" Louis Miller had "fixed" the matter correctly, though there was not the slightest truth to it.

The anarchists were also the first to organize the Jewish bakers in Philadelphia. Chaim Weinberg was most active and successful in this work; he spent his entire life in close proximity to this union and was considered its most prominent and beloved member. In his old age it provided him with a pension for his lifetime of good work. The same was done by the Cloakmakers' Union, for which he had done much useful work without remuneration.

Our comrades in Philadelphia were active in all areas of social life. They were the first to build cooperative organizations. Burgin, writing about the early 1890s, says that the anarchists at that time organized a "General

---

10. This quoted dialogue differs slightly from the version in Weinberg's published memoir, which reads: "As soon as Miller left the house, I asked Staller if he knew with whom he had been speaking. Staller answered that it was a reporter from the *Forverts*. I shouted out, 'Do you know who that is? That is Louis Miller, the editor of the *Forverts!*'" Weinberg, *Forty Years in the Struggle*, 80.

Cooperative Society," which opened stores that sold watches, shoes, hats, and other clothing. He adds, "They also kept a saloon. The profits of these enterprises went to the 'Knights of Liberty' group."[11]

I very much doubt the truth of that last claim about a saloon. In my many talks with old-timers, I have never heard them mention such a thing. Perhaps he meant a tearoom that the comrades had in their club, which was a mainstay of all socialist and anarchist clubs—the comrades had such tearooms in Philadelphia and other cities as well. To call it a saloon is, to put it mildly, an ugly slander.

Weinberg was a strong believer in cooperatives in all areas. His whole life he dreamed of a cooperative farm—the old dream of the Am Olam movement—and made several attempts to live in collective housing. He helped build much in the area of consumer cooperatives, but I will describe this later. Comrade Benny Moore related an interesting anecdote from those times. One bright morning he received an invitation to a mandatory meeting of the group. A matter of great importance was to be discussed. When he arrived at the appointed time at the hall on Pine and Second, he found most of the group present, about twenty Jewish workers. A guest was introduced, a delegate from Chicago, comrade Aria Feitelson (David Edelstadt's brother-in-law, later known as Robert Telson), who in earnest reported that Chicago was ready for the social revolution.[12] The comrades were only waiting for the groups in other cities to properly prepare. Then a signal would be given and the revolution would suddenly engulf the entire country. No comment is necessary here!

---

11. Hertz Burgin, *Di geshikhte fun der yidisher arbayter-bavegung in Amerike, Rusland un England* (New York: Fareynigte Idishe Geverkshaften, 1915), 341 [Cohen's note].

12. **Aria Feitelson** (Feytelson, 1865–1942) was a Russian-born Jewish salesman, anarchist, and later Communist. He immigrated to the United States in 1886, was soon involved in the anarchist movement, and married Sonia Edelstadt (1875?–1965). By 1900 the couple had moved to New York, and around the same time Aria Americanized his name to Robert Telson. He was a frequent contributor to the *FAS*, which in September and October of 1931 published a series of his articles about visiting the Soviet Union. His grandson and namesake, Robert Eria Telson, is a well-known composer.

CHAPTER 9

The Influence of London on Our Movement

For decades, until the First World War, London was the Mecca of our movement. There stood the cradle of the Yiddish socialist press. From there the
local socialists, as well as anarchists, attracted their first editors, writers,
and speakers. From there we received newspapers, pamphlets, and books
for many years—all the spiritual nourishment for our movement here in
this country.

The *Arbeter fraynd* began to appear in London in 1885 as a general
socialistic paper. The historic Berner Street Club included socialists, anarchists, and completely impartial members. It appears that the Jewish labor
movement in London was also under the influence of the German socialist
movement in its infancy. For the German workers in London, clubs were
a necessity due to the strong restrictions on the sale of beer and whiskey
in the evening and on holidays. However, members and their guests were
free from such restrictions in their own clubs. The whole German socialist
movement was organized into clubs in which they drank beer and carried on
their propaganda. The Jewish workers followed suit, and the Berner Street
Club became a historic landmark.

From London, the local Knights of Liberty group transferred comrade
Joseph Jaffa to New York to become editor of the first Yiddish anarchist
newspaper, *Di varhayt*, in 1889. After that, the local socialists imported Philip
Krantz from London in 1890 to edit the *Arbeter tsaytung*. From there they
imported Benjamin Feigenbaum, Morris Winchevsky, M. Baranoff, and
other spokesmen for their movement.[1] From there we imported the *Arbeter*

---

1. **M. Baranov** (1864–1924), real name Moyshe Gormidor, was a Russian-born Jewish
journalist and socialist. Arrested for his involvement in Narodnaya Volya, he fled abroad and

fraynd, Freedom with its voluminous essays, and the colorful *Zsherminal* (Germinal) with its rich offerings of European literature.[2] For a long time, all our Yiddish and English pamphlets came from London, and somewhat later also larger works on anarchism, natural science, and literature.

Until the First World War, all the leading spirits of our movement lived there: Kropotkin, Warlaam Tcherkesoff, Nikolai Tchaikovski, Stepniak, Errico Malatesta, Louise Michel, and dozens of other world-famous revolutionaries from Russia, Germany, Austria, and Spain.[3] The eyes of all the

---

in 1888 arrived in London, where he wrote for the *Arbeter fraynd* and sided with its social democratic faction. Baranov then migrated to Argentina and in 1895 to New York, where he wrote for several socialist publications including the *Tsukunft* and *Forverts*.

2. **Freedom** (1886–1928, 1930–36, 1945–2014), cofounded in London by Peter Kropotkin and produced by the Freedom Group, was the longest-running anarchist newspaper (with some interruptions) in the world. As of 2023 *Freedom* still exists as a website, a biannual journal, and a publishing house. **Zsherminal** (1900–1903, 1905–1908) was a Yiddish anarchist theoretical and literary journal edited in London by Rudolf Rocker.

3. **Nikolai Tchaikovsky** (1851–1926) was a Russian-born revolutionary. In 1868–69 he cofounded the eponymous Circle of Tchaikovsky, an important Narodnik group to which Peter Kropotkin and Stepniak belonged. Later he joined to the Freedom Group in London. From 1875 to 1879 Tchaikovsky lived in the United States, where he raised support for the Russian revolutionary movement and lived in a commune in Kansas, and he toured the United States again during the 1905 Revolution as a member of the Socialist-Revolutionary Party. After the 1917 February Revolution he was elected to the Petrograd Soviet and the short-lived Constituent Assembly and became an outspoken opponent of the Bolsheviks, briefly serving as head of an anti-Bolshevik government in northern Russia. **Stepniak** (1851–1895), real name Sergey Stepnyak-Kravchinsky, was a Russian-born revolutionary. He was arrested in 1874 due to his membership in the Circle of Tchaikovsky but escaped to the Balkans where he participated in guerrilla warfare against the Ottoman Empire. In 1877 Stepniak was in Italy and participated in the Benevento Uprising alongside Errico Malatesta and other anarchists. In 1878 he returned to Russia, where he promoted propaganda of the deed and assassinated the head of the secret police, General Nikolai Mezentsov (1827–1878). In 1890 Stepniak fled to Switzerland and then London, where he established the Society of Friends of Russian Freedom and joined the Freedom Group. He also toured the United States in support of the revolutionary movement in Russia. **Errico Malatesta** (1853–1932) was an Italian-born electrician, editor, agitator, and anarchist. He was a member of the First International and disciple of Mikhail Bakunin before becoming Italy's most well-known anarchist. Malatesta spent many years in exile in Europe, North Africa, and the Americas, including a brief residence in the United States in 1899–1900. He was one of the most respected and influential figures in the global anarchist movement up until his death. **Louise Michel** (1830–1905) was a French teacher and anarchist. The founder of a progressive school in Paris in 1865, she became involved in revolutionary politics and took a prominent role in the Paris Commune of 1871, leading to her deportation to New Caledonia until amnestied in 1880. In 1890–95 Michel lived in London, where she opened an International Anarchist School. Her

young comrades in America were drawn to London. Almost all of them dreamed of making the journey there—even in a cattle ship—in order to have the privilege of seeing and hearing the great theorists and leaders of our movement.

London was a kind of safe haven for the Jewish emigrants from eastern Europe. Without the means to travel to the faraway lands of the United States, South Africa, or Argentina, the Jews of Russia, Poland, and Galicia fled to London, where they stayed until they could make or receive more money or get a steamship ticket from a friend, for a further journey. During their temporary stay in London, they became acquainted with socialism and anarchism, and many of them remained radicals their entire lives. They carried with them the seeds of socialist ideas to all corners of the world, wherever fate led them, and looked back with much nostalgia on the short time they had spent in their youth in London, in its comradely atmosphere where the first rays of enlightenment had illuminated their spiritual horizons.

By the end of the 1880s many Londoners who had taken part in the anarchist movement were migrating to the United States. Among them there was a certain L. Rutenberg in New York who could not adapt to the American way of life and chose to return to London.[4] He had the idea of convincing Saul Yanovsky to leave the land of Columbus and go to London, where he could edit the *Arbeter fraynd*, or at least collaborate on it.

Yanovsky had come to the United States in 1885. For the first few years he struggled, throwing himself like a fish out of water from one job to another, never earning enough to live on. The Chicago tragedy of 1887 drew him into anarchist circles and placed him among the movement's speakers, debaters, lecturers, and writers. When the Pioneers of Liberty began to publish *Varhayt* and the arrival of its imported editor was delayed for several weeks, Yanovsky was hired as editor pro tem until Joseph Jaffa came. His duties were to sit in the editorial office, receive manuscripts when people brought them in, and answer questions, but it wasn't long before Yanovsky was doing real editorial work: correcting and "improving" the drafts that comrades had submitted, and he sometimes did so in their presence, with an article by

---

role as the "Red Virgin" of the Commune made her one of the most revered anarchists of her day.

4. **L. Rutenberg** was a member of London's Knights of Liberty group who immigrated to the United States in 1889.

Dr. Hillel Solotaroff, a report on a meeting by Roman Lewis, and others. A hew and cry arose that Yanovsky was taking too many liberties, and he was relieved of the office.

From an early age, Yanovsky possessed the ability to create more enemies than friends. His biting sarcasm and sharp wit irritated anyone who was not in total agreement with him. He very quickly became the Ishmael of the movement: "His hand will be against every man, and every man's hand against him!"[5] By the time the *Fraye arbeter shtime* began to appear in 1890, he was once again at loggerheads with the other comrades, although he still participated in the debates of the divided convention of 1889 and was the one to suggest the name of the newspaper. During one discussion he called out: "We need a newspaper which shall be the free voice of labor!" Those present took up this slogan enthusiastically as the proper name for a movement paper. However, Yanovsky did not take an active part in helping to publish the paper. Therefore, he was sympathetic to Rutenberg's suggestion. That very year, the Londoners sent two steamship tickets for him and his wife, and Yanovsky in a sense went against the current—he traveled to London from the United States to lead the movement there.

When he arrived in London, he found that the position he was intended to occupy was not vacant. The *Arbeter fraynd* was being edited by Konstantin Gallop, a sickly man, who did not want to give up his position.[6] The comrades still wanted to provide Yanovsky with an assignment, so they asked him to write a pamphlet, *Vos vilen di anarkhisten?* (What Do the Anarchists Want?), which was translated into many languages and has been distributed in many countries.[7]

In 1891 a split also occurred in London's historic Berner Street Club between the anarchists and the socialists. With a small majority of twenty-five votes to twenty-two, the comrades took over the management of the club and the newspaper and gave both an anarchist orientation. Yanovsky became editor of the *Arbeter fraynd* and tried to clean up the local labor unions and expel the useless, corrupt leaders who held the organizations in their hands.

---

5. Genesis 16:12.

6. **Konstantin Gallop** (Galop, 1862–1892) was a Russian-born Jewish editor and socialist. From 1890 to 1891 he edited the *Arbeter fraynd*, which he kept open to both socialist and anarchist perspectives. Gallop, who suffered from tuberculosis, died at the age of thirty.

7. S. Yanovsky, *Vos vilen di anarkhisten?* (London: Arbeter fraynd, 1890).

His activities did not stop there. In 1892 the comrades were compelled to appeal to the general labor movement to take over the club and the paper, believing they would be unable to continue under their own power.

The labor movement did not respond to the appeal. As Yanovsky explained in the very interesting first volume of his memoirs, the labor leaders hoped that the newspaper would collapse and that they would be free of its scathing critiques.[8] The *Arbeter fraynd* really did cease publication but not for long. The comrades could no longer go without a newspaper. They renewed their efforts and revived the *Arbeter fraynd* again under Yanovsky's editorship, though his name was not mentioned in the paper for some time. This, according to Yanovsky, had a positive effect.

Yanovsky then began arguing against "propaganda of the deed" as a means of bringing anarchism into existence. But he was not entirely consistent on the topic—he sang hymns of the highest praise for Alexander Berkman's attempt on the life of Henry Clay Frick. But in theory he strongly opposed the tactic, and because of this he made enemies and opponents of himself and the newspaper within the movement. In 1894 he was convinced that his usefulness to the movement in London was coming to an end, and when it was suggested that he should return to the United States and assume editorship of the *Fraye arbeter shtime*, he immediately agreed and set out on his way.

The *Arbeter fraynd* shut down again. Several attempts were made to revive the newspaper under the editorship of Jacob Caplan—who was a brilliant speaker but not a writer—and under William Wess and Abraham Frumkin, but they were all unsuccessful.[9] Finally the inspiration came to the

---

8. Saul Yanovsky, *Ershte yorn fun yidishn frayheytlekhn sotsializm: oytobiografishe zikhroynes fun a pioner un boyer fun der yidisher anarkhistisher bavegung in England un Amerike* (New York: Fraye Arbeter Shtime, 1948).

9. **Jacob ("Yud") Caplan** (Yakov Kaplan, died 1933) was a Russian-born Jewish tailor, labor organizer, and anarchist. A former *maggid* (Jewish preacher) and a talented speaker, he migrated to Leeds, England, in the mid-1880s and quickly became involved in both the Arbeter Fraynd Group and labor organizing among Jewish workers. He edited the *Arbeter fraynd* from 1894 to 1895. Obituary: *FAS*, May 19, 1933. **Woolf ("William") Wess** (Volf "Viliam" Ves, 1861–1946) was a Russian-born Jewish union organizer and anarchist. He immigrated to London in 1881 and became involved in the Jewish labor and radical movements. Wess was a cofounder of the anarchist Berner Street Club and edited the *Arbeter fraynd* from 1895 to 1896. He was also a member of the English-speaking Freedom Group, worked as a typesetter and manager for Freedom Press, and remained active in anarchist causes until his death. Obituary: *FAS*, July 18, 1947. **Abraham Frumkin** (1873–1940) was

comrades at the end of the 1890s to entrust the editorship of the Yiddish *Arbeter fraynd* to Rudolf Rocker, a German gentile, who with the help of comrade David Isakovitz as the paper's manager, proved able in a very short time to miraculously master the Yiddish language and all its characteristic idioms.[10] This time around the *Arbeter fraynd* "was here to stay," as the Americans say. Until the First World War, it served our movement and found support in all corners of the world.

Comrade Rocker united the comrades not only in London but also in most other countries. The comrades in London loved and respected Rocker personally and were attached to him as a good comrade (*khaver*) and teacher for whom they could not find enough words of praise. Those comrades who were not fortunate enough to know him personally were inspired by the revolutionary spirit that he breathed into his writings. The influence of the *Arbeter fraynd, Zsherminal,* and the books that appeared under his signature—the influence of these on all the comrades—was inspiring and

---

an Ottoman-born Jewish translator, journalist, and anarchist. Born in Jerusalem, he studied law in Constantinople, where he joined a radical Jewish group. In 1893 Frumkin visited New York and returned with a large amount of anarchist literature. In 1896 he immigrated to London, where he befriended Rudolf Rocker, helped edit the *Arbeter fraynd*, and married his wife, Sarah Frumkin. After relocating to the United States in 1899, Frumkin contributed to the *FAS* and many other Yiddish publications and became a prolific translator of European literature into Yiddish.

10. **Rudolf Rocker** (1873–1958) was a German-born bookbinder, writer, speaker, and anarchist. Born into a Catholic family, as a youth he became involved in labor organizing and the Social Democratic Party of Germany, then embraced anarchism. Rocker fled to France and then England to avoid arrest and was drawn to the radicalism of both cities' immigrant Jewish workers. He also became the companion and eventual husband of Russian-born Jewish anarchist Milly Witkop (1877–1955). Rocker edited the *Arbeter fraynd* from 1897 until 1914, when he was interned as an "enemy alien," as well as the journal *Zsherminal*. After returning to Germany in 1918, he took a leading role in the anarcho-syndicalist movement there. Rocker visited the United States for lecture tours in 1925 and 1930, then immigrated permanently in 1933 after fleeing from the Nazis. He remained one of the most respected figures in the international anarchist movement and published his best-known work, *Nationalism and Culture*, in 1937. **David Isakovitz** (Dovid Izakovitsh, c. 1874–1949) was a Russian-born Jewish printer and anarchist. In 1893 he migrated to London, where he joined the anarchist movement and helped produce the *Arbeter fraynd*. Isakovitz came to the United States in 1907 and worked as a printer for *Der tog*. In his later years he sympathized with the Poale Zion movement. His son, historian Henry David (1907–1984), wrote the first scholarly study of the Haymarket Affair (*The History of the Haymarket Affair*, 1958) and was president of the New School for Social Research.

Figure 15: Group of Jewish anarchists in London, 1912
Back row: Rudolf Rocker (second from left), Lazar Sabelinsky (second from right); front row: Milly Witkop (left), Milly Sabel (Sabelinsky) (middle); courtesy of Wikimedia Commons

revolutionizing. Each one was rousing call for struggle. Every issue of the newspaper brought news and notices of revolutionary struggles throughout the world, particularly in the Latin countries, which were for us a special source of inspiration and enthusiasm.

❋ ❋ ❋

In time, larger numbers of Londoners began to arrive in America and take part in our activities. And, remarkably, the most active of them embarked on a path of constructive, evolutionary activity here, at a time when we American anarchists, the younger ones at least, were trying with all our might to bring about the revolution. This is a bit of a puzzle, which can be partially explained by the general human weakness of throwing oneself from one extreme to the other. Children from conservative parents, brought up according to the Talmud, the Torah, and the yeshiva, or in monasteries, often pass to the camp of the heretics and reject all that they have been taught to worship in their youth; and children of radical parents often embark on the path of conservatism and become quite reactionary.

A number of the London comrades who came here immediately fell under the influence of Dr. Jacob A. Maryson and became devoted adherents of his teachings and the serious work that he later undertook to produce the classic works of anarchism and socialism in the Yiddish language. Comrades Sam Margolis and, in particular, David Isakovitz excelled in this regard.[11] From the first day he came here, Isakovitz took upon himself the difficult and thankless work of combating what Johann Most had described years earlier as the "childhood diseases" and currents in our movement.[12] He never missed an opportunity to speak out against "propaganda of the deed," against the irresponsible actions of individuals in the movement, and against the justification of antisocial acts in any area. His activity placed him in the quixotic position of tilting against the windmills of the small, organized circles in the movement, in which the word had replaced the deed. Talking and writing about revolution was considered by most of us in those years to be a revolutionary activity, although it remained mostly talk. We undertook no practical revolutionary work in this country, which would have been like beating our heads against a wall. Nevertheless, his work, as I have said, was difficult and thankless. More than once he even ran the risk of being beaten up after a tumultuous meeting by those who had failed to make logical arguments in defense of their position. But nothing frightened Isakovitz. Wherever the comrades discussed questions of tactics, comrade Isakovitz came with his word of warning and his demand that we do

---

11. **Sam Margolis** (1890–1964) was a Russian-born Jewish shoe cutter and anarchist. He immigrated to London in 1900 and became a member of the Arbeter Fraynd Group, then came to the United States in 1911. He belonged to the anarchist Naye Gezelshaft Group, the Kropotkin Literary Society, and the Boot and Shoe Workers' Union, and he later served as secretary of Jewish Anarchist Federation. His wife Goldie (Golde, c. 1897–1966) was likewise active in the anarchist movement. Obituary: *FAS*, March 15, 1964.

12. *Freiheit*, June 5, 1892 [Cohen's note].

something useful and constructive rather than contenting ourselves with just talking, and, more often than not, talking nonsense.

It was truly admirable: where did this man find so much courage, such an unwavering commitment to hammering, for years, against what was then the main current in our movement? The younger comrades wouldn't listen to him, and the older ones shrugged their shoulders, thinking: "Eh, he's a crank!" Yanovsky often edited his articles, changing their meaning, saying that he knew better than Isakovitz what Isakovitz meant to say! But nothing worked. Isakovitz went his own way, serving the movement as he understood it, and gradually he began to receive recognition and respect for his views, and he became an institution in the movement, one of the pillars upon which our activity stood.

Isakovitz was a busy man his whole life, a worker, a typesetter by trade, who suffered from the painstaking work of his craft but always found the time and patience to contribute enough to the field of writing, translating, debating, and popularizing ideas during the forty-odd years that he lived in this country. He faithfully translated Kropotkin's *Memoirs of a Revolutionist* into Yiddish for the Kropotkin Literary Society in 1912 and translated dozens of major works for the *Fraye arbeter shtime*, with which he was closely associated for many years as a member of the editorial board. In addition, he wrote hundreds of articles on movement issues, always in the same direction and with the sole intention of convincing the comrades to embrace constructive activities in the movement.

Comrade Isakovitz had two failings, both stemming from the same source. First, he was afraid of the specter of revolution, which was the soul of our movement; he sought to convince himself and others that not only is revolution not desirable from the standpoint of anarchism but also that it is absolutely not possible in our age—a prophecy that is not based on anything and that can only discourage the younger comrades. If the latter erred a little in attributing too much importance to the revolution, Isakovitz erred no less in his constant quest to bend the path entirely in the other direction and to question the possibility or desirability of a fundamental upending of the existing order.

His second weakness was that, in seeking another social force to take the place of revolution in future development, he embraced every new reform movement as an announcement of deliverance: Guild Socialism,

Technocracy, Social Credit—every single one of these movements in its turn received his whole-hearted support, as if it could truly bring redemption to the suffering of humanity.

These two small weaknesses somewhat lessened the extent of his influence, which should have had a wider affect in our circles, as his sincerity, seriousness, and devotion truly merited it. However, his contributions to our movement were nevertheless quite significant.

❀ ❀ ❀

Among all the other London comrades who contributed much to the development of our movement here in America, Aaron Mintz and Nathan Weinrich should be commended for their work for the *Fraye arbeter shtime*; Thomas B. Eyges, for his many lectures and his column "Korespondents fun a reyzenden" (Correspondence from a Traveler); Leon Baron, with his oppositional spirit that he brought from London and the magazine *Frayheyt* (Freedom), of which he published several issues, in addition to contributing much to the initial organization of the Amalgamated Clothing Workers of America; Abraham Greenstein, who published a few issues of *Der veker* (The Alarm); Sam Margolis, with his extensive work for the Kropotkin Literary Society and for the Jewish Anarchist Federation during his many years in New York; Dr. Benjamin Dubovsky, Tania Schapiro, Alexander Brown, and Simon Farber; Sam Mendelsohn, during his years in Baltimore; and finally Sol Linder, whom we have to thank for keeping the *Fraye arbeter shtime* going.[13]

---

13. **Aaron Mintz** (Ahrn Mints, 1870–1940), also known as "Der blinder Mints" (Blind Mintz) and A. Banov or Bonof, was a Russian-born Jewish cigarmaker and anarchist. After emigrating to London, he joined the Arbeter Fraynd Group and then the oppositional Frayheyt Group and became well-known as a radical *deklamator* (reciter of poetry). Mintz briefly came to the United States in 1888, then, after he began to lose his eyesight from nicotine poisoning, he returned permanently in 1905 in the company of Nathan Weinrich. In New York he began a long association with the *FAS*, as described later in this book. His younger brother Sam Mintz was also active in the anarchist movement. Obituary: *FAS*, July 12, 1940. **Nathan Weinrich** (Nokhum Vaynritsh, 1884–1970) was a Polish Jewish laborer, insurance agent, writer, and anarchist. In 1899 he migrated to London, where he took an active role in the anarchist movement. Weinrich also befriended Aaron Mintz, whom he accompanied to the United States in 1905 and for whom he became a guide and living companion after Mintz

A number of additional London comrades devoted the entirety of their
activities to the American labor movement and rose to high positions within

---

lost his sight. In New York he became a manager for the *FAS* and wrote for that paper, the *For-verts*, and other Yiddish publications. **Thomas B. Eyges** (Tuvye-Borekh Eyges, 1875–1960) was a Russian-born Jewish shoemaker, salesman, journalist, and anarchist. In 1889 he immigrated to London, where he worked in a shoe factory, became secretary of the Jewish Boot and Shoe Union, and joined the Arbeter Fraynd Group. Eyges moved to Boston in 1903 and worked for several years as a traveling clothing salesman, during which he lectured on anarchism and related topics and wrote about his experiences for the *FAS* and other newspapers. During the Great Depression he worked for the Federal Housing Administration and the Works Progress Administration and gradually became more politically moderate. In 1944 Eyges published his English-language memoir, *Beyond the Horizon: The Story of a Radical Emigrant*, in which he writes of himself in the third person as "Mot Segye" (an inverted spelling of Tom Eyges). Eyges's column "Korespondents fun a reyzenden" appeared regularly in the *FAS* from 1904 to 1906. **Leon Baron** (c. 1872–1914) was a Russian-born Jewish labor organizer and anarchist. He migrated to London around 1889, joined the anarchist faction of the Berner Street Club, and opposed *Arbeter fraynd* editor Saul Yanovsky's criticism of propaganda of the deed. Baron briefly coedited the *Arbeter fraynd* with William Wess after Yanovsky's departure, but he later clashed with Rudolf Rocker and in 1901 founded the oppositional Frayheyt Group. He was subsequently strongly influenced by French revolutionary syndicalism and participated in a Jewish tailors' strike in 1904 before he immigrated to New York around 1906. Baron became secretary of the United Brotherhood of Tailors and helped its 1913 strike but died shortly thereafter from a long illness. Obituary: *FAS*, May 23, 1914. *Frayheyt* was the name of two anarchist newspapers edited by Leon Baron, the first in London in 1902–1903 and the second in New York in 1913–1914. The **Amalgamated Clothing Workers of America** (ACWA) was a progressive menswear industrial union founded in 1914 by socialists and other radicals who broke away from the AFL's conservative United Garment Workers. In 1935 it was one of the founding organizations of the CIO. The ACWA dissolved in 1976 in the first of several union mergers that eventually produced the rival unions UNITE HERE and Workers United. **Abraham Greenstein** (Avrom Grinshteyn, 1880–?) was a Russian-born Jewish jewelry worker, labor organizer, and anarchist. In 1898 he migrated to London, where he became involved in the labor and anarchist movements, befriended Peter Kropotkin, and cofounded the paper *Frayheyt* with Leon Baron. Greenstein migrated to New York in 1906 and in 1916 helped reconstitute the International Jewelry Workers' Union, for which he served as secretary-treasurer for several years. His son, artist Benjamin Greenstein (aka Benjamin G. Benno), attended the Ferrer Modern School in New York. *Der veker* (1908), not to be confused with the paper of the same name published by the Jewish Socialist Verband, appeared around May 1908 and engaged in a brief debate with the *FAS* over each publication's stance on trade unions. No copies are known to have survived. **Benjamin Dubovsky** (Binyumin Dubovsky, 1888–1963) was a Russian-born Jewish doctor, writer, and anarchist. In 1900 he migrated to London, where he worked as a coat maker and became active in the anarchist movement. Dubovsky came to the United States around 1906 to continue his studies and earned a medical degree. He also began writing for the *FAS*, the *Arbeter fraynd*, *Der tog*, the *Forverts*, and other publications, and he published many pamphlets and

the ranks of its leadership: Morris Feinstone in the United Hebrew Trades; Morris Sigman and Israel Feinberg in the International Ladies' Garment Workers' Union; Osip Wolinsky in the Leather Goods Workers Union, Alex Cohen in the Amalgamated Clothing Workers, and probably many other who are unknown to me—a non-Londoner—as such.[14]

---

books in Yiddish and English on health, religion, and other topics. Obituary: *FAS*, October 1, 1963. **Tania Schapiro** (Tanya Shapiro, c. 1886–1960) was a Russian-born Jewish garment worker and anarchist. She migrated to London as a teenager and in 1905 joined a Russian anarchist group there. Tania married fellow anarchist Alexander Schapiro (c. 1882–1946), and the couple returned to Russia during the 1917 revolution, only to be expelled in 1922 for criticizing the Soviet government. They separated soon after and in 1923 Tania migrated to the United States, where she joined the Naye Gezelshaft Group and helped produce the *FAS*. Obituary: *FAS*, May 1, 1960. **Alexander Brown** (Aleksander Braun, 1883–1968) was a Russian-born Jewish brush maker and anarchist. As a teenager he joined the labor movement and organized on behalf of the Bund, for which he was repeatedly arrested. In 1902 Brown fled to London, where he became an anarchist and worked on behalf of both the *Arbeter fraynd* and *Freedom* and advocated anarcho-syndicalism. In 1913 he migrated to Philadelphia, where he became the longtime secretary of the Radical Library Group and helped found Philadelphia's Horse Hair Dressers' Union. His wife, Julia Brown, was also active in the Radical Library Group. See *FAS*, December 18, 1953. **Simon Farber** (Seymon or Shimeon Farber, 1887–1960) was a Russian-born Jewish garment worker, labor organizer, editor, and anarchist. At age eight he joined the Socialist-Revolutionary Party as a courier, and after emigrating to London in 1902 he became an anarchist. Farber moved to New York in 1904, and in the 1920s he served as chairman of Local 22 of the ILGWU's Dress Makers' Union, was a prominent member of the union's Anarchist Group, and edited the group's newspaper *Der yunyon arbeter* from 1925 to 1927. Farber later served on the editorial board of the *FAS*, as labor editor of the *Forverts*, and as editor of the ILGWU's paper *Gerekhtigkeyt* from 1936 until 1958. His wife Sonya Farber (1892–1983) was also active in the ILGWU and anarchist movement. Obituary: *FAS*, March 1, 1960. **Samuel ("Sam") Mendelsohn** (Shmuel "Sem" Mendelson, 1890–1952) was a Russian-born Jewish department store worker and anarchist. He immigrated to Baltimore with his mother and brother between 1895 and 1898 and by 1904 was a member of that city's anarchist Varhayt Group and in frequent correspondence with the *FAS*. **Solomon ("Solo" or "Sol") Linder** (Shlomo or Shoyel Linder, 1886–1960) was a Russian-born Jewish journalist and anarchist. In 1900 he immigrated to London, where he joined the labor and anarchist movements and corresponded with the *FAS*. Linder attended the 1907 International Anarchist Congress in Amsterdam, and from 1910 to 1914 he managed and coedited the *Arbeter fraynd*. He was interned in England during the First World War as an "enemy alien" (his home city of Zolochiv was then part of the Austro-Hungarian Empire) and in 1918 was expelled. In 1923 he migrated to New York, where he served as the *FAS*'s manager from 1940 to 1960 and editor from 1951 to 1958. Obituary: *FAS*, January 1, 1961.

14. **Morris Feinstone** (Moyshe Faynstoun, 1878–1943) was a Russian-born Jewish carpenter, labor organizer, and anarchist. As a student he joined the Polish Socialist Party and was arrested for his activities, then fled to England in 1898. There Feinstone joined the

The influence of London had a great effect on our movement in more than one branch of activity, and this positive influence increased after Rudolf

---

Woodcarvers' Union, of which he became president in 1895, and was involved in the British Labour Party in Birmingham before joining the Jewish anarchist movement. Feinstone immigrated to New York in 1906 or 1910 and became an organizer for the Umbrella and Cane Industry Union from 1913 until 1915. From 1915 to 1925 he served as assistant secretary of the United Hebrew Trades, then as its secretary-treasurer. Although Feinstone remained an anarchist and continued to financially support anarchist undertakings, by the 1930s he was also supporter of the socialist *Forverts* and *New York Call* (1908–1923), of the Labor Zionist movement Poale Zion, and of the American Labor Party. He also served on the boards of the National Labor Committee for Palestine, the Jewish Labor Committee, the Hebrew Immigrant Aid Society, the Rand School of Social Science, and the War Labor Board. **Morris Sigman** (Moris Zigman, 1881–1931) was a Russian-born Jewish garment worker, labor organizer, and anarchist. In 1902 he immigrated to London, where he joined the anarchist movement, then to the United States the following year. In 1904 Sigman organized the independent Cloak and Skirt Pressers' Union, which affiliated with the Socialist Trade and Labor Alliance and in 1905 was absorbed into the IWW. In 1908 Sigman gave up on the dual unionism of the IWW and joined the ILGWU, for which he served as chair of the picket committee during the 1910 Great Revolt, secretary treasurer (1914–1915), and vice president (1920–1923). Sigman was elected president of the ILGWU from 1923 to 1928, during which he headed a bitter campaign against Communist influence in the union and attempted to reorganize its unions along industrial lines. **Israel Feinberg** (Yisroel Faynberg, 1886–1952) was a Russian-born Jewish garment worker, labor organizer, and anarchist. He migrated to London with his parents in 1902 and took part in the anarchist and labor movements of both that city and, after 1908, Manchester. Feinberg came to New York in 1912 with his wife Nellie Feinberg and immediately joined the ILGWU, within which he held the offices of vice president (1922–1925, 1928–1952), general organizer for Canada, and then supervisor of the Pacific Coast. He soon gravitated toward the Socialist Party and later the social democratic Liberal Party of New York but maintained strong ties to the Jewish anarchist movement. In 1943 Feinberg negotiated the first union-run pension program in the United States. Obituary: *FAS*, September 26, 1952. See also Melech Epstein, *Yisrael Faynberg: kemfer far frayheyt un sotsyaler gerekhtikayt* (New York: Lerman Printing Company, 1948). The **International Ladies' Garment Workers' Union** (ILGWU) was founded in 1900 by predominantly Jewish workers in the women's clothing industry. As related later in this book, the union remained small until the massive garment strikes of 1909 and 1910, after which the ILGWU went on to become one of the largest unions in the United States. From 1908 onward the union's leadership was dominated by Jewish socialists, but the ILGWU was also the most significant stronghold of anarchism in the American labor movement, and from 1923 to 1928 its presidency was held by the anarchist Morris Sigman. **Ossip Walinsky** (Osip Volinsky, 1886–1973), real name Yosef Melekhinsky, was a Russian-born Jewish leather worker, poet, labor organizer, and anarchist. Around 1902 he joined the Bund and was repeatedly arrested in connection with radical activities. Walinsky fled to Germany in 1903 and made his way to London, where he was active in the Jewish labor and anarchist movements, wrote for the *Arbeter fraynd*, edited *Der idisher treyd yunyonist* (The Jewish Trade Unionist, 1907–c.

Rocker came to live in America, bring with him a spirit of revival wherever comrades had the privilege of encountering him.

1910), and in 1912 organized a London branch of the Workmen's Circle. He immigrated to the United States in 1914 and was immediately employed as an organizer for the ILGWU, then in 1918 for the Fancy Leather Goods Workers' Union, which after several mergers became the International Handbag, Leather Goods, Belt, and Novelty Workers Union, for which Walinsky served as president from 1951 to 1957. He wrote for and contributed funds to the *FAS* as late as 1965 and was a member of the Kropotkin Literary Society, however he also ran for the New York State Assembly in 1922, cofounded the Liberal Party of New York in 1944, and was a strong supporter of Labor Zionism and Histadrut. **Alex Cohen** (Aleks Kohen) was a Russian-born Jewish garment worker, labor organizer, and anarchist. He was involved in the labor and anarchist movements in Birmingham, England, before coming to the United States. Cohen helped lead the 1913 tailors' strike in New York that led to the formation of the ACWA, and was the longtime secretary-treasurer of the union's New York Joint Board. In 1917 he was prominently involved in the movement to prevent Alexander Berkman's extradition to California in connection with the Preparedness Day bombing.

CHAPTER 10

The Revival of the Anarchist Movement

In 1899 the Jewish anarchist movement began to show signs of revival. In London the *Arbeter fraynd* appeared again under the editorship of comrade Rudolf Rocker. In America too the comrades began to make serious preparations to revive their own newspaper. In the tenth anniversary issue of the revived *Fraye arbeter shtime* (October 2, 1909), Louis Finkelstein describes the struggle that took place for a number of years between two groups: "Proletariat"—composed mostly of comrades who wanted to publish a monthly journal—and the "Nayer Dur" (New Generation) group, which included many members who had emigrated from London and wanted to put out a weekly paper.

The "battle" lasted a long time. Gradually members of Nayer Dur joined the Proletariat group to bore from within. The united group put on the first *boyern* ball (peasants' ball) and raised a few hundred dollars for publishing propaganda material. In 1899 a convention convened in Brownsville, Brooklyn, attended by representatives from outlying areas but very few representatives from the New York groups. Dr. Michael A. Cohn was made secretary of the convention.[1] The delegates decided to publish a weekly

---

1. **Michael A. Cohn** (Maykl or Mikhael Kohn, 1867–1939) was a Russian-born Jewish physician and anarchist. After immigrating to the United States in 1886, he earned his medical degree at Baltimore's College of Physicians and Surgeons while working as a tailor. Radicalized by the Haymarket Affair, Cohn became a regular contributor to the *FAS* and was a delegate to the 1900 International Revolutionary Congress in Paris, where he presented a report, "The History of the Jewish Anarchist Movement in the United States." In 1931 Cohn became secretary of the Jewish Anarchist Federation. Throughout his career, he used the profits from his medical practice and real estate holdings to fund the anarchist movement.

newspaper and to invite Abraham Frumkin to come from London and be its editor. Frumkin accepted the invitation and came to New York, but before completing the preparations for the paper Frumkin "betrayed" the comrades—he joined the camp of the "journal-ists" who were endeavoring to resurrect the journal *Fraye gezelshaft*. The "newspaper-ist" faction then had no other choice than to send a committee to Saul Yanovsky, asking him to become editor of their paper. After a week, he sent a written statement to the group stating that he would accept the editorship providing he had a free hand in the editorial office: no one would tell him how to run the newspaper, and the comrades should know in advance that he would oppose "propaganda of the deed" and support active participation in the labor movement. But the paper under his editorship would be a free platform for the discussion of all social theories.

The group accepted Yanovsky's terms. On October 6, 1899, the first issue of the *Fraye arbeter shtime* under the editorship of Yanovsky made its appearance. The paper had sixteen pages and a smaller format than the *Fraye arbeter shtime* would later have. Five pages were filled with announcements. The masthead stated in big letters: "Anarchist-Communist Organ," and beneath it was the caption "Let the Voice of the People Be Heard! —A. Parsons."[2]

The second issue contained articles by two Philadelphians, Robert Wilson and Ephraim-Leib Wolfson. There were also reports from two Philadelphia groups: the Radical Debater Club and the Knights of Liberty group. The Philadelphia cloakmakers' and pants makers' unions also published reports in its first issues. Philadelphia was, in a word, very popular in the new paper. The comrades there donated $200 to the *Fraye arbeter shtime* and the *Fraye gezelshaft*.

The conflict between the two factions seemed to have abated. In almost every issue of the *Fraye arbeter shtime* there are advertisements for the *Fraye gezelshaft* signed by Abraham Frumkin. However, no description of the contents of the magazine are to be found in the newspaper.

The paper still makes a good impression. Besides Yanovsky, who often contributed translations and articles under different pseudonyms, there are contributions from Michael A. Cohn, Jacob Gordin, Shloyme Pres (the "Kleynshtedldiker"), Alexander Harkavy, Joseph Bovshover, J. S. Prenowitz,

---

2. These were the final words of Albert Parsons before his execution.

and Ozer Smolenskin, as well as David Moses Hermalin's sharp attacks against Zionism and religion.[3]

At the end of December there was an annual convention at which Philadelphia was represented by two delegates, Levene and Simon M. Dubin.[4] The entire first session and part of the second was taken up with discussions of the *Fraye arbeter shtime*'s ethos. The critiques of what it looked like and how it was managed were very sharp. At one point, Yanovsky himself suggested that Rudolf Rocker be invited to undertake the editorship, but the motion was rejected, as was another motion that Rocker be invited to

---

3. **Shloyme Pres** (1870–1961) was a Russian-born Jewish journalist and anarchist. He migrated to England in 1891 and wrote for the *Arbeter fraynd*, then moved to the United States in 1894 and became a regular contributor to the *FAS* under the pen name "A Kleynshtetldiker" (A Small-Towner). Based in Boston, Pres was prominent in that city's anarchist movement and in the Independent Workmen's Circle that formed there in 1906. **Alexander Harkavy** (1863–1939) was a Russian-born Jewish linguist, writer, and radical. He immigrated to the United States in 1882 as a member of Am Olam and began a long career of studying the Yiddish language and publishing multilingual dictionaries, language manuals, textbooks, and related materials. Harkavy rejected political labels but was affiliated with the anarchist Pioneers of Liberty and contributed to many radical Yiddish publications, including the *Fraye gezelshaft*, the *FAS*, *Tsukunft*, and the *Forverts*. In addition, he edited the short-lived radical paper *Der nayer gayst* (The New Spirit, 1897–1898), which published anarchist and socialist writings. Harkavy was also a member of Hovevei Tsion (Lovers of Zion), the Hebrew Immigrant Aid Society, the Workmen's Circle, the YIVO Institute for Jewish Research, and other prominent Jewish organization. **Joseph Bovshover** (Yoysef Bovshover, 1873–1915) was a Russian-born Jewish laborer, poet, and anarchist. He immigrated to the United States in 1891 and worked in a sweatshop before joining the anarchist movement and writing revolutionary poems for socialist and anarchist newspapers. Bovshover became a major figure of Yiddish "proletarian poetry" and also published poems in the English-language anarchist paper *Liberty* (1881–1908) under the penname "Basil Dahl." In 1900 he was permanently institutionalized for debilitating depression. **David Moses Hermalin** (Dovid-Moyshe Hermalin,1865–1921) was a Romanian-born Jewish journalist, translator, playwright, and socialist. He immigrated to the United States in 1885 and wrote for many leftist and mainstream Yiddish newspapers, including the *FAS*. In 1917 Hermalin belonged to the Jewish Socialist League, a short-lived breakaway faction of the Jewish Socialist Federation that favored the Allied war effort.

4. "Levene" is probably a reference to Moses Levene. **Simon M. Dubin** (1867–1919) was a Russian-born Jewish physician and anarchist. He earned his medical degree in 1896 in Berne, Switzerland, where he met and married his wife, Russian-born Jewish chemist and anarchist Minna Mandelston (c. 1863 or 1869–1946). The couple immigrated that same year to Philadelphia, where the Dubins' home became a hub for radical activity, including raising funds for the 1905 Russian Revolution. In 1900 Simon cofounded the Mount Sinai Dispensary, and in 1902 he testified as an expert witness at the trial of Herman Helcher.

become at least be a collaborator. The main objection was that the comrades did not want to undermine the London movement and the *Arbeter fraynd*, which Rocker had succeeded in revitalizing, and the London comrades were also preparing to reissue the journal *Zsherminal* under his editorship. So after all the debating and bitter criticism, Yanovsky continued as editor of the *Fraye arbeter shtime.*

The paper's financial situation, as reported at the convention, was not bad. There was $600 in the treasury. A collection made at the convention brought in another $160. Then the delegates allowed themselves the luxury of discussing publication of a supplement to the *Fraye arbeter shtime,* but the motion for creation of such a journal was turned down—the *Fraye gezelshaft* was filling this role very well. Therefore, the convention decided to create a propaganda fund, to publish pamphlets and at least one book on anarchism each year.

The convention also took up another important problem: what was to be done to gain Berkman's freedom? No public discussion could take place on this topic. The convention elected a committee of three to contact Berkman and find out what could be done on his behalf: Michael A. Cohn, Yanovsky, and Dr. Hillel Solotaroff. Several factors were involved here. A short time after Berkman's arrest in 1892, comrades Carl Nold and Henry Bauer, with whom Berkman had stayed the night before his deed, were arrested.[5] They had also distributed leaflets to the militiamen who had been sent in to break the strike. They were both given five-year prison sentences, which they served in the Western Penitentiary together with Berkman. In prison, the three men successfully produced a little newspaper, *Zuchthausblüten* (Prison Blossoms), for a time. Nold and Bauer were freed in 1897. The Pittsburgh comrades arranged a welcome party and picnic for them on a Sunday, and a number of people were arrested for breaking blue laws—by selling beer on the Sabbath. Comrade Harry Kelly, who at that time lived in St. Louis, heard

---

5. **Carl Nold** (1869–1934) was a German-born machinist and anarchist. He immigrated to the United States in 1883 and soon joined the anarchist movement, contributing to *Free Society, Mother Earth, Man!* (1933–1940), and other anarchist publications. After his release from prison, Nold was active in anarchist circles in Arkansas, St. Louis, and then Detroit up until his death. **Henry Bauer** (1861–1934) was a German-born carpenter and anarchist. He immigrated to the United States in 1880 and was radicalized by the Haymarket Affair. After his release from prison, Bauer served as secretary of the Berkman Defense Committee and became a distributor for numerous anarchist publications in the Pittsburgh region.

about the predicament of the comrades, and he wrote to Harry Gordon, then a resident of Pittsburgh, asking him to defend those detained.[6] Gordon gladly accepted, and when Kelly arrived he found that the comrades were already out of jail. He then went to all the English-speaking unions in the city to get them to take an interest in Berkman's situation. Kelly had good recommendations from the Central Labor Unions in Boston and St. Louis. He was active in the unions in both cities and held office in their central bodies. The American labor movement at that time was mostly in the hands of the Irish, who were disposed toward revolutionary politics, at least as far as their home country was concerned. The name Kelly (although Harry Kelly was not Irish) opened all doors for our comrade. He was able to interest the majority of unions in calling for a new trial or a pardon for Berkman. The secretary of the Pittsburgh Central Labor Union confided in Kelly that he had been a close friend of Albert Parsons in the early 1880s. He was now eager to get involved in the work to free Berkman.

This movement did not achieve any tangible results. The Pennsylvania State Board of Pardons replied to the unions' appeal by explaining that, although it was possible that the three-times-seven-years sentence was indeed beyond the scope of the law, since Berkman was still serving the first seven years that he undeniably, really deserved, it was premature to talk of a pardon!

One thing this movement did do was to arouse great interest among the working class in Berkman's plight. When Kropotkin was in America in 1898 he sent a letter to Berkman addressed "To the political prisoner Alexander Berkman." The prison officials were very offended. "We have no political prisoners in America," they wrote on the envelope and returned the letter. All

---

6. **Harry Kelly** (1871–1953) was an American-born printer, union organizer, and anarchist. After growing up in Missouri, in the 1890s he was involved in unionism and anarchism and became the companion of Jewish anarchist Mary Krimont. In 1898 the couple moved to London, where they joined the Freedom Group until their return to the United States in 1904. Kelly was a close friend of Emma Goldman. He and Alexander Berkman, with whom he cofounded the Francisco Ferrer Association in 1910, helped create several anarchist communes and schools in and near New York, including Stelton. Kelly also wrote for and helped to produce several English-language anarchist newspapers. **Harry Gordon** (1866–1941) was a Russian-born Jewish machinist and anarchist. After emigrating to Pittsburgh around 1890, he became involved in anarchist circles. In 1919 he and his family moved to the anarchist community of Stelton, New Jersey, and later to the Mohegan Colony. His wife, Lydia Gordon, was also an anarchist.

of this aroused great excitement in the movement all over the country, and this was the reason that the Berkman question was taken up by the unions.

Berkman, for his part, did not put much faith in all these appeals. He knew that for the time being Carnegie and Frick would never agree to his release, and, without their consent, nothing would be done in Pennsylvania. Berkman instead devised a plan to escape. In prison he had made friends with a fellow inmate in whom he had perfect confidence, and who was to be freed in 1899. He gave him the plan in full detail, worked out in a secret code that only they could read, and gave him Harry Gordon's address to get in touch with the comrades.

In the March 16, 1900, issue of the *Fraye arbeter shtime* we find a report that Harry Gordon came to New York in connection with the Berkman affair. For public consumption, the report states that there was reason to believe that there would be an opportunity for a new trial and that $1,000 was needed for hiring good lawyers and other expenses. The newspaper's appeal brought an amazingly warm and quick response. Money poured in from all sides. In the very short time, the *Fraye arbeter shtime* alone had raised more than a thousand dollars. In addition, a few hundred dollars was collected by the *Forverts*, and a smaller sum by the United Hebrew Trades.

The money collected went to renting a house near the penitentiary and to digging a tunnel under the street and the high wall of the prison. The work, as one can easily imagine, was torturous—digging a tunnel underground without the necessary tools, and with the participation of only two men laboring in the tunnel and one woman in the house to prevent suspicion. Not to mention the tremendous risk to those involved.[7]

The work could not be carried out according to Berkman's plans. The diggers encountered a gas main in the tunnel and had to curve to the left. In addition, a huge pile of building materials was just then dumped on the spot where the opening of the tunnel was supposed to be in the yard of the prison. The plan had to be abandoned. The comrades barely escaped in time. The tunnel was discovered and caused a big stir in the prison, though no one

---

7. The tunnel was dug by Harry Gordon, Norwegian-born anarchist Eric B. Morton (c. 1867–1930), and Berkman's former fellow prisoner and German-born anarchist Charles "Tony" Snyder (c. 1863–?), with the aid of unknown Italian anarchist miners. The woman Cohen mentions was Chicago-based anarchist Vella Kinsella, who played piano all day long to drown out the sounds of the operation.

knew exactly who had dug it, and for whom. The boldness and successful execution of such a difficult project aroused great admiration.

The *Forverts*, which was in financial straits at the time, was reluctant to turn over the money it had collected for the Berkman fund. It gave all kinds of excuses to the committee. The *Fraye arbeter shtime*'s fund had already reached $1,169.18—at no time before or after did an appeal create such a response. The comrades in England also sent contributions through David Isakovitz. But the *Forverts* responded that the appeal had only asked for a thousand dollars—why did they now need so much more money? They had probably gotten wind that the money was being used for illegal work and demanded an accounting from the committee of how the money was being used.

On the first of June the *Fraye arbeter shtime* published on its front page a demand that the *Forverts* hand over the money. They should send it directly to Berkman himself if they did not have confidence in the defense committee. This incident was drawn out until February 1901. The *Forverts* sent one check to Berkman but then stopped payment of it at the bank. To get the few dollars donated by socialist comrades took untold effort. On February 14, 1901, the *Forverts* sent Berkman five dollars; on February 28, it sent twenty-five; and on March 12, ninety-eight dollars.

The main reason and explanation was the terrible poverty of the *Forverts*, which every day seemed near death. In fact, at one point agents of the *Forverts* were ready to sell the newspaper to the *Yidishes tageblat* (Jewish Daily News), and it was only the fact that some people got wind of the deal and made a fuss that the *Forverts* was saved from ruin.[8]

Returning to the story of our movement, in March 1900 the Philadelphia Knights of Liberty group, of which Lubarsky was secretary, put on a *boyern* ball—the fifth annual one, according to the announcement—and raised seventy dollars for the *Fraye arbeter shtime*, which was considered quite a sum of money in those days and was received with great fanfare.[9]

---

8. New York's **Yidishes tageblat** (1885–1928) was one of the first Yiddish daily newspapers in the world and maintained a generally conservative stance.

9. **Morris Lubarsky** (1851–1906) was a Russian-born Jewish shopkeeper and anarchist. He was also an opponent of the Philadelphia shoemaking cooperative cofounded by Chaim Weinberg. See Chaim Leib Weinberg, *Forty Years in the Struggle: The Memoirs of a Jewish Anarchist*, ed. Robert P. Helms, trans. Naomi Cohen (Duluth: Litwin Books, 2008), 36.

In August 1900 Gaetano Bresci shot the Italian king Umberto I.[10] Bresci had traveled from Paterson, New Jersey, to Italy, to get revenge for the wantonly spilled blood of the Italian working people. The police and the American capitalist press were given a new opportunity to renew their agitation against anarchists in general and the anarchists in Paterson in particular. Americans do not have a king and in theory do not believe that God appointed one to rule over his fellow man, but the anarchists nevertheless are a danger to society—they seek to abolish authority and exploitation altogether—so we must crush them to save ourselves from their influence!

Bresci was sentenced to life imprisonment. He died, or was killed, in prison a short time afterward. On the hard, stone walls of his cell, he was able to scribble the word "Revenge." For many years, his portrait hung on the walls of anarchist meeting halls.

An international anarchist congress was to take place in Paris on September 19 of that year. Great preparations were made on a very large scale. The international anarchist press debated the issues that the congress should address. Ninety reports and statements were submitted. From America, Dr. Michael A. Cohn traveled as a delegate.

The French government, in which one of the ministers, Alexandre Millerand, was a socialist, outlawed the congress and harassed the delegates.[11] Two Italian delegates were given forty-eight hours to leave the country, and, when they did not obey the order, they were thrown into prison for several months and then expelled. For a long time after the planned congress, the police continued to persecute anarchists, especially foreigners. Finally the anarchists were forced to print a warning in Jean Grave's paper, *Les Temps nouveaux*, that they would use all methods to prevent the government from robbing them of their rights and freedom.[12] This had an effect. But the social-

---

10. **Gaetano Bresci** (1869–1901) was an Italian silk worker and anarchist. After joining the anarchist movement in Milan and being imprisoned for strike activity, he immigrated to Paterson, New Jersey in 1898. In 1900, outraged at the killing of dozens of protesters in Milan two years earlier, he returned to Italy and killed King Umberto I. Defended at his trial by former anarchist Francesco Saverio Merlino, he was sentenced to life in prison but died less than a year later under suspicious circumstances.

11. **Alexandre Millerand** (1859–1943) was a French editor and socialist who was first elected to the Chamber of Deputies in 1885. After becoming increasingly conservative, he was appointed prime minister in 1920 and served as France's president from 1920 to 1924.

12. **Jean Grave** (1854–1939) was a French writer, journalist, and anarchist. From Paris,

ist movement in France, which had at the time quite an influence, ignored the whole matter and did not mention it in its papers. They did not want to embarrass their socialist comrade Millerand.

Michael A. Cohn wrote a number of reports from France and Europe for the *Fraye arbeter shtime*.[13] When he returned, he gave a report on the planned congress and the work being done in France to publish the reports and materials that had been prepared. It was also decided to publish the materials here in Yiddish, and for this purpose a sum of twenty dollars was collected on the spot. But the money was swallowed up by the *Fraye arbeter shtime* a few months later, during a financially critical moment. The paper later published only one statement on women and their rights in society—a message from French students to the planned congress.

In New York, our movement suffered two great losses that year. Two of our most prominent and young comrades died. In July 1900, John H. Edelmann, a highly educated man and successful architect, passed away.[14] He was a devoted and active comrade, who together with Francesco Saverio Merlino had edited the anarchist newspaper *Solidarity* in English, and he often spoke at open-air meetings. Kropotkin, when he came to New York, was his house guest. His wife, Rachelle, was one of the four sisters of the Krimont family, who were devoted and active in our movement all their lives.[15] Anuta Krimont was the wife of Dr. Samuel Ellsberg; Mary Krimont, also very active, was the wife of Harry Kelly.[16] The fourth sister was the wife

he edited the influential anarchist newspapers *Le Révolté* (1879–1885), *La Révolte* (1887–1895), and *Les Temps nouveaux* (1895–1914) and corresponded with radicals around the globe.

13. *FAS*, October 12, October 26, and November 30, 1900.

14. **John H. Edelmann** (1852–1900) was an American-born architect and anarchist. The son of German immigrants, he worked for the architecture firm of Alfred Zucker. Between 1886 and 1892 Edelmann moved from the single-tax movement through the SLP to the anarchist movement. He contributed articles to several anarchist periodicals and married fellow anarchist Rachelle Edelmann.

15. **Rachelle Edelmann** (née Krimont, 1870–1952) was a Russian-born Jewish anarchist. In 1884 she immigrated to the United States with her mother and six siblings to join her brother at Am Olam's New Odessa Colony near Portland, Oregon. After the colony's collapse in 1886, the family resettled in New York, where Rachelle married John H. Edelmann in 1892.

16. **Anuta ("Anna") Krimont** (Anyuta Krimont, 1867–1933) was a Russian-born Jewish dentist, masseuse, and anarchist. She immigrated to Oregon with the rest of her family in 1884 and attended dental school in Switzerland in the 1890s. By 1910 Krimont had separated from Samuel Ellsberg, and she briefly married English anarchist William C. Owen. She was a cofounder of the Modern School Association and a manager of the Stelton Colony. **Samuel**

of comrade Alexander Kislik, a comrade in New York whose whole family was active in the Ferrer School.[17] After John Edelmann's untimely death, his wife emigrated to England, where she lived for many years in an anarchist colony.[18] Later she returned to the United States with their son, John W. Edelman, who taught at the Ferrer School for several years and became a prominent member of the CIO.[19]

In December 1900 Justus Schwab died. He was one of the most prominent anarchist activists in the German-speaking movement.[20] He was a giant of a man, very tall, with extraordinarily broad shoulders and a handsome, intelligent face topped with golden hair. He personified the legendary German heroes of yore. He was the owner of a New York saloon that he elevated and turned into a meeting place for all revolutionists, artists, writers, and labor leaders who came to discuss art, literature, and social problems. When Johann Most was sentenced to prison in London, Justus Schwab sent

---

Ellsberg (Shmuel Elsberg, 1871–1931) was a Russian-born Jewish physician and anarchist. He immigrated to the United States in the 1880s and earned his medical degree from New York University in 1895. In 1907 Ellsberg posted bail for Emma Goldman, Alexander Berkman, and John Coryell after their arrest following a meeting at New York's Clinton Hall. He supported the Russian revolutionary movement and later socialist territorialism, Poale Zion, and the Organization for Jewish Colonization in Russia. Obituary: *FAS*, May 29, 1931. **Mary Krimont** (1874–1922) was a Russian-born Jewish anarchist. She immigrated with the rest of her family in 1884, and in 1898 followed her companion Harry Kelly to London, where both were active in the Freedom Group. After the couple's return to the United States in 1904, she helped cofound the Ferrer Modern School and the Stelton Colony.

17. **Sophie Kislik** (Sofi Kisliuk, 1873–1945), née Krimont, was a Russian-born Jewish anarchist. She immigrated with the rest of her family in 1884 and in 1885 married **Alexander Kislik** (Kisliuk, 1861–?), a Russian-born Jewish machinist and anarchist, when both were still living at Oregon's New Odessa colony.

18. Following Edelmann's death in 1900, Rachelle Krimont moved with their two children to the Whiteway Colony, a Tolstoyan commune in Gloucestershire.

19. **John W. Edelman** (1893–1971) was an American-born radical educator and labor organizer. He returned to the United States with his mother in 1916 to help run the Modern School in Stelton. Edelman was later active in the Socialist Party in Reading, Pennsylvania, and then became an organizer for the CIO and its Textile Workers Union of America.

20. Cohen's original Yiddish text claims: "Justus was the son of a German revolutionist who was forced to flee his home and come to America in 1849 after the revolution in Germany failed. Young Justus was brought up and educated in America, but he remained a true German in his ways." However, according to most sources, Schwab's father served four years in a German prison for his part in the revolutionary uprising of 1848 (and therefore could not have emigrated in 1849) and Schwab himself did not come to the United States until 1868 or 1869.

$200 so that Most's paper *Freiheit* could continue publication without inter-ruption. When Most later came to America, Schwab supported *Freiheit* until it developed enough support and a sizable readership. Three or four years later, he grew apart from Most. An attitude of irresponsibility developed among a certain crowd which began to frequent his saloon. Schwab drove them out of his place and demanded that Most write against this antisocial element in *Freiheit*. Most refused. He considered these elements victims of our social order. For years Schwab was the center and the soul of the anar-chist movement in New York, among both the American and the German comrades. This giant of a man succumbed to the disease of the proletariat: consumption. Both were severe losses for our movement.

❄ ❄ ❄

The reorganized journal *Fraye gezelshaft*, under the editorship of Dr. Jacob A. Maryson, was an improvement over the magazine published under the same name years before. It had more original articles and serious studies of anar-chism and social problems. Frequent contributors included M. Leontieff (Leon Moissieff), Iser Ginzburg, Hillel Solotaroff, Moyshe Katz, Jacob Gordin, and Abraham Frumkin, who reported on the situation in Europe. Of course, there were also translations of informative writings. The journal was a great success. However, it did not last more than a year. It went under not for lack of readers or support but because of a remarkable event.

In the last number of the first volume, the editor, Dr. Maryson, wrote a review of the work that had been accomplished and concluded that the Jews would never by themselves bring anarchism to America. In his opinion, therefore, it would be more useful and practical to publish the journal in English and thereby reach a wider public.[21]

Without a doubt, Maryson was mistaken in the conclusion of his edi-torial. Many comrades have since made the same mistake, asking why we don't publish English books and newspapers instead of literature in Yiddish. At the time that Maryson wrote these words, there was already an English

---

21. "Di 'Fraye gezelshaft' tsu ihre lezer," *Fraye gezelshaft*, October 1900, 575–76. Cohen's original Yiddish text incorrectly claims this article was never published.

newspaper by the same name, *Free Society*, edited and published by Abe Isaak and his family.[22] Both before and since, there were many attempts to publish anarchist newspapers and journals in English, such as *The Alarm*, *Mother Earth, Solidarity, The Road to Freedom, The Blast*, and others.[23] Turning a Yiddish journal or newspaper into an English one would not change the situation. It is especially surprising that Maryson took this attitude, since he was a very logical thinker and spent his entire life strongly interested in enriching and improving the Yiddish language and its literature. This can be seen in his numerous translations into Yiddish of Kropotkin, Karl Marx, Darwin, Herbert Spencer, and others. The only explanation that I can find is the fact that he was convinced that all the original contributions to anarchist theory written and published in Yiddish remained unknown to the rest of the world and therefore did not bring the desired result. Even Dr. Max Nettlau, the great historian and bibliographer of the anarchist movement and its literature, who mastered many European languages, could only read the headings of Yiddish articles but not the contents.[24] He complained

---

22. *Free Society* (1897–1904), like its predecessor *The Firebrand* (1895–1887), was one of the foremost English-language American anarchist communist newspapers of its time. Its contributors included Emma Goldman, Michael A. Cohn, Harry Kelly, and Voltairine de Cleyre. **Abraham Isaak** (1856–1937) and his wife **Mary Dyck Isaak** (1861–1934) were Russian-born farmers and anarchists, both born and raised in a Ukrainian Mennonite community before moving to Odessa. There they became involved in radical circles, which forced Isaak to flee to Argentina in 1889. In 1891 he reunited with Mary in Portland, Oregon, where they launched *The Firebrand* in 1895. The couple's children also helped to produce the paper and its successor, *Free Society*, in San Francisco and Chicago.

23. *Solidarity* (1892–1893, 1895, 1898) was an important English-language anarchist newspaper aimed at an American working-class audience. Its contributors included Jacob A. Maryson, Emma Goldman, and Voltairine de Cleyre. *The Road to Freedom* (1924–1932) was published in Stelton and then New York City by the Road to Freedom Group and edited by Hippolyte Havel and American-born anarchist Warren Van Valkenburgh (1884–1938). As one of the country's only English-language anarchist periodicals of the era, it took a non-sectarian line and published articles by many Jewish anarchists, including Alexander Berkman, Emma Goldman, David Isakovitz, Shmuel Marcus, Samuel Polinow, and Anna Sasnovsky. *The Blast* (1916–1917) was a labor-oriented anarchist newspaper published by Alexander Berkman in San Francisco. Its contributors included Leonard D. Abbot, Sadakichi Hartmann, Harry Kelly, and Robert Minor.

24. **Max Nettlau** (1865–1944) was an Austrian-born linguist, historian, and anarchist. While studying Celtic he lived in London, where he joined the Freedom Group before returning to Austria. Beginning in the 1890s Nettlau dedicated his life to documenting the history of the anarchist movement, and his writings on anarchist history and theory appeared

to me many times and expressed the opinion that if only the Jews at least used Latin letters instead of the Hebrew alphabet, he and others would have learned the language and followed what we had to say. Thus, even to him, the original contributions of Dr. Maryson remained unknown.

---

in periodicals around the world, including the *FAS*. In 1938 he fled Nazi occupation to the Netherlands, where he died in 1944. Many of his works were not published until after his death, and most remain untranslated into English, including his seven-volume *Geschichte der Anarchie* (History of Anarchy).

CHAPTER 11

1901: McKinley's Assassination

At the annual convention held at the end of 1890, many problems had been listed on the agenda, but none were addressed. The whole time had been taken up with the comrades' criticism of the spirit and the content of the *Fraye arbeter shtime*. Discontent with the paper was great. It was smaller than before, only twelve pages, of which a third was taken up with advertisements.[1] From the end of its first year and through the whole of its second, the *Fraye arbeter shtime* was filled with endless translations, four or five in each issue. Original articles appeared only occasionally. Letters and reports had almost completely vanished. The financial condition of the paper was also very poor. It was on the verge of giving up the ghost. Every month some affair had to be held and appeals for money made. Only the stubborn determination of Yanovsky kept the paper alive. He not only filled the paper with his notes, translations, and articles signed with different pen names, he also did all the hard physical work that the newspaper required. He was editor, manager, bookkeeper, errand boy, and peddler—all in one.

Some thirty years later, a certain comrade Mitchell ("Baby Elephant," we used to call him, for his huge stature and large ears), related the following tale. Only once in his life had his conscience forced him to try his hand at physical labor. It happened one very cold winter's day when he met Yanovsky lugging a heavy pack of the *Fraye arbeter shtime* to be distributed to the newspaper stands. Poor Yanovsky was doubled over under the heavy load, dragging his

---

1. Unlike most other anarchist periodicals of the era, the *FAS* sustained itself partially through the sale of advertising space in its back pages. Over the years, its (sometimes unsuspecting) advertisers included national brands such as Camel cigarettes and Ex-Lax.

feet with difficulty. Mitchell, who on principle was perpetually lazy and an idler, was moved. He took the heavy pack of newspapers and let Yanovsky direct him to where he needed to go.

In February 1901, the office of *Fraye arbeter shtime* moved to 185 Henry Street, where it had facilities for a reading room and for holding small and frequent entertainments. But it was still forced to make appeals for money to comrades outside of New York to keep the paper going. A meeting and concert at the Windsor Theater, at which Johann Most, Yanovsky, Michael A. Cohn, Voltairine de Cleyre, and Rudolf Grossman spoke, failed to attract an audience and netted only twenty dollars.[2] The situation was very serious.

In March 1901 a small notice in the paper announced that Peter Kropotkin would speak in Boston on March 10 at Paine Memorial Hall, on "Anarchism: Its Philosophy and Morals." For some inexplicable reason, the *Fraye arbeter shtime* had otherwise ignored Kropotkin's second visit to the United States. However, in the April 5 issue there is a letter from Kropotkin in which he promised to write an article in the *Fraye arbeter shtime*, and there are notices of his lectures in New York.

That year Kropotkin gave a series of lectures on Russian literature at the Lowell Institute of Boston. Later these appeared in book form under the title *Ideals and Realities in Russian Literature*, and they were translated into all European languages, including Yiddish (by the Kropotkin Literary Society of New York).[3] Kropotkin also lectured at many colleges and universities and used every opportunity to lecture on anarchism in a number of large cities. His visit made a great impression on the country and did much to revitalize our movement. When he lectured in Carnegie Hall in New York, the audience was overflowing. In his column "Oyf der vakh" (On Watch) in the *Fraye*

---

2. **Rudolf Grossman** (1882–1942), later known as Pierre Ramus, was an Austrian-born Jewish journalist and anarchist. In 1898 he was expelled from school for undertaking socialist propaganda, and his parents sent him live with relatives in the United States. Grossman attended Columbia University and wrote for the socialist *New Yorker Volkszeitung*, then in 1900 he became an anarchist and began contributing to *Freiheit* and other anarchist newspapers. After fleeing to England to avoid arrest in connection with the 1902 Paterson silk strike (described in chapter 12), he resumed anarchist activities under his pseudonym and in 1907 returned to Austria, where he became a leading anarchist thinker, editor, and pacifist.

3. Peter Kropotkin, *Ideals and Realities in Russian Literature* (New York: Alfred A. Knopf, 1905). The Yiddish edition appeared as *Idealen un virklikhkayt in der Rusisher literatur*, trans. H. Rozenfeld (New York: Kropotkin Literatur Gezelshaft, 1922).

arbeter shtime, Yanovsky scolded those comrades who ran in the thousands to hear Kropotkin but did nothing for the anarchist movement. Yanovsky was less than enthusiastic over the whole affair, which had so thrilled and inspired the comrades.

But the vile and shameful behavior of Daniel De Leon was even worse. De Leon, spiritual leader and boss of the Socialist Labor Party, and his Jewish underling, Joseph Schlossberg,[4] in their paper foolishly declared, "Since the presidential election of last November, when the S. L. P. phalanx alarmed the capitalist class by its wonderful exhibition of invincibleness, the capitalists, have trotted out one decoy after another . . . to throw dust in the eyes of the workers. . . . Last Sunday afternoon they shoved out another juggler before the footlights—Prince Kropotkin, the Russian anarchist."[5] They ridiculed Kropotkin's personal appearance and ostensibly innocently asked what became of the $500 that Kropotkin and Professor George D. Herron (chairman of the Carnegie Hall meeting) had collected from the poor workers for the privilege of entering Carnegie Hall.[6] Joseph Schlossberg, the great sage and wise man, criticized Kropotkin's English pronunciation and the "junk" ideas expounded in his speech. This kind of Jesuitical article created a storm even among the ranks of their own followers (who were in reality already on the decline at the time).[7]

An incident at the beginning of September 1901 put not only the *Fraye arbeter shtime* but also the whole anarchist movement in jeopardy. On September 6, President McKinley came to the World's Fair in Buffalo and was given a hearty welcome by the public. From among the crowd a young

---

4. **Joseph Schlossberg** (Yoysef Shlosberg, 1875–1971) was a Russian-born Jewish garment worker, labor organizer, and socialist. He immigrated to the United States in 1888 and joined the SLP, which he stuck with after Abe Cahan and others split away in 1897 to form the *Forverts.* Schlossberg edited several Yiddish socialist and labor newspapers, and in 1914 he helped form the ACWA, for which he served as secretary-treasurer for more than two decades.

5. *Weekly People,* April 6, 1901.

6. **George D. Herron** (1862–1925) was an American-born minister, teacher, and Christian socialist. He was an advocate of the Social Gospel movement and belonged to the SLP and then the Socialist Party, but he supported the Allies in the First World War and in 1914 immigrated to Switzerland, where he worked for British and American intelligence services.

7. In the 1900 election that the *Weekly People* claimed was a "wonderful exhibition of invincibleness" for the SLP, the party's presidential candidate garnered 40,943 votes—just 0.29 percent of the total.

man with a bandaged hand approached him. As the president turned to shake his hand, he fired several shots from the bandaged hand and seriously injured McKinley. The man was, of course, immediately arrested, and mercilessly beaten. The newspapers immediately exclaimed in inflammatory articles that the assassin, Leon Czolgosz, had carried out his attack under directions given him by the anarchists.

An investigation showed that a short time before, Czolgosz had visited the office of the anarchist magazine *Free Society* in Chicago, where he introduced himself as Nieman and met Emma Goldman. What the capitalist press in all their inflammatory articles seemed to forget was that a notice had been printed in *Free Society* warning the comrades about a suspicious young man who called himself Nieman.[8] The press chose to ignore this entirely and clamored for the arrest of anarchists all over the country. In Chicago, all the comrades associated with *Free* Society were arrested—men, women, and children. The newspapers' main attacks were aimed at Emma Goldman, who happened to be in St. Louis at the time. Against the advice of her friends and comrades, she went back to Chicago to give herself up to the police.

In New York, a week earlier, Johann Most happened to reprint an article, "Mord contra Mord" (Murder against Murder) on the right to assassinate anointed rulers.[9] The original had been printed in America some fifty years before and was the work of Karl Heinzen.[10] For the crime of reprinting the article, he was arrested and incarcerated for a long time without trial. When McKinley succumbed to his wounds, the newspapers created a wild hysteria throughout the country. The office of the *Fraye arbeter shtime* was attacked by Jewish hoodlums, who carried out a pogrom there. The landlord forced the paper to move out. It took them a long time to find a space for new

---

8. *Free Society* editor Abe Isaak printed a warning on September 1, 1901, reading: "The attention of the comrades is called to another spy. He is well dressed, of medium height, rather narrow shoulders, blond and about 25 years of age. . . . His demeanor is of the usual sort, pretending to be greatly interested in the cause, asking for names or soliciting aid for acts of contemplated violence. If this same individual makes his appearance elsewhere the comrades are warned in advance, and can act accordingly."

9. *Freiheit*, September 7, 1901.

10. **Karl Heinzen** (1809–1880) was a German-born socialist, revolutionary, and abolitionist whose writings were criticized by Karl Marx as unscientific. He immigrated to the United States in 1848 to avoid arrest. The article in question was an extract from Heinzen's 1853 pamphlet *Mord und Freiheit* (Death and Freedom).

location at 105 Henry Street. And this despite the fact that the *Fraye arbeter shtime* had, from day one, been outspoken against Czolgosz and his *attentat*. The other Jewish newspapers meanwhile rivaled the English ones in their hysteria. Jacob Saphirstein advocated pogroms against, and murder of, the anarchists.[11]

Czolgosz was tried in secret and convicted. No one was allowed to enter. No word about his execution and what he had to say about it appeared anywhere. The State of New York wanted to extradite Emma Goldman from Illinois to Buffalo but did not succeed. After a thorough investigation, all the arrested anarchists of Chicago were freed. Only Johann Most, who was brought before a court of three judges, was sentenced to a year in prison. All the efforts of his defense lawyer, Morris Hillquit, could not help. Hillquit even managed to get an order from a higher judge for a new trial, but that was only a temporary relief. The verdict was upheld.

On Sunday May 5, 1902, a send-off party was held in New Irving Hall for Johann Most, who was going to jail for the third time in free America. At the meeting William MacQueen, an English anarchist, exclaimed during his speech, "The devil with the law!"[12] As they left the hall, MacQueen and Most were handcuffed and arrested—MacQueen for his outspoken statement, and Most for applauding it. They were each put under a thousand dollars bail. Most was freed by the judge, who ruled that applauding was not a crime.

As a result of all this, the *Fraye arbeter shtime* experienced trying times. Comrades from outside of New York, especially in Philadelphia and other cities, were frightened and left the movement. They withdrew from public life and tried to cover up their former connections with this dangerous cause. In response, a meeting of the Philadelphia comrades called by Benny Moore at comrade Moses Levene's restaurant on South Fifth Street raised twenty-six dollars for the *Fraye arbeter shtime*, which exclaimed in a headline,

---

11. **Jacob Saphirstein** (1853–1914) was the conservative Russian-born Jewish publisher of the *Nyu Yorker abend post* and *Morgen zshurnal*.

12. **William MacQueen** (1875–1908) was an English-born painter, editor, and anarchist. He became a well-regarded anarchist speaker in Leeds in the 1890s and immigrated to the United States in 1902. Fluent in German, he was friends and collaborators with both Johann Most and Rudolf Grossman. Press reports give several different versions of MacQueen's "seditious" statement at this event, but all are variations on the same sentiment. Later that same month MacQueen participated in the 1902 Paterson silk strike, discussed in chapter 12.

"Philadelphia Is Not Yet Dead!"[13] Moore promised in his report to raise more money, but the Czolgosz affair ended all activity.

In New York the opposite occurred. The comrades there rallied around the *Fraye arbeter shtime* and gave the newspaper their full support. The paper was truly revitalized. At its second anniversary celebration in early October, the police did not allow speeches, but they did not interfere with the entertainment. The next month the paper announced that it would be increased to sixteen pages and would be printed with better type so as to be easier to read. In December, Yanovsky's call for the annual convention reported that the paper had $350 in its treasury, and he waxed poetic about the way the movement had united in solidarity. "All together!" he exclaimed with great enthusiasm, "We will really get to work now." A few weeks later, for the New Year, he was able to report that the treasury contained $800, which put the *Fraye arbeter shtime* on a rock-solid foundation.

Legislative bodies all over the country were feverishly engaged in creating strict laws against anarchism and the anarchists. Teddy Roosevelt, instead of appreciating what Czolgosz had done for him—for without his help Roosevelt would never have had the honor of becoming president—spit fire and vitriol on the anarchists, demanding that Congress pass the harshest of laws against them. One clever senator, Joseph Roswell Hawley, said he would be willing to pay $1,000 to shoot at an anarchist.[14] Voltairine de Cleyre publicly announced that she was willing to be his target for free, on the condition that he first let her explain to him the meaning of anarchism.[15] She sent him her name and address. Émile Zola in France asked: Is there not a single reasonable person in America who can explain to the legislators that laws and oppression cannot suppress or eliminate ideas?

One such person was found in America. John P. Altgeld, the former

---

13. *FAS,* June 21, 1901.

14. **Jacob Roswell Hawley** (1826–1905) was an American former Civil War general, journalist, and Republican politician from Connecticut, who served in the US Senate from 1881 to 1905.

15. De Cleyre in fact proposed that, "if payment of the $1,000 is a necessary part of your proposition, then when I have given you the shot, I will give the money to the propaganda of the idea of a free society in which there shall be neither assassins nor presidents, beggars nor senators." Paul Avrich, *An American Anarchist: The Life of Voltairine de Cleyre* (Princeton: Princeton University Press, 1978), 136. Cohen's mistaken version of the offer is drawn from Goldman, *Living My Life,* 2:332.

governor of Illinois who had freed the remaining imprisoned Chicago anarchists of the Haymarket Affair, boldly pointed out in a speech to the Good Government Club at the University of Michigan how foolish and criminal the agitation against the anarchists was.[16] He discussed the topic from all angles and proved that all the arguments were without foundation. He retold the tragedy of the Chicago anarchists and reiterated that his studies of the case had proved to him their innocence.[17]

But his voice remained a cry in the wilderness. The lawmakers continued their terrible work. Anti-anarchist laws were passed in New York and other states. The *Fraye arbeter shtime* found it necessary, in April 1902, to remove the words "Anarchist-Communist Organ" from its masthead, so as to not be banned under that pretext. But the spirit and content of the paper were unchanged.

At the end of December, our annual convention was held. This time the atmosphere was friendlier, the criticism of the editor milder and more restrained. Yanovsky put out a proposal that there should be a daily paper. But the convention considered it too risky to undertake. The proposition to make the *Fraye arbeter shtime* a biweekly was also discussed, but no decision was reached. However, a resolution was passed to create a fund for the publication of pamphlets. The question of our attitude toward the labor movement brought forth a surprising declaration from Yanovsky. He stated that he was no longer as enthusiastic about the unions as he once was. There was nothing there but corruption and degeneration. But he saw no other arenas in which we would be able to develop our activities.

Yanovsky also raised the question of our relationship with the social democrats, noting that it had changed greatly. There was no longer the bitterness and hostility of previous years. He addressed the question: was this the result of a better understanding or simply the result of neglect and indifference? The discussion did not clarify the issue. Both questions were signs

---

16. **John P. Altgeld** (1847–1902) was a German-born lawyer and politician. A well-known Progressive and Democrat, as governor of Illinois in 1892–1897 he pardoned the remaining anarchists convicted in the Haymarket Affair (Samuel Fielden, Oscar Neebe, and Michael Schwab). Because of this decision he was widely admired by radicals and reviled by conservatives, and he lost his 1896 reelection campaign. Afterward he worked at the law firm of Clarence Darrow.

17. Altgeld's speech, on "American Ideals," is detailed in the Chicago *Inter Ocean*, December 15, 1901.

of the times. The Jewish unions were but shadows of their former selves. Quarrels and frequent splits in the SLP, and the founding of its Socialist Trade and Labor Alliance in opposition to the existing unions—all the upheaval and confusion in the socialist movement, which lasted for more than ten years—had completely ruined the labor movement and led it astray. The so-called general strike of the Jewish bakers in New York, which led to a boycott of the *Tageblat* in 1901, turned out to be a cheap maneuver of the *Forverts* to capture a few readers away from the *Tageblat*.[18] The whole movement was in a morass.

With the passage of time, relations with the social democrats had grown milder, simply because the socialists had channeled all their toxic hostility into the fraternal fighting in their own ranks, in which they themselves came out in favor of anarchistic demands for free expression and a little autonomy in their own party. Thus Abe Cahan and Louis Miller became champions of freedom and fighters against stricter discipline and dictatorship of the party under the leadership of Daniel De Leon. The social democrats had no more time or energy left for fighting anarchists.

---

18. During a strike of the East Side Bakers' Union in 1900–1901, the *Yidishes tageblat* published an article falsely claiming that a settlement had been reached and the strike called off; in response, an angry mob attacked the newspaper's offices. On the alleged role and motives of the *Forverts* in the strike, see *FAS*, May 11, 1901.

CHAPTER 12

1902: Anti-Anarchist Backlash

The new year of 1902 found our movement in excellent condition. The *Fraye arbeter shtime* had appeared as a sixteen-page paper in the middle of November with good, clear type, original articles, and correspondence, and was materially sound. The whole movement, especially in New York, came to life. In March 1902 John P. Altgeld died. The liberals in New York organized a memorial meeting at Cooper Union. The son of Henry George, who was named for his father, chaired.[1] Anarchists sold copies of an English-language pamphlet, *Roosevelt, Czolgosz and Anarchy*, at the meeting.[2] The chairman called the police and had the anarchists arrested. Afterward he got up and sang the praises of Altgeld, the sincere liberal and humanitarian. In the morning, realizing the contradiction between his action and his speech, he hired a good lawyer to defend the people whom he had had arrested.

The Congress of the United States, under the influence of the general hysteria and of the incitement of Teddy Roosevelt, passed a law prohibiting the entry of anarchists into this country. Much stricter measures had been proposed, such as banishing all anarchists to some desert island and the like, but the public had largely calmed down and forgotten the whole affair. Even immediately after McKinley's assassination, not everyone was particularly upset. One brave lawyer dared to suggest that perhaps Czolgosz committed a socially justifiable and useful act. He was deprived of the right to practice

---

1. **Henry George Jr.** (1862–1916) was an American-born journalist and Democratic politician. He served as a US representative for New York from 1911 to 1915.

2. Jay Fox, *Roosevelt, Czolgosz and Anarchy* (New York: New York Anarchists, [1902]).

his profession for this sin.[3] His comments, however, proved that not every-body in the country had lost their senses. The hysteria was artificially inflated by the press, and within a few months they found other sensations to feed their readers.

From Russia came new reports about the greatly stepped-up activities of the revolutionary movement. Stepan Balmashov shot the minister Dmitry Sipyagin, who had punished thousands of university students by conscript-ing them into the army.[4] Balmashov's daring and successful act aroused great enthusiasm in the whole radical movement in America. The Russian gov-ernment, incidentally, did not understand the dangers of sending so many radical students into the military. There they continued their revolutionary activity and undermined the morale of the entire army.

That summer in Paterson there was a general strike of the weavers in the silk industry. Comrades William MacQueen (an Englishman) and Rudolf Grossman (an Austrian, later known as Pierre Ramus), were active in that strike. After one of their rallies, there was a major clash between strikers and scabs under police protection. MacQueen and Grossman were arrested and placed under $5,000 bail for inciting to riot. The father of their defense lawyer put up the bail money. The comrades were both sentenced to five years in prison. The verdict was appealed, they were released on bail, and both fled the country. When a higher court reaffirmed the sentence, the lawyer's father was about to lose his whole fortune.

The *Fraye arbeter shtime* sharply criticized the behavior of the two com-rades. But in the wider movement there were different opinions. Regardless, the father who put up bail went to England and persuaded MacQueen to come back to the United States and serve his term so that he should at least get half his money back. MacQueen returned and served three and a half years in prison, where he contracted tuberculosis. After he was freed, he

---

3. Attorney William C. Buderus of Sturgis, South Dakota, was disbarred for stating, in reaction to McKinley's shooting, "I am glad of it, and I hope he will die, as there will be one more tyrant less." See *St. Paul Globe*, November 17, 1901.

4. On April 15, 1902 Russian university student and Socialist-Revolutionary **Stepan Bal-mashov** (1882–1902) killed Russia's minister of the interior, **Dmitry Sipyagin** (1853–1902), who had punished radical students by imposing military service on them. Cohen's original Yiddish edition mistakenly identifies the assassin as Pyotr Karpovich, another Socialist-Revolutionary student who had a year earlier assassinated Russia's minister of national enlightenment, Nikolay Bogolepov, in retaliation for the same policy.

went back to England and died shortly thereafter. He was a direct victim of the cruel judgement and propaganda of our press following his escape. Grossman, who remained in Europe, for several decades carried out a strong campaign on behalf of the anarchist movement.

After the failure of his attempt at escape through the tunnel, Alexander Berkman lived through a very difficult and melancholy time. He had fourteen years left to serve in prison. He doubted that he would survive those long years of terrible suffering. But a miracle occurred: one of the wealthiest cigar manufacturers in Pennsylvania began deceiving the government by printing his own excise stamps, for taxes that amounted to $3,000 on every thousand cigars sold since the Spanish-American War. He was arrested and sentenced to a long prison term. His family spent a fortune to get him out of the mess and was able to get a law passed by the state legislature that would remit a third of every prison sentence. They had tried to make it one-half, but the press did not allow this, because they were not brought into the debate as the legislators took up the issue. However, as it turned out, the wealthy manufacturer gained nothing: his crime was against the federal government, and state law had no jurisdiction over them.[5] Berkman and all other prisoners, however, found their sentences automatically shortened. Under the new law, Berkman had only a few years left on his sentence. This revived his spirit and gave him determination to survive until his release.

In Philadelphia, the movement had almost died out. The hysteria generated by the assassination of McKinley completely demoralized our comrades. The meetings in front of City Hall were discontinued. Thomas Earle White withdrew from any sort of anarchist activity. Among the Jews, people stopped coming to anarchist lectures and meetings. The only source of activity was the cooperative store into which Weinberg put his whole heart and soul. The cooperative organization bought a building on South Street and, when the store opened, the comrades held a grand parade with fireworks, enthusiastic speeches, and lots of ballyhoo. It seemed as if the movement was mushrooming, but this appearance was false, as will be seen.

Some weak attempts were made by a Frayheyt (Freedom) Group, which arranged a series of lectures by Ephraim-Leib Wolfson and Moses Levene

---

5. This likely apocryphal account of the origins of Pennsylvania's Commutation Act of 1901 is a variation of the version given in Berkman's own *Prison Memoirs of an Anarchist*. The act allowed for the reduction of sentences for good behavior.

without much success. In the beginning of September, Yanovsky visited and wrote a lengthy report on the cooperative society. According to his assessment, he saw great hope for the anarchist movement in this kind of activity.

A young comrade by the name of L. Lavrov, who knew not a word of Yiddish, was announced in the *Fraye arbeter shtime* as an official agent of the paper in Philadelphia. This was not the only time that such things happened in our movement; several times our Yiddish newspapers were distributed by people who did not speak the language.

In May 1902 news arrived of Hirsh Lekert's attempted *attentat* against General Viktor von Wahl, the governor of Vilna, Lithuania, who had ordered May Day demonstrators who had fallen into the hands of the police to be flogged.[6] Lekert, a member of the Bund and a simple laborer, a shoemaker by trade, sacrificed his young life to take revenge on the wild beast. This act stirred the radical movement not only in Russia but also in America. Meetings were called in every city and money was raised to take care of his family.

About this time, our movement in Philadelphia received a terrible blow. A mentally ill anarchist youth named Herman Helcher shot three bullets into Voltairine de Cleyre.[7] She was near death for a long time. The doctors were only able to remove two of the bullets; the third they dared not touch. Many different stories were told of what drove Helcher to commit this mad deed. As far as I was able to gather from among all the gossip, what happened was this:

In the years of great activity of our movement, Voltairine became a good friend of Dr. Samuel Gordon. The stagnation of the movement following the assassination of McKinley coincided with strained relations between the two. Helcher was deeply concerned about the movement's lack of activity; he longed for the big mass meetings and everything that went with them. He

---

6. **Hirsh Lekert** (1880–1902) was Russian-born Jewish member of the Bund. In 1900 he was internally exiled for taking part in an attack on a police station in Vilna but escaped in 1902. That same year he attempted to assassinate aristocratic general **Viktor von Wahl** (1840–1915). Lekert was tried in a military court and executed, and Von Wahl went on to become a member of Russia's State Council.

7. **Herman (Chaim) Helcher** (1878–1912) was a Russian-born Jewish cigarmaker and anarchist. He immigrated to the United States in 1888 and became involved in the anarchist movement in Philadelphia, joining the Social Science Club. His mental illness reportedly manifested following a severe fever.

developed the idée fixe that the cause of the inactivity was the strained relationship between Voltairine and Gordon, who no longer talked to each other, and for which she was entirely to blame. Helcher was one of Voltairine's pupils to whom she had taught English. He undertook the holy mission to bring her on the right path, to resume her friendship with Dr. Gordon and to lead the movement. When she could not convince him that her personal relationships were none of his concern, she was forced to send him away and forbid him from coming to her house. Helcher became bitter and melancholy; in addition, he was unemployed for a while—he was a cigarmaker by trade—and one fine day he followed Voltairine and shot her three times.[8]

Severely wounded, Voltairine could not get her poor, mentally ill attacker out of her thoughts. As soon as she was able to write, she penned an appeal to her comrades to do everything in their power to save him from the clutches of the police. Her attitude caught the fancy of the capitalist press, which exclaimed in astonishment: "The anarchist Voltairine de Cleyre behaves in real life in accordance with the teachings of Jesus!—Something more than many so-called devout Christians have shown."

Helcher was given six years. Voltairine was no Henry Clay Frick, no partner of Carnegie, that her assailant should be given twenty-two years. But it was immediately clear that Helcher was not in his right mind. He spent the rest of his life in asylums.[9]

For three or four years after the shooting, Voltairine was unable to do much for herself or for the movement. One of her first lectures after the assassination attempt was on "Crime and Punishment." It was a splendid analysis that was published as a pamphlet and later included in the volume of her collected essays.[10]

---

8. According to other accounts, Helcher had also long been sexually infatuated with De Cleyre and further believed that her Social Science Club was somehow responsible for his inability to secure a job.

9. Helcher's full sentence was six years and nine months, but he was soon transferred to an asylum and then released into his mother's care in 1907. He was in and out of institutions for the remainder of his life.

10. Voltairine de Cleyre, *Crime and Punishment: A Lecture Delivered before the Social Science Club of Philadelphia, March 15th, 1903* (Philadelphia: Social Science Club, [1903]), and "Crime and Punishment" in *Selected Works of Voltairine de Cleyre*, ed. Alexander Berkman (New York: Mother Earth Publishing Association, 1914), 173–204.

PART TWO

In Philadelphia, 1903–1913

CHAPTER 13

The Period of Revision in Our Movement

For a quarter of a century, the anarchists in most countries held to the most extreme revolutionary position adopted at the conference in London in 1881. Their main activity consisted of agitating for the social revolution, for propaganda of the deed and energetic attacks by individuals. The social significance of the movement faded into the background.

Most comrades truly and honestly believed that the social revolution was around the corner and would break out today or tomorrow all over the world. Every daring uprising of an individual would help bring closer the long-awaited final conflict for total liberation. On the other hand, every reform, every improvement in living conditions, even if acquired through the action of the working masses, was an obstacle to the arrival of the revolution and brought more harm than good. They worked under the notion *the worse the better*, that the greater the exploitation and oppression of the masses, the greater will be their revolutionary fervor and the sooner salvation will come.

But this theory did not fit with the facts of life. In their struggles, workers sought *improvement*, not complete liberation. They enthusiastically embraced anarchist agitation regarding methods of struggle and applauded the lofty goals of anarchism without seriously examining how and when it could be achieved. Our movement took on a romantic character—great enthusiasm for lightning-fast, heroic acts without deep roots in the daily realities of life.

✻ ✻ ✻

In France and a number of other countries, a slew of terrorist acts perpetrated by anarchists shook the world in the 1890s.[1] Some were appropriate, justified, and successfully defended in court by the defendants. But some were senseless and unjustified, like the assassination of the empress of Austria or bombings of public places, where the lives of many innocent people were endangered. Such acts gave the impression that the anarchists had declared war on the whole of society, rather than just the state, and sought to terrorize everything and everybody.

This impression was, of course, false. Some romantic individuals here and there may have fantasized about such activity and expressed this in a childish way. The thinking people in the movement as a whole always had the social character of anarchism in mind, the necessity of penetrating the broad mass of people, of teaching them, attracting them to our doctrines, and not frightening or repelling them. At the same time, however, they could not condemn those comrades who sacrificed their lives by committing acts that were not understandable or justified. They felt that, in a sense, our agitation and worldview were responsible for these acts. They tried to explain and, as far as possible, justify terrorist acts that had no real social significance.

Terrorism played a very insignificant role in the anarchist movement in general. With the exception of Russia during the revolutionary uprising of 1905, only a few dozen acts of terrorism were committed by anarchists around the world.[2] In comparison with other movements and parties, anarchism is, one might say, relatively free from such sins. The Church, for example, has far more heinous crimes on its conscience. The Socialist-Revolutionaries, the Republicans in Ireland, Spain, and other countries, the labor movement—not to speak of the capitalist and imperialist murderers and robbers—have

---

1. Acts of "propaganda of the deed" in this decade included the bombing of Barcelona's Liceu Theater and the bombing of the French National Assembly in 1893; the bombing of the Café Terminus in Paris and the assassination of French President Sadi Carnot in 1894; the bombing of a Feast of Corpus Christi procession in Barcelona in 1896; the assassination of Spanish prime minister Antonio Cánovas del Castillo and the attempted assassination of King Umberto I of Italy in 1897; and the assassination of Austro-Hungarian Empress Elisabeth in 1898.

2. According to the most comprehensive survey to date, "During the 1890s real or alleged anarchists in Europe, the United States, and Australia killed more than sixty and injured over 200 people with bombs, pistols, and daggers." Richard Bach Jensen, *The Battle against Anarchist Terrorism: An International History, 1878–1934* (Cambridge: Cambridge University Press, 2014), 36.

all used terror on a very large scale. Yet our movement was attacked, as if by a swarm of bees, to create the impression that anarchism and terrorism are synonymous, that the only task of an anarchist is to make bombs and destroy the whole world.

❉ ❉ ❉

However, we must admit that in those years our movement did not have a clear understanding of the question. Some lauded every deed and sought to explain and justify even for the most foolish acts, while others disavowed and condemned every terrorist act—even those that were socially justified—and later renounced revolution altogether. As it turns out, to further confuse people's thinking, in those same years our movement began to be influenced by the teachings of Max Stirner, who had died in 1856 and whose work, *The Ego and Its Own*, remained for half a century unknown to the wider world.[3] Shortly thereafter came Friedrich Nietzsche's Torah on the "superman," who does not recognize and does not have to accept any duty or social responsibility.[4]

Thus, under these influences our movement was beset with many questions: may anarchists be organized and accept certain responsibilities, such as paying dues, submitting to the decision of a majority, and so on? May

---

3. **Max Stirner** (1806–1856), real name Johann Kaspar Schmidt, was a German teacher and philosopher. He was a member of Berlin's "Young Hegelians" along with Karl Marx, Friedrich Engels, and Mikhail Bakunin. His major work, *The Ego and Its Own* (first published in German in 1844 as *Der Einzige und sein Eigentum*), is an extended post-Hegelian critique of Christianity, morality, capitalism, nationalism, liberalism, socialism, and all other forms of authority and abstractions. Stirner instead promoted "egoism," or the individual pursuit of freedom and happiness unfettered by artificial restrictions and doctrines. Although he never called himself an anarchist and the anarchist movement emerged after his death and independent of his ideas, Stirner's writings greatly influenced some of its later members, including many American individualist anarchists.

4. **Friedrich Nietzsche** (1844–1900) was a German philosopher. His controversial nihilist views rejected all religion and traditional morality, and in his 1883 book *Also sprach Zarathustra* (Thus Spoke Zarathustra) he presents the ideal of the *Übermensch*, or superman, who creates his own values free from superstition and out of love for the material world. Elements of Nietzsche's thought influenced many anarchists, including Emma Goldman, Alexander Berkman, and Gustav Landauer.

anarchists preside over meetings and adopt certain rules of conduct? A kind of code of conduct worked itself out, a sort of anarchist *Shulchan Aruch* [a guide to Jewish religious law], mostly a negative one that proscribed what anarchists should not do if they wanted to use that label for themselves. The emphasis was placed entirely on the individual and his free will, but even he was not free to act against the code's taboos and prohibitions.

❄ ❄ ❄

Such a state of affairs could not last long. After all, anarchism is fundamentally a social doctrine, not a religious belief by which the individual seeks to save his soul. Anarchism is built on the principle of the responsibility of each individual to his fellow man and to society, not on the capricious, irresponsible actions of an individual doing whatever comes into his head in the moment. In Jewish anarchist circles, the first signs of a change in anarchist tactics, and later even in anarchist theory, began to emerge in the 1890s.

This had caused the split in our movement between those who advocated for a newspaper and those who advocated for a journal. These differences of opinion confused even other comrades, to whom it seemed a petty quarrel. What did it matter if the publication was a newspaper or a journal? But the real causes lay much deeper, in differences of opinion that needed to be examined.

Saul Yanovsky was, as far as I know, the first in the Jewish movement of the 1890s to speak out publicly against agitating for "propaganda of the deed" and terror for the sake of terror. In 1893 in the *Arbeter fraynd*, which he edited in London at the time, he tried to clarify his position—a terrible apostasy for which we, the younger comrades, would not forgive him for many years. In all other matters of theory and tactics, Yanovsky remained religiously consistent. For many long years, he defended every part of the anarchist program in the *Fraye arbeter shtime*.

Dr. Jacob A. Maryson went a step further: in the *Fraye gezelshaft* he questioned the close connection between anarchism and revolution per se—as if the first was inevitably dependent on the second.[5] He also dared to question

---

5. Dr. M--n, "Es meg un es ken, nor muz nit," *Fraye gezelshaft*, September 1900, 481–87.

the dogmatic theory that anarchism will inevitably lead to communism. His compelling thesis—"It can and it may, but it does not necessarily!"—forced us all to think more seriously about the principles of our theory, even though the heresy of his ideas shocked us profoundly.

In the *Fraye arbeter shtime* in 1906, Dr. Maryson sought to remove the anarchist prohibition against participating in electoral politics. In this he was not entirely original. The Italian anarchist Francesco Saverio Merlino, who had carried on active propaganda in the United States for several years, first suggested the idea and defended it with the same arguments.[6] At one point he had proposed that the Italian anarchists nominate Errico Malatesta to parliament in order to remove the ban on the anarchist movement in Italy. Malatesta roundly rejected the offer.

Other non-Jewish anarchists also began to suggest changes in the theory and practices of our movement. Voltairine de Cleyre developed a unique approach—"anarchism, simply," with no adjectives or modifiers.[7] Dr. Max Nettlau strongly emphasized the idea of moral and social obligations of the individual, which require revolutionaries as well as workers in general to have a conscientious attitude toward everything they do and produce. They must always ask if their actions are beneficial or harmful to society. Leo Tolstoy, with his supremely creative ethical-Christian approach to the social question, gave our movement a sense of collective moral responsibility.[8] His teachings of passive resistance were later adopted by Gandhi in India and proved to be no weaker or less effective tactics than aggressive struggle.

The greatest contributor in this area, however, was Peter Kropotkin, who in the 1890s set out to establish an objective, scientific approach to anarchism by tracing the changes that have occurred in societies and the

---

6. Francesco Saverio Merlino, *Pro e contro il socialism: esposizione critica dei principii e dei sistemi socialisti* (Milan: Fratelli Treves, 1897).

7. Voltairine de Cleyre described herself as "an Anarchist, simply, without economic label attached" in her article "A Correction," *Mother Earth*, December 1907, 473. See also her essay "Anarchism," in *Selected Works of Voltairine de Cleyre*, ed. Alexander Berkman (New York: Mother Earth Publishing Association, 1914), 96–117.

8. **Leo Tolstoy** (Count Lev Nikolayevich Tolstoy, 1828–1910) was a Russian aristocrat, writer, pacifist, and antiauthoritarian. The author of such well-known novels as *War and Peace* (1869) and *Anna Karenina* (1878), in the 1870s he developed a radical interpretation of Christianity that rejected feudalism, capitalism, violence, and all worldly authority. Though Tolstoy never called himself an anarchist, he was widely admired by anarchists around the world, some of whom embraced his pacifism and adopted the label "Tolstoyan anarchist."

tendencies toward future developments that are already observable. In his many great works—*Mutual Aid: A Factor in Evolution,* as well as *Fields, Factories and Workshops, The Great French Revolution,* and other treatises such as *Modern Science and Anarchism, Anarchist Morality, The State: Its Historic Role,* and *Ethics*—Kropotkin built a monumental foundation for constructive anarchism, tracing the forces that have always operated and continue to contribute to the building of free institutions, the development of ever-increasing forms of solidarity and mutual aid, and the decentralization of industry and its linkage to agriculture. As illuminated by Kropotkin, anarchism took on a new appearance, a solid social significance.

In the United States, Dr. James P. Warbasse, in his great work *Co-operative Democracy,* established anarchism as the basis of the entire cooperative movement and its activity.[9] It helped to unleash a constructive social conception of anarchism, which did not include the fiery verbiage of the revolution but was firmly rooted in human nature and the development of social relationships between people.

❋ ❋ ❋

These theoretical considerations and developments were not unaffected by the practices of actual movements: in France, the anarchists began to build the revolutionary syndicalist movement—the synthesis of anarchism and practical activity in the labor movement, which was born here in America

---

9. **James Peter Warbasse** (1866–1957) was an American-born surgeon, writer, and radical. From a wealthy New Jersey family, he earned his medical degree at Columbia University in 1889. In the 1910s Warbasse wrote and spoke on behalf of many radical causes and organizations, including the IWW, the Socialist Party, the single tax, birth control, and cooperatives, as well as anarchism. He contributed articles to *Mother Earth* and taught for a time at the Ferrer School in New York, but by the end of the First World War he focused exclusively on the cooperative movement. In 1916 Warbasse cofounded the Co-operative League of the United States of America, and he served as its president until 1941. He argued, in the book Cohen mentions, "The Co-operative Democracy has no better champion of its fundamental principles than that remarkable book by the naturalist historian, Peter Kropotkin, entitled 'Mutual Aid'," and "The best way to abolish the State is to do a constructive piece of work that will make the State unnecessary. . . . The Co-operative Movement offers a libertarian philosophy." *Co-operative Democracy: Attained through Voluntary Association of the People as Consumers* (New York: MacMillan, 1923), 367, 370.

with the Chicago anarchists of the 1880s. The blood of the Haymarket martyrs nourished and sanctified this synthesis. At the beginning of the twentieth century, these ideas suddenly began to show great vitality in France. In the other Latin countries, as well as here in the promised land, revolutionary syndicalism, or industrial unionism, embodied the great liberatory ideal and led to a massive wave of organized mass strikes, huge demonstrations, and active methods of struggle that became a daily occurrence in many countries. Anarchism received a new impetus toward more suitable ground and moved away from the romantic, conspiratorial revolutionary activity of small groups and individuals. It influenced the broad masses of working people.

In Germany, Gustav Landauer was active in building the "free socialist" movement, which emphasized peaceful evolution through constructive activity.[10] In Spain, Francisco Ferrer began establishing Modern Schools, which were predicated on the principle of libertarian education.[11] After many years of revolutionary activity, Ferrer came to the conclusion that "time respects only those institutions which time itself has played its part in building up"—an idea that we all should reflect upon.[12]

With the exception of Russia and Mexico, where special conditions prevailed, the anarchist movement everywhere busied itself in a broad, public

---

10. **Gustav Landauer** (1870–1919) was a German-born Jewish writer, pacifist, and anarchist. Radicalized as a student in Berlin, he became editor of the newspaper *Der Sozialist* (1891–1899) in 1893 and turned it into an explicitly anarchist publication. Landauer's anarchism incorporated elements of Jewish and Christian mysticism as well as Stirner and Nietzsche's individualism, and it largely focused on self-transformation and living as an anarchist in the present. During the brief-lived Bavarian Soviet Republic of 1919 he was appointed commissioner of public enlightenment but resigned after the Communist Party of Germany gained control of the government. Shortly thereafter, Landauer was arrested and murdered by members of the right-wing Freikorps during the suppression of the Republic.

11. **Francsico Ferrer** (Francisco Ferrer i Guàrdia, 1859–1909) was a Spanish-born Catalan railway worker, educator, and anarchist. In 1885 he immigrated to France following his participation in a failed republican uprising and in Paris became an anarchist and was influenced by Paul Robin's (1837–1912) libertarian school at the Prévost orphanage. After returning to Spain in 1901, Ferrer founded the first anarchist Modern School (Escuela Moderna) in Barcelona. As Cohen relates in later chapters, Ferrer was arrested in 1906 and again in 1909 for alleged involvement in the violent acts of others, and his execution in 1909 turned him into an international martyr and spread the Modern School movement around the world, including to the United States.

12. The source of this quotation appears to be Joseph McCabe, *The Martyrdom of Ferrer: Being a True Account of His Life and Work* (London: Watts, 1909), 17–18.

way with constructive social activity, through education, organization, and popular struggles.

❋ ❋ ❋

Of course, this change did not come about all at once. Every new idea evokes opposition and sharp criticism among anarchists as well as in other circles. Every attempt to revise the tactics—and especially the theory—of anarchism has been fought with great bitterness. The debates in our publications have not always been conducted in the best manner. But time has a way of correcting matters, and almost imperceptibly our movement turned onto new paths.

Everywhere our comrades engaged in systematic educational work. They opened libraries, ran schools for adults as well as children, and published books, creating a rich literature. Above all, however, they sought to inspire the rank and file of the working class with the spirit of anarchism and of revolutionary syndicalism.

In many respects, this work was similar to the activity that our comrades had done from the very beginning in the 1880s, when they thought that the revolution was around the corner. At first glance, one would think no change had occurred. But in truth a fundamental change had taken place: little by little our movement freed itself from many dogmas and taboos. It was no longer afraid to carry on its work in an organized way, with deliberate planning, votes, and resolutions. The responsibility was put on every individual member of the organization to live up to his accepted obligations. He could no longer, like a will-o'-the-wisp, do whatever he pleased.

There were still many obstacles in the way. On the one hand, it was hard for the movement to throw off the fiery, demonstrative activities of the "good old days." Educational work had no fireworks in it, nothing flashy. It is systematic work that needs to be done day in and day out, in a relatively monotonous way. Such work cannot evoke lifelong enthusiasm and devotion in everyone.

On the other hand, our movement has always suffered from the weakness of accepting every new idea and making it part of our activity without critically analyzing it. Women's rights (*froyen-rekht*), free love, birth control, vegetarianism, spiritualism, psychoanalysis—things which had no direct connection to the fundamental problems of social coexistence, as long as they were new and spicy, would quickly find a place in the movement and become part of our program. This brought more harm than good to our movement. Instead of concentrating our efforts on the fundamental anarchist tasks, we have spread them out to include everything and everyone, as if we could solve all problems of the entire universe. As a result, we were often unwelcome guests at a stranger's wedding, while our own work was neglected.

Let us give one little example. When Margaret Sanger began her campaign for birth control and needed help getting a public hearing, she was a dedicated revolutionary.[13] On the masthead of her magazine was the slogan, "No Gods No Masters."[14] Emma Goldman took this new Torah of birth control to heart and spread it all over the country, as if in it really lay the solution to the social problem. Margaret's movement grew. She herself climbed high on the ladder of popularity. The revolutionary motto was removed from the publication. Margaret gained prestige, honor, and influence with the higher-ups. When Emma Goldman and Ben Reitman were arrested for advocating birth control, Margaret ignored their plight.[15] She

---

13. **Margaret Sanger** (1879–1966) was an American-born nurse, writer, birth control activist, and onetime radical. The daughter of Irish immigrants, she trained as a nurse before marrying and having three children. Around 1911 Sanger and her husband became involved in the Socialist Party as well as the IWW. By 1914 she had befriended Emma Goldman and was contributing to anarchist periodicals, and her children attended the Modern School in New York and then Stelton. Sanger opened the first birth control clinic in the United States in Brooklyn in 1916, leading to one of many arrests in connection with birth control advocacy. By 1921 she had distanced herself from radicalism and founded the American Birth Control League, which focused on a middle-class audience and eventually became the Planned Parenthood Federation of America.

14. *The Woman Rebel* (1914) was a monthly magazine published by Margaret Sanger that focused on birth control and other topics related to women's political and bodily autonomy. Eight issues appeared before it was suppressed for violating New York's obscenity laws. The slogan "No Gods, No Masters," although predating the modern anarchist movement, had by the 1890s been appropriated as a specifically anarchist catchphrase.

15. Sanger in fact was out of the country when Goldman and Reitman were arrested in Portland, Oregon, in September 1915 for distributing information on birth control. However, Cohen may have been thinking of Goldman's subsequent arrest on similar charges in New York in February 1916. **Ben L. Reitman** (1879–1942) was an American-born Jewish physician and radical. The son of poor Russian Jewish immigrants, he spent time as a hobo before earning his medical degree at the College of Physicians and Surgeons in Chicago in 1904.

was now very unhappy that her association with anarchists could compromise all her work!

❋ ❋ ❋

Under these and other hardships, the revision of anarchism occurred in the early years of the twentieth century, with debates over basic principles and, more generally, the methods and tactics to be used by the movement to spread and strengthen its ideals. Under these circumstances and in this atmosphere, our younger generation joined the movement and began to influence its direction. In most cities across the country, there were very active anarchist groups. In Philadelphia, the Radical Library was founded, which brought up a whole generation of active anarchists whose influence was felt in various circles of social life. A knowledge of this environment and these circumstances will make the activities and development of our movement in these years easier to understand.

Reitman offered medical care, including illegal abortions, to the poor, radicals, and other marginalized communities. In 1908 he met and became romantically involved with Emma Goldman and worked as her lecture tour manager until they separated in 1917.

CHAPTER 14

My First Years in Philadelphia

In the spring of 1903, I arrived in Philadelphia. The circle of people into which I fell was very conservative, nourished by Sarasohn's *Yidishes tageblat*, which was not to my liking from the start.[1] For a couple of years, around the age of twelve or thirteen, I had been part of a revolutionary group in Minsk. I became acquainted with socialist ideas as they were understood at that time in Russia. From a secluded corner of the Polesian Lowland I then followed the emergence and development of the Bund and the growth of the revolutionary movement among the Jewish people.

Three works, quite different in character, had strongly influenced my intellectual development in my younger years: as a boy at the great Mir Yeshiva, Kalman Schulman's description of the Paris Commune in his nine-volume *Divre yeme 'olam* (General History of the World) aroused my sympathy for the Communards.[2] The more the writer sought to depict them in an unfavorable light, the more I was attracted to them. I felt a close empathy with their desires and a personal sympathy for their martyrdom.

In the woods of Polesia, I later came across a bound volume of collected issues of *Ha-Melitz* (The Advocate) from 1881, which gave a detailed account

---

1. **Kasriel Hirsch Sarasohn** (1835–1905) was a Russian-born Jewish journalist and publisher who immigrated to the United States in 1866 and in 1886 founded the *Yidishes tageblat*, which reflected his conservative and Orthodox religious views.

2. The **Mir Yeshiva** was Jewish religious school founded in 1815 in the city of Mir in present-day Belarus. **Kalman Schulman** (1819–1899) was a Russian-born Jewish teacher, *maskil*, and prolific writer and translator. He published many popular Hebrew works on history, geography, and other topics, including *Divre yeme 'olam* (Vilna: Defus ha-Almanah veha-ahim Rom, 1867–1884).

of the historic trial of Andrei Zhelyabov, Sophia Perovskaya, and their associates for the assassination of Tsar Alexander II.[3] As you can imagine, the newspaper presented them in the worst possible light. The very idea of these renegades daring to raise their hands against the God-anointed ruler of Russia! My sympathy, however, definitively lay with those who committed the deed. I read the proceedings with the greatest interest, swallowing every word and reliving all their experiences.

The third work, which was in a way even more interesting to me, was a bound appendix to *Novoye Vremya* (The New Times), which contained Edward Bellamy's novel *Looking Backward*.[4] This appeared long before that newspaper became reactionary and antisemitic. I acquired this collection in the mid-1890s, and Bellamy's critique of present society in his first chapter, with the parable of the people harnessed to a heavy wagon, impressed me greatly.

Before coming to America, I spent a few years in the army in Grodno, where I had a good opportunity to study and read the best Russian classics nonstop, day and night in the local library. I was even able to organize a revolutionary circle.

I tell all this to point out that when I came to Philadelphia in the spring of 1903, I was well acquainted with socialist ideas. At this time, I considered myself a socialist and revolutionary. But I had never heard of anarchism; I had never even come across the term anywhere. A few years before, I had read some articles by Samuel H. Setzer in *Ha-Dor* (The Generation), I believe, about Stirner's teachings, but his extreme individualism, or egoism, did not appeal to me.[5]

---

3. **Ha-Melitz** (1860–1904) was the first Hebrew newspaper published in the Russian Empire and was strongly influenced by the Haskalah movement. **Andrei Zhelyabov** (1851–1881) and **Sophia Perovskaya** (1853–1881) were husband and wife and members of the Russian revolutionary group Narodnaya Volya. They were both executed by hanging for their roles in the assassination of Alexander II with a homemade bomb.

4. **Novaya Vremya** (1868–1917) was one of tsarist Russia's most popular newspapers. **Edward Bellamy** (1850–1898) was an American-born journalist, novelist, and socialist. His utopian novel *Looking Backward: 2000–1887* (1888), was one of the best-selling books of the nineteenth century. It depicts a future United States where all private property has been nationalized and all people's needs are met by a benevolent state. The novel briefly inspired a large-scale "nationalist" movement that advocated such a state-socialist system.

5. **Samuel H. Setzer** (Shmuel-Tsvi Zetser, 1876–1962) was a Russian-born Jewish journalist and Zionist who wrote for Hebrew and Yiddish publications in both Europe and the

Figure 16: Joseph Cohen, c. 1903
Courtesy of Jenny Schwartzberg

The backward milieu in which I found myself was quite shocking. I could not take the *Tageblat* in my hands, and the *Forverts* did not print what I expected to find in a socialist paper. Soon after, news of the horrific Kishinev pogrom reached us.[6] The Yiddish newspapers were filled with horrific descriptions. It was very striking that the *Tageblat* and *Forverts* were

---

United States. **Ha-Dor** (1901–1904) was a weekly Hebrew magazine published in Warsaw. It often carried articles summarizing works by European writers and philosophers.

6. The **Kishinev pogrom** was a violent antisemitic attack on the Jewish community of Kishinev (present-day Chișinău, Moldova) from April 12 to April 21, 1903. Inspired by blood libel rumors, rioters killed forty-nine Jews, injured and raped hundreds, and destroyed fifteen hundred homes, sparking a global outcry.

competing to reopen the deep wounds of the Jewish people in order to gain more readers. The *Forverts* won this race, beginning its phenomenal growth in readership that no other Jewish paper reached before or since. But for me the paper became even more odious than Sarasohn's officially nationalist sheet.

The anarchist movement in Philadelphia after the assassination of McKinley in 1901 and the attempt on Voltairine de Cleyre's life in 1902 was very weak. Chaim Weinberg was very occupied with work in the cooperative store on South Street, as well as with the cooperative house in which a number of young comrades lived, among them Benjamin Axler and I. Katz, saving money and dreaming of a communist farm colony.[7]

An attempt was made that year to carry out some anarchist educational work by the Frayheyt Group, whose secretary and most active member was Eliezer Landau (A. Wohliner).[8] But the group was not very successful. Its meetings and lectures did not attract an audience. It is clear from announcements in the *Fraye arbeter shtime* that the group did not have much confidence in its work.

My time that first year in Philadelphia was taken up with heavy labor during the day in a building supply yard where almost all the skilled workers were Germans, professionals, and where one only worked eight hours a

---

7. **Benjamin Axler** (Benyomin Aksler, 1887–1955) was a Russian-born Jewish printer, journalist, and anarchist. In 1903 he immigrated to the United States, where he became an anarchist and began contributing to the *FAS* and the *Arbeter fraynd*. In 1906 Axler edited the short-lived Philadelphia anarchist newspaper *Broyt un frayheyt*. He later moved to New York and joined the Naye Gezelshaft Group, Branch 364 of the Workmen's Circle. Axler also helped produce the *FAS* and served as the longtime secretary of the Jewish Anarchist Federation of America and Canada. Obituary: *FAS*, July 29, 1955. I. Katz appears to be **Isaac Katz** (Yitskhok Kats or Ketsenboym, died 1956), a Russian-born Jewish garment worker and anarchist who later lived in New York where he was active in the Anti-Conscription League and the Free Workers' Center and in the mid-1930s became secretary of the Jewish Anarchist Federation. In the 1940s Katz lived in Detroit and was a member of the Fraye Arbeter Shtime Group. Obituaries: *FAS*, September 21 and October 19, 1956.

8. **Eliezer Landau** (Leyzer Landau, 1877–1942), pen name A. Wohliner (Vohliner), was a Russian-born Jewish garment worker, writer, editor, and anarchist. A Zionist in his youth, he immigrated to Montreal in 1902 with a group hoping to form a commune and soon began to write for the *FAS*. Moving to Philadelphia, New York, and then back to Montreal, Landau was active in several anarchist groups, established himself as a well-known Yiddish writer, and became literary editor of the *Forverts*. In the 1920s he drifted away from the anarchist movement and became a member of Poale Zion. Obituary: *FAS*, April 24, 1942.

day. In the evening I was learning a trade, cigar making, at the Baron Hirsch School on Tenth and Carpenter. During the remaining time, on my rides back and forth from work and on my few free days, I was busy learning English, the language of the country. There was simply no time left for social activities.

But I could not continue this way for long. My urge to be among people, to start doing "something," was very great. One day I came across a handbill announcing a meeting at the cooperative society on South Street. It caught my attention immediately. When I attended the meeting, I found an intelligent circle of people there and became a member myself, paying five dollars out of my meager earnings.

Little by little I became acquainted with the work of the group, with its activists and leaders, among whom Chaim Weinberg was the head. He took me under his wing, spending every free moment with me before and after meetings, acquainting me with the entirety of his activities in the anarchist movement. It was through him that I learned of the history of our movement, its glorious activity among the workers, and the great ideal to which the anarchists aspire. Under his tutelage and with the help of the *Fraye arbeter shtime* I was gradually converted to anarchism and began devoting more and more time to reading anarchist literature.

The cooperative store, which sold shoes and hats—items that workers could only afford to buy once a year, giving them virtually no connection with the enterprise—was already going downhill. The cooperative bakery, organized a few years before, was already a shambles. Weinberg would relate to me with great enthusiasm the story of the huge parade they held upon the opening of their bakery, which was attended by thousands of people, all from the Jewish unions and societies. The bakers, in snow-white aprons, marched at the head of the parade, displaying on a cart a challah as big as a house. Next followed the other unions with bands of musicians. Money was collected in white sheets passed among the spectators, and, although there seemed mountains of it, when the copper coins were counted there was not enough to cover the expenses of the parade.

The bakery did achieve its goal in one regard: the strike and lockout that gave birth to its founding were soon settled. And only then did the troubles in the enterprise itself begin. Weinberg, who was a cigarmaker and did not have the slightest knowledge of baking, was himself hired as the bakery's manager. The workers were not the best in the trade, and, being members of the cooperative, they considered themselves the owners of the enterprise, at least insofar as no one could tell them when and how to work. Their pastries always came out late and were not always the best that the public expected. The management of the shoe and hat cooperative was also very inept. The first manager was comrade Ezekiel Edelstein, also a cigarmaker, an anarchist-nationalist, one of the first organizers of Poale Zion.[9] He was a good speaker but had no business management experience. When he gained a little knowhow, he was removed and another inexperienced man, comrade Sokolov, put in his place. Not only did they change the manager but also the location of the shop, which relocated to Fifth and South Streets, an area with many flourishing stores, but which was not suitable for a cooperative store. The private businesses on that street made their profits by swindling the neighborhood's Negroes—a source of income that the cooperative business could not use. When it moved to its new place, the comrades held another big parade, led by Joseph Barondess on a white steed. Everything was done with great enthusiasm and on a grand scale but to no avail.

Incidentally, Edelstein, the former store manager, opened up his own shoe store on Second Street, in the cooperative's old location, and did good business. He was a very gifted young man and an interesting personality, who dreamed of and promoted a paramilitary movement of Jewish youth around the world for the purpose of demanding a Jewish homeland and

---

9. **Ezekiel Edelstein** (Edelshteyn, died 1907) was a Russian-born Jewish cigarmaker, anarchist, and Labor Zionist. He had been a member of Hovevei Zion before emigrating around 1898 to Philadelphia, where he was soon involved in the Jewish labor and anarchist movements. In 1904 he formed the second American branch of Poale Zion and was the first manager of the organization's newspaper *Der idisher kemfer* (The Jewish Fighter, 1906–1923). Obituary: *Der shtern* (Philadelphia), August 11, 1907. **Poale Zion** (Workers of Zion; Po'alei Tsiyon in Hebrew) was a Labor Zionist movement that first emerged in Russia in the first years of the twentieth century, with the first US branch being formed in New York in 1903, followed by the founding of a national American organization (officially called the Labor Zionist Organization of America) in 1905. It advocated Jewish colonization of Palestine (its "minimum program") to be followed by class struggle resulting in the socialization of the means of production (its "maximum program"). According to Poale Zion founder Ber Borochov (1881–1917), a Marxist who described his own views on the topic as "anarchist-socialist," this would in turn lead to the abolition of the Jewish state. Such views provided enough common ground for many sympathetic Jewish anarchists to join the organization.

supporting that demand with terrorist acts. But an untimely death from an accident at the beach put an end to his plans and dreams.

At this time our movement was shaken up by the arrest of John Turner, an English anarchist, who had come to America for a short lecture tour. Turner was the organizer and secretary of the Shop Assistants' Union in London. He, like many others, had been converted to anarchism by the Chicago tragedy in 1887. He had visited America in the 1890s and lectured in all the major cities without any interference. But now, under the new anti-anarchist law, he was arrested at his first public appearance in New York City. Immediately, a Free Speech League formed, which many liberals joined, and with great difficulty it managed to get Turner out on bail until his case came before the highest court of the land.[10] Turner visited Philadelphia, where he addressed a huge gathering and made a wonderfully good impression. He also held lectures in many other cities and aroused great interest in the cause of free speech and the extent to which legislators were restricting it to prevent foreign anarchists from entering the country. The Supreme Court, as was expected, upheld the law: Congress had the right to pass such a law, even though it expressly went against both the spirit of the Constitution and its guaranteed freedoms.

April 10, 1904, was the first time I saw and heard Emma Goldman. A meeting was to be held in the Odd Fellows Temple at Broad and Arch, not far from City Hall. When we arrived, we found a cordon of police on the steps around the entire building. The street was full of people who were not allowed to congregate. The mounted police on the sidewalk kept pushing the crowd, just as the Cossacks in Holy Russia used to do. I stood there dumbfounded; I could not at first comprehend what was taking place. That here in America, in this free country, peaceful citizens should not be allowed to gather in a hall to hear a speaker—I just could not believe my eyes! But my complete ignorance of the English language prevented me from making an attempt to address the people around me and urging them to resist. I left dismayed and upset, determined to do whatever I could to fight such barbaric tyranny.

---

10. The **Free Speech League** actually formed in 1902 in response to the introduction of the Anarchist Exclusion Act. Its members included anarchists and other radicals, civil libertarians, and liberal sympathizers, and it published literature, organized meetings, and sponsored legal defense campaigns on behalf of a wide array of radicals before dissolving during the First World War.

Throughout the year 1904 we in the cooperative store struggled with problems we could not solve. The debts grew, and the possibilities of meeting them grew ever slimmer. We tried to interest more people in our undertaking by arranging lectures and meetings. For one of our lectures we brought down Yanovsky who, although he was not especially interested in cooperatives, agreed to come and help us.

After the meeting, Weinberg introduced the two of us, and we went to the cooperative house together. On the way, Yanovsky complained that the comrades in Philadelphia were neglecting the *Fraye arbeter shtime*. There were few subscribers there, and they weren't paying up. The retail sales at the newsstands were also negligible. Few people even knew that there was such a paper. Comrade L. Lavrov, the official local representative of the *Fraye arbeter shtime*, was a very fine person, but he didn't know Yiddish and didn't know what was going on in the paper. As a result of this conversation, I offered to take over representation of the *Fraye arbeter shtime* in Philadelphia.

Yanovsky was very happy with my volunteering. That was exactly his goal with the entire conversation. He knew me from my frequent correspondence that I sent to him. Now he had made me his lieutenant. In the following issue, in the historic "letterbox" (*brief-kasten*), he included the following notice:

> L. Lavrov, Philad.—Please be so kind as to act according to what we decided at the meeting. Pass on all lists, money, and bills to Joseph Cohen, who, we hope, will do his best so that Philadelphia too will do its part for the *F.A.S.*[11]

This struck me as strange. There had been no meeting, and no one but he had made the decision. Lavrov had no money or records to give me. The whole affair was a bit contrived, but—alas! I had undertaken an obligation, and I had to carry it through.

I became a very frequent correspondent for the newspaper. At election time that year, I wrote an article about the trained oxen who lead their herds to the slaughterhouses in Chicago to be butchered, and I compared this to the activities of the socialist politicians among the workers. Yanovsky

---

11. *FAS*, September 24, 1904.

published it in the first two columns on the front page, attracting much attention to its content.[12] My future friend William Zukerman considered it an undeserved assault on the socialists and sparked an interesting discussion on the whole matter.[13]

My work as an official representative put me in contact with all the comrades in the city. Every Sunday I would visit them, getting to know most of them and forming close relationships with many of the more active comrades. The condition of the movement was not great. Everyone talked of how Philadelphia was once a citadel of the anarchist movement, how it used to have many good speakers in English and Yiddish. The comrades had been active. They formed unions of cloakmakers, vest makers, bakers, and other trades. They used to hold rallies every Sunday near City Hall that drew large audiences. The Yiddish meetings were also well attended. But that was all long gone—now not trace of it was left. A couple of the speakers had died (Robert Wilson and Gretch), others left the anarchist movement and went their separate ways (Isidore Prenner and Dr. Samuel Gordon), still others became professionals, doctors, and pharmacists (Dr. Max Staller, Dr. Max Barbour, Dr. Leo Gartman, Dr. Julius Segal, George Seldes, Jacob L. Joffe, Natasha Notkin, etc.). They had become busy people leading respectable lives and more or less kept their distance. The only speakers left were Chaim Weinberg and old Moses Levene. In comparison with the old days, our movement was on its last legs.

Those are the conditions I found when I became official representative of the *Fraye arbeter shtime* in 1904. Visiting our subscribers and getting to know them personally, I found that they could be divided into certain categories. Some of the old guard, formerly speakers and now doctors, were dead to the movement. The most that could be expected from them was a few pennies

---

12. *FAS*, November 5, 1904.

13. **William Zukerman** or Zuckerman (Viliam Tsukerman, 1885–1961) was a Russian-born Jewish journalist, anarchist, and anti-Zionist. He immigrated to Chicago around 1900 and worked his way through college at the University of Chicago, where he majored in philosophy. Zukerman wrote for numerous radical periodicals, including the *Forverts* (the Chicago office of which he managed) and the *FAS*, and he was active in the Workmen's Circle. Zukerman lived in London after the First World War, then returned to the United States in 1940 and published the *Jewish Newsletter* (1948–1961), a prominent anti-Zionist publication that stridently criticized Israel's treatment of Palestinians. Obituary: *FAS*, January 15, 1962.

and a visit to a holiday gathering. The pharmacists, especially Jacob L. Joffe and Natasha Notkin, by contrast, gave their all to the movement. Joffe's drugstore, at Third and Bainbridge, was our main gathering place. There were also a few of the old guard scattered all over the city, like Chaim Weinberg, Moses Levene, William Eidelson, Abe Brandschain, Joseph Prenowitz, Ozer Smolenskin, David Apotheker, and Ephraim-Leib Wolfson—these last four, poets and writers with pen in hand.[14]

There were also a number of respectable Jews, shopkeepers, who were sympathetic to our movement: Riklin, Lubarsky, Morris Shtofman, Simon M. Dubin, the Agursky brothers, and others. There were also worker-intellectuals such as Menkin, Meyer Rosen, Jacob Lifshits, the Tsan brothers—people who longed for the good old days and wanted to see a general revival, if someone would just take the initiative to start the work.[15]

Among our readers I also found a small circle of young, lively workers who had thrown themselves into activity: I. Katz, Benjamin Axler, Joseph Washkowitz (Joe Wascow), Sembat, and especially Eliezer Landau (A.

---

14. **Abraham Brandschain** (Abraham Brendsheyn, c. 1882–1947) was a Russian-born Jewish cigarmaker and anarchist. In 1895 he immigrated to the United States with his family, and he contributed funds to the *FAS* in 1899. Brandschain joined the Social Science Club of Philadelphia after its formation in 1901 and was briefly romantically involved with its cofounder Voltairine de Cleyre.

15. **Riklin** was, according to Benny Moore's memoirs (*FAS*, September 15, 1944), an outspoken atheist who opened a general store and later became a Zionist and embraced religion. Census records suggest this may be Jacob Ricklin (1871–1956), who immigrated from Russia around 1889 and sold chinaware and furniture in Philadelphia. **Morris Shtofman** (c. 1872–1952) was a Russian-born Jewish tailor, department store owner, and anarchist. He immigrated to Philadelphia in 1889 and moved to Wilmington, Delaware, in the early 1900s. Shtofman later joined Poale Zion but donated money to anarchist causes at least as late as 1926. **Menkin**, according to Chaim Weinberg, briefly managed the Philadelphia anarchists' cooperative bakery. See Chaim Leib Weinberg, *Forty Years in the Struggle: The Memoirs of a Jewish Anarchist*, ed. Robert P. Helms, trans. Naomi Cohen (Duluth: Litwin Books, 2008), 38. **Meyer Rosen** (Mayer Rozen, 1876–1942) was a Russian-born Jewish cabinet maker and anarchist. He immigrated to Philadelphia in 1903 and married fellow anarchist Sarah Rosen. He later moved to Los Angeles, where he became a member of the Kropotkin Literary Society, Branch 413 of the Workmen's Circle. Obituary: *FAS*, July 24, 1942. **Jacob Lifshits** (died 1908) was a Russian-born Jewish worker, insurance agent, and anarchist. After immigrating to Newark and then moving to New York, he was radicalized by Johann Most in the 1880s. According to the *FAS*, Lifshits was "one of the first Jewish anarchists in America," and he briefly managed that paper after its revival in 1899. He later moved to Philadelphia, where he joined to the Radical Library Group. Obituary: *FAS*, August 8, 1908.

Wohliner), who at that time lived in Philadelphia, sewing shirts at Fagin's old shop and writing feuilletons in the *Fraye arbeter shtime*.[16] We became close friends and used to spend all our time together planning further activities.

The cooperative store slowly succumbed to its agony and died. A number of its devoted members formed a branch of the Workmen's Circle and named it "Cooperative Branch 81."[17] My humble self was among its first members. In closing the store, I served on a committee reviewing the accounts. There I found two interesting things: the organization had hundreds of members, but the entire capital from paid-up dues totaled less than $300. Most members paid not more than 25 or 50 cents. Only two newcomers—a woman and myself—had contributed the full five dollars each. By contrast, the enterprise's shining lights, the members of the board of directors, owed the organization over $226, which they never paid up. The store had been built and run without any capital of its own. It was destined to failure from the very start.

The liquidation of the cooperative store gave me the opportunity to devote all my free time to working for the movement and the *Fraye arbeter shtime*, which gave me much satisfaction. I also received much help and encouragement from two older comrades. The first was Harry Wolf, who

---

16. **Joseph Washkowitz** (Yosef Vashkovits, c. 1886–1930), who Americanized his name to Joseph Wascow, was a Russian-born Jewish paperhanger and anarchist. He joined Philadelphia's anarchist movement around 1903 and shortly thereafter cofounded the Radical Library. Washkowitz married fellow anarchist Rose Wascow, and the couple later helped establish and run Camp Germinal, discussed in chapter 43. Obituary: *FAS*, July 11, 1930. **Sembat**, according to the 1910 census, was likely Harry Sambat (1880–?), a Russian-born Jewish tailor who immigrated to the United States in 1902.

17. The **Workmen's Circle** (Arbeter Ring in Yiddish) is a secular Jewish mutual aid and educational organization founded in 1900. In its early decades it maintained a nonpartisan but generally socialist outlook, and at its height in the 1920s it included more than eighty thousand members in hundreds of branches. The Workmen's Circle opened more than a hundred Yiddish schools and cultural centers throughout North America. Many anarchists joined the organization, which included two dozen explicitly anarchist branches by the end of the 1920s, including Branch 92 (Washington, DC); Frayheyt Group, Branch 160 (Paterson); Ferrer Center (later the Ferrer-Rocker) Branch 203 (Bronx); Frayheyt Group, Branch 239 (Baltimore); Radical Library, Branch 273 (Philadelphia); Fraye Gezelshaft Branch 339 (Toronto); Branch 358 (San Diego); Naye Gezelshaft Group, Branch 364 (Bronx); Kropotkin Literary Society, Branch 413 (Los Angeles); David Edelstadt Branch 450 (Denver); Fraye Gezelshaft Branch 564 (Winnipeg); Branch 584 (Kansas City, Missouri); and Harmony Branch 693 (San Francisco).

devoted one day each week to distributing the *Arbeter fraynd* of London.[18] Every Friday he would come to town all the way from Manayunk to sell copies at the bakers' union meeting and visit some of the newspaper's regular buyers. The second was comrade Benny Moore, at that time a manufacturer of women's clothes, who was always willing to leave his little shop to do whatever was necessary for the movement.

The real work, however, was done from then on by the Three Musketeers: Axler, I. Katz, and myself, who were for a time inseparable in our friendship and our work. That winter we organized several meetings, lectures, as well as the traditional *boyern bal* (peasants' ball), for which we issued a *Boyern tsaytung* (Peasants' Newspaper) put together by Eliezer Landau and David Apotheker. The ball was a great success under the circumstances. It brought in over $200 in net profit for the *Fraye arbeter shtime* and created a good mood among the comrades.

Among our activities that year that should be noted is our active participation in the reception for "Babushka," Yekaterina Breshkovskaya, who came to visit America accompanied by Dr. Chaim Zhitlowsky.[19] The meeting was arranged for a Sunday afternoon at the Walnut Street Theater. When I

---

18. **Harry Wolf** (Volf, 1872–1957) was a Russian-born Jewish grocer and anarchist. He immigrated to London, where he may have first become an anarchist, and then moved to Philadelphia in 1897.

19. **Yekaterina Breshkovskaya** (1844–1934), also known at Catherine Breshkovsky, was a leading Russian radical, known as the Grandmother of the Revolution. Born into nobility, she was influenced by Mikhail Bakunin as a young woman and joined the Narodnik movement, later cofounding the Socialist-Revolutionary Party. Breshkovskaya was repeatedly imprisoned and exiled for her activities, which made her an international celebrity by the time of her 1904 US tour. She was again imprisoned in 1908 and not released until after 1917's February Revolution, at age seventy-three. Breshkovskaya supported the Provisional Government and opposed the Bolshevik seizure of power, and in 1918 she returned to the United States to appeal for intervention against the Bolsheviks in the Russian Civil War. She lived the rest of her life in exile. **Chaim Zhitlowsky** (Khaym Zhitlovsky, 1865–1943) was a Russian-born Jewish writer, Yiddishist, and socialist. Attracted to both radical and Zionist politics as a student, he dedicated his life to synthesizing socialism and Jewish nationalism. Zhitlowsky joined Narodnaya Volya and later was a founding member of the Socialist-Revolutionary Party, within which he promoted Jewish autonomy and the use of Yiddish. After the Kishinev pogrom he called for "progressive nationalism," or socialist territorialism—the pursuit of an autonomous territory to establish a Jewish socialist society, be it in Palestine or elsewhere—and eventually joined Poale Zion. Zhitlowsky visited the United States in 1904–1906 and 1908 and settled there permanently after the First World War, writing for *Der tog*, *Tsukunft*, and other Yiddish publications.

approached the place, I found the building packed with people, and on the street stood a huge crowd who could not enter. I conferred with comrade Moore, sending him to look for another meeting hall in the neighborhood, and I went to ask the speakers about addressing a second meeting. In a matter of minutes, everything was squared away. The crowd filled the big hall at nearby Eighth and Lombard, and the speakers all came from the theater to address the meeting. The speech that Weinberg gave at the Walnut Street Theater surpassed anything else I've ever heard from a platform.

After the meeting, a small group of comrades went to the anarchist communal house, where Babushka was staying. We spent the evening in an atmosphere of wonderfully intimate excitement. Babushka, despite her old age and hard, brutal time in a Russian forced labor camp, was young and cheerful in spirit. She sang Russian revolutionary songs with us, danced, and kissed all the young comrades, whose presence renewed her faith in the future of our ideal.

On another occasion, we in Philadelphia welcomed the gray-haired leader of the Russian Socialist-Revolutionaries, Nikolai Tchaikovsky. He was one of the oldest activists in the Russian revolutionary movement. When Peter Kropotkin returned to Russia from Europe in 1872, where he had become a member of the First International, he joined Tchaikovsky's group in St. Petersburg. We welcomed the eminent guest at Jacob L. Joffe's house, where we spent the whole night talking about the prospects for the coming revolution in Russia.

The official mission of Tchaikovsky's visit was to collect money for the movement. His true task, however, was to procure and deliver arms to the revolutionists in our old homeland.

CHAPTER 15

Discussions about Nationalism

The pogroms in Kishinev, and the others that followed, badly shook the spirits of radical circles all over the country. Dr. Hillel Solotaroff, an emotional person, wrote a series of articles for the *Fraye arbeter shtime* under the title "Serious Questions," in which he tried to show that we cannot and must not depend upon the fact that the social revolution will solve the Jewish question along with all other social problems. He pleaded that, while we wait for the revolution, our brothers and sisters will be murdered and violated without mercy. We cannot, therefore, dismiss with a wave of the hand the fact that we are Jews and are being persecuted and tortured as such across the whole world, wherever it benefits the ruling classes.[1]

What is to be done? For this question he had no clear-cut, practical answer. He was, as just noted, a man of feelings, of strong emotions, over which his intellect did not always have complete control. Once on a platform in Philadelphia, he was so carried away by his own speech about the social revolution that he lifted the hem of his doctor's coat and shouted, "We shall wade up to our ankles in the blood of our exploiters!" And this was said by a man who was kindness itself, a man who would have fainted at the sight of a drop of spilled blood. His conclusion was that we needed to return to the Jewish people (*folk*), unite with them and their past, comfort them and sympathize with them. Well, those are beautiful words, noble expressions of feeling, but they are not of any practical use to anyone. Of course we are part of the Jewish people, living among and with them, sharing all of their

---

1. *FAS*, May 23 and 30, 1903.

suffering and joy—all of our activity and our entire spiritual lives unfold within the context of the Jewish people. But what could, what should be done about the pogroms is a completely different question.

Dr. Solotaroff, the sentimental anarchist, simply got lost when faced with the serious question before him. He became a nationalist and later a Zionist, screaming and sighing about the terrible ruin visited upon the Jewish people, but he found no practical solution and no way out.[2]

---

2. Chaim Weinberg wrote, "In my opinion, Comrade Solotoroff's tragedy was that he couldn't go over to the nationalists wholeheartedly. . . . But at the same time, he separated himself more and more from the anarchists, because he felt that they disapproved of his nationalist inclinations. He was never really accepted by the nationalists as one of their own, and among us, the Jewish anarchists, he was gradually less and less remembered." Chaim Leib Weinberg, *Forty Years in the Struggle: The Memoirs of a Jewish Anarchist*, ed. Robert P. Helms, trans. Naomi Cohen (Duluth: Litwin Books, 2008), 112.

CHAPTER 16

The Birth of the Radical Library and the *Abend tsaytung*

On the afternoon of Sunday, January 22, 1905, we conducted a meeting in Garrick Hall at which Saul Yanovsky gave a lecture to a large audience of attentive listeners. While the lecture was in progress, a reporter from an English-language newspaper came in and told me the news that in St. Petersburg a certain priest, Father Gapon, had led a huge demonstration before the Winter Palace and that, at the command of Tsar Nicholas, soldiers had fired into the crowd, killing many people. St. Petersburg and all of Russia was in a state of disarray, and he expected more serious news to come any minute.

I mounted the platform and interrupted Yanovsky, sharing the important news I had just received. The effect on the audience was beyond description. "Bloody Sunday" in St. Petersburg momentarily resonated with us in Philadelphia.

At this same meeting young comrade Joseph Washkowitz came to me and presented the idea of establishing a library, where we could meet and spend our free time. The number of young newcomers had continued to grow, but we had no cultural center. The library of the Hebrew Literature Society was in an old, cramped room on Catherine Street, and people there were not overly eager to have our comrades as visitors. I liked the idea, and we began to take it seriously and think about the possibility of creating such an institution. This was actually the birth of the Radical Library—an idea that took an entire year to make a reality.

A short time after the *boyern* ball, our group sent David Apotheker and me as delegates to the annual *Fraye arbeter shtime* convention in New York.

We brought the $200 profit from the ball with us and left for New York, where our first visit was to the editorial office of our newspaper. The office was then located in a small, dark room, a kind of large closet without a window, on the fifth floor of a tenement building on Rutgers Street. There was a small desk and two chairs. One of us had to stand the entire time, while we presented the check and greetings from the comrades of Philadelphia to Yanovsky. We, of course, were his guests, and he invited us into his home on the same floor, in somewhat larger rooms, and had us stay to have a bit of herring and a glass of tea with him as an evening meal. Afterward, we went to the convention together.

The meeting took place on the top floor of Clinton Hall, in a huge room with a low ceiling, divided by thick, round columns which broke up the expanse of the space. The hall was crowded with people. The air was thick with cigarette smoke, and the mood was tense. As soon as the convention opened, there was a barrage of questions about and criticisms of the newspaper, mostly directed at the editor. Most of the speakers who asked for the floor spoke with bitterness and great indignation. A number of them stepped out from behind the big columns, angrily recited their bitter tirades, and darted back behind the columns. They gave the impression to me of rats who came out of their nests to bite and gnaw at the editor, then crawled back and hid in their dark holes. The meeting lasted until after midnight. During the last hours the talk was calmer and more straightforward. The older speakers, Dr. Michael A. Cohn, Dr. Hillel Solotaroff, Benjamin Saphir, and others, also had objections to the editorship and suggestions for improvement, but their criticism had always been friendly and constructive.[1]

After the meeting we headed off to Herrick's Café at 141 Division Street, where we spent several hours talking in small groups. Through the convention, I became acquainted with the most active comrades in New York and learned about the condition of our movement there. The next morning, at the second session of the convention, the atmosphere was entirely different, relaxed and reinvigorated. A motion was made to raise a fund of $5,000

---

1. **Benjamin Saphir** (Benyomen Safir, 1871–1928) was a Russian-born Jewish insurance agent, journalist, and anarchist. He immigrated to the United States in 1888 or 1890 and settled in Brooklyn, where for two decades he was an active member of the anarchist movement. Saphir was co-treasurer of the group that revived the FAS in 1899, and in the 1910s he became a manager of Der tog. Obituary: FAS, November 9, 1928.

with which to start our own daily newspaper. The proposal was received with great enthusiasm—$5,000 seemed an enormous sum of money, but, in our great excitement for the prospect of having our own daily paper, the difficulties of such an undertaking did not stop us. On behalf of the comrades from Philadelphia, I pledged to raise $500 for this purpose. Dr. Michael A. Cohn promised to donate an entire $1,000 himself. The whole movement in New York and the other cities, therefore, would have to raise no more than $3,500, which seemed to us a trifle. The decision was made with great enthusiasm. Ely Greenblatt was elected treasurer of the fund, and an on-the-spot collection raised $26 and another $27 in pledges.[2] The convention ended on a very positive, hopeful note. We drove home, very enthusiastic, and unwittingly engaged in a very wide range of activities.

In Philadelphia the idea of a daily was taken seriously. The members of our group decided to contribute a week's wages each and to recruit more members and, in general, more readers for the *Fraye arbeter shtime*, in order to create a solid base of readers for the proposed daily, which was to begin publication in the fall of that year.

It became necessary for our group to hold regular weekly meetings, so my small family decided to rent a larger apartment with one room that could serve as a meeting place. We found such a place at 830 South Fifth Street, on the second floor, with an entrance so narrow that only one person could enter at a time. There we carried out a wonderful range of activity. The comrades used to meet there a couple of times a week, and the inner core of activists—Axler, Katz, and a few others—seldom missed an evening to visit me.

We were all excited for a daily newspaper. The need for an honest, well-maintained newspaper was very great and was felt not only in our circles but also among the masses of young socialists and Bundists who had begun to immigrate from Russia in large numbers. The journalism of the *Forverts*

---

2. **Ely (or Eli) Greenblatt** (Ali or Eli Grinblat, 1865–1948) was a Russian-born Jewish farmer and anarchist. He immigrated to the United States in 1889 and was active in the Jewish anarchist movement in New York. After moving to Connecticut, Greenblatt was for many years president of the Federation of Jewish Farmers of America, an organization founded in 1909 to establish credit unions and cooperatives for Jewish farmers. He later moved to Detroit and was a founder of the Sunrise Colony along with Joseph Cohen, as discussed in chapter 53. Greenblatt is referred to as "Yoine" in Cohen's book about the colony, *In Quest of Heaven*. Obituary: *FAS*, December 24, 1948.

at this time was just as yellow as the most sensationalist English papers, and in those years it still did not have the reputable literary collaborators that it later attracted. There was no other decent Yiddish daily newspaper. This was our opportunity to fulfill a social need in a field where we had already done some work.

There were other calculations as well: we were all then devoted body and soul to the revolutionary uprising in Russia, where great, historical events were unfolding every minute. This required a well-maintained, honest newspaper to deliver the news from there without prejudice and without sensationalism.

In the labor movement, a daily newspaper is a powerful force. When you want to organize a union or especially when you have to lead a difficult fight, a strike, then a daily paper is simply a necessity of life. Such a publication must have integrity, consistency, and no intrigue behind the scenes. The *Forverts* in fact very seldom served the interests of the workers. The interests of its clique of leaders, of the party machine, of the trade unions, always stood above the interests of the workers. Very often in those days the *Forverts* printed announcements for scabs in the same issue in which it reported on a strike. Hostile labor demonstrations around the office of the *Forverts*, including attacks in which all its windows were broken, were not uncommon. Conditions required a new daily newspaper, an honest, sincere, and consistently socialist one.

Yet another consideration: a daily paper is a strong material force in a movement, even if only by providing employment and a livelihood for a good number of people: writers, typesetters, literary agents, and personnel in various cities. It also gives the opportunity for people to engage in movement activity; there are always tens of thousands who hope to find work in or around a publication over time, and this actively prepares them for such an opportunity. The influence of the *Forverts* in the workers' organizations, in the Workmen's Circle, and in trade unions was sustained by members of a machine that called the shots everywhere.

We never even dreamed of building our own "party machine" and imitating the harmful tactics of the *Forverts*. We sought to neutralize such poison, to wipe out the evil plague. But, on the other hand, there is no denying the fact that our movement lacked opportunities for paid activity. Our writers also contributed to the *Forverts* in order to make a living. Our intelligent youths had no prospect for making a living within the framework of our movement. At first the prospect of a daily publication of our own gave hope for such a possibility.

Eliezer Landau went immediately to New York, where he connected with a number of older comrades who took an interest in the business side of the *Fraye arbeter shtime* and the organization of its office. It turned out that although the new *Fraye arbeter shtime* had been in existence for five years, it had no bookkeeping records. Yanovsky did all the administrative work by himself in addition to the editing. The condition of the paper in its early years was not good. It was thanks to Yanovsky's unlimited dedication and boundless generosity that it survived until its readership was enlarged by the influx of new immigrants after the Kishinev pogrom. During the Russo-Japanese War (1904–1905) Yanovsky did not have an office assistant, and he did not hire an accountant. He recorded all income and expenses in his own illegible handwriting. When the comrades asked him for the first time about his bookkeeping, his answer, as recounted to me by Landau, was simple: he kept the incoming money in one pocket, and in the other he kept the few coins that were his salary. Most of the time, however, both pockets were empty—there was nothing to keep in them.

He then showed them the accounts, many lines of which he himself could not read. In addition to all his other activities, Yanovsky, as is well known, used to give lectures every Sunday afternoon, during which he gave an overview of the news of the week, followed by discussion of a particular topic. He donated the income from these meetings to the *Fraye arbeter shtime* for the first few years. After reviewing the accounts, the comrades found that they did not include the income from one Sunday meeting a year or two prior. They noted this and then at a meeting asked Yanovsky what he had done with the proceeds from that Sunday. At the time, Yanovsky could not recall and did not know how to answer; the question was recorded, and they moved on to other topics.

Only later, on the way home, did he recall that there had been no lecture that Sunday. He had left the city for a couple of days on some errand and was unable to return in time. However, this incident upset him so much that he decided not to contribute the income from these meetings to the newspaper any longer, which the comrades agreed he had the right to do. But he did not have the heart to use this money for personal purposes. (It was only later that he learned from other lecturers how to make profitable income from his speeches.) At the time being discussed here, he kept the money from his lectures in a separate fund. A few years later, when comrade Abe Isaak, the editor of the English-language weekly *Free Society*, decided to leave New York, he decided to sell his small house on Teller Avenue to Yanovsky. Yanovsky bought the house with money saved from his Sunday lectures, and there he lived for the rest of his life.

In 1905 an attempt was made to systematize the business of the *Fraye arbeter shtime*'s office. Louis Elstein, an active comrade, good speaker, and very capable man who had lately come from London, was employed as a manager.[3] Nothing of this was reflected in the newspaper; the only thing we noticed was that the *Fraye arbeter shtime* did absolutely nothing on behalf of the planned daily newspaper and did not even mention the whole matter, except when some group reported on its work in this area.

But we in Philadelphia energetically continued our work for this endeavor. Our group grew in size. We attracted a number of young comrades lately come from London or Russia: William Shulman, Israel Kaplan, Dave Cohen, Samuel Hindin, Harry Granet, Jacob (Jack) Bowman, Morris Deglin, and dozens of other less active members.[4] We arranged a big picnic that sum-

---

3. **Louis Elstein** (Luis Elshteyn, c. 1872–1946) was a Russian-born Jewish garment worker, labor organizer, insurance agent, and anarchist. He immigrated to London with his family as a child and was put to work in the garment trades at a young age. Elstein soon became a labor organizer and prominent anarchist speaker associated with the *Arebter fraynd* and was then active in Leeds. He was invited to Paris to help organize Jewish garment workers and there met his wife, anarchist Fannie Elstein (1882–1963). The couple immigrated to New York sometime before 1905 and in 1907 moved to Montreal, where they opened an anarchist bookstore. The Elsteins returned to the United States in 1919, settling in Whittier, California, where Louis opened a "notions store," became a social democrat, and was active in the Workmen's Circle. Obituaries: *FAS*, October 18 and November 1, 1946.

4. **William Shulman** or Schulman (1887–1935) was a Russian-born Jewish garment worker and anarchist. After immigrating to Philadelphia around 1903 he became an active and lifelong member of the Radical Library Group, and he served on the managing board of the Stelton Modern School. Obituaries: *FAS*, October 18, 1935; *Man!*, November–December 1935. **Oscar Sharlip** (1882–1956), **Israel Sharlip** (1884–1931), and **Samuel ("Muni") Sharlip** (1891–1955) were Russian-born Jewish brothers, garment workers, and anarchists. All three immigrated to Philadelphia between 1903 and 1906 and joined the Radical Library Group. Oscar later opened a drugstore and then a children's store, and Israel became a musician. Israel's wife, anarchist Fannie Sharlip (née Spivak, c. 1893–1964), was likewise a member of the Radical Library Group. Obituaries: *FAS*, April 24, 1931 (Israel); *FAS*, December 30, 1955 (Samuel); *FAS*, October 19, 1956 (Oscar). **Israel Kaplan** (c. 1884–1952) was a Russian-born

mer in a grove far outside of the city. We invited Dr. Hillel Solotaroff from New York to talk about the planned daily newspaper. He arrived the evening before the picnic, accompanied by Ely Greenblatt and Dr. Iser Ginzburg. We spent the evening at comrade Jacob L. Joffe's house, where the guests stayed the night. Dr. Ginzburg disappeared during the night and we never saw him in Philadelphia again. Dr. Solotaroff gave an inspiring speech at the picnic, and a considerable sum of money was raised.

From then on, we were successful in all our activities. For each endeavor we put in tons of work. We never depended on miracles or expected that our speakers or other forces would automatically bring us success, and in those years we never suffered any failures.

That summer there was a bakers' strike in Philadelphia to which we contributed much work and material assistance. We did not pass up any opportunity for activity.

A conference of radical labor leaders was also held that summer in Chicago to lay the foundations of the Industrial Workers of the World. Their program aroused much interest in our ranks, although we were adamant that "dual unionism" in the workers' ranks brings more harm than good. We in Philadelphia we were not so tempted to latch onto the new organization, but in New York our comrades made a considerable ruckus in this area. Nevertheless, these debates and discussions about forms of organization and methods of struggle in the labor movement gave us plenty of food for thought.

The Russian Tea Party that year brought in a $249.35 profit. The money was divided among the anarchist publications *Free Society, Freedom, Fraye*

Jewish tailor and anarchist. As a youth he joined the Russian revolutionary movement and participated in the 1905 Revolution. In 1906 Kaplan immigrated to Philadelphia, where he joined the Jewish anarchist movement and Radical Library Group. In 1921 he and his wife, anarchist Fannie Kaplan, moved to the anarchist colony in Stelton, New Jersey, where their children attended the Modern School. Obituary: *FAS*, November 21, 1952. **Samuel Hindin** (1886–1931) was a Russian-born Jewish garment worker and anarchist who immigrated to the United States in 1906. **Harry Granet** (1882–?) was a Russian-born Jewish printer and anarchist. He immigrated to the United States 1903 with his widowed mother, shortly after surviving the Kishinev pogrom. In 1908 Granet was arrested following the Broad Street Riot (described in chapter 22). **Jacob ("Jack") Bowman** (Boiman, c. 1885–?) was a Russian-born Jewish newspaper dealer and anarchist. He immigrated to the United States around 1905 and was a member of both the Radical Library Group and the Kropotkin Literary Society. **Morris Deglin** (1882–?) was a Russian-born Jewish bakery worker, newspaper carrier, and anarchist who immigrated to the United States around 1905.

arbeter shtime, Freiheit, Arbeter fraynd, Zsherminal, Khleb i Volya, The Demon-strator, and the planned daily newspaper.[5] A sum of seventy-five dollars was also sent to Peter Kropotkin for the anarchist movement in Russia. In Chicago the comrades had decided to publish an English-language paper, *The Liberator,* under the editorship of comrades C. L. James and Lizzie Holmes.[6] Lucy Parsons made a nationwide tour for the paper and spent some time with us in Philadelphia.[7]

---

5. ***Khleb i Volya*** (Bread and Freedom, 1905–1907) was a Russian-language anarchist newspaper published in Geneva and closely associated with Peter Kropotkin. ***The Demonstrator*** (1903–1908) was an anarchist newspaper published at the anarchist colony in Home, Washington, and edited for most of its run by Jay Fox.

6. ***The Liberator*** (1905–1906) was an anarchist newspaper published in Chicago and informally affiliated with the IWW. Lucy Parsons was listed as editor on its masthead. **Charles Leigh James** (1846–1911), who published under the name C. L. James, was an English-born grocer, insurance agent, writer, and anarchist. A highly educated son of historian George Payne Rainsford James, in 1865 he moved with his widowed mother and siblings to Eau Claire, Wisconsin, and soon became active in the Knights of Labor and wrote extensively for *The Alarm, Free Society, Mother Earth,* and other anarchist periodicals. Although he rarely left Eau Claire, James was a well-respected writer for the anarchist press and in 1902 published his massive *History of the French Revolution.* **Lizzie M. Holmes** (1850–1926), née Hunt, also known as Lizzie Swank, was an American-born teacher, garment worker, labor organizer, writer, and anarchist. Born and raised in the rural Midwest, she moved to Chicago in 1879 and soon joined the Knights of Labor, befriended Lucy Parsons, and met her second husband, English anarchist William T. Holmes. She joined the anarchist IWPA, worked as assistant editor of *The Alarm,* and contributed to many other American anarchist newspapers.

7. **Lucy Parsons** (c. 1851–1942) was an American-born garment worker, labor organizer, writer, and anarchist. Likely the daughter of an enslaved mother and white slave owner (though Parsons denied Black ancestry and instead claimed Mexican and indigenous heritage throughout her life), in 1871 she married Albert Parsons in Texas, and the couple fled to Chicago in 1873. There the couple joined the SLP and then the anarchist IWPA and began producing *The Alarm.* After her husband's execution Parsons wrote for numerous anarchist periodicals and dedicated much of her time to documenting and memorializing the Haymarket Affair. She was a delegate to the 1905 founding of the IWW, and beginning in the 1920s she worked with Communist-affiliated organizations, although she does not appear to have officially joined the Communist Party.

CHAPTER 17

A Strike against the *Forverts* and a Confrontation with Yanovsky

In February of 1905, a unique strike took place in Philadelphia. The Jewish news dealers (Yiddish newspapers were never sold by newsboys in Philadelphia but instead by special "carriers") went on strike. The newspaper publishers had raised the price from fifty cents to sixty cents per hundred papers, which sold for a penny a copy. It is interesting to note that the *Forverts* went along with the other capitalist publishers, joining forces with them. Their editorial board's position was that it did not interfere with the financial affairs of the paper. The publishers claimed they lost thirty-eight dollars a week in Philadelphia. However, they were apparently unaware that they received only forty-two cents per hundred papers in New York.

Through the *Fraye arbeter shtime*, we let all the facts of the case be known to the public. This upset the social democratic and workers' circles in the city. They convened a mass meeting, which moved that the *Forverts* should immediately grant the strikers their demands. If the other publishers succeeded in increasing the price, then the *Forverts* could do likewise, but it should not be a partner in the effort to implement them.

The *Forverts* for its part both agreed and disagreed. Its publishers insisted that the news dealers pay a higher price, with the understanding that if the other newspapers were not successful in getting the increase, it would return the extra ten cents. The dealers were happy to settle with the *Forverts*, with the understanding that each of them would immediately receive the same number of newspapers they had before the strike. Under the circumstances, they were able to sell many more copies of the *Forverts* to the readers of other newspapers, but the management of the *Forverts* did not want to even hear from them. The news dealers were dismayed when, after the settlement, they came to the office of the *Forverts* on February 15 to find—under police protection—the business agents of the *Tageblat* and the *Abend post* (Saphirstein's paper) distributing the *Forverts* to their scab dealers, leaving almost no papers for the dealers who had just settled the strike.[1] The story created tension in Philadelphia's labor circles for a long time. There was a great deal of resentment against the *Forverts*, and the time was ripe for the anarchists to come out with a decent daily newspaper.

Fund-raising, however, was very difficult for us. The *Fraye arbeter shtime* was, one might say, completely indifferent. On June 10 a lengthy notice appeared in the *Fraye arbeter shtime*, signed by the executive board—a new institution in our movement. It stated, among other things: Many of our older comrades have gradually fallen away. The young comrades did good work for the *Fraye arbeter shtime* and demanded a voice in its administration. Yanovsky was afraid to let them in. Now, after a meeting of the older comrades, things would change. Yanovsky would dedicate all his energy to editorial work. The administration and all matters concerning the movement would be in the hands of the executive board, which was convening a conference on June 17 to arrange for the daily newspaper.[2]

A short time before this we in Philadelphia had a small disagreement with Yanovsky. A large advertisement for a bank appeared in the *Fraye arbeter shtime*—the first to be printed in our paper.[3] To us naive people, this seemed not kosher: how can we advertise a bank, a capitalist institution that helps always to swindle workers, often robbing them of the few pennies they save? Several comrades who happened to meet that day wrote a short letter of protest, signing our names: Joseph Cohen, Benjamin Axler, I. Katz, Samuel Diskan, and Harry Wolf.[4] Yanovsky printed the letter—and how!—in his

---

1. **Nyu Yorker abend post** (New York Evening Post, 1899–1905) was a conservative daily Yiddish newspaper published by Jacob Saphirstein.

2. *FAS*, June 10, 1905.

3. *FAS*, May 20, 1905. The advertisement was for the Van Norden Trust Company.

4. **Samuel Rubin Diskan** (c. 1886–1950) was a Russian-born Jewish paperhanger, labor organizer, and anarchist. He immigrated to the United States around 1893 and joined Philadelphia's Jewish anarchist movement. He was a longtime member of the International Brotherhood of Painters, Decorators and Paperhangers of America and by 1914 was a district organizer for the AFL. In the 1937 Diskan became a full-time organizer for the AFL's National Council of United Cement Workers and a vice president of the subsequent United

column "Oyf der vakh," the showpiece of the newspaper.[5] He wanted to teach us greenhorns a biblical lesson (*parshat Balak*), showing that we did not need to worry about the kosherness (*kashrut*) of anarchism—he already took care of such things on his own. A bank, however, is not a non-kosher (*treyf*) thing; it performs a necessary function in society, et cetera. He skewered those of us who objected.

Comrade Axler then wrote an open letter, in his own name, to the publishers of the *Fraye arbeter shtime*—we in Philadelphia did not yet know about the new executive board—protesting against the behavior of the editor. Yanovsky never forgave Axler for his chutzpah. But he realized that he had been too hasty in his attack against us—a group of very active people—and he wrote to us asking to arrange a lecture for him on the subject, "Principles and Their Application," in order to give him an opportunity to explain his point of view. This we did. Yanovsky arrived on June 4, bringing with him Ely Greenblatt as a sort of bodyguard, and tried both in the lecture as well as later at my home to smooth over his overly sharp attack and reestablish friendly relations again.

Our group sent Axler and me as delegates to the June 17 conference. We made most of the trip on foot. Hitchhiking was still out of fashion, and we simply did not have money for train tickets. The special convention was a nightmare. The younger comrades came ready for a fight: they brought with them credentials from the groups to which they belonged, so that no one would be able to dismiss their opinions. The older comrades, Michael A. Cohn especially, disagreed with such an un-anarchistic approach. "All these credentials!" he cried sarcastically. "How can you represent anyone?"

Toxic criticisms of the editor took up two long meetings. When the long list of speakers finally ended and Yanovsky was called on to answer his critics, he was so depressed and upset that he could not speak. Tears began to pour from his eyes and his voice was caught in his throat. The entire audience remained glued to their chairs. Nobody moved a muscle.

As the saying goes, fools rush in where angels fear to tread. In my naiveté, I jumped up, asked for the floor, and chastised both the critics and Yanovsky

---

Cement, Lime and Gypsum Workers International Union, a position he held up until his death. Obituaries: *Philadelphia Inquirer*, June 19, 1950; *Voice of the Cement, Lime, Gypsum and Allied Workers*, July 1950, 146.

5. *FAS*, May 27, 1905.

alike. "What's going on here?" I cried out. "Why are we talking nonsense and fighting each other? And why are we crying like little children? We came to build a newspaper, to change the whole world, and here we are dealing with rubbish that makes no sense. Let's quit all this nonsense and get to the work that we actually came to do!"

And a miracle: my impudent words worked. The depressed mood seemed to disappear. We took seriously the tasks, opportunities, and difficulties that lay ahead of us. Since it was already the middle of June and virtually nothing had been done toward the publication of the daily paper, the conference decided to delay its appearance later than originally planned, but then the work should begin in earnest. The fund-raising soon raised quite a sum of money. Morris Weinberg, who later became part owner of *Der tog* (The Day), contributed $200 in cash and pledged another $100.[6] Ely Greenblatt, Isaac Hourwich, Isaac A. Benequit, and Yanovsky pledged $100 each.[7] It now seemed that there would be no more difficulties raising the funds to carry out our plans.

For Yom Kippur that year we arranged two antireligious meetings, one in Yiddish in the afternoon, and one in English in the evening. The first meeting was held in an enormous place on Bainbridge and Broad Street, where prize fights usually took place. The platform, encircled by ropes, stood in the middle of the hall, the audience facing it from all four sides in ascending rows, so that everyone could see the fight. But for a speaker, it was not very

---

6. **Morris Weinberg** (Moris Vaynberg, 1876–1968) was a Russian-born Jewish journalist. He immigrated to the United States 1894 and worked as a copy boy for the SLP's newspaper *Dos abend blat* before forming a newspaper delivery service in 1900. Weinberg cofounded *Der tog* in 1914 and served as its general manager until 1923. **Der tog** (The Day, 1914–1971) was a daily Yiddish newspaper published in New York. Founded as a "newspaper for the Jewish intelligentsia," it printed articles by nearly every major Yiddish writer of its day. Although not a radical publication, *Der tog* frequently included works by Jewish socialists and anarchists and employed a number of radicals on its staff.

7. **Isaac A. Benequit** (Yitskhok A. Benekvit, 1866–1934) was a Russian-born Jewish garment worker, labor organizer, business owner, and anarchist. He immigrated to New York in 1888 and began to read *Freiheit*, then joined the Pioneers of Liberty. During a brief residence in Philadelphia, Benequit also joined the Knights of Liberty group there. A lifelong anarchist, he once relinquished his ownership of a garment shop to rejoin the working class and was a frequent financial supporter of both the *FAS* and Johann Most. Benequit became a regular contributor to the *FAS* in the 1920s and wrote the autobiography *Durkhgelebt un durkhgetrakht* (1934). Obituary: *FAS*, April 13, 1934.

comfortable to show his back to a good part of his audience, yet Michael A. Cohn, the keynote speaker, was able to carry on his fight with the master of the universe (*Ribono shel olam*) brilliantly. The evening meeting took place in the Odd Fellows Temple at Broad and Arch Streets. The speakers were George Brown (the wittiest Irishman), James C. Hannon from the Free Thought Society, and Dr. Michael A. Cohn again.[8] Both meetings were a great success. Crowds filled both great halls and listened intently to the speakers.

Summer was on its leisurely way out. New publications were announced. The *Forverts*, jealous of the *Morgen zshurnal* (Morning Journal), came out with its own morning edition.[9] Louis Miller bought the printing press of the defunct *Jewish Herald* and published a competitor of the *Forverts*, with which he had crossed swords. The territorialists began to put out their own weekly paper, *Dos folk* (The People).[10] The radical milieu was alive with activity. Revolutionary events in Russia held us all in anxious attention. Only the collection of funds for our own daily paper moved at a snail's pace. It did not seem to move an inch.

In the middle of December, an announcement appeared in the *Fraye arbeter shtime* that the plan would be entirely abandoned. The group in New York could not see eye to eye with the editor and saw no path forward. What the dispute was about was not known to us then and is still not known to this day. The announcement, however, provoked widespread outcries among comrades all over the country. Many groups demanded that a conference be convened. We called for a convention to be held in Philadelphia, in order to avoid the New York rabble (*Erev Rav*), who were disrupting any planning for negotiations. These protests worked. In the second week in January 1906, the *Fraye arbeter shtime* announced that on Sunday, March 18, the daily paper would begin publication, and everything possible would be done to make up for lost time. The name of the paper would be the *Abend tsaytung* (The Evening Newspaper).

---

8. **James C. Hannon** (1858–1923) was an Irish-born housepainter and Freethought advocate who often spoke alongside Philadelphia's anarchists.

9. **Der morgen zshurnal** (1901–1971) was a conservative daily Yiddish newspaper published in New York by Jacob Saphirstein. In 1953 it merged with *Der tog*.

10. **Dos folk** (1906) was a weekly socialist territorialist periodical published in Philadelphia and edited by Chaim Zhitlowsky and anarchists Hillel Solotaroff and Moyshe Katz. Another socialist territorialist journal of the same name was edited by Nachman Syrkin in New York in 1907–1908.

The first Sunday of February we arranged a big meeting about the new newspaper with Yanovsky and Hillel Solotaroff as speakers. In the evening we met at the Radical Library and spent so much time there that our New York guests could not find enough words of praise for our good work. Dr. Solotaroff came up with the idea of selling the last bit of whiskey in the bottle for the newspaper's fund. That brought in $147.50. Dr. Staller, who joined our ranks for the last time, added another $100. Yanovsky later dedicated almost his entire "Oyf der vakh" column to praising our activities in Philadelphia, "where there was no movement at all a couple of years ago." Now, he wrote, the comrades there had already contributed $1,000 to the fund. We earned back for Philadelphia the title of the foremost city in the anarchist movement and have maintained a good reputation for years.

Philadelphia in these years created a unique anarchist milieu and educated a generation of workers not only in our movement but also in the labor movement in general, who were distinguished by their sincerity and devotion wherever they happened to be. And they were later scattered throughout the whole of America. In New York, Chicago, Los Angeles, Montreal, Stelton, and elsewhere, you could find former members of the Radical Library, in anarchist groups but also in unions, especially in the International Ladies' Garment Workers' Union, where they occupied important positions. The Radical Library left its mark on them all and gave a definite direction to their entire lives' activities. But let's not get ahead of ourselves (*farloyfn di fish farn nets*). Let us first examine how the Radical Library came about.

CHAPTER 18

The Opening of the Radical Library

In addition to our activities in the summer of 1905 and the heavy expenses incurred in raising funds for the daily newspaper, a smaller circle of comrades prepared to carry out the plan to open our own library [in Philadelphia], as first suggested by Joseph Washkowitz at the Bloody Sunday meeting. Twenty-six of us had pooled a dollar each from our meager earnings—five or six dollars a week on average, when we had work—and with the twenty-six dollars of capital, we decided to get to work and open the library on November 11, when we celebrate the memory of the Chicago tragedy and the martyrdom of our comrades on that date in 1887.

We had found two rooms on the second story of a building at 515 Pine Street, which we rented for fifteen dollars a month. With the remaining eleven dollars, we bought two old tables and a number of long, secondhand benches. This alone, of course, would not constitute a library. Fortunately, our movement had inherited two immense cupboards filled with good English- and Russian-language books from the good old days, which sat in Natasha Notkin's room just begging to be used again as soon as comrades were able to revive their activities and open a library once more.

I learned of the origin of the name "Radical Library" from an old issue of the *Pennsylvania Nationalist* from 1893, a publication of Edward Bellamy's movement to nationalize the country's industries. In this issue one finds an announcement for a Radical Library, at the corner of Fifteenth Street and Spring Garden, which had been around for a long time.[1] Meetings of

---

1. The following announcement appeared in the *Pennsylvania Nationalist* (Philadelphia)

the Ladies' Liberal League and four poems by Voltairine de Cleyre are also announced, which the editors offered to their readers for fifteen cents each and recommended as a good means of propaganda. This Radical Library was organized and maintained by Russian Jewish youths, a fact that can be seen in the great number of good Russian books which we inherited from it years later. Mary Hansen related in a 1925 anniversary booklet about our library that a young man named Steinberg came to a meeting of the Ladies' Liberal League and asked them to take over the library, which could no longer be maintained by its founders. The offer was accepted. The women ran the library for a number of years. When they were unable to continue their activities, they donated some of the books to the socialists, who had a library, and some to Natasha Notkin to keep until it was possible for comrades to again make use of them.

Our plan was largely based on the possibility of using this inheritance. We adopted the Radical Library name and asked Natasha Notkin to transfer the books to us. Natasha was not eager to part with the books, which were dear to her and for which she felt responsible. She worried that our group would not last, since we did not even have enough money for a second months' rent. She pleaded that we should first prove that we could carry on for several months, then she would feel justified handing over to us the assets that the movement had entrusted to her years before.

We worked with her for a long time, trying to convince her that without books we could not open and maintain a library. However, she insisted, and it was time for the library to officially open. Katz, Axler, and I decided that we would have to get the books, once for all. We declared a strike, coming to Natasha's apartment late in the evening, when she came home from work at the pharmacy, and sat down on the floor, explaining that we would sit there until she changed her mind. We would not leave until we received a promise that she would allow us to remove the bookcases the very next day.

It worked. After a couple of hours of discussion and argument, she finally gave her consent and the key to her room, so that in the morning we could remove the books and the cupboards in which they were held. That year the eleventh of November came on a Sunday. That afternoon we arranged a big

---

on December 23 and December 30, 1893: "Radical Library. Open Saturday evening only, 7:30 to 10 P.M. Free Reading. N.E. cor. 15th & Spring Garden Sts."

meeting in a hall. From the platform we announced the official opening of the Radical Library and invited the audience to come and bring a couple good books to donate if they could. The opening was a success. The place was filled with many visitors, and the mood was inspiring. Guest speakers spent the evening with us and contributed greatly to the momentousness of the event.

The two rooms of the library were quite separate and not equal in size. In the first, much smaller room at the entrance, we arranged the library, which grew and expanded after that first evening. The second room had a separate entrance and could accommodate fifty to sixty people, who could sit and read or hold a discussion or meeting and the like. The library was under my personal supervision. I spent every evening and every free day there. We considered the library a kind of preparatory school for our movement, where people could become familiar with our ideals, with the theory of anarchism and the history of our movement. And we did this carefully and systematically.

The library was open to everyone. We did everything we could to attract new visitors, new readers. My task was to get acquainted with each new visitor, to recommend to them the books that would help their development, and through brief lessons to guide them on the path we wished they would go. As these visitors became, over time, spiritually and intellectually mature, they would, without any effort on our part, enter our groups and take part in our activities.

Of course, not everything went as smoothly as we would have liked. Our movement has always and everywhere attracted the best, most highly developed people, as well as the worst, most irresponsible scoundrels, who rebelled against the existing order simply because they did not want to recognize any limits or responsibilities. Around the fringes of our movement there always hung people whose first concern was that no one should exploit them. Anarchism gave them a kind of theoretical justification for their laziness and parasitism—to live at the expense of other poor devils who were foolish enough to allow themselves to be exploited by capitalism. Parasites are always looking for a public place where they can use their radical phrases to deceive their victims. I abhorred those souls with absolute hatred. I could not be indifferent to their parasitic activity among people who worked hard for every penny and never had enough to cover their own expenses. Embezzling fifty cents or a dollar from such people in order to be able to walk around idly seemed to me to be the vilest form of exploitation.

As soon as we opened the Radical Library, these reptiles began to hang around it. Some members of this species were Philadelphia residents; others came from as far as Boston and similar places. There was a fellow by the name of "Dr." Tumarinson who came from London, England, who hung around our group one year. Later we found out that he was a spy for the Russian Okhrana (secret police) and had worked for them in London, Paris, and other cities.[2] I sought to expel these parasites from our circles. I said to them: first of all, go and take care of yourself; earn your own living—after that we will work together on behalf of the whole of humanity! Don't be parasites on the backs of your own brethren, who are poor devils the same as you.

This, of course, did not please these fellows. They called me bourgeois, middle-class, with petit bourgeois prejudices. They called me the dictator of the movement and carried on a campaign to discredit me and push me aside. When this failed, they combined themselves into a kind of a silent opposition, conducting anarchist activity in their own way. The leader of all this was a young Scottish Jew by the name of Jack Ryan, an excellent speaker in English with his Scottish accent. He was assisted by his friend Lieberman, old man Rom (*der alter Rom*), David Apotheker (who was smarting because he had not been elected manager of the forthcoming daily paper), and some other professional idlers who would today be very embarrassed to see their names on such a list.

---

2. **Mikhail Borisovich Tumarinson** (sometimes spelled Toumarinson, Tomarinson, or Tomarison, 1864–?), also known as Maurice Gabriel Tomarinson, was a Russian-born Jewish dentist, former radical, and police informant. In the 1880s he was active in revolutionary activities that resulted in exile to Siberia, and around 1890 he fled to England and then France, and became a paid informant for the Okhrana within the Yiddish-speaking anarchist movement in both countries. Tumarinson worked as a dentist in Argentina from around 1891 to 1895, then settled in London where he resumed spying and became a well-known anarchist figure. Abraham Frumkin recalled him as "energetic, very accommodating and interested in everything we did." Tumarinson was responsible for Rudolf Rocker's expulsion from France in 1904, and that same year he moved to Philadelphia and enrolled at the University of Pennsylvania's Department of Dentistry. In 1906 he returned to France where in 1909–1910 served as secretary of the new Jewish Anarchist Federation in Paris. As early as 1908, however, some radicals had begun to suspect Tumarinson, and in 1910 the Socialist-Revolutionary spy hunter Vladimir Burtsev (1862–1942) exposed him as the Okhrana informant code-named "Mechanic." Tumarison returned to Russia in 1911. See A. Frumkin, *In friling fun yidishn sotsyalizm: zikhroynes fun a zshurnalist* (New York: A. Frumkin yubiley komitet, 1940), 109–18; Sh. Fridman [Zosa Szaijkowski], *Etyudn: tsu der geshikhte fun ayngevandertn yidishn yishev in Frankraykh* (Paris: Fridman, 1937), 109–10, 168–69n9.

I must in all honesty confess that now, some forty years later, I am no longer so firm in my conviction on this matter. I know from experience that, over time, many of these youthful idlers and layabouts became very worthy and active people. One of them has become very prominent in the Poale Zion movement, another has for many years been the leader of a large labor union, and another eventually became a bank employee and held a prominent position in public life. Who can judge another person with certainty and condemn them?

In the winter of 1905–1906, the *Fraye arbeter shtime* convention was held in New York earlier than usual, in order to make final preparations for publishing the long-awaited daily newspaper. The delegates elected from Philadelphia were me and Benny Moore, who had been active in founding the Radical Library. His shop was just across the street. Almost every day he used to run in, sweep, dust the furniture, and see that everything was in order for the evening.

The meeting was peaceful and calm compared to the previous ones, although there was no dearth of criticism and attacks. I remember that after the convention, in one of his biting feuilletons, Dr. Iser Ginzburg, under the pen name "Oketz" ("Stinger"), chastised the comrades for their personal attacks on the editor and their constant repetition of the same complaints over and over. As he put it, even a turkey dinner becomes tiresome day in and day out, especially if you must pluck the feathers every day. And to pluck and tear at a human being is a practice that should have ended long ago.

After the first session of the convention and following a few hours at Herrick's Café, we delegates from Philadelphia went with Michael A. Cohn to his home in Brownsville for the night. The late-night trip by elevated train was long and tedious. The streets in Brownsville were not paved and after the rain that day were very muddy. But Dr. Cohn's home was new and comfortable, and his wife gave us a very friendly reception. Anna Cohn was the daughter of a comrade in New York, Jacob Netter, whose home and restaurant were always open not only to comrades but to anyone in need.[3] It was

---

3. **Anna Cohn** (Ana Kohn, c. 1870–1920), née Netter, was a Russian-born Jewish labor organizer and anarchist. She immigrated to the United States with her family in 1882 and became an active member of the Knights of Labor as well as one of the only female members of the anarchist Pioneers of Liberty. In 1891 she married fellow anarchist Michael A. Cohn.

said that her mother used to make every effort to feed David Edelstadt, the editor of the first run of the *Fraye arbeter shtime*, whenever he showed up. In his modesty and poverty, Edelstadt would order no more than a bowl of soup for a few cents, but Mrs. Netter saw to it that his soup included a substantial serving of meat.

At the convention, it was decided to try to interest Dr. Maryson in working on the daily paper. Yanovsky needed two or three writers to help him in the editorial office. Dr. Maryson, Dr. Solotaroff, and Dr. Ginzburg were asked to contribute a couple of articles each week. However, there was a shortage of good, capable administrators. The New York comrades were considering comrade William Lief, who was an agent for the *Forverts* at that time and later became a publisher of the *Yidishe velt* of Philadelphia.[4] He was present at all the sessions of the convention but refused to give a definite answer on the spot. The convention also ratified a motion to buy two new linotype machines and to approve naming the paper the *Abend tsaytung*. Even the name of the novel that Yanovsky had decided to translate and serialize in the paper was announced.

After the convention, we went to Max Maisel's bookstore, where at his own expense comrade Benny Moore bought fifteen prints of famous writers and artists.[5] He put them all in simple but nice frames and used them to

---

Abraham Jacob Netter (Avrom-Yankev Neter, 1842–1918) was a Russian-born Jewish teacher, grocer, and socialist. A former rabbinical student, he became radicalized as a young man and immigrated to the United States with his wife and daughter in 1882 as members of Am Olam. The family's apartment on Orchard Street in New York's Lower East Side became a center of early Jewish radicalism. Netter had close relationships to both anarchists and socialists and wrote antireligious articles for both the *FAS* and the *Forverts* (which he helped found in 1897). Obituary: *FAS*, January 19, 1918.

4. **William B. Lief** (Viliam B. Lif, 1872–1938) was a Russian-born Jewish journalist and socialist. He immigrated to the United States as a child and, after completing high school, became active in the Jewish labor movement and SLP. In 1897 Lief cofounded the *Forverts*, and he moved to Philadelphia in 1912.

5. **Max N. Maisel** (Maks N. Mayzl, 1872–1959) was Russian-born Jewish bookseller, publisher, and anarchist. He belonged to the socialist movement in Riga before emigrating to the United Stated in 1892. In New York, Maisel, whose first language was German, became an anarchist under the influence of Johann Most and then learned Yiddish. In 1905 he opened a radical bookstore in New York's Lower East Side, and he later ran a small publishing house that produced Yiddish translations of works by Peter Kropotkin, Oscar Wilde, Henry David Thoreau, and many others. Maisel was also a founding member of the Kropotkin Literary Society. Obituary: *FAS*, November 1, 1959.

decorate the walls of the Radical Library. They later hung in the Kropotkin Library in Stelton, New Jersey.[6]

On my return to Philadelphia, I had posters made announcing the appearance of the new daily newspaper. I included a few words about who the regular contributors would be, what sections it would have, and also indicated, among other things, that the famous novel by Eliza Orzeszkowa would appear in its pages.[7] However, this poster made a bad impression on my two closest collaborators, Axler and Katz, who found it a cheap ploy to gain subscribers, which, in their opinion, was not appropriate for a serious and quality publication such as ours. They refused to distribute the posters and left the task to other comrades, who weren't so piously scrupulous.

At the beginning of February, Johann Most turned sixty years old. Comrades in many cities throughout the country wished to celebrate the event and use it as propaganda for our movement by featuring Most as a speaker. In Philadelphia, the oppositional clique seized the opportunity and took over the arrangements. They organized the meeting for a Saturday evening in a small hall on Lombard Street, where the police captain was a fierce reactionary. All the preparations were done carelessly. Less than a hundred people came for the celebration, half of them Italians. Just as Most stopped speaking, the police captain entered the hall with a squadron of his men. The captain marched down the middle aisle to the platform, while the other police lined the walls on both sides and surrounded the small audience. I was sitting near the door, and I noticed that one of the Italians, comrade Dominic, moving quietly toward the captain with a stiletto in his hand.[8] I was scarcely able to grab him from behind and push him down into a seat, avoiding a foolish and dastardly act that would have ended in a horrible bloodbath. The captain, meanwhile, approached the platform. He ordered us all to leave the hall at once. He simply drove us out, without explanation, without a hearing, without cause.

---

6. The **Kropotkin Library**, also known as the Kropotkin Institute, was founded at the Stelton Colony by Joseph Cohen and Harry Kelly in 1922 in memory of Peter Kropotkin, who had died the previous year. It held a large collection of radical literature and hosted frequent anarchist conferences and classes.

7. **Eliza Orzeszkowa** (1841–1910) was a renowned Polish novelist. It is not clear which of her books Cohen refers to here, as none were ultimately serialized in the *Abend tsaytung*.

8. This is likely Dominic (or Dominick) Donelli, who was later arrested during the 1908 Broad Street Riot, described in chapter 22.

A few of us then took Most to David Apotheker's home, which was nearby. There we sat, drinking beer and bemoaning the backwardness of the American workers, who refused to join the ranks of our revolutionary movement. Most listened to our complaints for a long time, and then suddenly he stood up and began to speak, pointing out that our statements were unfair. The American worker, he said, knows his living conditions are incomparably better than those of workers in any other country. The American worker knows instinctively that he cannot fall far beyond the workers of other countries. But when the time comes for workers in other countries to live as well or better than those in the United States, then the American workers will not want to be left behind for a moment. They are used to protesting, to walking out spontaneously, without preparation, to fight in the streets. They are by no means as backward as we portrayed them.

These were insightful words that illuminated for us the clear view that Johann Most had of social development. These were the clear-sighted words of a prophet (*khozeh*), not an agitator, as most had imagined him to be. A week later, Johann Most died in Cincinnati in the midst of his lecture tour. The police would not allow his ashes to be brought back to New York, fearing this great rebel's spirit in death no less than in his stormy life. This ban inspired comrade Shloyme Pres ("Der Kleynshtetldiker") to write one of his most celebrated feuilletons in the *Fraye arbeter shtime*, "Ashes."

Comrade Benny Moore, at his own expense, had five thousand photographs of Johann Most printed, hoping that they would sell and bring in funds for the movement. Years earlier, a biography of Bakunin had created a demand for his image. A picture of the great rebel had hung in almost every immigrant's home. There was a similar demand for pictures of Kropotkin, Karl Marx, and others. Images of revolutionaries had long been in vogue. We tried our best to promote the photographs of Johann Most but to no avail. Benny Moore's hasty act cost him over $100.

CHAPTER 19

The *Abend tsaytung*

On the appointed day, March 18, 1906, the first issue of our new daily newspaper appeared. The *Abend tsaytung* was a kind of miniature *Fraye arbeter shtime*. The articles were serious, weighty—I dare say, perhaps a little too heavy, above the head of the average reader, but we were pleased with it because we wanted a serious paper that was worth reading.

We in Philadelphia opened an office in one corner of Mina Finkler's tiny cigar store on Fifth Street between South and Bainbridge. The place was convenient for news dealers and newsstand operators to come and pick up the newspaper on their way to get copies of the *Forverts* and the *Tageblat* in the same neighborhood. We were also able to convince a young comrade, Malamut, to give up his job as a dressmaker in order to go out and sell advertisements for our paper.[1] With the help of comrades, he was able to sell a whole page of ads, which would bring in a couple hundred dollars a month. We distributed fifteen hundred copies an issue, and the news dealers were happy to help us circulate the paper, for which there seemed to be quite a demand.

But you can imagine our annoyance and frustration when, from the very beginning, our newspaper began arriving from New York much later than the other Yiddish papers. First of all, we had to have a special courier travel by train to bring back the bundles of papers; secondly, the news dealers— several dozen individuals—could not sit around and wait for a couple of

---

1. This appears to be a reference to **Joseph Malamut** (Yoyel-Leyb or Yud Lamed Malamut, 1886–1966), who was briefly involved in Philadelphia's anarchist movement around this time and went on to become a well-known Jewish journalist for dozens of Yiddish publications, including the *FAS*. He later settled in Los Angeles and became a Labor Zionist.

Figure 17: A daily anarchist newspaper: *Di abend tsaytung*
First issue of *Di abend tsaytung*, March 18, 1906, featuring a
front-page obituary of Johann Most

hours for our paper. Not all of them were able to make a separate trip just
to pick up their copies. We felt that our opportunity was slipping away due
to such negligence, and when the ordeal was repeated over several more
days, we decided that I should go to New York and try to immediately correct matters.

I got up, left for New York, and arrived at the offices by 8:00 in the morning.
My friend Eliezer Landau and Menakhem-Mendl Tsipin, the editorial staff

member, were seated at their work desks, nervously biting their fingernails.[2] Yanovsky, they told me, needed to come with his editorial for the newspaper, which he wrote at home. However, he never arrived earlier than 9:00, and this prevented the paper from going to the printer on time. In New York, they told me, they had the same trouble distributing the newspaper in the outlying boroughs of the city for the same reason. Finally Yanovsky arrived. As soon as he saw me, he exclaimed, "What are you doing here so early?"

"Thief (*Gazlen*)!" I replied. "You are clearly ruining all our efforts! If the paper arrives two hours late, more than half of the copies remain unsold! The newspaper must arrive on the same train as the other Yiddish papers!"

Listening to me, he looked at me with his clever, squinting eyes and said, "So, for such a trifle, people run all the way from Philadelphia to New York at dawn; you could have just written a postcard! We'll see to it that the paper comes out a couple hours earlier."

This was, it seemed, obviously good. He saw for himself and admitted that the paper needed to be published on time! However, there was no noticeable improvement. The paper arrived late almost every morning and was a burning problem for us. I carried copies to the nearby newsstands and news dealers almost entirely by myself. For those farther away from our office, I was sometimes able to send their bundles of papers with someone. The rest of the papers lay around until the next morning. Certainly this was no way to launch a new daily newspaper.

By April, the comrades in New York had realized that all was not well with the paper. It had no manager. Yanovsky had fired Louis Elstein, thinking it would probably help him secure William Lief for the position. On April 14–15, a coalition formed the "Abend Tsaytung Association," whose members agreed to contribute six to twelve dollars annually for the support of the paper. They elected as secretary Harry Gordon, who did his work efficiently. Branches of the association were organized in a number of cities.

---

2. **Menakhem-Mendl Tsipin** (1874–1925) was a Russian-born Jewish garment worker, journalist, anarchist, and later Communist. After being expelled from high school for participating in a strike, he immigrated to the United States in 1902 and was active in the Jewish labor and anarchist movements, contributing to the *FAS*, the *Abend tsaytung*, and *Broyt un frayheyt*. Tsipin went on to work in several editorial positions for other Yiddish newspapers and traveled to Russia in 1917 after the February Revolution as a correspondent for *Der tog* and other publications. After returning to Philadelphia, he joined the Communist Party.

The list of members grew larger from week to week. Over time, things would work out, if only the paper appeared on time and was managed properly. But this did not happen. In the second week of May, the *Abend tsaytung* ceased publication. Writing in the *Fraye arbeter shtime* on May 13, Yanovsky tried to convince himself that it was only temporary, that the Abend Tsaytung Association would raise $1,500 and we would get back to work. But no one had confidence in his words.

This was a terrible blow to us. We had not been warned of it and were not prepared for such a catastrophe. Little by little it became clear to us that soon after the 1905 convention, Yanovsky had regretted the whole affair. By nature, it was difficult for him to work with other people on an equal basis, as one worker among many. In addition, he was close friends with the manager of the *Forverts*, with whom he often played dominoes at Herrick's Café, and who correctly warned Yanovsky of the many hardships and demands of publishing a daily paper. And this was the reason why the *Fraye arbeter shtime* did not agitate on behalf of the daily newspaper following the 1905 convention, and why he burst into tears at the special convention. He lacked the courage to come out against a decision for which everyone else was so enthusiastic, and at the same time he was unable to put all his heart and energy into the work of the daily paper. He made a weak attempt to carry out the will of the comrades, and with his own hands he throttled the infant before it had an opportunity to reach its potential.

This was to be his last deed in connection with our movement as an organized social force. There were no more conventions called by the *Fraye arbeter shtime*, and no more questions pertaining to the movement were addressed in the paper. The *Fraye arbeter shtime* became Yanovsky's newspaper, an expression of his opinions and his personality.

This was unfortunately at a time when our ranks were greatly expanded and enriched by new, young members who kept arriving from London and Russia. Around this time, comrades Benjamin Dubovsky, David Isakovitz, Sam Margolis, Aaron Mintz, Mina and Nokhum Vaynritsh, L. Baron, Alex Cohen, Lazar and Millie Sabelinsky, and dozens of other active comrades arrived from London.[3] From Russia we received Novomirsky, who did not

---

3. **Lazar (or Lazarus) Sabelinsky** (Zabelinsky, c. 1871–1928), also known as Lazar Sabel (Zabel), was a Russian-born Jewish jeweler and anarchist. He was a longtime member of London's Arbeter Fraynd Group and served as the *Arbeter fraynd*'s treasurer. In London he

stay long with us, Louis Levine, Alexander Mikhailovich Krasnoshchekov (Mikhail), and hundreds of lesser-known anarchists and sympathizers.[4] Never before or since did our movement have such a great opportunity to

---

met and married **Millie Sabelinsky** (1878–1972), née Green (Grin), a cigarette maker and fellow Russian Jewish anarchist. The couple came to the United States in 1904 and lived in New York's Greenwich Village but returned to London by 1906. After Lazar's death, the *FAS* established a fund to help support his family.

4. **Daniel Novomirsky** (Daniil Novomirskii, 1882–c. 1937), real name Yankel Isakov Kirilovsky, was a Russian-born Jewish anarchist. He became a social democrat at a young age and was arrested in connection with his politics in 1904, then fled to France where he studied law and became an anarchist and syndicalist. Around 1906 Novomirsky came to the United States, where he contributed to the *FAS*. After returning to Russia that same year and founding an anarcho-syndicalist group in Odessa, he was arrested in 1907 and served eight years in prison before being exiled to Siberia, but in 1916 he escaped to the United States where he wrote for both the *FAS* and the Union of Russian Workers' paper *Golos Truda*. Novomirsky returned to Russia following the February Revolution, joined the Communist Party, and worked for the Comintern but left the party in 1921 and was briefly imprisoned. He was again arrested during the purges of 1936–1937 and sent to Siberia, where he died. **Louis Levitzki Levine** (Luis Levitsky Levin, 1883–1970), who later changed his name to Lewis L. Lorwin, was a Russian-born Jewish economist, historian, and onetime anarchist. His family immigrated to New York in 1888, and from 1896 to 1906 Levine studied abroad in France, Switzerland, and Russia, where he became active in the Russian anarchist movement around the time of the 1905 Revolution. After returning to the United States in 1906, Levine became a regular contributor to the *FAS*, the *Fraye gezelshaft*, and other anarchist publications, writing on the labor movement as well as anarchist and socialist history, theory, and tactics. In 1911 he also coedited the short-lived Yiddish anarchist newspaper *Dos fraye vort* with Jacob A. Maryson. In 1912 Levine completed his PhD in political science at Columbia University, publishing his dissertation as *The Labor Movement in France: A Study in Revolutionary Syndicalism* and writing articles on syndicalism for several American magazines and journals, as well as lecturing on syndicalism at the anarchist Ferrer Center. He became a professor of economics and was fired from the University of Montana in 1919 for publishing a book advocating higher taxation of mining corporations. In 1920 Levine married Russian-born Jewish socialist and feminist Rose Strunsky (1884–1963), and in 1924 he published *The Women's Garment Workers*, a well-received study commissioned by the ILGWU. Levine was subsequently hired by the Brookings Institution and began to actively conceal his radical past. In the 1930s and 1940s, under the name Lewis Lorwin, he became a prominent advocate of economic planning—something he first became interested in through syndicalism—and was appointed to several posts in Franklin D. Roosevelt's administration, where he helped draft the Marshall Plan. He was also instrumental in facilitating the immigration of leftist Jewish intellectuals from Germany's Frankfort Institute for Social Research who were fleeing Nazism. Between 1947 and 1951 Levine was investigated as an alleged Communist by the House Un-American Activities Committee and the FBI, leading to his resignation from the Commerce Department. His eldest son, Valentine ("Val") Rogin-Levine (later Lorwin, 1907–1982), was a student at the Modern School in Stelton and likewise became

develop wide-ranging organized activity as in those years. Unfortunately, the rift between the newspaper and the movement hampered any undertaking.

The wider anarchist movement at that time, in the spring of 1906, was full of vitality. Emma Goldman, with the help of a number of American comrades—Harry Kelly, John R. Coryell, Max Baginski, and others[5]—began publishing a monthly magazine, *Mother Earth*, in anticipation of Alexander Berkman's release from prison. For twelve years it carried out a vigorous propaganda campaign on behalf of our ideas. In Chicago, the comrades chose to publish another English-language journal, *The Liberator*. At the Home Colony, on the Pacific Coast, Jay Fox began publishing a small English magazine called *The Demonstrator*.[6] In London, Freedom Press put out a weekly

---

a historian of the French labor movement, a civil servant under Roosevelt, and a subject of anti-Communist investigations. **Alexander Mikhailovich Krasnoshchekov** (1880–1937), also known as Mikhail Tobinson and Abraham Stoller Tobinson, was a Russian-born Jewish painter, lawyer, anarchist, and later socialist. As a teenager he joined an underground revolutionary group in Chernobyl and was repeatedly arrested, leading him to immigrate to the United States in 1903. Krasnoshchekov joined the Jewish anarchist movement in Brooklyn, and around 1910 he moved to Chicago, where he earned his law degree at the University of Chicago, became a socialist, and organized on behalf of both the IWW and the AFL. Krasnoshchekov became superintendent of Chicago's Workers' Institute in 1916 but returned to Russia following the February Revolution. He immediately joined the Communist Party and was appointed president of the Far Eastern Soviet of People's Commissars until its overthrow; he then became minister of the Far Eastern Republic from 1920 to 1921. Krasnoshchekov was arrested in 1924 on charges of corruption and convicted in one of the first Soviet "show trials" (during which his old anarchist comrades staunchly defended him in the pages of the *FAS*). He was released in 1925, but arrested and executed during the purges of 1937. See *FAS*, October 12, 1923.

5. **John Russell Coryell** (1851–1924) was an American-born writer, educator, and anarchist. Creator of the dime-novel detective Nick Carter, he contributed to *Lucifer, the Light Bearer, Mother Earth*, and other anarchist publications (often under the pen name Margaret Grant), and briefly edited his own anarchist journal, *The Wide Way* (1907–1908). He and his wife Abby Hedge Coryell were the first teachers at New York's Ferrer Modern School. **Max Baginski** (1864–1943) was a German-born editor and anarchist. A former member of the Social Democratic Party of Germany, he was an admirer of Johann Most and joined the anarchist movement in Germany, leading to a thirty-month prison sentence for publishing radical literature. Baginski immigrated to the United States in 1893 and settled in Chicago, where he edited the *Chicagoer Arbeiter-Zeitung* for many years. He later edited *Freiheit* after Johann Most's death, as well as *Mother Earth*, and was an American delegate to the 1907 International Anarchist Congress in Amsterdam.

6. **Home Colony** was an anarchist community founded on Puget Sound near Tacoma,

paper called *The Voice of Labour*.[7] In Switzerland, the Russian comrades published two magazines, *Burevestnik* (Petrel) and *Chernoye Znamya* (Black Flag). In addition to London's *Arbeter fraynd* and *Zsherminal*, then enjoying their heyday under the editorship of Rudolf Rocker, an opposition group there also began publishing a new Yiddish weekly called the *Fraye arbeter velt* (Free Workers' World).[8] There was no dearth of newspapers, magazines, pamphlets, and major works in the languages familiar to us.

The *Fraye arbeter shtime* also contained rich, interesting content. In honor of the appearance of the short-lived *Abend tsaytung*, Dr. Jacob A. Maryson, Dr. Hillel Solotaroff, and Dr. Iser Ginzburg were added as regular contributors—and after the demise of the daily paper they remained as writers for the *Fraye arbeter shtime* for some time. The Russians Novomirsky and Louis Levine were both prolific writers. For many months they debated among themselves over the condition and spirit of the contemporary anarchist movement in Russia, greatly interesting readers in this country.

In the spring of that year, there was a debate between Dr. Maryson and Dr. Chaim Zhitlowsky on the topic of territorialism, which was then very much in vogue in Jewish circles.[9] At first glance, the debaters seemed an unevenly matched pair. Dr. Zhitlowsky was widely considered one of the very best Jewish speakers, while Dr. Maryson was by no means a speaker. He had to read every lecture from notes and usually did so sitting down. That he agreed to debate with Zhitlowsky was truly a wonder. And the wonder

---

Washington, in 1898. It officially dissolved in 1919, though many former residents continued to reside there. **Jay Fox** (1870–1961) was an American-born worker, journalist, anarchist, and later Communist. The son of Irish immigrants, he grew up in Chicago, where he joined the Knights of Labor in 1886 and was present at the Haymarket bombing. In the 1890s Fox collaborated on the anarchist paper *Free Society*, and in 1905 he was a delegate to the founding of the IWW. In 1908 he moved to the Home Colony and founded the paper *The Agitator* (1910–1912), then moved to Chicago where he edited *The Syndicalist* (1913) and joined William Z. Foster's Syndicalist League of North America. In 1924 he joined the Communist Party.

7. **The Voice of Labour** (1907) was an anarcho-syndicalist paper that John Turner helped to produce.

8. **Fraye arbeter velt** (1905–1906) was edited in London by noted Hebrew writer Yosef Haim Brenner (1881–1921) during his brief affiliation with anarchism.

9. **Jewish territorialism** sought to create an autonomous territory for the Jewish people, but unlike Zionism it did not focus on Palestine as the location, and it did not necessarily advocate the creation of an independent Jewish state. Chaim Zhitlowsky was a prominent representative of the movement's socialist wing.

became even greater once it became clear that Maryson's prepared, logically written arguments were, to us at least, much more convincing than Zhitlowsky's polished phrases and flowery oratory. Maryson's logical arguments about territorialism were indisputable. His talk was published in the *Fraye arbeter shtime* and created a sensation.[10]

❀ ❀ ❀

In May 1906 an anarchist bomb exploded in Spain. King Alfonso XIII was celebrating his marriage with great pomp and ceremony, as befits a king. Madrid's streets were decorated with flags. The wedding procession was adorned with flowers. The bomb was wrapped in a bouquet and exploded with tremendous force. The blast resonated around the world, scaring law enforcement to death and sowing confusion in quite a few minds.

A young man named Mateo Morral, son of a wealthy family and a very intelligent fellow, threw the bomb.[11] For a time he had collaborated with Francisco Ferrer in publishing schoolbooks for the students of Ferrer's Modern School. When the police attempted to arrest him a couple of days later, he committed suicide.

Francisco Ferrer was arrested and accused of being responsible for the attack. The trial took place in a civilian court, and, as the prosecution possessed no evidence to support the charges, he was released.

The trial brought the name of Francisco Ferrer to the attention of the world. It was then that we first learned about the man and his great life's work, the Modern School. Socialist and anarchist circles were interested in the issue of children's education, and the first socialist Sunday schools had opened in various cities, where, once a week, children were taught a bit about socialism and the history of the struggle for liberation. In Philadelphia, comrade Benny Moore, with the help of Mary Hansen and Mina Finkler, opened a Ferrer Sunday school, which they led for some time. In New York, Alexander Berkman was one of the teachers at a Sunday school run by the

---

10. *FAS*, February 10, 1906. Over the following decade, Maryson himself embraced territorialism.

11. **Mateo (or Mateu) Morral** (1879–1906), son of a textile factory owner, was a Spanish anarchist and a librarian at Francisco Ferrer's Modern School.

Workmen's Circle. The writer Eugene Lyons received his education in socialism in one of these schools.[12]

Dr. Maryson wrote a number of articles for the *Fraye arbeter shtime* on
the subject of "tactical questions," in which he strongly criticized the belief in
"propaganda of the deed," individual acts for the sake of precipitating revolution and the like.[13] At the end of his critique, he advised that instead of all of
the actions that harm the movement, frighten people, and put the anarchists
on the fringes of the mainstream, we, truly as anarchists, should participate
in political elections and parliamentary activities, in order to preach anarchism from the highest platform in the land.

To us younger comrades, this sounded so crazy, so contrary to all that
we understood by the word anarchism, that we attacked him like a swarm of
bees. Criticisms and polemics erupted on all sides. As far as I can recall, not
one among the dozens of writers who took part in that discussion accepted
Maryson's ideas. However, we all treated him with great respect, knowing his
sincerity as an anarchist and his willingness to participate in any discussions
pertaining to our movement.

Yanovsky at first let the discussion take its course. Maryson would occasionally respond to a couple of opponents, and then the discussion would
continue until Yanovsky at last could not restrain himself. In a long editorial
note, in small font, he treated Maryson in his usual sarcastic manner. The
debate continued in London's *Zsherminal*, where comrade Rudolf Rocker
was Maryson's only opponent.

The discussion was extremely useful. It touched on one of the fundamental principles of our movement. The arguments, in favor of and against,
made readers think seriously. Wherever anarchists congregated, at meetings,
at gatherings, in the parks that summer, or in private homes, they earnestly
discussed and delved into the problems of our movement. This alone was
already a significant revitalization.

---

12. **Eugene Lyons** (1898–1985) was a Russian-born Jewish journalist. He immigrated
to New York with his parents at a young age and as a teenager joined the Young People's
Socialist League. After graduating from Columbia University, Lyons became a professional
journalist while also writing for the *New York Call*, *The Liberator*, and other radical publications. He became a "fellow traveler" of the Communist Party, but six years of living in
Moscow turned him into an outspoken anti-Communist, and thereafter his political views
moved increasingly to the right.

13. *FAS*, June 9 through June 23, 1906.

CHAPTER 20

The Release of Alexander Berkman and His Return to the Movement

The name of Alexander Berkman was, for us younger comrades, a kind of talisman, a source of inspiration and encouragement. We did not know him personally, and we had some vague knowledge of the act that brought about his martyrdom. All we knew was that a brave young man, an anarchist, who had risked his life to avenge the spilling of striking workers' blood, had been languishing in the Western Penitentiary of Pennsylvania, in Pittsburgh, since 1892. We also knew that a daring, heroic attempt had been made to free him by way of a long, cleverly dug tunnel, which in our eyes gave a romantic aura to the whole story.

In the spring of 1906, his long and cruel punishment finally came to an end. The gates of the prison opened for Berkman. Out in the free world his longtime friend Emma Goldman had been the only person who knew about his deed before he committed it and who in spirit did not leave him throughout the long years of his martyrdom. It was difficult for Berkman to readjust to his new condition of freedom. His hellish nightmare shadowed him everywhere he went. His long incarceration and the many months spent locked up in solitary confinement made it impossible for him to tolerate being around people, to put up with their nonsense and petty preoccupations.

He came to us in Philadelphia after the entire Jewish labor movement had welcomed him with a ceremonial reception in New York City. Upon his arrival in Philadelphia, we hastily called together a number of guests in a room on the third floor of comrade Ozer Smolenskin's print shop, across the street from Joffe's drugstore, in which we had never met before. We spent several hours there on a very hot evening. A most eloquent speech was given by Baruch Zuckerman, a Poale Zionist who, like all active people at the time, hung around our circle.[1] The entertainment part of the program was brilliantly performed by Sam Shore, who outdid himself.[2]

A few days later we held a picnic in honor of Berkman's liberation in the historic forest in Ogontz. There comrade Jack Ryan got well and truly drunk and shouted that he was going to shoot me! I do not know if he really had a gun with which to shoot, but he made no small noise until we managed to put him under a bush and hold on until he fell asleep. After the picnic, he disappeared, vanished. He was probably ashamed of his behavior and left the city.

A few days later we received a communication from New York telling us that Alexander Berkman had suddenly disappeared. He had last been seen in Cleveland, where he had received an enthusiastic welcome and been taken to spend the night at a comrade's home on a farm not far from the city. But when the host awoke in the morning, there was no sign of Berkman, and he could not be found.

It is impossible to describe our anxiety. We imagined the worst. The capitalist press wrote shortly after his release that the steel magnate Frick, whom Berkman had attempted to assassinate fourteen years earlier, was displeased with the idea that Berkman was free. Was there any limit to what people such as Frick were capable of? He had proven more than once that he could hire murderers to do his bloody work for him and kill innocent people! We did not rule out the possibility that Berkman had been abducted and taken back to Pennsylvania to the penitentiary. After all, he had only

---

1. **Baruch Zuckerman** (Borekh Tsukerman, 1887–1970) was a Russian-born Jewish garment worker, writer, and Labor Zionist. He embraced his radical and nationalist ideas shortly before immigrating to the United States in 1904, and the following year he cofounded the Labor Zionist Organization of America (the American branch of Poale Zion), of which he later became president. In 1956 he moved to Israel.

2. **Samuel Shore** (Shmuel Shur, 1888–1946) was a Russian-born Jewish garment worker, labor organizer, and anarchist. In 1904 he immigrated to Philadelphia with his family and soon joined the anarchist movement, contributing his first piece to the *FAS* in 1907. Shore became an organizer for the Bakers' Union in Philadelphia and then in Baltimore, and in 1911 he moved to New York, where he was made manager of the ILGWU's White Goods Workers' Union (later renamed the Undergarment and Negligee Workers' Union) Local 62. He was an instrumental organizer of the 1912 New York tailors' strike and became an international vice president of the ILGWU. Shore drifted away from anarchism and near the end of his life served as treasurer of the social democratic Liberal Party of New York.

served two-thirds of his term. This meant that he was free under parole, which could be revoked.

We spent days weighted down with such terrible worry. I spent all night at the telephone at Natasha Notkin's drugstore in Richmond, waiting for a call from New York. When I left for home in the morning, broken and beaten, I had to walk through the streets of the slums in that area, where people were sleeping in the gutter and on the sidewalk, where the police patrolled the streets two or three abreast for fear of walking around alone. The image was horrible; it exposed the foundation of our decaying society and displayed what was happening under the lid of the great sewer that calls itself civilization.

On the third day, at last, we received word that Berkman was back in New York unharmed. He simply could not stand the pressure of so many people around him, and for the previous few days had wandered among people who did not know him. We all breathed easier and realized the depth of Berkman's suffering, which was now being made worse by the martyr's own comrades. His announced tour was canceled. It was a long time before Berkman could shake off the nightmare of his fourteen years in hell, until he finally managed to exorcize the whole experience artistically, on paper, in his famous book, *Prison Memoirs of an Anarchist*, which is recognized by friends and foes alike as a masterpiece on a par with Dostoevsky's descriptions of Russia's Katorga system of penal labor.[3]

❄ ❄ ❄

A few years after all this, the aforementioned Jack Ryan came to visit me. He was well-dressed, traveling from Pittsburgh to Atlantic City for vacation. He came to thank me for criticizing his idleness years before. This, he said, drove him to return to his trade as a machinist in one of the largest factories in Pittsburgh and earn a living as a worker and anarchist agitator.

---

3. Russian novelist **Fyodor Dostoevsky** (1821–1881) portrayed life in a tsarist prison camp in his semi-autobiographical novel *The House of the Dead* (1862).

CHAPTER 21

Broyt un frayheyt

Later that same summer we held another picnic in the same woods for our own circle. There we spent a nice day sitting in the sun on the green grass discussing the condition of our movement. I gave a speech, calmly and logically, about the issue and concluded that under the circumstances, there remained one thing for us to do—to create a movement newspaper, which should be maintained and controlled by the organized movement, not by an individual.

The younger comrades were thrilled with the idea. But the old-timer Chaim Weinberg sighed. He recalled the factionalism in the movement between the "journal-ists" and "newspaper-ists" in the 1890s and tried to dissuade us from taking such a step. To his question, "What will a newspaper be able to accomplish for the movement?" one of the younger comrades gave a characteristic answer: "Our paper will not be as watered-down as the *Fraye arbeter shtime*. We shall write revolutionary articles, the police will arrest us, we will resist them strongly, and it will bring life to the movement!"

After thorough discussion, it was decided to raise a fund of $500 to start publishing an anarchist paper in Philadelphia. We planned the newspaper, of course, not as a local Philadelphia enterprise. We were just the initiators. We wanted the publication to represent the organized anarchist movement of the whole country. We communicated with comrades in every city and received a surprisingly enthusiastic response in New York, with comrades Benjamin Dubovsky, Mikhail (Alexander Krasnoshchekov), and Louis Levine very cooperative. We held two conferences in our city, to which they and other comrades came as delegates. After one of the conferences, when we accompanied one of the other delegates to the station, as we passed Wanamaker's department store, he suddenly exclaimed: "If anyone could explain to me how an anarchist society could manage an enterprise as big as Wanamaker's, I would feel much more confident in the possibility of realizing our idea." This sparked a heated debate in the Broad Street Station, standing in a closed circle, which caused the New York comrades to miss one train after another.

The practical decisions of the conference were that the newspaper would bear the name *Broyt un frayheyt* (Bread and Freedom) and that it would publish a statement of principles in the first issue, which we worked out at the conference. It would appear on November 11, 1906, the anniversary of the deaths of the Chicago martyrs. The editorship would be headed by a committee. The writers would include Menakhem-Mendl Tsipin, who had settled in Philadelphia and was working at his trade in a knitting factory, and Benjamin Axler.

During the summer the *Fraye arbeter shtime* carried a few reports from the Broyt un Frayheyt Group in Philadelphia about its activities and the preparations being made for publishing a new paper. Relations with the *Fraye arbeter shtime* were very friendly. We continued to distribute that paper and to collect advertisements and subscriptions for it, as in previous years.

On the first of September, however, a lengthy appeal for the new paper, almost filling a column, appeared, signed with my name and address for correspondence. The principles of the new newspaper were listed in the appeal as follows:

1. Immediately awaken the degraded and oppressed to struggle against all that degrades and oppresses humanity.
2. Encourage and develop the anarchist and revolutionary movement among all peoples and nations.
3. Educate and enlighten the labor movement everywhere, especially in America.
4. Maintain and further develop the militancy and fighting spirit which our young comrades brought with them from cold Russia, and their contempt for the submissive indifference of the bourgeoisie and the slavish patience of the workers.

After this declaration, an editorial of over two columns of small type followed, in which Yanovsky endeavored to give us a harsh lesson (*hot mit undz gelernt Balak*). He tore asunder every phrase, every sentence, to show that we did not have the least bit of knowledge about the art of writing or the ability to express our ideas adequately, and so on and so forth, as only he could. We could no longer speak of any peaceful cooperation or further support from the *Fraye arbeter shtime*.

This response provoked outrage in many groups. An invitation appeared in the *Fraye arbeter shtime* to open a discussion on the matter, but the damage was already done.

Suddenly, unexpectedly and unannounced, a few days before November 11, we received from New York two large bundles of a new newspaper, *Lebn un kamf* (Life and Struggle), edited, written, and published by Julius Edelsohn.[1] The issue, printed on slick, glossy book paper, was published in such a hurry, with so many typographical errors, jumbled lines, and twisted sentences, that it was impossible to read and make out the intentions of this publication.

The Edelsohns were an interesting family in New York City. There were three brothers and a sister, Becky, all of them very active in the movement.[2] Julius, the smallest and the youngest, was a true dynamo of energy, a person with a mercurial nature: always high-strung, ready to undertake the most difficult task of the moment. Two things he lacked kept him from being a real asset to the movement: initiative and perseverance. He tried to imitate everything we were doing in Philadelphia. He revived the defunct Progressive Library in New York after we founded our Radical Library here in Philadelphia, which under his leadership was nothing more than a caricature of our institution.

---

1. **Julius Edelsohn** (Edelson, c. 1886–?) was a Russian-born Jewish anarchist. He immigrated to New York with his family in the 1890s and later moved to California, where he continued to be involved in anarchist activities.

2. **Rebecca ("Becky") Edelsohn** (Edelson, 1892–1973) was a Russian-born Jewish anarchist. She immigrated to New York with her family a year or two after her birth, and as a teenager she became an anarchist, lived in Emma Goldman's home, and was romantically involved with Alexander Berkman. Edelsohn was arrested several times for her activism and in 1914 conducted one of the first hunger strikes in the United States (lasting twenty-seven days) while being held in Blackwell's Island for "disorderly conduct" after giving an antiwar speech. She later married fellow anarchist Charles Plunkett.

I once paid a visit there on a Sunday evening. The place was packed with people who talked so loudly, laughed, and made so much noise that no pretense was made of reading. Also, the place was very dirty, full of dust and trash piled in every corner. Julius suddenly ran into the room, sized up the place, and began to clean up for a lecture that was soon to take place that evening. He brought in a pail of water, splashed it on the floor, and began helter-skelter to sweep dirt, visitors, and anything in his way. On the cold winter days, he complained to me, visitors fueled the stove by burning the best Russian classics, and whole sets of good books were thus destroyed.

Now that we were preparing to publish a new newspaper, he suddenly knew he could do it faster and better. His family and his small group of followers gave him courage, and, in a few days, the thing was finished, done. Naturally the paper did not last long. Only three or four issues appeared. But the harm to our project was very great. It confused people, proving how irresponsible some of our young comrades were, so that you never knew from one minute to another what adventure they would embark on.

Broyt un frayheyt came out on time as planned, carefully edited and compiled. It contained serious articles, as well as good feuilletons written by Menakhem-Mendl Tsipin, but the paper had no income. We did not accept advertisements on principle. Very little money came in. The comrades now were not in a hurry to send contributions. Dr. Michael A. Cohn contributed an article for the fourth or fifth issue but gave us no material support. With the thirteenth issue, all the funding was used up, and we were forced to suspend publication. We just could not go on. But the thirteen issues of *Broyt un frayheyt* left a good impression. Many years later, when Yanovsky left the *Fraye arbeter shtime* to become editor of *Gerekhtigkeyt* (Justice) and Dr. Jacob A. Maryson took over the editorship of the *Fraye arbeter shtime* for a few months, he organized the paper, in appearance as well as content, along the same lines as our former *Broyt un frayheyt*.[3]

The year 1906 ended on a crazy note for us. Even before *Broyt un frayheyt* launched and Edelsohn's *Lebn un kamf* appeared in early October, Edelsohn decided to celebrate the anniversary of Leon Czolgosz's death. He wrote the *Fraye arbeter shtime* announcing a celebration on October 27

---

3. **Gerekhtigkeyt** (1919–1969) was the weekly Yiddish newspaper of the ILGWU.

at the Progressive Library. The police were on alert after the bomb incident in Madrid and burst into the library during the meeting and took it upon themselves to expel the audience of several dozen people. Becky Edelsohn, who was then very young, honored one policeman with a pair of slaps, which added some color to the incident. A number of youths, among them Harry Lang, who was then active in our movement, were arrested, together with Becky Edelsohn.[4]

A few days later, on November 5, a rally was held to protest the behavior of the police, and more people were arrested. The judge in front of whom they appeared took the matter very seriously. He put them all under $1,000 bail each and referred the case to a grand jury to pursue criminal charges.

At first Yanovsky reprimanded the "boys" for their foolishness and childish irresponsibility. But a week later he published a front-page, serious editorial by Alexander Berkman appealing for support for the defendants. The situation appeared to be serious in nature, with a defense committee, lawyers, and so on. The girls were immediately released on bail, while the young men were kept in jail pending the grand jury proceedings, which, a week or two later, threw out the entire case. The mountain, this time, gave birth to a mouse.

On the first of December, the following statement appeared on the front page of the *Fraye arbeter shtime*, in big letters:

> We the "F. A. S." Group declare, that not only do we have nothing to do with what various young people have been up to lately in the name of anarchism, such as publishing newspapers, distributing leaflets, organizing meetings, etc., but we simply think that these boys' reckless

---

4. **Harry Lang** (Hertz Lang, 1888–1970) was a Russian-born Jewish garment worker, paperhanger, union organizer, journalist, anarchist, and later socialist. In 1903 he immigrated to New York, where he became a labor organizer and joined the anarchist movement, contributing regularly to the *FAS* beginning in 1908. In 1912 Lang cofounded the Kropotkin Literary Society, but that same year he joined the Socialist Party. He also became secretary of the International Brotherhood of Painters, Decorators, and Paper Hangers of America and in 1913 was hired as an organizer for the ILGWU, of which he became executive secretary. Lang wrote for *Tsukunft*, *Gerekhtigkeyt*, the *Forverts*, and other Yiddish radical and labor papers, was the first editor of the Jewish Socialist Verband's weekly *Der veker* (The Alarm, 1921–1985), and became a longtime editor of the *Forverts*. In 1932 he married fellow former anarchist Lucy Fox Robins (1884–1962), the ex-wife of *FAS* manager Bob Robins.

Figure 18: Philadelphia's *Broyt un frayheyt*
First issue of *Broyt un frayheyt*, November 11, 1906, featuring a
front-page memorial to the Haymarket Martyrs

activity is a disgrace and harmful to anarchism and puts our whole
movement in danger.

That same month there was talk in the *Fraye arbeter shtime* that at the yearly
convention an attempt would be made to work out a new declaration of
principles. For the previous twenty-five years, Yanovsky declared, since the
last declaration of principles had been adopted in Pittsburgh, much had been

learned. It was time to formulate a new document based on our experiences. However, no convention was convened that year or in any of the subsequent twelve years that Yanovsky remained editor of the *Fraye arbeter shtime*.

❀ ❀ ❀

After the demise of *Broyt un frayheyt* and all the tumult of the last months of 1906, our movement was in a depleted state. A year earlier, the Radical Library had moved into two large, comfortable rooms at 229 Pine Street. The building belonged to an influential politician. The upper floors of the building housed an artificial flower factory. In the evening and on holidays we had the whole building to ourselves. We were free to do whatever we wanted. Once a month I would meet with the landlord and pay him his rent, and that was it. At one of these meetings, he introduced me to the police captain of that district, who seemed to be a gentle, kind, and friendly person in private.

Throughout the winter of 1906–1907, we continued our library work, lectures, discussions, and classes every Tuesday evening to study anarchism, et cetera. The only broader activity that I can remember was agitation against the arrest of Charles Moyer, George Pettibone, and William Haywood.[5] As the time for their trial approached, protests and demonstrations intensified all over the country. We convened a demonstration one Saturday in May near City Hall, in conjunction with a protest march of the downtown Jewish working-class community.

The reaction was grand. Thousands of workers gathered at Third and Catherine at the appointed time and from there marched to City Hall in closed ranks. It began to rain on the way. Most of the workers, dressed in their best clothes, ran for shelter against the downpour. Only the young women remained, their thin blouses clinging to their bodies and showing off their figures. The cold rain could not dampen their enthusiasm. Our elaborate demonstration marched through the quiet, empty streets to City

---

5. **Charles Moyer** (1866–1929) was an American-born miner, socialist, and president of the Western Federation of Miners. He was arrested in 1905 for alleged involvement in the assassination of former Idaho governor Frank Steunenberg and later acquitted. That same year he cofounded the IWW, but in 1908 he led the Western Federation of Miners out of that organization and subsequently affiliated it with the AFL.

Hall, where we held our protest meeting to an audience consisting of several hundred young women.

That summer, our movement began to prepare for the International Anarchist Congress to be held in Amsterdam the last week in August.[6] Alexander Berkman also gradually began to become active in the movement. He organized an Anarchist Federation, composed largely of individuals with membership cards.[7] This was a novelty in our movement—the beginning of a systematic way of organizing, albeit not in an entirely systematic way. What good is a federation of individuals, rather than groups? But it was a start.

For our part, we held to the idea of organizing groups. We had no membership cards. We gradually developed the idea of consolidating our organizations by turning our groups into branches of the Workmen's Circle. A number of us had already joined branches as individuals, and now we thought to organize our own, anarchist branches, in order to better maintain their memberships and carry on our anarchist activities more systematically through the branch organizations.

There were two incidents that caused us to think this way. In New York, not long before, a child born of radical parents who had not had him circumcised died.[8] Then when the child was buried, the burial society performed the barbaric ritual on his dead body. This provoked an uproar in radical circles, as can easily be imagined, forcing us to think about the mortal remains of every one of us.

Here in Philadelphia, a comrade by the name of Jacob Lifshits died. He was one of the most remarkable individuals of our time, an intelligent man, a scientist, a handsome, capable speaker and everything one could want, but a man who could not, or did not want to, face the harsh realities of life. He

---

6. The **1907 International Anarchist Congress** brought together delegates representing the anarchist movements of twelve countries, including two delegates from the United States: Max Baginski and Emma Goldman. Discussion centered on questions of anarchist organization and anarchism's relationship to syndicalism but brought about few concrete results.

7. The **Anarchist Federation of New York**, founded in 1908, included Yiddish-, German-, and English-speaking branches, among them Julius Edelsohn's Progressive Library, the Mother Earth Group, and the Frayheyt Group of Paterson, New Jersey. Its assistant secretary was future ILGWU president Morris Sigman.

8. Cohen elsewhere names the boy's father as Landau, possibly referring to Eliezer Landau.

was a life insurance agent and was always talking about the big premium he was about to get since he was negotiating a policy with John Wanamaker.[9] On the basis of this expectation he kept borrowing sums of money, which he never paid back. When he died without a penny, as he had lived, we were left with the responsibility of burying him. It is easy to say, "Throw my carcass to the dogs when I die," as he and other comrades used to. But comrades and friends could not bring themselves to take the body to the Jewish burial society or to the city morgue. We ran around like crazy trying to raise money to pay for the cremation and make arrangement that were completely foreign to us. We did not wish to repeat such experiences.

The Workmen's Circle was close to our hearts. For several years Leo Rosenzweig was general secretary of the organization. He had a permanent section in the *Fraye arbeter shtime* where he presented the activities of the organization in a highly attractive light—as a body for mutual aid, solidarity, education, and enlightenment. Rosenzweig was a distinguished lecturer, a highly educated man and a good orator; he specialized in scientific lectures on astronomy, physics, and similar topics, in order to fight against religious superstition and fanaticism. He was our regular "master of prayer" (*bel tfile*) at our anrireligious gatherings on Rosh Hashanah and Yom Kippur, which used to draw large audiences every year. However, the implementation of our plan to become a branch of the Workmen's Circle was delayed because of the crisis that was raging across the country.

---

9. **John Wanamaker** (1838–1922) was an American-born businessman and founder of Wanamaker's, Philadelphia's first department store. He was a fierce opponent of organized labor and a Republican appointee to postmaster general from 1889 to 1893.

CHAPTER 22

A Quiet Crisis and the Broad Street Riot

In the middle of the summer of 1907, a quiet crisis occurred throughout the country. No one noticed its arrival, and no one could tell exactly when it began. There were not even many bank failures in the beginning. Quietly, little by little, wheels in the factories ceased to turn. Here and there, manufacturers would suddenly shut down entirely, and only then did banks gradually begin to close, never to open again. People first began to feel its effects late in late autumn, when the streets of the big cities became filled with camps of the unemployed. One could recognize these poor creatures from a mile away by their shiftless gait, by the frightened look in their sad eyes filled with despair and worry.

By winter, these camps had grown exponentially in every major city. There was a disturbing misery everywhere you looked. Endless breadlines formed—a genuinely American institution that gathers the unfortunate in the street, in long lines, before the whole world, rain or shine, for a piece of bread and a cup of coffee.

The younger ones among us, who had been in this country a short while and had never seen such a spectacle before, were appalled by the humiliation and insult to which the unemployed masses were exposed so brazenly and shamelessly. Many were personally affected by unemployment and, in their helplessness, could give no advice to others. We felt that something had to be done to draw the attention of public opinion to this terrible phenomenon.

We called a rally at the new Pennsylvania Hall, at Sixth and Carpenter Streets, for January 23, 1908. We announced that Emma Goldman would

239

speak about the crisis. By this time Emma Goldman was widely known throughout the country. The Philadelphia police would not permit her to appear in public, but this time we announced the meeting only in the Yiddish papers, and the meeting was held in the heart of the Jewish ghetto. The police did not notice us and did not disturb the meeting.

On the appointed evening, the huge hall was filled with a great crowd of people—more than fifteen hundred had paid their admission fees, and a large number of the unemployed had entered without paying. To our chagrin, Emma Goldman did not come as announced to address the meeting. Instead, Alexander Berkman came, which disappointed us to a certain extent. Berkman was much beloved by us, like Goldman, but as a public speaker he could not compare to her. Besides, Berkman had already been to Philadelphia in the previous six months, since emerging from his living grave; Emma had not come to Philadelphia for many years, and the people came to see and hear her, not Berkman. Naturally, he could feel our disappointment. Every comrade with whom he shook hands in greeting asked, "What is the matter, why did Emma not come?" He became embarrassed and lost his ability to establish a rapport with his audience, which is very important in creating the necessary impression. Another handicap was that Berkman, not being fluent in Yiddish at the time, spoke in English, and the vast majority of listeners did not understand English well enough to follow his thinking.

In the course of the evening, a reporter from an English newspaper related to me the news that in Chicago, a big demonstration of the unemployed led by Dr. Ben Reitman had taken place. The police had attacked, brutally beating the demonstrators and arresting Reitman. As soon as Berkman finished his speech, I came onto the platform and relayed the news to the audience, adding that small demonstrations, which literally placed the heads of the unemployed under the heavy clubs of the police, did not make sense and did not bring results. The unemployed had to first be well organized in every city and then demonstrate simultaneously across the entire country in such large numbers that there could be no thought of attacking and dispersing them.

After the expenses of the mass meeting were paid, $100 was cleared. We decided to use the money to help organize the unemployed in our city. Our plan was to call meetings in the middle of the day, when only the unemployed could afford to come, and at each meeting to organize the unemployed from that section of the city. When such sections had been formed throughout the city, it would be possible to carry out a demonstration that, with its large size, would arouse public opinion.

❄ ❄ ❄

In Chicago the effects of the demonstrations were quite sensational. The well-known socialist lawyer Seymour Stedman took up the defense, and Dr. Reitman and the other imprisoned demonstrators were freed.[1] The vicious police attack on helpless unarmed protesters was not forgotten.

A few weeks later, on a Sunday, a young man presented himself at the home of the chief of police and asked to see him, but the chief was not at home. Early the next morning the young man again called on the chief at home. The door was opened by the chief himself, George M. Shippy, who was ready to go to his office and was waiting for his chauffeur to drive him there. Seeing the young man in front of him, who had called on him the day before, the chief invited him into the vestibule of his house, then grabbed him by both arms and yelled for his son and his wife. His wife was the first to enter and, at the command of the chief, she searched the young man's pockets for weapons. Meanwhile, the chief's son and, soon after, his chauffeur came in. All three— the chief, his son, and the driver—fired their guns and slightly wounded each other. This did not stop them from beating the young man with their revolvers, fists, and boots. He died on the way to the station or hospital.

There was an outcry in the city. The police found out who the young man was and first arrested his sister, a young girl and worker, and then raided the rooms of the Edelstadt Club, where they carried out a pogrom, seized everything, and closed the club.[2] The police sought to give the impression that there was a terrible anarchist conspiracy to kill the chief of police as revenge for his goons' brutal treatment of the unemployed demonstrators.

---

1. **Seymour Stedman** (1871–1948) was an American-born attorney who cofounded the Socialist Party of America and was its vice presidential nominee in 1920.

2. The **Edelstadt Club** was the meeting place of the David Edelstadt Group, an organization founded in memory of poet David Edelstadt by his brother, anarchist shoemaker Abe Edelstadt (c. 1859–1945).

The arrest of the sister, Olga Averbuch, a quiet and poor laborer, caught the attention of the editors of the *Idisher kurier* (Jewish Courier), a highly conservative Yiddish newspaper in Chicago.[3] The paper sought to bring the case to public attention.

It turned out that the young man, Lazarus Averbuch, had been born and brought up in Kishinev, where he had experienced the terrible 1903 pogrom. Afterward his family fled, trying to find a haven. The parents settled in Vienna. Olga came to the United States and brought over her brother a year later. He was still very young, only nineteen years old. In Chicago he found a job in a store and became active in Labor Zionist circles. What made him go to Chief Shippy's house, and what he intended to do there, was never made clear. But one thing made clear from the chief's own statement was that the unfortunate fellow had no opportunity to do anything. As soon as he crossed the threshold, the chief, who was twice as large and ten times as strong, took his arms in a vise grip. With the help of his wife, son, and chauffeur, he could have taken him wherever he wanted. There was no reason to begin shooting in the small vestibule and kill the man.

The *Idisher kurier* was able to interest a number of radical papers in the case. Outstanding among them was *The Public*, a single-tax weekly edited by Louis Post, which provided all the details.[4] The paper, however, was unable to enlist the interest of any of Chicago's prominent lawyers in taking up the case against the police chief and charging him with murder. The only attorney who came forward to defend Olga Averbuch was the young, then-unknown Harold Ickes, who later became famous as secretary of the interior.[5] He was unable to do anything. The coroner's verdict was that Lazarus Averbuch died of wounds inflicted by the chief of police in *self-defense*. The police absolved themselves of the whole affair, and the incident was soon forgotten.

---

3. **Der idisher kurier** (1887–1944) was a daily paper published by Kasriel Hirsch Sarasohn.

4. **Louis F. Post** (1849–1928) was an American-born journalist and reformer. He was an ardent single-taxer, and his weekly newspaper *The Public* (1898–1919) became that movement's leading advocate. Post later served as assistant secretary of labor from 1913 to 1921, and at the height of the First Red Scare he canceled thousands of deportation warrants for real and alleged alien radicals.

5. **Harold Ickes** (1874–1952) was an American-born Progressive politician who directed the Public Works Administration under Franklin D. Roosevelt.

❊ ❊ ❊

In Philadelphia our work among the unemployed caused great excitement and serious results. We started out with a meeting in our own section of the city, in the new Auditorium Hall at Third and Catherine Street, on a Thursday afternoon, and our leaflets strongly emphasized that this meeting was only for the unemployed. Those with employment should go to their jobs as they did every other day. This meeting was only for those who had been affected by the crisis and lost their jobs.

In accordance with this decision, I did not attend the meeting. I personally was not hit by the crisis. But my wife, not expecting any trouble, attended and brought our three-year-old child to the meeting.

Long before the hour for which the meeting had been called, the entire area around the hall was filled with people, mostly unemployed Italians. They filled two huge halls and listened to the speakers: Voltairine de Cleyre, George Brown, and Chaim Weinberg, whose languages they hardly understood. Philip Finkler chaired the meeting.[6]

When George Brown paused in the middle of his speech, a young man suddenly jumped up onto the platform and began shouting to those assembled in Italian, which our comrades could not understand. But the crowd was aroused by his words, as if an electrical current had passed through their collective body. They stood up from their seats and shouted, "To City Hall, to City Hall!"

Like a torrent of water rushing through a dam, the audience poured into the street from the two packed halls and marched through the Italian quarter toward Broad Street. Hundreds of small red flags appeared, leading us to suspect that the Italian comrades, without our knowledge, had planned the demonstration in advance and carried it out, though not one of the few among them whom we knew personally owned up to it or knew the fellow who had mounted the platform.[7]

---

6. **Philip Finkler** (1872–1934) was an Austrian-born Jewish shopkeeper and anarchist. He immigrated to the United States in around 1890 and in 1894 participated in Coxey's Army, a group of the unemployed who marched on Washington, DC. Finkler then became an active member of Philadelphia's anarchist movement and Camp Germinal. Obituaries: *FAS*, April 6, 1934; *Man!*, June–July 1934.

7. Other sources identify the Italian agitator as Eligio Strobino (1884–1982), a silk

In the Italian quarter, the marching crowd grew many times larger. The demonstration reached Broad Street and turned toward City Hall, and the crowd filled the wide street and stopped traffic. The crowd was peaceful, good-natured, and enthusiastic about its own grand scale. The unemployed in its ranks joked and sang Italian songs, and then suddenly, when they had almost reached City Hall, they were attacked by a squadron of mounted police who rode into the crowd with their horses, swinging their clubs right and left and chasing people into side streets and alleys.

In a flash, nothing was left of the large-scale demonstration. Bloodied, startled, and shocked, the demonstrators fled wherever they could find shelter. No serious resistance was made. There were no fights or rioting anywhere; the battle was entirely one-sided: the well-armed policemen beat and killed unarmed men, who did not even attempt to resist their brutality. Four Italians, beaten and bloodied, were arrested.[8]

Because the demonstration had occurred in the center of the city, it drew much attention. The evening papers came out with big headlines like "Riot on Broad Street!" and spread wild stories about a crowd of savage, lawless Italians who in the middle of the day had attempted to seize City Hall and, on the way, drove everyone out of Broad Street, threatening wealthy locals and businessmen there that they would soon take over. Only the brave and fearless actions of the vigilant policemen had saved the city from falling into the hands of the savage, predatory anarchists. The police were now going to eradicate all anarchist nests in the city and put an end to their criminal activity!

On Saturday morning, before we had an opportunity to prepare a proper defense for the four arrested Italians, they were brought before a judge. Comrade Dominic Donelli was sentenced to five years in prison. The other three got terms of one to two years.[9] The two who received the greatest

---

weaver and organizer for the IWW and the syndicalist Federazione Socialista Italiana (Italian Socialist Federation) who lived in Paterson, New Jersey, and was in the midst of a lecture tour through Pennsylvania.

8. The arrested men were Michael Costello, Dominic (or Dominick) Donelli, Francesco Piszicallo (or Piziscalo), and Angelo Troi (or Troy); of the four, only Donelli is known to have been an anarchist. A fifth man, Pietro Conello, was also arrested but released without charges.

9. Troi was sentenced to two years, Costello to eighteen months, and Piszicallo to one year. All were released early, however, including Donelli, who in 1909 was declared insane

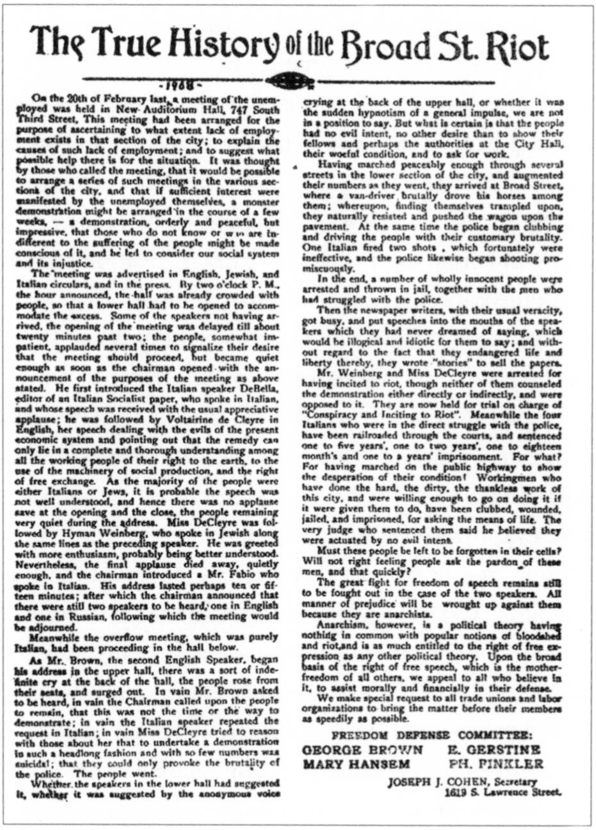

The True History of the Broad St. Riot

-1908-

On the 20th of February last, a meeting of the unemployed was held in New Auditorium Hall, 747 South Third Street. This meeting had been arranged for the purpose of ascertaining to what extent lack of employment exists in that section of the city; to explain the causes of such lack of employment; and to suggest what possible help there is for the situation. It was thought by those who called the meeting, that it would be possible to arrange a series of such meetings in the various sections of the city, and that if sufficient interest were manifested by the unemployed themselves, a monster demonstration might be arranged in the course of a few weeks, — a demonstration, orderly and peaceful, but impressive, that those who do not know or who are indifferent to the suffering of the people might be made conscious of it, and be led to consider our social system and its injustice.

The meeting was advertised in English, Jewish, and Italian circulars, and in the press. By two o'clock P. M., the hour announced, the hall was already crowded with people, so that a lower hall had to be opened to accommodate the excess. Some of the speakers not having arrived, the opening of the meeting was delayed till about twenty minutes past two; the people, somewhat impatient, applauded several times to signalize their desire that the meeting should proceed, but became quiet enough as soon as the chairman opened with the announcement of the purposes of the meeting as above stated. He first introduced the Italian speaker DeBella, editor of an Italian Socialist paper, who spoke in Italian, and whose speech was received with the usual appreciative applause; he was followed by Voltairine de Cleyre in English, her speech dealing with the evils of the present economic system and pointing out that the remedy can only lie in a complete and thorough understanding among all the working people of their right to the earth, to the use of the machinery of social production, and the right of free exchange. As the majority of the people were either Italians or Jews, it is probable the speech was not well understood, and hence there was no applause save at the opening and the close, the people remaining very quiet during the address. Miss DeCleyre was followed by Hyman Weinberg, who spoke in Jewish along the same lines as the preceding speaker. He was greeted with more enthusiasm, probably being better understood. Nevertheless, the final applause died away, quietly enough, and the chairman introduced a Mr. Fabio who spoke in Italian. His address lasted perhaps ten or fifteen minutes; after which the chairman announced that there were still two speakers to be heard, one in English and one in Russian, following which the meeting would be adjourned.

Meanwhile the overflow meeting, which was purely Italian, had been proceeding in the hall below.

As Mr. Brown, the second English Speaker, began his address in the upper hall, there was a sort of indefinite cry at the back of the hall, the people rose from their seats, and surged out. In vain Mr. Brown asked to be heard, in vain the Chairman called upon the people to remain, that this was not the time or the way to demonstrate; in vain the Italian speaker repeated the request in Italian; in vain Miss DeCleyre tried to reason with those about her that to undertake a demonstration in such a headlong fashion and with so few numbers was suicidal; that they could only provoke the brutality of the police. The people went.

Whether the speakers in the lower hall had suggested it, whether it was suggested by the anonymous voice crying at the back of the upper hall, or whether it was the sudden hypnotism of a general impulse, we are not in a position to say. But what is certain is that the people had no evil intent, no other desire than to show their fellows and perhaps the authorities at the City Hall, their woeful condition, and to ask for work.

Having marched peaceably enough through several streets in the lower section of the city, and augmented their numbers as they went, they arrived at Broad Street, where a van-driver brutally drove his horses among them; whereupon, finding themselves trampled upon, they naturally resisted and pushed the wagon upon the pavement. At the same time the police began clubbing and driving the people with their customary brutality. One Italian fired two shots , which fortunately were ineffective, and the police likewise began shooting promiscuously.

In the end, a number of wholly innocent people were arrested and thrown in jail, together with the men who had struggled with the police.

Then the newspaper writers, with their usual veracity, got busy, and put speeches into the mouths of the speakers which they had never dreamed of saying, which would be illogical and idiotic for them to say; and without regard to the fact that they endangered life and liberty thereby, they wrote "stories" to sell the papers. Mr. Weinberg and Miss DeCleyre were arrested for having incited to riot, though neither of them counseled the demonstration either directly or indirectly, and were opposed to it. They are now held for trial on charge of "Conspiracy and Inciting to Riot". Meanwhile the four Italians who were in the direct struggle with the police, have been railroaded through the courts, and sentenced one to five years', one to two years', one to eighteen month's and one to a years' imprisonment. For what? For having marched on the public highway to show the desperation of their condition! Workingmen who have done the hard, the dirty, the thankless work of this city, and were willing enough to go on doing it if it were given them to do, have been clubbed, wounded, jailed, and imprisoned, for asking the means of life. The very judge who sentenced them said he believed they were actuated by no evil intent.

Must these people be left to be forgotten in their cells? Will not right feeling people ask the pardon of these men, and that quickly?

The great fight for freedom of speech remains still to be fought out in the case of the two speakers. All manner of prejudice will be wrought up against them because they are anarchists.

Anarchism, however, is a political theory having nothing in common with popular notions of bloodshed and riot,and is as much entitled to the right of free expression as any other political theory. Upon the broad basis of the right of free speech, which is the motherhood of all others, we appeal to all who believe in it, to assist morally and financially in their defense.

We make special request to all trade unions and labor organizations to bring the matter before their members as speedily as possible.

FREEDOM DEFENSE COMMITTEE:

GEORGE BROWN   E. GERSTINE

MARY HANSEM   PH. FINKLER

JOSEPH J. COHEN, Secretary
1619 S. Lawrence Street.

Figure 19: The Broad Street Riot

"The True History of the Broad Street Riot," leaflet produced by the Freedom Defense Committee (Joseph J. Cohen, Secretary), 1908

punishments left behind families for whom we felt obligated to provide the necessary food. We created a fund of recurring weekly payments, which some people undertook collections for every week, and for two and a half years the comrades helped support the families with three and a half dollars each week.

and placed in an asylum but released in October 1911 and returned to Italy. In December 1918 the home of the trial judge, Robert von Moschzisker, was bombed by Italian anarchists, presumably in retaliation for his role in this case.

Warrants were issued for the arrest of the speakers at the meeting, but police were in no hurry to carry them out and may not have known where to find the speakers (as they told the newspaper). On early Friday morning, a police guard was placed at the door of the Radical Library and did not allow anyone to enter. City Hall issued an order that no more anarchist rallies be held in Philadelphia. And who would dare defy City Hall?

On Sunday evening, we gathered in a big room above the Colonial Restaurant on Fifth Street, not far from the Radical Library. We organized a defense committee and hired the services of a good lawyer. We drafted a statement to the public, stating that the so-called riot had never occurred. Only the police had rioted, no one else. We openly declared that we would continue with our work and would not be intimidated by the unlawful actions of the police.

That same evening we actually called reporters from various newspapers and let them in on our secret: we had held a meeting under the very noses of the police, in spite of the strict ban. The next morning, the liberal newspapers came out with humorous stories describing how the anarchists played cat and mouse with the police, holding large gatherings while a lone policeman stood guard outside a building to which no one came. It worked. The guard from the Radical Library was immediately removed. We were free to use our own club rooms. When the speakers were subsequently arrested, we were prepared with a lawyer and enough bail money to release them immediately.

The hearing against the three speakers took place months later. They were freed without trial. No one served as a witness against them.

Substantial measures were required to prepare for the other defense campaign, in addition to the support we gave to the two families of those convicted. We left no stone unturned. As soon as the other accused were released, we set to work to obtain a new trial for the convicted Italians. We appealed the case all the way to the Supreme Court of the United States, which did not see any wrong in convicting innocent people without, in effect, a hearing—without a proper defense and without any factual evidence against them.[10] For us, there was no choice but to enter into a deal with

---

10. Cohen was secretary of the men's defense committee, which appealed the case to the Pennsylvania Board of Pardons. If it was indeed then appealed to the Supreme Court, the justices declined to hear the case.

the prosecutor to release the two Italians and allow them to return to Italy. The arrestees and their families were satisfied with such an arrangement. We covered their travel expenses, and they were released after serving two and a half years.

Immediately after the speakers' trial, Voltairine de Cleyre addressed an open letter to the public in which she discussed the whole episode: the plight of the unemployment, the brutality of the police, the injustice built into an entire society that makes such incidents possible, and the solution that we anarchists propose. We printed fifty thousand copies and distributed them one night in every corner of the city. Every member of the Radical Library participated in this worthwhile work.

Philadelphia was not the only city shaken by the crisis. In New York, the unemployed would assemble in Union Square and hold meetings there every Saturday afternoon. Week by week, the number of unemployed increased, and the speakers at the open-air meetings became more serious. The police soon prohibited the unemployed from using the space for their rallies and brutally broke them up. One Saturday afternoon a young comrade of ours, Selig Silverstein, was mortally wounded by a bomb he had intended for the police.[11] In his pocket was found a membership card for the Anarchist Federation, signed by its secretary Alexander Berkman. This was just what the police needed to start new raids on the anarchists. Although Selig lived for a few days after the incident, he did not incriminate anyone else for his deed.

---

11. **Selig Silverstein** (Zelig Zilbershteyn, 1889–1908), real name Selig Cohen (Zelig Kohen), was a Russian-born Jewish cloakmaker and anarchist. He immigrated the United States around 1899 and became an anarchist in New York. Silverstein suffered from an incurable heart condition and had been beaten by police at a protest in Union Square the previous week.

CHAPTER 23

Voltairine de Cleyre's Lectures and the Execution of Ferrer

Sometime after the police guard had been removed from the Radical Library and we were able to resume our activities, Voltairine de Cleyre prepared four lectures that we announced on a poster and made known throughout the city.

We had an easy and good way of distributing our advertisements. The radicals of Philadelphia were great lovers of music and opera, year in and year out. At a concert of the symphony orchestra or at an opera performance, we used to find our whole "family" gathered at the Academy of Music. The night before an opera, even in the middle of winter, our people would wait in line until the big day, when the sale of tickets for the gallery would begin. At a concert when seats were not reserved, our comrades would stand in line for half a day to get into the Academy before it was filled. Abe Brandschain, who took care of our publicity for many years, not only provided everyone with a flyer but also told them not to miss the announced meeting. If he did not encounter someone at the Academy, he did not mind visiting them at home or at work.

The first lecture was to take place in the big Washington Hall on Fourth and South Streets. When a few friends and I arrived, we found "our" police captain and a few of his aides standing at the door. He declared that he had an order from City Hall not to let anyone enter for the lecture. So I sent my friends away to both ends of the street, to tell everybody who was coming to the lecture to go to the Radical Library, and I was left alone with the police captain. I told him that I was waiting for Voltairine in order to escort her home.

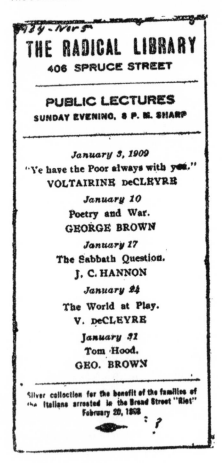

Figure 20: Lectures at the Radical Library
Flyer for lectures benefitting "the Italians
arrested in the Broad Street 'Riot,'" 1909

And so we stood conversing for quite a while. The captain began to wonder why no one was coming to the lecture, not even the speaker. I assured
him that it was still early—they would all come at once in a few minutes'
time. We stood around until half past nine at a door that nobody approached.
I excused myself to go home, leaving the police at the door of the hall for
another hour. But the captain insisted on following me. We came to the
Radical Library, which was then at 229 Pine Street, not far from the police

station, and found that the place was crowded with people. Voltairine had already finished her lecture and the audience was asking questions, as was our custom.

The captain was very much amused. He entered the library with me and sat down in a corner with a cigar in his mouth, listening to everything that was going on. He seldom missed coming to our classes on Sunday evenings and already had a usual spot by the wall where he used to sit and listen attentively to the speakers.

Voltairine's speeches were always erudite. She was one of the best speakers in our movement and used to prepare her lectures carefully on paper and read them aloud. Her lectures could be sent to the to the printer immediately for publication as good pamphlets. The series of lectures she presented for us consisted of:

1. "Anarchism and American Traditions," in which she proved that anarchism is not an imported ideology, but a product of American development since the Revolution.

2. "The Dominant Idea," in which she proved that in every epoch in history, one idea dominates the minds of the best and most talented people. At one time it was religion; at another time, it could be patriotism, imperialism, or the exploration of new, unknown regions of the world. The dominant idea of our time is the accumulation of wealth by any means possible—a clumsy materialist idea without any spiritual content.

3. "Direct Action"—a term that was then very much in fashion and that she translated into the correct anarchist viewpoint, as a way of life that encompasses all activities in which more and more people are interested.

4. "Ye Have the Poor Always with You"—a verse from the Torah, "for the poor shall never cease out of the land," that was used by robbers and rulers as a justification for their antisocial behavior.[1] In this lecture, Voltairine demonstrated how false and unfounded this view was in our time, when we already know how to create

---

1. Deuteronomy 15:11: "For the poor will never cease out of the land; therefore I command you, You shall open wide your hand to your brother, to the needy and to the poor, in the land."

abundant food and all other things. All of her lectures were a great success.[2]

❀ ❀ ❀

During the years of which I am writing, Voltairine was a teacher. Two nights a week I would go to her room after hours, get an hour-long lesson in English, and then spend the rest of the night discussing the movement and our activities. At that time Voltairine did not put much importance on revolution. She argued that the only means of uplifting and freeing people was education and enlightenment. I, in my naive Russian enthusiasm for revolution, tried to persuade her to my way of thinking. These discussions were long and lively. She was deeply interested in the details of the Russian revolutionary movement. All of my "compositions" in English needed to be written on that subject. In the summer, in addition to my lessons twice a week, she often accompanied me and my small family to Wissahickon, spending a day in the woods, and taking a seven- or eight-mile hike from Fairmount Park to Chestnut Hill, through wonderful forest trails with which she was very familiar. And the whole time we would discuss and debate revolution and evolution.

In 1910 Voltairine left Philadelphia. She undertook a lecture tour from New York to Chicago and all the cities in between, and she settled for a time in Chicago. There she became interested in the revolutionary activities of the Mexican anarchists, the Flores Magón brothers, who published the revolutionary anarchist newspaper *Regeneración* (Regeneration) in Los Angeles, and who were being hounded by the local authorities for their activity.[3] The paper contained an English page, edited by William C. Owen,

---

2. Versions of each of these lectures were later published in the *Selected Works of Voltairine de Cleyre* (1914).

3. **Ricardo Flores Magón** (1874–1922) and **Enrique Flores Magón** (1877–1954) were Mexican-born journalists and anarchists. Facing repression due to their opposition to President Porfirio Diaz, they fled to the United States in 1904 and in 1905 established the Partido Liberal Mexicano (Mexican Liberal Party, or PLM) which, despite its name, soon assumed an anarchist orientation. The brothers were repeatedly arrested for organizing uprisings in Mexico from afar, and in 1910 the PLM helped orchestrate the beginning of the Mexican Revolution, including a cross-border invasion of Tijuana in which dozens of American

which exuded revolution and fierce activity.[4] In our frequent correspondence, a complete change took place in our respective positions. Voltairine was resurrected, bursting with revolutionary zeal, while I approached the revolutionary outbursts of the inconsistent Mexicans coolly and skeptically. I was then engaged body and soul in educational work, in our Sunday school and planning to open a day school for children according to the model of Francisco Ferrer. I fully expected Voltairine to return to Philadelphia and take on the role of principal at the school. But her untimely death on June 20, 1912, ended those plans.

But I am getting ahead of myself. In the summer of 1909, the revolutionary situation in the world changed for the better. The Mexican Revolution, which in the beginning we did not take seriously, took on an anarchist tenor. The people began moving in a direction that was not acceptable to the politicians there and the rich oil companies here.

The Spanish government was conducting a war in Morocco, for which the workers and the masses, especially in Catalonia, saw no justification. Demonstrations against the war took place in some parts of Spain. The women in many cities lay down on the railroad tracks and tried to prevent the passage of trains transporting soldiers. In Catalonia, the demonstrations evolved into open rebellion against the government. And as was the fashion in Spain at the time of the uprising, the people turned their wrath on the Catholic churches and monasteries, which possessed the black power that held Spain in ignorance. When the uprising was suppressed, the government arrested Francisco Ferrer and blamed him for the whole insurrection, which

---

and European anarchists and IWW members participated. In 1918 the Flores Magóns were arrested for opposing the First World War and sent to Leavenworth Federal Penitentiary, where Ricardo died after a long illness. Enrique was released in 1923 and returned to Mexico, where he remained active in radical politics. *Regeneración* (1904–1906, 1910–1918) was the official organ of the Partido Liberal Mexicano and had a circulation of over twenty thousand copies at its height. By 1911 it had become an explicitly anarchist publication.

4. **William C. Owen** (1854–1929) was an Indian-born English journalist and anarchist. He immigrated to the United States in 1884 and quickly became involved in a succession of radical movements in California, eventually embracing anarchism in the 1890s. Owen became a staunch supporter of the Mexican Revolution and edited the English-language section of *Regeneración* as well as his own anarchist paper, *Land and Liberty* (1914–1915). He was briefly married to fellow anarchist Anuta Krimont. During the First World War, Owens supported the Allied war effort, but in 1916, facing possible deportation in connection with his involvement in *Regeneración*, he returned to England and joined the Freedom Group.

spread his name throughout the world and interested every radical person in his life and activity.

When the uprising began in Barcelona in 1909, Ferrer was in London. When he heard what was happening back in his home, he returned there and was arrested and imprisoned for several days in the Montjuïc Castle. This time the government made sure that he would not be able to get out of its clutches.

The court-martial selected as defense attorney a young officer who took an interest in his client and approached his job as defense counsel seriously, with the result that he was severely punished for his efforts. Ferrer was tried behind closed doors and had no opportunity to directly hear the witnesses who testified that they had seen him lead the uprising and set fire to churches. He was not given the opportunity to call witnesses to prove his innocence. He was sentenced to death, and before the wider world could protest this crime, the verdict was upheld. On October 13, 1909, Francisco Ferrer was put before a well-armed squadron of soldiers. His only request was not to have his eyes covered. Until his last breath, he wanted to view the world and the beauty of nature. His last words to the soldiers were: "Aim well, my friends. You are not responsible. Long live the Modern School!"

Ferrer's martyrdom shook the whole civilized world. Strong protests came from all countries, from the best sons of all nations, but to no avail. A few years later, when Ferrer's heirs sued the government for his property, which it had confiscated, a civil court took up the issue and ruled that the money had to be returned by the government. In other words, the civil court openly confirmed that the execution was an illegal murder by the state.

Understandably, our movement took part in the protests and held large demonstrations in every big city. In Philadelphia, these coincided with a fight we were then waging against the police for the right of Emma Goldman to speak in our town.

Goldman was already associated with Dr. Ben Reitman, who had become known to the radical world in 1908 when he organized a demonstration of the unemployed in Chicago. Ben was a very interesting guy: tall, large, and wide. With his head covered in thick black curly hair, on top of which sat a wide-brimmed hat, with a large, heavy cane in his hand, he drew attention to himself wherever he went. In his youth he had been a hobo riding the freight trains, tramping all over the country to the most abandoned places where the waste of society gathered. Later he studied medicine and became a physician and opened an office in Chicago. His patients were the poor, the neglected, the dejected, and the unwanted. Now he was intimately connected with Emma, traveling with her across the country on her lecture tours, selling literature at meetings, and bringing the spirit of American "ballyhoo" into the anarchist movement.

In a number cities across the country, Emma Goldman had difficulties with the police. In New York she was not bothered as much as elsewhere, but she had incidents there too. In the summer of 1909, Emma was scheduled to speak in West Orange, a small town in New Jersey. Local police intimidated the owner of the hall where the lecture was to be held and ordered him to lock the doors and not let anyone inside. Alden Freeman, a wealthy resident who had come to hear the terrible Emma, was upset by such outrageous behavior and on the spot invited the audience to go with him and hold the lecture in the large, comfortable garage that he had for his automobiles.[5] The lecture was held there. The police did not dare to interfere, for Alden Freeman was the son of the first treasurer of Standard Oil. Freeman then revived the Free Speech League and defended the right of Emma Goldman to speak in every city in the country.

Emma and Reitman came to Philadelphia, where for years the police had not allowed her to appear in public. They rented the Odd Fellows Temple, a large hall in the center of the city. The proprietor could not be intimidated to lock the doors and not permit anyone to enter. Here the police had to do their dirty work out in the open for everyone to see. On the eve of the rally, a squadron of police officers stood like a wall on the long flight of steps which led up to the entrance of the Odd Fellows Temple, right across from Broad Street, not far from City Hall, and did not allow Emma to enter the hall where a thousand people were waiting to hear her.

Some of us went to the hotel where Emma was staying to talk about the situation and her experiences with similar incidents. There we found quite a few single-taxers, distinguished gentlemen of Philadelphia who suggested that we anarchists apply a political-judicial strategy in this case: we should demand from the civil equity courts an injunction against the

---

5. **Alden Freeman** (1862–1937) was an American-born architect, philanthropist, and reformer. He later helped to fund the Ferrer Modern School in New York City.

police to prevent them from disturbing our business. The question, that is to say, should not be on the issue of free speech and the right of free assembly, which no court would want to hear, but on the accepted American basis of business. Emma was a lecturer, earning money from her speeches. Reitman was her manager, a businessman who invested money in renting halls, announcing the lectures, and similar expenses to make a profit—what could be more legitimate and honorable in America than profit? How dare the police interfere!

Such a case must be accepted by a court of equity (a court that deals exclusively with matters of money between two parties), and as it was simply a question of getting an injunction, the case would not drag on long.

We listened to the crazy plan, and at first we all arose in anger: What do you mean, we're going to tell on the devil to his mother-in-law (*onklogn dem tayvl far zayn shviger*)? How can we, anarchists, go to court, to a state institution, to ask for its protection and support! Emma was even more outraged and opposed to the plan than the rest of us. Gradually, however, the humor that could arise from the situation began to appeal to many of us. We let the matter hang in the air, and the end result was that a few days later Emma agreed to the plan of the single-taxers, and the lawyers began preparing the legal papers to present to the court.

Meanwhile, the Radical Library had moved to a big building at 424 Pine Street that housed the library, a larger lecture hall, and meeting rooms that were accessible. The library was not quite set up in the early fall of 1909, when we were dragged into protest meetings against the arrest and subsequent execution of Ferrer. After that came the conflict with the police because of Emma's visit, so we were overwhelmed with work. But until the court would accept our case, we decided to do our duty, and to do it our way, by calling a big protest meeting against the police, where prominent Philadelphians, not Emma, were invited to speak from the standpoint of free speech and free assembly. We rented the huge Industrial Hall on Broad Street and called the meeting for Sunday evening. Emma left for New York for a few days and Reitman remained to help us with the work.

Sunday evening I was standing near the new headquarters of the library when the captain of the police precinct passed by and greeted me. "What's taking place here tonight?" he asked me, to which I answered: "Nothing, the place is closed today." A few hours later, as I approached Industrial Hall,

I found a squadron of policemen blocking the entrance and "my" captain in civilian clothes directing the whole affair. In the street, hundreds of people soon gathered, having come for the rally, but the police did not allow anyone to loiter. I decided to lead the audience to the Radical Library and conduct the meeting there. I sent a message to Voltairine de Cleyre to go straight to the library and told all of the comrades that they should follow me and Reitman.

Past City Hall, through Broad and Pine Streets, we led a demonstration of five hundred people to the Radical Library, where the limited space was soon filled with people, shoulder to shoulder, standing in the hall and entrance (there were no more benches or chairs left in the building), and half of the audience stood in the street. Without a speaker, Reitman and I struggled to keep the audience together until Voltairine arrived. Thus, I gave my first talk in English to a large crowd. I quoted from the immortal words of John Milton, that one who suppresses the free expression of thought commits a crime worse than one who murders a man.[6] The Spanish government had murdered Ferrer's body, but it did not touch his spirit. The Philadelphia police were committing a great crime when they tried to oppress the free spirit of all those who seek a new world, a new idea. The next morning the liberal press took a serious stand on these points and considered them from all sides.

Suddenly the police appeared, with our captain at their head. Someone had let him know what was taking place, or he himself had noticed that no one was coming to Industrial Hall, and he permitted himself to leave. At any rate—here he was with his thugs. The police could not enter the building because it was too crowded; he divided his forces into two, one section going through the back alley into the courtyard of the library, and both groups physically dragged the assembled people one by one into the street and then drove them away. His explanation was that the floor of the building could not hold the weight of such a crowd. A great disaster could occur, and he needed to protect us from it.

I stood and watched the saboteurs at work. They did not injure anyone, but in a matter of minutes they were able to disperse the audience. The

---

6. **John Milton** (1608–1674), the English poet, wrote in his *Areopagitica* (1659): "And yet on the other hand, unlesse warinesse be us'd, as good almost kill a Man as kill a good Book; who kills a Man kills a reasonable creature, Gods Image; but hee who destroyes a good Booke, kills reason it selfe, kills the Image of God, as it were in the eye."

captain then asked me: "Why did you tell me that nothing was taking place today?" To which I answered: "You forced us to do it yourself. You did not let us enter Industrial Hall on Broad Street, so we had to come here, to our own home!" The inauguration of our new quarters was a great celebration—we were simply expelled from it.

A few days later, the hearing for an injunction against the police took place. We had one great satisfaction: we forced the mayor, John E. Reyburn, to come to court and explain why he ordered the police to prevent Emma Goldman from speaking in Philadelphia. The poor mayor was sweating profusely. He stated that on the day of the meeting he was riding home from New York, when someone told him that Emma Goldman was traveling to Philadelphia on the same train. "I sat down," said the mayor, "and thought: Philadelphia is a great city, quiet, peaceful. And here comes a woman from a foreign city, and she is able to upset peaceful people, causing the police to have to intervene, fight, crack skulls, and arrest people. Why do we need this? I saw no other way than to protect our city so that it could not happen!"

However, the court also questioned Emma, not so much about the riots she might have caused but instead about her ideas on law, the courts, and government institutions in general. The judgment of the court was that in a court of equity people must arrive with clean hands, with the clear intent to follow its judgement, to which they are entitled. In this instance, the court explained, this was not the case. "Those who turn to us do not believe in our justice or our right to judge. We cannot act on this matter!"

Regardless, at least we didn't go down without first explaining ourselves. But we did make fools of ourselves!

CHAPTER 24

The Radical Library Becomes a Branch of the Workmen's Circle

In 1908 all our plans to organize our own branch in the Workmen's Circle came to fruition. At the end of that year, there had been a lull in our activity. The Broad Street Riot, the victims of which we had to support and care for, overwhelmed us. We moved the Radical Library to 406 Spruce Street, the home of Dr. Segal's father, which was not very conducive to our general activity.[1] So we implemented the plan to establish our own Workmen's Circle branch.

This was not an easy task for us. The more established and prudent of us already belonged to various branches in the city. It was not easy to find, among the younger generation, twenty-five new members, as required by the Workmen's Circle. Besides, the local representatives of the organization, petty politicians, put all kinds of impediments in our path, in the hope that we would be discouraged and would then remain scattered and separated among in the general branches in which we, anarchists, were insignificant.

But we overcame all these hardships and, gathering our few pennies, we joined as the Radical Library, Branch 273 of the Workmen's Circle, which had definite rules for the payment of dues and expenses. We felt it would allow us to undertake greater work and develop a wider range of activities. Breathlessly, our perpetually impoverished comrade Samuel Hindin came running to join at the last moment. He was able to scare up the two dollars so that he would be counted among the organizers of the branch. For the first

---

1. **Aaron Segal** (1850–c. 1920), father of anarchist Julius Segal, was a Russian-born Hebrew teacher and widower. He and several of his children lived at 406 Spruce Street beginning around 1901.

time in her life, Voltairine de Cleyre formally joined an organization. She was older than the age limit set for joining, but, since we were organizing a new branch, this privilege was allowed.[2] We rented the big building at 424 Pine Street for fifty dollars a month and set up the library as well as meeting rooms that could by rented to friendly labor organizations.

The efforts of the fall of 1909, with the Emma Goldman riots and anxieties about the execution of Francisco Ferrer, undermined my health, and I was forced to spend several weeks in bed at my home in Fairmount Park, which was some distance from the Jewish section of town. Louis Segal and his family moved into the library to take care of the building and keep the books in order.[3]

A short time later, we accepted Benny Moore through a transfer from another branch. This almost caused a revolution within the branch. He was by then a boss, a bourgeois, who employed workers. The younger, doctrinaire comrades did not want him in their ranks as an equal member. It was kosher to work in his shop, learning a trade and making a living—many of them had been rescued by him during times of need. But to be a member of our branch, they argued, that was something else!

I stood up for him because I had never been a follower of the class struggle theory and, in this case, I recognized and appreciated his devotion to our movement and activity. He had remained an active member all those years and later became a bourgeois. And, as fate would have it, life later threw him back into the ranks of the proletariat, and who can say with certainty whether his activity in the movement played a role in undermining his position as a businessman?

Our branch prospered. The older comrades transferred from their general branches to our anarchist branch. A large number of young workers also joined our ranks. The International Ladies' Garment Workers' Union was well represented—cloakmakers, skirt makers, and ladies' waist makers—by

---

2. As a mutual aid society that provided healthcare, life insurance, and burial assistance, the Workmen's Circle required all new members to be between the ages of eighteen and forty. De Cleyre was forty-two years old at the time.

3. **Louis Segal** (Luis Sigel or Segal, 1877–1942) was a Russian-born garment worker, shopkeeper, and anarchist. He immigrated to Philadelphia in 1904 or 1905 and became a longtime member of Philadelphia's Radical Library, along with his wife Sarah (1869–1953). The couple's son, Louis Segal Jr. (1898–1978), attended the library's Sunday school. Obituary: *FAS*, September 11, 1942.

the Tsan brothers, I. Katz, William Puzis, Yossel Bluestein, Isidore and Sarah Kaplan, Samuel Hindin, Hyman Weinstock, Jack Bowman, Dave Cohen, Celia Melman, Dora, Yetta, Ada, Mina, and many others whose names I cannot now recall.[4] The very active Dave Forman, a cloakmaker, brought in members Sam Rothman, Bernard Shane, Louis Levy, Max Sandler, and many others.[5] We also had many tailors who joined the branch: William

---

4. A waist or shirtwaist was a popular style of blouse. **William Puzis** (Velvel Puzis, 1888–1976) was a Russian-born Jewish tailor and anarchist. He immigrated to the United States in 1907 and was, along with his wife Frances Puzis (née Ratner, 1891–?), a lifelong anarchist. The couple were active members of the Radical Library and subsequently in the anarchist colony at Stelton, the Sunrise Colony in Michigan, and the Kropotkin Literary Society, Branch 413 of the Workmen's Circle, in Los Angeles. Obituary: *FAS*, May 1, 1976. **Joseph ("Yossel") David Bluestein** (Yoysef "Yosel" Dovid Blushteyn, 1885– or 1890–1962), also known as David Bluestein, was a Russian-born Jewish garment worker, labor organizer, and anarchist. He was a member of New York Dressmakers' Local 22 of the ILGWU and the brother of anarchist Mendel Bluestein. Joseph married Mendel's ex-wife, anarchist Esther Bluestein (née Melman, c. 1890–?), and became the stepfather of her and Mendel's children, Abe (1909–1997) and Minnie Bluestein (1911–1971), both of whom were active members of New York's anarchist Vanguard Group in the 1930s. Joseph and Esther also had a daughter, May, and the couple moved to the Stelton Colony so that all three children could attend the Modern School there. Obituary: *Central New Jersey Home News*, January 7, 1962. **Isidore (or Israel) Kaplan** (Yisroel Kaplan, 1880–?) was a Russian-born Jewish housepainter and anarchist. In 1904 he immigrated to Philadelphia with his wife and fellow anarchist **Sarah Kaplan** (c. 1881–1935), née Schwartz. **Hyman Weinstock** (Vaynstok, c. 1886–1971) was a Russian-born Jewish tailor, grocer, and anarchist. He immigrated to the United States in 1903 and was soon involved in Philadelphia's Jewish labor movement, which led him into the anarchist movement and the Radical Library. He married fellow anarchist Minnie Weinstock. **David Cohen** was briefly arrested in 1908 following the Broad Street Riot (described in chapter 22). See *Philadelphia Inquirer*, February 22, 1908. **Celia Melman** (Sile Melman, c. 1891–1975) was a Russian-born Jewish garment worker and anarchist. She immigrated to the United States around 1907 and, along with her husband Harry Melman, was a member of the Radical Library and helped run Camp Germinal, which their daughter Ethel (1913–?) attended. Obituary: *FAS*, September 1, 1975. "Yetta" and "Mina" probably refer to Yetta London and Mina Finkler.

5. **Dave Forman** (Deyv Forman, 1882–?) was a Russian-born Jewish cloakmaker and anarchist who immigrated to the United States in 1894. **Sam Rothman** (Sem Rotman, c. 1885–1946) was a Russian-born Jewish cloakmaker, labor organizer, and anarchist. He immigrated to Philadelphia between 1900 and 1910 and became very active in the labor and anarchist movements. Rothman cofounded the Philadelphia Cloakmakers' Union in 1911–1912, and after moving to New York he remained an active rank-and-filer in both the anarchist movement and ILGWU Local 1 (later reorganized as Local 117) until his death. He was a member of the Anarchist Red Cross, the board of directors of the *FAS*, and the Ferrer Center Branch 203 of the Workmen's Circle. Obituaries: *FAS*, March 22 and April 19, 1946; *Justice*,

Shulman, Oscar and Muni Sharlip, Charles Saltz, Nathan Miller—all pants makers.[6] We also had wallpaper hangers Joseph Washkowitz, Samuel Telepman, the Lieberson brothers, Samuel Diskan, and Isaac Radinowsky.[7] There were also cigarmakers—Chaim Weinberg, my humble self, Nathan Navro, Aaron Miller, Sam Klonin, Abe Brandschain—and workers of other professions: Mendel (Max) Bluestein, Benjamin Axler, Harry Melman, Max

March 15, 1946. **Bernard Shane** (Sheyn, 1890–1975) was a Russian-born Jewish garment worker, union organizer, and anarchist. He immigrated to the United States in 1906 and was soon active in Philadelphia's anarchist movement and the ILGWU and later moved to New York where he helped with publication of *FAS*. Shane was sent as an ILGWU organizer to Chicago in 1931 and to Canada in 1934, where he remained until 1970. In Montreal he combated Communist garment trade unions, headed the Jewish Labor Committee of Canada, helped Jewish refugees immigrate after the Second World War, and became an ILGWU vice president in 1950. **Louis Levy** (Luis Livay, 1892–1951) was a Russian-born Jewish garment worker, labor organizer, and anarchist. He was working as a tailor by age ten and was radicalized during 1905 Russian Revolution. After immigrating to the United States in 1907, Levy joined the Radical Library and the ILGWU. In 1911 he moved to New York, where he married fellow anarchist Yetta Levy and served as manager of ILGWU Local 117 from 1930 to 1939. Levy became a vice president of the union in 1932, and from 1939 to 1949 he served as head of the ILGWU's Pacific Coast district. In Los Angeles, both he and Yetta were active members of Kropotkin Literary Society, Branch 413 of the Workmen's Circle. Obituary: *FAS*, June 22, 1951. **Max Sandler** (Maks Sendler, 1878–1953) was a Russian-born Jewish garment worker, labor organizer, and anarchist. He immigrated to the United States in 1904 and joined the Radical Library and the ILGWU. Throughout the 1910s Sandler was secretary or secretary-treasurer of Philadelphia's Cloak and Shirtmakers Union, and he remained active in the Radical Library until at least as late as 1936.

   6. **Charles Saltz** (Khone Zalts or Tsharls Saltz, 1882–1962) was a Russian-born Jewish tailor, butcher, and anarchist. He immigrated to the United States around 1901 and by 1930 had opened his own butcher shop, some of the proceeds of which he used to fund institutions in his hometown of Pochaiv (in present-day Ukraine). In 1908 he married fellow anarchist Rebecca Saltz. Following the Second World War, Saltz helped to produce the *Pitshayever yizkor bukh* (Pochaiv Memorial Book, 1960). **Nathan Miller** (Miler) was an official in the Pants Pressers' Union.

   7. **Samuel Telepman** (1871–1934) was a Russian-born Jewish paperhanger and anarchist. He immigrated to the United States around 1900 and by 1910 owned his own wallpapering business. Telepman was active in the anarchist movement from at least 1906 until 1928. **Isaac Lieberson** (Liberson, c. 1889–1961), **Samuel Lieberson** (c. 1892–1967), and **Hyman Lieberson** (1895–1968) were all Russian-born Jewish paperhangers and anarchists who immigrated to the United States between 1903 and 1909. **Isaac Radinowsky** (Yitzhak Radinovsky, c. 1892–1960) was a Russian-born Jewish paperhanger, construction foreman, and anarchist. He immigrated in 1907 and was active in the Jewish anarchist movement in Philadelphia and then New York and belonged to the Varhayt Group, the Union of Russian Workers, and later the Fraye Arbeter Shtime Group. Radinowsky cofounded the anarchist

Prussak, Gerson Goldstein, Harry Plotnick, and many others.[8] It was a real proletarian branch, representative of a variety of skills and occupations.

In June 1909 we experienced a streetcar strike in Philadelphia. It was a prelude to a bitter struggle barely a year later. This strike was settled quickly.

Stelton Colony, where his daughter Edith attended the Modern School; was treasurer of the United Libertarian Organizations during the Spanish Civil War; partnered with fellow anarchist Alexander Schapiro to send aid to Russia following the Second World War; and was president of the Fraye Arbeter Shtime Association at the time of his death. He eventually owned an apartment construction company in New York that specialized in building cooperative housing. Obituary: *FAS*, June 1, 1960.

8. **Nathan Navro** (1876–1947) was a Russian-born Jewish cigarmaker, cellist, and anarchist. He immigrated to the United States in 1893, became a close friend of Voltairine de Cleyre, and married Bessie Gerstine (1880–?), a nurse and fellow anarchist. The couple later moved to Manchester, New Hampshire, and then the single-tax colony at Arden, Delaware, where they ran the summer Hillside Nutrition Camp for children. **Aaron Miller** (Ahrn Miler, 1876–1954) was a Russian-born Jewish cigarmaker. He immigrated to the United States in 1895 with his wife and fellow anarchist Rebecca Miller. In 1931 the couple moved to New York, where Aaron served on the board of directors of the *FAS* and both were members of the Naye Gezelshaft Group, Branch 364 of the Workmen's Circle. Obituaries: *FAS*, July 2 and June 18, 1954. **Oscar Samuel ("Sam") Klonin** (Oskar Klanin, 1888–1969) was a Dutch-born Jewish cigarmaker, chemist, and anarchist. His Russian Jewish parents brought him from the Netherlands to the United States in 1891. Klonin and his wife Sarah (née Kaplan) later lived at the Stelton Colony, where their children attended the Modern School. In 1963 he moved to the Amalgamated Cooperative Apartment House in the Bronx and became a member of Ferrer-Rocker Branch 203 of the Workmen's Circle. Obituary: *FAS*, April 1, 1969. **Mendel ("Max") Bluestein** (Mendl Blushteyn, 1890–1957) was a Russian-born Jewish garment worker, labor organizer, and anarchist. Active in Russia's revolutionary movement at a young age, he fled to the United States in 1906 following the failed revolution and participated in the anarchist and labor movements in Philadelphia and later New York. He was the father of Abe and Minnie Bluestein, whose mother, anarchist Esther Bluestein (née Melman), later married Mendel's brother, Joseph David Bluestein. Mendel subsequently married anarchist Celia ("Shaindel") Kaplan (1895–1985), and the couple were founding members of the Stelton Colony, where their daughter Diana (1922–2003) was born and attended the Modern School. He wrote regularly for the *FAS* on labor matters and became manager of New York Dressmakers' Local 22 of the ILGWU. Mendel and Shaindel left Stelton in 1933 to help found the Sunrise Colony, where they oversaw the children's Living House. At the time of his death Mendel was still an anarchist and assistant manager of Local 22. Obituary: *FAS*, June 14, 1957. **Harry Melman** (c. 1889–1974) was a Russian-born Jewish news carrier and anarchist. He immigrated to the United States around 1910 and, along with his wife Celia Melman, became an active member of the Radical Library and Camp Germinal. Obituary: *FAS*, August 1, 1974. **Max Prussak** (Maks Prusak, 1886–?) was a Russian-born Jewish grocer, weaver, and anarchist. He immigrated to the United States in 1907 and later lived in Los Angeles, where he was a member of the Kropotkin Literary Society, Branch 413 of the Workmen's Circle.

The company gave in to the most important demands, but immediately after the settlement it began to organize its own union and to harass the workers who had been active in the strike.

One Saturday afternoon, Jack Bowman came to me and demanded to know what was going on: the library was not maintained as it should be, activities were neglected—how long could we continue like this? He had a plan: I would move into the library with my family, take over its supervision as in previous years, and revive the movement.

His words had an effect on me. We went immediately to the library to speak to Louis Segal, who was enthusiastic about the idea—he was already tired of living amid the tumult and was not satisfied with the condition of things. At a meeting that same week, the branch seized upon Bowman's proposal. We closed the library for a bit, cleaned and scrubbed the building from top to bottom with the voluntary labor of our members; carpenters, painters, and paperhangers came, and comrades washed the windows, floors, and every piece of wood throughout the building. The library was moved into the best rooms on the second floor, with better light for reading, and we celebrated the beginning of the winter season with extraordinary success.

From that day on, the library was abuzz with life for many years. The reading room was always full, except for the evenings when Enrico Caruso sang at the Academy of Music—with him we could not compete.[9] We held well-attended Yiddish lectures on Friday evenings, and lectures in English on Sunday evenings. A couple of other evenings in the middle of the week we had special classes to study English, Esperanto, and anarchism, and philosophy courses taught by Will Durant.[10] We paid him seven and a half

---

Gerson Goldstein (Gershon Goldshteyn, c. 1878–1936) was Romanian-born Jewish furniture worker and anarchist. He immigrated to the United States in 1910 and was active in the anarchist movement until his death. Obituary: *FAS*, November 6, 1936. **Harry Plotnick** (c. 1883–1957) was a Russian-born Jewish tailor and anarchist. He immigrated to the United States around 1903 and by 1920 had opened his own tailor shop. Plotnick was later active in the Jewish anarchist movement in Washington, DC, and died in Los Angeles.

9. **Enrico Caruso** (1873–1921) was an internationally famous Italian tenor and opera singer who made multiple tours of the United States.

10. **Will Durant** (1885–1981) was an American-born philosopher, historian, teacher, and socialist. He taught at the Ferrer Modern School in New York City from 1911 to 1913, until he fell in love with and married one of his students, Ariel Durant. He then served as director and lecturer at the Labor Temple School from 1914 to 1927 and completed a PhD in philosophy at Columbia University in 1917. Durant was later best known as the author, together with

dollars per lecture in those years, including his travel expenses from New York and back.

The work of the branch was well distributed among us. Abe Grosner devoted himself to giving the Sunday evening lectures in English and donating his musical talents for concerts.[11] Brandschain took care of publicity, announcements, and placing notices in the English newspapers. Every Saturday the *Philadelphia Bulletin*, the largest newspaper in the city, carried announcements of our library's events between notices for all the Sunday sermons in the churches and temples. A special committee oversaw the lectures in Yiddish. Still another committee had the responsibility of coordinating all these events. My task was to coordinate the work, clearing up misunderstandings between the committees and individual activists, and to see that everything ran smoothly, in addition to running the library. My wife Sophie was in charge of the building and the couple of meeting rooms that were used by the United Hebrew Trades and a number of other unions, as well as other Workmen's Circle branches.

The branch had officers as well as active members. The first secretary was comrade Charles Saltz, of whom the comrades, before they knew him well, were quite suspicious. He was tall and always neatly dressed, looking like he came from an entirely different world than men like Hindin and Dave Cohen, whose shoelaces never seemed to be tied. Saltz was precise and careful in his manners, as in everything he did. When he married and did not want to spend so much time on branch work, Gershon Goldstein took over the office, and as secretary for many years he carried out his duties in a highly satisfactory manner.

Ariel, of the eleven-volume *The Story of Civilization* (1935–1975), for which the couple won a Pulitzer Prize in 1968.

11. **Abraham ("Abe") Grosner** or Grossner (1892–1946) was a Russian-born Jewish teacher and anarchist. In 1906 his family immigrated to Philadelphia, where he began working as a language teacher and was an early member of the Radical Library, where he ran the radical Sunday school. In 1916 Grosner interrupted his graduate work in philosophy at the University of Pennsylvania to become a teacher and temporary principle at the Stelton Modern School. In 1924 he coedited *The Guardian: A Literary Monthly Published in Philadelphia*, for which he translated Yiddish poetry and wrote book reviews. Grosner subsequently moved to New York, where he became the manager of the *FAS* in 1929, associate editor of the anarchist paper *The Road to Freedom* in 1931, and taught at the Workmen's Circle school in nearby Lakewood, New Jersey. He also translated Jacob A. Maryson's *The Principles of Anarchism* (1935) into English. Obituary: *FAS*, July 26, 1946.

Branch meetings were held every week and were well attended. In a short time our branch numbered over a hundred members, and we became the most active cultural organization in Philadelphia. The only body to rival us in activity at that time was the Socialist Literary Society, under the leadership of a man who had the same name as me, Joseph E. Cohen.[12] People used to mix up our names and couldn't figure out who was who. On Sunday afternoons, the Socialist Literary Society held lectures in a theater much larger than ours. But we had a variety of activities that they did not even dare to attempt. The other Joseph Cohen's sister-in-law, Tema Camitta, was an important teacher in our Sunday school.[13] She openly admitted that she felt closer in spirit with our comrades than with the people of her husband's crowd.

We reestablished the Sunday school after the brief experiment initiated by comrades Benny Moore, Mary Hansen, and Mina Finkler sometime earlier. In our hands, the school grew and became a vibrant area of activity. Over a hundred pupils, many of them children of conservative parents in the neighborhood, used to regularly spend the whole day with us, attending various classes.

A few comrades did not see any sense or logic in us trying to educate the children of conservative parents. Most of us, however, came to understand that these children were, in a sense, more important for us to reach than children of radical parents who enjoyed a favorable radical environment at home. The children enjoyed almost the entire day. First was assembly, with the singing of songs by William Morris, and then there were special classes in drawing, sculpting, hygiene, et cetera.[14] Afterward, the older children had their own discussion group, led by their own chairman and organizer. Often

---

12. **Joseph E. Cohen** (1883–1950) was an American-born Jewish printer, labor organizer, and socialist. He was a member of the International Typographical Union, wrote for several Socialist Party publications, and authored the book *Socialism for Students* (1910). Beginning in the 1930s Cohen was involved in the CIO and campaigned on behalf of Franklin D. Roosevelt's reelection. The similarity between his and Joseph J. Cohen's names confused even the Bureau of Investigation, which believed both to be the same man.

13. **Tema Camitta Cohen** (1890–1977), later Tema Camitta Caylor, was the American-born wife of socialist George N. Cohen (who later went by George N. Caylor), the brother of Joseph E. Cohen. In 1912 she traveled to Lawrence, Massachusetts, during the IWW-led strike there and helped organize the transportation of strikers' children to stay with sympathizers outside of that city, and she later testified about her experience before Congress (where she coyly described herself as "a Sunday school teacher").

14. **William Morris** (1834–1896) was an English craftsman, poet, writer, and socialist.

I would attend the meetings, sitting among the children in a small chair and listening to the discussion, not interfering except when the conversation was running out of steam or getting off track. Then I would say a few words to get the ball rolling again down its desired path. It was one of the greatest pleasures to watch the development of the children. Among them were Ray Miller, Matthew Moore, Emma Avedon (Bessie Yelensky's sister), Heloise Brown, Yetta Kaplan, Louis Segal Jr., Dora Druker and her sister, my own daughter Emma Cohen, and dozens of others.[15]

Never missing a Sunday, older comrades, some of the students' fathers, and some other young people would come to help clean the classrooms and then the whole building for the evening, for the big gatherings and lectures

He was a major figure of the Arts and Crafts Movement and cofounded the Socialist League in 1884. Although a Marxist, Morris befriended anarchists like Peter Kropotkin and Stepniak, and his socialism bore a strong libertarian streak.

15. **Ray Miller** (1903–?), later Ray Shedlovsky, was the daughter of anarchists Aaron Miller and Rebecca Miller. She later attended the Ferrer School in Stelton. **Matthew T. Moore** (1902–1997) was the son of anarchists Sarah Moore and Benny Moore. He became a physician and professor of neurology at Temple University. **Emma Avedon** (1901–1977), later Emma Favia, was a Russian-born Jewish anarchist. She immigrated to Philadelphia with her siblings and widowed mother in 1908. By the 1920s Avedon was living in Chicago, where she belonged to the Anarchist Red Cross and married Italian anarchist tailor Domenic (or Dominick) Favia (1902–1980). In the 1940s and 1950s the couple was active in the Alexander Berkman Aid Fund. She was the sister of both Bessie Yelensky and Endel ("Anna") Weinberg. **Bessie Yelensky** (1889–1968), née Avedon, was a Russian-born Jewish anarchist. She joined the Bund at age fourteen and then in 1908 immigrated with her siblings and widowed mother to Philadelphia, where she joined the Radical Library Group and Anarchist Red Cross. She married fellow anarchist Boris Yelensky, and the couple moved to Chicago in 1913; they returned to Russia in 1917 following the February Revolution but in 1923 came back to Chicago. There Bessie participated in the Alexander Berkman Aid Fund and served as secretary of the Free Society Group and the women's auxiliary of Chicago's Branch 65 of the Workmen's Circle. Yelensky moved to Miami in 1959. She was the sister of Emma Avedon and Endel ("Anna") Weinberg. Obituary: *FAS*, July 1, 1969. **Heloise Hansen Brown** (1904–1975) was the daughter of anarchists Mary Hansen and George Brown. She later attended the Ferrer Modern School in New York and then Stelton, worked as a waitress at one of Romany Marie's cafés, and briefly married the socialist writer Berkeley Greene Tobey (1881–1962), whose numerous other ex-wives include Margaret Sanger and Catholic anarchist Dorothy Day (1897–1980). According to census records, **Dora Druker** (1896–?) was one of seven Russian-born daughters of Jewish immigrants Nathan Druker (Drukerowitz or Drukerovits, 1865–?) and Yetta ("Ida") Druker (1865–?), née Katz. **Emma Cohen** (1904–1986), later Emma Cohen Gilbert, was the daughter of Joseph and Sophie Cohen and was named after Emma Goldman. She later attended the Ferrer Modern School in New York City and then Stelton and eventually became a child psychologist.

that used to have music from a good quartet as an introduction. Later we introduced Saturday afternoon classes for the children in dance and the dramatic arts. The library was full of life from Friday night until Sunday after midnight, as well as every weekday evening. In addition to members, we had many library subscribers, who could borrow books to read for twenty-five cents a month. We also began to sell books and art postcards, which were then in vogue.

Among the lecturers we often hosted were professor Scott Nearing, who was later dismissed from his university for his radicalism, and other professors, as well as our own lecturers from New York: Leonard D. Abbot, Harry Kelly, John R. Coryell, Bolton Hall, Sadakichi Hartmann (who was half German, half Japanese), James F. Morton Jr., Hippolyte Havel, and others.[16] Our library was famous throughout the country for its good facilities, organization, and successful activity.

---

16. **Scott Nearing** (1883–1983) was an American-born economist, writer, pacifist, and socialist. He lost his professorship in economics at the University of Pennsylvania's Wharton School of Business in 1915 due to his radical ideas and became a prominent public intellectual. Nearing joined the Socialist Party in 1917 then in 1927 joined the Communist Party but was expelled in 1930 for deviating from party orthodoxy. He later advocated self-sufficient rural homesteading as an alternative to capitalism. **Leonard D. Abbott** (1878–1953) was an English-born editor, single-taxer, and anarchist. His parents were American expatriates, and in 1897 he immigrated to the United States, where he joined the Freethought movement and Socialist Party and subsequently became an anarchist. Abbott served as president of the Free Speech League, coedited the anarchist paper *Free Comrade* (1910–1912), and cofounded the Francisco Ferrer Association and the Stelton Colony. His wife, Rose Yuster (1887–1930), was a Romanian-born Jewish anarchist and sister of Romany Marie. **Bolton Hall** (1854–1938) was an Irish-born attorney, writer, single-taxer, and anarchist. After his family immigrated to the United States in 1868, he earned his law degree from Columbia University and became an official in the short-lived American Longshoremen's Union. Hall wrote widely on land reform and the single tax, and in 1910 he founded Free Acres, a single-tax colony in Berkeley Heights, New Jersey. He was also strongly influenced by American individualist anarchist Benjamin Tucker and became a member of the Free Speech League and the Francisco Ferrer Association as well as a close friend of Emma Goldman and a supporter of the anarchist journal *Man!* **Sadakichi Hartmann** (1867–1944) was a Japanese-born art critic, poet, playwright, and anarchist. The son of a Japanese mother and a German father, he was raised in Germany before immigrating to the United States in 1882. Hartman became a well-known modern art critic and poet (penning some of the earliest haiku to be written in English), while also contributing to *Mother Earth* and other radical publications. He moved to Los Angeles in the 1920s and had a small role in the 1927 film *The Thief of Baghdad*. **James F. Morton Jr.** (1870–1941) was an American-born journalist, civil rights advocate, and anarchist. A college classmate and friend of W. E. B. Du Bois, he was a member of the National Association for

Expenses for rent, heating, lighting, and cleaning the building, and paying teachers for the Sunday school and lecturers and the like, came to over $300 a month, and for many years this sum was raised from entrance fees, rent, and other ventures. We were successful in every respect. Most important was the friendly spirit. The work was a success in all regards.

The spirit that prevailed among the members was generally satisfactory. They were like one big family in the best sense of the word. Most called each other by their first names. There were no serious quarrels, no cliques, no factions or opposition. Some devoted themselves to circulating the *Arbeter fraynd*, some worked for *Mother Earth*, some for the *Fraye arbeter shtime*, or even the "Fraye Gezelshaft Clubs"—Yanovsky's special creation. Everyone, however, worked in solidarity for the library and responded to every appeal.

At one branch meeting, I said that Voltairine de Cleyre had told me she needed money for an important purpose. I had not asked what the purpose was, and the comrades at the meeting did not ask me either, but they emptied their pockets on the spot and we collected over $100. For a small gathering of workers, that was a hefty sum in those years.

Once on Yom Kippur at our Kol Nidre meeting at Odd Fellows Temple, I had an unusual experience. The large auditorium was filled with people. The massive doors to the auditorium, where there were tables with our literature for sale, were wide open. Voltairine was sitting on the platform, waiting to speak. Suddenly the head of the Philadelphia police, Mr. Stone, appeared and asked me: "Who is that woman seated on the platform, and what is she doing here?"

I explained to him: "She is the main speaker of our evening."

---

the Advancement of Colored People, spoke and wrote widely on racism, and published the antiracist pamphlet *The Curse of Race Prejudice* (c. 1906). Morton also lectured on women's rights and anarchism, contributed to anarchist publications including *Free Society, Lucifer, the Light Bearer,* and *Mother Earth,* and was an editor of *Free Society, The Demonstrator,* and *Discontent* (1898–1902). He lived for a time in the Home Colony in Washington and later in life became a close friend of writer H. P. Lovecraft and a member of the Bahá'í faith. **Hippolyte Havel** (1869–1950) was an Austrian Bohemian-born activist, writer, editor, and anarchist. He joined the anarchist movement in Bohemia as a teenager and was arrested multiple times for his activities before relocating to England. In 1899 Havel met and began a relationship with Emma Goldman and came to the United States with her the following year. He was a prolific writer for radical publications, edited *The Revolutionary Almanac* (1914) and *Revolt* (1916), and helped produce Goldman's *Mother Earth, The Social War* (1917), and *The Road to Freedom.* From 1925 until his death Havel lived at the Kropotkin Library in the Stelton Colony.

With all his effort, he commanded me in a very firm tone: "Go, tell her not to talk; I will not allow it!"

I looked him square in the eye and said: "I shall not do so under any circumstances. You go tell her yourself."

He began to argue. "You certainly do not want any disturbance at such a big meeting! Tell her that she cannot speak, and then you can continue peacefully with your meeting. Otherwise, I will be forced to shut down this whole meeting."

"Of course," I explained to him, "I do not want the meeting to be disrupted, and from our side, as far as I can see, nothing is being done that would lead to such an event. The meeting is peaceful and orderly; what more can you ask of us? We can't stop you from breaking up the assembly—the power is in your hands—but it is impossible for me to carry out your command. All these people have come to listen to Voltairine, and they have every right to hear what she has to say."

The chairman of the evening, George Brown, noticed our conversation in the foyer from the platform and hurriedly opened the meeting and introduced Voltairine, who was received with great enthusiasm. Mr. Stone waived his hand and left without a sound. He did not have the courage to break up such a large gathering.

❋ ❋ ❋

At that time in Philadelphia there was a revival of the Jewish social democratic movement. B. Charney Vladeck was sent from New York to run the local office of the *Forverts*, bringing life and activity back to their ranks. Every Sunday afternoon he conducted an open forum in a big movie theater on South Street owned by a comrade, A. J. Margolin, a wealthy real estate man.[17]

---

17. **Abraham J. Margolin** (1863–1917) was a Russian-born Jewish real estate broker, attorney, and socialist. Active in revolutionary circles as a teenager, he was arrested at age nineteen and sentenced to Siberian exile, escaping to the United States around 1891. Margolin became a successful businessman in Philadelphia but remained a radical until his death; he was a longtime member of the Socialist Party, lectured on radical topics, founded the North American Co-operative League, and was active in the Cooperative League of America. He also donated money to *Mother Earth*, and Cohen's description of him as "a comrade" suggests he was affiliated with Philadelphia's anarchists. In 1917 Margolin, in declining health, took his

Vladeck used to bring good lecturers from New York and was himself one of the best speakers of the Jewish working-class movement—he was called the "Young Lassalle."

One winter, he came up with the idea that he and I should have a debate on the question: "Can parliamentary action benefit the labor movement?" I told him the truth, that I had no desire to debate with him, especially in his own church (*shul*), where he had his own community of religious followers (*Hasidim*). I knew that I could not compare to his great oratorical talent, but I was simply ashamed to refuse his challenge. On the bright side, he was the first to present his arguments to the huge crowd of people, and stated, among other things, that politics, especially here in this country, is a dirty business in which few decent persons are willing to participate, yet workers could gain something from it, et cetera.

This provided me with an effective introduction to my response, which provoked considerable applause from those present and put him in a defensive position, having to defend and explain his own previous statements. It reiterated and confirmed the old tradition of the working masses in Philadelphia being more inclined to the anarchist way of thinking than to the state-socialist way.

---

own life, leaving behind an estate said to be worth over a million dollars. Obituary: *Forverts*, January 31, 1917.

CHAPTER 25

The Streetcar Strike and Its Consequences

On February 19, 1910, the Philadelphia Rapid Transit Company laid off six hundred active union members.[1] A new streetcar strike broke out, this time a very serious one. Streetcar strikes always and everywhere evoke great excitement—the shameful scabbing is done publicly, for all to see, and this sours the mood.

The police could not handle the unrest. At first the militia was called out, composed of young men from the city, many of them only workers, who were not enthusiastic about their task. They would let the girls surround them on all sides while the men took care of the scabs trying to run the streetcars. The city government then brought in the Pennsylvania Constabulary, well-to-do mounted Cossacks, who kept order in the mine districts, a few of whom paid with their lives for their energetic efforts during that strike.

Then Mr. Henry Clay, director of public safety, himself a partner in the streetcar company, came up with a brilliant idea: he hired a couple thousand Negroes as policemen, gave them clubs and guns, and filled the streets with them to keep order.[2] This brought the issue of race to the forefront and made the situation even more serious. Hundreds of earnest men were arrested every day, and Mr. Clay had them brought before a very strict judge—one who could not be bribed or swayed by political leverage.

---

1. Cohen's figure is inflated; the actual number of union members reported to have been fired was 173.

2. **Henry Clay** (c. 1850–1926) was an independent politician who served as Philadelphia's director of public safety from 1907 to 1911. In 1909 he had barred Emma Goldman from speaking in the city, and in 1911 he would be convicted of conspiracy to embezzle city funds from public building projects, though the verdict was overturned on appeal.

One evening, Mrs. Segal came to me with a small child in her arms and wept, crying that her husband, Louis Segal, had been arrested on charges of participating in a riot and assaulting a policeman. I had to save her husband for her! In ordinary times this would have been not too difficult a task. "My" police captain would gladly help me in such a case. Even then, in this most serious moment, he made an attempt. He took me to a political club, introduced me to a very powerful boss of the Republican Party machine, and asked for a personal favor on my behalf. But the boss, after listening to me, ashamedly told me that even he could not help. Mr. Clay had too much interest in the streetcar company. He followed every aspect of the strike, and he had no pull with either Clay or Judge Scott with which to help a friend.

I tried to get an appointment with the judge through his lacky—an ambitious Jewish politician. I offered him $200 for this small favor. He answered quite simply that he would gladly "earn" a few dollars, but it would be a wasted effort. Neither he nor anybody else could help. Our lawyer friends did not want to be involved the case. For two days and nights I worked tirelessly on the case, running from one politician to another for further recommendations and advice, but to no avail. In the last hour before the hearing, I went to a famous criminal lawyer in the *Bulletin* building, near City Hall, and told him the story. I had never met the man before and had no recommendation for him. But he became interested in the case and went immediately to City Hall with me, to the hearing.

There, my comrade Segal, bandaged and beaten, was soon brought before the stern judge. The police had wreaked their vengeance once they got their hands on him. Three large, fat policemen, of the old-fashioned type, stood up one after the other, swearing and testifying that the defendant had stopped them from doing their duty, had struck them with murderous blows, torn at their uniforms, and delivered beatings they were still recovering from.

Our lawyer listened to them, and did not ask any questions, but when all three of them were finished, he stood up and addressed the judge with the words: "Your Honor, can you believe that this little Jew"—Segal was a middle-aged man, and in court he sat huddled in a heap from the blows he had received—"struck these three large, healthy, armed policemen holding large clubs in their hands? They ought to be ashamed to come here and tell us such a story. If it is true, then it proves that none of them is suitable for holding his job as a law enforcement officer!"

The stern judge agreed with him, reprimanded the officers, and let Segal go home. He only told him to avoid falling into the clutches of the police a second time.

※ ※ ※

Meanwhile, agitation grew in working-class circles. There was talk of a general strike of all the workers in the city. Such a thing had happened in Philadelphia in 1835 and had brought the desired results.[3] On the Sunday afternoon of February 27, thousands of workers converged on the headquarters of the cigarmakers' union at 232 North Ninth Street (which a few years later became the headquarters of the Cloakmakers' Union), where the Central Labor Union was then meeting.[4] After a long wait outside, we learned that the Central Labor Union had decided to call a general strike, but there was a hitch: it had decided to begin the strike the following Saturday, the fourth of March.

During the week, I had an unhappy experience with my peers: I had called together some of our most active comrades, pointing out that under the circumstances it was necessary to distribute a large leaflet in which we should explain the character and goal of a general strike, in order to lead the popular movement in a revolutionary direction.

The comrades listened to me and rejected my proposal. The situation was too dire, and Segal's experience was fresh in their minds. They refused to take such dangerous steps.

I was more successful in my union.[5] I brought with me a number of young workers from the shop I worked in, the largest in town, and we were placed at the head of the meeting at which we kept hammering home, one after the other, the necessity of showing our solidarity with the strikers and obeying the call for a general strike, despite the fact that our union's

---

3. The 1835 Philadelphia general strike, considered by many historians to be the first general strike in North America, won all its demands, including a ten-hour workday.

4. The **Central Labor Union of Philadelphia and Vicinity** was a progressive local labor body founded in 1902, composed of local affiliates of both the AFL and non-AFL unions.

5. Cohen was a member of the Cigar Makers' International Union.

constitution prohibited such strikes. We won. The union thus voted in support by a large majority.

But here too I was doomed to be disappointed: a few days later, in the course of the general strike, when the excitement in the city was even greater than before, I came upon a large cigar factory that employed several hundred girls at machines. I got to work and soon told the girls to join the strike. Every single one left work together in the middle of the day and followed me to the union hall.

Imagine my disappointment when I was reminded that cigar machine workers were not accepted as members of our union! Our brilliant leaders, Samuel Gompers among them, had decided many years before, when Oscar Hammerstein first invented the cigar-making machine and offered control over it to the union, to refuse to have machines in their aristocratic profession.[6] The result, of course, was that the machines took over the industry and took away the work of the aristocrats. Now I was forced to tell hundreds of young women to return to work during a general strike. The union did not want to include them or have contact with them.

The general strike was a failure. The Central Labor Union's most important sectors—heating, lighting, water, and food—remained at work. The printers, bricklayers, and others refused to strike because it was against their contracts. Only the nonessential trades, without which one can go on for many months, went entirely on strike. One afternoon an attempt was made to lead a protest demonstration of fifty thousand strikers through Broad Street to Shibe Park on Lehigh Avenue. When the demonstration passed through Hahnemann Medical College, the students hooted and hollered like wild animals. They applauded the brutal attacks of the police, who attempted

---

6. **Samuel Gompers** (1850–1924) was an English-born Jewish cigarmaker and union organizer. After his family immigrated to New York in 1863, he joined the Cigar Makers International Union, of which he became a vice president in 1886. That same year Gompers helped found the AFL, of which he served as president virtually uninterrupted until his death. Despite an early attraction to Marxism and the single tax, Gompers became a conservative labor leader who eschewed political affiliations, opposed immigration, promoted class harmony, and prioritized protecting the job security and wages of skilled, white, male workers. Oddly, anarchist Dyer D. Lum and former anarchist Lucy Fox Robins (later Lucy Robins Lang) both worked stints as his personal secretary. **Oscar Hammerstein** (1846–1919) was a German-born Jewish cigar manufacturer and patron of the arts. He was the father of producer and songwriter Arthur Hammerstein and grandfather of lyricist Oscar Hammerstein II.

to disperse the march. This was also attempted when the demonstration reached Columbia Avenue. Small groups were forcibly driven down side streets by mounted police and not allowed to return to Broad Street.

The strike, however, was settled very soon with a compromise that was only partially beneficial to the workers. The famous "Mitten Plan" was established, which was supposed to make the workers part owners of the company and give them "seniority" rights.[7] The old-fashioned open platform cars, on which the motormen and conductors used to stand in the worst weather, exposed to cold and moisture, were done away with. And most importantly, it eliminated the split shift, which would keep a worker all day in the car barn in order to get four or six work hours of work in separate installments of an hour or two. The general strike had its effect but not the effect we expected.

Voltairine de Cleyre discussed the good and bad sides of the general strike in *Mother Earth* in April 1910, concluding that the workers needed to change their tactics: instead of going out on strike, they needed to enter the factories and sit there at their machines, so that no scabs could take their places.[8] This is, as far as I know, the first mention of the effectiveness of a "sit-down strike," which emerged from our ranks and which, twenty-five years later, proved to be so effective in the struggles of the automobile workers in Michigan.[9]

---

7. Named for Philadelphia Rapid Transit president Thomas Mitten (1862–1929), the **Mitten Plan** combined welfare capitalism, employee stock ownership, and a company union, and it remained in place until the Great Depression.

8. Voltairine de Cleyre, "A Study of the General Strike in Philadelphia," *Mother Earth*, April 1910, 39–44. De Cleyre wrote: "Do they perceive, do the workers perceive, that it must be the strike which will stay in the factory, not go out? which will guard the machines, and allow no scab to touch them? which will organize, not to inflict deprivation on itself, but on the enemy? which will take over industry and operate it for the workers, not for franchise holders, stockholders, and office-holders? Do they? Or will it take a few thousand more clubbings to knock it into their heads?"

9. There are earlier examples of sit-down strikes in the United States, including a 1906 IWW strike at a General Electric plant in Schenectady, New York.

CHAPTER 26

Two Conventions of the Workmen's Circle

In the spring of 1909 I was sent by our branch as a delegate to the Workmen's Circle convention in Baltimore. Along with the other Philadelphia delegates, I boarded a train that carried delegates from New York and New England in two separate cars. It was lively and noisy in them, like a small village fair. Jeheil Weintraub, then the general secretary of the order, who later proved to be a petty thief, was busy gossiping with the delegates.[1] Harris Goldin, the president and an employee of the *Forverts*, was circulating here and there with a bottle of liquor.[2] There was tension in the air. The writers for the *Forverts* were on strike, and the publishers warned in advance that the question of the strike would not be brought up at the convention.

Baltimore did not make a favorable impression upon me. Compared to Philadelphia, it looked like a dilapidated village. The streets in the impoverished neighborhoods around East Baltimore Street, where the convention was being held, were not paved, and there were no sewers. Waste was poured into open gutters along the sides of the streets. Every third or fourth house was a saloon where women, many of them Jewish, sold beer and whiskey to Negro patrons. The whole atmosphere of the Jewish quarter was old-fashioned, a retrogression.

---

1. **Jeheil Weintraub** (Yekhiel Vayntroyb, 1879–1938) was a Russian-born Jewish weaver, journalist, and socialist. He was general secretary of the Workmen's Circle from 1905 to 1913 but resigned after he was found to have embezzled funds. Weintraub later became a silk factory owner.

2. **Harris Goldin** was president of the Workmen's Circle from 1905 to 1908.

Baltimore had occupied a prominent place in our movement years before, in the 1890s. Dr. Michael A. Cohn had studied medicine at the university there and led a strong movement through which he had clashed with the Orthodox Jews and even the law. He carried on vigorous propaganda, especially an antireligious campaign, which caused a furor in the city. There used to be a joke that he was once arrested after an antireligious gathering and spent a night in the police station. This gave him enough material to write a long series of articles about his "experiences in prison." Around 1904, comrade Sam Mendelsohn came to Baltimore. A London comrade who was then active in New York for a couple of years, Mendelsohn had rolled a push-cart piled with bundles of the *Fraye arbeter shtime* from the print shop on Duane Street to the office at 24 Rutgers Street. In Baltimore, he sought out two comrades, Bayer and Ratkowitz, and together they recruited members for a group.

The group used to organize lectures and sell a lot of literature. In the winter of 1906–1907, Mendelsohn and Michaelson were arrested for selling *Broyt un frayheyt* at a large Sunday evening lecture by Emma Goldman. A Jewish policeman by the name of Barnett Berman, who was a former presser, arrested them for selling a newspaper that preached violence and revolution. The two comrades were held in jail for a day, naturally creating quite a bit of anxiety. The judge in front of whom they were tried ruled that a salesman is not responsible for the contents of the paper he sells. From this group later grew Branch 67 of the Workmen's Circle, which did much good work for our movement.

The group was able to attract some the older comrades: Shaltiel, Zeligman, Hyman Yaffe, Fox, and others.[3] There were also new, younger comrades—Reuben Feldman (who moved to the Deep South), Max Radin (who later lived for many years in San Diego), Slavin, Saltz, Berlinger, Harry Plotnick, Landau (whose son the pious rabbis had circumcised after his death), and Benjamin (Boris) Surasky.[4]

---

3. **Hyman Yaffe** (Hayman Yafe, 1880–1959) was a Russian-born Jewish shoemaker and anarchist. He was active in the Jewish anarchist movement in London before immigrating to the United States, where he was a member of Baltimore's anarchist Educational League. He later lived in Los Angeles, where he was an active member of the Rocker Publications Committee and the Sh. Yanovsky Kultur-Komitet. Obituary: *FAS*, January 1, 1960.

4. **Reuben Feldman** (died 1948) was an official in the Workmen's Circle of Maryland,

The latter was still a green, young, unassuming worker, in whom I saw great potential for development and activity. I encouraged him; he wanted to read and learn, so that he could be useful to the movement. This group gathered together the anarchist delegates from various cities and provided us with accommodations for the week and, during our free evenings, with meetings regarding our movement.

The convention was a tense one. The participants sought to give the impression to the outside world that everything was peaceful and tranquil within the order. The inaugural parade through the streets, the opening of convention, and the banquets were carried on with great fanfare, but at the business meetings the mood was belligerent. Morris Winchevsky came to address the convention on behalf of the striking writers of the *Forverts*; but he, the "grandfather" of the Jewish socialist movement, was not allowed to speak. This angered the younger delegates. They arranged another meeting for him in a separate location, but officially the question of the strike was banned at the convention.

That convention was historic in one regard. There, against the wishes of the conservative, frightened elements in the organization, it was decided to open a sanatorium for members suffering from the terrible proletarian disease [i.e., tuberculosis]. The opposition to the plan stemmed from fears that the Workmen's Circle would not be able to sustain such an institution, which required huge expenditures and costly medical equipment. At the time of its founding and for many years afterward, the sanatorium was the exemplar of the Workmen's Circle and a lifesaver for many members.[5]

A year later, in 1910, I was again a delegate to the convention in New York. This time I was elected not by my branch but by the Philadelphia

and later lived in Atlanta. Obituaries: *FAS*, October 15 and November 17, 1948. **Max Radin** (died 1944) was a Russian-born Jewish tailor and anarchist. He immigrated to the United States around 1906. In Baltimore Radin joined the Frayheyt Group and helped form a tailor's union and a branch of the Workmen's Circle. In San Diego, he opened a department store and was an active member of Los Angeles's Kropotkin Literary Society, Branch 413 of the Workmen's Circle. Obituary: *FAS*, September 29, 1944. **Benjamin ("Boris") Surasky** (1889–1972) was a Russian-born Jewish garment worker, labor organizer, and anarchist. He lived at various times in Baltimore, New York, Israel, and Los Angeles. Surasky was an agent for the *FAS* and an organizer for the ILGWU, and he belonged to the Kropotkin Literary Society, Branch 413 of the Workmen's Circle. Obituary: *FAS*, April 1, 1972.

5. The Workmen's Circle opened its sanitarium in Liberty, New York, in 1910.

membership in general. The convention was considered a small one, composed of 110 delegates. Philadelphia was entitled to send five delegates, representing all the branches combined, and, of all the nominated candidates, I received the highest number of votes. In those years I was very active in the Workmen's Circle and quite popular among the membership.

At the convention it was evident that more than half the delegates were directly associated with the *Forverts*, acting as a single body under the leadership of Abe Epstein and steamrolling their way through the proceedings, which was not so easy this time.[6] The two most important questions before the convention provoked sharp differences of opinion and lengthy debates: the question of publishing a monthly magazine, which was opposed by those affiliated with the *Tsukunft*, who feared competition from a new publication, and the question of renting a main office for the Workmen's Circle in the ten-story *Forverts* building, which was then under construction.

This second question provoked a great deal of discussion, which led to an extraordinarily long afternoon meeting. A number of delegates objected to the close collaboration between the Workmen's Circle and the *Forverts*; others dreamed of our own Workmen's Circle building in New York, which would serve the libertarian movement. For many years Leo Rosenzweig had campaigned for the construction of a Freethought Temple in New York. We saw in the Workmen's Circle the capacity to undertake such an endeavor. The meeting decided by a majority vote against renting an office in the *Forverts* building.

Imagine our frustration and disappointment when we later found out that this decision had been changed! This was done in a very simple way: at the second session, the following morning, the *Forverts* group showed up and convened the proceedings exactly on time—something that rarely happened—when a large number of delegates were not yet present, moved to reconsider the question, and officially amended the decision!

On Friday night my colleagues noted that none of the Philadelphia delegates had the honor of chairing a session. How could they return home

---

6. **Abraham Epstein** (Avrom Epshteyn) was a Jewish garment worker and socialist. In the 1890s he was a leader of the Waist and Wrapper Makers' Union, and he served as president of the Workmen's Circle from 1916 to 1920. During the 1921 split in the Jewish Socialist Federation, Epstein sided with the pro-Communist faction, and in 1922 he cofounded the Communist-affiliated International Workers Order.

and show their faces to their members after such an insult? They went to Abe Epstein, the head of the *Forverts* faction that year, and asked him how this was possible. He admitted that it was not right and asked who among us was capable of chairing a session of the convention. They gave him my name, and the slight was soon forgiven: Epstein raised his hand, and the whole convention voted that I should chair the Saturday morning session, when the delegates would have to hurriedly finish up all the business that had been left to the last minute.

The task was not difficult for me. The delegates had done enough talking and debating throughout the week. They were exhausted and anxious to leave. At half past eleven all questions had been answered and resolutions voted upon—all that remained was to close the convention and introduce some speakers to deliver closing sermons to which no one listened. But this required a special ritual at Workmen's Circle conventions—closing the convention is an honor that an ordinary delegate cannot enjoy as chairman. This was a privilege of the two or three people who always fought for the title of president of the Workmen's Circle—only Joseph Weinberg, Nathan Chanin, and Reuben Guskin had the eternal power to open and close the convention.[7] So an afternoon meeting had to be convened, the appropriate chairman elected, and the procedure carried out properly, even though half of the delegates had already left the convention before the meeting had begun.

I had the opportunity to participate as delegate at two or three additional conventions of the Workmen's Circle, but they were unexceptional. The two I have described give a brief idea of how the Workmen's Circle conducted its affairs.

---

7. **Joseph Weinberg** (c. 1877–1955) was an Austrian-born Jewish socialist, a staff member of the *Forverts*, and nine-time general secretary of the Workmen's Circle. **Nathan Chanin** (Nakhum Chanin, 1885–1965) was a Russian-born Jewish garment worker, labor organizer, and socialist. A former member of the Bund, he escaped Siberian exile and immigrated to the United States in 1912. Chanin became a leader of the Jewish Socialist Verband and vice president of the Cloth Hat, Cap and Millinery Workers International Union, and he served the first of several terms as general secretary of the Workmen's Circle from 1930 to 1932. **Reuben Guskin** (Ruven Guskin, 1887–1951) was a Russian Jewish labor organizer and socialist. A member of the Bund, in 1904 he immigrated to the United States, where he became an official in the Barbers' Union and then head of the Hebrew Actors' Union, president the United Hebrew Trades, and a member of the administrative board of the *Forverts*, and he served multiple terms as general secretary of the Workmen's Circle.

CHAPTER 27

Our Conventions in New York and Philadelphia, and the *Fraye vort*

In June 1910 the *Fraye arbeter shtime* published a report from the New York Anarkhie (Anarchy) Group calling for a convention of all organized groups in the country. Yanovsky dedicated nearly the entirety of his "Oyf der vakh" column to the matter, explaining that the *Fraye arbeter shtime* had not called a convention for a few years because there was no clarity within the movement. The comrades had become dissatisfied with the newspaper, but the newspaper did not know what the comrades wanted. Now we would see what a convention could accomplish!

The *Fraye arbeter shtime* was now well established. Its readership in the Jewish community had increased tremendously in recent years. Newspapers and magazines of all kinds had appeared: *Dos naye lebn* (The New Life), *Dos naye land* (The New Country), *Unzer gezunt* (Our Health), *Der groyser kundes* (The Big Stick/The Big Prankster), *Der kibetser* (The Kibitzer).[1] The *Fraye arbeter shtime* did not lag behind; it also began to publish a monthly magazine, *Di fraye gezelshaft* (Free Society), in a large format and with a wide circulation, with worthwhile articles by well-known writers.[2] Yanovsky

---

1. ***Dos naye leben*** (1908–1914, 1922–1923) was a socialist territorialist newspaper founded by Chaim Zhitlowsky. Anarchists Hillel Solotaroff and Jacob A. Maryson helped to produce it. ***Dos naye land*** (1911–1912) was a literary magazine founded by socialist Abraham Reisen. ***Unzer gezunt*** (1910–1917) was a radical health magazine founded by anarchist Benzion Liber. ***Der groyser kundes*** (1909–1927) was a left-leaning satirical journal founded by poet Yoysef Tunkel (1881–1949). ***Der kibetser*** (1908–1913) was another satirical journal founded by Tunkel.

2. *Di fraye gezelshaft* (1910–1911) featured contributions from many of the era's most prominent Yiddish writers and radicals and reached a circulation of eight thousand copies.

set out to organize his own movement of "Fraye Gezelshaft Clubs," which would discuss the articles that appeared in the magazine, thus crystallizing a clear public opinion among Jewish workers. Over time, Yanovsky was able to organize fifty such clubs—two of them with us in Philadelphia—with comrade Y. Fin as general secretary of the whole organization.[3] The reports of the clubs, arranged in their own column, were quite impressive, but no life or activity was in evidence. The existing anarchist groups in each city did not seem to have contact with the Fraye Gezelshaft Clubs.

The Anarkhie Group of New York, which soon became the Naye Gezelshaft (New Society) Group, Branch 364 of the Workmen's Circle, largely consisted of newly arrived comrades from London. They were all good, hardworking anarchists who wanted to not only do active work but also seek clarity in the movement. Comrade Sam Margolis was very active in it for many years, as were Morris Shutz and Tania Schapiro.[4] All through the years Max Horowitz served as secretary of the group.[5] We also had a representative in that group: comrade Benjamin Axler had moved to New York at that time and joined what was the most active group there.

The called-for convention met on July 2, in the hottest weather, and lasted for three days. The organizations represented were the Philadelphia Radical Library, by delegates Jack Bowman, Cohen, and Joseph Washkowitz; the Anarkhie Group, by Benjamin Axler, David Isakovitz, Sam Margolis, and Dreen; Baltimore's Frayheyt Group, Branch 239 of the Workmen's Circle, by Benjamin Surasky; Paterson's Frayheyt Group, Branch 160 of the Workmen's Circle; Boston's Zelbst-Bildung (Self-Education) Group; and groups from Winnipeg and St. Louis represented through proxies.

---

3. **Y. Fin** (died 1920) was a former member of the Jewish anarchist Berner Street Club in London and in the United States belonged to the Fraye Arbeter Shtime Association. Obituaries: *FAS*, May 20 and 27, 1921.

4. **Morris Shutz** (Moyshe Shuts, 1888–1968) was Russian-born Jewish garment worker and anarchist. He immigrated to Argentina but was expelled as an anarchist following the "Red Week" of 1909 and ended up in France and then London, where he joined the Arbeter Fraynd Group. He immigrated to the United States around 1913 and remained active in the anarchist movement, serving as a member of New York's Kropotkin Literary Society, the editorial board of the *FAS*, and the Kropotkin Literary Society, Branch 413 of the Workmen's Circle.

5. **Max Horowitz** (Maks Horovits, 1893–1957) was a Russian-born Jewish department store clerk and anarchist. He immigrated to the United States in 1890 and around 1930 became secretary of the Bronx's Naye Gezelshaft Group, Branch 364 of the Workmen's Circle, a position he held until his death. Obituary: *FAS*, January 25, 1957.

There were long agendas for each day. The meetings were serious and to the point. Dr. Maryson and Louis Levine attended the meetings and participated in the discussions. Everything went smoothly.

Yanovsky printed the report of the convention in the July 18 issue of the *Fraye arbeter shtime* under the heading: "What Was Said at the Meeting of a Few Anarchist Branches of the Workmen's Circle." The report took up three columns of the paper and was signed by Benjamin Axler as secretary of the newly formed federation. As one can see, the resolutions were quite important, and the explanation of our goals was stated very clearly:

> Our goal is the reconstruction of all relevant social institutions on the foundation of anarchist principles.
>
> 1. A social system in which private property is abolished in all natural resources, the means of production, and transportation, which will become community property;
> 2. A social system in which the central authority of the state and of the majority over the individual and the minority is abolished, in which federalism is the form through which unification is achieved;
> 3. A social system in which the freedom of movement and action of an individual cannot be violated by society or other individuals in any area of life.

Following an introduction by Dr. Maryson and a lengthy discussion on the question of participation in political and social reform movements, the following resolution was adopted: "We recognize the need to participate in all relevant political, economic, and social problems of the city and country, and to work for their resolution in the direction that is nearest to our goal. An exact program should be worked out at the next convention."

A number of resolutions were then made in favor of cooperatives, Ferrer schools, and the formation of a federation and publication of a periodical. Regarding this last question, the decision was to turn to the *Fraye arbeter shtime* and see what we could do through it to strengthen our movement.

The convention stated that "violence cannot propagate an idea; violent measures are the exact opposite of anarchism and cannot be used by anarchists. Expropriation means the social takeover of all properties; individual seizure of property is nothing more than theft and has nothing to do with anarchism." Resolutions were passed regarding the relationship of individual groups to the federation, whose office would be in New York, and it was also decided that the next convention would take place in Philadelphia.

The newly formed federation was very active, convening many meetings in certain parts of New York and organizing new groups in Harlem and downtown, but the suburbs responded poorly.

The secretary, comrade Axler, recounted a curious experience he had with the comrades at the first executive meeting, which was held in his home. The members were all in a big hurry and rushed through the meeting as quickly as possible. He wondered where they were heading in such haste. He had prepared refreshments for the meeting and was sure it would continue until after midnight, as was often the case in Philadelphia, yet here they were rushing as though to escape a fire!

Immediately after the meeting, they brought out a deck of cards and began to play pinochle. He stared at them as if they had gone crazy. He had never seen such a thing in our movement. The Philadelphia comrades had always been an exception. In the forty years during which I have been familiar them, I have never seen a card game at a meeting at a comrade's home. In New York in 1910, however, the members of the executive committee were all Londoners, active and intelligent people, who spent every free moment playing cards. Axler's protests had no effect that evening, but at future meetings of the federation's executive there was no card playing—the Philadelphia tradition prevailed.

That autumn, we began preparation for the convention that was to be held in our city. We conducted some business during the summer. We used to meet every Sunday at George's Hill Park, to spend time together and discuss movement issues. For Rosh Hashanah, as in previous years, we were preparing to hold a lecture in Washington Hall on the afternoon of the second day, after the observant Jews had finished their prayers in the same hall. At the time, the owner of the hall told us that the religious Jews wanted to get even with us—they planned to refuse to leave the hall for anything.

I attempted to intercept our speaker, Leo Rosenzweig, but it was too late. He was already on his way from New York. In a hurry, we tried to find another venue in which to hold the meeting and were able to obtain the club rooms of a branch of the Grand Army of the Republic. The walls were covered with flags and trophies of the Civil War. Every brick of the building exhaled

Figure 21: Jewish anarchist group in Chicago, 1910s
Standing: Luba Fagin (far right); front row: Aron Baron (center) and Fanya Baron (far right); courtesy of Elijah Baron

patriotism and militarism. There, in that incredibly conservative environment, Rosenzweig delivered a great speech against religion and superstition in front of a crowd of people that filled every inch of space. It truly was not an easy task to arrange and coordinate all this in less than two hours.

After the holidays we had four more lectures by Rosenzweig on these topics: "The Story of Creation"; "The Shape and Movement of the Earth"; "The Four Seasons"; and "Meteorology." All the lectures, illustrated with stereoscopic images, were well attended.

At the end of November, on Thanksgiving eve, we held our yearly *boyern bal* in the New Lyric Hall with great success.

On the tenth of December, the *Fraye arbeter shtime* carried an announcement of the convention of the federation, which would take place in Philadelphia during Christmas week. In the same issue there was also an announcement from the newly renamed Naye Gezelshaft Group that it was undertaking the publication of a new periodical, *Dos fraye vort* (The Free Word), edited by Dr. Maryson, Louis Levine, and Dr. John Weichsel.[6]

The convention was held at the Radical Library on Saturday, Sunday, and Monday, December 24 through 26, with delegates from the same groups as in New York. New groups included the Fraye Gezelshaft Group in Winnipeg (through correspondence) and the David Edelstadt Group in Chicago, which was unable to send a delegate due to the great tailors' strike taking place in that city, which later led to the formation of the Amalgamated Clothing Workers of America.

From the very long report in the *Fraye arbeter shtime*, signed by me as the new secretary of the federation, one can see that the proceedings were very serious.[7] On the question of participating in reform movements, no single decision could be reached. It was finally decided to publish two opposing resolutions for groups to discuss. The first said:

> We recognize the need to participate in all progressive reform movements, agitating among the people for the same, in order for the pressure of the people to be exerted on legislative bodies to force them to carry these out.

The second resolution read:

> We recognize the need to participate in all progressive movements through direct action, through economic action, and through the establishment of free institutions, which should organize the oppressed masses and improve their circumstances, but not through parliamentary methods.

---

6. **John Weichsel** (1870–1946) was a Russian-born Jewish mechanic, art critic, and anarchist. Born into a merchant family and educated in Berlin, he immigrated to the United States in the early 1890s and completed a doctorate in engineering at New York University. He later taught at the anarchist Ferrer Center and in 1915 organized the People's Art Guild, a cooperative of modernist artists.

7. *FAS*, January 7, 1911. The new organization adopted the name Federated Anarchist Groups in America (Federirte Anarkhistishe Grupen in Amerika).

Figure 22: *Dos fraye vort*

First issue of *Dos fraye vort*, February 1911, featuring a front-page article by Hillel Solotaroff on "The Young and the Old" in the anarchist movement

One important new aspect of previous practice had been adopted. The federation had been bound by a decision to not take an action unless all groups voted in favor of it. This was precisely why the former Anarkhie Group undertook publication of *Dos fraye vort* on its own initiative. The consent of *all* groups, it turned out, was almost impossible to obtain for any new venture. The Philadelphia convention adopted the position that when three groups decided to take up a new activity, the federation should take up and carry out the work on behalf of the movement. This was a practical decision, which removed a great deal of difficulty, but it did not lead to any effective activity whatsoever.

Our movement suffered from a peculiar disease: in Yiddish, Yanovsky led the *Fraye arbeter shtime* and *Fraye gezelshaft*, with a large number of clubs and successful endeavors, for which he had to thank, in particular, the activity of two comrades, Aaron Mintz and Nokhum Vaynritsh, who used to visit literally every union and other organization to sell tickets.

In English, Emma Goldman published *Mother Earth*, as well as a series of pamphlets and books. Every year she made a lecture tour all over the country, accompanied by Dr. Ben Reitman, who was well-versed in the art of American publicity and sold mountains of literature.

But there was no American anarchist movement in the true sense of the word. Yanovsky ridiculed Emma's activities, searching out her weak points: she made a little money, quarreled with the police, and a great "ballyhoo" surrounded her public appearances. The comrades meanwhile ignored Yanovsky's activity, changing the title of one of his pamphlets, *What Do the Anarchists Want?*, by placing the question mark after the last word on the title page, so it read *What Do the Anarchists Want from Sh. Yanovsky?*[8] And truly, what did they want from him, when he and his expenses no longer depended on their support and assistance? He could now stand on his own two feet without having to cater to their opinions.

One can see from its articles that *Dos fraye vort* was a serious magazine, which dealt with the problems of our movement. The *Fraye arbeter shtime* did not say a word about it.[9] The only response is found in old letter columns: "I am interested to see what will come out of such a movement." In a second reply to a letter in a later issue:

1) Why are we content with only a brief notice about *Dos fraye vort*? Our answer is that according to our view it does not deserve more. 2) Why do we speak of [Mayor William Jay] Gaynor, of the police commissioner, of theater and the like? Because we consider them very important. 3) Why do we not discuss whether the anarchists should participate in political action? Our answer is that this question cannot be on our agenda, because we believe that those who advocate

---

8. This is a pun that works in Yiddish but not English—the words "*fun Sh. Yanovsky*" can be read as either "by Sh. Yanovsky" or "from Sh. Yanovsky."

9. The *FAS* did in fact print a brief critique of *Dos fraye vort* in Yanovsky's column "Oyf der vakh" on February 18, 1911.

political action are no longer anarchists. . . 4) Why is there no movement? Our answer is that there is indeed a movement. . . 5) What are the Jewish anarchists doing? Before all else worthy anarchists (*anarkhisten mentshen*), it turns out, need to live and to make a living. . . 6) Do the anarchists have an ideal? . . . Our answer is: yes. . . 7) But are the anarchists not satisfied with every step forward? Are they not evolutionists? Yes, they are. . . But for the sake of a hundred and one reasons they cannot . . . take part in political action. . . 8) What is the position of the *Fraye arbeter shtime*? Read our answers above again and read the *Fraye arbeter shtime* every week.[10]

This is, of course, just the gist of the reply, which took up almost a whole column of small print. One week later, Yanovsky decided to acquaint all of us with the anarchist Torah according to his conception. He began to print a series of articles under the heading "Principles and Methods of Anarchism," which lasted for months, continuing for as long as the Jewish exile itself. They are all written in a polemical tone and in accordance with Abe Cahan's method of making a mountain out of a mole hill. In the same issue of June 10, 1911, there is a suggestion in the letter column that the *Fraye gezelshaft* would have to be discontinued. The clubs had already ceased to exist. The journal was no longer published after that month. The letter column promised to thoroughly discuss the whole issue of the clubs and their downfall.

On July 15, it was announced that the *Fraye arbeter shtime* had taken out a charter from the government. "[This was done] because evil tongues swore that the newspaper belonged to Yanovsky. Now the charter will prevent them from saying it again."[11] The paper promised that a short program would soon be published, but, needless to say, it never appeared.

---

10. *FAS*, June 3, 1911.

11. This document legally established that ownership of the newspaper was held by the editorial board, of which Yanovsky was not a member, and that Yanovsky was merely an employee of the paper.

CHAPTER 28

The McNamara Case

The years 1910–1911 were rich in important and serious events in the American labor movement. On October 1, 1910, the building of the very reactionary *Los Angeles Times* was blown up by dynamite, killing twenty-one employees, workers, and leading to one of the most tragic episodes in the history of the American labor movement.

Detective William J. Burns assumed the job of finding the culprits, digging deep into the McNamara brothers and the organization behind them.[1] It is highly amusing to read Burns's account of how he spent months spying around the Home Colony in Washington State.[2] He was sure that since dynamite had been used, there must be anarchists involved, and where can anarchists be found if not in an anarchist colony? He engaged some men to present themselves as surveyors, surveying the land near the colony. He would come twice a week to pick up reports and leave instructions. They watched Jay Fox and a number of other anarchists, reading every letter received or

---

1. **William J. Burns** (1861–1932) was the American-born founder of the William J. Burns International Detective Agency, which specialized in investigating labor unions and radical groups. He served as director of the Bureau of Investigation from 1921 until he was forced to resign in 1924 amid a corruption scandal. **John J. McNamara** (1876–1941) and **James B. McNamara** (1882–1941) were American-born labor organizers for the International Association of Bridge and Structural Iron Workers, of which John was elected secretary-treasurer in 1905. Soon after, in the face of an effective open-shop campaign in Los Angeles, members of the union orchestrated a series of bombings targeting the property of anti-union employers, with the aid of a small group of Bay Area anarchists. James McNamara placed the bomb at the *Los Angeles Times* building in retaliation for the paper's support of the open-shop movement.

2. William J. Burns, *The Masked War: The Story of a Peril that Threatened the United States, by the Man who Uncovered the Dynamite Conspirators and Sent them to Jail* (New York: George H. Doran, 1913).

sent, recording exactly what each one did from morning until they went to bed, with whom they spoke or had contact. This continued for a few months. Nothing was discovered there, at least as of the time he published his book, a year or two after the trial; he could not yet indicate any results from his surveillance there. His work, however, was not entirely in vain. He did manage to win over to his service a young man, the son of a well-known anarchist, and with his help a few years later was able to locate Matthew Schmidt.[3]

The arrest of the McNamara brothers shook up the whole working-class movement. Their union was a member of the American Federation of Labor, which took up their defense. Clarence Darrow was retained as the chief lawyer for the defense.

Lincoln Steffens was instrumental in bringing about a guarantee that if the McNamara brothers confessed they would receive prison terms and no one else would be prosecuted.[4]

Their confession struck the entire labor movement like a thunderbolt. Samuel Gompers wept like a child, complaining that he had been misled, deceived, and exploited. The socialists and the *Fraye arbeter shtime* attacked the McNamara brothers, calling them common criminals, outcasts, and every other insult. The resentment of the socialists was understandable. One of their members, Job Harriman, a lawyer associated with the defense, was running for mayor of Los Angeles, and in the context of the trial, he had a good chance of being elected.[5] Their confession killed his prospects. The *Fraye arbeter shtime* did not have such a reason, naturally. It was due to Yanovsky's offended sense of virtue, which often led him to chastise people

---

3. This was Donald Vose (1892–1945), the son of anarchist Gertie Vose (c. 1854–1926) of the Home Colony. **Matthew Schmidt** (1882–1955) was an American-born carpenter, mechanic, and anarchist. Raised in Wisconsin and a former member of the Chicago Woodworkers' Union, he was active in anarchist circles in San Francisco. Schmidt helped the McNamara brothers obtain dynamite and allegedly served as James McNamara's getaway driver.

4. **Lincoln Steffens** (1866–1936) was an American-born journalist and Progressive. The editor of *McClure's* and a prominent muckraker, he was best-known for exposing political corruption. Steffens traveled to Los Angeles to cover the McNamaras' trial and aided their legal defense.

5. **Job Harriman** (1861–1925) was an American-born former minister, attorney, and socialist. He ran for several political offices as a member of the SLP and then the Socialist Party of America, including governor of California in 1898, vice president of the United States in 1900, and mayor of Los Angeles in 1911 and 1913. Harriman was serving as an assistant defense attorney for the McNamara brothers at the time of the 1911 election.

for things he himself did not refrain from doing. He had the ability to put himself on a pedestal and let lofty morality drip from his pen.

In our circles too we were agitated and embittered, not so much because the McNamara brothers had committed the act but rather because they had confessed. I strongly suspect that Gompers wept over the same catastrophe. Since the stupid crime had already been committed and the trial had taken on the character of an attack on the organized labor movement, they had no right to make the confession. Even if dozens of witnesses testified at the trial that they had committed the crime, the workers would not have believed it and would not have allowed them to be executed. The labor movement was already powerful enough to protect its victims and would never permit important union officials to be hanged.

But alas. They confessed, and after much anticipation, got off with relatively light sentences.[6] However, the authorities did not make good on the second part of the bargain. Dozens of labor leaders in San Francisco and the Midwest were arrested, charged, and sentenced to prison. Burns was looking for Matthew Schmidt and David Caplan, who had helped supply the "stuff" [dynamite] in Los Angeles, and here the young man whose acquaintance he had made at the Home Colony now came in handy.[7] In 1914–1915 the young man went to New York and was kindly received by Emma Goldman, who was a close friend of his mother, and became a regular at the office of *Mother Earth*. He hung around for several months, until one Saturday afternoon Matthew Schmidt came to visit Emma Goldman to spend a few hours with her.

By that time, I was residing in New York, living in the Ferrer Center, where I oversaw various activities. After midnight that Saturday, the telephone woke me from my sleep. Emma spoke, saying that she had reason to

---

6. James B. McNamara, who admitted to placing the bomb, was sentenced to life in prison and died in San Quentin in 1941; John J. McNamara was sentenced to fifteen years, of which he served nine.

7. **David Caplan** (c. 1870–1933?) was a Russian-born Jewish laborer, barber, and anarchist. He immigrated to the United States around 1887 and was active in Philadelphia's Jewish anarchist movement before departing around 1910 for the West Coast, where he spent time in both San Francisco and the Home Colony. Caplan helped the McNamara brothers obtain dynamite and plan the bombing and went into hiding afterward. Finally arrested in 1915, he was convicted of manslaughter and sentenced to ten years. Following his release in 1923 Caplan went to Soviet Russia but became disillusioned and eventually made his way to Paris where, destitute, he reportedly committed suicide in 1933.

believe that Matthew Schmidt had been arrested and was in danger of being extradited to California without a hearing. For fear of compromising the case, she could not personally intervene. She wanted me to find a lawyer and see what could be done. In the middle of the night I woke up Simon O. Pollock, a socialist attorney, and we went to the Tombs to find out what we could do.[8] There we were told that Schmidt was in their hands, locked in a cell. The lawyer could see him in the morning, not then.

We spent the night wandering through the streets, stopping for coffee wherever a restaurant was open, until 7:00 or 8:00 in the morning, when Pollack was allowed to see the prisoner. Schmidt told him that his friend Donald Vose, whom he had met at the office of *Mother Earth*, had betrayed him. When Schmidt went down into the subway, the young man winked at a detective, who followed Schmidt and arrested him at the exit. He was of the opinion that it would be a wasted effort to try and keep him from being taken back to California. They had the "goods," he pleaded, and it was foolish to pretend otherwise. "I will have to take my medicine!"

Matthew Schmidt was highly intelligent worker, a good machinist by profession, and a quiet man. He was sentenced to life in prison and continued his trade in San Quentin, until he became foreman of the car shop there. Years later, when Tom Mooney was incarcerated in the same prison and was agitating for his freedom, Matthew Schmidt once turned to John McNamara and said, "Us, John, we're lucky. At least we're not innocent!"[9] Schmidt was freed by Governor Culbert Levy Olson, who was elected on Roosevelt's New Deal ticket.[10]

---

8. **Simon O. Pollock** (c. 1868–1934) was a Russian-born Jewish lawyer and socialist. He was expelled from Moscow University in 1887 for his radical activities and immigrated to the United States in 1890. Pollock was counsel for the Political Refugees' Defense League, wrote for *Tsukunft*, and was author of *The Russian Bastille* (1908), an exposé of Russia's imprisonment of political dissidents.

9. **Tom Mooney** (1882–1942) was an American-born iron worker, labor organizer, socialist, and syndicalist. After moving from Indiana to California in 1908, he joined the Socialist Party, the IWW (briefly), and the Syndicalist League of North America. In San Francisco Mooney published the newspaper *Revolt* (1911–1912), which represented the left wing of the Socialist Party and was sympathetic to the IWW, and he was a prominent organizer for the International Molders' Union. His arrest and trial are discussed in chapter 37.

10. **Culbert Levy Olson** (1876–1962) was an American-born attorney and Democratic politician who served as governor of California from 1939 to 1943. Sympathetic to the labor movement, he commuted Matthew Schmidt's life sentence in 1942.

CHAPTER 29

The Uprising of the 20,000, the Cloakmakers' Great Revolt, and Emma Goldman

The uprising of the waist makers in New York in the winter of 1909–1910 was of the utmost importance. On November 22, 1909, over twenty-thousand workers, three-quarters of them young women who had just come from Russia, left their jobs and went out to fight for better conditions.

It seemed to be the fate of the waist makers that all their struggles took place in winter, the worst time of year, when picketing the shops meant coming out in freezing weather, under inhuman conditions. The Jewish working-class community had never seen such a struggle before. The employers, most of them Jewish immigrants themselves, hired gangsters to beat up the pickets. The police, as is the custom, also stood firmly on the side of the employers. Violence occurred outside the shops every day. Hundreds of strikers were arrested. The struggle looked hopeless.

The union that called the strike was an organization only on paper. It had no members. It certainly didn't control any shops. It even lacked the capacity to accommodate the influx of new members. The officials of the union, Abraham Baroff, Samuel Schindler, and the others, were drowning in the great flood of new members for the first few days.[1] They received assistance from Morris Sigman, John Dyche, and Herman Grossman from

---

1. **Abraham Baroff** (Avrom Barof, c. 1872–1932) was a Russian-born Jewish garment worker, labor organizer, and socialist. He immigrated to the United States in 1893 and by 1909 was organizing on behalf for Ladies' Waist Makers' Union Local 25. Baroff served as general secretary-treasurer of the ILGWU from 1915 to 1929 and was also the first provisional secretary of the Workmen's Circle. **Samuel Schindler** was secretary of Ladies' Waist Makers' Union Local 25.

the International Ladies Garment Workers' Union, and from all the socialist and anarchist speakers of the East Side.[2]

The real strength of the strike, however, came from the militancy of the girls, their revolutionary enthusiasm and dedication, which never wavered. The reports in the English-language newspapers about their heroic behavior caught the attention of many liberal women in high society. They organized the Women's Trade Union League and went out on the picket line to help the strikers.[3] A number of them got a taste of being beaten and arrested, insulted and physically abused, which had a profound effect on public opinion. Huge demonstrations in the streets and rallies in the Hippodrome Theater added color to the movement. Negotiations for a settlement began, in which John Mitchell, president of the United Mine Workers union, was active.[4]

At the end of December the strike spread to us in Philadelphia, where the bosses were trying to help their colleagues in New York by supplying scab labor. Abraham Rosenberg and John Dyche came and called the girls to action.[5] I shall never forget the fighting spirit the girls displayed then, the hardships they had to endure from bad weather, hired hoodlums, and the police. Many times I was called at night to bail strikers out from Moyamensing Prison. The focus of the country, however, was on New York.

At the end of December, John Mitchell managed to work out a

---

2. **John Dyche** (Dzshon Daytsh, 1867–1939) was a Russian-born Jewish garment worker and labor organizer. In the 1890s he immigrated to England, where he was active in the Jewish socialist and labor movements, then in 1901 he moved to New York, where he was active in ILGWU Local 23. Dyche contributed to many Yiddish labor and radical newspapers and served as general secretary of the ILGWU from 1904 to 1914. Over time, however, he embraced antiradical views, and later became a businessman. **Herman Grossman** (1867–1934) was an Austrian-born cloakmaker and labor organizer. He cofounded the ILGWU and served as its first president from 1900 to 1903 and again from 1905 to 1907. Grossman subsequently sat on the New York Joint Board of the Cloakmakers' Union.

3. The **Women's Trade Union League** (1903–1950) was an independent, cross-class coalition of women and men seeking to aid the unionization of female workers and to support women's strikes. It played a prominent role in rallying public support for the ILGWU's strikes of 1909 and 1910.

4. **John Mitchell** (1870–1919) was an American-born miner who in 1890 cofounded the United Mine Workers of America, of which he served as president from 1898 to 1908.

5. **Abraham Rosenberg** (Avrom Rozenberg, 1870–1935) was a Russian-born Jewish garment worker, labor organizer, and socialist. He immigrated to New York in 1883 and quickly joined the Jewish labor movement and the Knights of Labor. In 1900 Rosenberg cofounded the ILGWU, of which he served as president in 1908–1914.

Figure 23: Striking garment workers during New York's "Uprising of the 20,000," 1910
Courtesy of the Library of Congress

compromise settlement, similar to the one he made with the mine owners in 1902. The employers agreed to a number of demands regarding shorter hours, paying for needles and thread, work sharing, and four paid holidays, but under no circumstance would they recognize the union. The girls almost unanimously voted down the pitiful settlement.

The fight continued. Public sympathy for the strikers was so great that the *Evening Journal* published a special edition in favor of the strike and donated fifty thousand free copies. The female students of Wellesley College raised and sent to the strikers thousands of dollars, and settlements were made with individual owners and contractors. In mid-February, the strike was declared officially ended, although a small number of shops with about thirteen hundred workers held out. This was, in fact, really the beginning of the powerful International Ladies' Garment Workers' Union. Young women—girls—with their enthusiasm and determination laid the foundation of the whole organized Jewish labor movement of which we are all now so proud.

❀ ❀ ❀

The male workers, of course, could not long lag behind the girls. A few months later, the cloakmakers began their historic strike, which attracted sixty thousand workers into its ranks. Today we cannot imagine the slavery people endured before the great strikes. Cloakmakers had to buy their own machines and move them from one shop to another while looking for a job. They had to pay for supplies, for thread, out of their meager earnings. The employer and the manager were all-powerful in the shop and did what they wanted, insulting and even beating up workers. The exception was a small number of privileged people in every shop: contractors who hired newly arrived immigrants and exploited them most shamelessly.

The cloakmakers went on strike against these dire conditions in the summer of 1910. Our comrade Chaim Weinberg, who had moved to New York for this purpose, contributed greatly. When he became seriously ill, the work was taken over by Meyer London and Max Pine.[6] The anarchists Sol Polakoff, Abraham Mitchell, Morris Sigman, and many other lesser-known comrades were themselves very active and prominent among the workers.[7] The American Federation of Labor gave a lot of support. Gompers addressed a giant mass meeting in Madison Square Garden that inspired great enthusiasm. The *Naye post* (New Post), in red letters, appealed to the workers in Yiddish, Italian, and English to leave their shops on July 7 at 2:00 in the afternoon and join the strike.[8]

The reaction among the workers far exceeded all expectations. All the workers—operators, tailors, cutters, pressers, finishers, designers, masters,

---

6. **Max Pine** (Maks Payn, 1866–1928) was a Russian-born Jewish printer, garment worker, journalist, labor organizer, and socialist. He immigrated to the United States in 1888 and became an official in the Knee-Pants Makers' Union, joined the SLP and then the Socialist Party of America, and in 1897 cofounded the *Forverts*. Pine served as secretary of the United Hebrew Trades in 1906–1909 and 1916–1926 and sat on the executive committee of the Workmen's Circle in 1922–1924.

7. **Sol Polakoff** (Polakov, c. 1875–1935) was a Russian-born Jewish cloakmaker and labor organizer. He immigrated to the United States in 1897, cofounded the ILGWU in 1900, and later occupied a number of official positions in the union, including vice-president. **Abraham ("Abe") Mitchell** (Avrom Mitshel) was a Romanian-born Jewish tailer, labor organizer, and anarchist. He served as vice president of the ILGWU from 1912 to 1914.

8. *Di naye post* (1910–1919) was the official newspaper of the ILGWU's New York Joint Board of the Cloakmakers' Union.

examiners, and all the rest—answered the call of the union and joined the struggle together. In less than thirty minutes after 2:00, the streets in the garment district were flooded with striking workers.

The experience of the waist makers' strike was put to good use. This time everything was prepared properly. Each group of workers from each shop knew exactly where to go, in which hall to register. Committees had been established in advance for all tasks. Morris Winchevsky was appointed to oversee the accounts. During the strike, the activities of each member were properly overseen. Everything was set up correctly to conduct the strike as well as for the settlement.

In the first three weeks of the strike, 350 of the smaller manufacturers settled with the strikers. But the larger manufacturers, organized into a "protective association," remained obstinate. Through the intervention of Lincoln Filene, a liberal owner of a large department store in Boston, Louis Brandeis became interested in the strike and, after lengthy negotiations, reached a whole new kind of settlement.[9] A "Protocol of Peace" was created, with rules for settling grievances in the shop through negotiations between union representatives and representatives of the employers' association. If the two parties were unable to reach an agreement, the matter would be submitted to a board of arbitration.

The strike was ended on September 2. During the course of the struggle, there were many confrontations with scabs and police. The workers fought with great determination and bravery. Decades later, dozens of cloakmakers and pressers still suffered from the wounds they received in that fight. The employers were able to get an injunction against the union. One scab was killed, and four years later, Morris Sigman, Saul Metz, and a number of other union members were charged with murdering the scab Herman Liebowitz during the 1910 strike.[10] The union was able to exonerate all of the defendants in court.

---

9. **Abraham Lincoln Filene** (1865–1957) was an American-born Jewish businessman and reformer, and son of William Filene, the founder of Filene's department stores. **Louis Brandeis** (1856–1941) was an American-born Jewish attorney and Progressive who in 1916 was appointed to the US Supreme Court.

10. **Solomon ("Saul" or "Sol") Metz** (Mets, 1883–1947) was a Russian-born Jewish cloakmaker, labor organizer, and socialist. He belonged to the Bund before emigrating in 1904 to the United States, where he joined the Socialist Party and later became manager of Cloak Pressers' Union Local 35, a vice president of the ILGWU (1914–18), and president

The cloakmakers' union became big and mighty, but there were still many conflicts in the shops. The Protocol's machinery did not work satisfactorily. This created a bitter confrontation between Isaac A. Hourwich, chief clerk of the Cloak and Skirt Makers' Unions of New York, and senior officials of the union's Joint Board. The members of the Cloakmakers' Union Local 1 were solidly on the side of Hourwich and against the other leaders.

This is not the place and it is not my task to try to unravel all of the tumultuous events of that time, which led to the exclusion and reorganization of Local 1, an action in which many of our comrades played a prominent part. Suffice it to say that the birth pangs of the now mighty ILGWU were difficult and painful.

Our comrades were active in every area and in all the struggles that were waged in New York, Cleveland, Boston, Chicago, Baltimore, and other cities. The cloakmakers' strikes reached us in Philadelphia in the summer of 1913, but that is a chapter in itself.

❀ ❀ ❀

On March 25, 1911, a fire broke out in a ladies' shirtmakers' shop situated on a high floor of a tall building in New York. The shop doors were locked so that no union organizers could contact the workers; 146 girls were killed in the fire. Some jumped from the windows to certain death, others were crushed against the locked doors that could not be opened in the panic. All died in the most horrible agony imaginable.[11]

❀ ❀ ❀

---

of the United Hebrew Trades. **Herman Liebowitz**, a tailor employed as a strikebreaker, was attacked by unknown assailants and died from a skull fracture. The ILGWU members belatedly charged and then acquitted in "The Trial of the Seven Cloakmakers" were John Aspitz, Solomon Metz, Morris Sigman, Max Singer, Morris Stupnicker, John Wedinger, and Julius Woolf.

11. Cohen refers here to the Triangle Shirtwaist Factory fire. Although most of the victims were young women, 23 of the 146 dead were male garment workers.

In our movement at this time, questions arose about the changed methods of anarchist propaganda that Emma Goldman had employed since her association with Dr. Ben Reitman. The first hint really came from Reitman's own pen. In 1910 he wrote in *Mother Earth* about his experiences in London, where he visited the most prominent leaders of the anarchist movement. The kind-hearted, gentle, and hospitable Peter Kropotkin, Reitman reported, received him quite coolly. Kropotkin kept repeating that our propaganda needs to be conducted among the workers. This was his polite hint that he was dissatisfied with the sensational methods Reitman used and with Emma's efforts to reach the ladies and gentlemen of the leisure class with her lectures on drama and art.[12]

A couple of months later, a more direct criticism appeared in the *Fraye arbeter shtime* and in *Mother Earth*, written by Voltairine de Cleyre, who had just made a lecture tour from Philadelphia to Chicago. Along the way, she became acquainted with the methods used by Reitman and the general scope of Emma's lecture tours, and she openly stated her opinion—which was not at all favorable—on the issue.[13]

Emma did not notice—or at least did not mention—Kropotkin's remarks published in her own magazine. However, she could not ignore a direct criticism from Voltairine de Cleyre. She cut Voltairine's report in two, leaving half for later due to "lack of space," and occupied three full pages with a reply that did not do her any great credit. She sought to prove that anarchism was not dependent only on the workers, who are in no hurry to take up our doctrines; that the workers had, in her opinion, simply betrayed the Haymarket Martyrs, who spent their whole lives serving only the workers; that Johann Most was in the last years of his life in danger of starving after dedicating his whole life to the workers; et cetera. Anarchism, she

---

12. Ben L. Reitman, "A Visit to London," *Mother Earth*, October 1910, 250–54. Reitman wrote: "Kropotkin expressed his fears that some of the Anarchists in America lean towards respectability and utilitarianism. He strongly urged the necessity of carrying the message of Anarchism to the workingmen" (252).

13. Voltairine de Cleyre, "Tour Impressions," *Mother Earth*, December 1910, 322–25. De Cleyre wrote: "My impression is that our present propaganda (if there is any) is a woeful mistake. I am more than ever convinced that our work should be with the workers, not with the bourgeoisie. If these latter choose to come, very well, let them. But I should never approve of this seeking after 'respectable halls,' 'respectable neighborhoods,' 'respectable people,' etc., etc., into which it appears we have somehow degenerated" (324).

concluded, gives everyone the freedom to choose for themselves their own method of action. Who then has the right to dictate to another which way they should go?[14]

※ ※ ※

Among the other important events of that year was the struggle for free speech and free assembly that the Wobblies (the IWW) carried on in the Far West. The struggle began in 1909 in Spokane, Washington, and spread to California, first in Fresno and then San Diego. Hundreds of workers were arrested and beaten; others, however, stepped in immediately to take the place of the arrested speakers. The Wobblies sought to organize the workers in the fields, forests, and harbors in the regions along the Pacific Ocean. This provoked the wrath of the wealthy employers there, who, with the help of the press, managed to incite the population against the terrible bindlestiffs. In most cities, "vigilante" committees were organized that took the law in their own hands, established "mob rule," and committed pogroms (*pogromirt*) against the Wobblies' offices, pouring hot tar and feathers on the naked bodies of active members. Reitman experienced such terrible treatment in San Diego in 1912. Some Wobblies were simply lynched by mobs, including Frank Little, Joseph Mikolasek, and others.[15] The lawlessness of the rich and powerful knew no bounds, yet no member of the respectable mob was ever charged or punished.

In this area, Emma Goldman's activity coincided with that of the Wobblies. She too had fights for free speech and free assembly in quite a few cities. The only difference was that her fights always had the character of a personal fight—it was Emma who was not allowed to speak; no other speaker was harassed—and under the circumstances the fight had to be

---

14. Emma Goldman, "A Rejoinder," *Mother Earth*, December 1910, 325–28.

15. **Frank Little** (1879–1917) was an American-born miner and IWW organizer who was lynched by vigilantes in Butte, Montana, while helping to lead a strike of copper miners. **Joseph Mikolasek,** sometimes spelled Mikolash or Mikolasch (Josef Mikolášek, c. 1882–1912), was an Austrian Bohemian-born anarchist and IWW member. He contributed to the Czech-language anarchist newspaper *Volné Listy* (Loose Leaves, 1890–1917) and was beaten and then shot to death by police during the IWW's free speech fight in San Diego.

taken up by liberals, single-taxers, prominent bourgeoisie, and often liberal clerics, while the Wobblies' struggle was everywhere a collective one, a labor struggle carried on by broad masses, the people who placed their own bodies before the clubs of the police and the wild mob.[16]

16. Cohen seems to forget here that Goldman and Reitman were in San Diego in 1912 to support the IWW's free speech fight.

CHAPTER 30

The Anarchist Red Cross

At the end of 1910, the world was shaken by the tragic news that Igor Sazonov and five of his comrades had committed suicide in a penal camp in Akatuy, Siberia.[1] They could not bear the humiliation of seeing their comrades, political prisoners, subjected to the brutal punishment of flogging. When their protests to the administration went unheeded, they decided to get the attention of the world by committing suicide. They achieved their goal. All of Russia and with it the whole civilized world was shocked. Students from every university in Russia staged huge demonstrations against the barbarous methods of the bloodthirsty autocracy.

Here in this country, in the years 1909–1910, a new organization was formed in our movement: the Anarchist Red Cross. It was founded in New York by a number of recently arrived anarchists, most of them from Bialystok, Krynki, and other towns of that region, with the aim of raising support for anarchists who had fallen into the clutches of the Russian government and languished in prisons, labor camps, and remote corners of Siberia. Two comrades, Jacob (Yankel) Katzenelenbogen and Harry Weinstein, were the initiators.[2] They had experienced prison in Russia, where the socialists' Political Red Cross had refused to give them any aid because they were

---

1. **Igor (or Egor/Yegor) Sazonov** (1879–1910) was a Russian student and a member of the Combat Organization of the Socialist-Revolutionary Party. He assassinated Russia's brutal minister of the interior, Vyacheslav von Plehve, with a bomb on July 15, 1904.

2. **Jacob Katzenelenbogen** (Yankl Ketsenelenboygn, 1882–?) was a Russian-born Jewish cigarmaker and anarchist. He was active in the anarchist movement in Bialystok before immigrating to the United States in 1906. **Herschel (Harry) Weinstein** (Hershl Vaynshteyn, died 1964) was a Russian-born Jewish tailor and anarchist. He was active in the

anarchists.[3] They set out to provide assistance to their close associates in Russian prisons.

Although the members of the Red Cross were all young, many of them women in their twenties, they had already experienced plenty in the inferno of the fight against tsarism, and they threw themselves entirely into the relief work with the enthusiasm of young souls: Feygel Rotberg, Izzie Wishnack, Joe Radding, Zalman, Shlomke, Niomke, Ostrovsky, Morris Weitzman (Granberg), Sam Klatchko, Barukh Yelin, Miller, and dozens of others worked with all their means to gather support for arrested comrades in Russia.[4] They organized the first *arestantn-bal* (prisoners' ball),

---

anarchist movement in Bialystok, leading to his arrest in 1906. He immigrated to New York around 1907 and was later active in the ILGWU. Obituary: *FAS*, January 1, 1965.

3. The **Political Red Cross** was formed in Russia in the 1870s to raise funds for, and sometimes plan the escape of, imprisoned radicals.

4. **Isadore (Izzie or Iza) Wishnack** (Izidor or Izy Vishnyak, 1891–1952) was a Russian-born Jewish garment worker and anarchist. He was active in the anarchist movement in Bialystok, for which he was sentenced to Siberian exile. Wishnack subsequently immigrated to the United States around 1908 and was later a member of the anarchist Broyt un Frayheyt Group, the Bronx's Amshol Group, and Krinker Branch 389 the Workmen's Circle. His wife Feygel (Fannie) Wishnack (Feygl Vishnyak, c. 1891–1986), née Alpert, was likewise a Jewish anarchist from Bialystok and belonged to the board of directors of the *FAS* at the time of its closure in 1977. The couple's home in the Bronx was known as "Hotel Wishnack" due to the number of comrades who visited and stayed with them. Obituary: *FAS*, March 14, 1952. **Joseph (Joe) Radding** (Yosef Rading, c. 1890–1950) was a Russian-born Jewish salesman and anarchist. He was active in the anarchist movement in Bialystok before immigrating to New York in 1905. His wife, Esther Radding (c. 1889–1962), was a Polish Jewish anarchist. The couple were members of the short-lived Jewish agricultural Clarion Colony in Utah in the 1910s and briefly returned to Russia after the 1917 February Revolution. They subsequently lived in Detroit, the Sunrise Colony, and finally Los Angeles. Obituary: *FAS*, April 28, 1950. Morris Weitzman (Moyshe Vaytsman) was the pseudonym of **Morris Granberg** (Moyshe Granberg, 1888–1979), a Russian-born Jewish factory worker and anarchist. He became an anarchist as a teenager in Khotyn, participated in the 1905 Revolution, and in 1906 cofounded the Anarchist Red Cross in Bialystok with Bayrekh Yelin. Granberg immigrated to Argentina in 1909 to avoid arrest and relocated to the United States in 1910. In 1917 he returned to Russia and fought against Whites forces in the Russian Civil War, then in 1920 returned to America, where he lived in the Bronx and sat on the board of directors of the *FAS*. Granberg published firsthand historical accounts of the Anarchist Red Cross in the *FAS* (February 10, 1956, and January 15, 1966). **Samuel (Sam) Klatchko** (Shmuel Klyatshko, 1895–1987) was a Russian-born Jewish printer and anarchist. He was active in the revolutionary movement in Bialystok, leading to several years of imprisonment. Klatchko immigrated to the United States in 1913 and belonged to New York's small Jewish IWW group in the 1910s. **Bayrekh (Barukh or Bernard) Yelin** (1891–1970) was a Russian-born Jewish cloakmaker

which attracted much attention and became an annual institution in our movement in cities across the country until the outbreak of the Russian Revolution in 1917.

Yanovsky, who had an inborn distrust of young comrades, initially approached them with suspicion. He even allowed himself to make a couple of public statements casting unfounded aspersions on their work. With the help of Alexander Berkman, however, they managed to get Yanovsky to hold a meeting and review their accounting. This convinced him that these young people were doing a wonderful job and doing it in a very systematic and honest way. He found an accurate receipt for every penny they collected and hundreds of letters from arrested anarchists in Russia showing how much money was being sent. The evidence was so clear that Yanovsky was completely convinced. He apologized publicly to the youths, and from that time on he did all that he could to help the Anarchist Red Cross in all its undertakings.

In Philadelphia our movement was enriched by the arrival of comrade Morris Beresin, a very intelligent fellow and anarchist, who had been sentenced to many years in prison in Russia.[5] After enduring that martyrdom he was lucky enough to have been locked in the same cell as Sazonov. He managed to escape from the prison camp and described his experiences in the book *Fun keyten tsu frayheyt* (From Chains to Freedom).[6]

---

and anarchist. He was active in the anarchist movement in Bialystok and then imprisoned, and after his release in 1906 he cofounded Anarchist Red Cross with Morris Granberg. After immigrating to New York, Yelin became an active member and secretary of the ILGWU's Local 35. He later moved to Los Angeles, where he belonged to the Kropotkin Literary Society, Branch 413 of the Workmen's Circle, then relocated to Elsinore, California, and donated funds to the *FAS* up until his death. Obituary: *FAS*, December 1, 1970.

5. **Morris Beresin** (Moyshe Berezin, 1888–1973) was a Russian-born Jewish dentist and anarchist. He grew up in Kishenev, where he witnessed the 1903 pogrom, and by 1905 was active in the Russian anarchist movement, leading to him being arrested and sentenced to a forced labor camp in Siberia in 1906. Beresin escaped and in 1911 immigrated to the United States where he became active in the Radical Library Group. In 1917 he moved to Baltimore, where he joined Union of Russian Workers and was arrested in 1921 during the Palmer Raids and nearly deported. Beresin then returned to Philadelphia and became a contributor to the *FAS*. His wife, Rebecca G. Beresin, was also an active member of the Radical Library Group. Obituaries: *FAS*, April 1, 1973; *The Match!*, April 1974.

6. M. Berezin, *Fun keyten tsu frayheyt: fertseykhenungen fun an antlofenem politishen katorzshnik* (From Chains to Freedom: Notes from a Fugitive Political Hard-Labor Convict) (New York: Anarkhistishen royten kreyts, 1916).

Arriving in Philadelphia, he joined our ranks and began working hard for the cause of the martyrs in Russian prisons. His activity found great sympathy in the hearts of Bessie Yelensky and her sister Emma Favia, recently arrived Russian anarchists, who had lived through a very interesting period in Krynki before coming here, as well as Boris Yelensky, who was then still a very young man who spoke no Yiddish because he was born in the Caucasus and raised in a Russian milieu, with White Russians and others.[7] They had, of course, our full sympathy and support. The first *arestantn-bal* in Philadelphia was held in the winter of 1910–1911 and was a great success.

---

7. **Boris Yelensky** (Borekh Yelensky, 1889–1974) was a Russian-born Jewish paper-hanger and anarchist. As a teenager he joined the Maximalist wing of the Socialist-Revolutionary Party and fought in the 1905 Russian Revolution, and in 1907 he fled to the United States, where he had to learn both Yiddish and English. In Philadelphia Yelensky joined the Radical Library, met and married fellow anarchist Bessie Yelensky (née Avedon), and became secretary of the local Anarchist Red Cross. In 1913 the couple moved to Chicago, where Boris joined the Union of Russian Workers, and in 1917 they returned to Russia on the same ship as Leon Trotsky and John Reed. He was a leader in the factory committee movement in his native city of Novorossiysk and twice imprisoned by Bolsheviks before returning to Chicago in 1923. There Yelensky became secretary of the Alexander Berkman Aid Fund and founded the Free Society Group.

CHAPTER 31

The Kropotkin Literary Society

In 1912 our movement began preparing to celebrate Peter Kropotkin's seventieth birthday. The *Fraye arbeter shtime* arranged a big meeting and concert in Carnegie Hall. We, the members of the movement, felt that the celebration needed to have a more concrete character. After some discussion, it was decided to publish Kropotkin's autobiography in a good translation. The book had been hurriedly translated years earlier by Dr. Michael A. Cohn for serialization in the *Fraye arbeter shtime* during Yanovsky's first two years as editor and later published in book form in London.[1] But the book had long been sold out, and the translation, as mentioned, was done too hastily. We therefore decided to publish a new edition in an accurate translation made by comrade David Isakovitz.

The work met with great success. This led to the idea of publishing more books, Kropotkin's as well as others', in Yiddish translations. The result was the formation of the Kropotkin Literary Society, which in a short time became the most important publisher of social science works in the Yiddish language.

Most of the credit for the success of the enterprise must be given to the dedication and willingness of Dr. Jacob A. Maryson, who was the society's treasurer for many years and the principal figure in all branches of the work that it undertook. He was assisted in this work by comrades David Isakovitz, Max Maisel, Shtam, and Sam Margolis, who made several tours across the

---

1. Peter Kropotkin, *Kropotkin's lebens-beshraybung*, trans. M. Cohn (London: Grupe Frayheyt, 1904–1905).

country to recruit member-subscribers and to distribute the works that had been published. In almost every small city there were individual comrades who devoted themselves to the work of recruiting members, distributing the books, and so on.

The society consisted of members all over the country, who paid a dollar a year. For this fee, they received the book that the society published that year. Later, when the society numbered just over 3,000 members, they were able to receive two books for that dollar.

Once a year, the society held a meeting, along with a dinner, at which its officers reported on the work accomplished and suggested a number of new books from which the meeting would choose which ones to publish the following year. At these annual meetings, it later became customary to have an important original presentation on a social issue. Such lectures were given by Dr. Chaim Zhitlowsky, Isaac Hourwich, Shmuel Niger, and others.[2] Over time, the dinners and lectures became an institution in themselves.

The society grew, publishing seven volumes by Kropotkin; one volume of the writings of Bakunin; Karl Marx's *Das Kapital* in three volumes; Sidney and Beatrice Webb's *The History of Trade Unionism* in two volumes; one volume of Ferdinand Lassalle's writings; Pierre-Joseph Proudhon's *What Is Property?*; Max Stirner's *The Ego and Its Own*—sixteen books in all, over seven or eight years. There were many other classic works of socialist and anarchist thinkers on the list, but the Russian Revolution and the Communist "Left" in the labor movement put an end to this wonderful work. The Jewish radicals were afterward not able to publish so many and such well-chosen books in the field of social research.

The founding of the Kropotkin Literary Society, with its unique work, brought about two significant changes in the field of producing literature for our movement. Up until then, this work had been done on the side by our newspapers. Larger treatises used to be serialized in the newspapers and later

---

2. **Shmuel Niger** (1883–1955), real name Samuel Charney (Shmuel Tsharny), was a Russian-born Jewish writer, editor, literary critic, and Labor Zionist. The older brother of B. Charney Vladeck and Daniel Charney, in 1904–1905 he helped found the territorialist Zionist Socialist Workers Party and was imprisoned several times for his political activities. Niger also became a prolific Yiddish writer and essayist and immigrated to the United States in 1919. He wrote for the *Forverts, Der tog, Tsukunft* (which he coedited from 1941 to 1947), and the *FAS*, among other publications.

collected into a pamphlet. Johann Most published a number of pamphlets along the way in his paper *Freiheit*: *Die Gottespest* (The God Pestilence, 1906), *Die Eigenthumsbestie* (The Beast of Property, 1887), *Die freie Gesellschaft* (The Free Society, 1884), *Revolutionäre Kriegswissenschaft* (The Science of Revolutionary Warfare, 1885), and many others, as well as Yanovsky's pamphlet *Vos vilen di anarkhisten?* (What Do the Anarchists Want?), which was reprinted in the *Freiheit* many times. All these pamphlets have been translated into most European languages. Yanovsky's second pamphlet, *Der olef beys fun anarkhizmus* (The ABCs of Anarchism), was widely circulated in many countries. In 1905 we find a note in the almanac of the Russian anarchist movement that *Azbuka Anarkhizma* by "Yanovskaya" is widely used in Russia as a means of propaganda.[3]

In London, *Freedom* and later the *Arbeter fraynd* used the same method and published an entire series of instructive pamphlets and books. Here in America, *Free Society*, during its run at the turn of the twentieth century, published several good pamphlets. But rarely did one of the newspapers publish a large and thorough book. Among the local Philadelphia periodicals, such publications can be counted on the fingers of one hand.

The successful work of the Kropotkin Literary Society encouraged the *Fraye arbeter shtime* to publish several good books: Kropotkin's *The Great French Revolution*, Tolstoy's social writings, and Joseph Bovshover's poems.[4] In its early years under the editorship of Yanovsky, the *Fraye arbeter shtime* was an exception in the sense that it did not publish any pamphlets or books. It left the entire task to the Londoners, the comrades of the *Arbeter fraynd* and the oppositional Frayheyt Group. *Mother Earth*, on the other hand, published a large number of pamphlets and books in its eleven years of activity between 1906 and 1917, in addition to the publications of *Freedom* from London, of which it made free use. Its major works included Alexander Berkman's *Prison Memoirs of an Anarchist* and Voltairine de Cleyre's *Selected Works*, Emma Goldman's *Anarchism and Other Essays* and

---

3. *Almanakh: sbornik po istorii anarkhicheskago dvizheniia v Rossii* (Paris: n.p., 1909), 37.

4. Peter Kropotkin, *Di groyse Frantsoyzishe revolutsyon: 1789–1793*, 2 vols., trans. S. Yanovsky (New York: Fraye Arbeter Shtime, 1912); Leo Tolstoy, *Di sklaferay fun unzer tsayt, un andere geklibene shtriften*, trans. S. Yanovsky (New York: Fraye Arbeter Shtime, 1912); Joseph Bovshover, *Gezamelte shriften (poezye un proza)* (New York: Fraye Arbeter Shtime, 1911).

The Social Significance of the Modern Drama, and many other individual treatises.[5]

The growth of the anarchist press in the first quarter of the twentieth century should also be noted. In the mid-1890s, there were sixty newspapers in the world that spread our ideas: thirteen Italian, eleven French, eleven Spanish, ten German, five English, five Czech, two bilingual Italian-Spanish, two Portuguese, and one Yiddish. In 1925 comrade Diego Abad de Santillán, editor of the anarchist paper *La Protesta* in Buenos Aires, compiled a list of 104 publications, forty-two of them in Spanish (from the various Latin American republics), sixteen Italian, ten French, eight German, two English, three Portuguese, three Yiddish, one Polish, four Scandinavian, six Dutch, three Russian, two Japanese, and four Chinese.[6]

---

5. For a complete list of books and pamphlets published by *Mother Earth,* see Rachel Hui-Chi Hsu, *Emma Goldman,* Mother Earth, *and the Anarchist Awakening* (Notre Dame: University of Notre Dame Press, 2021), 317–21.

6. Cohen's source for these figures is *The Road to Freedom,* December 1926. Diego Abad de Santillán's original article, however, actually undercounted the number of anarchist periodicals being produced; for example, in 1925 there were at least four English-language anarchist periodicals appearing in the United States alone. **Diego Abad de Santillán** (1897–1983), real name Sinesio García Hernández, was a Spanish-born writer, editor, syndicalist, and anarchist. He was a prominent labor and anarchist organizer in both Spain and Argentina, a longtime editor of *La Protesta,* and translated a number of Rudolf Rocker's works into Spanish. Abad de Santillán was deported from Argentina in 1931, and during the Spanish Civil War he (controversially) served as Catalonia's minister of the economy as a representative of the anarchist Federación Anarquista Ibérica (Iberian Anarchist Federation). *La Protesta* (Protest, 1897–2015), which until 1903 bore the title *La Protesta Humana* (Human Protest), was a major Spanish-language anarchist newspaper published in Buenos Aires.

CHAPTER 32

The General Strikes of 1912 and 1913 in New York and Philadelphia

During the great tailors' strike in New York in 1912, a large number of our comrades, many of them newly arrived from London, plunged into the battle with great enthusiasm and unwavering generosity, including L. Baron, Alex Cohen, Solomon, and dozens of others. Under their leadership, the strike took on the character of a true uprising and brought about the organization of strong union locals.

The leaders of the United Garment Workers could not bear the thought that so many radicals had become well regarded by the workers. They unequivocally refused to allow delegates from New York City to attend the 1914 convention in Nashville, Tennessee, a city chosen to guard against the rebellious spirit of the tailors in the large industrial cities. This led to the organization of the Amalgamated Clothing Workers of America (ACWA) as an independent national organization, in opposition to the United Garment Workers.

The new labor organization aroused great hope and anticipation among the thousands of tailors and menswear workers. Sidney Hillman was elected as president, and Joseph Schlossberg was elected general secretary.[1] The

---

1. **Sidney Hillman** (1887–1946) was a Russian-born Jewish garment worker, labor organizer, and onetime socialist. As a teenager he became an organizer for the Bund and participated in the 1905 Russian Revolution. Hillman immigrated to Chicago in 1907 and briefly worked for the ILGWU before becoming president of the ACWA. In the 1930s he played a major role in the formation of the CIO and was a strong supporter of the New Deal. **Joseph Schlossberg** (1875–1971) was a Russian-born Jewish cloakmaker, labor organizer, socialist, and Labor Zionist. In 1888 he immigrated to the United States, where he was involved in

317

ACWA soon established a reputation as a radical organization and gained the upper hand in the Jewish labor movement. Whether it was able to live up to these expectations and maintain its good reputation is another question. But in 1912, and the years that followed, it undoubtedly brought life and enthusiasm to the ranks of the Jewish workers.

In our circles, agitation for direct action, sabotage, and the general strike was popular. The *Fraye arbeter shtime* was opposed to the idea of sabotage as unsocial and immoral. The Socialist Party went a step further. At its annual convention in Indianapolis, it passed a resolution that all members who publicly opposed political action, or who advocated the idea of direct action and sabotage, should be expelled from the party.

With this resolution, the Socialist Party signed its own death warrant. The party was then at the height of its popularity, numbering 120,000 members throughout the country, and publishing many newspapers and magazines. Shortly after the convention, members began leaving the party— William D. Haywood and his supporters, against whom the resolution was primarily aimed, and masses of others who until then had believed that the Socialist Party still had a revolutionary purpose. The decision opened their eyes, proving that the party was in the hands of politicians and careerists like Victor Berger, Morris Hillquit, and similar leaders, who were completely alienated from the workers' lives and struggles. Thus the party began to decline in members and influence.[2]

In the four years following the uprising of ladies' waist makers in 1909, the International Ladies' Garment Workers' Union grew to become one of the largest and most powerful unions in the country. The "Protocol" that was introduced as a result of the big cloakmakers' strike was gradually imposed on the owners of the other branches of the women's clothing industry. By

---

the Jewish labor movement and joined the SLP, becoming an editor of its papers *Das abend blat* and *Der arbeter* (The Worker, 1904–1911). Schlossberg was a leader of the opposition movement within the United Garment Workers that led to the formation of the ACWA. In 1940 he resigned to focus on Labor Zionist causes.

2. **Victor Berger** (1860–1929) was an Austrian-born Jewish teacher, editor, and socialist. His family immigrated to the United States in 1878, and in 1881 he settled in Milwaukee where he joined the SLP and began editing a series of socialist newspapers. In 1901 Berger cofounded the Socialist Party of America, and in 1910 he was the first socialist to be elected to the House of Representatives. He was elected again in 1918 and 1920 (but Congress refused to seat him both times), and yet again in 1924 and 1926.

1913 the ILGWU numbered a few hundred thousand members and was well established in many cities.

In mid-July of that year, it was the turn of the cloakmakers in Philadelphia, Baltimore, and St. Louis to be called out on strike. Some of us had secret suspicions that the main goal was to strengthen the market in New York, but that was nothing more than a suspicion, about which we did not even want to speak with each other. A strike is a strike; one must not dig deep into its causes.

The leader of the union in Philadelphia was Max Amdur, a comrade.[3] The executive board of the union included many comrades, like Max Grishkan and others.[4] From New York came Abraham Mitchell, also a comrade and a union vice president, with a heavy cane and a bodyguard—a man experienced in strikes—to help lead the fight, which soon spread like wildfire.

Nobody was living at the library at 424 Pine Street during the summer months. The building, located right near a cemetery, was generally in the right location for certain kinds of activity. The strike committee used the building for as long as necessary. Our library members who were cloakmakers were all, without exception, active in the strike and did everything possible. The branch helped the striking members financially, according to their needs, throughout. The strike was a lengthy one, a losing one. The business world was already feeling the effects of the severe crisis that was looming. The workers struggled for twenty-six weeks, with great sacrifice. The union spent a quarter of a million dollars and became embroiled in a series of serious lawsuits due to the many assaults and attacks on scabs. As a result of one such lawsuit, a very serious one, alleging that several union leaders had fired revolvers at a bunch of scabs from a moving automobile,

---

3. **Max Amdur** (Maks Amdur, c. 1878–1940) was a Russian-born Jewish garment worker, labor organizer, and anarchist. He immigrated to London, then in 1905 moved to Philadelphia, where he was active in the Cloakmakers' Union and became manager of its Philadelphia Joint Board. Amdur served as a vice president of the ILGWU in 1908–1920 and 1924–1932. In 1928 he relocated to Boston. Obituary: *Gerekhtigkeyt*, October 1940.

4. **Max Grishkan** (Maks Grishkan, 1885–1960) was a Russian-Jewish garment worker, labor organizer, and anarchist. In 1904 he immigrated to London, where became an anarchist and was associated with the *Arbeter fraynd*. Grishkan came to the United States in 1906 and joined the Radical Library as well as the Cloak and Dressmakers' Union, of which he became secretary. In 1940 he was elected secretary of Jewish Anarchist Federation, and he was a member of New York's Ferrer-Rocker Branch 203 of the Workmen's Circle at time of his death. Obituary: *FAS*, June 1, 1960.

my wife and I were forced to come from New York a year later as witnesses to rescue the accused.

The strike had to be called off. A number of workers, our active comrades, were blacklisted by the bosses and had to leave the city to find work elsewhere. Both sides, however, had learned a lesson from the strike. When Benjamin Schlesinger, who was elected president of the ILGWU in 1913, came to Philadelphia a year later and worked a little on public relations, he was able to come to an understanding with the bosses without a strike.[5] The union lost the battle in 1913 but not the broader war. It continued to function in a weakened condition, and, at the first opportunity, as soon as industrial conditions in the country began to improve, the union returned to its vital activity and influence.

5. **Benjamin Schlesinger** (1876–1932) was a Russian-born garment worker, labor organizer, and socialist. He immigrated to the United States in 1891 and, beginning at age sixteen, held several offices in the Chicago Cloakmakers' Union. Schlesinger joined the SLP and then the Socialist Party of America and was business manager of the *Forverts* from 1907 to 1912. He served multiple terms as ILGWU president: 1903–1907, 1914–1923, and 1928–1932.

CHAPTER 33

Our Movement in Philadelphia after 1913

My departure from Philadelphia at the end of 1913 did not weaken our movement there. On the contrary, in some respects, it intensified the activity of a number of comrades, who felt that they now needed to devote more time to movement work. The Radical Library was put under the supervision of a committee: Samuel Hindin, Israel Kaplan, Harry Melman, Muni Sharlip, and a few others—each rotating in for one week, with the understanding that if they did not fulfill their obligation the specified week, they had to pay two dollars. The Sunday school was led by Abe Grosner, with the help of some of the children. All other jobs were done in a similar fashion.

Emma Goldman again attempted to address a meeting in Philadelphia, without success. As far as I know, Goldman never had the opportunity to speak publicly in Philadelphia, the city that was the cradle of American liberty.[1] In 1893 she was arrested before she could enter the hall. In 1904 the police did not let the audience into Odd Fellows Temple. In 1909, during a second attempt to hold a meeting at the same hall, the police let the people enter but did not let Emma in. Now, in 1914, the comrades had arranged a series of lectures at the Labor Lyceum. Emma was announced among the list of speakers. Berkman arrived a few days beforehand and announced that Emma Goldman would be giving a lecture. He called all the editors of the English-language newspapers to deliver the spicy news over the phone—a

---

1. Cohen is incorrect; Goldman successfully delivered talks in Philadelphia on multiple occasions between 1896 and 1917, as well as during her return visit in 1934. See Candace Falk, Stephen Cole, and Sally Thomas, "Chronology (1869–1940)," in *Emma Goldman: A Guide to Her Life and Documentary Sources* (Alexandria, VA: Chadwyck-Healey, 1995), 37–116.

עמא גאָלדמאָן די גראַגערקע און פרייע רעדע אין אמעריקא.

Figure 24: Emma Goldman cartoon from *Der groyser kundes*
"Emma Goldman, the noisemaker, and free speech in America," from the Yiddish satirical magazine *Der groyser kundes*, June 4, 1909

kind of challenge to the police for an open confrontation. The police took up
the challenge and did not permit Emma to enter the hall. She and a number
of comrades at the Radical Library decided to hold her lecture no matter
what. In order to prevent the police from interrupting the talk, Emma tied
herself with ropes and chains to the platform on which she stood and to
the windows and the iron fence separating the library from the neighboring
cemetery. Until the police managed to cut all the ropes and chains, she would
be able to continue with her performance. The scenario was easy to imagine.
But all this effort was in vain—the police did not show up. Emma, bound in
chains, was undisturbed and delivered her lecture to a circle of her comrades.

About a year later, the comrades were forced to look for a new location for the Radical Library. The owner of the building, a former radical who now was a rich real estate agent, insisted that they either buy the building or vacate it. This was a tactic often used in Philadelphia. Most people there lived in small single-family homes and were forced to buy the houses for very high prices with small down payments, and a few years later the houses would be foreclosed on for nonpayment on the mortgage.

The comrades were not prepared at that time to buy the building. For one thing, they had already concluded that the neighborhood was not the best place for a library. They found a building in the Uptown area, one of the larger buildings belonging to the Girard Estate, and settled on North Sixth Street.

In their new home, the comrades carried on with their former activities, with the addition of a new venture: a cooperative grocery store under the supervision of Max Prussak. It was a unique store, open only in the evening when comrades and their wives came to the library for all sorts of other purposes. Few of them lived close enough to come to the store to buy all the little things that are sold in such a store every time a housewife finds that they are missing something in the kitchen. The store was not a great success.

The building was overseen by the likes of Fannie and Israel Kaplan.[2] All her life, Fannie excelled in keeping her home clean. At her house, everything shone. It was said that Fannie would stand at the entrance of the library with a clean white cloth in her hand, and as soon as anyone entered, stepping up the white stairs with which the old houses in Philadelphia are adorned, she'd begin to wipe the steps clean and let them shine again in their full glory. This was, of course, just a jest, but under her supervision the building really was kept in the best order—something that can rarely be said about a radical institution.

Eventually the time came when America was drawn into the First World War, and the wild hysteria of patriotic bloodlust overtook the country. A large number of comrades had to withdraw from public life in order to avoid

---

2. **Fannie Kaplan** (c. 1875–1956) was a Russian-born Jewish garment worker and anarchist. She immigrated to the United States in 1911 and married fellow anarchist Israel Kaplan. In 1921 the couple moved to the Stelton Colony, where their children attended the Modern School. Obituary: *FAS*, July 27, 1956.

the military draft. Maintaining the library became too difficult. In addition, one fine evening, when the comrades were all gathered for the Russian Tea Party, they learned that a fire had broken out in the library's building and caused much damage. Luckily, the room that housed the books was not badly damaged. The other rooms, however, were ruined. The comrades had to again find a new location, and, under the greatly aggravated circumstances caused by the war, they packed up the books, put the boxes in a cellar, and wandered about like neighbors in busy meeting halls.

The longing for a home of their own and for a wide range of activities, however, was very great. One evening during Passover, comrades gathered at Charles Saltz's place for a "seder" and argued that this could not continue; they had to figure out how to revive the activity of the Radical Library. Everyone agreed, they absolutely had to! Times were better now in America; there was what people called prosperity, and comrades were able to talk not only about reopening the library but also about purchasing a building in which to do so. They collected $2,000 among themselves and after a short search bought a large building on North Franklin Street, where the Radical Library carried out many activities for more than ten years.

The work there shifted to a larger scale than during the library's best years on Pine Street. Comrade Beresin spent one summer vacationing at Unity House, where he met Will Durant, a frequent lecturer at the Radical Library in previous years.[3] They, of course, discussed the possibilities for activity, the need for educational work among adults, and so on, until they arrived upon the idea of opening a "People's University" in the Radical Library's new building. Durant consented to take on the role of director, for a relatively good salary. He would come from New York and hold a series of his own lectures on philosophy—which he had already worked on for a number of years, preparing to publish them in the form of a book that later made a big impression and was distributed in huge numbers.[4] He would also obtain lecturers and arrange classes on various other subjects.

The comrades agreed to the plan with great enthusiasm, despite the enormous expenses involved. Every lecturer was to receive twenty-five

---

3. **Unity House** was a health resort and educational center run by the ILGWU in the Pocono Mountains for its members between 1919 and 1990.

4. These lectures were the basis for Durant's best-selling book *The Story of Philosophy: The Lives and Opinions of the Greater Philosophers* (1926).

dollars plus travel expenses. But the prospects were so large, and the reaction of the public was so enthusiastic, that nothing would stand in the way of their plans. Among the lecturers—each of whom led a series of discussions on a particular issue—were professors Harry Allen Overstreet, Charles Loomis Dana, Everett Dean Martin, John Cowper Powys, and others, in addition to Durant's long series of lectures.[5] The audience was very large. People stood shoulder-to-shoulder, in the foyer, on the stairs, and wherever they could find a spot as they rushed in to hear the speakers. The debts were also large every week and were partially covered by comrades Beresin and Harry Melman, who did not want the other comrades to realize the extent of the expenses. In addition to spending all his free time at the building, Melman saw to it that everything was kept in order and negotiated with the tenants—such as the Russian anarchist group, which occupied a large room and could not or would not pay the rent; the Workmen's Circle school, which demanded a great deal of space for very little rent; and other such comradely occupants.

With the great success of the activities of the People's University, and the limitations of the space, the idea arose to remodel the building, especially the second floor, to create a larger auditorium there with a stage and other improvements. Some practical comrades, including Saltz, were opposed to going into greater debt. As it stood, the building was financially in good condition, with a mortgage of only $5,000, on which they had to pay twenty-five dollars a month. The taxes to the city were taken care of by comrade Harry Wolf for four years, who paid $100 a year. Yet the expenditures for heating, lighting, cleaning, and managing the activities were much greater than the income from the building and all the events throughout the year. The branch had been carrying the load and was often behind on its payments to the main office of the Workmen's Circle.

---

5. **Harry Allen Overstreet** (1875–1970) was an American-born liberal philosopher and psychologist who taught at the City College of New York and is best known for his book *The Mature Mind* (1949). **Charles Loomis Dana** (1852–1935) was an American-born doctor and professor at Cornell Medical College who specialized in neurological disease. **Everett Dean Martin** (1880–1941) was an American-born social psychologist, writer, educator, and champion of adult and liberal arts education who taught at the New School for Social Research and Cooper Union's People's Institute. **John Cowper Powys** (1872–1963) was an English-born novelist, poet, critic, and anarchist. He was a friend of Emma Goldman and a talented public debater.

An aside: Comrade Harry Wolf was one of the most interesting figures in our movement in Philadelphia. For a half a century, he devoted himself to selling our literature and generously supporting the movement. He seldom missed a meeting. He traveled to all the major happenings in New York and Stelton, and he seriously discussed every issue and expressed a logically minded opinion on every activity. In public, however, in all those years, he never said a word or took part in any discussion. No amount of coaxing would succeed in making him express his views at a meeting on an issue of great importance. For many years he supported the *Fraye arbeter shtime*, until an advertisement appeared in it for "Kosher Passover Matzos"; he stopped giving a cent to the newspaper beyond the price of a subscription. Far from being a capitalist in the true sense of the word, he gave his relatively large donations to all movement pursuits anonymously. When one well-known anarchist lecturer first came to Philadelphia, Wolf greeted him and slipped a hundred-dollar bill into his hand, and this was not an isolated case. He was a very good person (*mentsh*) all his years.

Returning to our story: the movement demanded larger facilities, and so they had to be obtained. The library took out a second mortgage on the building for another $3,000 and rebuilt the second floor, making it into a larger auditorium—but not very successfully, as the ceiling was low and the room long and narrow, though there was space for a considerable number of people. Lessons and classes could be held there on a larger scale. The expenses for keeping the building in order also increased greatly. Comrade Moore, who by now could no longer be classified as bourgeois, moved into the library to take charge of the building, to be secretary of the Workmen's Circle branch, and to carry on its activities, which had not been very strongly maintained. When Abe Grosner moved to New York to manage the *Fraye arbeter shtime*, the People's University, with its horribly large expenses, could not be sustained or developed.

The most active Radical Library members in those days were Morris Beresin, Alexander Brown, Harry Melman, Benny Moore, Max Grishkan, Louis Segal, Hyman Weinstock, Sarah Greenberg, and a few young people who arrived after I had already left Philadelphia.[6] Beresin was a very mod-

---

6. **Sarah Greenberg** (Grinberg, 1891–1959) was a Russian-born Jewish cloakmaker and anarchist. She immigrated to Philadelphia around 1907 and by 1911 was an active rank-and-file

est, reserved, and gifted man. At one point he wrote a lengthy play, which through the efforts of Abraham Frumkin was performed by the famous actors Samuel Goldenberg and Celia Adler, with a professional troupe, in the Arch Street Theatre rather than the Radical Library.[7] During the war hysteria and Palmer raids, Beresin stayed in Baltimore, where he had the misfortune of falling into the hands of patriotic government officials. Their behavior was no better than in tsarist Russia, where he had been sentenced to years in a prison camp. Here, in free America, after his arrest with a large number of other members of the Union of Russian Workers, he was beaten mercilessly and held for several months.[8] Fortunately, local officials in Baltimore did not have the heart to break up his family and take away the father of small children who were born here and therefore American citizens. He was not sent to Ellis Island like the others, and after a few months he was released on bail and then kept under police surveillance for a long time. In comparison with the other radicals arrested, he made it through those difficult times much more easily.

The Radical Library attracted a number of talented new people. In 1913 comrade Alexander Brown came from London. A good speaker, a practical activist in the labor movement, he soon joined the foremost ranks of the active members of the library. He became active in the Workmen's Circle and in the unions and rendered much service to the branch as secretary for many years. His name was well known in Philadelphia as a representative of the Radical Library and among our comrades across the country as one

militant in Philadelphia's Cloakmakers' Union Local 69 and a member of the Women's Trade Union League. Obituary: *FAS*, November 15, 1959.

7. The unpublished play, titled *Der falsher emes* (The False Truth), was staged in 1924. **Samuel Goldenberg** (Goldnburg, 1886–1945) was a famous Russian-born Jewish actor of the Yiddish theater. **Celia Adler** (1889–1979), was the American-born daughter of Russian Jewish actors Jacob Adler and Dina Shtettin Adler, and like her parents she became a famous actress of the Yiddish stage.

8. The **Union of Russian Workers of the United States and Canada** (Federatsiia Soiuzov Russkikh Rabochikh Soed. Shtatov i Kanady) was an anarcho-syndicalist federation founded in 1914, bringing together several preexisting groups of Russian workers that had formed over the previous few years. It supported both the revolutionary movement in Russian and labor struggles in North America and was closely aligned with the IWW. The Union of Russian Workers included a disproportionately large number of Jewish radicals among its Russian-speaking membership, which reached over ten thousand before the organization was repressed by the US government in 1919.

of the most active members of our movement. The comrades sent him as a delegate to all our conferences and conventions, at which his remarks were listened to with great care.

Some of the younger comrades advanced very well intellectually and contributed much to the success of the library. William Shulman excelled in this regard. He read and studied assiduously, becoming, in spirit, a leader among the comrades with his frequent lectures, introductory discussions, and participation in all activities. His passionate approach to society and his serious approach to social questions placed him high in our ranks. For a time he was engaged as a paid organizer for his union, the pants makers, but the work did not appeal to his philosophical-intellectual inclinations and did not match his worldview, so he resigned and devoted all his free time to the service of our movement. Death tore him from our ranks at a young age.

In these years, the library had a number of people who were capable of giving a good speech, presenting our point of view, and seriously engaging with the problems of the social movement. Grosner, Shulman, Brown, Beresin, Samuel Polinow, Moore, Segal, and Grishkan kept the branch meetings interesting and engaging for its members.[9] Old Chaim Weinberg seldom missed a gathering or lecture. His presence always added a certain distinction to the event.

Among the active members we must also note the following comrades: Charles Saltz, Gershon Goldstein, and the Sharlips (Oscar and Sam). Over the years, some of the well-known comrades carried the burden of caring for the library, maintaining its very existence. Special acknowledgment must be given to comrades Melman and Brown. The former never tired of waking others up, alerting them to their responsibilities, and instilling in them a spirit of unlimited optimism in the work. He seldom held an official office, but unofficially, practically, his work almost always bore fruit.

The position of the branch's official representatives was difficult. The secretaries had to take care of the financial side of the work. They had to be a kind of opposition to the members, who at meetings were generous with

---

9. **Samuel Polinow** (Semuel Polinov, 1892–1973) was a Russian-born Jewish accountant and anarchist. He joined the Radical Library Group after immigrating to Philadelphia around the turn of the twentieth century and in the 1920s and 1930s became a regular contributor to Yiddish and English-language anarchist publications, including the *FAS*, *The Road to Freedom*, and *Man!* In 1949 Polinow married fellow anarchist Rose Wascow.

their decisions and free in their willingness to help everything and everyone. No appeal to the branch was ever turned down. No member was ever
dropped for nonpayment at a meeting. They certainly never abandoned
activities because of heavy expenses. The financial secretary went crazy trying to meet all these generous resolutions.

For many years comrades Goldstein, Brown, Polinow, and Bernard
Shane performed this unenviable service. Nobody was envious of their fate.
There were times when the branch was drowning in debts. The central office
of the Workmen's Circle was owed a large sum of money. For a while, it
seemed that the branch would have to be dissolved. But the organization
dealt with the Radical Library like the branch dealt with its members: recognizing the good work and pure intentions of the branch, the national
executive board canceled a large portion of the debt and made it possible
for the branch to continue its work.

A prominent place in the activity of the Radical Library was occupied by
the wives of its members: Celia Melman, Minnie Weinstock, Ethel Finkler,
Sonia Grishkan, Gussie Beresin, Julia Brown, Rebecca Saltz, Rose Wascow,
Anna Matusow, Rachel Gosfield, Sarah Moore, Sophia Mariella, Sarah
Greenberg, and Becky Stein.[10] The latter two were almost like twins and were
inseparable for years.

---

10. **Minnie Weinstock** (Vaynshtok, 1890–1970), née Wedman, was a Russian-born
Jewish anarchist. She immigrated to the United States in 1909 and married fellow anarchist
Hyman Weinstock in 1916. Obituary: *FAS*, September 1, 1970. **Ethel Finkler** (1895–1966),
née Cohen, was a Russian-born Jewish clerk and anarchist. Her family immigrated to the
United in 1898 when she was a small child, and she joined the anarchist movement in 1921,
marrying fellow anarchist Philip Finkler. At the time of her death Finkler was remembered
as "the liveliest part" of the Radical Library Group. Obituaries: *FAS*, April 15 and May 1, 1966.
Sonia Grishkan (1885–1965), née Katzman, was a Russian-born Jewish anarchist. She came
to the United States in 1905 and married anarchist Max Grishkan. For two summers she was
the manager of Camp Germinal. Obituary: *FAS*, October 1, 1965. **Rebecca G. ("Gussie")
Beresin** (Berezin, c. 1891–1964), née Roitman, was a Jewish anarchist born in either Russia or Romania. In 1906 she immigrated to the United States, where she married anarchist
Morris Beresin, taught at the Radical Library's Sunday school, and assisted at Camp Germinal. Obituary: *FAS*, March 15, 1964. **Julia Brown** (Braun, c. 1882–1968) was a Russian-born
Jewish anarchist. She was active in the Jewish anarchist movement in England before immigrating to Philadelphia around 1912, and she married fellow anarchist Alexander Brown the
following year. Obituary: *FAS*, July 15, 1968. **Rebecca ("Becky") Saltz** (1888–1964), née
Kochensky, was a Russian-born Jewish anarchist. She came to the United States around 1905
and married fellow anarchist Charles Saltz in 1908. She was an active member of the Radical

I could mention dozens of women from the early years—Natasha Notkin, Mary Hansen, Yeta Bok, Sophie Cohen, Sarah Neper, Yetta London, the Kutin sisters, Rose Levenson, Olye Boyman—to show how large the contributions of women were to our movement.[11] This was a kind of tradition in Philadelphia, a legacy of the Ladies' Liberal League, from which we inherited the name and the foundations of our library.

In the hot summer months, our circle used to gather every Sunday afternoon in Fairmount Park near George's Hill. Over the years, this became an

---

Library Group up until her death. Obituary: *FAS*, February 1, 1965. **Rose Wascow** (Vasko, 1892–1977) was a Russian-born Jewish anarchist. She immigrated to the United States around 1907 and was the wife of fellow anarchist Joseph Washkowitz (Joseph Wascow). Following Joseph's death, she married anarchist Samuel Polinow in 1949. **Anna Matusow** (Matusov, c. 1884–1978) was a Russian-born Jewish anarchist. She immigrated to the United States in 1904 with her husband, Abraham Matusow (c. 1874–1945), who was not an anarchist but financially supported the *FAS* and local anarchist causes on behalf of his wife (see his obituary in *FAS*, February 9, 1945). Anna remained active in the Radical Library, where she ran a Yiddish literature discussion group, into her nineties. She also became a strong supporter of Labor Zionism. Obituary: *Philadelphia Inquirer*, July 31, 1978. **Rachel (Rose) Gosfield** (Rokhl Gosfild, 1882–1956), née Kaufman, was a Russian-born Jewish garment worker and anarchist. She joined the labor movement in her native Vilna (present-day Vilnius, Lithuania) and at age sixteen immigrated to England, where she became involved in the anarchist movement and met her first husband, anarchist Edward Gosfield. The couple immigrated to the United States in 1902 and joined the Radical Library Group, where Rachel was active in women's reading circles and the Modern School movement. In 1945, following Edward's death, she married widower Max Zebine, another member of Radical Library. Obituary: *FAS*, December 28, 1956. **Sarah Moore** (Mur, c. 1879–1966) was a Russian-born Jewish anarchist. She immigrated to Philadelphia in 1899 and married anarchist Benny Moore the following year. Around 1944 the couple moved to Los Angeles, where they were active in the Kropotkin Literary Society, Branch 413 of the Workmen's Circle. Obituary: *FAS*, July 1, 1966. **Sophia Mariella** (Mariela, 1886–1965), née Peel (Pil), was a Russian-born Jewish garment worker and anarchist. She immigrated to England before coming to the United States around 1910 and joining the Radical Library Group. Her husband, Angelo Mariella (c. 1888–?), was an Italian-born cement worker. Mariella helped run Camp Germinal and was active in the anarchist movement at least as late as 1945. **Becky Stein** (Beki Steyn, c. 1893–?) was a Russian-born Jewish garment worker, labor organizer, and anarchist. She immigrated to Philadelphia with her mother and siblings in 1907 and began working in a garment shop in 1909. Soon Stein was an active rank-and-file militant in the Cloak and Skirt Finishers' Union, Local 69, and a member of the Women's Trade Union League. She testified about conditions in the garment trades before the congressional Commission on Industrial Relations in 1914.

11. **Yetta London** (1886–1942), also known as Yetta Weinberg, was a Russian-born Jewish labor organizer and anarchist. She immigrated to the United States around 1896, was an organizer for the cloakmakers' and cigarmakers' unions, and became fellow anarchist Chaim Weinberg's lifelong companion.

institution in and of itself. The members and sympathizers of our movement would come there in huge numbers. There, on the green grass under
the open sky, discussions were held in small circles, and quite often—when
a serious question interested the public—the small circles would merge
into one large gathering of hundreds of people, for whom our speakers—
George Brown, Max Grishkan, Morris Beresin, and Shmuel Marcus—would
appear.[12] These Sunday meetings became famous throughout Philadelphia.

---

12. **Shmuel Marcus** (Markus, 1893–1985), also known as Marcus Graham, Fred S.
Graham, and Robert Parsons, was a Romanian-born Jewish garment worker, egg candler,
writer, editor, and anarchist. After his family immigrated to Philadelphia in 1907, he joined
the Socialist Party and then the anarchist movement. Marcus went to Canada during the
First World War to avoid registering for the draft, and in 1919 he settled in New York where
he anonymously edited the underground papers *Anarchist Soviet Bulletin* (1919–1920) and
Free Society (1921–1922), which advocated immediate insurrectionary action. He was arrested
in 1919 and held for deportation as an alien anarchist but refused to divulge his given name
and country of birth and was eventually released on bail. In 1924 Marcus joined the Road to
Freedom Group, but he found it too moderate and left for the Stelton Colony the following
year, then relocated to San Francisco in 1932 to edit *Man!* under the pseudonym "Marcus
Graham." From the First World War onward he was a vocal critic of the *FAS* (and of Joseph
Cohen in particular), as well as of labor unions of all stripes, which aligned him more closely
with many Italian anarchists than most of his fellow Jewish anarchists. After repeated arrests
by immigration authorities, in the 1940s Marcus began living clandestinely, though he continued to contribute to anarchist publications until his death.

PART THREE

In and around New York, 1913–1932

CHAPTER 34

In New York

I left Philadelphia on Monday, December 1, 1913. The day before, the children of our school took leave of me with songs mixed with tears. In the evening, the members of the Radical Library wished me good luck as I set out into the wider world.

A few months earlier, I had moved out of the library building, where I had lived for three years amid constant turmoil and perpetual exertion. Now a call had come from New York to take over the Ferrer Center and school there.

The center had been organized at the end of 1910, a year after the martyrdom of Francisco Ferrer. Emma Goldman and Alexander Berkman had initiated it. They first opened the center on St. Marks Place, in downtown. John R. Coryell and his wife Abby were the first teachers.[1] At its opening the school had a single student, but over time the number of children increased to reach a couple of dozen. In 1911 Alden Freeman pledged $100 a month to pay for the salary of a teacher, and he recommended his protégé, Will Durant, for the position.

Durant was then a very young man, and he looked even younger. He had been educated in a Catholic university, from which he emerged as a staunch freethinker with a strong desire to enlighten people, to open their eyes and help them think critically about the order of the world and their many superstitions.

---

1. **Abby Hedge Coryell** (1858–1957) was an American-born poet, educator, and anarchist and a close friend of Emma Goldman.

Figure 25: Will Durant and students at the Ferrer Modern
School, 1912
Courtesy of Wikimedia Commons

In those years he was very shy, and he used to give his lectures sitting
behind a table. This, together with his youthful appearance, made an unusu-
ally good impression on his listeners. He was a natural orator, and the Jesuit
teachers in the university had acquainted him well with the philosophical teachings of the great thinkers. He was well equipped for his work as a
teacher, especially for teaching adults.

So the school was provided with a salaried teacher. The center had
enough income to cover all other expenses, but there was no order in and

around the school. Comrade Harry Kelly had been dealing with its management for a while—for half a day, only—without success. Then Alexander Berkman took on the responsibility for a while and gave up on it after a short trial. Dr. Paul Luttinger also quickly tired and left with a bang: a lawsuit against the members and the entire institution.[2] The poet Lola Ridge held the job of organizer longer than the others, but she too grew tired of the struggle with the delinquent element that hung around the center.[3]

By 1913 the school was located on 107th Street in Harlem, near Central Park. Will Durant had left after he was forced to marry one of his students, a fifteen-year-old girl.[4] His place was taken by a middle-aged woman (Cora Bennett Stephenson), who took two younger women as her assistants to help with the teaching of twenty-five children of different ages.[5]

My first impression of the center was not at all favorable. The building was shabby, dirt was piled in every corner, and the dust was thick on all the cabinets and shelves. In one room a group of "spittoon philosophers"

---

2. **Paul Luttinger** (1885–1939) was a Romanian-born physician, writer, and Marxist. He was educated in Bulgaria, Turkey, Palestine, Germany, and the United States, to which he immigrated with his family in 1901. Luttinger was an advocate of "rational education," but after leaving the Ferrer Modern School he claimed it was "a notorious educational swindle" and "the most colossal fake ever perpetrated on any community" (*The Burning Question: Rational Education of the Proletariat* [Rational Education League, 1913], 38, 41). He later joined the Communist Party, writing a health column for its *Daily Worker* (1924–1958) and publishing the radical medical magazine *Health* (1934), but by 1936 Luttinger was affiliated with the Trotskyist Socialist Workers Party.

3. **Lola Ridge** (1873–1941), born Rose Emily Ridge, was an Irish-born factory worker, artist, poet, editor, and anarchist. As a child she emigrated with her widowed mother to New Zealand and Australia, then came to the United States in 1907 after her mother's death. Ridge published her radical poetry in *Mother Earth*, *The New Masses*, *The New Republic*, *The Saturday Review of Literature*, and other outlets, and is best-known for her collection *The Ghetto and Other Poems* (1918).

4. The student was **Ariel Durant** (1898–1981), born Chaya ("Ida") Kaufman. Her family immigrated to London in 1900 then in 1901 to the United States, where her mother Ethel Kaufman (née Appel) was involved in the anarchist movement and she began attending the Ferrer Modern School in 1912. Cohen's claim that Will Durant was forced to marry her is misleading; by all accounts, the pair were happy to wed, despite their thirteen-year age difference. They would go on to collaborate on the prize-winning *The Story of Civilization* (1935–1975), as well as *A Dual Autobiography* (1977).

5. **Cora Bennett Stephenson** (1872–1958) was an American-born teacher, novelist, Latin teacher, and socialist. She left the Ferrer Modern School following the Lexington Avenue explosion of 1914.

gathered, chewing tobacco and incessantly criticizing everyone and every-thing.

In the evening, Leonard D. Abbott conducted a class on literature. A number of prominent people attended: Stewart Kerr, Manuel Komroff, Carl Zigrosser, and others.[6] I knew them all and held them in high esteem for their sincerity and devotion. When they asked me for my impressions of the situation, I answered very briefly, "The place needs a proper cleaning up!"

Stewart Kerr sprang up. "There's an idea!" he exclaimed enthusiastically. "Why did it not occur to us before? You are just the man to do it. We shall help you with everything!"

But this was easier said than done. Much tact and effort was necessary to prevent the idle loafers, the "spittoon philosophers," from coming there in the daytime when the children occupied the place. It was also necessary to fire the janitor, a comrade Elliott, who had no regard for cleanliness or responsibility but had behind him a whole "mob" of supporters, ostensibly members of the Ferrer Association.[7] The organization was anarchist in the primitive sense of the term. Meetings were held every week. Anyone who wanted to come did so and gave their opinion. The members had no defined responsibilities to the organization, and the decisions reached at the meet-ings were disregarded. Each meeting took up whatever topic was brought up in the moment.

My efforts to make changes, to eliminate the loafer element, provoked a full-fledged revolution against me. At one of the meetings Emma Goldman

---

6. **Stewart Kerr** (1868–1949) was a Scottish electrician and anarchist. He immigrated to the United States in 1888 and was a founding member of Francisco Ferrer Association and the Stelton Modern School's managing board. Kerr was a friend of Emma Goldman and wrote for *The Modern School* (1912–1922), which he briefly edited, as well as *Mother Earth*. **Manuel Komroff** (1890–1974) was an American-born journalist, playwright, novelist, and anarchist. He was an art critic for the socialist *New York Call* and an active member of the Ferrer Center. Komroff traveled to Russia during the 1917 revolution as a journalist and went on to become a successful writer, remaining an anarchist until the end of this life. **Carl Zigrosser** (1891–1975) was an American-born art dealer and anarchist. He was later involved in the Modern School at Stelton and edited *The Modern School*. Zigrosser went on to become a curator for the Philadelphia Museum of Art.

7. This may be the same janitor, known as Frank the Crank, who, according to former student Révolte Bercovici, once "chopped a cat's head off to teach . . . [the students] 'about life.'" Paul Avrich, *Anarchist Voices: An Oral History of Anarchism in America* (Princeton: Princeton University Press, 1995), 198.

appeared. This was a miracle to me; she had no time for such things, although she was one of the initiators of the Modern School movement and was genuinely interested in the development of the school. As soon the meeting opened, the reason became clear to me: she had learned that the comrades wanted to have me sent back to Philadelphia, whence I had come to join them. Dozens of good speakers, one after another, attacked my bourgeois-dictatorial ideas and actions. Everyone demanded my resignation. Then Emma took the floor, chastised them all in her incomparable way, and the "revolution" ended with a complete victory for my efforts to clean up the school and elevate it to the proper level. I had no more difficulties with the membership.

I tried to get to know everyone who was interested in the school, or could be useful to it, and there were many such people in New York. I convinced Will Durant to lecture for adults, and with the help of Leonard D. Abbott, I became acquainted with Henrietta Rodman, one of the most distinguished and influential high school teachers in the city; with Robert Henri and George Bellows, two great painters and members of the American Academy of Arts and Letters; with Dr. John Weichsel and Dr. Benzion Liber, Bolton Hall, Alden Freeman, Rose Pastor Stokes, William English Walling, and dozens of others influential figures who had something to contribute in the field of education.[8] All these efforts yielded results over time.

---

8. **Henrietta Rodman** (1877–1923) was an American-born teacher, feminist, and pacifist. She was a member of Greenwich Village's feminist Heterodoxy group, the Liberal Club, and the Women's Peace Party. **Robert Henri** (1865–1929) was an American-born painter and anarchist. He cofounded the Ashcan School of social realist art and taught painting classes at the Ferrer Center. **George Bellows** (1882–1925) was an American-born painter and anarchist. A protégé of Henri, he taught art classes at the Ferrer Center and contributed drawings and prints to the socialist magazine *The Masses*, on whose editorial board he sat. Unlike most fellow radicals, Bellows strongly supported US intervention in the First World War. **Benzion Liber** (Ben-Tsien Liber, 1875–1958), born Ben-Tsien Libresko or Librescu, was a Romanian-born Jewish physician, psychiatrist, writer, and anarchist. Educated in Paris, Bucharest, and Vienna, he joined the Romanian socialist movement and was imprisoned for his subversive writings. Liber immigrated to the New York in 1904 and became a prominent advocate of vegetarianism, sex education, and birth control, and an opponent of circumcision. He wrote on these topics in the *FAS*, the *Forverts*, and in many books and pamphlets, as well as in his own radical journals *Unzer gezunt* and *Rational Living* (1920–1928). Liber was also treasurer of the New York Anarchist Red Cross and a cofounder of the Ferrer Modern School, where his son, Amour Liber, was the first student to enroll. In 1910 Liber moved to the single-tax colony Free Acres in Berkeley Heights, New Jersey, and after the Russian

Among other things, I paid a visit to Yanovsky to win the support of the *Fraye arbeter shtime* for our work. He greeted me kindly and promised he would do everything possible to help. But he also told me that it was a mistake for me to have left Philadelphia, where I did good work and everyone knew me and followed my activities. "Who here, in Babylon, will pay attention to you?"

I assured him that I did not care if anyone paid attention to me or not. There was more than enough work to be done in New York, I added, and I didn't need anything more.

In the thirty years that I came into contact with Yanovsky, my relationship with him was always remarkably friendly, despite our differences of opinion and clashes. I had affection for him, for his sharp intellect, his humor, even his biting sarcasm. I enjoyed spending hours with him and had many opportunities to convince myself that this feeling was reciprocal. But when I returned to New York a second time, six years later, to take over the editorship of the *Fraye arbeter shtime* six months after he had resigned, he told me quite frankly that had he known that I would consent to come work for the paper, he would not have taken the step of stepping down as editor. But more about that later.

That winter the Ferrer Center flourished. Bessie Dunn, a mother of two children at the school, voluntarily took on the task of ensuring that the building was immaculately clean.[9] The next day, the kindergarten was run

---

Revolution he became a supporter of the Soviet Union, though he did not join the Communist Party. During the Spanish Civil War he conducted health exams of volunteers for the International Brigades. In 1956 Liber published his memoir, *A Doctor's Apprenticeship*. **Rose Pastor Stokes** (1879–1933) was a Russian-born Jewish cigarmaker, journalist, socialist, and later Communist. Her family immigrated to the United Sates in 1891, and she joined the Socialist Party of America in 1905, soon becoming a prominent writer and lecturer on socialism and birth control. In 1919 Stokes cofounded the Communist Party of America, and she sat on its executive committee. **William English Walling** (1877–1936) was a wealthy American-born settlement house worker, journalist, and socialist. Best known for his reporting on the Russian Revolution of 1905, he also cofounded the Women's Trade Union League and the National Association for the Advancement of Colored People. Walling married socialist Anna Strunsky (1879–1964) in 1906, joined the Socialist Party of America in 1910, and became a regular contributor to *The Masses*, but his support of the Allied war effort resulted in his resignation from the Socialist Party in 1917 and the breakup of his marriage.

9. **Bessie Dunn** (Besi Don, 1888–?), née Markowitz, was a Romanian-born Jewish anarchist. She immigrated to the United States in 1901 with her husband, Romanian-born Jewish roofer Newman Dunn (1884–?), and the couple had two daughters: Luna (1906–1964) and

as planned, without any problems. In the evening, all the rooms were filled with adults in various classes and meetings.

The winter was severe, critically so, and masses of the unemployed filled the streets of the city. Under the influence of Alexander Berkman, the "spittoon philosophers" embarked on the task of addressing the street meetings of the unemployed. Gradually, an army of several hundred unemployed people formed, which served as the "nucleus" holding together the movement.

One of the speakers, Sam Hartman, came up with the idea of leading the unemployed to churches to ask for food and lodging from the followers of Jesus, who had called on all who were hungry and suffering to come to him and be saved.[10] The idea caught on with his comrades. They paid their first stop not to a church but to the *Forverts* building on East Broadway. There the management fed them and gave them money for a night's lodging in a cheap hotel. The next day, they gathered at the Russian Orthodox Church, with the same result. Then, for a week, they went to the Protestant churches, where they were also received more or less humanely. Finally they came to the Catholic church, the Church of Saint Alphonsus Ligouri on Canal Street and West Broadway, where they met with strong resistance. God's representatives called the police and insisted that they arrest the unfortunates and put a stop to these newfangled demonstrations, which were beginning to attract a lot of attention.

The police, of course, did not need much coaxing. They dispersed the unemployed and arrested leaders and brought them to justice. Frank Tannenbaum was given a year in prison.[11] Isidore Wisotsky was given two

---

Estelle ("Stella," 1909–1996). They later lived at the Stelton Colony, where the girls attended the Modern School, Bessie sometimes cooked for the children, and Newman sat on the managing board of the Modern School.

10. **Samuel (Sam) Hartman** (c. 1895–?) was a Russian-born Jewish IWW member and anarchist. He was a member of the Ferrer Center and arrested along with Becky Edelsohn in Park Row in 1914 for giving a speech in which he declared, "The United States flag isn't worth fighting for" (*Evening World* [New York], April 22, 1914). In 1918 he was a member of the militant Frayheyt Group, and he participated in the Second Anarchist Conference at Croton-on-Hudson, New York, held by the Road to Freedom Group in 1926.

11. **Frank Tannebaum** (1893–1969) was an Austrian-born Jewish laborer, historian, criminologist, IWW member, and anarchist. His family immigrated to the United States in 1905, and he subsequently ran away from home, working odd jobs and joining the IWW and the anarchist movement. Following Tannenbaum's imprisonment for leading New York's

months, and several others received smaller sentences.[12] For Wisotsky, this was the beginning of a period of arrests and persecution that lasted for years. He was identified by the police and the newspapers as a "young William Haywood" and was the first to be arrested at any opportunity. While in prison, Frank Tannenbaum studied for his college entrance exams and later earned a PhD, devoting his talents to improving the situation of those who fell into the hands of justice and languished in prisons.

Two anecdotes in connection with this movement deserve to be noted. One evening I was with Jack Bowman, who had come from Philadelphia for a visit, down in the Bowery to visit the breadline there. We dressed in old clothes, to not draw attention to ourselves. We wanted to be treated like all the other beggars. The night was terribly cold, and the missionaries took pity on the hungry and did not keep them outside but allowed the people in line into the large building to sit on long benches. Despite our efforts, the supervisors recognized us and put us on a separate bench and did not allow anybody to come near us. After sitting for a few hours, a well-groomed man mounted the platform and gave a pious sermon about God and his righteous ways, which we could not understand. He prayed for all those hungry and suffering and urged the assembled to sit down and sing a few hymns and psalms with him. Then the crowd was led through a narrow passage with iron stairs and grating where only one person at a time could pass. The railing extended along the long walls on both sides of the basement. At one spot, everyone was presented with a burned little roll, and at the end of the passage to the large open area, everyone was given a cup of coffee.

The people, several hundred of them, stood while they ate the roll with their coffee. There were no benches. Here the people were permitted to talk to each other for the length of time they were allowed to remain. Their words were wild, lacking a shred of understanding of the causes that had reduced

unemployed movement in 1914 he drifted away from radicalism and attended Columbia University, eventually becoming a prominent professor of criminology and Latin American history.

12. **Isidore Wisotsky** (Izidor Visotsky, 1895–1970) was a Russian-born Jewish laborer, union organizer, and anarchist. His family immigrated to New York when he was fourteen, and in 1912–1913 he joined the anarchist movement and the IWW. In the 1920s Wisotsky served as secretary of the International Pocketbook Workers' Union, and in the 1960s he became editor of the *FAS*.

them to such an awful state. It was pitiful to watch and hear the depths to which humanity can sink.

The second experience was of a different sort. The United Hebrew Trades and the *Forverts* could not idly watch the plight of the unemployed. They called a conference in the huge Beethoven Hall to discuss what could be done in the current situation. Naturally, we also sent delegates to the conference—yours truly and Manuel Komroff. The great hall was packed with delegates, several hundred in number. The socialists nominated Efim H. Jeshurin for chairman.[13] I nominated my fellow delegate, Komroff. To everyone's surprise, Komroff received more votes than Jeshurin. It was probably one of those cases where the people voted not for the love of Mordecai but for hatred of Haman.[14] Most of them did not know Komroff, but Jeshurin, they knew, represented the will of the *Forverts*, and they did not want that. The votes had to be counted three times until a few more were found for Jeshurin, and then the conference began.

The socialists had a ready-made proposal—to open soup kitchens downtown, for which committees would go to the bakeries, butcher shops, and groceries to ask for donations. For our part, we did not see any value in such an undertaking. In 1905 the socialists in New York had opened a public kitchen where one could buy a whole meal for five cents. They were enthusiastic about the undertaking, but shortly afterward the waiters went on strike and were arrested, and Jacob Saphirstein, owner of the *Morgen zshurnal*, had to bail out the victims of the socialist enterprise. We now insisted that we had best leave soup kitchens to the charities. An alliance of hundreds of workers' organizations had to undertake something more effective in such a situation. In the vote, our motion received such a large majority that it would not have helped to count them ten more times. The chairman left the podium and urged the socialist delegates to demonstratively leave the

13. **Ephim H. Jeshurin** (Yefim Yeshurun, 1885–1967) was a Russian-born Jewish pharmacist, writer, and socialist. He was active in the Bund before immigrating in 1907 to the United States, where he joined the Socialist Party. Jeshurin was a contributor and longtime treasurer of the *Forverts* and served as president of the Workmen's Circle in 1920–1921 and 1946–1950.

14. This colloquialism is a reference to the Book of Esther, in which the Persian King Ahasuerus contravenes a royal order issued by his viceroy Haman, who had been angered by the Jew Mordecai's refusal to bow to him, to kill all Jews. The king instead has Haman hanged on the gallows intended for Mordecai.

conference. So they, these believers in majority rule, did not follow their own Torah when the vote was against them. This is an old story.

The next day, the *Forverts* shrieked that the anarchists were trying to "capture" the conference and destroy the good work that the socialists had chosen to do. Nevertheless, no soup kitchens were opened.

One Saturday afternoon we held a huge mass meeting in Union Square, with Emma Goldman as the principal speaker. A collection taken up for the unemployed raised more than $100. We invited all the unemployed to march to the Ferrer Center at 107th Street and prepared a meal for them.

The jobless marched a few miles up Fifth Avenue to the center. The police—wonder of wonders!—didn't harass the assembly in Union Square or the march up Fifth Avenue. At the center, each unemployed person received food and twenty-five cents for a night's lodging, until the entirety of the money raised had been dispensed. The newspapers reported the whole story in a friendly tone the following day.

CHAPTER 35

Ludlow, Tarrytown, and Lexington Avenue

Toward spring, when the sufferings of the unemployed lessened somewhat, we received news of the bitter miners' struggle in Ludlow, Colorado. The natural resources of the region belonged to a few big companies, among which Rockefeller's holdings were the most extensive. He, the great philanthropist, who gave billions of dollars to charity, exploited his wage slaves in the most outrageous manner. He robbed them at work, fleecing them for rent on company-owned housing, for groceries at company-owned stores, and at every other turn.

Now that their patience was running out and they could no longer endure the horrific exploitation, he evicted them from their homes, forcing them into the freezing cold, to literally live on bread and water furnished by the union.

When this too did not break the miners' fighting spirit, Rockefeller took more active measures. Hired thugs attacked the camp of the strikers, shot at the defenseless men, women, and children, and set fire to their tents.[1]

The horrific murders shook public opinion throughout the country. Upton Sinclair began to picket Rockefeller's New York office at 26 Broadway.[2] We decided to picket Rockefeller's home in the hills near Tarrytown, New York, and to convene a protest rally in that town. For this purpose, we printed a series of five leaflets in which the entire history of the strike was accurately

---

1. Company guards and National Guardsmen killed approximately twenty people, including twelve children and two women, during the Ludlow Massacre of April 20, 1914.

2. **Upton Sinclair** (1878–1968) was an American-born journalist, novelist, and socialist, best known for his novel *The Jungle* (1906) and his 1934 campaign for governor of California.

described. A committee of young comrades began distributing the first leaflets in Tarrytown and was expelled from the city. A second group, a day later, was also arrested. On the third day a number of comrades—Romany Marie, Sophie Cohen, and others—handed out the flyers.[3] They were not arrested, but the police followed their every step. On the fourth day, Leonard D. Abbott, William Shatoff, and I did the work without incident, but no rally was possible.[4] The comrades who had been arrested—Isadore Wisotsky, Arthur Caron, David Sullivan, Jack [Isaacson], Maurice Rudome, Joseph Secunda, and a number of others—were given thirty days in the workhouse by the court in White Plains.[5]

---

3. **Romany Marie** (1885–1961), real name Marie Marchand (née Yuster), was a Romanian-born Jewish restaurateur and anarchist. She immigrated to the United States in 1901, and her tearooms and cafés became central hubs of Greenwich Village's bohemian and radical circles. Marie was active in the Ferrer Center and Modern School, and her sister, anarchist Rose Yuster, married Leonard D. Abbott.

4. **Vladimir ("William" or "Bill") Shatoff** (or Shatov) (1887–c.1938) was a Russian-born Jewish laborer, union organizer, administrator, and anarchist. A veteran of the 1905 Russian Revolution, in 1907 he fled to the United States, where he worked a variety of jobs in cities throughout the Northeast and Midwest, agitating as he went. Shatoff cofounded the Ferrer Modern School and the anarcho-syndicalist Union of Russian Workers and organized on behalf of the IWW. In 1917 he returned to Russia and was one of four anarchist members of the Petrograd Soviet's Military Revolutionary Committee that orchestrated the October Revolution. Although never renouncing anarchism or joining the Communist Party, Shatoff believed that cooperation with the Bolsheviks was necessary to preserve the revolutionary gains of the Russian workers, and he served in a number of official posts in the Soviet Union before he was arrested and shot during Stalin's purge of "Old Bolsheviks" in the late 1930s.

5. **Arthur Caron** (1883–1914) was French Canadian-born engineer, mill worker, IWW member, and anarchist who claimed Native American ancestry on his mother's side. He was active in the Ferrer Center and the Anti-Militarist League. **David Sullivan**, who was either Irish or Irish American, was beloved by the students at the Ferrer Modern School and became Becky Edelsohn's lover. He was also, Cohen neglects to mention, an undercover detective for the New York City Police Department. After serving thirty days in jail to maintain his cover, he delivered an incendiary speech at the memorial for the anarchists killed in the Lexington Avenue explosion that was published in *Mother Earth* (July 1914, 151–53). Sullivan's cover was later blown, however, by his aggrieved wife. **Jacob ("Jack") Isaacson** (Yakov Itzikson, 1896–1946), also known as Jack Denenberg, was a Russian-born Jewish laborer, union organizer, and anarchist. He immigrated to New York in 1908 with his mother and sister and became active in the Ferrer Center as well as in publishing the anarchist papers *Revolt* (1916) and *Freedom* (1919). Isaacson was arrested when authorities raided the offices of *Freedom* following its publication of an antiwar article and deported in 1922. He returned to the United States in 1924 under the maiden name of his wife, anarchist Gussie Denenberg (1895–1983), and opened a grocery store in Washington DC while remaining involved in the

At the same time, mass protest meetings were held every Saturday after-noon in New York's Union Square. The number of attendees grew week to week and reached tens of thousands. The police were wild with rage. At every meeting, detectives dressed in civilian clothes would single out a few active young comrades and beat them mercilessly. They did not touch the movement's speakers and leaders. I used to be accompanied to the meetings every Saturday by a certain Spivak, an official in the IWW's waiters' union.[6] He used to follow me like my shadow. Berkman and a few others also had similar companions. For the Fourth of July, we planned an excursion to Westfield, New Jersey, where Leonard D. Abbott and J. William Lloyd had a comfortable place for a picnic.[7] As I sat in a barber's chair on 107th Street, I heard a loud explosion not far from the area. I had a hunch that some of our people might be involved in the incident. Out on the street, I discovered that a bomb had exploded in a tenement house on Lexington Avenue. My suspicion grew stronger. A couple of our comrades lived in that house. One could not get near the place, but police and firefighters surrounded the area, roaming around like scurrying mice. I then went to the police station and asked at the desk if I could visit the wounded. The sergeant shouted that he had no time for such nonsense. He literally chased me out of the station.

When I got home to the Ferrer Center, my wife told me that Michael Murphy, one of the very young transient comrades, had just been there, dressed in an old police coat.[8] The night before, after a very late meeting in the center, he had spent the night at a comrade's apartment on Lexington

---

anarchist movement. Cohen's original Yiddish edition refers to him only as "Jack," as Isaacson was living illegally in the country at the time of its publication. In 1946 Isaacson committed suicide while once again under investigation by federal authorities for possible deportation. **Maurice ("Morris") Rudome** was a French-born Jewish anarchist who immigrated to New York in 1907 with his brother, anarchist Jacques ("Jack") Rudome (c. 1893–1985), and was active in the Ferrer Center. **Joseph Secunda** (c. 1891–1973) was a Russian-born Jewish pocketbook maker and anarchist who arrived in the United States in 1906.

6. This is probably a reference to the IWW-affiliated Hotel Workers' International Union, which included restaurant workers who had led a dramatic but failed strike in New York in 1912.

7. **J. William Lloyd** (1857–1940) was an American-born poet, writer, free-love advocate, and anarchist. He wrote for anarchist periodicals including *Liberty, Lucifer, the Light Bearer*, and *Free Society*, and published the magazine *Free Comrade* (1900–1902 and 1910–1912).

8. **Michael Murphy** was an anarchist who had previously been active in the IWW in Stockton, California.

Figure 26: Damage caused by the Lexington Avenue
explosion, 1914
Courtesy of the Library of Congress

Avenue. The explosion threw him out of the fifth-floor window and left him
unharmed, but naked, outside, where the police found him, took him to the
station, gave him some old clothes, and let him go. He was now at the office
of *Mother Earth*.

I was not happy with this story. I was sure that Michael did not know
anything about what was happening in the apartment. At the same time,
however, I was sure that the police would soon regret having let the boy go.
They would arrest him and with a little pressure could get him to say whatever
they wished. Who knows what kind of rubbish they could cook up about us!

I called Alexander Berkman immediately and found out that Michael was
there with him, telling of his miraculous escape and letting his imagination

run free to embellish the story. I advised him to send the boy to Westfield, from whence I would make certain that he would not fall into the hands of the police. I also told Berkman of my visit to the police station and what I had experienced there. He was upset: "Why put yourself in danger when you don't have to?" he asked me. My answer was that it is better to go to them than to have them come to us.

While I was talking to Berkman on the telephone, two policemen came to ask if Michael was with us at the center. My wife assured them that no one except us was in the building, and they headed off to the office of *Mother Earth*, but Michael was no longer there.

In Westfield I found Michael surrounded by a large number of comrades, with whom he had already been photographed, telling tall tales about the bombing and his escape. I found a suit for him and sent him with a trust-worthy committee to a local train station where they put him on a train going to Philadelphia. A letter to the comrades, which I had given him, warned them to keep a tight watch on him, to never let him out of their sight.

As soon as Michael had left, newspaper reporters began to inquire about him. Among them, especially among the reporters from the *World* and *America*, we knew that there were people who worked undercover for the police. But they were too late. I had enough time to destroy the film of the photos in which Michael was included, so that no trace of him remained. From Philadelphia, after a few weeks, the comrades sent him to London, where he remained for a couple of years and then returned.[9]

In the evening, my wife and children and I left for New York, to open the center as usual for the evening's activities. On the ferry, I found copies of newspapers full of fear-mongering headlines about the anarchist conspiracy to destroy Rockefeller's residence. Their analysis was correct. The bomb, assembled in the tenement house, was to be transferred that day to another place that Spivak, my shadow, had open access to. The bomb was placed under a bed on which two men slept without an inkling of what was under

---

9. According to Joseph Cohen's daughter Emma, Murphy did not actually return to the United States. Instead, "He wrote to Father from England shortly before the Second World War asking, 'Is it safe for me to come back?' Dad did a double-take when he read that, and figured that if he had to ask such a question after all that time he had better stay there, so he answered no." Paul Avrich, *Anarchist Voices: An Oral History of Anarchism in America* (Princeton: Princeton University Press, 1995), 226.

them. Louise Berger, the woman from the apartment, had left early in the morning to make final arrangements for the transfer of the bomb.[10] Before Louise Berger had walked three short blocks, she heard the explosion. It is possible that the men may have engaged in a little horseplay on the bed and jostled it, causing the detonation. Three men—Charles Berg, Arthur Caron, and Berger's half-brother Carl Hanson—were torn to pieces.[11] It was a miracle that Michael was spared.

The bomb was in fact intended for Rockefeller, but it was not meant to kill him or anybody else. Rockefeller's home in the mountains was inaccessible. The grounds had a very high fence around them and were well-guarded. The intention was for the bomb to tear up a corner of the fence to intimidate the great philanthropist.

I contacted Berkman and found out that, after my departure, he had reconsidered and followed my example, going to the police station and demanding to see the wounded and the dead. He had the same luck as me. He too was simply thrown out and sent home.

The ensuing uproar, the horror in the newspapers, the huge rallies in Union Square, the ban on arranging a public funeral for the ashes of the dead, and Berkman's determination to hold such a funeral, kept the entire city abuzz for weeks. Berkman was successful, and at the memorial meeting in Union Square the entire area was packed with people. More than fifty thousand came to the rally that Saturday afternoon.[12] The speeches were extremely radical. Charles Plunkett, a young comrade, recited the words of Louis Lingg, one of the Haymarket martyrs: "If you cannonade us, we shall dynamite you!"[13] The assembly was too large, the crowd too volatile, for the police to interrupt.

---

10. **Louise Berger** (died 1921) was a Russian-born anarchist. She immigrated in 1911 to New York, where she joined the Lettish Anarchist Group, the Lettish branch of the Anarchist Red Cross, as well as the Ferrer Center. Berger was the half-sister of Carl Hanson, and in 1917 she returned to Russia and reportedly joined a group of anarchist "expropriators" before dying of typhus.

11. **Charles Berg** (1891–1914) and **Carl Hanson** (died 1914) were Russian-born sailors and anarchists. Radicalized as teenagers, both took part in the 1905 Revolution and emigrated in 1911 to New York, where they joined the Lettish Anarchist Group and the Lettish branch of the Anarchist Red Cross. Hanson was the half-brother of Louise Berger.

12. This is an exaggerated figure; according to the account in *Mother Earth* (July 1914, 136) the crowd numbered eighteen thousand to twenty thousand.

13. **Charles Plunkett** (1892–1981) was an American-born labor organizer and anarchist.

The next day, the ashes of the deceased were placed in a beautiful urn fashioned by Adolf Wolff in the shape of a clenched fist, in the yard of the Ferrer Center.[14] All day long an endless stream of people came to honor the memory of the victims.

Soon thereafter, the First World War broke out. Alexander Berkman organized an Anti-Militarist League and steered the activities of the younger comrades and their street meetings toward agitating against the war, militarism, and imperialism.

The address for the Anti-Militarist League was the office of *Mother Earth*, but the meetings to prepare its activities took place in our center. One fine morning, Berkman came to see me. He was very agitated. In his hand he held a report written by a spy, sent from his office, with all the details of our activities and signed with a number. The report had been sent in an envelope of the Anti-Militarist League but without a stamp, so the post office sent it back to the address on the envelope.

We knew that spies circulated among us. A number of American youths were under suspicion, but the handwriting in the report belonged to someone who had used the Russian form of many letters. This reduced the pool to a very small number of people. Our suspicions rested on Spivak. It was necessary to get a sample of his handwriting to confirm these suspicions. For this purpose, that same evening, I asked a comrade with whom Spivak was intimate friends to obtain a handwritten letter. I had full confidence in her, a devoted Russian revolutionary, yet I could not tell her what this was all about. But she became upset, turned pale as chalk, thought for a minute, then said, "Okay, I will do it."

After graduating from Cornell University, he joined the Socialist Party and then the anarchist movement and became an organizer for the IWW's Marine Transport Workers. Plunkett later became a professor of biology at New York University. **Louis Lingg** (1864–1887) was a German-born carpenter and anarchist. He joined the anarchist movement in Germany before immigrating to the United States in 1885, and in Chicago he belonged to the militant anarchist North Side group and manufactured homemade bombs. Lingg was sentenced to death in the Haymarket trial but committed suicide in his cell the morning of the executions. Plunkett's speech at the Lexington Avenue memorial, as printed in *Mother Earth* (July 1914, 164–66), slightly misquotes Lingg's actual words, saying instead: "If they attack us with cannon, we will attack them with dynamite."

14. **Adolf Wolff** (1883–1944) was a Belgian-born sculptor and anarchist who immigrated to the United States as a child. He taught classes at the Ferrer Center and in 1927 also sculpted the urn that held the ashes of executed anarchists Sacco and Vanzetti.

Two days later, she brought me such a letter written on her behalf to one of her girlfriends, under the pretext that an injured finger made it impossible for her to hold a pen in her hand. The evidence was clear. We made quick work of him. No one saw him again.

The public outcry and publicity in connection with the bomb episode caused a great deal of damage to the Ferrer school. Alden Freeman withdrew his contribution of $100 a month. It looked as if the project would have to be abandoned. We were able to maintain the center by charging entrance fees, membership fees, and some other activities. But the expenses of the school were beyond our means. At our meetings, most of the members came to this sad conclusion with heavy hearts. But I could not accept the idea that the actions of one man, who might withdraw his support of $1,200 a year, should determine the fate of a collective enterprise. I suggested that we create a fund from small contributions, enough to cover the loss, and increase the activities of the school instead of abandoning it.

This the comrades did, issuing an appeal for a $3,000 fund, and this gave me a free hand to prepare the building for the winter season. The work with adults never stopped at the center. In the summer we held classes under the open skies in our large yard. In addition to our winter audience, the whole neighborhood showed up. The neighbors used to sit on fire escapes and at open windows to listen to the lectures and our discussions. One family tried to disrupt the proceedings a couple of times during a presentation. One of our comrades went up on the roof and poured a bucket of cold water on the entire family. Residents from the whole area warmly applauded the act. We had no more trouble.

But the school was closed that summer, and we were looking for a principal. We were luckier than we expected. From far off New Zealand, we received a letter from a young American couple wanting to come and work in our community as teachers. Further correspondence revealed that they were well prepared and properly equipped for such work. So Robert Hutchinson and Delia Dana Hutchinson, a granddaughter of the poet Henry Wadsworth Longfellow, came and took over management of the school.[15]

---

15. **Robert ("Bob") Hare Hutchinson** (1887–1975) was an American-born writer, educator, and radical. In 1913 he married American-born nurse and educator **Delia Dana Hutchinson** (1889–1989), a fellow graduate of Harvard University. The couple was honeymooning in New Zealand and doing research for Robert's book, *The "Socialism" of New*

Henrietta Rodman, Dr. John Weichsel, and Dr. Benzion Liber worked hard to find a few more teachers and worked out the curriculum. When the school opened, we had more teachers and pupils than ever before.

Our appeal did not bring in $3,000, but enough money came in to start. After that, it turned out that the Hutchinsons did not need the salary we were paying them. They returned the check in order to improve the condition of the building. This led to us having to close the school for a week for the new year, buy paint and wallpaper, and, with the volunteer labor of a number of painters and paperhangers whom comrade Isaac Radinowsky brought in from his union, have the whole place renovated from top to bottom. During Christmas week we celebrated with an international bazaar: each evening featured a program about, and the costumes and food of, a particular nationality. It was a marvelous success and brought in a considerable sum of money.

Sometime later we organized a public debate between Emma Goldman and Isaac Hourwich with the goal of raising money. The debate brought in more than $300 above expenses. Through these and other measures we were able to raise three times as much money as we had lost by Alden Freeman's resignation.

The center was full of life and activity that year. Our lecturers included Clarence Darrow, Edwin Markham, Joseph McCabe from London, Lincoln Steffens, Emma Goldman, William English Walling, and many other celebrities, in addition to our own lecturers.[16] Two or three classes on various subjects were held each evening. Nathaniel Buchwald and Robert Minor, both of whom later became Communists, were among the teachers, and art classes were conducted by Robert Henri and George Bellows.[17] Among

---

Zealand (1916), a left-wing critique of that country's Liberal Party government. The Hutchinsons subsequently moved with the Ferrer School from New York to Stelton, New Jersey, but in 1915 they left to establish the Stony Ford School in upstate New York, which closed when the couple divorced in 1918. Robert Hutchinson later wrote detective novels under the name Robert Hare.

16. **Edwin Markham** (1852–1940) was a celebrated American poet who often wrote on social and populist themes. **Joseph McCabe** (1867–1955) was an English-born former priest who wrote and spoke widely on Freethought and rationalism.

17. **Nathaniel Buchwald** (Naftoli Bukhvald, 1890–1956) was a Russian-born Jewish writer, Yiddish theater critic, socialist, and later Communist who wrote for the *Forverts* and then the Communist press. **Robert Minor** (1884–1952) was an American-born cartoonist, journalist, anarchist, and later Communist. A successful political cartoonist for mainstream newspapers, he joined the Socialist Party in 1907 and subsequently became an anarchist and

the art teachers and students were Adolf Wolff, Ben Greenstein (Benjamin Benno), William Zorach, and a whole host of others who have made great names for themselves.[18] Isadora Duncan took a keen interest in our work and used to invite the entire school as her guests to her every performance in New York.[19] At that time, Ruth Pinchot and Mabel Dodge were flirting with the radical movement and visited us several times.[20] Margaret Sanger's children and Harry Glantz's son were among our pupils, as were Konrad Bercovici's children, who were not unfamiliar to us.[21] His daughter later married Leonard D. Abbott's son.

----

a close friend of Alexander Berkman and Emma Goldman. Minor contributed articles and cartoons to radical publications like the *New York Call*, *The Masses*, *Mother Earth*, *Revolt*, *Frayheyt*, and *The Blast* (which he helped to produce in San Francisco). In 1918–1919 he traveled to Russia as a correspondent for the *Call* and published articles critical of the Bolshevik consolidation on power, but by 1920 he had reversed himself and joined the Communist Party. Minor became a prominent party leader and unsuccessfully ran for several political offices as a Communist candidate. During the Spanish Civil War, he served as a political commissar for the Communist-organized International Brigades.

18. **Benjamin Greenstein** (1901–1980), known professionally as Benjamin G. Benno, was an English-born Jewish sailor and artist. His father was the anarchist Abraham Greenstein, but his parents separated when he was two years old, and he remained in London with his mother, living for a few years in the home of Peter Kropotkin. Greenstein immigrated to New York in 1912 and attended art classes at the Ferrer Center where he became a protégé of Robert Henri. He went on to become a well-known abstract painter and sculptor. **William Zorach** (1889–1966), born Zorach Gorfinkel, was a Russian-born Jewish painter and sculptor best known as one of the first artists in America to embrace cubism.

19. **Isadora Duncan** (c. 1877–1927) was an American-born dancer and choreographer. Duncan was a pioneer of modern dance and sympathized with radical politics; she lived in Soviet Russia in 1921–1924 and later befriended Emma Goldman in France.

20. **Ruth Pickering Pinchot** (1893–1984) was an American-born writer, feminist, birth-control advocate, and radical who wrote for *The Woman Rebel*, *The Masses*, *The Liberator*, *The Nation*, and other leftist and liberal publications. **Mabel Dodge** (1879–1962) was an American-born heiress and patron of the arts who hosted weekly salons in her Greenwich Village home featuring prominent radicals and artists, including Emma Goldman, Margaret Sanger, William Haywood, and John Reed.

21. Margaret Sanger's children Stuart, Grant, and Peggy continued to attend the Ferrer Modern School after its move to Stelton, New Jersey, where in 1915 Peggy caught pneumonia and died at age five. **Harry Glantz** (c. 1896–1982) was a famous Russian-born Jewish trumpet player and first trumpeter for the New York Philharmonic. **Konrad Bercovici** (1882–1961) was a Romanian-born Jewish capmaker, organist, writer, journalist, and anarchist. His family immigrated to France after his father was killed in a pogrom in their village of Galați. There Bercovici met and married the sculptor Naomi Librescu, the sister of anarchist Benzion Liber. The couple moved to Montreal and then New York, where he wrote for

The children used to come from all corners of the city to spend the whole day in school and in the park. Instead of bringing lunch from home, we suggested that they should bring what few cents they could and anonymously contribute it. One or two mothers used to come in and, for the pennies brought, prepare a well-cooked meal that the children served themselves. It was a wonderful start to the season.

We introduced another novelty. Upon my arrival, I had found the floor-to-ceiling windows covered with a thick wire mesh, which kept the light out of the rooms and added to the appearance of a prison. I was told that this was necessary for protection from the rocks that children in the neighborhood threw at the windows. I could not tolerate such a relationship with the neighbors. I made one small change: in the large backyard of the school, I placed exercise and playground equipment. Then all the children from the street were invited to come and play and spend their free time with us. Within a couple of weeks we were friends with all the children and had full control over their games. We no longer needed any protection on the windows.

Life at the center proved too hectic for child-rearing activities. The idea arose to move the school to the country, following the model of Sébastien Faure's "Beehive" (La Ruche) in France.[22] Comrade Harry Kelly spent his free time that summer at a socialist colony, Fellowship Farm, in New Jersey.[23] He had the good idea to buy a farm nearby, establish an anarchist colony, and set aside enough land and the old farmhouse for a school. I backed the idea and supported it with all my might. Thus, the Ferrer Colony of Stelton, New Jersey was born.

Thirty-two children under the supervision of several teachers and five caregivers left New York on May 16, 1915, to settle in their new home. The

---

the Yiddish- and English-language press and was involved in the Jewish anarchist movement. Their children were named Hyperion, Gorky, and Révolte. Bercovici went on to become an established figure in literary and Hollywood circles. In 1941 he published his memoir, *It's the Gypsy in Me.*

22. **La Ruche** was an experimental anarchist school near Rambouillet, France, that ran from 1904 to 1917 and attracted much attention in international radical circles.

23. **Fellowship Farm** was an agrarian colony founded in 1912 in Stelton, New Jersey, by predominantly German socialists from New York. Harry Kelly's companion, Mary Krimont, owned a cabin there that was later moved to the Stelton Colony. Never financially stable, Fellowship Farm dissolved around the time of the Second World War.

dormitory for the children was built hastily with the voluntary labor of Morris Papagailo and a few other Brownsville comrades whom William Judin was able to interest in our work.[24] A new, unfamiliar life, with new problems and difficulties, began to unfold for a large group of people.

24. **Morris Papagailo** or Popugailo (Moyshe Popugaila, 1890–?) was a Russian-born Jewish carpenter and anarchist. He lived at Stelton with his wife Sylvia, a dressmaker, and their son Benny, who attended the Modern School. In the 1920s the entire family moved to the Soviet Union. **William Judin** or Yudin (Viliam Yudin, c.1887–?), also known as William ("Bob") Parker, was a Russian-born Jewish housepainter and anarchist. He immigrated to the United States in 1904 and belonged to the anarchist Friends of Art and Education Group in Brownsville. Judin later moved to Chicago, where he was secretary of the International Propaganda Group that published *The Alarm* (1915–1916), *The Social War*, and *The Social War Bulletin* (1918). He was arrested for distributing the *Bulletin* and held for deportation but ultimately released, and in the 1930s he ran the Central Dinner Club in New York, which advertised in the pages of the *FAS*.

CHAPTER 36

Sasha Is Leaving!

A Sunday evening. A large circle of us gathered in a wine cellar on the East Side; we drank wine and sang. The crowd was sentimentally dominated by a kind of sad joy, which gnawed and soothed at the same time. We were meeting with Alexander Berkman, who was leaving for San Francisco where he would publish an anarchist newspaper. Berkman was a great favorite among us young comrades; everyone felt him to be a close, dear companion. We said goodbye to him as if he were a brother, without any speeches or formalities. We drank wine and sang the refrain, "Sasha is leaving!"

Late in the night, the last of us, fifteen to twenty people, left with Berkman out into the street and wandered toward the elevated train on Third Avenue. The streets were empty, the night silent; we walked in one mass and sang softly. Entering St. Marks Place, we met a policeman who did not enjoy our singing. He undoubtedly was right: we were disturbing the peaceful sleep of the inhabitants around us, but he was also right that not everyone wanted, or could, be under the influence of wine and good company. Little Helen of Troy began to jump up, arguing with the policeman in a high tenor, with the latter raising his club, as if trying to convince her of his authority.[1] It happened that I was standing behind him, so I grabbed the

---

1. **Helen Goldblatt** (1897–1963), nicknamed "Helen of Troy," was a Russian-born Jewish hatmaker and anarchist. She had been involved in revolutionary politics in Warsaw before immigrating to New York with her family in 1910 and participated in the 1914 protests against John D. Rockefeller in Tarrytown. Goldblatt was the girlfriend of Arthur Caron at the time of his death, and she later married French Jewish anarchist Jacques Rudome and moved to the Mohegan Colony. She was the sister of anarchist Lillian Goldblatt.

police club and ripped it out of his hand. This, of course, made him furious and perhaps frightened him, although none of us had the least thought of harming him. He began to use his whistle and call for help, and within a few moments several police came running from all directions. By that time I had already returned his club to him and we all stood quietly, calmly, watching to see what would happen. Little Helen was hanging onto Berkman's arm and was still arguing with police. When the law enforcement officers arrived, our adversary laid his hands on Berkman and arrested him, taking him to a police station not far from the scene. Helen and her sister Lillian were arrested and taken to night court, where they were sentenced to pay a ten-dollar fine or ten days in the workhouse.[2] They opted for the latter, not allowing their father to pay the fine. A number of us went along with Berkman, demanding that he be released or that all of us be arrested. They laughed at us, detaining Berkman and kicking us out and locking the door behind us. As the comrades went home feeling as if they had been beaten up, William Shatoff and I sat up on the steps of the police station and stayed there all night. We picketed the police, who did not disturb us and did not care about us.

In the morning, Berkman was brought before a judge. The policeman accused him of horrific crimes: disturbing the peace, obstructing a representative of law and order from carrying out his duty. Also, he had robbed the police officer of his symbol of authority—his heavy club. Our lawyer did not find it necessary to delve into the case, and Berkman was released under nominal bail, and we left for home. Berkman soon left for San Francisco, and the case was never called up in court.

---

2. **Lillian Goldblatt** (1895–1967) was a Russian-born Jewish hatmaker and anarchist. She had been involved in revolutionary politics in Warsaw before immigrating to New York with her family in 1910, and she participated in the 1914 protests against John D. Rockefeller in Tarrytown. In 1918 Goldblatt attempted unsuccessfully to return to Russia, and she later married Howard Buck (c. 1891–?), a single-taxer who taught mathematics at Commonwealth College in Arkansas and moved to the Mohegan Colony. She was the sister of anarchist Helen Goldblatt.

CHAPTER 37

The Tom Mooney Case in San Francisco

In the summer of 1916, our superpatriots held what they called a "prepared-ness parade" in San Francisco—the first of a series to be carried out in all the major cities—on a Saturday afternoon. Everything proceeded as planned, until one little thing ruined its success: a bomb went off, wreaking havoc on the patriotic mood of the procession.[1]

This launched a hunt for radicals, revolutionaries, and all who had the audacity not to be inspired by the bloody war mood. The police did not know who threw the bomb, and did not wish to find out. They took the opportunity to get even with people they already had an eye on. There are always and everywhere such people. In this instance, the police arrested Tom Mooney—a labor agitator, who a short while before had led a bitter strike against the city's immensely rich gas company. Mooney, his wife Rena, Warren Billings, Israel Weinberg, and a few other people were arrested and charged with the crime.[2]

---

1. The Preparedness Day bombing of July 22, 1916, killed ten people and injured dozens more.

2. **Rena Mooney** (1878–1952), née Brink, was an American-born music teacher and socialist. She married Tom Mooney in 1911 and was active in his defense campaign until his eventual release. **Warren K. Billings** (1893–1972) was an American-born laborer and radical. He was sympathetic to, but not a member of, the IWW and in San Francisco worked closely with Tom Mooney on behalf of various local labor struggles. **Israel Weinberg** (1884–?) was a Russian-born Jewish carpenter, jitney driver, and radical. He immigrated to the United States around 1901 and organized Cleveland's Jewish Carpenters' Union the following year. A few years later Weinberg moved to San Francisco, where he was elected to the executive board of the Jitney Bus Operators' Union and subscribed to Alexander Berkman's anarchist paper *The Blast*.

Alexander Berkman had by then lived in San Francisco for a couple of years. He published an anarchist weekly, *The Blast*, and did good educational work. Recognizing the great danger those accused were facing, he set out across the country to bring public attention to the case and organize the defense for the detainees.

In San Francisco the police created an atmosphere of terror. The trial was conducted even more dishonorably and hideously than the notorious Chicago trial of 1886—which had sent the anarchists to the gallows. The prosecutor, Charles Fickert, stopped at nothing.[3] His witnesses were all criminals, degenerates, and prostitutes. They contradicted each other at every step. Fickert, however, was able to wangle a verdict of guilty from the jury, which ruled that Mooney and Billings should pay with their lives for a crime for which the perpetrator had not been determined.

The prosecutor's appetite grew. He got the devious idea that he could actually kill two birds with one stone; his bribed witnesses would not demand much more money to claim another victim: Berkman. He had Berkman arrested in New York and demanded that he be extradited to California and delivered into the hands of the angel of death. But the organized labor movement, the Socialist Party under the leadership of Morris Hillquit, and public opinion stood up for Berkman, sent delegates to the governor of New York, and led a vigorous campaign in his favor. Berkman's life hung by a thread.

What saved him were the huge demonstrations of Petrograd's revolutionary workers in front of the American Embassy in that city. The American government was keenly interested in maintaining the friendship of revolutionary Russia. President Wilson had two reasons for this: he wanted to become the advisor and the spiritual leader of the newly formed Russian republic; and, perhaps more so, he wanted Russia to continue its involvement in the war against Germany. When his ambassador in Petrograd informed him the extent of Russia's opposition to the San Francisco travesty and the attempt to involve Berkman in the trial, Wilson began to use his influence to quench the thirst of the murderous patriots in California.

---

3. **Charles Fickert** (1873–1937) was an American-born lawyer and Republican politician who served as district attorney of San Francisco from 1909 to 1920. Revelations of his underhanded prosecution of the Mooney-Billings case undermined his political career, and he unsuccessfully ran for governor of California in 1920.

He publicly called for the governor of California to pardon Mooney and Billings.

There would be no more talk of extraditing Berkman and having a new murder trial.

The enormous protest demonstrations in Petrograd took place in the nick of time and at the right psychological moment, it seems. Among the protesters was a large, well-organized group that had for years published the Russian anarchist weekly *Golos Truda* (The Voice of Labor) in New York.[4] They had not yet established themselves properly in Russia or obtained a specific mailing address. Letters to them were sent to the American embassy. When the demand for Berkman's extradition became strong, the New York comrades sent a cable to address of the American embassy which read: "SASHA IN GRAVE DANGER, DOCTORS WISH TO SEND HIM TO CALIFORNIA. WE ARE HELPLESS, WHAT CAN YOU DO?" The comrades in Russia understood the meaning behind these innocent words and immediately carried out the work, with the desired results.

---

4. *Golos Truda* (1911–1918) was a Russian-language anarchist newspaper. It was one of the first publications in the world to describe itself as anarcho-syndicalist and became the official paper of the Union of Russian Workers of the United States and Canada after that organization's formation in 1914. Following the February Revolution, its editorial staff returned to Russia and reestablished the paper in Petrograd and then Moscow as the organ of the new Anarcho-Syndicalist Propaganda Union until it was suppressed by the Bolsheviks in 1918.

CHAPTER 38

The Ferrer School and Colony

Reestablishing the Ferrer School in the country turned the institution into a national undertaking. The first to show interest in its fate and work were the comrades from Philadelphia. We had few children from that city in the first year; no more than two: Aaron and Rebecca Miller's daughter Ray, and Louis Segal's son—but all the comrades showed great interest.[1] They understood that it was no longer a local New York enterprise but merited the help of all those who wanted to see Modern Schools established throughout the country. The same attitude was found among the comrades in Brownsville, who helped us greatly, as well as the group in Newark, from which Morris Lipshitz and the Dreskins were very active in this work, and the comrades in Paterson, New Jersey.[2]

The setting of the school was a very poor one—an old farmhouse, the ceiling of which collapsed in two rooms the day before the children were to arrive. Through the efforts of comrade William Judin, a number of

---

1. **Rebecca ("Bella") Miller** (1882–?) was a Russian-born Jewish anarchist. She immigrated to the United States in 1895 with her husband and fellow anarchist Aaron Miller, and in 1931 the couple moved to New York, where they became members of the Naye Gezelshaft Group, Branch 364 of the Workmen's Circle.

2. **Morris Lipshitz** (Moyshe Lipshits, died 1957) was a Jewish anarchist who briefly taught at Stelton's Modern School. He and his wife Minnie later lived in the Amalgamated Cooperative Apartment House in the Bronx. Obituary: *FAS*, December 27, 1957. **Benjamin Dreskin** (1901–1990) and **Morris Dreskin** (c. 1887–1962) were Russian-born Jewish carpenters and anarchists. Morris immigrated to the United States around 1903 and lived in California before moving to Newark in 1912. The brothers helped build the schoolhouse at Stelton, and Morris sat on the school's managing board.

Brownsville comrades—painters and paperhangers—made up for the loss during the night. We took an old building apart and used the wood to construct a long dormitory—a sleeping place for some thirty children, with a larger room in the center in which we hoped to soon install water, baths, and other amenities to keep the children clean.

The dormitory was constructed from thin beams covered with paper. The front wall facing the sun was completely open, for sunshine and air. The plan for the structure was made by a well-known German architect from New York, Max Heidelberg, who commented, "This is an important, historical experiment. At a time when the Kaiser seeks to spread the spirit of Prussian Junkerdom over the whole world, you are starting to build a school in which children will be raised free, without any discipline. It seems to me that you will be more successful than the Kaiser."[3]

His voluntary help and encouragement were very important to us, but we did not have the means to build the school. All the work was done entirely by volunteers, by comrades to whom we could offer only food. The building was, as mentioned, made of paper and open. We very quickly found out that in New Jersey, people could not sleep in such buildings. The mosquitoes there are the largest and the most poisonous in the country. We had to cover the openings and protect the children with cheesecloth.

We had one other building—an old stable, a large one, which we cleaned out and made into a playroom for the children and a meeting room for the adults. This was the extent of our facilities.

The school was built by poor people for poor people. The parents of the children were all workers and could pay only very little for the upkeep of their children. The teachers and caretakers were all volunteers: the Hutchinsons, Helen Lund, Sophie Cohen, Gusta Goldman, Mary Hansen, Sophie Margolies, and Jacques Dubois comprised the staff to feed the children, keep them clean, look after them, and teach them.[4]

---

3. **Max G. Heidelberg** (1878–?) was an American-born architect and socialist. He was a son of German immigrants, a member of the Cooperative League of America, and sat on the executive board of the National Birth Control League, of which his wife, Virginia Heidelberg (née Newbold), was chair.

4. **Helen Lund** was an educator and anarchist from Chicago. A former church worker turned individualist anarchist, she was a practitioner of Montessori teaching methods. An article in *Mother Earth* (June 1915, 148) described her as "a level-headed woman well adapted for the career she has chosen. . . . She understands child-psychology, and she is an

The parents paid—or rather, were supposed to pay—three dollars a week for one child, and five dollars a week for two. We had one family of five small children, the oldest a thirteen-year-old girl, whose mother had died that winter and left them orphans with a father who had to work in a shop to feed them. From him, we asked $7.50 a week for the whole family. Altogether, the children were supposed to bring in about seventy-five dollars a week, which would probably have been sufficient to sustain them all if all the parents had been punctual with their payments. But this was not the case.

Our friend Bolton Hall warned us from the beginning that we were making a mistake to organize a school where the parents were not obliged to pay for their children's food, let alone the labor. He understood that such an undertaking could not sustain itself. However, we had great confidence in the voluntary activity of the comrades and the support that the movement would give us. In spite of great hardships, we kept the school running for several years until wartime prosperity made it possible to increase the tuition.

In the first summer, there were no buildings in the colony other than the school. Every week a large number of people from all the nearby towns and cities came out to spend the weekend with us. They ate as much food as we could prepare, but we had no sleeping quarters. So we would build a huge bonfire on Saturday night, sit in a large circle, listen to a lecture, and, after the discussion, sing and have fun all night.

There was great enthusiasm. Inquiries about land in the colony grew weekly. We bought another stretch of land nearby and created what was called the Second Tract, which could accommodate thirty new families. This

uncompromising libertarian." After leaving Stelton, Lund taught at the Stony Ford School. **Gusta Goldman** (c. 1889–1974), born Gittel Levine, was a Russian-born Jewish dairy farmer, anarchist, and later Communist. She immigrated to the United States in 1906 and was the wife of Sam Goldman (c. 1883–?), with whom she ran a dairy business from their plot in Stelton. They named their first child, born in 1910, Lucifer, and later joined the Communist Party. Obituary: *Central New Jersey Home News* (New Brunswick), March 10, 1974. **Sophie Margolies** (1887–?) was a Russian-born Jewish anarchist. Her son, Herman, attended Stelton's Modern School. **Jacques Dubois** (1888–1976) was a French-born jeweler and anarchist. As a teenager he joined the Parisian anarchist L'Endehors Group, and around 1905 he immigrated to England where he was affiliated with the Freedom Group. Dubois immigrated to the United States in 1910 and joined the Mother Earth Group, then moved to Stelton and later the Mohegan Colony, where his children attended the Modern School.

brought the school an income of $1,500. A year later, we found it necessary to buy another strip of land, the Third Tract, which provided the school another $1,500 in revenue.

The colony members began to build houses, to settle. The first winter we had four families in the colony outside of the school. Our conditions deteriorated horribly. Our guests stopped coming, the voluntary teachers and caretakers disappeared. Some parents fell behind in their payments. There was no furnace in the building, no way to heat it. Robert Minor came to our rescue with a loan of $100, for which he never asked repayment, and Minna Lowensohn with fifty dollars, which she had collected from among her friends.[5]

At the end of the summer, we were able to engage Dr. Henry Schnittkind of Boston—a young man who was a born teacher—as well as his young wife Sarah, whom he had just married, and their friend, Joseph Gershenzwit, an agronomist who taught the children about earthworks and natural sciences, as teachers.[6] All was well, but there was no space in which to teach the children. During the cold, rainy fall days, the teachers began to complain about the lack of a classroom, a place to study. I tried to comfort them by pointing out that we had the best and biggest classroom in the world—all of the land around and the sky overhead, but in my heart I knew that this was nothing more than a beautiful phrase. In the dry, cold days we could hold a class around a bonfire in the woods; but on the very rainy days there was no shelter.

At the end of November, our teachers left us. Dr. Schnittkind's young wife, a city girl, could not stand the rigors of primitive country life. We were able to enlist Abe Grosner to come from Philadelphia to take on the job. We were able also to obtain a small printing press as a gift from Dr. Charles

---

5. **Minna Lowensohn** (1880–1958) was a Russian-born Jewish garment worker and anarchist. She was a longtime friend of Emma Goldman and active in the Ferrer Center, the Stelton Colony, and later the Mohegan Colony.

6. **Henry T. Schnittkind** (1888–1970) was a Russian-born author, editor, translator, and socialist who had previously taught at socialist Sunday schools in Boston. He was a founder and longtime president of the Stratford Publishing Company. **Joseph Lippe Gershenzwit** (c. 1895–1968), who also went by Joseph Austin, was a Russian-born agronomist and socialist. His family immigrated to the United States around 1904, and in 1914 he graduated from Cornell University, where he was secretary of the Cornell Socialist Study Club, with a degree in agriculture.

Kuntz, who at one time had a school in Iselin, New Jersey, not far from our colony.[7] Joseph Ishill, a member of our colony who was a printer and an artist, became interested in teaching the children and publishing a children's journal, *The Path of Joy*.[8] It was a splendid edition, written, printed, and put together by the children themselves, and one of the most successful publications our movement created. In addition there was *The Modern School*, a monthly magazine for adults, edited by Carl Zigrosser and printed by Ishill. The artist-illustrator Rockwell Kent designed wonderful large initials, or drop caps, for our magazine, which Ishill and the children used to decorate it.[9] Our publications, with their content and craftsmanship, gained a good reputation and gave us great satisfaction.

The students that winter excelled in performing an anti-militaristic play called *Shambles*, composed by Henry Schnittkind.[10] They performed in New York before a large audience, which welcomed them. Then on April 26, 1916, they performed the same play, with a series of suitable musical numbers, at Philadelphia's Eagle Hall, before an enthusiastic audience. They repeated their performance in Newark and New Brunswick too, with great success. Our new life in the country was a mixture of joy and sorrow, with enthusiastic activity and very difficult circumstances—a real pioneer life, which has a great appeal, despite all the inconveniences.

---

7. **Charles Kuntz** (1870–?) was a Russian-born Jewish agronomist, sociologist, and radical. He attended university in Kiev, Vienna, and Zurich before immigrating to the United States in 1894 to go to Columbia University. Kuntz then established an experimental poultry farm in Iselin, New Jersey. Cohen later refers to Kuntz as "[one of] our former comrades," indicating he was close to the anarchist movement during this time. But following the Russian Revolution, Kuntz worked for the Commissariat of Foreign Affairs of the Soviet government and in 1928 became head of the Organization for Jewish Colonization in Russia. He taught at the Rand School of Social Science and Columbia University and twice visited the Soviet Union to advise the Soviet government on agricultural practices in the Jewish settlement of Birobidzhan.

8. **Joseph Ishill** (1888–1966), born Joseph Ishileanu, was a Romanian-born Jewish printer and anarchist. He became an anarchist while working in Bucharest, then immigrated to the United States in 1909 and moved to Stelton in 1915. Ishill published the anarchist journal *Open Vistas* (1925) and his Oriole Press produced limited editions of writings by and about prominent anarchists such as Peter Kropoktin and Elisée Reclus.

9. **Rockwell Kent** (1882–1971) was an American-born artist and socialist. He was later active in the Artists' Union of America, the Artists' League of America, and the American Labor Party.

10. Henry T. Schnittkind, *Shambles: A Sketch of the Present War* ([New York]: n.p., [1916]).

We celebrated our first anniversary in the country with a big parade. A huge crowd of people came to share in our happiness. The comrades from Philadelphia came as a group, in two crowded trucks, which in those days were not so sturdily built as they are today. The road was also a primitive, not completely paved one. As a result, the trucks suddenly broke down, and the comrades finally reached the colony just after dinner.

On a later occasion, an outing of all the New Jersey branches of the Workmen's Circle brought together a few thousand people in our fields. By that time the school was under the care of William Thurston Brown, a Unitarian schoolteacher who became a freethinker, a socialist, and an extreme radical in his educational ideas.[11] We had organized the Modern School Association of North America, and with the help of our active union members we had interested a large number of labor unions in joining the association and paying annual dues. The yearly conventions of the Workmen's Circle also regularly provided support for the school. The parents took on the responsibility of contributing a dollar a week in tuition for each child. Many families settled in the colony, and their children received their education from us at the school. We instituted annual conventions over Labor Day weekend, during which the school's administrators for that year were elected. At the end of every May, we celebrated the creation of our community. The school and the colony grew and received a great deal of attention.

The colony underwent a remarkable development. It had never been purely anarchist, in the sense that only anarchists could become members. We did not ask new members for a passport or letter of recommendation. On the other hand, it was no secret that the colony was organized by anarchists and conducted in an anarchist spirit. In its first years, newspapers in the surrounding towns and even in New York gave considerable space to descriptions of the new colony where anarchism, free love, and other such beautiful things, as capitalism's hired pens understood them, were practiced in life.

---

11. **William Thurston Brown** (1861–1938) was an American-born writer and Christian socialist. A former clergyman and onetime member of the Socialist Party, he directed Modern Schools in Portland and Chicago before arriving at Stelton, where he served as principal and briefly edited *The Modern School*. Brown supported American intervention in the First World War and left Stelton to direct the Walt Whitman School in Los Angeles from 1919 to 1924.

An interesting discussion took place our first summer one Saturday night around a large bonfire: a couple of doctrinaire (*frume*) comrades bitterly criticized our conduct, having seen with their own eyes an old Jew wearing a *tallit* and *tefillin*, saying his prayers in one of the first houses in Stelton. What kind of anarchists were we, to allow such a thing in our colony![12]

The discussion dragged on for hours. Most comrades held the belief that this was true anarchism—the individual has the right to act according to their will and understanding. No one has the right to tell anyone how they should behave or what they should believe. The old Jew, whose praying had provoked the discussion, was a guest in the colony, visiting his son, a certain Silverman who had been the first to settle in the colony. Even before he knew which piece of land was his, he had bought a prefabricated home from a mail-order catalog and set it up—a canvas house with a wooden floor—as soon as he was shown his lot. In the fall, when the heavy winds came, they carried away his house and everything in it.

The colonists were all, if not outspoken anarchists, radicals of various kinds who were interested in the maintenance of the Ferrer School, which was the center and the soul of the whole enterprise. A conservative would have had no interest in settling with us in the colony. We had trouble enough with our own radicals in organizing the collective affairs of the colony. Even before we settled on the land, we decided to provide running water to every house. Sometime later, the question arose as to how the streets, paths, and entrance, which were impassable on rainy days, were to be repaired and paid for. This required collective action and pitching in for the cost on the part of every member, to which some did wish to agree, on principle. They considered it coercion, especially those who were not in a hurry to settle in the colony. When developing the other two tracts, we therefore decided that instead of water pipes, part of the money should be used for improving the roads. Other problems in dealing with collective issues were never completely resolved. There is a certain difficulty and misunderstanding of our anarchist views that is a major obstacle to the development of social coexistence.

---

12. **Tefillin** are small boxes with straps that contain verses from the Torah and are worn by Orthodox Jews during morning prayers.

Still, the colony grew. Life there was interesting and very exciting. The school held us together and gave us much satisfaction. In and around the school there were a wide range of lectures, discussions, entertainments, conventions, conferences, and annual gatherings of many comrades. Stelton was the Mecca of our movement for many years. All roads led there, and visitors came from all corners of the country.

CHAPTER 39

The First World War and Its Impact

The outbreak of the First World War shook the ranks of the socialists in countries all over the world. From the very first day, the powerful socialist parties stood behind their governments and supported the war with all their might. Of course, there were individual exceptions here and there. Jean Jaurès in France paid with his life in the first days of the war.[1] Karl Liebknecht, in Germany, had the courage to stand up in the German Reichstag against war credits.[2] Lenin, Trotsky, and other Russian emigrants in Europe held to their principled opposition to the war.[3] But the majority of socialists, the leaders

---

1. **Jean Jaurès** (1859–1914) was a leader of the French Socialist Party who was assassinated by a French nationalist on July 31, 1914, due to his opposition to the First World War.

2. **Karl Liebknecht** (1871–1919) was a prominent member of the left wing of the Social Democratic Party of Germany and a member of the Reichstag from 1912 until 1916, when he was expelled from the party for opposing its support for the German war effort. Liebknecht later cofounded the Spartacist League and the Communist Party of Germany and was assassinated by soldiers during the suppression of the German Revolution of 1919.

3. **Vladimir Lenin** (1870–1924), real name Vladimir Ilyich Ulyanov, was a Russian-born Communist leader. He went into European exile in 1900 and led the Bolshevik faction within the Russian Social Democratic Labor Party. In 1917 Lenin returned to Russia, where he orchestrated the October Revolution, became head of the Soviet state, and launched the international communist movement. Most anarchists never forgave him for the Soviet government's repression of rival radicals, including anarchists, beginning in 1918. **Leon Trotsky** (1879–1940), real name Lev Davidovich Bronstein, was a Russian-born Communist leader and writer. After escaping from Siberian exile to Western Europe, he initially sided with the Menshevik faction of the Russian Social Democratic Labor Party. Trotsky lived in New York for two months in 1917, during which he visited the anarchist Ferrer Center, but returned to Russia following the February Revolution. There he joined the Bolshevik faction and helped coordinate the October Revolution, after which he became commissar

of the big parties, were swept up in the storm of patriotism in every country and forgot everything they had preached about internationalism, antimilitarism, and brotherly love. In no country was there an attempt to stop the epidemic of war by calling for a general strike—as had been promoted in radical circles for many years. Even the world-famous antimilitarist Gustave Hervé, who suffered persecution and years in prison for his activities, was transformed into a chauvinistic patriot at the time of the war.[4]

The situation in our ranks was no better. We did not have well-organized parties in individual countries that could give expression to the sentiments of the movement. But there were some prominent people whose words had always been taken as the expression of our movement. Among them, Peter Kropotkin had held the highest and most prominent place in our movement for over thirty years. Immediately after the outbreak of war, he openly declared that if he were younger, he would have gone to great lengths to defend the freedom-loving traditions of the French people.[5] Some well-known French anarchists like Jean Grave took a similar stand.

This provoked a great commotion in our ranks. Kropotkin's position on a question could not be ignored and silenced. The vast majority of anarchists, however, could not and did not want to accept Kropotkin's new message. Comrades in England issued a manifesto signed by Kropotkin's closest friends and students expressly lamenting his un-anarchistic stance and expressing the firm conviction that under no circumstances can anarchists support a capitalist war.[6]

The anarchist press throughout the world was opposed to the war. The *Fraye arbeter shtime* not only agitated against the war but also showed contempt for Kropotkin and his views. The *Fraye arbeter shtime* pretentiously,

---

of foreign affairs and head of the Red Army during the Russian Civil War (1917–1923). After Stalin's rise to power, Trotsky was exiled and eventually settled in Mexico City. Trostky's role in commanding the repression of the Krondstadt revolt and of the partisan army of Nestor Makhno especially embittered the anarchists.

4. **Gustave Hervé** (1871–1944) was a French former pacifist and socialist who in 1914 supported the French war effort and in 1919 cofounded the quasi-fascist Parti socialiste national (National Socialist Party).

5. *Freedom* (London), October 1914. Kropotkin's statement was translated in the *FAS*, October 24, 1914.

6. **The International Anarchist Manifesto on the War** (1915) was signed by Leonard D. Abbott, Alexander Berkman, Emma Goldman, Hippolyte Havel, Saul Yanovsky, and Joseph Cohen himself, among others.

one might say maliciously, gave Kropotkin lessons on the doctrine of anarchism and its principles, in the same way that it had taught us youths, from time to time, what anarchism is.

Most of us were not pleased with the attitude of the *Fraye arbeter shtime*. We were all against the war and wholeheartedly supported Alexander Berkman and Emma Goldman in their antimilitarist activities, but despite Kropotkin's stance we had no interest in portraying him as a transgressor or a traitor to anarchism. We sought to find an explanation and justification for his position and found it in his long-standing enthusiasm for the libertarian (*frayheytlikhe*) ideas that France had spread throughout the world. Even the years of imprisonment that he had suffered in that country, and the ban on him visiting it, never dampened his enthusiasm for the French people. He considered France the embodiment of the spirit of freedom in Europe, as opposed to the barracks-discipline spirit of militarist-Prussian-German Junkerdom. When the French government several years earlier had lengthened the term of military service from one year to two, Kropotkin had publicly advised the French workers not to oppose the bill. German militarism was for him, as for Bakunin many years before, the worst danger threatening not only Europe but also the whole world.

We did not then realize the correctness of his view of the situation. As anarchists we allowed each his own judgment, but we could not and did not want to dismiss him out of hand.

In the spring of 1917, when President Wilson made an about-face in his diplomacy and allowed the newspapers to build up the war hysteria here in America, the situation suddenly changed sharply in the country's socialist ranks as well as in our movement. The American Socialist Party then had a unique relationship to the war. It had developed under the spiritual influence of the Social Democratic Party of Germany and remained under its sway. Nevertheless, like all of us, it was hostile toward Russia's tsarist regime. In the first years of the war, its press made no secret of its friendship with Germany and hatred of Russia. It did not take a principled stand against the war and militarism in general but reported on daily events and particular battles in the light of Germany's victories and Russia's defeats. However, when it came to US involvement in the war, the party suddenly remembered its internationalism and antimilitarism. At its convention that year in St. Louis, it adopted an extremely revolutionary stand, when there was still no danger in taking such a stance: if we cannot be for Germany, then we are against war in general.[7]

The naive Debs took this seriously. He had little understanding of the political games of the party leaders like Morris Hillquit, Victor Berger, Abe Cahan, and others. He worked in the spirit of the convention's decision and was sentenced to many years in prison.[8] A number of other naive socialists made the same error and were punished severely, but not the leaders of the party, who knew when to turn the cart around to avoid a collision with the war hysteria.

At this time, the *Fraye arbeter shtime* was already strongly influenced by the spirit of the Socialist Party in this country. It was also a well-established, respectable, practical, and prudent paper. As soon as America entered the war, our paper "stood behind the president" and supported him without hesitation. Forgotten were all the arguments the newspaper had previously used against Kropotkin, all the principled insights and calculations: Wilson was declared to be the leader and savior of all mankind. The absurdity peaked with the *Fraye arbeter shtime* admonishing the waves of the Atlantic Ocean to be proud that they were carrying Woodrow Wilson when he boarded the ship for his triumphant voyage to Europe![9]

Emma Goldman, Alexander Berkman, and a small group of comrades around the Anti-Militarist League remained true to their principles. Until the end, they carried on a vigorous campaign against the war, against conscription, and against the hypocrisy of the whole blood-soaked game. The response of the masses was tremendous. Thousands of people, who were not intimidated by the attacks of riotous, hysterical patriotic hoodlums

---

7. "The Socialist Party and the War," Marxists Internet Archive, https://www.marxists .org/history/usa/parties/spusa/1917/0414-spa-stlouisresolution.pdf.

8. **Eugene V. Debs** (1855–1926) was an American-born railway worker, union leader, and socialist. The former head of the Brotherhood of Locomotive Firemen, Debs was imprisoned for six months for leading the 1894 Pullman Strike. Radicalized by the experience, he became a socialist and in 1901 cofounded the Socialist Party of America, standing as its presidential candidate five times. He was sentenced to ten years in federal prison for his statements against the war, of which he served nearly three.

9. *FAS*, December 7, 1918. Cohen mischaracterizes the cause of *FAS* editor Saul Yanovsky's about-face on the war, which was primarily motivated by the threat a potential German victory posed to the gains of Russia's February Revolution. But Yanovsky did praise Woodrow Wilson and the principles for maintaining a postwar peace laid out in Wilson's "Fourteen Points."

in military uniforms and civilian clothes, attended their rallies. The brave activities in New York of these two great individuals (*mentshn*), Berkman and Emma, resonated throughout the country. The US government found it necessary to declare war on these two brave anarchists before it could successfully fight the German army.

On June 15, 1917, Alexander Berkman and Emma Goldman were arrested on the charge of conspiracy to obstruct the government's registration of young men for military service. The office of *Mother Earth* at 20 East 125th Street was overrun by an entire squadron of government agents who ransacked the whole building, without a search warrant, and took with them everything they found there, as well as everything that was in the office of *The Blast* a floor above in the same building. They were held in the Tombs overnight and in the morning were placed under $25,000 bail. In addition, the government rejected offers of real estate worth $300,000 as bond, insisting on the whole amount in cash. It took five days to manage to raise the money for Emma's release, and another five days to raise the other $25,000 for Berkman. He was released on bail from the Tombs on June 25.

Two days later, the court heard the case against them before Judge Julius M. Mayer, a typical Prussian Junker who made no pretense of impartiality. Emma and Berkman decided to go it alone, without the help of a lawyer. They knew that the trial was a farce, and they decided to use the opportunity to explain their views on society and its institutions in court, to make as much propaganda for anarchism as possible, and to suffer the consequences whatever they might be.

The trial took ten days. The official charge was that they had formed a conspiracy to obstruct the registration of young men for conscription. During the trial, however, the prosecutor did not even attempt to substantiate his charges. He highlighted the political beliefs of the defendants, accusing them of preaching violence and at every step hindering the government from keeping order in the country. His principal witness was a policeman who claimed that at a huge mass meeting in the Harlem River Casino the night before the law was signed by the president, he was standing at a table writing a stenographic report of Emma's speech, in which there was a sentence that read, "We believe in violence, and we shall use violence!"

This, in fact, was irrelevant to the indictment and should have been stricken from the proceedings by the court; but Judge Mayer did not stop the prosecutor's unlawful act, and the entire trial revolved around this accusation. The defendants had no difficulty proving that the self-anointed stenographer was not able to write down what Emma was saying. He could not even do that in court, where Emma spoke more slowly than before a large, enthusiastic audience. They called a number of prominent witnesses: Bolton Hall, John Reed, Leonard D. Abbott, Helen Boardman, and other celebrities, all of whom confirmed that Emma simply could not have used such language regarding violence.[10] They read lengthy excerpts from Goldman and Berkman's writings on violence, anarchism, and war that stated the exact opposite of such assertions. It made no impression on the jury or the judge.

The prosecutor found a passage, in an issue of *Mother Earth* from 1914, from Charles Plunkett's speech in Union Square at a memorial for the three victims of the Lexington Avenue explosion, in which he had repeated the words of Louis Lingg about answering police violence with dynamite, and repeated the phrase to make a stronger impression on the jury.

At the end of the trial when the defendants addressed the jury, Alexander Berkman took on the role of a lawyer, analyzing everything the prosecutor and the witnesses had said during the entire trial. He was interrupted a couple of times by the judge and prosecutor. His speech lasted for two hours but did not have the effect that it needed in this situation.

Emma Goldman's speech was a true masterpiece—short, sharp, and to the point. There was not a single unnecessary word or phrase.[11] And the whole thing was so magnificently put together, with so much dignity and consistency, that it made a deep impression on all listeners. The prosecution

---

10. **John Reed** (1887–1920) was an American-born journalist, socialist, and later Communist. A friend of many anarchists and supporter of the IWW, he was best known for his coverage of the Mexican and Russian revolutions, and as a writer for the socialist magazine *The Masses*. In 1919 Reed cofounded the Communist Labor Party of America and then returned to Russia, where he worked on behalf of the Comintern before dying of typhus. **Helen Boardman** was an American-born social worker and reformer. In the 1910s, on behalf of the National Association for the Advancement of Colored People, she investigated lynchings. During the First World War Boardman was a member of the No-Conscription League, and in 1919 she cofounded the short-lived interracial Libertarian International School in Newburgh, New York. She subsequently became a social worker at the Children's Hospital of Los Angeles and a prominent advocate for child welfare.

11. "Emma Goldman's Address to the Jury," in *Trial and Speeches of Alexander Berkman and Emma Goldman in the United States District Court, in the City of New York, July, 1917* (New York: Mother Earth Publishing Association, 1917), 56–66.

and the judge could not refrain from praising the speech and expressing sympathy for this heroic woman whom they sought to condemn. They succeeded in doing so. The jury was out for less than forty minutes and returned a verdict of guilty, which sent the two brave freedom fighters to two years in the penitentiary, with the addition of a fine of $10,000 and the prospect of being deported back to Russia after finishing their terms.

The judge was so unfriendly that he gave them no opportunity to appeal to a higher court or to properly adjudicate their affairs. He immediately handed them over to the marshal on the spot, and that very evening they were taken to prison; Emma was sent to Jefferson City, Missouri, and Berkman to Atlanta.

Harry Weinberger then took up the case, appealing to the Supreme Court of the United States on the grounds that the judge had so openly stated his prejudice against the defendants.[12] In his appeal, Weinberger emphasized the unconstitutionality of the conscription law, which violates citizens' rights as guaranteed by the Constitution. His appeal, printed and circulated in pamphlet form, is a highly interesting document.[13] However, the appeal did not help the defendants.

---

12. **Harry Weinberger** (1886–1944) was an American-born Jewish attorney, civil libertarian, and single-taxer. Born to Hungarian Jewish immigrant parents, he became a close friend of Emma Goldman's and was sympathetic to anarchism. Weinberger's clients included Goldman, Alexander Berkman, Ricardo Flores Magón, Tom Mooney, and numerous lesser-known radicals.

13. *Emma Goldman and Alexander Berkman, Plaintiffs-in-Error, vs. the United States, Defendant-in-Error* (New York: Weinberger, 1917), available online at Hathi Trust Digital Library, https://catalog.hathitrust.org/Record/100883694.

CHAPTER 40

The Russian Revolution and its Effect on Our Movement

In the spring of 1917 the long-awaited news of the collapse of the Russian autocracy arrived. Tsar Nicholas II was arrested. The country was free!

Who can describe the joy that enveloped us Russian emigrants in those glorious days! The impossible had finally occurred!

The tsar arrested! How was it possible? Who dared to place a hand on the absolute ruler of 150 million people and say to him, "You are no longer in charge! You are a common criminal who now must answer for all your heinous crimes!"

However, it had happened. The fierce wrath of the people, who had gathered for generations and fought, suffered, and made the greatest sacrifices for a hundred years, since the Decembrists—that fierce wrath had finally boiled over and at once washed away all the filth and injustice.[1]

And it happened without bloodshed and without resistance.[2] The countless victims of the war all made clear the rottenness of the government. The vile adventures in the imperial court, the promiscuity and negligence, the Rasputin scandal and the criminal mischief of the generals, the great grudges—all of these things, the internal turmoil of the system, made the whole government collapse like a house of cards. The people were freed and began to build a new life.

---

1. In December 1825 liberal members of Russia's military, known as the **Decemberists**, staged a failed coup in support of a constitutional monarchy and the abolition of serfdom.

2. Cohen is incorrect; although the February Revolution was relatively bloodless, according to official figures 1,443 people were killed or injured in Petrograd. Orlando Figes, *A People's Tragedy: The Russian Revolution, 1891–1924* (New York: Penguin, 1998), 321.

With great joy and revolutionary enthusiasm, the Provisional Government freed all political prisoners, emptied all the terrible prisons and Siberian labor camps, where thousands of freedom fighters had languished for years. It invited all émigrés to return home from all corners of the earth to help build the new, free Russia of the future.

A series of migrations began. Hundreds and then thousands of Russian revolutionaries, socialists, and anarchists set out to return to Russia, at the expense of the Russian people, who opened not only the gates of that country but also their sincere, welcoming arms.

From our circles whole groups departed: the Broyt un Frayheyt Group of New York, with its printing press and equipment; the *Golos Truda* editorial staff, with its press, typewriters, speakers, and organizers—all returned enthusiastically. Peter Kropotkin, now almost eighty years old, returned to his old home after forty years of exile.

For those of us who were rooted here in America and could not, or did not want to, join the new migration and transplant ourselves and our children into another land and environment, it was a bitter mercy. Our hearts were torn; we were pulled there, to the land of revolution, but our intellect told us that there was plenty of work to be done here in this country for the same lofty ideal.

Of all the enthusiastic goodbyes and farewells with close comrades and intimate friends, such as Bill Shatoff, Manuel Komroff, Maxim Rayevsky, and others, the farewell of Alexander Krasnoshchekov is sharply etched in my memory.[3] I had not seen the man in almost ten years. He had settled in Chicago, become a lawyer, and did good educational work at the Workers' Institute.[4] And now, one fine morning, he came specially from New York to

---

3. **Maxim Rayevsky** (c. 1882–1931), real name Lev Josifivich Fishelev, was a Russian-born Jewish editor and anarchist. He immigrated to Germany in the 1890s to study and became an anarchist, collaborating on several Russian-language anarchist newspapers published in western Europe between 1906 to 1914. Rayevsky was strongly influenced by syndicalism while living in Paris, and in 1914 he immigrated to the United States and became a leading figure in the Union of Russian Workers, editing its paper *Golos Truda* from 1914 to 1917. He returned to Russia in 1917 and helped reestablish *Golos Truda* in Petrograd but soon withdrew from the anarchist movement and took a nonpolitical government position.

4. The **Worker's Institute** was a nonpartisan labor education center founded in 1915 by a coalition of radical and labor groups. It held classes and lecture series for adults and catered to unionists, socialists, syndicalists, and anarchists alike before closing in 1920 during the First Red Scare.

my house in Stelton to say goodbye to me, and his first words of greeting were, "You know, I became a social democrat!" The matter seemed to bother him, and he wanted to get it out of the way.

I wished him luck in his new ideological orientation. From the long conversation that we had after that it became clear to me that here was a person who would go far in Russia. He was young, full of life, well educated, and brimming with energy. He would not stop for anything.

We lived and breathed the events in Russia: The upheavals in governmental circles, the elevation of Alexander Kerensky into power, the continuation of the war despite the will of the people, the disorganization in the country, the famine in the cities and the uprising of the peasants in the villages.[5] My friend Manuel Komroff, who was brought up here, went to Petrograd with Shatoff, despite the fact that he knew no Russian, and sent me his drawings of a baker and big loaves of bread, about which they all dreamed both in their sleep and also while awake.

We began to hear stories of expropriations that our comrades made there, not always for the greater good. It was said that one of them, a certain Caplan who used to hang around the Ferrer Center and did not have a good reputation, had lost all his teeth during an "ex" [expropriation] because of a cigarette case. He and a comrade entered an aristocratic club in Petrograd and found a large group of aristocrats playing cards. He commanded them to hold up their hands, and emptied their pockets. There was no resistance. Completing their mission, the pair saw themselves out. Caplan stood near the door with his revolver, protecting their retreat. Suddenly, he observed one of the aristocrats taking out a gold cigarette case, which aroused in him a desire to take it as a souvenir. He went back to the table, forgetting he was now alone among a crowd of enemies. So entranced was he with the golden cigarette case that he forgot to use his revolver properly.

Don't even ask what they did to him then!

---

5. **Alexander Kerensky** (1881–1970) was a Russian attorney and socialist. A former member of the Narodnik movement and a veteran of the Revolution of 1905, he was elected to the Russian Duma in 1912 as a member of Trudovik Group, an agrarian socialist breakaway from the Socialist-Revolutionary Party. Kerensky played a prominent role in the February Revolution and served as head of the new Russian Provisional Government until the Bolshevik seizure of power in the October Revolution forced him to flee. He later settled in France and then the United States.

Of course, there was other, more encouraging news: Raymond Robins, head of the American Red Cross expedition sent by President Wilson, let it be known that the real power in Russia lay in the hands of the soviets of workers, peasants, and soldiers and not in the hands of the Provisional Government.[6] Bitter experience had taught him that when there was a need to do something, such as transfer food and medicine from a port, he could move from one government office to another without any results. A visit to the local soviet, however, always brought immediate results.

It became clear that in Russia a new way of life came with terrible birth pangs. The new order had to combat all kinds of destructive forces, which put large obstacles in its way.

In July there were reports of a new revolutionary uprising in Petrograd, which was easily repressed. Lenin and Trotsky had to hide to avoid arrest. The peace between the government and the soviets was no longer secure. The political parties were campaigning for representation on the proposed Constituent Assembly, which would have to decide what form of government and organization the country should have.

That summer we heard that Kerensky had unofficially consulted with prominent individuals concerning the situation in Russia, and that Kropotkin had participated and had suggested that the country should be organized on a federal basis, following the model of the United States. This consultation brought no results.

In November we learned Russia was facing a new upheaval. The Constituent Assembly was dispersed without any resistance. Government power was seized by the Bolsheviks, who established themselves in the Smolny Institute, and this new government was led by Lenin and Trotsky.

❀ ❀ ❀

We, the younger comrades, were all overjoyed. Our enthusiasm knew no bounds. We saw in the new developments the arrival of the social revolution, against which nothing could stand and that would not be satisfied with paper

---

6. **Raymond Robins** (1873–1954) was an American-born miner, social worker, writer, labor activist, and Progressive who advocated for diplomatic relations between the United States and Soviet Union.

freedoms and political promises but would make fundamental changes, uproot the old order, and build a truly new, free world.

Among the older comrades there were some skeptics. Yanovsky and Dr. Maryson, whose approaches to social issues had always been opposed, took one and the same view of the matter: It is no good! It's not anarchist; not kosher. It will lead to bloodshed, dictatorship, and worse that we can only imagine.

Yanovsky had been greatly discredited in our eyes by his position on the war, first supporting Kropotkin and then President Wilson. We did not take his opinion at all seriously. On the other hand, Dr. Maryson's ideas had always been incomprehensible to us. We had never been able to follow his line of thinking clearly. We immediately asked, what were they supposed to do in Russia? Let the Constituent Assembly produce a constitution like the one in France, let's say, and establish a bourgeois-capitalist system— imposing new governmental fetters on the people and enslaving them to the bourgeoisie?

This is where the ambiguity in our ranks regarding the Russian Revolution became apparent. For two or three generations straight we had been preaching revolution, and now, when the opportune moment had come, our trailblazers were telling us that the revolution may not be allowed to reach the point of giving power to the economic organizations of the workers instead of to the bourgeois political parties. Something was amiss here!

Such an attitude was incomprehensible to us.

The *Fraye arbeter shtime* was getting ready to celebrate its twentieth anniversary in 1919. There was prosperity among the Jewish working class due to the war. Someone had the bright idea that on such an occasion and under such circumstances, it would be a good idea to raise a fund of $20,000 to buy the *Fraye arbeter shtime* a building of its own and ensure its continued existence. The United Hebrew Trades endorsed the idea. The unions opened their purses. The International Ladies' Garment Workers' Union and the Amalgamated Clothing Workers each gave $1,000, the smaller unions likewise gave relatively large sums. The celebration in Carnegie Hall was also splendid; one could not have imagined a better one.

But $20,000 was not raised. No building was purchased. Instead of all these good things, six months later came Yanovsky's resignation, after twenty years of editing the newspaper.

He took another job, editing the journal of the ILGWU, where he would have an audience, as he said, of 50,000 readers and could accomplish more.[7] He introduced his replacement, Dr. Maryson, with many words of praise in his final "Oyf der vakh" column, despite having never previously uttered a kind word about him.

Maryson made radical changes in the *Fraye arbeter shtime*'s appearance, content, and direction. The paper immediately changed to a tabloid format, without any announcements, and was completely filled with anarchist treatises. It was strictly anti-Bolshevik, to the extent that no favorable opinion of them could even be published in a letter to the editor. Under Yanovsky's editorship the newspaper had been open to anyone to express their views, but now that policy had abruptly been abolished. The comrades, the vast majority of whom were sympathetic to the Bolsheviks at that time, could not express their thoughts in their own paper.

For the preceding five years, since I had tied my fate to the Ferrer School and colony, I had been estranged from the Jewish anarchist movement, seldom coming into contact with the activities of Jewish groups, although I remained a member of the Radical Library of Philadelphia the entire time. During the war years I even stopped reading the *Fraye arbeter shtime*, unable to stomach "standing behind Wilson." But, of course, I kept track of what was happening in our movement. My friends Sam Rothman, Harry Gordon, Isaac Radinowsky, and others used to keep me apprised of every little thing. In midsummer of 1920, Harry Gordon came to me with a demand: I must come to New York for a meeting of the *Fraye arbeter shtime*. A sharp quarrel had developed between Maryson and the comrades. They could not agree on anything. Gordon argued that my presence would perhaps help settle the dispute.

---

7. From 1919 to 1925 Yanovsky was managing editor of the ILGWU's new weekly newspaper *Justice*, as well as editor of its Yiddish edition, *Gerekhtigkeyt*. (The union also published an Italian edition, *Giustizia*, and the three papers carried many of the same articles in translation, as well as original material in each language.) He later privately reflected: "For almost seven years, I edited an ILGWU rag, and put up with as much as I could bear. How many abominations did I gloss over, how much filth did I try to justify and defend! And all this I did—not for the big bucks I got—but because each time I persuaded myself that this was necessary, that the workers' cause required it, that if I didn't keep my mouth shut and speak out strongly against these things, I would be doing more harm than good." Dmitry Ivanovich Rublyov, "'No Anarchist Should Take . . . Part in This Wretched and Insane War': A Letter by Saul Yanovsky to Marie Goldsmit in 1915," Kate Sharpley Library, https://www.katesharpleylibrary.net/cfxqzs.

I went to the meeting. For three years, since America had entered the war and unleashed poisonous hysteria, I had not been to New York. At the meeting the following comrades were present: Aaron Mintz, Nokhum Vaynritsh, Morris Shutz, Louis Finkelstein, Maryson, Gordon, myself, and a few others. At issue was an article that Dr. Michael A. Cohn, then a fervent Bolshevik, had submitted praising Bolshevism, and Maryson refused to print it. The atmosphere was tense. Maryson refused to listen to anyone. "You need to listen and learn from me!" he shouted in one comrade's face. My attempt to mediate and settle the dispute did not yield any results. We left having accomplished nothing. That week's was the last issue edited by Maryson. The newspaper was suspended and did not appear again that summer.

In the fall, the comrades regrouped and decided to resume the *Fraye arbeter shtime*. For the following year, they hired Mosheh Kats, a Communist who had worked for the *Forverts*, as editor.[8] He received a salary of seventy-five dollars a week. Haim Kantorovich, also a Communist at the time, was hired as his assistant for a couple of days a week, with a salary thirty-five dollars a week.[9] Menakhem Boreysho was hired as a theater critic at $7.50 a week.[10] The business manager received fifty dollars a week. As you

8. **Mosheh Kats** (Moyshe Katz, 1885–1960) was a Russian-born Jewish writer, editor, and Communist. He was involved in socialist and Zionist organizations in his youth, for which he was arrested multiple times. Kats spent time in Palestine, Egypt, and the United States before settling in the US in 1920 and, in 1921, joining the Communist Party. Katz wrote for many Yiddish publications, including the *Forverts* and the *Morgn-frayheyt*. He should not be confused with the anarchist Moyshe Katz.

9. **Haim Kantorovich** (Khayim Kantorovitsh, 1891–1936) was a Russian-born Jewish writer, teacher, and socialist. He was active in radical circles in Russia before immigrating to the United States in 1907, and he wrote for many radical Yiddish publications, including the *Arbeter fraynd* and *FAS*, and taught at Workmen's Circle schools. Kantorovich briefly joined the IWW, then Poale Zion, and then the Communist Party, but subsequently became a critic of the Soviet Union and joined the Jewish Socialist Verband. Upon his death, the editors of the *FAS* noted: "Haim Kantorovich always stood at a distance from the libertarian-socialist worldview. But he not infrequently found the most generous hospitality in the columns of our newspapers" (*FAS*, August 21, 1936). Obituary: *American Socialist Monthly*, October 1936, 2–5.

10. **Menakhem Boreysho** or Boraisho (1888–1949), born Menakhem Goldberg, was a Russian-born Jewish writer, poet, and socialist. He joined the Labor Zionist movement as a teenager and was already an accomplished poet when he immigrated to the United States during the First World War. Boreysho became a teacher for the Workmen's Circle and contributed to the *FAS*, *Der tog*, and other Yiddish papers, and was a writer for the Communist *Frayheyt* until it defended the 1929 anti-Jewish riots in Palestine.

see, the enterprise was quite expensive. There was already not a penny in the treasury, so people first decided to hold a proletarian reception for the first issue at Beethoven Hall, charging a dollar a head. About six hundred people gathered. Second, five-dollar bonds were sold, of which Michael A. Cohn promised to buy a few hundred.

Cohn was always, since 1899, the most active of the comrades working to ensure the publication of the paper. When I asked him, "How can it be, that one could put a Communist in charge of editing an anarchist newspaper?" he answered me and explained, "We are not just anarchists; in addition, we are also communists and revolutionaries. Mosheh Kats is both a Communist and a revolutionary. He is only one third of the way from being completely kosher. And, well, in a time of need, one should not be too picky!" "We had no other choice," he added. We would soon see that there was no lack of anarchism in the newspaper.

A few weeks later, Harry Gordon came to me with a new complaint. The business manager of the *Fraye arbeter shtime*, Bob Robins, was leaving for Russia, and nobody wanted the job.[11] The editorship was already what it was. The paper came out every week, but there was no one to oversee the business end. The paper would have to be shut down again.

The manager had always been a sort of fifth wheel. They had little to do with the anarchist movement. Often they were people that none of us knew. Robins, the last manager whom Yanovsky had left behind, was a very capable man, but he could not read a word of Yiddish. And he was supposed to reply to letters and deal with Yiddish readers. Now he wanted to go to Russia, leaving the paper in God's hands.

My comradely heart began to pound. Suspending the newspaper for a second time in a year would mean its end. How could this be tolerated? After all, the *Fraye arbeter shtime* was an institution in the movement, for which a

---

11. **Bob Robins** (c. 1874–c.1933) was a Russian-born Jewish printer and anarchist. After immigrating to the United States with his family, he lived in Chicago where he worked on the anarchist paper *Free Society* and in 1904 married fellow anarchist Lucy Fox. The couple moved to San Francisco, where they opened that city's first vegetarian restaurant, then to the Home Colony, then traveled across the country in a homemade mobile home. Robins went to Russia in 1917 but was soon disillusioned and, after much difficulty, was able to depart using a fake passport. He returned "a tired, sick, and low-spirited man" (Lucy Robins Lang, *Tomorrow Is Beautiful* [New York: Macmillan, 1948], 215) and soon separated from Lucy due to political differences.

whole generation of anarchists had put in a world of effort. It could still be used to benefit the movement. It had to be saved from destruction.

At the time, I was free in the sense that the Ferrer School and colony were not my responsibilities. The school was in the good hands of Elizabeth and Alexis Ferm, and the colony was by now fully established.[12] I offered my services as business manager of the *Fraye arbeter shtime*, and this offer was accepted. Beginning in December 1920, I took over the office.

There was not enough money left in the coffers for the week's expenses. Where the $16,000 or $17,000 collected a year earlier had disappeared to, I was never able to trace. Part of the money was spent on books to sell, which filled the office. However, small sums of money did trickle in each week, and the paper continued without too much difficulty.

In February 1921 we received a cable from Moscow stating that Kropotkin had died. We tried to send a cable requesting details, but no company would undertake the job. Soviet Russia, due to an iron blockade of the Allied Powers, was cut off from the rest of the world.

We released a special issue of the *Fraye arbeter shtime* and organized a rally at the Manhattan Opera House on a Sunday evening. Unfortunately, there was a blizzard that Sunday, making it impossible for people from further afield in Brooklyn to attend the meeting. However, the huge opera house was filled with people who came to pay their respects to the memory of the great freedom fighter. The speakers were Michael A. Cohn, B. Charney Vladeck, Bob Minor, Mosheh Kats, and others. They were listened to attentively. But when I introduced Yanovsky as the last speaker, a barrage of protest erupted. No amount of pleading, no reminder of the sanctity of the occasion, helped; the Bolshevik-minded comrades would not allow him to speak. Such was the Bolshevik sentiment in our ranks.

In the editorial office of the *Fraye arbeter shtime*, I was a foreigner. I used to debate with Haim Kantorovich from time to time, enjoying his torment as he, a devout Marxist, tried to explain why the social revolution had come

12. **Elizabeth Ferm** (1857–1944), born Mary Elizabeth Byrne, was an American-born educator and single-taxer. **Alexis Ferm** (1870–1971) was a Swedish-born educator, single-taxer, and individualist anarchist who immigrated to the United States with his family at age two and was influenced by Benjamin Tucker. The couple led Stelton's Modern School from 1920 to 1925, and again from 1933 to Elizabeth's death in 1944, after which Alexis continued as principal until 1948, when he retired to the Fairhope single-tax colony in Alabama.

in a backward country like Russia and not in a highly industrialized country where the economic process had properly prepared the ground.

In March we received reports of the uprising of the sailors in Kronstadt.[13] I spoke to Mosheh Kats, the editor, about it, and expressed the opinion that we must be careful in interpreting the event. After all, we did not know exactly what was really happening there. Maybe it was a true revolutionary uprising!

He listened to me but wrote an editorial under the heading "Soviet Russia on Guard!," in which he attacked the sailors and sang the praises of the Soviet government for drowning the uprising in blood.[14] That was already a little too much for me. I wrote an article entitled "Anarchism and Dictatorship," demonstrating how inconsistent we were in our sympathies with the Russian régime.[15]

The article caused a heated debate that lasted for months. It was reprinted in *Der Syndikalist* in Berlin and reached a wide readership in Europe. Alexander Berkman, in a private letter from Russia, sent me greetings and said that I had hit the nail on the head. The result of the discussion was that the individual elements separated from each other. Those anarchists who were completely swallowed up by Bolshevism became outright Communists. Only those in whom anarchism was deeply rooted in their hearts and their beliefs remained in the movement. The paper lost many readers but it remained anarchist and was not drowned in the "leftist" flood.[16]

I consider this to be the most important contribution of my longstanding activity in the anarchist movement. It was my fate to prevent the newspaper and the movement from being swallowed up by a foreign, hostile ideology and movement.

---

13. In March 1921 soldiers and sailors stationed at the Kronstadt naval base on Kotlin Island, in response to the centralization of Bolshevik rule and a strike wave in nearby Petrograd, formed a new soviet and issued a set of demands that included new elections for representation on soviets, equalization of rations, freedom of speech for anarchists and other radicals, and the release of left-wing political prisoners. Soviet troops stormed and retook the base after sixteen days, and executed more than one thousand of the rebels.

14. *FAS*, March 26, 1921.

15. *FAS*, May 20, 1921.

16. Within the Jewish labor movement, members of the Communist Party referred to themselves as "the Left" (*di linke*). Anarchists like Cohen often placed the term within sarcastic quotation marks to signal that they, and not the Communists, truly represented the far left of the political spectrum.

That summer, at a three-day convention in Philadelphia, I proposed and carried a resolution that the *Fraye arbeter shtime* be owned and published by the Jewish Anarchist Federation of America and Canada, not by a single organization.[17] Instead of a single editor, the convention chose a collegium of five: David Isakovitz, Louis Finkelstein, Michael A. Cohn, Benjamin Axler, and myself. Axler went to work in the printing house of the paper, so as to be on hand at the office at all times. We shared the work of putting together and managing the paper.

---

17. The Jewish Anarchist Federation of America and Canada (Yidishe Anarkhistishe Federatsie fun Amerike und Kenede), discussed by Cohen in greater detail in chapter 50, had twenty-one affiliates at its founding in 1921, and survived into the 1970s.

CHAPTER 41

Emma Goldman and Alexander Berkman Are Deported

On September 19, 1919, Emma Goldman was freed from the federal penitentiary in Jefferson City, Missouri. On the recommendation of Judge Mayer, who had sentenced her, the government demanded $15,000 bail pending a Bureau of Immigration hearing. The bail money was raised. For the moment, Emma was free again.

Berkman was released from the Atlanta Penitentiary on October 1. The federal government seemingly made him suffer greater and worse tortures in those two years there than he had lived through in the Western Penitentiary in Pennsylvania in fourteen years. For months he was held in solitary confinement on a diet of bread and water for standing up for fellow prisoners. When he once came to the aid of a Negro prisoner, he was thrown into a "tomb"—a hole measuring two feet wide by four and a half feet long, in which a man could not stand up or extend to his full height. There was neither light nor air in the tomb. He had to lie on the ground with his mouth open near the door to catch some air through the gap underneath it. The last seven months he was held in solitary confinement. He emerged physically broken, more dead than alive, but they could not suffocate his rebellious spirit.

Before he was released, he was taken to court, on the recommendation of the judge, to be expelled from the country. Berkman refused to appear for trial. He provided a written statement in which he declared:

The purpose of the present hearing is to determine my "attitude of mind." It does not, admittedly, concern itself with my actions, past or present. It is purely an inquiry into my views and opinions.

I deny the right of any one—individually or collectively—to set up an inquisition of thought. Thought is, or should be, free. My social views and political opinions are my personal concern. I owe no one responsibility for them. Responsibility begins only with the efforts of thought expressed in action. Not before. Free thought, necessarily involving freedom of speech and press, I may tersely define thus: no opinion a law—no opinion a crime. For the government to attempt to control thought, to prescribe certain opinions or proscribe others, is the height of despotism.

This proposed hearing is an invasion of my conscience. I therefore refuse, most emphatically, to participate in it.[1]

Berkman also had to pay $15,000 in bail. When he was released, detectives from San Francisco tried to arrest him in connection with the Mooney case, but federal agents prevented this.

Returning to New York, Emma and Berkman found their former home and office in shambles. The government had demolished everything, confiscated all the old newspapers and the masses of books they had for sale. In their absence, Eleanor Fitzgerald, Berkman's secretary and girlfriend, had continued to support the large number of political prisoners and to work on the Mooney case.[2] With the help of Minna Lowensohn, Hilda and Sam Adel, Pauline Turkel, and a few other comrades, Fitzgerald was able to do a great deal of work, but the movement as a whole was severely damaged.[3]

---

1. Quoted in Emma Goldman, *Living My Life*, vol. 2 (New York: Alfred A. Knopf, 1931), 703.

2. **Mary Eleanor ("Fitzie") Fitzgerald** (1877–1955) was an American-born teacher, editor, theater director, and anarchist. She was a romantic companion of Ben Reitman and then Alexander Berkman and worked as assistant editor of *Mother Earth* and *The Blast*. Fitzgerald cofounded the Political Prisoners Amnesty League and later directed the Provincetown Players.

3. **Hilda Adel** (1892–1984), née Kovner, was a Russian-born Jewish anarchist. Her family immigrated in 1906 to Boston, where she became an anarchist in 1912 and met her husband **Sam Adel** (1891–1960), a Russian-born Jewish cabinetmaker and anarchist who likewise immigrated in 1906. He was involved in the anti-conscription movement during the First World War, and in 1917 the couple moved to New York, where they participated in the Mother Earth Group and the Frayheyt Group. In 1927 they moved to the radical enclave of Mount Airy, New York, where they lived the remainder of lives in a cabin Sam built. **Pauline Turkel** (1899–1987) was an American-born Jewish secretary, editor, and anarchist. The

Mollie Steimer and a number of other comrades were charged and received long sentences.[4] Their crime consisted of protesting Wilson's deployment of troops to Murmansk, Soviet Russia, without a declaration of war.

This was the policy of the Allied governments at the time: France, England, and the United States all sent troops and ships to Russia to help the reactionary generals there in their fight against the Soviet government. By law, President Wilson had no right to send troops and wage a war in Russia without a congressional declaration. Yet it was not the criminals who were punished but the young comrades who dared to protest against this: Mollie Steimer, Jacob Abrams, Samuel Lipman, Hyman Lachowsky, and Jacob Schwartz were arrested, betrayed by a purported comrade.[5] They were

daughter of immigrants from Russian Galicia, she became Emma Goldman's secretary and was active in the Mother Earth Group, the No-Conscription League, and the League for the Amnesty of Political Prisoners. Turkel visited Goldman in Europe after the latter's deportation, and from 1937 until her retirement in 1964 she was managing editor of the *Psychoanalytic Quarterly* (1932–present).

4. **Mollie Steimer** (1897–1980) was a Russian-born Jewish garment worker and anarchist. In 1912 her family immigrated to New York, where she became an anarchist and joined the Shturem Group, which in 1918 became the Frayheyt Group, as well as the Union of Russian Workers. Steimer was arrested in 1918 while distributing leaflets protesting American intervention in the Russian Civil War and, along with Jacob Abrams and other members of the Frayheyt Group, was sentenced to fifteen years in prison under the Espionage Act and then deported in 1921. In Russia she worked to aid imprisoned anarchists, leading to multiple arrests and her eventual expulsion in 1923. Steimer settled in France until the Nazi occupation, then fled to Mexico.

5. **Jacob Abrams** (Yankel Abramovsky, 1883–1953) was a Russian-born Jewish bookbinder and anarchist. He immigrated to the United States in 1908, was active in the International Brotherhood of Bookbinders, and cofounded the militant anarchist Shturem Group and Frayheyt Group. After his deportation he joined the Golos Truda Group, then immigrated to France and Mexico in 1925–26. Abrams joined the Spanish anarchist exile group Tierra y Libertad in Mexico City, where in 1939 he cofounded the Yiddish antifascist newspaper *Di shtime* (The Voice). **Samuel Lipman** (1888–1930s) was a Russian-born Jewish furrier and socialist. He immigrated to the United States in 1913, and, although a socialist rather than an anarchist, he was strongly influenced by Leo Tolstoy and belonged to the Frayheyt Group. After his deportation he became a professor of agronomy and in 1928 joined the Communist Party but was arrested and executed during Stalin's purges of the 1930s. **Hyman Lachowsky** (Hayman Lakhovsky, 1894–?) was a Russian-born Jewish bookbinder and anarchist. He immigrated to the United States in 1907 and was a member of the Shturem Group and Frayheyt Group. After his deportation he withdrew from radical politics and started a family in Minsk (in present-day Belarus). **Jacob Schwartz** (Dzsheykob Shvarts, 1887–1918) was a Russian-born Jewish bookbinder and anarchist. In 1910 he immigrated to New York, where he belonged to the International Brotherhood of Bookbinders and the Frayheyt Group.

given twenty-year sentences. Mollie, because she was so young, was given fifteen years. The recommendation was that they be deported as soon as they finished their prison terms. In prison they were beaten mercilessly. Jacob Schwartz died a day before his trial. In his cell, these few words were found: "Farewell, comrades. When you appear before the court I will be with you no longer. Struggle without fear, fight bravely. I am sorry I have to leave you. But this is life itself. After your long martyr—" Here, it seems, he was unable to finish. He died, a victim of criminal, reactionary behavior that nothing could justify.[6]

Berkman and Emma, in the brief time left to them, organized and addressed huge meetings in New York, Detroit, and Chicago; on December 5, they were told in Chicago to report to Ellis Island, whence they would be deported to Soviet Russia.

They both protested their deportations as long as possible, although in reality they were happy to return to Russia to take part in the revolution. At the time, they were in complete sympathy with the activities of the Bolshevik government, insofar as we were aware of them here. Emma strongly opposed "Babushka" Yekaterina Breshkovskaya when the latter came to America to accuse the Bolsheviks of murder and dictatorship. In the opinion of Emma, and of all of us, many things were justified that would not have been tolerated in peaceful times.

At Ellis Island, they found many friends and acquaintances. Hundreds of revolutionaries were detained there. The war was long over. The armistice had been celebrated with indescribable enthusiasm some thirteen months earlier, but A. Mitchell Palmer, Wilson's attorney general, did not stop his raids against radicals.[7] His agents and bloodhounds roamed all the industrial cities. They broke up meetings, broke into private homes, and arrested anyone they suspected of sympathy toward the Bolshevik government. The arbitrary behavior of the police here in America at that time had

---

6. Schwartz's official cause of death was pneumonia, but most believed that the brutal beating he had received at the hands of police seven weeks earlier was the true cause.

7. **A. Mitchell Palmer** (1872–1936) was an American lawyer and Democratic politician who served as US attorney general from 1919 to 1921, during which he coordinated the massive federal campaign against left-wing radicals known as the First Red Scare. Palmer, a former congressman, unsuccessfully attempted to secure the Democratic Party's presidential nomination in 1920.

reached the same degree of brutality as that of Tsar Nicholas's government in benighted Russia.

Two small examples out of many will suffice: In Stelton we were subjected to some severe hearings. One day a US district attorney named Stone held us for a five-hour cross-examination. I took the opportunity to accuse the government of engaging in a witch hunt, similar to that which had occurred in Salem, Massachusetts, many generations ago. They persecuted people who had not committed any crimes against the laws of the land—if they had broken the law, they could be tried and punished here, and imprisoned—but instead they were breaking up families, deporting fathers whose children were born here and were American citizens, because the fathers had dared to have different political opinions about the social order, though they had never committed an unlawful act.

Mr. Stone was upset and warned me that this hearing was official: I had better be careful what I said. He had come to interrogate me, not to answer my questions and suggestions. Nevertheless, he allowed himself to be drawn into long discussions more than once. His main argument was that they did not punish innocent people. They just did not want "foreigners" telling them how to run the country. Those who were in sympathy with Soviet Russia were being sent there. No families were broken up. He, as well as I, knew that this was a lie. In Stelton he was after comrade Bernard Sernaker, to deport him and leave his two small children behind.[8]

We learned the result of this hearing after Berkman managed to obtain a copy of it: the entire population of Stelton should be sent to Ellis Island for rigorous individual hearings, with the intention to deport us. What saved us from this recommendation was the fact that we, more than a hundred families, all owned property and held debts with many local companies and banks. So the higher authorities did not accept Stone's

---

8. **Bernard Sernaker** (1884–1971) was a Russian-born Jewish machinist and anarchist. He was a member of the Polish Socialist Party and arrested in 1905 before migrating to Argentina and then England, where he was active in Jewish anarchist circles. Sernaker and his family immigrated to the United States in 1909 and later moved to the Stelton Colony, where his two daughters attended the Modern School. A pacifist, he joined the Shturem Group and the Conscientious Objectors League and was deported as an anarchist in 1920. In Russia Sernaker worked as an engineer and in 1949 was sent to a prison camp for six years for having "subversive" foreign connections. He was able to reestablish contact with his American-born daughters only in 1956, thirty-six years after his deportation.

recommendation. This little bit of sacred property kept us from being deported.

Patriotic hoodlums under the leadership of Mr. Johnson of New Brunswick—owner of the famous Johnson & Johnson pharmaceutical supply company, which had made millions in the war—came to the Stelton Colony armed to the teeth, to remove the red flag that waved over the colony after the defeat of Germany, briefly frightening the women and children in the colony. There were no men in the colony at the time, in the middle of a workday.

In Philadelphia two detectives came to arrest Jack Bowman at his home one evening. By chance, he saw them in the street and suspected that they were looking for him. The detectives made themselves comfortable while they waited for him. Convinced that he was correct, he, of course, did not hurry home. The detectives sat down on his porch, waiting for him to return. My daughter Emma and a couple of friends happened to be there. When the detectives heard that one of those present was named Emma they believed that God had sent a real prize into their hands. In the dark, they could not see who Emma was—they thought they had found Emma Goldman, who was sitting behind bars in Jefferson City. They turned on all the lights and discovered a young girl of thirteen before them.

Bowman remained in hiding for a few days, until he could arrange for a lawyer and sufficient bail. This saved him from being taken to Ellis Island, from which very few managed to escape. Dozens and hundreds of workers—Russians and Jews—who had been arrested in the police raids on radical meetings and organizations in the big cities were held on Ellis Island for months.

In the middle of the night on December 21, 1919, detainees on Ellis Island were dragged from their beds and told to get ready to leave. In haste they were put on barges and taken to the ship *Buford*, an old rust bucket that had been used as a transport in the Spanish-American War and was totally unsuited for a long ocean voyage. Two hundred forty-nine political prisoners, with no hearing or trial, people who had not committed any crime, were sent under heavy military guard out of free America. After twenty-eight days of torment and suffering, they were put in sealed train cars through Finland to the border of Soviet Russia, the entrance into a new world.

CHAPTER 42

Reaction at Home and around the World

In no other country did the First World War engender such a dark reaction as in America. Our president, Woodrow Wilson, author of the book *The New Freedom*, seems to have felt uncomfortable leading the nation into a bloody foreign war far across the sea.[1] So he encouraged the press to stir up a crazy, hysterical chauvinism and gave his attorney general, A. Mitchell Palmer, a free hand to ruthlessly persecute anyone who dared express an opinion against the war. Raids were carried out all over the country. Thousands of people were arrested, beaten, and tortured. Conscientious objectors, people who refused to join the military and take part in the slaughter, crowded the prisons. Roger Baldwin, the son of a businessman and a well-known person in his own right, was sentenced to a year in prison for his courageous declaration that he would not take part in the war under any circumstances.[2] But others were not so lucky. They received sentences as high as ten, fifteen, and twenty years in prison.

---

1. Woodrow Wilson, *The New Freedom: A Call for the Emancipation of the Energies of a Generous People* (New York: Doubleday, 1913).

2. **Roger Nash Baldwin** (1884–1981) was an American-born social worker, attorney, pacifist, and onetime anarchist. During the First World War he was a member of the American Union Against Militarism and became an anarchist, befriended Emma Goldman, and joined the IWW. Baldwin cofounded Civil Liberties Bureau in 1917, which in 1920 became the American Civil Liberties Union (ACLU), and helped launch the International Committee for Political Prisoners in 1924. In 1927 he edited the book *Kropotkin's Revolutionary Pamphlets*, and that same year he visited the Soviet Union and published a book defending the Soviet government. Baldwin soon grew disillusioned with Soviet communism, and in the 1940s he expelled Communist Party members from the ACLU.

William Haywood received a sentence of twenty years. Eugene V. Debs: ten years. Kate Richards O'Hare, Rose Pastor Stokes, and hundreds of others were likewise sentenced to long terms.[3] But the Justice Department's outrage centered mostly on the Wobblies. A hundred members were tried along with Bill Haywood, and all received sentences from one to twenty years. Our democratic government unleashed a real reign of terror throughout the country, which was no milder than the terror of the Bolsheviks during the revolution, except that the hypocritical domestic newspapers inveighed against the Russian terror, while they concealed or approved of the crimes committed by the government here.

As soon as the United States entered the war, the post office imposed censorship on the press, the likes of which had never been seen. Foreign-language publications were subjected to terrible difficulties. Every article concerning a political or social issue had to be accompanied by a literal translation into English. No matter how faithfully newspapers tried to conform to the government's regulations during the bloody war, often entire issues were held up by the post office, simply confiscated without explanation. This happened not only during the war, when it was shamelessly excused as protecting oneself from the enemy, but long after as well. In my time as manager of the *Fraye arbeter shtime*, in late 1920 and early 1921, several issues of the paper were held up. I went to the head official at the post office to find out why, but to no avail. The big official pleaded his case: that he wasn't obliged to tell us what they didn't like in the publication. We ourselves needed to figure out how to keep from being censored. Only after Warren G. Harding and his "Ohio gang" of racketeers and thieves took over the government in March 1921 did the new postmaster general, William H. Hays, suspend censorship and let the press breathe freely again.

Wilson paid the appropriate penalty for his reactionary policy in the United States. When he came in conflict with the Republican politicians concerning the League of Nations, he went out of his way to appeal to public opinion. When he came to Seattle, Washington, the Wobblies and their

---

3. **Kate Richards O'Hare** (1876–1948) was an American-born journalist, editor, and socialist. She spoke and wrote widely on behalf of the Socialist Party, which nominated her for federal office multiple times. In 1919 she was sentenced to federal prison for speaking against the First World War, and she befriended Emma Goldman in the Missouri State Penitentiary before her sentence was commuted in 1920.

sympathizers filled the sidewalks of many streets along the route of the cav-
alcade and stood silently with their arms folded over their hearts, looking
him squarely in the eyes in sharp rebuke.

When Wilson, in his open car and surrounded by his retinue, reached
these streets, with his top hat in his hand and a sweet smile plastered on
his face to greet his admirers, he was stunned by the piercing glare of the
assembled people, who were standing still, not moving, and looking at him
with hostile eyes. The smile disappeared from his face. The hand with the
hat dropped helplessly, never to rise again. It was as if he had been hit by a
bullet. He called the Wobbly leaders to his hotel room to find out the reason
for this hostility. It was not hard for them to explain. His Justice Department
had criminally persecuted their organization. In Seattle, Spokane, and other
towns in the area, patriotic vigilantes had carried out pogroms on the offices
of their unions, killing and molesting innocent people. How could they be
friendly to the overlord of those murderous hoodlums?

Earlier, while he was in France, Wilson sent an unofficial commission
to Russia to find out what was going on and whether it would be possible
to come to an understanding with the Bolsheviks. The head of the committee was William Bullitt, a young Philadelphia millionaire aristocrat and
diplomat.[4] Lincoln Steffens accompanied him. Their impressions of Russia
were favorable. They were able to come to an understanding with Lenin
about the important issues of the day. When the commission returned to
Versailles with its report, Wilson did not respond or listen. By that time, he
had already agreed to French prime minister Georges Clemenceau's policy of encircling Russia with an iron cordon of small nations to isolate the
revolution.

In Russia, Lincoln Steffens met William Shatoff on a train going from
Moscow to Petrograd. They had known each other in America. Shatoff was
interested in our school. He had been a member of the Ferrer Colony, and
for a time before his departure he had lived at the Ferrer Center and super-
vised its activities. He emptied his pockets, handing over all the money he
had to Lincoln Steffens for our school here in America. This amounted to a

---

4. **William Bullitt Jr.** (1891–1967) was an American-born journalist and diplomat.
From 1924 to 1930 he was married to radical journalist Louise Bryant (1885–1936), and in
1933–1936 Bullit served as the first US ambassador to the Soviet Union but subsequently
became a strident anti-Communist.

staggering one thousand American dollars and served to inaugurate a fund to build a new school building.

In the first year after the Bolshevik Revolution, before learning what was really taking place there, the working masses' enthusiasm for Bolshevism was great. When the Bolsheviks issued a call for the unification of all the workers in the Third International, they gladly included anarchists and all other revolutionary parties, and pressure from its membership forced the American Socialist Party to consider the issue and look for a way to become involved.

They probably would have joined had the Bolsheviks not been so assured of their victory and so dogmatic in their approach. Many in Moscow thought the socialist movement was under their thumb, and they issued a twenty-one-point list of conditions that each party had to accept and sign onto before it could be admitted to the Third International. Of the twenty-one points, they would not concede on a single one. They were like Moses when he came down from the mountain, telling the global socialist movement: "Either you accept our Torah, or we will reduce you to dust!" Such an attitude, of course, could hardly elicit a friendly response. With a heavy heart, the Socialist Party of America, under the leadership of Morris Hillquit, declined the invitation.

The younger socialists in the party's Jewish federation, who had always been somewhat more left leaning, took a different position, a Bolshevik one. The energetic activist Jacob Salutsky and others of the most important contributors to the *Forverts*—Hillel Rogoff, Zivion, Moissaye Olgin, and more—left the newspaper and joined the "Left" movement.[5] True, Zivion

---

5. **Jacob Benjamin Salutsky** (Yankev Binyamin Salutsky, 1882–1968), also known as J. B. S. Hardman, was a Russian-born Jewish journalist, union organizer, and socialist. He was active in the socialist movement and joined the Bund, leading to numerous arrests, and fled to France in 1908. In 1909 he immigrated to the United States, where he cofounded and became general secretary of the Socialist Party's Jewish Socialist Federation. Salutsky joined the Communist Party in 1921 but was expelled in 1923 for refusing to accept party control. In the 1930s he helped form the CIO and joined the Democratic Party. **Hillel Rogoff** (Hilel Rogof, 1882–1971) was a Russian-born Jewish journalist and socialist. After immigrating in 1906 he became active in the Socialist Party and worked and wrote for the *Forverts*. Rogoff also contributed to the *FAS* and *Tsukunft* and briefly joined the Communist Party in 1921. In 1926 he stood as a Socialist Party candidate for Senate. **Zivion** (Tsvien, 1874–1954), real name Ben-Tsien Hoffman, was a Russian-born Jewish engineer, journalist, and socialist. At age eighteen he was ordained as a rabbi but shortly thereafter became a socialist and later

and Rogoff did not stay there for long. Bolshevik discipline and methods were not to their liking. They returned to the socialist movement and the *Forverts*. But Olgin felt like a fish in water. His name and enormous journalistic talents put him at the forefront of the movement, and he held onto his high status with all his might and in the face of all the perverse and bizarre changes of the party line until his dying day.

Remarkably, during his first visit to Soviet Russia not long after the Bolshevik Revolution, he had not found a single ray of light there. He was then the only writer for the *Forverts* who opposed the general enthusiasm for Bolshevism. This was, incidentally, also the case with Robert Minor at that time. Later, back here in America, they both became leading spokesmen for Bolshevism.

Other people began to return from Russia. Mosheh Kats and our comrade Menakhem-Mendl Tsipin returned as full-fledged Bolsheviks and agitated for their new Torah in the *Forverts*. Comrade Morris Weitzman (Granberg), an ordinary worker, came back and told completely different stories about the Bolsheviks and how they hunted down anarchists in Ukraine. Grigory (Grisha) Raiva, a member of the editorial board of the Russian anarchist paper *Golos Truda,* wrote a series of articles in the *Fraye arbeter shtime* reporting what had happened there.[6] Boris Yelensky from

---

a Labor Zionist and Bundist. Zivion attended university in Germany and was a European correspondent for the *Forverts* and *Tsukunft* before immigrating to the United States in 1908. He wrote for various Yiddish socialist and labor papers, including *Der tog* and the ILGWU's *Gerekhtigkeyt*, which he began editing in 1929. Zivion joined the Communist Party in 1921 but left it the following year to rejoin the *Forverts*. **Moissaye Olgin** (1878–1939), born Moyshe-Yoysef Novomirski, was a Russian-born Jewish writer, journalist, and socialist. He was involved in the Russian revolutionary movement as a university student in Kiev and joined the Bund before emigrating to Germany and then the United States at the outbreak of the First World War. Olgin wrote for the *Forverts* and *Tsukunft*, but in 1921 he joined the Communist Party and helped to produce its papers *Morgn-frayheyt* and *Der hamer* (The Hammer, 1926–1939) and became a contributor to the *Daily Worker* and Moscow's *Pravda*. He also stood as a Communist Party candidate for Congress and New York State Assembly multiple times.

6. *FAS*, February 14 and February 21, 1920, September 9, October 7 through October 28, and November 11, 1921. **Grigory ("Grisha") Raiva** (Rayva, c. 1893–?) was a Russian-born Jewish anarchist. He belonged to the Union of Russian Workers, the Anarchist Red Cross, and the IWW and returned to Russia after the February Revolution with the rest of the *Golos Truda* editorial staff, including his brother, Mikhail ("Misha") Griva, who died either during the voyage or shortly after arrival. Raiva returned to the United Sates in 1920 and began

Chicago and Joseph Radding from Detroit brought personal greetings from the Bolshevik paradise.[7] Ben Agursky and the former business agent of the *Fraye arbeter shtime*, Bob Robins, scarcely escaped with their lives.[8] Later, Abba Gordin and then I. N. Steinberg, the first minister of justice in the Soviet government, also came and explained the situation to us.[9]

regularly writing for the *FAS* (usually under the signature "Gr. R."). In 1922 he was elected to the paper's editorial board.

7. Yelensky returned from Russia in 1923 after being twice imprisoned by the Bolsheviks, and he later wrote of his time there in the book *In sotsyaln shturem: zikhroynes fun der rusisher revolutsye* (In the Social Storm: Memoirs of the Russian Revolution, 1967), which is available in English on Libcom at https://libcom.org/article/boris-yelenskys-memoirs-russian-revolution. Radding's experiences in Russia remain obscure.

8. **Benjamin Agursky** (c. 1878–1946) was a Russian-born Jewish shoemaker, garment worker, and anarchist. He immigrated to England, where he immediately became active in the Jewish anarchist movement in Leeds, then came to the United States in 1903 and settled in Chicago, where he joined the IWW and wrote for the *FAS*. Agursky continued to financially support the paper until his death but became a supporter of Histadrut in the 1940s. His younger brother Samuel Agursky (1884–1947) was also an anarchist in Chicago but in 1917 returned to Russia where he joined the Communist Party and became a commissar and later historian who helped lead the Communist campaign against the Bund until his arrest in 1937. Obituary: *FAS*, December 27, 1946.

9. **Abba Gordin** (1887–1964) was a Russian-born Jewish teacher, writer, editor, and anarchist. As a teenager he was a Labor Zionist and briefly imprisoned for participating in the 1905 Revolution. He and his brother Velvel (Wolf) Gordin (1885–1974) subsequently became prominent, if iconoclastic, members of Russia's anarchist movement and edited the Moscow Federation of Anarchist Groups' daily newspaper *Anarkhiia* (1917–1918). After the October Revolution the Gordin brothers attempted to reconcile Bolshevism and anarchism within a new "Anarchist-Universalist" tendency but were nevertheless repeatedly arrested. Abba fled and around 1927 arrived in the United States, where he wrote for the *FAS* (of which he briefly served as a coeditor), the *Forverts, Tsukunft*, and many other publications, and founded his own periodicals, *The Clarion* (1932–1934) and *Yidishe shriftn* (Yiddish Writings, 1941–1946). Abandoning class struggle for an individualist and religiously inflected anarchism, he founded the Jewish Ethical Society and authored dozens of books and pamphlets about the libertarian core of Judaism and Jewish culture, as well as a biography of Saul Yanovsky. Around 1957 Gordin immigrated to Israel, where he founded the bilingual Yiddish-Hebrew anarchist magazine *Problemen/Problemot* (Problems, 1959–1989). **Isaac Nachman Steinberg** (Yitskhok-Nakhmen Shteynberg, 1888–1957) was a Russian-born Jewish lawyer, journalist, writer, and Socialist-Revolutionary. From a wealthy family and a lifelong Orthodox Jew, he became a leader of the Socialist-Revolutionary Party and in 1917 aligned with its left wing. After the October Revolution Steinberg served as the people's commissar for justice until February 1918 and attempted to rein in the Cheka and prevent summary executions. He was arrested in 1919 and fled the country in 1923, living in Germany, England, Australia, and Canada before coming to the United States around 1943. In 1935 Steinberg founded the

Emma Goldman, Alexander Berkman, Alexander and Tania Schapiro, Volin, Efim Yarchuk, Peter Arshinov, Gregori Maximoff, Mark Mratchny, and other well-known comrades managed to escape or be expelled from Russia and reported on the real situation there.[10] We learned all about the baseness and falseness of the Bolsheviks, about their criminal behavior toward the anarchists and the Left Socialist-Revolutionaries, who together with

Freeland League, a territorialist organization that sought to secure a place to resettle European Jews threatened by the rise of Nazism. He was also a frequent contributor to the *FAS*, *Tsukunft*, *Der tog*, and other Yiddish publications, and worked closely with Jewish anarchists in both Toronto and New York.

10. **Volin** or Voline (1882–1945), real name Vsevolod Mikhailovich Eikhenbaum, was a Russian-born Jewish labor organizer, writer, and anarchist. He joined the Socialist-Revolutionary Party in 1904 and participated in the 1905 Revolution, during which he participated in the St. Petersburg Soviet and was then arrested. In 1907 Volin fled to France, where he became an anarchist and a syndicalist and in 1915 was interned as an enemy alien. He escaped to the United States and immediately joined the Union of Russian Workers and the editorial board of *Golos Truda*, and in 1917 returned to Russia where he cofounded the Petrograd Union of Anarcho-Syndicalist Propaganda and the Nabat Confederation of Anarchist Organizations. In 1919 Volin joined the Cultural-Educational Commission of Ukrainian anarchist Nestor Makhno's partisan army, leading to his imprisonment and then 1921 expulsion by the Bolsheviks. He lived the rest of his life in Germany and France and dedicated himself to documenting the history and persecution of Russia's anarchists. **Chaim ("Efim") Yarchuk** or Yartchuk (Khaym "Yefim" Yartshuk, c. 1882–1937) was a Russian-born Jewish tailor and anarchist. He cofounded the Chernoe Znamia (Black Banner) anarchist group in Bialystok in the early 1900s and participated in the 1905 Revolution, resulting in five years of Siberian exile. In 1913 Yarchuk immigrated to the United States, where he was active in the Anarchist Red Cross and the Union of Russian Workers. He returned to Russian in 1917 and was elected to the Kronstadt Soviet (prior to the rebellion of 1921, during which he was in prison). Yarchuk edited the successor to *Golos Truda*, *Volnyi Golos Truda* (1918) and was arrested by the Bolsheviks at least six times before being expelled from the country in 1922. However, in 1925 he returned to Russia and joined the Communist Party, only to be executed in 1937. **Peter Arshinov** (1886–1937) was a Russian-born factory worker, historian, and anarchist. During the revolution of 1905 he belonged to the Bolshevik faction of the Russian Social Democratic Labor Party and then became an anarchist and participated in bombings and expropriations, leading to multiple arrests. In 1911 Arshinov met fellow anarchist Nestor Makhno in prison, and after their release during the 1917 February Revolution he joined Makhno's army, the history of which he later documented. He fled Russia in 1922 but later embraced Bolshevism and in 1933 returned to the Soviet Union, where he was arrested and executed around 1937. **Gregori Maximoff** (1893–1950) was a Russian-born agronomist, paperhanger, syndicalist, and anarchist. He was radicalized as a student and in 1917 he joined the Anarcho-Syndicalist Propaganda Union, helped produce its transplanted paper *Golos Truda*, and was a leading figure in the Nabat Confederation. Maximoff was arrested in 1921 and expelled from Russia the following year. He immigrated in 1925 to Chicago, where he joined the Free Society Group

them had carried out the October Revolution and made it possible for the Bolsheviks to seize power.

We were able to get details on the military pogrom perpetrated on the Anarchist Club in Moscow; the mass arrests of anarchists in Ukraine who had been given permission to convene a conference in Kharkov; and the brutality at the funeral of Peter Kropotkin, where only a few incarcerated anarchists in the Butyrka Prison were given permission to attend the burial of their spiritual leader, and this on the condition that they immediately return to prison. We learned of the martyrdom of Lev Chernyi, of Aron Baron, of Maria Spiridonova, and dozens of lesser-known individuals.[11] The horrible picture of a dictatorship based on terror, of *"zalozhniki"*—human hostages for the actions of others—of torture chambers, of the confiscation of monies sent in letters from the United States, arrests and deportations

---

and edited the Russian-language IWW paper *Golos Truzhenika* (Worker's Voice, 1918–1927) and the anarchist *Delo Truda—Probuzhdenie* (Worker's Cause—Awakening, 1939–1950). **Mark Mratchny** (Mratshny, 1892–1975), real name Mark Klavansky, was a Russian-born Jewish teacher, psychiatrist, editor, and anarchist. He became an anarchist as a student and during the Russian Revolution joined the Nabat Confederation and the Cultural-Educational Commission of Makhno's army, leading to his arrest in 1920 and expulsion in 1922. Mratchny immigrated to the United States in 1928 and taught for Workmen's Circle schools in Los Angeles and Detroit before serving as editor of the *FAS* from 1934 to 1940, after which he withdrew from radicalism.

11. **Lev Chernyi** (1878–1921), real name Pavel Dimitrievich Turchaninov, was a Russian poet, writer, and anarchist. An individualist anarchist strongly influenced by Max Stirner and Friedrich Nietzsche, he was arrested and exiled to Siberia for his radicalism but after the February Revolution became secretary of the Moscow Federation of Anarchist Groups. In 1919 Chernyi joined the anti-Bolshevik Underground Anarchists, leading to his arrest and summary execution in 1921. **Aron Baron** (1891–1937) was a Russian-born Jewish labor organizer, syndicalist, and anarchist. As a teenager he was involved in the Kiev Bakers' Union and the 1905 Revolution, leading to his exile to Siberia in 1907. Baron escaped and immigrated to Chicago, where he became an organizer and lecturer for both the IWW and the Union of Russian Workers and coedited the anarchist paper *The Alarm*. He returned to Russia after the February Revolution and was elected to the Kiev Soviet by the bakers' union, fought in the Russian Civil War, and helped form the Nabat Confederation of Anarchist Organizations. Baron was arrested repeatedly beginning in 1919 and served numerous sentences in prison, labor camps, and internal exile before being executed in 1937. **Maria Spiridonova** (1884–1941) was a Russian Socialist-Revolutionary. Her imprisonment and torture after assassinating a security officer in 1906 earned her widespread radical sympathy, and she played a prominent role at the head of the Left Socialist-Revolutionaries during the 1917 revolution. In 1918 she openly opposed the Bolsheviks and took part in a plot to sabotage Russia's peace talks with Germany by assassinating German officials, leading to the first of many arrests that culminated in her execution in 1941.

without any charge or trial—this picture, with all of its hideous baseness, unfolded before our eyes.

A bitter conflict developed between the "Left" and the "Right" in the Workmen's Circle, in the unions, in the fraternal organizations, in families, everywhere where people came into contact with one another. Quarrels and violence broke out at meetings, rallies, and conventions. The labor movement the world over was transformed into a battlefield on which brother fought against brother, and intimate friends became the bitterest enemies.

We did not want to take part in that bitter struggle. But the poison of "Leftism," like Hitlerism later, was, in a sense, aimed at our worldview, at the notion of freedom and the belief that the human personality must be respected and defended. So we took up the fight. At a public rally in New York, Bolshevik disrupters had to be thrown headfirst down three flights of stairs, so that they would not have the strength to crawl up them again. In Philadelphia, at a big meeting on Snyder Avenue, there was a fight with chairs, in which Sarah Greenberg greatly excelled. Quite often the disruptors were our former comrades.

In 1921 Emma Goldman and Alexander Berkman succeeded in exiting Soviet Russia. They were allowed to attend an anarcho-syndicalist congress in Berlin.[12] It was very difficult for them to get permission from the Soviet government to leave, and it wasn't much easier for them to get permission from the socialist government in Germany to enter that country. Comrade Harry Kelly went from the United States to attend the congress and to meet with our friends and other older comrades in Europe.[13] During his stay in Berlin, a strike of electrical workers broke out. Friedrich Ebert's government immediately confiscated the union's funds and suppressed the strike with the same brutality used by other governments.[14]

---

12. The **International Anarchist Conference** convened in Berlin from December 25, 1921 to February 2, 1922, to formulate a united response to the Russian Revolution and the Communist International, and it laid the basis for the creation of the anarcho-syndicalist International Working Men's Association in December 1922.

13. Harry Kelly, although a gentile, represented the Jewish Anarchist Federation of America and Canada at the congress. Russian-born anarchist Vasili ("William") Dodokin (died 1972) also attended as a delegate for the anti-syndicalist Federation of Anarchist Communist Groups of the United States and Canada.

14. **Friedrich Ebert** (1871–1925) was a leader of the Social Democratic Party of Germany and president of Weimar Germany from 1919 to 1925.

We had become disillusioned with our enthusiasm for the Bolshevik revolution—many of us had lost faith in revolution in general, wherever it took place and whomever its leaders. Our movement entered a new phase of activity.

CHAPTER 43

Camp Germinal

For many years, in addition to the Radical Library in Philadelphia, there existed another organization, the Modern Home and School Association, which collected funds and dreamed of opening a school for children, perhaps even establishing a colony with a school, modeled after Stelton.[1] In 1924 its dream began to come true. A group of people bought a farm about twelve miles from Willow Grove with the idea of establishing a colony there.[2] The work involved comrade Edward Gosfield and a number of new people, radicals, but not from our narrow circle: Sophia Mariella, Daniel Weinstock and his wife Bessie, Marcus and Clara Woro, Alexander Drossin, and many others.[3] Their plans were not entirely clear or defined. The drive to the farm was inconvenient. You needed your own car to get there without wasting time. By train it took more than half a day to travel from Philadelphia. There was no other way to get there. The location, on the other hand, was wonderfully beautiful and nice. The farm was situated on a hill, high above the whole area. The land was good, and the buildings, considerable in number, were not even in bad condition. It was a very attractive place for a colony or school, if people really wanted to settle on the land, which was not the case among that circle.

At that time there was a movement among radical circles to establish summer camps, both for children and adults. I left Stelton around this time

---

1. The **Modern Home and School Association** was founded in Philadelphia around 1910.

2. Willow Grove is a suburb north of Philadelphia.

3. **Edward Gosfield** (Edvard Gosfild, c. 1883–1937) was a Russian-born Jewish tailor, manager, and anarchist. He immigrated to England, where he became involved in the

and settled in Cambridge, Massachusetts. I could not free myself from my work for the *Fraye arbeter shtime*—there was no one to take over the office. One winter, I divided my time every week between New York and Cambridge, a distance of 230 miles. I did not enjoy the prospect of spending the summer with my family in the city. We were by then used to living in the countryside, surrounded by children, flowers, trees, and a free environment. I had the idea to volunteer my services to the comrades in Philadelphia to organize the summer camp for children on the newly acquired farm.

The comrades gladly accepted the offer, and in the spring of 1925 I partially moved back to Philadelphia to do the work and build the new institution. The first meeting I attended brought together a great many people who received the plan enthusiastically. Among them, I was especially happy to see my old friend Joe Wascow (Joseph Washkowitz), who had not appeared among our ranks for some ten or twelve years. He was a paperhanger, worked for himself, and employed several workers, union members, and was very busy with his work and his family of three small children. However, he attended the meeting and reentered the movement, devoting all his free time until his untimely death in July 1930.

Preparing the farm for this purpose, rebuilding a couple of the buildings,

---

anarchist movement and met his wife, anarchist Rachel ("Rose") Gosfield. The couple immigrated to the United States in 1902 and joined the Radical Library Group. Obituary: *FAS*, May 28, 1937. **Daniel ("Dan") Weinstock** (Vaynshtok, 1892–1956) was a Russian-born Jewish jeweler, and **Bessie Weinstock** (Besi Vaynshtok, 1899–1984) was a Russian-born Jewish garment worker. They both immigrated around 1910 and were members of the Radical Library Group. Obituary for Daniel: *FAS*, July 13, 1956. **Marcus Woro** (Markus Voro, 1888–1953) was a Russian-born Jewish photographer and socialist. He joined the Bund at age fifteen and immigrated to Philadelphia three years later, where he joined the Socialist Party and Branch 12 of the Workmen's Circle. Although Woro called himself a social democrat, he was an active member of the Radical Library. His wife, **Clara Woro** (Klara Voro, c. 1886–1954), was a Russian-born Jewish anarchist who immigrated to the United States in 1906. In 1931 the couple moved to Los Angeles, where they were active in the Kropotkin Literary Society, Branch 413 of the Workmen's Circle, up until their deaths. Obituary for Marcus: *FAS*, March 27, 1953; Clara: *FAS*, January 14, 1955. **Alexander Drossin** (Aleksander Drozin, 1893–1931) was a Russian-born Jewish upholsterer and anarchist. He immigrated to Philadelphia in 1909 and became secretary of the Modern Home and School Association. Drossin, a married man, had an affair with Rose Buchin, the wife of his employee Andrew Buchin (Anshil Bukhin, 1887–1960) and sister of fellow anarchist Marcus Woro. At the Woros' going away party on December 4, 1931, Andrew Buchin shot and killed Drossin in a jealous rage—an event Cohen makes no mention of. Obituary: *FAS*, January 8, 1932. On the murder, see also *FAS*, December 11, 1931; *Philadelphia Inquirer*, December 5, 1931, and February 28, 1932.

and acquiring all the necessary tools required a world of work. Edward Gosfield was born for this kind of activity: the man was a dynamo of restless energy. Although heavily engaged in his own business—he was manager of a women's clothing store and also rebuilt houses under his own supervision— he still somehow found time and energy to undertake the preparations, which required great effort.

Among my friends and acquaintances, I managed to gather a whole staff of "counselors," teachers, and caretakers for the children, all volunteer workers. The camp opened on the appointed day with about fifty children and was a wonderful success from that first day on. The camp's life and activities attracted a lot of attention in the city and brought many visitors. The most active people around the camp were Harry Melman, Joe Wascow, Daniel Weinstock, Sophia Mariella, Marcus Woro, Alexander Drossin, Alexander Brown, Benny Moore, Moris Beresin, and Gosfield. With the latter, peace did not last through the summer. In addition to his virtues, he possessed certain qualities that made it difficult to work harmoniously with him. But the enthusiasm and satisfaction were so great that we did not dwell on the inconveniences. Everyone was satisfied with the accomplishment, and the reputation of Camp Germinal was firmly established in the city.

But the second summer, parents' desire to send their children to our camp was so great that we had to make room for them to sleep in large sheds as well as reconstruct other buildings. Some 120 children, some from Wilmington and even a few from New York, lived in joy and freedom that summer in Camp Germinal. The farm was full of life and activity. During the bitter strike of the textile workers in Passaic, New Jersey, we took in five children of the strikers, who rotated out every two weeks.[4] Evening gatherings with games around a large bonfire every Wednesday brought crowds of people from the city. Children's performances of the highest art on Saturday and Sunday, under the direction of Molly Gilbert Hoffman, were always a tremendous success.[5] Every activity was very gratifying.

---

4. The **1926 Passaic textile strike** was the first major struggle led by the Communist Party's Trade Union Educational League, which after more than six months had to cede leadership to the AFL. The Passaic strike leaders emulated the IWW's tactic of sending strikers' children to live with sympathizers outside of the city.

5. **Molly Gilbert Hoffman** (c. 1898–?), née Gaylburd, was an American-born Jewish artist and actress. She ran the Molly Gilbert Hoffman Studio of Dramatic Art in Philadelphia

However, there was also friction among the membership. Life became full, as it does with people. In addition to the Philadelphia comrades, men and women, who helped with the personal and manual labor, we had Tanya Schapiro as a nurse, and Ida Cohen worked as a chef—both from New York.[6] Among the female comrades from Philadelphia who worked at the camp during these two summers were Celia Melman, Bessie Weinstock, Julia Brown, Sarah Moore, Fannie Kaplan, Gussie Beresin, and Sophie Cohen.

All this work was done voluntarily, without pay. This made it possible to admit children for a very small fee and, in general, added the grace and satisfaction of free labor to the whole enterprise.

I stayed at the camp from Wednesday evening until Monday morning; then I went to New York for three days. My friend and comrade Joe Wascow served as my chauffeur for two summers, meeting me at the train station and taking me back to it. He never failed me, was never late even by a minute, even though he was a very busy man. His dedication and precision were greatly satisfying to me.

On the last Wednesday of the second season of the camp, when we had just gathered around the campfire in the field for the evening's program, a fire broke out in the large barn where our theater was and where a considerable number of older children had their dormitory. It also housed the generator that produced electric lighting for the farm, and the fire was probably started by the generator and quickly engulfed the entire building and threw flames high into the clouds. Dozens of firefighters from miles around gathered and prevented the flames from engulfing the other buildings. Our members and most of the parents had come that evening to watch the program and witnessed the uproar and catastrophe caused by the fire. The closing of the

---

(which advertised in the pages of the *FAS*) and, together with her husband Samuel S. ("Seth") Hoffman (1895–1948), later joined the Woodstock Artists Association and taught art classes for members of the ILGWU.

6. **Ida Cohen** (Ayda Kohn, 1885–1972), later Ida Galloway (Galovey), was a Russian-born Jewish anarchist. She joined the Bund as young girl and then fled to the United States, where she became an anarchist and a member of Harlem's Likht Group. Cohen was a cofounder of the Stelton Colony and later of the Free Workers' Center in New York, where she ran a vegetarian diner. In the 1940s she belonged to the Naye Gezelshaft Group, Branch 364 of the Workman's Circle, and around 1955 she moved to Brighton Beach, California, and became an active member of the Kropotkin Literary Society, Branch 413 of the Workmen's Circle. Obituary: *FAS*, April 1, 1972.

camp season, which was to be carried out with a grand parade and rich entertainment programs, was, under the circumstances, tense and depressed. That successful summer deserved a better, more solemn end, but the accident dictated otherwise. For me and my family, participation in the camp came to an end.

The comrades carried on the children's camp for a few more summers, under the supervision of Harry Potamkin, Abe Grosner, Abe Goldman, Schneider, Dr. Benjamin W. Barkas, John Scott, and others, but it was no longer a great success.[7] It never rose to the level of that second summer, 1926, again. It eventually died on its own. The site was transformed from a children's camp into a summer home and camp for adults, without great success.

---

7. **Harry Alan Potamkin** (1900–1933) was an American-born Jewish social worker, poet, critic, and Marxist. The child of Russian Jewish immigrants, he graduated from New York University with an English degree in 1921, lived at the Stelton Colony for a time, and was a social worker in Philadelphia. In 1925–1929 Potamkin traveled to Paris and Russia, where he embraced Marxism and began a career as a film critic. **Abraham Leib Goldman** (Avrom Leyb Goldman, c. 1888–1971) was a Russian-born Jewish tailor, educator, and anarchist. In 1898 his family immigrated to England, where he became involved in the Jewish socialist movement. In 1907 Goldman moved to Toronto and was involved in the socialist territorialist movement before becoming an anarchist around 1908. He was an advocate of Esperanto and vegetarianism and came to the United States around 1917. Goldman taught at some of the first Workmen's Circle schools before moving to Stelton, where his daughter attended the Modern School and he served as principal in 1926–1927. In the 1930s he ran a weekend Modern School in New York City, where he was also a member of the Naye Gezelshaft Group, Branch 364 of the Workmen's Circle. See *FAS*, March 15, 1963. **"Schneider"** may be a reference to New York anarchist and ILGWU member Joseph Schneider. **Benjamin W. Barkas** (1897–1977) was an American labor educator. From 1925 to 1931 he taught at the Philadelphia Labor College, and in the late 1920s he briefly served as principal of the Mohegan Modern School. Barkas was later a teacher in the Philadelphia public schools, at Temple University, and for the Pennsylvania Federation of Labor, and from 1944 to 1965 he was the assistant director of the Philadelphia School District's Division of School Extension. Obituary: *Philadelphia Inquirer*, October 8, 1977. **John G. Scott** (1879–1953) was an American-born educator and onetime anarchist. A former member of the Socialist Party, around the First World War he began to describe himself as a "Thoreauvian anarchist." Scott taught at the anarchist Walt Whitman School in Los Angeles before being hired at the Stelton Modern School in 1915 and the Mohegan Modern School in 1926. In 1933–1934 he published the agrarian anarchist magazine *Mother Earth* with his then-companion Jo Ann Wheeler Burbank. Scott later became a Quaker and a member of the Christianity-based Social Credit movement before drifting into Christian nationalism and joining the fascist American Nationalist Party in 1945. He edited the journal *Money* (1936–1953), in which he republished the notorious antisemitic forgery *The Protocols of the Elders of Zion*.

In 1925 we held the annual convention of our movement there, for which the facilities came in handy. But the movement and the comrades were not overly impressed, and the comrades did not enjoy the farm. A beautiful place, a good one, but ill-fated—it stands largely empty at the time of this writing.

CHAPTER 44

The Radical Library and the People Around It

Through the years the Radical Library continued with its work. Of course, all the conflicts around Camp Germinal, and the enormous effort that went into it every year, taking up many hours—none of this contributed to the health of the library. After all, it was the same people who did the work there and in the camp, or in the Modern Home and School Association. For this reason, the work of the library was carried on every winter, with more or less success. It was there that the comrades had a great time celebrating my fiftieth birthday, on which occasion they showed me such friendship and comradely appreciation that I was moved to my very soul. My parents, very pious and conservative people in their old age, were both present and pleased with their son, whom the rabbi in their little shtetl had once prophesied would become a "great man of Israel." His prophecy was not fulfilled, but that certainly was not their fault and perhaps not even mine!

In the 1920s the Radical Library was no longer as unified as in the early days. Officially the library was affiliated with the Jewish Anarchist Federation of America and Canada; however, a number of members at one meeting managed to pass a motion for it to join the Anarchist Communist Groups of the United States and Canada—a body that was critical of the official labor movement and often strongly opposed to union practices.[1] This provoked

---

1. **The Anarchist Communist Groups of the United States and Canada** was a loose-knit alliance of insurrectionist, anti-syndicalist Jewish anarchists formed in 1921. It promoted underground revolutionary work, published the illegal anarchist paper *Free Society* edited by Shmuel Marcus, and was closely aligned with the similarly oriented Federation of Russian Anarchist Communist Groups of the United States and Canada. Confusingly,

strong dissatisfaction among the active union members in the library, who demanded that the organization openly declare that the library had nothing to do with that body. When these demands were not met, some members withdrew from the library in protest.

In the 1920s our movement in Philadelphia enjoyed the friendly support of Moyshe Katz, editor of the *Yidishe velt*, a local daily, and especially the close cooperation of Abraham Frumkin and his wife Sarah, who had lived in Philadelphia for a long time.[2] The Frumkins were an institution in our movement. Abraham Frumkin had joined the movement in England at a young age and tried to publish a newspaper on his own, acting as editor, writer, typesetter, printer, and manager. He describes this admirably in his book *In friling fun yidishn sotsyalizm* (In the Springtime of Jewish Socialism), which deserves to be read by everyone.[3] After that he worked for many years on the *Arbeter fraynd* and *Zsherminal* in London, as well as on the second series of the *Fraye gezelshaft* here in America. He translated more good books from other languages into Yiddish than anyone else. In addition to his great knowledge of languages, he had a serious interest in and knowledge of European and Yiddish theater. A quiet, modest man, he seldom spoke in public debates and was what people might call an old-fashioned aristocratic intellectual, who enhanced all our gatherings.

His wife Sarah was, in some respects, an even more interesting personality. A kind-hearted woman, she always cared about the movement and the individuals who comprised it. Though she became very nearsighted, she did not fail to read every word printed in our periodicals and to respond to every question posed in a newspaper or at a meeting. She had a weakness for the needs of poor Yiddish writers—likely an echo of her own bitter

---

the Jewish Anarchist Federation initially bore a similar name: the Anarchist-Communist Groups of America.

2. **"Moyshe Katz"** refers to the former anarchist Moyshe Kats, not the Communist Mosheh Kats who briefly coedited the *FAS* in 1920–21. **Sarah Frumkin** (1873–1940), née Kroyn, was a Russian-born Jewish garment worker, proprietor, and anarchist. Raised in a strict Orthodox family, she ran away to England in 1889 and after a few years became active in socialist circles in Leeds and Glasgow, then joined the anarchist movement after moving to London in 1894. There she met and married Abraham Frumkin, with whom she immigrated to the United States in 1899. Obituary: *FAS*, February 9, 1940.

3. A. Frumkin, *In friling fun yidishn sotsyalizm: zikhroynes fun a zshurnalist* (New York: A. Frumkin yubiley komitet, 1940).

experiences in London and Paris. In her old age she was very worried about her husband's work, with his own poor eyesight, and she was busy helping him out by running a restaurant where she had to work extremely hard. She had neither business skills nor any capital. As a result, he had to borrow and borrow to make up for her debts. But the entire Jewish writers' community of New York and Philadelphia frequented her restaurant and summer camp at Sea Gate, in New York, in a large villa leased from Dr. Michael A. Cohn at a sizable rent. Sarah Frumkin's place was a household topic in the literary world.

In the mid-1920s the Radical Library added a new branch of activity—an "Art Corner" (*kunst-vinkl*), which engaged in performing literary plays and proper concerts. These attracted a circle of talented young people who excelled in these fields. From the reactions and serious reviews in the local press of that time, it can be seen that these activities were carried out with a wide scope and found a warm response among the radical public. From the programs and circulars that were kept by Arn Kanyevsky, one can see that Moyshe Katz and all the active members of the Radical Library were earnestly devoted to this new endeavor.[4]

The Great Depression, which began at the end of 1929 and continued to deepen and worsen, robbed the comrades of their home, and it ended their wide-ranging and successful activities. The books, paintings, and exhibits were moved to Stelton, to the Kropotkin Library. The branch had to go into exile, looking for a place to hold meetings and lectures wherever it could. Its tradition continued but without a home. Rarely did a winter pass without activity in the form of lectures, entertainment, and the like.

Yet one must never give up hope. Who can say with certainty what the future will bring? The people who, in the early 1890s, handed over the first Radical Library to a women's group certainly did not expect that another group would carry on their work, and even the same name, for over forty years, and on a much larger scale than the original group. But that did happen and may happen again. Dissatisfaction with the condition of things as they are is no less now than it was then. Social progress has not stopped forever.

---

4. **Arn Kanyevsky** (1890–1960) was a Russian-born Jewish writer, educator, and anarchist. He was active in Jewish revolutionary circles before emigrating in 1908 to the United States, where he wrote on the Yiddish theater for *Der tog* and other publications. Kanyevsky made financial contributions to the *FAS* up until his death.

In and around the Radical Library there were always individual comrades who, for one reason or another, never became as integral a part of the library as the others. In the early years, we had a considerable number of such people who spent all their time at the library, participating in every enterprise, yet more or less stood on the sidelines. Outstanding among them were Jacob Lifshits, Morris Shtofman, Ephraim-Leib Wolfson, and Sam Shore—all four were excellent dramatic readers, most notably the latter, who was the most beloved by audiences. Sam Shore was then young, handsome, lively, and engaging in every one of his performances. There are still legends about him reading every book in the library; how when he was a car conductor in Fairmount Park, he avoided collecting fares from comrades; and more. He left a fond memory behind in Philadelphia, although he has long since been away from there and distanced himself from our movement.

Others around at that time were Baruch Zuckerman, M. Rozumovsky, Meyer Rosen, Menkin, Averbakh, Sokolov, Leybovits, Isidore Prenner, and dozens of others, people from various radical circles.[5] But even our own good anarchists were at the periphery of our movement for many years.

Old Weinberg, for example, never missed our events or meetings and was always ready to mount a platform as speaker whenever and wherever we required, but he never was a member of our organization. In later years, he was in a sort of competition with our outings to the country. He owned his own piece of a farm, near Willow Grove, where he tried to do two things without much success: breed chickens and rent rooms to summer boarders. His hens, he used to say, lay down but never got up! And his summer boarders—paupers, usually—didn't pay their rent money and made his life miserable. At his farm, he used to host small meetings and discussions. The comrades often went out to spend hours with him and listen to his delightful stories, which he related wonderfully. He and his wife Yetta dreamed all their lives of two things: living in a commune and turning their small farm into a school for children. But the farm was unsuitable for such purpose. Small, with no more than two acres of low, wet soil, it did not suit a hen, let alone a large number of children. Their first and main dream—to live on a commune—they were destined to get a taste of. They enthusiastically embraced

---

5. **M. Rozumovsky** occasionally corresponded with the *FAS* between 1904 and 1907.

the idea of settling in the Sunrise Colony and spending their years there.[6] They joined and encouraged others to become members, lent me thousands of dollars above their membership fee, and were, in a word, enthralled. It did not last long, however. After seven or eight months, Weinberg left our communistic paradise—he was, in fact, the first anarchist to leave the battle-field—and his tales about life in the colony did not do it any good. In his own way, however, he was serious and sincere, serving our movement for over fifty years with considerable success, greatly helping to spread our teachings, to build cooperatives, and to organize unions. His memory is revered throughout our movement.[7]

A somewhat different kind of personality was Shmuel Marcus, who grew up in our circle. He came to us as a very young boy and lived and worked in and around the Radical Library for many years, without being or becoming a member. Nature endowed him with a measure of obstinacy, *chutzpah*, and a hot revolutionary temperament. In his younger years, he attacked Yanovsky in a childish manner and was scolded as he deserved. Not only Yanovsky but also Rudolf Rocker's anarchism in those years was not kosher in the eyes of Marcus, and when he took a dislike to someone in the movement, there was no restraint in his attacks. He formed his own circle of Russian and Italian anarchists who hardly understood English and carried on his revolutionary agitation among them. At one meeting, Weinberg tells us by way of Marcus's pen, Marcus, as chairman, declared that if he had ten other men like himself they could make the revolution in this country and lead it to anarchism.[8] At the time of the Palmer Raids, he was arrested, beaten, tortured, and threatened with deportation and what have you. He endured persecution for many years. When I was editor of the *Fraye arbeter shtime* he began to present his views, for which I gladly

---

6. The Sunrise Colony is discussed in detail in chapter 53.

7. Weinberg did not reciprocate Cohen's graciousness and omitted any mention of Cohen, his former friend and protégé, in his own memoir, *Forty Years in the Struggle*.

8. Weinberg dictated his memoir to Marcus in 1930, when he was seventy-eight years old. According to Weinberg, "The chairman was from the new young generation.... He spoke very briefly, and said approximately the following: The history of the world shows that all revolutions begin with a minority. The rank and file follows after. If I were able to have 50 people who are willing to start the revolution, I would leave here immediately and begin working on it." Chaim Leib Weinberg, *Forty Years in the Struggle: The Memoirs of a Jewish Anarchist*, ed. Robert P. Helms, trans. Naomi Cohen (Duluth: Litwin Books, 2008), 124.

gave him space.[9] But he didn't last long. He became angry at me and at the newspaper. Instead of writing about principles and methods, he engaged in personal attacks, which I would not tolerate. He then made a special tour throughout the country to criticize and undermine our paper. In a moment of frustration, I committed a great wrong against him, repeating a rumor about suspicions as to his honesty and sincerity as a revolution-ist—a rumor that circulated in certain circles of our movement without sufficient evidence. This put an immediate end to his harmful activities, but this left a bad aftertaste in the mouths of many comrades as well as myself. Under a different name, Marcus published a large anthology of revolution-ary poetry in English, and up until the Second World War he also put out an English-language periodical called *Man!*, in which he continued his revo-lutionary agitation without much respect for, or benefit to, our movement.[10]

A paradoxical case, of a completely different sort, was comrade William Chidekel, an older member who was very active in our organization and especially in his union, the Amalgamated Clothing Workers, where he pro-moted anarchist ideas without success.[11] He was a product of the Russian anarchist movement in this country and lacked the opportunity to make himself understood by his Jewish comrades in the movement or in the union. He was an honorable man but like someone from another, foreign world.

The composition of the people who led the movement's work in Philadelphia was very diverse, colorful, and rich. On average, we had intelli-gent people and honest workers. For example, there was Max Grishkan, for many years the secretary of our federation, and for even more years secretary of the Cloakmakers' Union; Joseph Dudnick, who loved to delve into the smallest details, and translated and self-published one of Freud's treatises; Max Zebine, a Jew with a deep knowledge of the Torah and a serious man;

---

9. *FAS*, December 2 and December 9, 1921. These articles were blistering critiques of the Jewish Anarchist Federation's "Anarchist-Communist Manifesto," a document coauthored by Cohen (see appendix).

10. Marcus Graham [Shmuel Marcus], ed., *An Anthology of Revolutionary Poetry* (New York: Active Press, 1929). *Man! A Journal of the Anarchist Ideal and Movement* (1933–1940) was an iconoclastic and militant paper that, although bitterly critical of both Cohen and the *FAS*, was also one of the most important American anarchist publications of the 1930s.

11. **William Chidekel** (Volf or Viliam Khidekel, 1875–1960) was a Russian-born Jewish tailor and anarchist. He immigrated to Philadelphia in 1904, joined the Radical Library Group and the ACWA, and supported the *FAS* and other anarchist publications into the 1950s.

the Guralnicks, who were a little swept up in nationalism and Yiddishism; Dinov, a quiet, loving, and devoted comrade; the Sharlip brothers, Oscar and Muni, who were active in the library for so many years; Nathan Miller, who served as chairman of the Pants Pressers' Union for many years.[12] None drew special attention to themselves, but they were the rank and file who built the library and helped create the spirit that reigned within it. Also noteworthy is comrade Harry Teitelman, a social democrat who was a member of the branch in his later years.[13] His wife Masha had helped keep the Pine Street library location clean during its golden years.[14] In her old age, she returned and brought along her husband, a good, sincere, and active man. They never gave up hope for a better future.

---

12. **Joseph Dudnick** (Yosef Dudnik, 1886–1959) was a Russian-born Jewish grocer and anarchist. The brother of anarchist Pearl Guralnick, he was involved in the revolutionary movement in Russia before immigrating to the United States in 1910 and joining the Radical Library. In 1917 Dudnick briefly returned to Russia, then settled in Cleveland. In 1934 he and his family moved to the Sunrise Colony, then returned to Philadelphia where he rejoined the Radical Library Group and was a member until his death. The volume that Cohen mentions—and which his original Yiddish text mistakenly describes as a "book about Freud's life and teachings"—is Sigmund Freud, *Di tsukunft fun an iluzye*, trans. J. Dudnik (Cleveland: n.p., 1932), a translation Freud's *The Future of an Illusion* (1927). Obituary: *FAS*, September 15, 1959. **Max Zebine** (Maks Zebin, 1880–1959) was a Russian-born Jewish laundry worker and anarchist. He immigrated to Philadelphia in 1904 and joined the Radical Library Group. In 1945 he married anarchist Rachel ("Rose") Gosfield. Obituary: *FAS*, January 1, 1960. **Louis Guralnick** (Luis Guralnik, c. 1888?1973) was a Russian-born Jewish garment worker, store clerk, and anarchist who immigrated to Philadelphia in 1912. His wife **Pearl Guralnick** (Poyrl or Perl Guralnik, 1888–1952), née Dudnick (Dudnik) was a Russian-born Jewish domestic worker and anarchist. She was involved in the revolutionary movement in Russia before immigrating to the United States in 1910 and becoming active in the Jewish anarchist movement in Philadelphia. The couple moved to Cleveland and then the Sunrise Colony before returning to Philadelphia, where they both joined the Radical Library Group. Pearl was active in aiding orphans and formed a "women's reading group" in Philadelphia. Louis moved to Miami after her death and continued contributing to the *FAS* into the 1960s. Obituary for Pearl: *FAS*, September 26, 1952.

13. **Harry Teitelman** (Hershl "Heri" Taytlman, 1884–1968) was a Russian-born Jewish merchant, newspaper manager, and socialist. He was a member of the National Executive Committee of Jewish Socialist Verband, a founder of the Central School Committee of the Workmen's Circle, and worked for the *Forverts* for forty years. Although a socialist, he joined the Radical Library Group, financially supported the *FAS*, and was close friends with many anarchists. Obituaries: *Philadelphia Inquirer*, May 31, 1968; *FAS*, August 1, 1968.

14. **Masha ("Mary") Teitelman** (Taytlman, c. 1886–?), née Kushin, was a Russian-born Jewish housewife and radical. She immigrated to the United States in 1905 and was active in the Radical Library Group.

CHAPTER 45

Differing Opinions and Misunderstandings in the Movement

I left Stelton in 1924. The previous five years had been bursting with life and activity, ever since the Ferms had settled there and taken over management of the school. The new school building, which was erected during the First World War, cost more than $15,000 and was splendid. Most of the construction was done by volunteers. The gatherings in the big auditorium every Saturday and Sunday evening, the frequent "community dinners," the dramatic performances by children and adults, all brought life and energy to the colony and maintained a very high level of sociability.

The Russian Revolution had halted further development and growth of the colony. We had already purchased another adjacent farm for a fourth tract, but since a good number of colonists left for Russia, we felt that there was no good way to increase membership. We were able, however, to delay the epidemic of upheavals between the "Left" and the "Right" by avoiding heated political discussions. We all agreed on the school's mission, and even the ardent "Communists" agreed that it had to be conducted in a purely libertarian way. The recognition that our school received from the Bolshevik government helped greatly in this regard. A letter written on the tsar's official stationary and signed by Lenin's wife arrived with warm greetings and inquiries about our methods, experiences, and achievements. This bestowed great prestige upon us in the eyes of the fanatical "Communists."

To avoid clashes and misunderstandings, we decided not to use the school for purely anarchist undertakings and activities, as we had done in previous years. The school had to remain nonpartisan enough to be able to have the support and cooperation of all the elements in the radical

421

movement and the colony. We acquired a piece of land near the school to construct our own building, the Kropotkin Library, in which to conduct our own activities. In the summer of 1936, the comrades conducted a systematic seminar there to study anarchism, its history, its different tendencies, and its influence on literature, art, education. Comrade Anna Sosnofsky was secretary of the Kropotkin Library at that time.[1]

Our domestic tranquility (*sholem-bayes*) lasted for quite a few years. Everyone collaborated not only on the school but also in our cooperative ventures, a grocery store and a jitney service, that served the colony. Opinions differed from time to time, especially when it came to a celebration in connection with the Russian Revolution, or the fund-raisers that the Communists held every Monday and Thursday, but no serious conflicts arose until long after I had left the colony.

I left the Ferrer colony, as well as New York, for a few reasons. My life took shape in such a way that I never stayed in one place for more than ten years. Differences of opinion had developed at the Ferrer school between me and the principals, Elizabeth and Alexis Ferm. I insisted that the school's activity be broadened and improved. They were satisfied with things as they were. No compromise or understanding was possible.

We all agreed that libertarian education means giving children the greatest possible opportunity to develop their inherent capacities and interests, and not forcing any knowledge or discipline on them that is not sought by their inner desire to learn or achieve something. The children in our school were free to learn or not to learn, to play by themselves or in a group, to do what they pleased, as long as it did not disturb the other children in their work. We did not worry if a child did not learn to read or write by a certain

---

1. **Anna Sosnovsky** (1900–1949), born Anna Luchkovsky, was a Russian-born Jewish garment worker, labor organizer, and anarchist. She immigrated to New York with the rest of the Luchkovsky family in 1913 and at age sixteen began working in a sweatshop. Sosnovsky joined the Ladies' Waistmakers' Union Local 25 of the ILGWU and in 1919 was active in the shop steward movement. She became an anarchist during the First World War and joined the Frayheyt Group but had to flee the city and change her name to avoid deportation. Sosnovsky married anarchist Abe Winokour and lived at the Stelton Colony, where she was active in the Modern School and organized a cooperative dress factory. She also became a regional organizer for the ILGWU in New Jersey and was active in the Sacco-Vanzetti defense campaign. Sosnovsky and her family moved to Mohegan around 1941, then to Los Angeles in 1948. Obituaries: *FAS*, May 13 and June 10, 1949.

age; we knew that when the time came for the child to need this knowledge, they could without difficulty teach themselves even the Torah. This was confirmed by many cases. Children who were not able to read, write, or do arithmetic at the age of nine or ten were able in two or three years' time to complete entrance exams for a city high school and excel there compared to children who attended elementary school for a full eight years. We could afford to give the children complete freedom in all respects, without a shred of discipline or attempts to influence them.

So far, so good.

Our school day began with an assembly of all the children in a big auditorium, with singing and folk dancing, in which a large number of adults often participated. After the assembly, the children went to different rooms for special activities—weaving, spinning, printing, carving, welding, woodworking, reading, writing—[or engaged in] playing outdoors, working in the nearby garden, or going where they wished—to catch fish, to play Indians in the small forest—to do, in a word, exactly what they wanted and what their heart desired.

In most rooms an adult, a teacher, worked on projects, serving as the center of activity. Children who were interested in such work came, watched, and participated in the activity as long as they remained interested. When they became bored, they stopped and left, returning to finish when their own will led them to do so. The older children, with the help of a couple of teachers, built a good, long building for the workshops, which was in no way inferior to the buildings constructed by professional craftsmen.

The most exciting activities for the children were in the printing shop, which they used to print their own compositions of prose or poetry, and to illustrate them with woodcuts or linocuts, which all became their own children's magazine.[2] Many of the children showed unusual talent long before they were able to read and write properly. The very young children used to imitate the older ones, inventing their own fairy tales, which an older child would put into writing for them, then they would illustrate these with their own carvings and assist with the printing according to their abilities.

Joseph Ishill, a well-known artistic printer, led this work for two long

---

2. Twenty-one issues of **Voice of the Children** were published between 1921 and 1935, entirely produced by students of the Modern School.

periods. But for most of the time the printing press was managed by Paul Scott, an ordinary worker who was wonderfully well-suited for such a role.[3] The older children also were able to produce all the printing work that the school and colony needed.

A second popular activity took place in the art studio conducted by Hugo Gellert, where the children drew and painted pictures according to their imaginations and tastes.[4] You could always find a large number of children at work there, many of them with considerable talent. Their drawings adorned the walls of the great auditorium and drew much enthusiasm from visitors.

A third craft was weaving, directed by Anna Koch, a highly educated woman, a born teacher, who later worked in the same job for many years at Antioch Preparatory School.[5] Under her supervision, many children made large articles woven from cotton and wool in different colors on looms of all sizes. The older children were able to weave pieces of cloth for clothes, drapes, and other useful things.

The metal and wood workshops, under the care of "Uncle" Alexis Ferm, were very popular with the children, who built chairs, tables, boats, and

---

3. **Edward Paul Scott** (1880–1963), real name William Frederick Hays, was an American-born laborer, printer, and anarchist. Born one of twelve children in Missouri, in the 1910s he went AWOL from the US Army with guns that he intended to smuggle to Emiliano Zapata's forces in Mexico. Scott made his way to Mexico City, where he worked on the anti–Porfirio Diaz daily newspaper *El Diario* until his expulsion two years later. He married Russian Jewish anarchist Edith ("Polly") Chary and the couple moved to Stelton, where their two daughters attended the Modern School and he coedited *The Modern School* and taught English and printing. Scott later taught at the Walden School in New York.

4. **Hugo Gellert** (1892–1985) was a Hungarian-born lithographer, socialist, and later Communist. In 1906 his family immigrated to the United States, where he studied art and joined the Socialist Party. Gellert contributed illustrations to socialist publications like *The Masses* and *The Liberator* and taught art at the Stelton Modern School from 1920 to 1922. After the Russian Revolution, Gellert became a lifelong supporter of the Soviet Union and contributed lithographs to Communist periodicals while also working for mainstream publications like *The New Yorker* and *New York Times*. In the 1950s he was blacklisted after refusing to testify before the House Un-American Activities Committee.

5. **Anna Koch** (c. 1894–?), née Riedel, was a German-born weaver, educator, and anarchist. After immigrating to the United States in 1905 she became a supporter of *Mother Earth*, cofounded the German-language anarchist paper *Das freie Wort* (The Free Word, 1907), and married German anarchist architect and publisher Hans Koch (died 1948). The couple moved to Stelton, where their children attended the Modern School, and in 1921 Anna coedited the brief-lived paper *Action*.

airplanes. They repaired broken furniture and made all kinds of toys from iron and other metals.

In the well-stocked library sat Jimmy Dick, an Englishman, ready to help any child with reading, writing, and arithmetic.[6] The children came and went—book learning did not hold great interest for them. Jimmy was more successful in assembly and on the sports field playing ball, which was very popular.

The younger children spent their time in the large auditorium under the personal supervision of "Auntie" Elizabeth Ferm—the most gifted woman I had the good fortune to meet in my life. She was sixty-six years old when she came to us in 1920 to take over the care of the children's dormitory. She was young in spirit despite her age, lively and cheerful in everything she did, and gifted by nature with a good intellect, strong willpower, and what we might call personal influence.

Born of Irish parents here in America, she was imbued with the best revolutionary traditions that her people had maintained for generations against English oppression. Personal freedom and humanitarianism were her religion. Brought up in a convent and trained to be a teacher, she soon realized that the methods used in the primary schools were not the right ones. Children were treated like instruments into which school had to infuse a certain amount of knowledge, about everything, regardless of the abilities and inclinations of particular students. She began to seriously study theories of education until she sought out the ideas of Friedrich Fröbel, who for years had insisted that the child was a personality, an adult in miniature, who had rights that needed to be respected by anyone who came in contact with them.[7]

---

6. **James ("Jim") Dick** (1882–1965) was an English-born educator and anarchist. While attending the University of Liverpool in 1907 he met Francisco Ferrer and the following year opened the Liverpool Communist School, which lasted until 1911, and then London's International Modern School in 1913. **Nellie Dick** (1893–1995), born Naomi Ploschansky, was a Russian-born educator and anarchist. When she was a young girl her family immigrated to London where her father was active in the Jewish anarchist movement. In 1912 she cofounded London's International Modern School with Jim Dick, whom she married in 1916. The following year the couple immigrated to the United States and taught at the Stelton Modern School in 1917–1924 and 1928–1933 and the Mohegan Modern School in 1924–1928, before founding their own Modern School in Lakewood, New Jersey, which ran from 1933 to 1958.

7. **Friedrich Fröbel** (1782–1852) was an influential German pedagogue and teacher who founded the first kindergartens.

The function of education is to help the child develop their innate abilities, not to impose on them the wills and whims of adults. The child must be treated with care, with full respect and complete freedom.

These concepts of education were in harmony with her own on character and worldview. She left her job and opened her own kindergarten for young children, where she applied Froebel's theories in practical life. Her school was a huge success. Ernest Crosby—the American Tolstoy, as he was called—was interested in her method of teaching and made them well-known in various circles.[8]

An article had appeared in the *Fraye arbeter shtime* many years previous written by Thomas B. Eyges in his successful column called "Correspondence from a Traveler," describing the Ferms' remarkable school in Dyker Heights, Brooklyn. This article had made a huge impression in our circles. When we found it impossible to solve the difficulties of running the children's dormitory on our own, we asked Elizabeth and Alexis Ferm to come and take over this work.

They brought new life and a great deal of order to the whole colony. They soon changed not only the name but also the content and spirit of the institution they ran: the dormitory was transformed into a "Living House"—a place of life and lively activity. It was quickly filled with children, over fifty in number, and was equipped with the complete means for maintaining itself—a garden, cows, chickens, et cetera—which the older children looked after. The elderly Elizabeth Ferm would get up early in the morning and begin her piano exercises for an hour, waking up the children and the inhabitants of the colony with the sweet sounds of good music.

All day long, activity in the Living House was conducted systematically, albeit freely, in the fullest sense of the word. In the evening, after a long day of hard work with so many children, Elizabeth would gather a number of parents and colonists in the Living House to discuss all kinds of problems they encountered with the children.

---

8. **Ernest Howard Crosby** (1856–1907) was an American-born pacifist, radical, and writer. A former member of the New York State Assembly and a respected poet, he became an advocate of Leo Tolstoy's anarchist pacifism and a proponent of the single tax. Crosby was a member of the Friends of Russian Freedom and president of both the New York Anti-Militarist League and the New York Anti-Imperialism League. He counted many anarchists among his friends and admirers and published poetry in *Mother Earth*.

We developed a friendship and mutual respect for each other. I persuaded the parents and the school administrators to leave the running of the school entirely in their hands. For four or five years, the work was carried out according to plan, with great satisfaction in all regards. As chairman of the administrative board and the big annual meetings, I heartily endorsed their activities and the way in which they led the work.

With the passage of time, however, differences of opinion arose. Their educational method was well-suited for very young children, up to the age of ten, let's say. But children have a bad habit of growing up and getting older. Before they reach their teenage years (*bar mitzvah yorn*), most of them have far outgrown such an approach to education. They then need to be encouraged to take up serious academic instruction and planned activities. This also can and must be done in a libertarian way, but the schoolwork must be organized in such a way that the child is encouraged and guided in the desired direction. There must be an atmosphere of learning, just as we had created an atmosphere of work activities for the younger children. The Ferms refused to accept such ideas. The result was that most of the children, when they reached the age of ten, were withdrawn and sent to public schools. Their places were taken by new youngsters, and they began all over again. I became convinced that under such a system our school had no future. It was destined to remain a kindergarten every year.

There was a second difficulty concerning the composition of the children. Fifty children resided in the Living House, mostly from New York. There were twice as many children in the colony, composed of colonists' children and strangers who stayed with colonists because there was no room for them in the Living House. Unconsciously and reluctantly, Elizabeth had developed a different relationship with the children in the Living House (she had no children of her own) than with the other children who lived in the colony. I tried to settle the matter in a practical, educational way, by introducing a new arrangement in which all children would spend the entire day in school and have their lunch together, which would lead to a wide-ranging, new activity for the children, producing food in the garden in the summer, preserving it for winter, preparing and serving meals, managing the kitchen and dining rooms, and tidying them up—in a word, a whole range of self-directed activities in which all children would participate equally. But the Ferms would not accept the plan.

Another thing struck me as important: our school was then very popular among teachers and educators all over the country. Tons of people, teachers and professors, would visit us to acquaint themselves with our school's methods. At the same time, however, we had difficulty finding teachers for our school when it was needed, or recommending teachers to those who wanted to organize similar schools in other parts of the country. And there were many. A number of comrades in Los Angeles ran such a school for some time.[9] In Philadelphia, there was a special organization for this purpose. The same situation existed in a number of other cities. Something had to be done to prepare a cadre of teachers suitable for such work.

I suggested we open summer courses for teachers to introduce them to and teach them our methods, so that a circle of willing teachers for Modern Schools would develop among them. In addition, every summer we had an influx of children, and the public-school teachers had their summer vacation. A number of them were willing and able to take such courses. But Elizabeth Ferm would not hear a word of it.

We discussed these three problems for a year with no results. I could not remain at the colony and continue to help lead its work in the same old way. I did not want to initiate a public movement in favor of my views, as this would lead to conflict and personal grievances. To remain at the colony and resign from the administrative work for the school was impossible for me. My only solution was to move out of the colony and settle in Cambridge, Massachusetts, where my children were studying at Harvard University. My plan was to settle down there and take up some studies in my old age, instead of teaching others. For this purpose it was necessary, of course, to find someone who would take over the editorship of the *Fraye arbeter shtime*, and who would be more suitable for this job than comrade Rudolf Rocker, who had experience in such work and was so highly regarded and loved by comrades all over the country?

In 1925, when we began to consider how we could celebrate the anniversary of the *Fraye arbeter shtime*, we had the idea to invite comrade Rocker to come and elevate the occasion, help with the celebration, and make a cross-country lecture tour along the way. We had a strong desire to hold the

---

9. The **Walt Whitman School** was a Modern School that operated in Los Angeles's Boyle Heights neighborhood from 1919 to 1924, directed by William Thurston Brown.

celebrations in the larger cities throughout the country all at the same time, in October, when the rejuvenated *Fraye arbeter shtime* would appear, and conduct its annual fund-raising. It was necessary to have several prominent speakers for this purpose, so that they could cover the whole field in one month's time. Yanovsky volunteered to help out in and around New York. I chose to visit Cleveland, Detroit, and Chicago. For other cities as well as for New York, Rocker's presence would be a great help to us. I also hoped to suggest to Rocker, when he came, that he should stay and take over the editorship of the *Fraye arbeter shtime*.

Such was my plan. We corresponded with Rocker, securing a visa for him with the help of Morris Sigman and other labor leaders. Our suggestion to Rocker was that he should come to our annual celebration in early October and then do a winter lecture tour here. We would pay his travel expanses both ways and also compensate him for all of his time.

Rocker arrived for our celebrations after a very long delay. He was welcomed with great respect and affection. His first reception at the Manhattan Opera House drew an enormous crowd. For me and thousands of others, it was our first meeting with a man whom we had known through his writings for decades. Comrades who had emigrated from London, his students and personal friends, were overjoyed. We all could not to get enough of his splendid lectures and evocative speeches. We were all convinced that his devoted followers had not exaggerated his talents as a speaker and his personal magnetism. He was a God-gifted orator with a wonderful memory, and possessed a world of knowledge.

In private talks, however, we found that he was not willing to engage in his lecture tour under the direction of the *Fraye arbeter shtime*. He preferred to arrange and carry it out on his own accord. A number of his close friends formed a Rocker Lecture Committee that took on responsibility for everything.

Naturally, I and a number of other comrades close to the *Fraye arbeter shtime* were a bit disappointed in the turn that his lecture tour had taken, but we had no complaints about him. He was free to decide how and under what conditions his personal activity should be conducted. Comrade Morris Shutz, the manager of our paper for the previous few years, resigned in order to devote his time to the tour, accompanying Rocker across the country and taking care of the financial problems of the enterprise.

The tour was a great success. The lectures were well attended. At the reception banquets, money was raised to publish Rocker's writings. The tour brought in several thousand dollars but not much more than the amount we estimated we would have needed to give him. Of course, the *Fraye arbeter shtime* would probably have also raised a bit of money from direct appeals to the comrades attending the celebrations. But not all was lost! It was a real victory for the movement. A few appearances at large gatherings in New York had brought in a considerable sum of donations for the *Fraye arbeter shtime*.

When Rocker returned to New York from his tour, Yanovsky invited him and me to his house to discuss the *Fraye arbeter shtime* and my plan to have Rocker become editor. Yanovsky was familiar with the plan and tried to help me as much as possible. Over a good meal, we discussed the question from all angles. Rocker did not give us a definite answer. He needed to consider it, to consult with his closest friends, and write us his decision from Berlin.

His answer, which came later, was negative. He saw no way to break away from the great work with which he was associated in Germany and could not accept our offer.

Rocker, as many know, had returned to Germany in 1918, at the end of World War I, after being held in a concentration camp in England for almost four years. His old-new home was foreign to him. He had been away from Germany for about thirty years, living most of that time among the Jewish workers in London. The free atmosphere in Germany following the "revolution" gave him an opportunity for wide-ranging activity in the syndicalist movement. With his help, a significant syndicalist organization quickly grew, which put out a good weekly publication called *Der Syndikalist*, which had a huge circulation.[10] It also created a significant publishing house to bring out books and pamphlets on anarchism and syndicalism.

In 1921 a syndicalist International with branches in many countries was organized in Berlin. At that time, Berlin was the transit point between Soviet Russia to the rest of Europe, where final permission to enter the Soviet Union was obtained. All the traveling anarchists from England, France, Italy,

---

10. **Der Syndikalist** (1918–1932) was the official organ of the anarcho-syndicalist Freie Arbeiter Union Deutschlands (Free Workers' Union of Germany). It was coedited by Rudolf Rocker and in 1920 had a circulation of 120,000.

Spain, and elsewhere stopped in Berlin, visited the Rockers on the way to and, above all, on the way back from the Bolshevik paradise. His location was important to him and perhaps later for the movement.

It was no secret to us, however, that he was unhappy and dissatisfied in his new-old home. We learned that he was not exactly happy with the anarchist-communist movement in Germany, with its federation and newspaper *Der freie Arbeiter*.[11] Life there was not at all pleasant for him. We were convinced of that. Sooner or later, we felt, he would come to us, to our group, where he would live his life appreciated and satisfied.

In 1930 he came to America for a second lecture tour. In his speech at our welcoming celebration, he gave us an enthusiastic account of Germany, of the freedoms that they enjoyed there, about the many kinds of activity that the syndicalist wing of our movement conducted, and especially about the youth movement that was growing there day by day and developing in a libertarian direction. This tour was also a great success. On the initiative of the Toronto group, the comrades had already during his first lecture tour formed a Rocker Publication Committee, which had published his memoirs of the concentration camp, *Hinter shtekhige droht un grates* (Behind Barbed Wire and Bars), and now planned to publish his other great works.[12]

When he came back to New York after the second tour, the comrades called together an intimate gathering at the Free Workers' Center to hear a report on the movement around the country. The small place was overflowing with comrades, the most active members of our movement. But the news Rocker brought was sad: he had found no movement in this country! This was not news to us. We knew our weaknesses. What was new were the impressions and conclusions he drew from his observations. He accused us of being responsible. We, who were exerting ourselves beyond capacity to sustain what there was of our movement, who were in this respect more

---

11. The **Föderation Kommunistischer Anarchisten Deutschlands** (Anarchist Communist Federation of Germany) was founded in 1919 and revived the paper *Der freie Arbeiter* (1904–1914, 1919–1933), which had been banned during the First World War. The federation, which counted only several hundred members, suffered from sectarianism and had an antagonistic relationship with the anarcho-syndicalist Freie Arbeiter Union Deutschlands. Both it and its paper were banned by the Nazis in 1933.

12. Rudolf Rocker, *Hinter shtekhige droht un grates: erinerungen fun der krigs-gefangenshaft* (Behind Barbed Wire and Bars: Memoirs of War Imprisonment) (New York: Rudolf Rocker shriften komitet, 1927).

successful than the other language groups in this country—we were responsible for the fact that in America the anarchist movement was not as big and strong as we all would like to see it!

There were sharp answers from David Isakovitz, Dr. James Globus (my assistant in the editorial office at that time), and me.[13] The celebration broke up. The mood among those present became very tense. People left embittered and disappointed.

That could have been the end of it. But at the time it seemed to me that this could not be the end. Around a 150 people had witnessed the clash, which under the circumstances could not be fully resolved on the spot. I covered the entire affair from our point of view in a couple of articles in the newspaper. This did not make me any friends in the movement, especially among Rocker's supporters, who did not like me. Rocker himself did not respond with a word. He was more experienced and more self-restrained than I was. After nearly ten years, his cooperation with the *Fraye arbeter shtime* ceased. In time the whole episode was forgotten.

Toward the end of 1933, after Hitler had seized total power in Germany, Rocker was able to escape to America to settle. He was received everywhere with great respect and affection. For a time he made a lecture tour of the country every year. In the spring of 1934 he visited us at the Sunrise Colony and spent a few days among us. He also began to again collaborate with the *Fraye arbeter shtime*, where he published many series of interesting articles. Of course, he did not—could not—create an anarchist movement in this country, just as we had not been able to in previous years. This is not within the power of just one person or a few people.

It was deeply moving to see the great friendship and sincere devotion that the comrades and the organized labor movement showed to comrade Rocker on the occasion of his seventieth birthday, when he was seriously ill. The response across the country was wonderful. A fund was created,

---

13. **Isaac ("James") Globus** (Ayzik Globus, 1873–1950) was a Russian-born Jewish pharmacist, dentist, and anarchist. He was involved in radical politics as a teenager and fled to the United States in 1890. Globus studied pharmacology and opened a drugstore in Brooklyn, then became a dentist. A nondogmatic radical, he was an admirer of Marx and Labor Zionism and wrote for the *FAS*, *Problemen/Problemot*, *Der tog*, *The Road to Freedom*, *The Clarion*, and *Man!* In 1933–1934 he was a member of the *FAS*'s editorial board. Obituary: *FAS*, October 13, 1950.

which made it possible for him to carry on his literary work without any worries. During the years he lived here in America, a number of his important works were translated and published in English. *Nationalism and Culture* aroused great interest in intellectual circles.[14] *The Six* attracted attention in literary and artistic circles.[15] Comrade Rudolf Rocker was the last of the giants in our movement, which the previous generation possessed in such large numbers.

In 1937 Rocker made his home at the Mohegan Colony. Many years earlier comrade Harry Kelly had withdrawn from the Stelton Colony, with the idea of establishing a second, larger colony in a beautiful and more pleasant place, by a lake for bathing—the lack of which we in Stelton had suffered from greatly. He organized a new settlement outside of New York, the Mohegan Colony, purchasing a large farm that had previously belonged to the Baron de Hirsch Fund, which used it as an agricultural college for Jews. The large farm had about five hundred acres of land and was located only forty miles from New York City in a very beautiful and nice area.[16] Kelly's plan was to build another libertarian colony with a Modern School. The price of lots was set much higher than in Stelton. The place attracted more affluent, middle-class people, professionals and better-paid workers, some of them former Stelton colonists. They managed to erect an unfinished building and ran a school out of it for several years. However, the school did not have deep roots there. Most of the colonists were not really interested in the school, they were instead attracted to the beauty and convenience of the place. A considerable number of them, it turned out, were "Lefts," with all the trimmings. The colony developed well, much better than Stelton. But the school disappeared without a trace. There were a considerable number of comrades there: Jacob Mont, Lydia Gordon and her daughters, Moyshe

---

14. Rudolf Rocker, *Nationalism and Culture*, trans. Ray E. Chase (Los Angeles: Rocker Publications Committee, 1937). The book's admirers included Louis Adamic, Will Durant, Albert Einstein, Lewis Mumford, and Bertrand Russell. See *Impressive Opinions by Important People about a Significant Book: Souvenir of Bertrand Russell–Rudolf Rocker Reception and Banquet* (Los Angeles: Rocker Publications Committee, 1939).

15. Rudolf Rocker, *The Six*, trans. Ray E. Chase (Los Angeles: Rocker Publications Committee, 1938). In this allegorical novel, six figures from Western literature must work together to solve a sphinx's riddle after failing to do so individually.

16. The **Mohegan Colony** was established in Westchester County, New York, in 1923, and lasted into the 1950s.

Morris, William Puzis, Morris Freeman, Bertha Chazick, and many others.[17] There were also a number of French and American comrades. Many visitors from other cities, when they came to New York, would also visit Rocker there.

17. **Jacob Mont** (1888–1959) was a Russian-born Jewish carpenter and anarchist. As a teenager in Lodz he participated in the socialist movement and the 1905 Revolution, leading to a life sentence of Siberian exile. Around 1913 he escaped to the United States with the aid of false documents provided by the Anarchist Red Cross. In New York Mont was active in both the Anarchist Red Cross and the Ferrer-Rocker Branch 203 of the Workmen's Circle. His family was one of the first to settle at the Mohegan Colony, where his nephew, future sociologist Daniel Bell (1919–2011), stayed with them for a time. They later moved to the Amalgamated Cooperative Apartment House in the Bronx. Obituary: *FAS*, June 1, 1959. **Lydia Gordon** (1875–1960), née Landau, was a Russian-born Jewish anarchist. After immigrating around 1896 she was active in the anarchist movement in Chicago and then New York, where she was a friend of Emma Goldman and custodian of the Ferrer Center. She married fellow anarchist Harry Gordon, and the couple moved to Stelton and then Mohegan, where their three daughters attended each colony's Modern School. **Moyshe Morris** (Moris, c. 1883–1959) was a Russian-born Jewish anarchist. He was involved in the anarchist movement in England before coming to the United States and was one of the first residents of the Mohegan Colony, where he lived until his death. Morris's wife was reportedly a militant member of the Communist Party until the Hitler-Stalin Pact. Obituary: *FAS*, August 15, 1959. **Morris (or Maurice) Freeman** (Friman, c. 1891–?) was a Russian-born Jewish painter and anarchist. He immigrated to the United States in 1913 and lived at Mohegan with his wife Lena. **Bertha Chazick** (Berta Tshezik, 1881–1982) was a Russia-born Jewish capmaker and anarchist. Her family immigrated to the United States around 1893, and after the death of her first husband she married anarchist printer Marc Epstein (c. 1885–?). The couple lived at Stelton and then Mohegan, where in 1936 she hosted a lawn party fund-raiser for the journal *Vanguard*.

CHAPTER 46

The Shop Stewards Movement and the Free Workers' Center

In the early days of the Russian Revolution, when the slogan "All power to the soviets!" was on everyone's lips, here in America, as well as in England, the idea of establishing soviets in the factories was widespread.[1] In the English-speaking countries, the concept was modified under the title "shop stewards"—that is, elected representatives of the workers in each department in a factory would form a council to protect the interests of the workers and study the relevant conditions and technical requirements of production.

This idea was revolutionary and very relevant. The intelligent workers realized that if their organizations were to take over the industries, they would not have the experience and technical know-how required to undertake the complex process of obtaining raw materials, producing the necessary products correctly and efficiently, and distributing them appropriately. This needed to be learned, studied, and planned systematically.

The intelligent workers had also learned that the unions, when they grow to become too large and powerful, become bodies *above* and *over* the workers. The direct bond between worker and union is lost. Shop floor concerns become foreign to union officials, who hold their offices for years and quickly forget the experience of working in the shops. For the union and its officials, it is impossible to keep track of everything happening in every shop and to see to it that union conditions are properly observed.

For these reasons, we then believed, it was necessary to establish a system of workers' control, with management in the direct control of the

---

1. The Russian word *soviet* literally means "council."

435

workers, who would thus be involved in the activities of the union, becoming active, effective components of a revitalized labor movement. Comrade Simon Farber was the main figure in this movement. For a time we gave much space in the *Fraye arbeter shtime* to discussion and agitation, convened meetings, and formed anarchist groups in various industries, to campaign for limiting the terms of union officials and, above all, for maintaining idealism, purity, and honesty in the labor movement.

The need for frequent gatherings of small groups of workers led comrades Morris Michael and Isaac Radinowsky to the idea of opening a Free Workers' Center at 176 Second Avenue.[2]

Starting as a very small and modest backroom with a narrow entrance, the center immediately demonstrated the possibility for broader, more fruitful activity. After moving to 219 Second Avenue, the center served our movement for several years as a gathering and meeting place for small meetings, lectures, conventions, and entertainment. A large number of comrades grouped around the center: Meyer and Sarah Rosen, Tania Schapiro, Hannah Lake, Jack Borodoulin, Benjamin, Hershel Pinchuk, Ida Cohen, Hirsh Reiff, and dozens of others who were less active.[3] But Radinowsky and

---

2. **Morris Michael** (Moris Maykel or Maykl, c .1890–1972) was a Russian-born Jewish bookbinder, butcher, and anarchist. In 1909 he immigrated to New York, where he was an active member of Local 119 of the International Brotherhood of Bookbinders, secretary of the Free Workers' Center, and later a member of the Rocker Publications Committee and the managing board of the *FAS*. Obituary: *FAS*, August 1, 1972.

3. **Sarah Rosen** (Sore Rozen, 1877–?) was a Russian-born Jewish anarchist. She immigrated to the United States around 1903 and married anarchist Meyer Rosen. A mother of three, in 1913 Rosen published a letter in the *FAS* defending working-class women's decision to have children (*FAS*, February 22, 1913). **Hannah Lake** (Khane-Leyke, died 1960), real name Anna Block (Blok), was a Jewish garment worker and anarchist who was active in the anarchist movement and ILGWU in New York, then in the Kropotkin Literary Society, Branch 413 of the Workmen's Circle in Los Angeles. Obituary: *FAS*, February 1, 1960. **Anna Goldstein** (Goldshteyn, c. 1886–1969) was an active member of New York's Jewish anarchist movement. Obituary: *FAS*, July 1, 1969. **Jacob ("Jack") Borodoulin** (Dzshek Borodulin, 1873–1925) was a Russian-born Jewish machinist and anarchist. He immigrated to Paris, where he was involved in the Jewish anarchist movement and met his wife, anarchist Anna Borodoulin (1876–1951). The couple moved to London and then came to the United States in 1907. Obituary for Anna: *FAS*, December 7, 1951. **Hershel Pinchuk** (Hershl Pintshuk, 1880–1964) was a Russian-born Jewish brush maker and anarchist. As a teenager he was active in the labor and anarchist movements in Bialystok and then London. Pinchuk immigrated to the United States in 1906, became secretary of the Free Workers' Center, and sat on the board of directors of the *FAS* at the time of his death. Obituary: *FAS*, April 1, 1964.

Michael were the center's main caretakers. Their work yielded good results and was very important to all of us.

In the struggle against the "Left," the center served as the headquarters for our side. There comrade Farber published *Der yunyon arbayter* (The Union Worker)—a small newspaper that caused the "Left" plenty of headaches.[4] The tactics of this struggle were carried out in and around the shops of the city's garment district. *Der yunyon arbeter* appeared regularly for eighteen months.

For our movement, the Free Workers' Center always served as a home, an enjoyable gathering place to meet friends, spend free time, and attend meetings or entertainments. Comrades from out of town knew that when they came to New York they had to visit the office of the *Fraye arbeter shtime* in the afternoon and the center in the evening in order to get acquainted with the development of our movement. In the winter months lectures were held at the center every week in Yiddish and often in English as well. However, we were not able to set up a library at the center, despite several attempts.

After ten years of existence, the center faced a bit of competition from the Clarion Group, organized by Abba Gordin, which had its own English-language journal and meeting place. The result was that both social centers closed, and the movement remained without a home of its own.

Hirsh Reiff (Rayf, 1887–1948) was a Russian-born Jewish floorer, humorist, and anarchist. He immigrated to the United States in 1903 and joined the Jewish anarchist movement. In his later years Reiff began to write humorous sketches, which were collected and published posthumously as *Lehayim Yidn (Humor on Gal)* (Cheer Up, Jews [Humor without Malice], 1948). Obituary: *FAS*, May 7, 1948.

4. ***Der yunyon arbayter*** (sometimes transliterated as *Der yunyon arbeter*, 1925–1927) was a weekly newspaper published by the Anarchist Group of the ILGWU. Much of its content was dedicated to combating Communist influence in the union and supporting union president and anarchist Morris Sigman, although its writers also criticized the socialist "machine" that dominated the ILGWU's administration.

CHAPTER 47

Saul Yanovsky and Abe Cahan

One fine day in 1926, Saul Yanovsky came into my office on Canal Street. He slowly began to tell me that he had been invited to become a contributor to the *Forverts*. He was on his way there to have a meeting with Abe Cahan about the details and conditions. Yanovsky would suggest that he be made the labor editor, in charge of labor news. Of course, he would not go to union meetings and offices to collect the news himself; the *Forverts* would have to give him two young men to do the legwork. He would oversee the presentation of this news in the *Forverts*, track the policies of each union, and see to it that they followed the right path. Not a bad idea!

He also had another plan for the *Forverts*—to introduce a letters page (*briv-kastn*), as he formerly had in the *Fraye arbeter shtime*, which had long ago been the most popular feature of that newspaper.

Also quite an idea!

He had other good plans for how to make the *Forverts* a respectable newspaper. He just needed to see that Cahan would give him a free hand, and he would show them what he was capable of.

I sat and listened to him, not saying a word. I did not see any crime in joining the *Forverts*. Other anarchists had done so before him. Moyshe Katz was the only real journalist who stuck with the newspaper in the early years of the *Forverts*. And Abraham Frumkin was Cahan's right-hand man for quite some time. Gottlieb, Harry Lang, and many other collaborators there began their careers as anarchists.[1] Why should Yanovsky not do the same?

---

1. "Gottlieb" appears to be a reference to Leon Gottlieb (Leybush-Arn Gotlib, 1878–1947), a Russian-born Jewish socialist who after immigrating to the United States from

Still, it was not to my liking. I listened to his plans and kept quiet. He stopped and asked me: "Well, why are you silent? Why do you say nothing?"

I answered that I had nothing to say. "You didn't come to me for advice, you came to tell me something. All that I can say is mazel tov, may it last a long time—and that is all I will say since you have made all your plans."

"And what would you say if I asked for your advice?"

"Oh, then I would have much to say. I do not like your entire plan. I would not have done the same in your place."

My answer interested him. He wanted to know my reasons for such a wondrous answer. I told him: A few years earlier, Philip Krantz, then a contributor the *Forverts*, had lost his faith in the social democratic Torah. He became interested in syndicalism. He often came to us, read syndicalist newspapers, and discussed socialism, anarchism, syndicalism, and similar questions. He never mentioned his work with the *Forverts*, but it was clear that he was not liking it there. One Friday he came in agitated, sat for a while, and in his stuttering way, very agitated, said: "C-Cahan, I've h-had it up t-to here"—he pointed to his neck—"I c-can't t-take it an-anymore!" He left and died of a heart attack a day or two later!

Then there was the story of Isaac Hourwich. The *Forverts* hired him as a staff writer, and Abe Cahan drove him to an early death. Hourwich was a very proud man, and he never mentioned a word about what he suffered there. Every time Abe Cahan rejected one of his articles, Hourwich brought it to me at the *Fraye arbeter shtime*, where it was always received by readers with appreciation and interest. Later, the rejections became too frequent for the *Fraye arbeter shtime* to be able to use. He was suffocating, and the wound became deeper and more painful, until his proud nature could no longer bear it. As a result of his contact with the *Forverts* and its editor, his life was shortened.

I listed a few other incidents that everyone in the world of Jewish writers knew, and I ended with these words: "I know Abe Cahan only from afar, but I am convinced that he is a tyrant, a sadist, who cannot, in general, tolerate a person with knowledge, dignity, and self-respect. If I were in your place, I would have nothing to do with him."

London became a regular contributor to the *Forverts* and the sometimes secretary of Abe Cahan. No other sources on Gottlieb, however, mention an anarchist period in his life, although he did have a brother who was an anarchist (see *FAS*, January 13, 1956).

Yanovsky listened to me, thought for a while, then remarked, "Eh, what foolishness! He'll never be able to pull such tricks on me! Krantz and Hourwich were softies (*lemeshkes*). Cahan will not be able to boss me around."

What more could I say? I wished him luck, and he was gone.

❋ ❋ ❋

His first piece in the *Forverts* was scandalous. Yanovsky was an extremist and a passionate person. He did not always have control of his tongue or his pen. When he began to praise the virtues of the *Forverts* and its editor—his justification for becoming a contributor—he poured such sweet words into hymns of praise that it was painful to behold.[2]

Of course, all his idealistic plans came to nothing. Cahan wanted nothing to do with them. He allowed Yanovsky to publish several articles but very quickly reduced him to writing about how fat girls milked cows naked, and other such important subjects.

This arrangement did not last for long. Yanovsky by that time was not dependent on his earnings as a writer. That was his good fortune. He spit on the swamp, whose hymns of praise as the source of life and light he had sung only a few months before, and withdrew.

On his deathbed, a few days before he died, Yanovsky told Samuel Freedman, then the manager of the *Fraye arbeter shtime*, of the following incident.[3] The first time Cahan rejected one of his articles, he went to save

---

2. *Forverts*, March 1, 1926.

3. **Samuel Freedman** or Friedman (Shmuel Fridman, c. 1887–1941), born Samuel Reichgold and also known as Shmuel Mezeritsher, was a Russian-born Jewish garment worker, labor organizer, and anarchist. Orphaned at age six, he joined the Bund in Warsaw and was sentenced to death at age fourteen for his role in a garment workers' strike but was liberated during the 1905 Revolution. Freedman fled to London and then Paris, where he was involved in the Jewish anarchist movement and led a successful shoemakers' strike in 1910 before returning to England. Writer B. Rivkin described him as a "man of extraordinary courage and daring deeds" (*FAS*, July 31, 1942). Freedman met his wife, anarchist Rose Burack (Borak, c. 1893–1958), after returning to London, and the couple immigrated to the United States in 1912. In 1921 they moved to Stelton where their three children attended the Modern School. Samuel was meanwhile an active member of the ILGWU's Waterproof Garment Workers' Union Local 20 in New York (resulting in at least one arrest for strike

his creation. Cahan insisted—the article was not suited for the *Forverts*, so there was nothing to talk about. After the meeting, as Yanovsky stood in the open door of Cahan's office, he was suddenly asked a question: "Just tell me, Yanovsky, do you know for whom you are writing?" Yanovsky looked at him: "What do you mean, for whom am I writing? I write for the intelligent readers of the *Forverts*, for people who understand what they are reading!" "Aha!" Cahan exclaimed, triumphantly, "that is where you are mistaken. You are writing for a bunch of illiterate swine, who in America learned from me how to read romances and the *'Bintel brief.'*[4] You write for pushcart peddlers, old women, illiterate shopkeepers and all kinds of ignoramuses. Do you understand me?" Yanovsky looked at him and asked, "Comrade Cahan, would you like me to repeat these words at your funeral, 120 years from now?" Enraged, Cahan murmured through his teeth, "You'll never see the day!" and slammed the door behind him.

And now, with the angel of death standing beside his bed, Yanovsky recalled the incident and regretted that Cahan's wish was coming true. He would not be able to speak Cahan's well-earned praises after his death.

---

activity), served as manager of the *FAS* in 1930–1939, and was elected secretary of the Jewish Anarchist Federation. He and Rose also joined the Naye Gezelshaft Group, Branch 364 of the Workmen's Circle in the early 1930s. Obituary: *FAS*, August 1, 1941.

    4. **"A Bintel Brief"** (A Bundle of Letters) was Abe Cahan's popular advice column in the *Forverts*.

CHAPTER 48

The Struggle against the "Left" and Zionism

Throughout the time I was associated with the *Fraye arbeter shtime*, the "Left" epidemic drove us to engage in stressful activity. First, it weakened our ranks by causing the great split in 1921, when we formulated a consistent anarchist path for ourselves. Second, it bothered and hurt us very much to see that the leaders of the "Left" movement were, in fact, almost all our former comrades: Bob Minor and Menakhem-Mendl Tsipin—two close personal friends of mine—as well as William Z. Foster, Israel Amter, Jay Fox, Charles Kuntz, Mrs. Parsons, and dozens of others.[1]

---

1. **William Z. Foster** (1881–1961) was an American-born worker, labor organizer, syndicalist, and later Communist. He joined the Socialist Party in 1901 but left it in 1909 to join the IWW. In 1912, influenced by French syndicalism, he withdrew from the IWW to form the Syndicalist League of North America to advocate "boring from within" existing mainstream unions. Foster gravitated toward anarchism at this time, marrying Russian-born Jewish anarchist Esther Abramowitz (died 1965) and writing that "syndicalism has placed the Anarchist movement upon a practical, effective basis" (Earl C. Ford and William Z. Foster, *Syndicalism* [Chicago: William Z. Foster, [1912], 31). After the league dissolved in 1914, Foster became an organizer for the AFL and led the failed steel strike of 1919. That same year he founded the Trade Union Educational League, which became the official US affiliate of the Profintern, and in 1921 he joined the Communist Party. Foster quickly ascended to the party's leadership, sitting as its candidate for president of the United States in 1924, 1928, and 1932, and serving as its general secretary in 1945–1957. **Israel Amter** (Yisroel Amtur, 1881–1954) was an American-born Jewish musician, socialist, and later Communist. He joined the Socialist Party in 1901 and from 1903 to 1914 lived in Germany where he belonged to the Social Democratic Party. Amter became a Communist in 1919 and held several important posts within the Communist Party over the following decades. If he had early connections to the anarchist movement, as Cohen suggests here, these are not evident in the existing record.

In the early years, I had a couple of interesting experiences with Bob Minor. We often met and spent time together, not entering into political discussions. One day, we both had the idea to arrange a debate between him and comrade Harry Kelly. Such a debate at that time would certainly have attracted a large audience and raised substantial funds, which our movement could have made good use of. So we discussed all the details: who to invite as chairman, how to divide the revenue, when and where it should be held. Every detail was worked out properly. A few days later, Minor told me shamefacedly that the debate could not take place: the party refused to let him participate. I couldn't believe my ears—"What do you mean, the party won't allow it? Since when have you become a slave of the party, with someone else deciding what you can or cannot do?" Bob blushed, his face changed color. But he stubbornly held his position: the party would not allow it. He could not participate!

Another time, he called me on the phone: he needed to see me as soon as possible. I met him that very day and heard from him the following story: They had in their hands one of the witnesses who had testified against Tom Mooney and helped get him condemned to death. Now the scum was willing to recant his testimony and tell how the prosecutor, Fickert, had fixed the trial. Until the California courts heard him out, he had to be kept under lock and key so that he did not disappear and change his mind again. Bob Minor wanted me to take on the task of caring for him until he was needed.

This question, of course, interested me very much. Indeed, something had to be done. And I could have done such a thing without too much difficulty. But then I was struck by the fact that he had turned to me. Could they, within their "Left" circle, not find a way to provide such a small thing?

I asked him: "Just tell me, my friend, what is the problem here? What must one have, or do, to hold this soul for a little while?"

Unashamed, Bob Minor answered that you do not need much: "Plenty of food, whiskey for him to drink, and beautiful girls to keep him entertained!"

This upset and angered me. I dispelled all the base fantasies in his head on this issue, that we should furnish whomever it was with "beautiful girls." We quarreled and never met again.

The poisonous activity of the "Left" in the Workmen's Circle and in the unions was even worse. At a convention of the Workmen's Circle in New York, Moissaye Olgin had the audacity to demand that he be given a chance to address the delegates and publicly denounce the entire order. Meyer London actually spat in his face, which cooled his zealotry.

In the ILGWU and the furriers' union, a life-and-death battle ensued between these two wings. I recall a large meeting held by the "Left" in Madison Square Garden on a Saturday afternoon. I traveled into the city to witness the event and report on it in detail for the *Fraye arbeter shtime*. There was a terrible crush at the entrance, through the only door. In the great vestibule stood two rows of commissars, who examined each and every person who entered. Police were everywhere, scanning the room. Before I had passed halfway through the crowded foyer, one of the commissars instructed the police to take me outside and send me back home. Morris Sigman, the president of the ILGWU, insisted on his right as a worker to attend a meeting about his industry, but his arguments were in vain. He was removed from the hall. The police were under the supervision of the famous underworld leader Arnold Rothstein, the worst racketeer that New York has ever seen. The "Left" revolutionaries had succeeded in making him their protector and assistant in their dirty work.[2]

This reminds me of the sad 1926 convention of the ILGWU, at which the "Left" had a majority of delegates. How they tore apart Sigman, a man who had dedicated his entire life to the labor movement and was the most honest and sincere leader the ILGWU ever had—a man who had stood under the shadow of a death sentence because of his activities during the Great Revolt of 1910; a president who had earnestly tried to rid the union of the corruption that had accumulated over the previous years, to get rid of the union's unscrupulous elements and their harmful practices—now the vile plotters Julius Portnoy, Louis Hyman, Joseph Boruchowitz, and their supporters tortured and tormented him as if he was one of them.[3]

---

2. **Arnold Rothstein** (1882–1928) was an American-born Jewish racketeer and organized crime boss. In 1924 the Communist Party began paying tens of thousands of dollars to retain his services, including access to the network of New York police officers on his payroll, to protect the activities of its members in the garment workers' unions.

3. **Julius Portnoy** (1887–?) was a Russian-born Jewish garment worker, labor organizer, and Communist. He was a leader of the Communist faction within the ILGWU, and secretary of its Cloak, Suit, Dress, Skirt and Reefer Makers' Union Local 22. Portnoy was elected to the ILWU's General Executive Board in 1926 and served as treasurer of the strike committee during the disastrous Communist-led 1926 general strike. **Louis Hyman** (1888–1963) was a Russian-born Jewish garment worker, labor organizer, and Communist. In 1902 he

And how obscenely did they conduct their assault on him in their filthy rag, the *Morgn-frayheyt* (Morning Freedom)![4] His personal life, his wife, and anything that had anything to do with him was deluged with the filthiest slanders that these shameless people could devise.

At that convention, Saul Yanovsky resigned from his post as editor of *Gerekhtigkeyt*. Sigman remained with the union, despite the "Left's" bacchanalia, in order to prevent the organization from collapsing. The convention was the most depressing and saddest I have ever experienced. One saw with their eyes and felt with every nerve that a great working-class body, an organization that had taken decades to build, was being consumed by filthy little vermin (*sherets*) and torn to pieces.

These armchair heroes, who were so ferocious when it came to fighting the leadership and breaking up the unions, were powerless and helpless when it came to fighting the employers. They looted the ILGWU funds, squandered everything they could, and paralyzed the strike they themselves had called. No better results could be expected from them.

I remember an evening meeting of the Joint Board of the Cloakmakers' Union, in which three "Left" locals were accused of betraying the ILGWU. The indictments in all three cases, made by Israel Feinberg, manager of the Joint Board, in the same dry, legalistic style as those prepared by lawyers, were not too convincing, but this did not matter. After each indictment, a motion was made to expel and reorganize the respective local. All should agree to this. And dammit if that's not what happened! This comedy was

---

immigrated to England, where he joined the socialist movement and wrote for the *Arbeter fraynd*, then came to the United States in 1911. Hyman was a leader of the Communist faction in the ILGWU and served as business agent, executive board member, and president of Cloak and Suit Tailors Local 9, and was elected to the ILGWU's General Executive Board in 1926 after unsuccessfully challenging Morris Sigman for the union's presidency. He then served as president of the breakaway Communist-led Needle Trades Workers Industrial Union but left the Communist Party after the Hitler-Stalin Pact and rejoined the ILGWU, serving as a vice president of the union from 1949 until his retirement in 1956. Hyman also contributed articles to the *FAS* and other Yiddish publications. **Joseph Boruchowitz** (Yosef Borukhovits, 1891–1943) was a Russian-born Jewish garment worker, labor organizer, and Communist. He immigrated to the United States in 1905 and became a leader of the union's Communist faction. Boruchowitz was an ILGWU vice president and elected to the union's General Executive Board in 1926. He remained with the ILGWU after the 1926 split.

4. *Morgn-frayheyt* (1921–1988) was the daily Yiddish newspaper of the Communist Party. It was edited by Moissaye Olgin until 1939.

repeated three times, all decisions being unanimous. The "Left" delegates, who were present at the meeting, were conspicuous by their silence. The matter was settled without interruption.

After the meeting I went with Sigman up to his office on the top floor of the same building, where we discussed the situation. He assured me that everything was conducted properly. The offices of the relevant locals, their records and property were protected so that the "Left" could not seize and exploit them. This was Friday after midnight.

But a few days later we found out that only the offices of the finishers local and the cloakmakers local were "taken care of." Dressmakers' Union Local 22 was neglected; those assigned to take care of it had left for the weekend "to rest" at Unity House. When they came back to the city on Monday morning, the "Left" was already in full control of the office and all that belonged to it. To dislodge them now was impossible.

I also have many memories of the "Right" clique that, with the help of the *Forverts*, orchestrated the expulsion of Sigman from the union to make way for Benjamin Schlesinger, who was at that time manager of the Chicago office of the *Forverts* and very unhappy with his work there.[5] We naturally took up this subject in the *Fraye arbeter shtime* and complicated their plans.

I met Schlesinger in a restaurant once, and he was very happy to see me. "Good that I find you here!" he exclaimed. "I wanted to call you on the phone last week from Chicago, to tell you that your analysis of the situation in the ILGWU and in the *Forverts* is not correct. But I realized that it would be impossible on the telephone. Let's just sit here and talk."

So we sat down and talked. That is, Schlesinger talked. Such was his habit, in a conversation with him one could seldom get a word in edgewise. He feigned ignorance of my offer in the *Fraye arbeter shtime* for him to openly discuss the matter from all points of view. Talk is cheap, but to write things down in black and white, making it possible analyze arguments, is another matter altogether.

The intrigues continued and achieved their goal. Sigman returned to his farm in Iowa, and Schlesinger, who had assured me that he did not want

---

5. The "Right" within the ILGWU refers to members of the Socialist Party aligned with the *Forverts*, many of whom later became New Deal Democrats. Morris Sigman and most of the anarchists in the union maintained an uneasy alliance with the much larger Right faction against the Communists.

to and would not go back to the now devastated union, became its president again.

I can still envision Morris Sigman's impressive funeral in July 1931, in Forverts Hall, where the leaders of the "Right" clique mourned the loss of a great man and labor leader with crocodile tears, where they praised to heaven his great feats and his beautiful, fruitful life, which they had themselves embittered to death. To this day, I can't shake off the disgust aroused in me by the saccharine, false sermons at the pompous funerals held in our radical circles.

I am also reminded of the impressive funeral for Joe Schneider, a young active comrade, who fell victim to the quarrels and bad blood within the union.[6] A young life was cut short without reason or cause.

I spent many days and evenings in those years in the Fur and Leather Workers Union, in the conflicts and fights between the "Left" and the "Right," in the intrigues surrounding Morris Kaufman, Oizer Shachtman, and Ben Gold and his friends.[7] We had a large number of good, active comrades in

---

6. **Joseph ("Joe") Schneider** (died 1933) was a Jewish garment worker, labor organizer, and anarchist. He was active in New York's Free Workers' Center and business agent of the ILGWU's New York Dressmakers' Local 22. On May 29, 1933, union member Benjamin Marder shot and killed Schneider in the offices of Local 22, claiming that Schneider had caused him to lose several jobs due to political differences. Obituaries: *Forverts*, June 2, 1933; *FAS*, June 9, 1933.

7. The **International Fur and Leather Workers Union** (IFLWU) was formed in 1913 and an affiliate of the AFL. In the 1920s it became a stronghold of Communist influence in the labor movement. The union joined the CIO in 1934 but was expelled in 1950 during the CIO's Cold War purge of Communist-dominated affiliates. **Morris Kaufman** (1884–1960) was a Russian-born Jewish furrier and socialist. He had been a Bundist before immigrating to the United States around 1902, and he joined the Socialist Party and the International Fur and Leather Workers Union upon its founding in 1913. Kaufman served as the union's president in 1918–1925 and 1929–1932 and, backed by the *Forverts*, opposed Communist influence within it. In 1935 he was convicted on corruption charges. **Oizer Shachtman** (1889–1955) was a Russian-born Jewish fur worker and union official. In the IFLWU he led the anti-Communist and anti-Kaufman "Progressive" tendency and served as the union's president in 1925–1929, during which he expelled numerous Communist members. **Benjamin Gold** (1898–1985) was a Russian-born Jewish fur worker, labor organizer, and Communist. A former member of the Socialist Parry, in 1919 he cofounded the Communist Labor Party of America. Gold first joined the IFLWU in 1912 and became a prominent leader in it, leading to repeated confrontations with the union's non-Communist leadership as well as with the national leadership of the AFL. In 1929 he left to help form the rival Needle Trades Workers Industrial Union, which in 1935 re-merged with the IFLWU. Gold served as president of the reunified union from 1937 until 1955.

that union: Sam Glassman, Fishkin, Moyshe Reitman, and many others, who had their hands full with the Communist bacchanalia there.[8]

We also spent much time occupied with the Fancy Leather Goods Workers' Union.[9] Ossip Walinsky, a comrade from London, and a good speaker albeit with a German accent, worked strongly for the union. Due to entanglements with the underworld during a difficult strike, he decided to withdraw and made the foolish mistake of finding a job with one of the big manufacturers before leaving the union. The *Forverts* spread rumors that Walinsky had become a partner of the rich boss. A thorough investigation proved this wrong, but the doubt that these lies engendered was enough to rattle the union, leading it to the brink of collapse. Little Isidore Wisotsky was then active in the union, trying to heal the wounds, and we helped him as much as possible. He went to almost all the big meetings, to get all the facts, and spent a lot of time on these problems.

For a long time, we were heavily involved with the confusing ups and downs of the Bakery and Confectionery Workers International Union, with hearings before the executive board of the United Hebrew Trades.[10] Among the bakers we always had good, dedicated comrades: Meyer Pollack, Sheynman, Morris Gross, Barnett Heller, and many others.[11] Their difficul-

---

8. **Sam Glassman** (Sem Glazman, c. 1893–?) was Russian-born Jewish fur worker and anarchist. He immigrated to the United States in 1915 and was affiliated with the "Progressive" faction in the International Fur and Leather Workers Union. **Moyshe ("Mack") Reitman** (Ritman, c. 1885–1950) was a Russian-born Jewish fur worker and anarchist. He had been active in the labor movement in Warsaw before fleeing to London after leading a furriers' strike. Reitman immigrated to the United States in 1920 and became secretary of Cutters Local 101 of the IFLWU. He aligned with the anti-Communist "Progressive" Group after Ben Gold became union president. Reitman later committed suicide following many years of worsening epilepsy and arthritis. Obituary: *FAS*, July 7, 1950.

9. The **Fancy Leather Goods Workers' Union** was an independent union formed in New York in 1910 by the United Hebrew Trades as an industrial union with socialist leadership. After several mergers it became the International Handbag, Leather Goods, Belt, and Novelty Workers Union, and in 1996 it was absorbed into the Service Employees' International Union.

10. The **Bakery and Confectionery Workers International Union of America** was founded by German immigrants in 1886 and affiliated with the AFL the following year. It had a close relationship with the United Hebrew Trades. After a series of mergers, in 1999 it became the Bakery, Confectionery, Tobacco Workers and Grain Millers International Union.

11. **Meyer Pollack** (Polak, c. 1888–?) was a Russian-born Jewish baker and anarchist. He immigrated in 1910 to Brooklyn, where he became a member of and business agent for Local 87 of the Bakery and Confectionery Workers International Union of America. In the

ties were always very close to our hearts. Together with their distinguished national organizer, Jacob Goldstone, and the secretary of the United Hebrew Trades, Morris Feinstone, we held meetings week in and week out for a long time.[12]

Feinstone was an interesting personality: an anarchist, a comrade originally from London, for years he managed through dedication and sincere work to maintain the highest office in the United Hebrew Trades, within which the *Forverts* machine was strong, as in all the high offices of the Workmen's Circle and in the unions under its supervision. In spite of this, Feinstone remained an anarchist his entire life and was closely interested everything our movement undertook. At the same time, he was involved in helping the Jewish workers in Palestine and carried out this activity on a very high level.

1920s he was arrested multiple times for strike activity. **Morris Gross** (Moyshe Gros) was a Russian-born Jewish baker and anarchist, and a member of Local 87 of the Bakery and Confectionery Workers International Union of America. **Barnett Heller** (Barnet Heler, 1891–?) was a Russian-born Jewish baker and anarchist. He immigrated to London before coming to the United States in 1912 and likewise became a member of Local 87, where he was known as "The Anarchist."

12. **Jacob Goldstone** (1871–1940), born Jacob Goldstein (Yankev Goldshteyn), was a Russian-born Jewish garment worker, labor organizer, and socialist. He immigrated to Scotland in 1887 and then to Boston in 1895. Goldstone was active in the Jewish labor and socialist movements and in 1903 was hired as the business agent of Hebrew Bakers Local 45. In 1908 he was elected general organizer of the Bakery and Confectionery Workers International Union, a position he held until his death, and he also aided the 1909 New York garment workers' strike.

CHAPTER 49

The *Fraye arbeter shtime*: Its Publishers and Staff

Throughout the years that I was associated with the *Fraye arbeter shtime*, we often designated our circle as the *Fraye arbeter shtime* "family." We all felt that we—the publishers, contributors, and readers—treated one another as members of one family, with the fullest respect and a great deal of friendship. It is worth saying something about the circle that worked together harmoniously for so many years.

The publication, for most of its years, had an editorial board of four members with whom I consulted on important matters. Through the years, the following individuals sat on the board: David Isakovitz, Benjamin Axler, Dr. James Globus, Simon Farber, Dr. Benjamin Dubovsky, Aaron Mintz, Louis Finkelstein, Dr. Michael A. Cohn, Hirsh Reiff, and a couple of others. All of them, with the exception of comrade Mintz (which is a long story [*parashah*] in itself), were steadfast coworkers, especially Axler and Isakovitz, my close friends throughout the years. During my twelve years with the newspaper, they contributed a great deal of work as writers in all areas. In addition, within our circles of comrades we had help from Dr. Jacob A. Maryson, William Nathanson, Dr. Herman Frank, Abba Gordin, Grigory (Grisha) Raiva, S. Retap, S. Davidson, William Shulman, Abe Frumkin, Yerakhmiel Lazarson, and the younger comrades, who took up every question of principles and tactics.[1] Comrade Simon Farber was, for most of this

---

1. **William Nathanson** (Viliam Natanson, 1883–1963) was a Russian-born Jewish teacher, writer, philosopher, and anarchist. He was active in the Bund as a student in Zhytomyr before immigrating around 1903 to the United States, where he studied medicine, philosophy, and psychology at the University of Illinois. Nathanson joined the anarchist movement

time, our expert and consultant on labor issues. From abroad, we had the cooperation of comrades Rudolf Rocker, Maria Korn, Dr. Max Nettlau, Dr. Israel Rubin, Dr. I. N. Steinberg, Alexander Berkman, Volin, and William Zuckerman.[2]

---

in Chicago and married fellow anarchist Dr. Miriam ("Becky") Yampolsky (c. 1882–?), a prominent birth control advocate. The couple were members of the David Edelstadt Group, hosted Emma Goldman's visit to Chicago in 1906 (during which they introduced her to Ben Reitman), ran a Modern School in 1910–1911, and in 1923 cofounded the Naye Gezelshaft Press. Nathanson was a regular contributor to the *FAS*, *Tsukunft*, and *Der tog*, as well as to the English-language magazine *Open Court* (1887–1906) and published numerous books on philosophy, the best-known being *Kultur un tsivilizatsye* (Culture and Civilization, 1923). Later in life Nathanson was affiliated with the Labor Zionist movement. Obituary: *FAS*, November 1, 1963. **Herman Frank** (1892–1952) was a Russian-born Jewish sociologist, writer, editor, and anarchist. He became a Zionist while a student in Kiev and was then active in the labor and anarchist movements in his hometown of Bialystok. Frank earned a PhD in sociology in Berlin before immigrating to the United States in 1923. An admirer of Gustav Landauer, he wrote on anarchism and many other topics for the *FAS*, *Gerekhtigkeyt*, *Tsukunft*, and the *Forverts*, and he edited the *FAS* from 1941 until his death. Frank also authored many books and pamphlets, including *Anarkho-sotsyalistishe ideyen un bavegungen bay yidn: historishe un teoretishe aynfirung* (Anarcho-Socialist Ideas and Movements among Jews: Historical and Theoretical Introduction, 1951) and a number of works on the history of Bialystok. **S. Retap** wrote regularly for the *FAS* from 1922 to 1936, mostly on cultural topics, and described himself as "a Russian journalist." **Simon Davidson** (Saymon Davidson, 1888–1963) was a Romanian-born Jewish garment worker, labor organizer, and anarchist. He immigrated to the United States in 1905 and became secretary of the ILGWU's Philadelphia Joint Board of the Cloak and Skirt Makers' Union. **Yerakhmiel Lazarson** (1893–1964) was a Russian-born Jewish writer, teacher, and anarchist. He was active in the Polish Socialist Party before emigrating in 1914 to New York, where he worked in a sweatshop, graduated from high school, and attended the Workmen's Circle's teachers' school, while also participating in the Jewish anarchist movement. In 1922 Lazarson moved to Atlanta and then lived in Dallas before returning to New York in 1931. He published articles in the *FAS*, *Forverts*, *Tsukunft*, *Der tog*, and other Yiddish periodicals.

2. **Maria Korn** (1871–1933), real name Marie Goldsmith, was a Russian-born Jewish scientist, writer, and anarchist. Her parents were both radicals who in 1884 fled to France, where Marie earned a PhD at the Sorbonne in 1915 and became a respected biologist. She belonged to the Socialist-Revolutionary Party as a teenager but in Paris became an anarchist and began to correspond with Peter Kropotkin and write for the *FAS* and other international anarchist publications. She committed suicide shortly after the death of her mother. **Israel Rubin** (1890–1954) was a Russian-born Jewish teacher, writer, and anarchist. In his youth he was active in the Bund, the Labor Zionist movement, and finally anarchism. Rubin worked as a teacher in Minsk, Vilnius, and Warsaw, and earned a doctorate in education. He immigrated to Germany in 1926 and to Palestine in 1929 and published articles on pedagogy and philosophy in the international Yiddish press, including the *FAS* and Joseph Cohen's *Der frayer gedank* (Free Thought, 1949–1962).

From non-anarchist circles we could always depend on collaboration from A. Almi, Abraham Bookstein, Benjamin Jacob Bialostotzky, Lazar Borodulin, Baruch Glasman, B. Y. Goldstein, Isaac Hourwich, Dr. Rafael Seligmann, Morris Jonah Chaimowitz, Daniel Charney, Leibush Lehrer, Hayim Lieberman, Jacob Milch, Leib Malach, Nakhmen Mayzil, Reuben Fink, Alter Epstein, A. M. Fuchs, Osher Kartozshinsky, Yekhezkl Kornhendler, Leon Krishtol, Melech Ravitch, Joshua Rappaport, Barukh Rivkin, and Dr. Jacob Shatzky.[3] At celebrations we enjoyed the friendly

---

3. **A. Almi** (1892–1963), real name Elyahu-Khayim ben Shloyme-Zalmen Sheps, was a Russian-born Jewish writer, poet, satirist, and agnostic. After immigrating to the United States in 1912 he became a contributor to the *FAS*, *Forverts*, *Tsukunft*, *Der tog*, and *Der groyser kundes*. **Abraham Bookstein** (Avrom Bukhshteyn, 1877–1958) was a Russian-born Jewish journalist and writer. In 1914 he immigrated to the United States, where he studied sociology and statistics at Columbia University. Bookstein published articles on political and economic topics in the *FAS*, *Der tog*, and other Yiddish periodicals. **Benjamin Jacob Bialostotzky** (Binyumen-Yankev Bialostotsky, 1892–1962) was a Russian-born Jewish writer, teacher, and Labor Zionist. He belonged to the territorialist wing of the Zionist movement in Kovno as a youth and in 1911 emigrated to the United States, where he joined Poale Zion and became a pioneer of Yiddish-language schooling. Bialostotzky wrote for the *Forverts*, the *FAS*, and other papers, and he edited the *Dovid Edelshtat gedenk-bukh* (David Edelstadt Memorial Book, 1953). **Lazar Borodulin** (1879–1947) was a Russian-born Jewish teacher and writer. He immigrated to the United States in 1907 and wrote popular articles on science and nature for the *FAS*, *Tsukunft*, *Der tog*, *Grekhtigkeyt*, and other outlets. **Baruch Glasman** (Borekh Glazman, 1893–1945) was a Russian-born Jewish housepainter and fiction writer. He immigrated to the United States in 1911 and published his first story in the *FAS* in 1913. Glassman also contributed fiction to *Tsukunft*, *Der idisher kemfer*, and other publications. **B. Y. Goldstein** (Borekh Y. Goldshteyn, 1879–1953) was a Russian-born Jewish writer, editor, and theater critic who lived in Montreal and Detroit. **Rafael Seligmann** (Refoel Zeligman, 1875–1943) was a Russian-born Jewish writer. He studied in Switzerland and then lived in Germany, and after the First World War began writing on Jewish social and cultural topics for the Yiddish press, including *Tsukunft* and the *FAS*. **Morris Jonah Chaimowitz** (Moyshe-Yoyne Khaymovitsh, 1881–1958) was a Russian-born Jewish tailor and writer. He immigrated to the United States in 1902 and published his first story in the *FAS* in 1905. Although he lived in relative poverty throughout his life, Chaimowitz became a leading Yiddish fiction writer and essayist. **Daniel Charney** (Tsharny, 1888–1959) was a Russian-born Jewish poet and writer. The youngest brother of Shmuel Niger and B. Charney Vladek, he wrote extensively for the international Yiddish press. Following the 1917 Russian Revolution he became secretary of the Folkspartei (Jewish People's Party), a liberal political party that advocated diasporic Jewish cultural autonomy, before briefly joining the publishing division of the Commissariat for Jewish National Affairs and then editing several Yiddish Communist journals. In 1924 he immigrated to Germany and from there attempted to come to the United States but was refused entry due to chronic health problems. In 1934 Charney fled to Latvia, Poland, and then France, and in 1941 he finally succeeded in coming to the United States, where he became secretary of the Y. L. Peretz

cooperation of Joseph Opatoshu, Ben-Zion Goldberg, A. Glanz-Leyeless, Dr. Chaim Zhitlowsky, H. Leivick, Dr. A. Mukdoyni, Shmuel Niger, Zivion,

---

Writers' Union and the Yiddish PEN Club. **Leibush Lehrer** (1887–1964) was a Russian-born Jewish garment worker, poet, writer, and teacher. He joined the Labor Zionist movement as a teenager and in 1909 immigrated to the United States, where he published poetry and prose in the *FAS, Fraye gezelshaft, Der tog, Tsukunft,* and other papers. Lehrer became a teacher at the Workmen's Circle's schools in New York and cofounded the Sholem Aleichem Folk Institute and Camp Boiberik, as well as the US branch of the YIVO Institute for Jewish Research. **Hayim Lieberman** (Khayim Liberman, 1889–1963) was a Russian-born Jewish writer, teacher, and Labor Zionist. He came to the United States in 1905 and wrote for the *Forverts, FAS, Der groyser kundes,* and other papers. A proponent of "radical education," Lieberman was in 1913 elected to the education committee of the Jewish National Labor Alliance. He wrote and translated numerous books on Jewish literature, life, and politics. **Jacob Milch** (Yankev Milkh, 1866–1945), born Yankev Zoyermilkh, was a Russian-born Jewish woodcutter, candy manufacturer, writer, and socialist. In 1891 he immigrated to the United States where he joined the SLP and helped publish its *Arbeter tsaytung.* Milch briefly became secretary of the United Hebrew Trades in 1893, and published articles and stories in the *FAS, Tsukunft* (which he briefly edited), *Forverts,* and elsewhere, as well as in English-language publications. He later became a successful businessman, joined the Communist Party, and sat on the executive board of the Organization for Jewish Colonization in Russia. **Leib Malach** (Leyb Malack, 1894–1936), real name Leyb Zaltsman, was a Polish-born Jewish poet, playwright, and Labor Zionist. He immigrated to Argentina in 1922, then to the United States, Israel, and France, and contributed to Yiddish publications throughout the world, including the *FAS.* **Nakhmen Mayzil** (1887–1966) was a Russian-born Jewish writer, editor, and publisher. He was a prolific contributor to the Yiddish press, often on the topic of Yiddish and Hebrew literature, and immigrated to the United States in 1937. **Reuben Fink** (1889–1961) was a Russian-born Jewish teacher, writer, and Labor Zionist. He immigrated to the United States in 1903 and became a prominent Yiddish journalist as well as manager of the Labor Zionist paper *Di tsayt* (The Times, 1920–1922). **Alter Epstein** (Epshteyn, 1879–1959) was a Russian-born Jewish journalist and critic. He was active in the Bund before emigrating in 1908 to the United States, where he contributed to the *Forverts, Tsukunft, Der tog,* and the *FAS,* among other papers, often on the Yiddish theater. **A. M. Fuchs** (Avrom-Moyshe Fuks, 1890–1974) was an Austrian Galician-born Jewish journalist, fiction writer, and socialist. He was active in the Galician Bund and the Labor Zionist movement and lived in New York in 1912–1914 before returning to Europe. Fuchs worked as a correspondent for the Austrian Yiddish press and later the *Forverts,* and was arrested by the Nazis in 1938 but was able to make his way to western Europe. **Osher Kartozshinsky** (1882–1933), also known as Oscar Carter, was a Russian-born Jewish writer, playwright, and theater producer. He immigrated to the United States in 1914 and was an occasional contributor to the *FAS, Forverts, Tsukunft,* and other papers until the mid-1920s. **Yekhezkl Kornhendler** (1899–1984) was a Russian-born Jewish writer. He immigrated to Germany and then France, where he wrote fiction, history, and articles on contemporary topics for Yiddish publications in both France and the Americas. **Leon Krishtol** (1894–1954) was a Russian-born Jewish journalist, critic, and translator. He immigrated to New York in 1914 and became manager of the Yiddish Art Theatre as well as a theater critic for the *FAS* and a

Dr. Abraham Coralnik, Hillel Rogoff, and Abraham Reisen.[4] The number of essayists and poets are too numerous to count—Rachel Okrent, Fishel

---

contributor to the *Forverts* and other Yiddish publications. In 1956, after traveling to the Soviet Union, he helped break the story of the secret 1952 executions of thirteen Yiddish writers who had belonged to the Jewish Anti-Fascist Committee. **Melech Ravitch** (Meylekh Ravitsh, 1893–1976) was an Austrian Galician-born Jewish essayist and poet. In the 1920s he became a contributor to Yiddish papers in the United States and elsewhere, and beginning in the 1930s he traveled extensively across the globe. **Joshua Rappaport** (Yeshue Rapaport, 1895–1971) was a prominent Russian-born Jewish literary critic, a prolific translator, and a Labor Zionist. **B. Rivkin** (1883–1945), real name Borekh-Avrom Vaynrib, was a Russian-born journalist, literary critic, and anarchist. He joined the Bund in 1903 and was arrested the following year for revolutionary activity, leading him to flee to western Europe in 1905. In 1908 Rivkin began writing for anarchist publications in Geneva, followed by contributions to London's *Arbeter fraynd* and *Zsherminal*. In 1911 he immigrated to New York, where he became a prolific writer for the Yiddish press and an editor of *Tsukunft*. Much of Rivkin's writings developed the idea of the liberatory and messianic role of Yiddish literature that he argued had functionally replaced both Judaism and a Jewish homeland. Nevertheless, Rivkin was an eclectic thinker and was also sympathetic to Labor Zionism and socialist territorialism. In the words of Melech Ravitch, Rivkin was "a mystical-naturalist, a pious-religious-heretic, a socialist-communist, anarchist-democrat, liberal-reactionary, yiddishist-hebraist, [and] assimilationist-chauvinist" ("B. Rivkin—Portret," in *B. Rivkin lebn un shafn*, ed. Mina Bordo-Rivkin [New York: Aber Press, 1953], 76). This ideological promiscuity is likely the reason Joseph Cohen here categorizes Rivkin as a "non-anarchist." **Jacob Shatzky** (Yankev Shatsky, 1893–1956) was a Russian-born Jewish teacher and historian of Jewish life, literature, and philosophy. After serving in the Polish Legions in the First World War, he immigrated in 1922 to the United States where he cofounded the American division of the YIVO Institute for Jewish Research and wrote hundreds of articles for the Yiddish press (including a scathing review of this book).

4. **Joseph Opatoshu** (1886–1954), real name Yoysef-Meyer Opatovsky, was a Russian-born Jewish teacher and writer. In 1907 he immigrated to New York, and in 1910 he began publishing short stories and serialized novels in Yiddish publications, including the *FAS*, *Tsukunft*, and *Der tog*. Opatoshu was a prominent member of the Yiddish literary movement known as *Di yunge* (The Young Ones.) **Ben-Zion Goldberg** (1895–1972), real name Ben-Tsien Veyf, was a Russian-born Jewish psychologist and journalist. He was the son-in-law of celebrated Yiddish writer Sholem Aleichem (1859–1916) and a columnist for *Der tog* who wrote on a wide variety of topics. Goldberg later became a Communist fellow traveler. **A. Glanz-Leyeless** (Arn Glants-Leyeles, 1889–1966) was a Russian-born Jewish poet, journalist, literary critic, and socialist territorialist. In 1905 he immigrated to London, where he was active in the Zionist Socialist Workers Party, and then in 1909 he moved to New York, where he joined the socialist territorialist movement and contributed to territorialist publications as well as to publications like *Tsukunft*, *Gerekhtigkeyt*, and the *FAS*. Glanz-Leyeless cofounded several Yiddish schools in the United States and was a member of many Yiddish literary and cultural institutions, including the modernist literary magazine *In zikh* (1920–1939). **H. Leivick** (1888–1962), real name Leyvik Halpern, was a Russian-born Jewish poet, novelist, and playwright. In 1905 he joined the Bund, resulting in multiple arrests and sentences

Bimko, Shmuel Deiksel, David Gisnet, Shimen Yudkov, Menashe Zinkin, and dozens of others published their work in our newspaper.[5]

In my time, at least, the *Fraye arbeter shtime* never had the money to pay its contributors. There could be no question of commissioning articles and determining their content in advance. What we did have, on the one hand, was the friendship and goodwill of the writers, and on the other, we had the help of Aaron Mintz, which was exceedingly important to us.

Mintz was, for many years, a unique institution in the Jewish literary and publishing world. He was from a prominent family in Poland, came to America as a young boy in the 1880s, and became active in our movement. His brothers were the publishers of the *Yidishe folkstsaytung* and other papers.

---

to hard labor and Siberian exile. Leivick escaped to the United States in 1913 and began contributing poems, often on political and autobiographical themes, to the *FAS*, *Tsukunft*, and other publications. In the 1920s he became a Communist fellow traveler and wrote for the Communist *Frayheyt* until it defended anti-Jewish riots in Palestine in 1929. Leivick then became a writer for *Der tog* and cut all ties to radicalism following the Hitler-Stalin Pact. **A. Mukdoyni** (Mukdoni, 1878–1958), real name Aleksander Kapel, was a Russian-born Jewish journalist, critic, and Labor Zionist. By the time to immigrated to the United States in 1922 he was already well known as one of the first theater critics in Yiddish journalism. **Abraham Coralnik** (Avrom Koralnik, 1883–1937) was a Russian-born Jewish journalist and Zionist. He immigrated to New York in 1915 and became a regular writer for *Der tog*, occasionally contributing to other papers as well, including the *FAS*. **Abraham Reisen** (Avrom Reyzen, 1876–1953) was a Russian-born Jewish poet, writer, and socialist. Following two earlier stays, he settled permanently in the United States during the First World War and contributed to many radical Yiddish periodicals.

5. **Rachel Okrent** (Rokhl Okrent) was a Jewish poet, fiction writer, essayist, and anarchist who lived in Glasgow and contributed regularly—and seemingly exclusively—to the *FAS* between 1930 and 1945. **Fishel Bimko** (1890–1965) was a Russian-born Jewish fiction writer and playwright who had been arrested for revolutionary activities as a teenager, immigrated to the United States in 1921, and was known for his social realism. **Shmuel Deiksel** (Shmuel Dayksel, 1886–1975) was a Russian-born Jewish fiction writer. He participated in the revolutionary movement before emigrating to the United States in 1911, and in 1915 he debuted as a writer in the *FAS*, to which he contributed regularly into the 1920s. **Shimen Yudkov** (1889–1959) was a Russian-born Jewish writer and playwright. He moved to the United States in 1907 and from 1919 to 1940 published a series of stories and one-act plays in the *FAS*. **Menashe Zinkin** (Tsinkin, 1880–1969) was a Russian-born Jewish garment worker, journalist, writer, and anarchist. After coming to the United States in 1910 he was active in the Jewish anarchist movement and ILGWU and contributed autobiographical sketches about working-class life to the *FAS*, *Gerekhtigkeyt*, *Der yunton arbeter*, and the *Forverts*. A collection of his writings was published as *In shap un oysern shap: bilder un skitsen fun dem arbeyters leben* (Inside and Outside the Shop: Pictures and Sketches of Working Life, 1951), and in English as *Through the Eye of a Needle: Shop Sketches* (1955).

Keni Liptzin was married to one of his brothers and brought the family into the wonderful world of theater.[6] In the 1890s Aaron Mintz went to London, where he worked in the Jewish anarchist movement there and caused an upheaval. He took over part of the editorial work of the *Arbeter fraynd*, organized the Frayheyt Group, and published a series of pamphlets that sold in the thousands. He adorned them all with attractive title pages and saw to it that the printing was beautifully done. Among the pamphlets he published were Kropotkin's memoirs, with a series of splendid pictures. Before leaving London in 1905, he returned this valuable property, with profits, to the Arbeter Fraynd Group.

He was tall in his youth, handsome in appearance, a good orator and skilled speaker. Shortly after his return to the United States, he lost his vision and for thirty-five years relied on the help of Nokhum Vaynritsh, who became an almost indivisible part of him. Mintz and Vaynritsh were like Siamese twins. Where you saw one you were certain to see the other. They were inseparable all those years.

The *Fraye arbeter shtime* became the center of Mintz's universe. He spent all day at its office. With Nokhum Vaynritsh's help, he kept track of everything printed in Yiddish, everything that was performed on the stage and in the moving pictures. He was acquainted with all the Yiddish poets and writers, recognized them by their voices, and could tell by the sound of their voice how they felt, and even how they looked. Over the years his spirit developed wonderfully, and he became a true encyclopedia of the Yiddish literary world. He knew everyone, and they knew and respected him. His opinion mattered, and through his efforts a Yiddish writer could find employment or an introduction to the public.

In Yanovsky's day, Mintz had to use diplomacy to persuade a famous writer to do a favor, pen an article, or write a poem for the *Fraye arbeter shtime*, and at the same time to make Yanovsky feel that he was doing the writer a favor by publishing it. He didn't need to play at diplomacy with me. We knew each other well and understood each other perfectly. We did not always agree on everything. Mintz was at times a difficult person to bear having in your company day after day, but his devotion to the *Fraye arbeter*

6. **Keni Liptzin** (1856–1918) was a Russian-born Jewish actress and star of the Yiddish theater in England and the United States. Her husband was newspaper editor and stage manager Michael Mintz (Mikhl Mints, 1858–1912).

shtime, his sincere love for the newspaper, and his helpfulness atoned for everything.

Vaynritsh also possessed many virtues, as well as the ability to write a good feuilleton when the spirit moved him to take the pen in hand, which was not often enough—a great virtue among those closely associated with the paper. He was always ready to do what he could for the *Fraye arbeter shtime*.

Also characteristic was the collaboration and work of Isaac Hourwich. He was the best friend that we had at that time, always encouraging and helping us. Whenever there was trouble, I would seek him out, saying that we needed an article. He would come up to the office with me, and I would give him a mountain of paper, the kind used to print proofs, as well as a pen, a pot of glue, and a brush. His handwriting in Yiddish was chicken scratch (*kakshers mit lopetes*) in crooked lines. For a paragraph of several sentences, he needed a large sheet of paper which he usually cut with scissors like a jigsaw puzzle and glued back together on another sheet of paper. One article of two columns written in Yiddish used up a ream of paper.

Another collaborator I happily received and often spent hours with was Jacob Milch. A wise Jew, a scholar, an orthodox (*frumer*) Marxist, and a worldly man, he was part of the Yiddish socialist literary family for all of his years but reached beyond it. It was always interesting to discuss and debate our differences between Marxism and anarchism, between the theory of class struggle and the concept of mutual aid. We learned much from each other.

❊ ❊ ❊

For its first five years of existence the *Fraye arbeter shtime* did not have a manager. After that Louis Elstein had the pleasure of doing the job for a short time. Following the demise of the *Abend tsaytung*, Louis Finkelstein managed the paper for several years, and Benjamin Dubovsky helped him out with all the bookkeeping.

Shloyme Pres ("Der Kleynshtetldiker") was for a time associated with our office. Nokhum Vaynritsh was also manager for many years—but the newspaper, in black and white, never mentioned who the manager, with whom subscribers actually had to deal, was.

In my time, Axler and I co-managed the office together for about two years. But neither of us had time for the work. I was busy with editorial work, and Axler worked on the press. We brought in a second linotype machine, and, after putting in a lot of work, we were able to engage comrade Bernard Shane, who had just been released from his job as manager of the Cloakmakers' Union. He ran the shop, increasing the printing work, until he was burned out after two years of effort. Comrade Morris Shutz took his place and continued the same work—maintaining close relations with the printers' unions, in particular—and helped put on the twenty-fifth anniversary celebrations, for which we released a much-expanded issue of the *Fraye arbeter shtime* with almost a hundred articles by the best Yiddish writers. But by the end of 1925 he was also tired out.

We then managed to entice comrade Abe Grosner to come from Philadelphia to take over the management. He too managed to endure for about two years—there was no more strength, neither in him nor in the newspaper. We sank more and more into debt. The last manager during my tenure was Samuel Freedman, with whom there was no longer any question of becoming exhausted or leaving the job. He was a man of extraordinary endurance. During his many years as business manager in the Raincoat Makers' Union, it was said, he wore down the bosses during negotiations until they gave into the union's demands. He broke the curse of the two-year term for managers. He outlasted me at the paper, as well as the next couple of editors.

Abe Grosner had the good idea of hiring a young, intelligent, lively girl, Sima Rosen, a daughter of comrades in Winnipeg.[7] She was a graduate of the Peretz School there, and could speak, read, and write Yiddish well, both by hand and on the typewriter.[8] Her presence cheered up the office, bringing purity and vitality to its atmosphere.

---

7. **Sima Rosen** (1908–1993) was a Canadian-born Jewish bookkeeper and anarchist and the daughter of anarchists William and Rebecca Rosen. She came to the United States in 1930 to help manage the *FAS* and a few years later moved to the Sunrise Colony, where she married anarchist Aaron Kitzes (1900–1964). The couple later settled in Los Angeles and were active in the Kropotkin Literary Society, Branch 413 of the Workmen's Circle.

8. The **I. L. Peretz School** (originally called the Jewish Radical School) was a secular Yiddish day school founded by the Workmen's Circle in Winnipeg in 1914. Anarchist Feivel Simkin was one of its directors. Through a series of mergers, the school evolved into the Gray Academy of Jewish Education, which still exists as of 2023.

All those active around the *Fraye arbeter shtime* were, of course, comradely collaborators, like those I have mentioned above. All the members of the board of directors were delegates from the New York groups, including Tania Schapiro, Sam Rothman, Morris Shutz, Max Horowitz, Sam Margolis, Hannah Lake, Benjamin, and Isaac Radinowsky, who were the most active members. In addition, we had a number of individuals who were always ready and willing to help—V. Polyak, Jacob Genn, Fayn, Leibush Frumkin, Isidore Wisotsky, and many others.[9]

For example: during one of the many crises that the publication went through in those years, we, as always, appealed to the comrades and readers, asking them for three things: to pay their debts, to make a donation of whatever they could, and to lend us a little money until things improved. A man in work clothes, whom I had never met before, came into the office and said that he wished to pay his debt—he thought he owed us seven and a half dollars, for three years of the paper.

Very well, that would come in handy for us.

Before we could ask him his name in order to check our records and make a receipt, he said: "I see you need money, that you're asking for donations, so I'll give you twenty-five dollars!"

Well, this was, of course, even better. That was a bundle of cash in those troubled times. But he was not done yet: "If you want a loan," the unknown man said to us, "I'll lend you a hundred dollars!"

Said and done. He wrote out a check for $132.50. Half a week of life! He was comrade A. Y. Shapiro, the plumber, who afterward became a frequent visitor.

I don't want to leave the impression that we had many such friends,

---

9. **Jacob Genn** (Gen, 1886–1953) was a Russian-born Jewish garment worker and anarchist. In 1910 he immigrated to New York, where he sold copies of *FAS* on the street. His children Sally Genn (Sore Gen, 1920–1985) and Irving Genn (Yitskhok Gen, 1925–1991) also became anarchists, and the whole family belonged to the Amshol Group in the Bronx. **David ("Leibush") Frumkin** (1886–1964) was a Russian-born Jewish garment worker, labor organizer, and anarchist. He was involved in the anarchist movement in Warsaw and participated in the 1905 Revolution before immigrating to England and then to the United States in 1912. Frumkin became an executive board member of ILGWU Local 22 and helped to produce the *FAS*, and his children, including Rose Frumkin Pogrebysky, attended the Stelton Modern School. He was an active member of Ferrer-Rocker Branch 364 of the Workmen's Circle up until his death, and in 1957, at the age of seventy-one and retired, he was arrested for picketing a New York factory on behalf of ILGWU. Obituary: *FAS*, November 1, 1965.

who could write hundred-dollar checks, but there were a few: Isaac A. Benequit, Harris Mindlin, Dr. Michael A. Cohn, and even Yanovsky, at one of our anniversary banquets.[10] But in large part the *Fraye arbeter shtime* was financed by contributions from ordinary workers, who gave a proportionately much larger share of their earnings and wealth than our rich and respectable friends.

Another source of support came from donations from the unions and the Workmen's Circle. Over the years, they always contributed a considerable amount of money. Our mainstay was the International Ladies' Garment Workers' Union, whose Joint Boards and various locals were always ready to help us no matter the circumstances, even though they were often quite dissatisfied with our viewpoint. The Amalgamated Clothing Workers of America supported the *Fraye arbeter shtime* with a generous hand in its early years, but after Sidney Hillman came back from Soviet Russia as a Communist fellow traveler, he would not allow old Chaim Weinberg, our messenger, to address the union's convention. We were not kosher enough for Hillman's political orientation at that time, and we never really found favor in the eyes of His Royal Highness (*dem groysn prits*).

But as the prophet says somewhere: *Merubbim tzarechei ammecha veda'tam ketzarah!* (Many are the needs of your people but their mentality is shrunken!)[11]—the needs of a radical newspaper are great, and the income is always too small. In 1905 the paper cost $8,000. One-third or more of that amount had to be collected through donations and fund-raising. Twenty years later, in 1925, spending had increased by more than 100 percent—the cost was $18,000 that year, and once again more than a third, a total of $7,000 to $8,000, had to be generated on the side. Our summer fund-raiser, the famous "excursion," had long been abandoned. There were a couple of unhappy experiences. But we usually had three events a year: an anniversary banquet, a *boyern bal* (peasants' ball), and a theater benefit.

---

10. **Harris Mindlin** (c. 1867–1933) was a Russian-born Jewish manager and anarchist. After immigrating to New York in 1883 he became, according to the *FAS*, "one of the first Jewish anarchists in America" and a member of the Pioneers of Liberty. Mindlin was publisher of the first *Fraye gezelshaft* and financially supported the *FAS* up until his death. Obituary: *FAS*, April 14, 1933.

11. Cohen here quotes a Hebrew line from a closing prayer (Ne'ila) for Yom Kippur. This English translation is taken from Sefaria, https://www.sefaria.org/.

The best event for a while was the anniversary banquet. In New York, we could always get a large audience. We did well in good times, raising from $1,500 to $2,000 in donations, all of it pure income. However, the *boyern bal* required a lot of work and was not always a great success. For a few years we put on the ball in the Armory on Thirty-Fourth Street. Five or six thousand people would not feel crowded in there. There two incidents were etched into my memory.

When Sam Margolis and I went to the Armory one evening to pay the $600 rent for the hall, the manager, a colonel, told us: the police and the firemen have a nasty habit—as soon as the general public begins to arrive (and they all arrive within about an hour's time), a couple of police or firemen would show up, take a look at the hall, and order the doors closed, not allowing any more people in, to prevent a fire hazard. Until you straightened the matter out with them and got them to shut their mouths and look the other way, the entrance would remain blocked!

We had heard of and seen such things happen at large events and our excursions. It is not at all pleasant to face such an obstacle. So we asked him: "How can we avoid it?"

Without a trace of embarrassment, he said: "Go see the police captain of this district. Put something in the palm of his hand, and everything will be all right!"

Well, what won't one do for the movement? We went to the police station and into the captain's office and began telling him: "Today we are going to have a ball in the Armory. . ."

He looked at us sternly and began to give us quite a scolding. But as soon as he saw dollar bills rolled up like a cigarette coming across his desk, he became soft as butter. He stood up and asked in a friendly tone if there was anything he could do for us, assuring us that there would be no trouble.

He kept his word. He sent a sergeant to stand at the door and not let anything interfere.

The second incident concerns protecting the money that such evenings brought in, several thousand dollars, from misfortune (*beyz oyg*). Not only could it be stolen but a life could be taken for it. Such things happen in America.

We found out that some banks have safe deposit boxes which are accessible all night. You can come at any time, bring whatever you want, and leave it in a locked box. No one asks you who you are, what you brought, or where you got it. The whole thing cost a dollar a day to keep it there. The only problem was getting the money there. This was not too difficult. Sam Rothman and Morris Weitzman (Granberg) came along as bodyguards, with kosher mezuzahs in their hands.[12] They escorted me there, where a heavy iron door opened when we rang the bell and closed by itself behind us. Downstairs, in a deep cellar, a second heavy iron door opened and let us into the sanctorum (*mokem-kodesh*), where we no longer had any worries or fears. Two little old men in slippers took care of everything.

Oh boy, America is a blessed land! Everything is taken care of. After a successful theft or a deadly hold-up, even a robber can put the loot in a safe place for a dollar a day. And only they will to able to access it.

The *boyern bal* usually generated an income, but it had long since outlived its day as entertainment. The whole thing seemed too childish to spend so much time on. One year we decided—Enough! What does Mitchell Kaplan say? "An end should take it!"[13] We needed to find another kind of entertainment more suited to the commercial spirit of the times. We started holding bazaars, which for a time were an annual institution and were also associated with a lot of work and difficulties but were somewhat more satisfying.

These were the means by which the *Fraye arbeter shtime* was sustained all the years of its existence. The theater benefits were never a great success financially and often not in terms of morale either. Something was missing in the Yiddish theater; the atmosphere around it was a barrier to the satisfaction of the intellectual people who came out for an evening's entertainment.

We never learned how to be successful as businesspeople. We expanded the print shop, the sale of books, and the circle of subscribers through all sorts of premiums, but there was little blessing in all of this. At Mintz's suggestion we persuaded Benequit to buy us a third linotype machine—at a cost

---

12. **Mezuzahs** are small cylinders that hold pieces of parchment inscribed with verses from the Torah and are affixed to the doorposts of Jewish homes or worn as lockets. They were popularly thought to ward off ill fortune, which may be why the two men carried them. Alternatively, mezuzahs are often made of metal and could have been clutched to add weight to the (presumably atheist) anarchists' punches in the event of an attempted robbery.

13. **Mitchell (Mikhl) Kaplan** (1882–1944) was a Russian-born Jewish poet who immigrated to the United States in 1905. However, this phrase actually seems to have been coined by one of Kaplan's contemporaries, poet and *Der groyser kundes* founder Yoysef Tunkel, in his 1924 story "A teater fun kaptsonim" (A Theater for Beggars).

of several thousand dollars—but it was not of great benefit to us. The *Fraye arbeter shtime*'s debt grew larger and larger. Those to whom we owed money were some of our own people employed in our own office and printshop; others, outsiders, had to be paid on time. By 1932 the compositors, Axler and Senderov, were owed by the office over $1,000 each, as was I. In my case, that meant almost a year's salary at $35 a week. Only thanks to the hard work of my wife Sophie was it possible for us to endure. Sometime later, when I was still living at the Sunrise Colony, I calculated that the debt of $1,200 that the *Fraye Arbeter Stime* still owed me could be considered a reduction in my wages of two dollars a week for the twelve years that I had worked there. It was not much of a sacrifice. I let Sam Freedman, the manager, wipe my debt from the books and forget the whole thing. The compositors, I heard through the grapevine, were given a linotype machine as payment. The bottom line is that the *Fraye arbeter shtime* never stole anything from anyone, no matter its difficulties and crises, and did not remain in debt to anyone.

We made a few attempts to deal with the deficit in a systematic way. The amount was constant, around $7,000 to $8,000 a year. We tried to introduce a quota of a certain amount for each group to contribute regularly every month, and to do so without waiting for appeals or calls. The women's group in Detroit was the only one that took this suggestion seriously and paid more.[14] For decades, they made monthly contributions in addition to other donations throughout the year. None of the other groups passed this test. Some contributed more than their quota each year. Los Angeles and Philadelphia excelled in this area, but even they did not send the money until they were convinced that the paper was in dire need.

We found it necessary to send someone all over the country to visit readers and subscribers. We also tried to send speakers, lecturers—old Comrade Weinberg, Simon Farber, and Alexander Brown—and once even persuaded comrade Shulman to travel across the country. They were not successful. Finally, we sent out comrade Benjamin Surasky, a simple worker, an active man, and remarkably he excelled at the task. He circled the entire country back and forth several times, and though the comrades in many cities

---

14. The **Froyen Grupe "Fraye Gezelshaft"** ("Free Society" Women's Group) was active from around 1932 to 1947 and held annual fund-raising "bazaars" on behalf of the *FAS*. Other Jewish anarchist women's groups subsequently formed in Miami, the Bronx, and Philadelphia (including one affiliated with the Radical Library).

grumbled loudly, he did much for the newspaper and increased its circle of readers.

Under the management of comrade Sol Linder, the financial condition of the *Fraye arbeter shtime* improved, I have been told. The paper was able to pay its employees every week and to meet all its expenses each year. Of course, wartime prosperity likely helped to some extent, but much of the credit undoubtedly goes to Linder for his dedicated and successful activity. He materially placed the newspaper on solid ground.

It is much more difficult to evaluate and record the spiritual state of the paper, its accomplishments and failures. No publication can please all its readers all the time. Certainly, the *Fraye arbeter shtime* is no exception. On the contrary, the *Fraye arbeter shtime* had a readership of highly intelligent people with well-honed political, social, and national views. The greatest sage (*goen*) would not be able to satisfy them all—especially after the newspaper so many years ago fell into the hands of me, a man who did not possess any of the qualities which a truly good editor can claim. I lacked a lot of knowledge and perhaps determination. Born and raised in Lithuania, in a cold, skeptical atmosphere, I did not have the kind of fiery enthusiasm that flares up and ignites others. I am by nature cautious, skeptical, and cool-blooded—I always see both sides of the coin, the good as well as the bad, and I seldom get hung up on one thing. In addition, among the comrades I was my own man, a "rank-and-filer" with no title and, above all, no ambitions—a very important quality for a community activist (*klal-tuer*), a leader in a movement. I did not impress my comrades, nor did I arouse in them any reverence for the high office that I held. It also did not help that I replaced a man like Saul Yanovsky, who was arguably the most successful editor of a weekly newspaper. I find myself empathizing with Truman, whom fate placed in the shoes of the great President Roosevelt. There is no comparison with the predecessor.

The comrades and readers put me under a microscope (*leyener mir gekukt oyf di finger*), watching every expression and criticizing every turn of phrase. Some did not like my praise of Lenin after his death. Others did not agree with my position on Bolshevism—in Russia, not in America—or on nationalism, on Palestine, and similar issues. Others thought I was a heretic based on my criticism of many anarchist views, and almost all of them demanded more sharpness, that I "show more teeth," as they used to put it, be more partisan, more relentless in relation to opponents.

The only small virtues I possessed were ingenuity, perseverance, and the willingness to do the work to build the movement. For me and the comrades around me, it was an important duty to publish the newspaper every week, even if there was no money in the coffers and no opportunity of getting any. We never entertained the idea of closing the paper or even skipping a single week. When a fire destroyed everything in the basement office at 23 Division Street and severely damaged the typesetting machines, the *Fraye arbeter shtime* did not fail to appear with its usual format and content. And filling out an issue of the paper in those years was a chore, as it was at least twice the size that it would later become. The paper had only six pages, but it contained more reading material than in its previous eight pages, of which three had been taken up with advertisements. It took ten articles, in addition to the front page, serialized stories, letters, and other items to fill out an issue. This necessitated and was made possible by a wide selection of contributions such as "Philosophical Discourses" (*Filozofishe shmuesn*) by Dr. Mem (Jacob Milch), "Spinoza's Life and Ideas" by Dr. Jacob Shatzky, and other long treatises from which intelligent readers learned so much.

Among the features I was able to publish, which in a more favorable time and in a more widely used language would have been worthy of being put out in book form, I will mention just two: the biographies of great revolutionary leaders, in a series on which Abe Frumkin worked long and hard, and the series "Social Credos" (*Sotsiale ani-maymen*), which was of great significance and rich in original contributions.

I did my work to the fullest, according to my limited abilities and under the difficult circumstances of those times. I approached my duties seriously and found great satisfaction in them. I considered it a great honor and an undeserved happiness to be able to serve the movement in this area. I was truly convinced that to be the editor of the *Fraye arbeter shtime* one must, first, be able to write; and second, be an anarchist, active and experienced in the movement, familiar with its history and steeped in its traditions. Life has since shown me that not one of these things is absolutely necessary. One can get on without them. But life teaches us many things, and my disappointment in this respect did not come as a great surprise.[15]

---

15. This is a veiled reference to Mark Mratchny, who edited the *FAS* from 1934 to 1940 and whom in Cohen's opinion met neither criterion.

I had a very unfortunate experience as editor with Yanovsky's autobiography. I would have been very happy to publish it in the *Fraye arbeter shtime*, but he had other plans. During his lecture tours, he solicited subscriptions of five dollars toward publishing his memoirs in three volumes. He expected at least a few thousand subscribers; but his friends, with great difficulty, could only sign up five hundred—too few to publish three books and have any income from them. I persuaded him to let us start serializing in the paper the volume containing his experiences as editor of the *Fraye arbeter shtime*.[16] But the spirit moved him to touch on the time when Chaim Zhitlowsky came to America and began his work here on behalf of Jewish nationalism. Speaking about Zhitlowsky, Yanovsky described him as a great figure with feet of clay.

Well, that did it! I received protests from all sides. Dr. Jacob A. Maryson was especially angry with me. How could I allow such a thing?

I was adamant that I was not responsible for what Yanovsky—or anyone else like him—wrote, despite the fact that I was the editor. To me, to edit or censor the writing of Yanovsky, Zhitlowsky, or Dr. Maryson himself would have taken enormous chutzpah. They were adults who could take responsibility of their own words and opinions.

The situation became very unpleasant for me.

Yanovsky realized this and sent no further chapters. He expected a large number of readers to demand their continuation. This, however, did not occur. His memoirs were not destined to see the light of day.

We negotiated with him several times about publishing the books. He rejected the suggestion that he give us the money he had collected and we would publish all three volumes, no matter the cost. We then offered to let him hire a typesetter to set type and use our press, lead, and gas, without charging him a cent; he would only have to pay the typesetter, which would cut his costs in half. He really liked this idea, but he did not hurry to start the work, and then the crash on Wall Street wiped out everything that Yanovsky owned, including his property and the subscribers' money. There was nothing left to talk about or negotiate.

To tell the truth, I strongly suspect that he did not have all three volumes written. The project was, apparently, clear in his mind, and he spoke of them as though they was already finished. In reality, he did not finish anything.

16. *FAS*, October 19, 1928, and February 1 through June 28, 1929.

During the few months that his memoirs were published in the newspaper, he held onto the manuscript, typed on large sheets of cheap paper, and brought in just enough each week for the following issue. After his death, only the manuscript of the first volume was discovered in the office of the *Fraye arbeter shtime*, which briefly describes his childhood, his experiences in America in the 1880s, and the time he spent in London. It is a very interesting account, written as best as Yanovsky could. There is a wealth of material on the history of our movement there.[17] But Yanovsky took to his grave the rich memories of the later era in which he played no small role.

---

17. Saul Yanovsky, *Ershte yorn fun yidishn frayheytlekhn sotsializm: oytobiografishe zikhroynes fun a pioner un boyer fun der yidisher anarkhistisher bavegung in England un Amerike* (New York: Fraye Arbeter Shtime, 1948).

CHAPTER 50

Our Movement: The Federation and Its Work

From the time of Bakunin, anarchists in all countries and in all periods organized in the same way. Wherever a number of anarchists wanted to do something to spread their ideal, they organized themselves into a group under a certain name and conducted their activities quite independently. In larger cities, where there were several groups, they united in a citywide federation to carry out larger projects. In most countries, there were national federations—loose associations for consultation, without any jurisdiction over the activities of the individual groups.

Here in America, where there were so many different national and linguistic groups, most federations were created according to the language in which groups carried out their activity. In the larger cities, there were a number of federations with no direct links to each other. For a time, there was a tendency in our movement to create conspiratorial cells, even when there was no basis for it. Comrade Simon Farber recounts, for example, that in 1904 or 1905, when he arrived in New York, he joined such a group, which was intent on having its own underground printing press. One of the members built a primitive press entirely in the Russian style, though there was no need for it at the time. Similar attempts were made in later years by small groups. The last secret printing operation, as far as I know, was set up during the First World War, when A. Mitchell Palmer actually drove the movement underground.

At the end of 1913, when I first moved to New York, our movement had a large number of groups active in various languages. In our Jewish circles there was a group in Brownsville called the Friends of Art and Education, which led a wide range of activities; in Harlem there was the Broyt un Frayheyt (Bread and Freedom) Group with its own small printing house that published a few pamphlets and began printing a Yiddish edition of *The Famous Speeches of the Eight Chicago Anarchists*; the Anarkhie Group, founded in 1910 by comrades who came from London and by this time had renamed it the Naye Gezelshaft Group, Branch 364 of the Workmen's Circle, which sought to lead the movement to undertake constructive activity; the Arbeter Fraynd Group, which was mainly concerned with the distribution of pamphlets and newspapers published in London; the Anarchist Red Cross, with its broad relief effort on behalf of comrades imprisoned in Russia; the Zsherminal (Germinal) Group (a unique body that undertook revolutionary agitation by distributing large numbers of a free leaflet every month); the Ferrer Association, with its school and center; the Mother Earth Group, with its publications, lectures, and other activities; and the Syndicalist Educational League and later the Anti-Militarist League, which did good work.[1] The Russian anarchists, likewise, had a large number of groups associated with the Union of Russian Workers, which put out the weekly newspaper *Golos Truda*. The Spanish, Italian, and French anarchists also had their own newspapers and organizations. Many groups held their meetings in the Ferrer Center, creating a truly international movement.

In the summer of 1914, we celebrated the hundredth birthday of Mikhail Bakunin with a huge mass meeting to which admission was free. We published a large pamphlet on Bakunin's life, ideas, and activities for the occasion, thousands of copies of which were distributed for free.[2] The united groups covered all the expenses and carried out the whole thing in a grand manner.

When I came to New York City for the second time in late 1920, there was no trace of any of these groups and activities. Some had left for Russia

---

1. The Zsherminal Group's publications included Katherina Yevzerov, *Di froy in di gezelshaft* (Woman in Society) (New York: Grupe Zsherminal, 1907) and Peter Kropotkin, *Tsum yungen dor* (An Appeal to the Young), trans. A. Frumkin (New York: Zsherminal Pub. Association, 1915). The **Syndicalist Educational League** was formed in October 1912 by anarchists affiliated with New York's Ferrer Center, including Hippolyte Havel and Harry Kelly. Its founding manifesto, published in *Mother Earth* (November 1912, 307–8), declared its intention of "spreading the idea of Syndicalism, Direct Action, and the General Strike among the organized and unorganized workers of America." The organization was defunct by the time of the First World War.

2. Hippolyte Havel, *Bakunin* (New York: Centenary Commemoration Committee, 1914).

in 1917 to take part in the revolutionary reconstruction of that country; others were victimized (*pogromirt*) by the Palmer Raids, driven underground or broken up. The only two organizations I found were the Fraye Arbeter Shtime Association, consisting of a few comrades, and the Naye Gezelshaft Group, which remained as a branch of the Workmen's Circle. A couple of foreign-language newspapers also maintained their existence with great hardship. No one even dared to speak about widespread, public activity in our circles.

At the first annual convention of the Jewish Anarchist Federation of America and Canada in Philadelphia in late 1921, we adopted a declaration of principles and organized a federation of existing Jewish groups in the different cities [see appendix]. Harry Gordon was the secretary. He made great efforts to organize new groups all over the country. In those days this was not an easy task. The struggle between the "Left" and the "Right" was in full swing. A large number of our former comrades were seized by the "Left" fever. The apparent success of the revolution in Russia blinded them. The working masses had many grievances against the *Forverts* and the union bureaucracy, who were certainly not without sin. They flocked to the "Left," filling its meetings, at which revolutionary phrases thundered like a mighty storm. We found ourselves caught between two warring camps. Our opposition to the "Left" made us appear in an unfavorable light as supporters of the "Right" clique, who were not much better, more honest, or more consistent than their opponents. It was, after all, the corruption of the "Right" and their "machine" in the unions that had produced the swamp in which the "Left" reptiles thrived.

Our organizational work was difficult and met with little success. Through the efforts of comrades Surasky, Hirsh Reiff, and Max Wolman, a group called Likht (Light) was organized in Harlem that held a series of lectures and meetings in that neighborhood.[3] In particular, there was a debate between me and Dr. Benzion Liber about Bolshevism, which led to unpleasant events: I wrote my introductory speech in advance and read it aloud. Hirsh Reiff attempted to record Dr. Liber's so that we could publish both parts in the *Fraye arbeter shtime*. But he was unable to accomplish this because of the

---

3. **Max Wolman** (Maks Volman, c. 1899–1955) was a Russian-born Jewish hatmaker and anarchist. He joined the anarchist movement in 1913 and was active in the Frayheyt Group and later the Free Workers' Center.

frequent interruptions and commotions in the hall. I published my manuscript and asked Dr. Liber to submit his arguments, which he did. He insisted on being given the last word in the discussion, to which I argued he was not entitled. This led him completely away from our movement. The Likht Group dissolved shortly after, when comrades Surasky and Reiff left town.

Comrade Sam Rothman was more successful with the Ferrer Center Group that he organized in the Bronx and that eventually became a branch of the Workmen's Circle. This group systematically organized lectures for many years, published many copies of Kropotkin's *Appeal to the Young*, and in cooperation with Naye Gezelshaft Group also published a volume of Dr. Jacob A. Maryson's essays on anarchism.[4] Active members in the Ferrer Center included Rothman, Nicholas Kirtzman, Morris Goodfriend, Adolph Karpoff, and others.[5]

Around this time the Free Workers' Center was established, which I have described elsewhere. For a while, we also had the idea of building a

---

4. J. A. Maryson, *Di teorye un praktik fun anarkhizm: geklibene shriften* (The Theory and Practice of Anarchism: Collected Writings) (New York: "Naye Gezelshaft" un "Ferer Senter" brentshes fun Arbeter Ring, 1927).

5. **Nicholas ("Kalie") Kirtzman** (Nikolas Koyrtsman, 1896–1963) was a Russian-born Jewish garment worker, labor organizer, and anarchist. He participated in revolutionary activities in Russia before emigrating in 1913 to the United States, where he was active in the Jewish anarchist movement and the ILGWU. Kirtzman was elected to the executive board of Cloak Finishers' Union Local 9 in 1921 (which he later managed) and in 1932 became a vice president of the ILGWU. He resigned from his post in 1937 and temporarily retired following the union's disastrous "civil war" with Communist members, then returned in 1945 and in 1950 became general manager of the Ohio-Kentucky Region and moved to Cleveland. Obituaries: *FAS*, April 15, May 1, and June 15, 1963. **Morris Goodfriend** (Moyshe Gutfraynd, c. 1896–1962) was a Russian-born Jewish bookbinder and anarchist. As a youth in Warsaw he joined the Bund and took part in a strike, leading to his imprisonment. In 1913 Goodfriend immigrated to Chicago, where he became an anarchist and joined both the Anarchist Red Cross and the International Propaganda Group. He then moved to New York, where he met his wife, anarchist Gussie "Gitl" Goodfriend (1895–1966) and joined the Ferrer-Rocker Branch 364 of the Workmen's Circle and then the Amshol Group and took an active part in the Jewish Anarchist Federation. Goodfriend was a longtime member of the International Brotherhood of Bookbinders, and his daughter, Audrey Goodfriend (1920–2013), was also an anarchist and a member of Vanguard Group in the 1930s and the Why? Group in the 1940s. Obituary: *FAS*, October 15, 1963. **Adolph Karpoff** (Adolf Karpov, 1885–1950) was a Russian-born Jewish sign painter and anarchist. He immigrated to the United States in 1904 and cofounded the Ferrer-Rocker Branch 364 of the Workmen's Circle and the Amshol Group. Obituary: *FAS*, October 13, 1950.

Kropotkin Institute in New York. We even started to raise a fund for this purpose and collected several hundred dollars, but the response was far from sufficient for an undertaking worthy of bearing our great teacher's name.

We dreamed for a time of building our own cooperative housing for the enjoyment of our movement, but this enterprise too was beyond our means. And before long, some comrades found apartments in the Amalgamated Clothing Workers' Sholem Aleichem cooperative houses.[6] This led to the organizing of the Amshol Group—the name was derived from the first syllables of "Amalgamated" and "Sholem Aleichem"—which became the largest and most active group in the city. The number of active members is too large to enumerate. It was supported in its work by many comrades who belonged to other groups but lived in the cooperative houses or nearby.

The persecution of the anarchists in Soviet Russia made it necessary to revive the Anarchist Red Cross, which had ceased to function in 1917. Now it was more difficult to provide assistance to our comrades in Russia. The Bolshevik rulers were well acquainted with the conspiratorial methods of radical movements and how to thwart such relief work. But the need was great, and Alexander Berkman demanded that under no circumstances should we forget the martyrs of our movement. The active comrades in the Anarchist Red Cross were Yetta Levy, Rose Mirsky, Anna Sosnovsky, Rose Pesotta, Barukh Yelin, Moshe Levin, Sam Rothman, the Wishnacks, the Luchkovskys, and many others.[7]

---

6. The **Sholem Aleichem Houses** (sometimes spelled "Shalom Aleichem"), also known as the Yiddish Cooperative Heimgesellschaft, were built in the Bronx in 1926–1927 by the Workmen's Circle for residents with an interest in preserving secular Yiddish culture and are named for famed Yiddish writer Sholem Aleichem.

7. **Yetta Levy** (Yeta Livay, 1893–1968) was a Russian-born Jewish anarchist. She had been involved in the revolutionary movement in Bialystok, leading to her imprisonment, before emigrating to New York in 1909. There she joined the Anarchist Red Cross and married anarchist and ILGWU organizer Louis Levy. After moving to Los Angeles, both she and Louis were active members of Kropotkin Literary Society, Branch 413 of the Workmen's Circle. Obituary: *FAS*, March 15, 1968. **Rose Mirsky** (1893–1948), real name Rose Bernstein (Bernshteyn), was a Russian-born Jewish garment worker, labor organizer, and anarchist. She immigrated to New York in 1910 and joined the ILGWU's Ladies' Waistmakers' Union Local 25. Mirsky also became an anarchist and joined both the Shturem Group and Frayheyt Group, as well as the Anti-Militarist League. During the First Red Scare her younger sister, anarchist Ethel Bernstein (1898–?), was deported, and Rose fled New York and changed her name to avoid a similar fate. In the 1920s she returned to the city and was active in the Political Prisoners' Defense Committee, the Sacco-Vanzetti defense movement,

In Chicago, comrade Boris Yelensky conducted widespread activity for the same cause under the name of the Alexander Berkman Aid Fund.[8] With the help of Gregori Maximoff and other Russian comrades, he was able to establish direct links with the anarchists imprisoned in Russia and develop

---

and the Anarchist Group of the ILGWU and became a paid negotiator for the union. Mirsky married fellow anarchist Moshe Levin. Obituaries: *FAS*, August 27 and September 10, 1948. **Rose Pesotta** (Rouz Pesota, 1896–1965), born Rokhl Peysoty, was a Russian-born Jewish garment worker, labor organizer, and anarchist. She was involved in the radical movement in Ukraine before emigrating to New York in 1913 to avoid an arranged marriage. Pesotta quickly joined ILGWU Local 25 and the anarchist movement, and she belonged to the Union of Russian Workers, the Anarchist Group of the ILGWU, and the Road to Freedom Group, of which she was secretary. In the 1930s she became an ILGWU international organizer and vice president, which took her as far as California, Puerto Rico, and Montreal, and she helped organize the wives of striking automobile workers during the famous Flint sit-down strike of 1936–1937. Pesotta resigned from the ILGWU's executive board in 1944 to protest the fact that she was its only female member, and she became an active supporter of Histadrut. She published two volumes of memoirs, both of which unfortunately avoid discussion of her involvement in the anarchist movement: *Bread upon the Waters* (1945) and *Days of Our Lives* (1958). **Moshe Levin** (c. 1895–1952) was a Russian-born Jewish garment worker and anarchist. He was a member of the Anarchist Red Cross and ILGWU Locals 60 and 66 and lived for a time at Stelton, where his children from his first marriage attended the Modern School. He later married Rose Mirsky. Obituary: *FAS*, August 1, 1952. The Luchkovsky (Lutshkovsky) family consisted of Jewish anarchist **Zipporah ("Sarah") Luchkovsky** (c. 1872–1951), née Burlakov, and her five daughters, at least four of whom were active in the anarchist movement: **Fanny Breslaw** (Feni Breslav, 1898–1987), Anna Sosnovky, **Esther Luchkovsky** (1903–1947), and **Liza ("Lisa") Luchkovsky** (1908–1989). The family's home in the Ukrainian town of Talne had been a center of Jewish radicalism, and they had to flee to the United States in 1913 because Zipporah's husband, shopkeeper Gershon Luchkovsky (died 1914), was discovered hiding illegal radical literature. Gershon died the following year, but the widow Luchkovsky's home on Grand Street in Manhattan became "a kind of institution" among radical Jews. Her daughter Fanny Breslaw was a garment worker, a member of the Frayheyt Group, the Anarchist Communist Groups of the United States and Canada, and the Anarchist Group of the ILGWU, and she later worked on the anarchist journal *New Trends* (1945–1946). Esther, a librarian, was peripherally involved in the *FAS* but less visible in the movement than her sisters. Liza contributed to the anarchist publications *Challenge* (1938–1939) and *New Trends* and became the companion of radical American-born journalist John Nicholas Beffel (1887–1973). Lisa and Fanny both also financially supported the *FAS* until its closure in 1977. Obituary for Zipporah: *FAS*, August 31, 1951.

8. **The Alexander Berkman Aid Fund** began in Chicago in 1924 and went under several names in its early years: the Russian Political Relief Committee, the Committee to Aid Political Prisoners, and the Chicago Aid Fund. In 1932 it became an official branch of the Relief Fund of the International Working Men's Association (IWMA) for Anarchists and Anarcho-Syndicalists Imprisoned or Exiled in Russia, which was itself renamed the Alexander Berkman Aid Fund in 1936. The Chicago organization continued to operate through the 1950s.

wide-ranging systematic activity in that country, which yielded good results. This sometimes led to jurisdictional quarrels in the movement, which did not please anyone. In 1927 these questions took up considerable time and discussion in the groups, as well as a lot of space in the *Fraye arbeter shtime*. A proposal from the Detroit group that all major activities should be led by the Jewish Anarchist Federation provoked heated debate. And despite the fact that most comrades agreed that the proposal was practical and logical, it did not lead to any practical results. Our movement is deeply imbued with the idea that each individual and each group is free to do whatever they wish, and the fear of centralization is so great that there is no way to change it. Relief work, publishing activities, and even such work as maintaining a social center in a city is often duplicated, without any benefit to the movement.

In addition to the systematic collection and distribution of funds, the Alexander Berkman Aid Fund of Chicago also published Maximoff's large work about the Russian Revolution and the fate of the anarchists there, *The Guillotine at Work*, in English.[9] In New York, Henry Alsberg also published, in English, *Letters from Russian Prisons*, which made a big impression in our movement.[10]

In 1926 there was a long and earnest debate in the *Fraye arbeter shtime* about changing our position on Soviet Russia. Our bitterness against the scandalous activity of the "Left" in the labor movement outside of Russia united us all behind the decision to fight their work with all our might, but regarding Russia itself some of us felt we had gone too far in our opposition. We saw only the evil that was happening there—which was striking—but we ignored or forgot the historically important changes the revolution had brought: the abolition of private property, equal rights for all nationalities,

9. G. P. Maximoff, *The Guillotine at Work: Twenty Years of Terror in Russia (Data and Documents)* (Chicago: Chicago Section of the Alexander Berkman Fund, 1940).

10. International Committee for Political Prisoners, *Letters from Russian Prisons* (New York: A. & C. Boni, 1925). **Henry Alsberg** (1881–1970) was a gay American-born Jewish journalist and "philosophical anarchist." He was a correspondent for mainstream publications such as the *New York Evening Post*, New York *World*, and *The Nation* and befriended Emma Goldman and Alexander Berkman in Russia while reporting on developments there in 1919–1921. After returning to the United States, Alsberg cofounded the International Committee for Political Prisoners on behalf of imprisoned radicals in Russia. From 1935 to 1939 he was director of the Federal Writers' Project but was fired after being called before the House Un-American Activities Committee. Most of the documents included in *Letters from Russian Prisons* had been collected anonymously by Alexander Berkman and Mark Mratchny.

and so on. The discussion was very interesting, but it did not change our attitude. Most of the comrades were so strongly embittered and determined to oppose all that was taking place there that they could not mitigate their hatred and opposition to everything the Bolsheviks were doing. Comrade Grisha Raiva was the only one who never gave up hope that he could persuade the comrades to be more objective.

About this time, we found it necessary to help a number of anarchists outside of Russia, who were not in prison but had no means to make a living. Such comrades, who were elderly and had given their all to the movement, could be found in Austria, Germany, France, and a few other countries. We therefore organized the International Aid Fund (Internaid Fund), which I consider to be our movement's most important act of solidarity.[11] Through this fund we for many years supported many destitute, deserving comrades and later had the apparatus ready to aid an increasing number of refugees who depended on our movement.

A number of attempts were made to organize occupational groups in the various professions. Many meetings were held in the Free Workers' Center for this purpose but without much success. There had always been a large number of active comrades in the International Ladies' Garment Workers' Union, who exerted an influence on their locals. We also had a number of active members among the furriers' union, who suffered plenty at the hands its "Left" administration. We were well represented among the bakers, the fancy leather goods workers, the capmakers, and a couple of other unions, but we were unable to establish coordination between these groups.

We had no better luck in other parts of the city. To the best of my knowledge, we were not able to establish functioning groups in Brooklyn, Brownsville, and the like. There was a Rudolf Rocker Group in Coney Island for a time, conducting a number of lectures and small entertainments, but their work was without results.

Our endeavors in outlying areas were also more ambitious than our results. Over the years, the Jewish Anarchist Federation hosted a number of regional conferences to which we would send the secretary of the federation and the editor of *Fraye arbeter shtime*. A number of these conferences

---

11. **The International Aid Fund** was founded in 1925 by the Jewish Anarchist Federation and published regular reports in the *FAS* beginning in 1929. It continued to operate into the 1970s.

were held not far from New York, in Stelton, at the Mohegan Colony, and at Camp Germinal near Philadelphia. At those conferences, usually held in the middle of summer, many comrades came from New York and Philadelphia, and from the colonies, and they were very successful. People debated serious questions, which led to better understanding among the comrades. In 1925 the annual convention was held in Philadelphia and was highly productive.

Chicago and Detroit also held exceptional regional conferences. In the twenties, we had a very good group in Detroit with a lot of intelligent, active comrades: the Zubrins, the Raddings, the Smiths, the Rosenbaums, Louis Tucker, Feybusovits, Abe Zweig—all smart and hardworking people.[12] Each enjoyed a wider circle around them, which devoted itself to movement activity and occupied a prominent place in the social life of the city. They took part in the work of the unions and all the cultural organizations and seriously discussed every question that was raised in our newspaper. Everyone respected their opinions. Their conference was a great success and made a good impression.

---

12. **Abraham ("Abe") Zubrin** (1893–1946) and **Sonia Zubrin** (1898–1960), née Olansky, were Russian-born Jewish anarchists. They both immigrated to the United States around 1904 and became members of the Fraye Arbeter Shtime Group in Detroit, where Abe opened a dry goods store. Obituary for Abe: *FAS*, July 26, 1946. **Joseph Smith** (Yoysef Smit, c. 1895–1962) and **Lena Smith** (Line Smit, c. 1899–1983), née Kreczmer or Kretzmar, were Russian-born Jewish anarchists. They immigrated in 1913 and initially settled in New York, where Joseph worked as a printer and became secretary of the Ferrer-Rocker Branch 203 of the Workmen's Circle. By 1930 the couple was living in Detroit, where both belonged to the Fraye Arbeter Shtime Group. Obituary for Joseph: *FAS*, January 1, 1963. **David Rosenbaum** (Dovid Rozenboym, 1893–1972) and **Malka ("Molly") Rosenbaum** (1902–1965), née Schwartz, were Russian-born Jewish anarchists. David, an iron worker, immigrated in 1913, and Malka arrived in 1920. Both were members of Detroit's Fraye Arbeter Shtime Group and remained active in the anarchist movement until their deaths. **Louis Tucker** (Luis Toker, 1882–1947), born Levi Tukerchinsky, was a Russian-born Jewish tailor, candy seller, and anarchist. In 1902 he immigrated to England before coming to the United States, where he became an anarchist and the longtime secretary of Detroit's Fraye Arbeter Shtime Group. Influenced by Max Stirner and Friedrich Nietzsche, he began writing on philosophical and political topics for the *FAS* in the early 1930s. His wife, **Rose Tucker** (1886–1932), cofounded the Froyen Grupe "Fraye Gezelshaft." Louis committed suicide after a long period of poor health. Obituary for Louis: *FAS*, June 13, 1947. **Abraham ("Abe") Zweig** (Avrom Tsveyg, 1893–1958) and **Celia Zweig** (1895–1949), née Dokser, were Russian-born Jewish anarchists. Both immigrated in 1914, and Abe worked as a machinist at the Packard auto plant. Obituary for Abe: *FAS*, August 1, 1958; for Celia: *FAS*, December 9, 1949.

We had a large number of good, active comrades in Chicago as well: Boris Yelensky, Morris Krupnick, Alexander Peck, A. M. Weinberg, Joseph Goldman, Sam Kagan, Katie Piconi, Irving Abrams, Jacob Livshis, Levin, Maximiliano Olay, Gregori Maximoff, and dozens of other militants.[13] They

---

13. **Morris Krupnick** (Moris Krupnik, 1884–1946) was a Russian-born Jewish anarchist. In 1904 he immigrated to Chicago, where he met Voltairine de Cleyre and joined the Anarchist Red Cross, the David Edelstadt Group, and then the city's Anarkhie Group. In 1933 Krupnick moved to the Sunrise Colony and served as its president for three years. Cohen refers to him as "Mendl" in his book *In Quest of Heaven*. Krupnick then moved to Los Angeles, where he joined the Kropotkin Literary Society, Branch 413 of the Workmen's Circle. He was a lifelong member of the International Brotherhood of Painters, Decorators and Paperhangers of America. **Sender Alexander Peck** (Aleksander Pek, 1884–1958) and **Fanny Peck** (Faiga Lea Pek, 1888–1964), née Kirszenberg, were Russian-born Jewish anarchists. They were both active in the revolutionary movement in Warsaw and both fled to England, where they joined the Jewish anarchist movement in Leeds and London. The couple married in England before immigrating to the United States in 1911. In Chicago, Sender worked as a watchmaker and secretary of an anarchist group. In the 1940s the Pecks moved to Los Angeles and joined the Kropotkin Literary Society, Branch 413 of the Workmen's Circle. Obituary for Sender: *FAS*, August 15, 1958; for Fanny: *FAS*, November 1, 1964. **Abraham Maishel ("Morris") Weinberg** (Avrom Moshe Vaynberg, c. 1891–1978) was a Russian-born Jewish garment worker and anarchist. He immigrated to Chicago in 1910 and became a well-known anarchist lecturer, a member of the Fraye Arbeter Shtime Group and Cutters' Local 61 of the ACWA, as well as president of the Workmen's Circle schools in Chicago. His wife **Endel ("Anna") Weinberg** (Entl Vaynberg, 1895–1947), née Avedon, joined the anarchist movement in her hometown of Krynki (in present-day Poland) when she was a young teenager and immigrated to Philadelphia and then Chicago with her widowed mother and siblings in 1908. She was the sister of anarchists Emma Avedon and Bessie Yelensky. Several of the couple's children and grandchildren inherited their anarchist beliefs, including their son Arthur Weinberg (1915–1989), a well-known journalist and historian. Obituary for Endel: *FAS*, April 25, 1947. **Joseph Goldman** (c. 1880–1972) was a Russian-born Jewish garment worker and anarchist. He was a member of the Free Society Group, the Anarchist Red Cross, and the Alexander Berkman Aid Fund and a friend of Alexander Berkman and Emma Goldman (to whom he was not related). After the Second World War, Goldman moved to Los Angeles, then Florida. Obituary: *FAS*, November 1, 1972; see also *FAS*, March 1, 1965. **Samuel ("Sam") Kagan** (1896–1986) was a Russian-born Jewish laborer, garment worker, grocer, and anarchist. He immigrated to Chicago in 1912 and worked a variety of jobs before becoming a millinery worker and joining the Cloth Hat, Cap and Millinery Workers International Union. Kagan distributed copies of London's anarchist journal *Zsherminal* and was a member of a "Russian Club" that was raided during the First Red Scare, after which he temporarily relocated to Harlem and participated the Likht Group. In the 1930s he and his wife Pauline (c. 1891–1985) joined the Sunrise Colony, where he became a leader of the opposition to Joseph Cohen's leadership. (Cohen refers to Kagan as "S." in his book *In Quest of Heaven*.) Kagan later moved to Rockville, Maryland, where he wrote and self-published a few copies of his own account of Sunrise, *The Rise and Fall of the Sunrise Commune* (1979),

opened the conference with a large meeting in the Labor Lyceum and arranged all sessions appropriately. Chicago had been sanctified in our movement with the blood of the martyrs of 1887 and evoked in each of us a whole series of reminders and suggestions for further activity.

In Montreal our conference was only a partial success. We had few active comrades there: Max Bernstein, Abraham Baron, and the amiable Shlakmans, who always did the most work for our paper, even though comrade Louis Shlakman considered himself a socialist—perish the thought (*nit far keyn*

---

and supported the *FAS* until its closure. **Katherine** (**"Katie"**) **Piconi** (Keyti Pikoni, c. 1895–1955), née Kunkin, was a Russian-born Jewish laborer and anarchist. In 1909 she immigrated to New York, where she joined the Likht Group, and she later moved to Chicago, where she was a member of the Free Society Group. In 1913 she married Luigi ("John Louis") Piconi (1891–1954), an Italian miner, salesman, and anarchist. The couple raised funds for the anarchists in the Spanish Civil War and were both members of the Alexander Berkman Aid Fund. Obituary: *FAS*, November 4, 1955. **Irving S. Abrams** (1891–1980) was an English-born Jewish garment worker, labor organizer, attorney, and anarchist. His German father and Polish mother were both Christian converts to Judaism who met and married in Lodz and then migrated to London and Germany before coming to the United States in 1901. As a teenager, Abrams joined the Socialist Party, the Workmen's Circle, and an American branch of the Bund in Rochester, New York, then relocated to Chicago, became an anarchist, and joined the IWW, the Free Society Group, the Anarchist Red Cross, the Alexander Berkman Aid Fund, and Local 61 of the ACWA. He became a popular radical speaker and was arrested dozens of times for strike activity, while also earning a law degree in 1920 from John Marshall Law School. In addition Abrams was an officer in the Hebrew Immigrant Aid Society, the Jewish Labor Committee, and both the Independent Workmen's Circle and then the Workmen's Circle. He wrote a memoir that was published after his death: *Haymarket Heritage: The Memoirs of Irving S. Abrams* (1989). **Jacob** (**"Jack"**) **Livshis** (1861–1925) was a Russian-born Jewish cigar manufacturer and anarchist who immigrated to Chicago in 1881. He wife Anna Livshis (c. 1868–1953), née Mindlin, was active in the Free Society Group and Alexander Berkman Aid Fund and became known as "Mother Livshis" (*muter Livshis*) within the movement. Obituary for Jacob: *FAS*, October 2, 1925; for Anna: *FAS* June 5, 1953. **Maximiliano Olay** (1893–1941) was a Spanish-born cigarmaker, translator, journalist, and anarchist. He immigrated to Cuba in 1908 from there to the United States in 1911 and joined the anarchist movement and the IWW in Tampa, Florida. Olay was deported as an anarchist but returned to the United States in 1913 and settled in Chicago in 1919. There he became a leading figure of the Free Society Group and wrote for New York's *Cultura Obrera* (Workers' Culture, 1911–1927), *Vanguard*, and other anarchist publications. Olay also married Russian Jewish garment worker and anarchist Anna Edelstein (Ana Edelshteyn Oley, 1898–1957). During the Spanish Civil War, at Emma Goldman's recommendation, Maximiliano was appointed the official US representative of Spain's Confederación Nacional del Trabajo–Federación Anarquista Ibérica (CNT-FAI), and the couple temporarily moved to New York to run the Spanish Labor Press Bureau and cofound the United Libertarian Organizations to aid the CNT-FAI. Obituary: *FAS*, April 11, 1941.

yidn gedakht)!¹⁴ Of the other large cities in Canada, the sole representative was Toronto, which was home to a large number of comrades organized into the Fraye Gezelshaft (Free Society) branch of the Workmen's Circle. The other major cities did not send delegates—it was too far to travel. Only a few comrades from the smaller towns and cities came. Montreal made a bad impression on us. Wherever you turned, you felt the influence of the Catholic Church, the cathedral, which is a poor copy of Notre Dame of Paris.¹⁵ A curious gloom poured out onto the people of the whole city, especially in the poor neighborhoods, of course.

A conference in our own capital brought quite a few comrades. There we had an interesting family—the Kisliuks—who formed the center of the movement wherever they lived.¹⁶ For example, when they resided for a long period in Atlantic City, there was an active group around them.

---

14. **Meyer ("Max") Bernstein** (Bernshteyn, died 1944) was a Russian-born Jewish anarchist. He had been active in the anarchist movement in London before immigrating in 1907 to Montreal, where he joined the Workmen's Circle and the Jewish Labor Committee. Obituary: *FAS*, March 10, 1944. **Abraham Baron** (c. 1883–1970) was a Russian-born Jewish tailor and anarchist. He was active in the anarchist movement in London before immigrating to Montreal in 1905. Obituary: *FAS*, September 1, 1970. **Louis Shlakman** (1875–1954) was a Russian-born tailor, foreman, and socialist. He immigrated to London and then New York. **Lena Shlakman** (c. 1873–1975), née Hendler, was a Russian-born Jewish garment worker and anarchist. As a teenager she had been active in the socialist movement in Vilna (present-day Vilnius), and in 1897 she immigrated to New York, where she became an anarchist and met and married Louis. In 1901 the couple moved to Montreal, but they eventually returned to New York and supported the *FAS* until its closure. Their daughter, economist Vera Shlakman (1909–2017), was fired from New York's Queens College in 1952 for refusing to testify before the anti-Communist McCarran Commission. Obituary for Louis: *FAS*, November 5, 1954.

15. Cohen refers here to Montreal's Notre-Dame Basilica, a Gothic Revival church constructed between 1829 and 1879.

16. **Max Kisliuk** (Kisluk, c. 1862–1938) was a Russian-born Jewish cabinet maker and anarchist. He immigrated to London and joined the anarchist Berner Street Club, becoming a lifelong rank-and-filer in the anarchist movement. **Leonora Kisliuk** (c. 1868–?) was a Russian-born Jewish anarchist who likewise immigrated to London, where she met and married Max. The couple immigrated to the United States around 1894 with their English-born daughter, **Lillian ("Lily") Kisliuk** (1888–1970), who became a stenographer, teacher, and anarchist. Lillian contributed to *Mother Earth*, supported *The Blast*, worked on behalf of imprisoned radicals, and married American-born Jewish anarchist **Israel Philip ("Phil") Dinowitzer** (Dinovitser, 1882–1949). In the 1920s and 1930s the couple's home in Washington, DC, was both a progressive nursery and a radical center. Obituary for Max: *FAS*, November 11, 1938; for Lillian: *FAS*, July 1, 1970; for Philip: *FAS*, April 1, 1949.

When the family moved to Washington, DC, the activity in Atlantic City died out, but here they found a broader field for activism. They grouped around them the Denison brothers (active, old-time comrades involved in the local Workmen's Circle branch), Harry Plotnick, Jack Dennenberg [Jacob Isaacson], Sidney Zigmond, and many others, whom they encouraged to become more active.[17] Their group enjoyed the support of a number of non-anarchist intellectuals. Lillian, the Kisliuks' daughter, continued to serve as a focal point for our movement and helped every undertaking. A number of comrades from Baltimore, Bayer and others, attended the conference. The results were quite satisfactory.

The best period in the field of organizational work and planning activity lasted for four years, from 1927 to 1931, when Benjamin Axler was elected secretary of the Jewish Anarchist Federation year after year. He carried out the work systematically, aroused and encouraged comrades to be active, raised serious questions for discussion, and conducted the Internaid Fund in a very satisfactory manner. If one reads an issue of the *Fraye arbeter shtime* from that period, one will see how wide-ranging our activities were. In New York not a week passed without notices of lectures to be held in different parts of the city. In Philadelphia, the Radical Library was highly active with lectures, classes, and dramatic performances in the "Art Corner," and in the summer it led a wide range of activities at Camp Germinal. In Chicago, the Free Society Group held a regular open forum with lectures and discussion, to which large numbers of people came.[18] It was the same in Detroit and many other cities. Not a winter passed that we did not have a good speaker on a lecture tour across the country. A few of these tours were organized privately, by special committees (such as Rudolf Rocker's tours in 1926 and 1930), or by

---

17. **Max Denison** (c. 1871–?), **Louis Denison** (1873–1954), and **Nicholas ("Nick") Denison** (c. 1875–1940) were Russian-born Jewish anarchists whose family immigrated to the United States around 1888. Max became a salesclerk and secretary of Branch 92 of the Workmen's Circle; Louis was a cigarmaker and butcher; and Nicholas was a grocer. Obituary for Nicholas: *FAS*, February 9, 1940. **Sidney Zigmond** (1893–1988) was a Russian-born Jewish tailor and anarchist. He was active in the anarchist movement in Russia before immigrating to the United States in 1922 to flee mounting Communist repression and financially supported the *FAS* from his arrival until its closure.

18. Chicago's **Free Society Group** (Grupe Fraye Gezelshaft in Yiddish) was founded in 1923 as a Yiddish-language group but subsequently switched to English to reach a larger audience and incorporate non-Jewish members, including Maximiliano Olay and Gregori Maximoff. The organization lasted into the 1960s.

Figure 27: The Free Society Group
Free Society Group, Chicago (with Rudolf Rocker and Milly Witkop seated in the third row, fourth and fifth from the left), date unknown; courtesy of Tamiment Library, New York University

the speaker directly (such as Saul Yanovsky's two lecture tours), but the federation also helped to do everything possible to make them successful.

Three or four tours were arranged directly by the federation. Chaim Weinberg went back and forth across the country. Abba Gordin made two tours all the way to California and back, organized by the federation. Yours truly also, in the fall of 1929, visited California and most of the towns in between on the initiative of the federation. At the time, we were also involved in all other anarchist endeavors, even if they were not directly related to our own work. We helped to establish and support the publication *The Road to Freedom*, and through a special International Relations

Committee we maintained direct contact with the comrades of the other language groups and their activities through open-air meetings and lectures at the International Center on Broadway, and we raised funds to publish Alexander Berkman's book *Now and After: The ABC of Communist Anarchism*, as well as to aid Emma Goldman on her lecture tour through Canada.[19]

One winter we were able to bring together a large group of young people, children of comrades, every Sunday afternoon at the home of Tania Schapiro on Union Square, where we spent hours in informal discussions together. Some of these youths developed very well that winter and later became the leading spirits of the young Vanguard Group, which along with its eponymous magazine made a name for itself through its activities.[20] We even tried to publish a special monthly English supplement to the *Fraye arbeter shtime* called *The Free Voice of Youth*, but the post office concluded that this was a separate publication that could not be mailed together with our newspaper.[21]

Those few years under the leadership of comrade Axler were the heyday of the federation. But within four years there were complaints, criticisms, and dissatisfaction that led to his resignation in 1931. At a very stormy meeting at the Free Workers' Center, the convention elected Dr. Michael A. Cohn secretary of the federation. Abba Gordin could not understand how an anarchist federation could entrust its work to a man who had a reputation as a capitalist and was far removed from the labor movement.[22] This provoked a heated discussion and a series of questions and answers, which concluded that such a thing was allowable.

It was not the best choice. The new secretary was unable to establish close relationships with the active comrades across the country. The terrible

---

19. Alexander Berkman, *Now and After: The ABC of Communist Anarchism* (New York: Vanguard Press and Jewish Anarchist Federation, 1929). This book has subsequently been reprinted numerous times, in part or in whole, under slightly different titles.

20. The **Vanguard Group** formed in 1932 out of the preexisting Bronx-based Friends of Freedom. Its members were largely the college-aged children of Jewish and Italian anarchists, and the group adhered to an explicitly anarchist-communist and pro-syndicalist standpoint. It dissolved around 1939. *Vanguard* (1932–1939) was a bimonthly magazine published by the Vanguard Group and edited by Abe Bluestein. It was sharply critical of the ILGWU and the moderate tone of the *FAS* and instead supported the syndicalist IWW.

21. Only two issues of ***The Free Voice of Youth*** appeared, in April and May 1928. Despite the name, its content was almost entirely written by older anarchists like Joseph Cohen, Leonard D. Abbott, and Alexander Berkman.

22. As noted earlier, Michael A. Cohn was a successful doctor and real estate investor.

economic crisis that was raging across the land at the time also, apparently, helped to weaken the activity of our groups. A year later, comrade Hirsh Reiff, a proper (*kosher*) proletarian, was elected secretary and held the post for a short time. He did not improve the situation but rather in many respects made it worse. The Internaid Fund was mismanaged. In the Free Workers' Center and the *Fraye arbeter shtime*, behind-the-scenes politics were introduced that did a lot of damage. After six months, comrade Axler had to be appointed to take the position of secretary again to oversee the work. A family illness later forced him to step down. The federation was never able to reach the previous level of activity and prestige that it had enjoyed. Comrades Isaac Katz, Max Grishkan, and Tania Schapiro subsequently held the office.

Returning to my description of our movement in particular cities in the twenties: One of the other cities in which our movement had an active presence was Cleveland, where we had a most interesting family, the Dudnicks—three sisters and a brother, all committed to our movement— who were almost a group in themselves.[23] However, they also had the cooperation of a number other fine comrades, among them Sam Mintz (a brother of the New York Mintz family, who was active as a speaker and activist), Herman Carter, Julius Seigel, and a number of others.[24] The distributor of our pamphlets and newspapers was comrade Fred Dan, a Russian, who was married to one of the Dudnick sisters and knew only a little Yiddish.[25]

23. The Dudnick (Dudik) family consisted of the Russian-born Jewish anarchist siblings Joseph Dudnick, Pearl Guralnick, **Gite ("Gertrude") Dudnick** (c. 1884–1942), and **Sarah Dan** (c. 1890–1962), who all immigrated to the United States between 1910 and 1912 and settled in Cleveland, where Gite was a garment worker. Sarah and her husband, anarchist Fred Dan, attempted to return to Russia around 1918 but were arrested and expelled for criticizing the Bolsheviks. Obituary for Sarah: *FAS*, July 1, 1962.

24. **Sam Mintz** (died 1943) was a Russian-born Jewish anarchist and the younger brother of anarchist Aaron Mintz. He was a member of Cleveland's Fraye Arbeter Shtime Group, campaigned on behalf of Sacco and Vanzetti, and helped arrange Rudolf Rocker's lectures. Obituary: *FAS*, September 10, 1943. **Herman Carter** (Karter, 1879–1989) was a Russian-born Jewish shoe store manager and anarchist. His family immigrated to the United States in 1890, and he became a member of Cleveland's Fraye Arbeter Shtime Group and corresponded regularly with *FAS* through the 1940s. **Julius Seigel** (Sigel, 1896–1970) was a Russian-born Jewish tailor and anarchist. He immigrated to Cleveland in 1914 and in 1934 moved to Los Angeles where he was active in the Kropotkin Literary Society, Branch 413 of the Workmen's Circle until his death. Obituary: *FAS*, June 1, 1970.

25. **Fred Dan** (1884–?) was Russian-born garment worker and anarchist. He immigrated to Cleveland in 1909 and married fellow anarchist Sarah Dudnick.

However, he was well informed of their contents through the mediation of his intelligent wife.

In St. Louis we had a number of devoted comrades at that time: Jacob Handshear, Gutman Levin, Hyman Samuels, Joe Rothstein, Morris Taylor, and also a number socialists, like Abe Filler, who helped out with the work.[26] It was always a pleasure to go and spend a few days in that hospitable environment. The Handshears were some of the most interesting people in our movement. Jake and his wife worked at home as tailors, a profession at which he was an artist—they did not have to work in a shop or employ any workers.[27] They devoted their free time entirely to the radical social activity in which they found satisfaction for decades.

In Kansas City we had a few good comrades at this same time: the Zoglins, the Tupmans, and a couple of others who responded to every national call for activity.[28] They mostly took upon themselves the respon-

---

26. **Jacob ("Jake") Handshear** (Handshier, 1886–1964) was a Russian-born Jewish tailor and anarchist. In 1907 he immigrated to London before coming to the United States, where he was an active member of the Fraye Arbeter Shtime Group in St. Louis and married fellow anarchist Fannie Handshear. **Gutman Levin** was a Jewish anarchist in St. Louis who helped organize protests against Ukrainian pogroms in 1919, and in 1933 coordinated Saul Yanovsky's local lectures. **Hyman Samuels** (Heymi Semuels, 1886–1969) was a Russian-born Jewish foreman, shopkeeper, and anarchist. He immigrated to St. Louis around 1907 and corresponded regularly with the *FAS* between 1933 and 1956. **Joseph ("Joe") Rothstein** (Rotshteyn, c.1860–1939) was a Russian-born Jewish shoemaker and anarchist. His wife, Sarah Rothstein (died 1959) was also an anarchist. Obituary: *FAS*, December 8, 1939. **Morris Taylor** (Moris Teylor, 1880–1952) was a Russian-born Jewish shoemaker and anarchist. He immigrated to St. Louis in 1904, began reading the *FAS* from his very first day in the country, and contributed funds to the paper up until his death. Obituary: *FAS*, February 29, 1952. **Abraham ("Abe") Filler** (Avrom Filer, 1885–1959) was a Russian-born Jewish insurance agent and anarchist. He immigrated to St. Louis in 1906 and in the 1930s relocated to Los Angeles, where he was active in the Kropotkin Literary Society, Branch 413 of the Workmen's Circle until his death. Obituary: *FAS*, January 1, 1960.

27. **Fannie Handshear** (c. 1888–1978) was a Russian-born Jewish dressmaker and anarchist. She immigrated to the United States in 1907 and married anarchist Jacob Handshear in St. Louis around 1910.

28. **Isaac ("Izzie") Zoglin** (1885–1976) was a Russian-born Jewish metal worker, building contractor, and anarchist. He joined the anarchist movement in Russia as a teenager and was arrested prior to immigrating to the United States in 1903. **Bessie Zoglin** (1892–1985), née Raskin, was a Russian-born Jewish garment worker and anarchist. Her family immigrated to Kansas City in 1909 after surviving two pogroms in their hometown of Gomel. She met and married Isaac Zoglin in Kansas City, where the couple helped arrange local anarchist lectures and belonged to the Workmen's Circle. During the First Red Scare Bessie organized

sibility of documenting and supporting political prisoners in the federal penitentiary in Jefferson City. In the hysterical period following World War I, Emma Goldman, Kate Richards O'Hare, and others were incarcerated there, some of the most prominent radicals in America.

In Denver, comrade Bernard Rose and the Chalefmans carried on the earlier work of Max Spanier, who had been active there for many years.[29] There is a fine monument in the cemetery at the grave of the prematurely deceased David Edelstadt, which every comrade felt the need to visit and honor with a bowed head.[30] Too often we also found someone in the magnificent Spivak Sanitorium for victims of the white plague [tuberculosis].[31] Denver has a rich history of great labor struggles and interesting memories,

---

the "Women's Tea Club" to support radicals imprisoned at Leavenworth Federal Prison. In the 1920s she became a Labor Zionist and was the founder and president of the Kansas City chapter of Na'amat (Pioneer Women), a Labor Zionist women's organization with the goal of forming women's cooperatives in Palestine. Obituary for Isaac: *FAS*, July 1, 1976; for Bessie: *Kansas City Times*, February 16, 1985.

29. **Bernard Rose** (Roz, 1878–1961) was a Russian-born Jewish tailor, manager, and anarchist. He immigrated to London, where he joined the militant Frayheyt Group, before coming to the United States in 1914. In Denver, Rose became an active supporter of the *FAS* and helped arrange Rudolf Rocker's visits to that city. Obituary: *FAS*, April 15, 1961. **Boris Chalefman** (Barukh Khalifman, 1878–1947), a salesman and fruit grower, and his wife **Rebecca (Rivke) Chalefman** (1879–1941), were Russian-born Jewish anarchists. They both immigrated in the 1900s and actively supported the *FAS* from 1920 until their deaths. **Max Spanier** (Maks Shpanier, 1874–1954) was a German-born furrier and anarchist. The son of German Lutheran parents who emigrated from Berlin to London and then, in 1890, to New York, he became an anarchist in 1892 and joined Johann Most's Freiheit Group. He also met and married Florence ("Fanny") Samburg (1880–1954), a Russian-born Jewish garment worker and anarchist, who introduced him to the Jewish anarchist movement and taught him Yiddish. In 1899 the couple helped to relaunch the *FAS*, of which Max became manager, and both joined the Nayer Dur (New Generation) Group. In 1907 they moved to Denver where Max, a talented speaker who was widely beloved in the Jewish anarchist movement, helped organize a furrier's union and founded both the Denver Labor Lyceum and the David Edelstadt Branch 450 of the Workmen's Circle. In 1930 the Spaniers relocated to San Francisco, where they joined the anarchist Harmony Branch 693 of the Workmen's Circle and Max helped produce the *Dovid Edelshtat gedenk-bukh* (David Edelstadt Memorial Book, 1953). Obituary for Max: *FAS*, November 19, 1954; for Florence: *FAS*, July 2, 1954. See also *FAS*, March 12, 1954.

30. David Edelstadt's headstone was erected in 1915 at Golden Hill Cemetery by the Workmen's Circle, at the initiative of Max and Florence Spanier. It is inscribed with Edelstadt's poem "Mayn tsavoe" (My Testament).

31. The **Jewish Consumptives' Relief Society Sanitorium** opened in 1904 and was also known as the Spivak Sanatorium after its founder, Russian-born Jewish physician and former anarchist Charles (Khayim) Spivak (1861–1927).

in addition to its extraordinarily rich natural environment. We could always find a crowd of sympathetic listeners and willing helpers there.

Denver stood above the American prairielands to its west in a social as well as topographical sense. There was no reason for our people to stop anywhere there—not even in big, rich Salt Lake City, which the Mormons built in the middle of the desert—until they reached California. There, on the shores of the Pacific Ocean, rose before us a new world with our people in every city. In San Francisco we had a small group of very devoted friends. There was Max Spanier, Bernard Blumberg, John J. Nathan, David Gisnet, Becky Poyzner, Becky Yeszin, and many other comrades in and around town, in Oakland, Petaluma, et cetera.[32] In the twenties we had reason to visit San Quentin, the huge prison in which Tom Mooney, Warren Billings, Matthew Schmidt, and the MacNamaras wasted away in those years. People also used to sail on a small boat to the island of Alcatraz, where the federal government detained those who fell into the clutches of its justice system on a desolate rock.

---

32. **Bernard Blumberg** (1881–1946) was a Russian-born Jewish laundry worker, plumber, and anarchist. He immigrated to the United States in 1900 and married fellow anarchist Ethel Snyder (1888–1960). Their home in San Francisco became a center of radical activity. Obituary for Bernard: *FAS*, December 13, 1946; for Ethel: *FAS*, March 15, 1960. **John J. Nathan** (Y. Y. Natan, 1887–1960) was a Russian-born Jewish insurance agent, editor, and anarchist. He immigrated to London, where he joined the Arbeter Fraynd Group, then to Buenos Aires, where he took an active role in both the Spanish-speaking and Yiddish-speaking anarchist movements and edited the Yiddish page of the anarchist paper *La Protesta* in 1908–1909. Nathan relocated to San Francisco in 1915 and remained active in both Spanish-speaking and Jewish anarchist circles. Obituary: *FAS*, November 1, 1960. **David Gisnet** (1881–1947) was a Russian-born Jewish sailor, garment worker, labor organizer, writer, editor, and anarchist. He first came to the United States at age seventeen but migrated to London and then Paris where he lived for five years and joined the Jewish anarchist movement. Gisnet also traveled to Italy and Egypt as a sailor before returning to the United States in 1909. In St. Louis he was prominent anarchist speaker, and in 1918 he moved to San Francisco where he was active in the radical People's Institute, led weekly discussions at the William Morris School, cofounded Harmony Branch 693 of the Workmen's Circle, and became an organizer and manager for the ILGWU. Gisnet was a journalist for California's Jewish press and later joined the Jewish National Workers Alliance (Yidish Natsionaler Arbeter Farband), a Labor Zionist mutual aid society founded in 1912. Obituaries: *FAS*, August 1 and October 3, 1947. **Becky Poyzner** or Pevzner (died 1935) was a Jewish anarchist active in the Bay Area and, after 1928, Los Angeles. Obituary: *FAS*, August 9, 1935. **Becky Yeszin** (Yezshin, 1889–1935) was a Russian-born Jewish anarchist who lived in Berkeley and regularly donated funds to the *FAS* in the 1920s and 1930s.

The City of Angels (Los Angeles) in Southern California was much larger, sunnier, and at the same time much more socially backward. Rapidly expanding, spreading out for miles and miles, Los Angeles had not yet had time to properly shape itself and develop a character (*fizionomie*) of its own. The vast city was sprawled out like a large village warming itself in the bright California sun. Our group there, the Kropotkin Literary Society, Branch 413 of the Workmen's Circle, quickly grew to become our largest group in the whole country, and it did much work for our movement specifically and also for other causes. It gave much support but lacked a scope and mission of local educational work. The number of active members there was so large that I cannot begin to list them all: Isaac Isgur, Barukh Yelin, Benjamin Surasky, Abe Filler, Morris Krupnick, Israel Slakter, Yetta Gordin, Yaffe, Dr. Joseph Holtz, the Hermans, B. Greenfield ("the Brownsville carpenter"), Silverman, and many others.[33] Los Angeles attracted many members from other cities: comrade Benjamin Moore had come from Philadelphia, the

---

33. **Isaac Isgur** (Yitskhok Izgur, 1881–1969) was a Russian-born Jewish capmaker, labor organizer, dentist, and anarchist. He was "born into the greatest poverty" and active in the Jewish revolutionary movement in Vilna (present-day Vilnius) and Minsk, leading to his imprisonment and then exile to Siberia. Izgur escaped to the United States and in New York became an organizer for the United Cloth Hat and Cap Makers of North America and worked for the *FAS*. After becoming blacklisted for his union organizing, in the 1910s he lived at the Jewish agrarian Clarion Colony in Utah with his wife, Russian-born Jewish anarchist Anna ("Annie") Isgur (c. 1886–1960). The couple then moved to Los Angeles where they joined the Arbeter Fraynd Group, Branch 512 of the Workmen's Circle, and then cofounded the Kropotkin Literary Society, Branch 413, after Communists gained control of Branch 512. Isaac also became an active supporter of Histadrut. Obituary: *FAS*, January 1, 1970. **Israel Slakter** or Slecter (Slekter, 1886–1976) was a Russian-born Jewish metalworker, hardware store owner, apartment manager, and anarchist. He immigrated to Detroit in 1904 and in the 1930s moved to Los Angeles where he belonged to the Kropotkin Literary Society, along with his wife Cecile (Silia, 1892–1981). **Joseph Holtz** (Yoysef Holts, 1888–1946) was a Russian-born Jewish laborer, dentist, and anarchist. In Warsaw he was a member of the Polish Socialist Party and then became an anarchist, and in 1909 he fled to London to avoid persecution. Holtz joined the Arbeter Fraynd Group and helped to produce the journal *Zsherminal* before emigrating to the United States in 1911. He lived in New York and Chicago, then settled in Los Angeles around 1924 and was active in the Kropotkin Literary Society, as well as the Russian Aid Fund. Obituary: *FAS*, November 1, 1946. **Bernard Greenfield** (Ber Grinfeld, 1868–1948), who wrote under the name "Der Bronzviler stoler" (The Brownsville Carpenter), was a Russian-born Jewish carpenter, humorist, and anarchist. He immigrated to New York in 1887 and began writing humorous sketches for the *FAS* in 1902, encouraged by editor Saul Yanovsky. Greenfield became a well-known Yiddish writer and moved to Los Angeles in the 1920s. His collected works were published as *Hubelshpener: oytobiografishe skitsen*

Keysers, Weisses, Aranoffs, and Zelda Kobrin were from Stelton, and so on.[34] They all came with a history of activity in other cities and were experienced fighters in our movement.

In close proximity to them was our very small group in sunny San Diego, where Max Radding lived and received guests most of his years. There were also the Feinbergs—really nice people who did not pass up any opportunity to do something for our movement and to bring in a good crowd to listen to our lectures.[35]

---

un geklibene shriften fun Bronzvviler stoler (Wood Shavings: Autobiographical Sketches and Collected Writings of the Brownsville Carpenter, 1933–1946). Obituary: *FAS*, May 28, 1948.

34. **Dora Keyser** (Kayzer, 1899–1983) was a Russian-born Jewish garment worker and anarchist. The seventeenth of eighteen children, at the age of six she helped smuggle radical literature and witnessed pogroms during the revolution of 1905. Keyser immigrated to the United States in 1912 after the death of her father and joined the anarchist movement two years later, taking part in the Francisco Ferrer Center and the Zsherminal Group, as well as Local 22 of the ILGWU. She also married fellow Jewish anarchist **Louis (Lyova) Keyser** (c. 1895–1955), a member of the Union of Russian Workers. Around 1920 the couple moved to Philadelphia and joined the Radical Library, then relocated to the Stelton Colony in 1922 and the Sunrise Colony in 1934, before finally settling in Los Angeles in 1938. Both were active in the Kropotkin Literary Society, Branch 413 of the Workmen's Circle, and in the 1970s and 1980s Dora worked on behalf of the United Farm Workers of America. Obituary for Louis: *FAS*, December 16, 1955. **Max Weiss** (c. 1897–1937), according to his obituary in *Man!* (February-March 1937), "was active in the Jewish, Russian, and English Anarchist movement in New York, Philadelphia and Los Angeles." He had been a member of the Union of Russian Workers in New York and was imprisoned during the First Red Scare, during which time he contracted the illness that ultimately killed him. In 1922 Weiss moved to Los Angeles and was active in the largely Jewish Libertarian Group in Boyle Heights. Obituary: *FAS*, January 15, 1937. **John Aranoff** (Dzshon Aranov, 1895–1983) was a Russian-born Jewish hardware store owner, repairman, and anarchist who immigrated to the United States in 1915. **Sarah Aranoff** (c. 1904–?), née Golokow, was a Russian-born Jewish anarchist who immigrated with her family around 1905. In 1930 the couple lived in Stelton, where their children attended the Modern School, and they later moved to Los Angeles. **Zelda Kobrin** (1889–1979) was a Russian-born Jewish garment worker and anarchist. She joined the revolutionary movement in Grodno as a young girl, then immigrated to United States where she joined the Jewish labor movement, and her home in Harlem became an anarchist meeting place. Kobrin was active in the Consumers League of Harlem and later moved to the Stelton Colony where her daughter Charlotte attended the Modern School. In Los Angeles she became "one of the most active members of the Kropotkin Branch" of the Workmen's Circle, of which she served as secretary, and was a longtime financial supporter of the *FAS*. See *FAS*, November 5, 1954.

35. **Nellie Feinberg** (Neli Faynberg, c. 1888–1956), née Weisman, was a Russian-born Jewish labor organizer and anarchist. She immigrated to Manchester where she joined a branch of the Bund, then met her husband Israel Feinberg and became an anarchist. In 1912

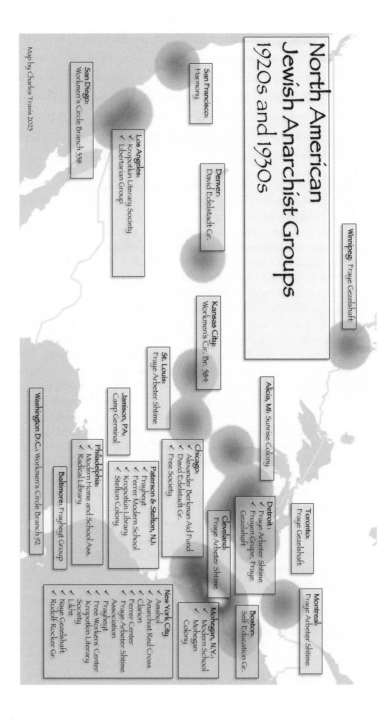

Figure 28: Map of anarchist groups

This map includes all groups referenced by Cohen in this chapter, including some, like Chicago's Free Society Group, that were not exclusively Jewish but within which Jews predominated

North American Jewish Anarchist Groups 1920s and 1930s

Map by Charles Travis 2023

Winnipeg: Fraye Gezelshaft

San Francisco: Harmony

San Diego: Workmen's Circle Branch 358

Los Angeles:
✓ Kropotkin Literary Society
✓ Libertarian Group

Denver: David Edelstadt Gr.

Kansas City: Workmen's Cir. Br. 584

St. Louis: Fraye Arbeter Shtime

Jamison, PA: Camp Germinal

Washington D.C.: Workmen's Circle Branch 92

Baltimore: Frayheyt Group

Philadelphia:
✓ Modern Home and School Ass.
✓ Radical Library

Paterson & Stelton, NJ:
✓ Frayheyt
✓ Ferrer Modern School
✓ Kropotkin Library
✓ Stelton Colony

Chicago:
✓ Alexander Berkman Aid Fund
✓ David Edelstadt Gr.
✓ Free Society

Cleveland: Fraye Arbeter Shtime

Alicia, MI: Sunrise Colony

Detroit:
✓ Fraye Arbeter Shtime
✓ Frayen Grupe, Fraye Gezelshaft

Toronto: Fraye Gezelshaft

Montreal: Fraye Arbeter Shtime

Boston: Self Education Gr.

Mohegan, N.Y.:
✓ Modern School
✓ Mohegan Colony

New York City:
✓ Amshol
✓ Anarchist Red Cross
✓ Clarion
✓ Ferrer Center
✓ Fraye Arbeter Shtime Association
✓ Frayheyt
✓ Free Workers Center
✓ Kropotkin Literary Society
✓ Likht
✓ Naye Gezelshaft
✓ Rudolf Rocker Gr.

This concludes the list of cities that were well represented in our ranks here in America. Boston always had a small group, which did good work from time to time, but, considering the possibilities in such a large city with such a large population, it was of a very small scope. Those active in this period were Isidore Garber, Thomas B. Eyges, Morris Tubiash, Goldberg, and a few others.[36]

In a number of smaller towns scattered across the country, we had some individuals ready to undertake certain work: Ben Swire in Albany, Max Rosenbaum in Wilmington, Paul T. Goodwin in Pittsburgh, Bayer in Baltimore, L. Finkel in Buffalo, et cetera.[37]

---

the couple immigrated to New York where Nellie became a member of the New York Joint Board of the Cloakmakers' Union, and then they moved to Canada in 1928, Boston in 1931, and finally Los Angeles in 1933. Obituary: *FAS*, June 29, 1956.

36. **Isidore Meyer Garber** (1886–1944) was a Russian-born Jewish ironworker, shoe worker, and anarchist. He immigrated to the United States in 1905 and lived in New York City, Boston, and Chelsea, Massachusetts, before becoming the longtime secretary of Malden, Massachusetts's Chenstochover Branch 261 of the Workmen's Circle. Garber was also active in the shoemakers' union and moved to Los Angeles around 1934. Obituary: *FAS*, May 5, 1944. **Morris Tubiash** (c. 1880–1961) was a Russian-born Jewish printer and anarchist. He was active in London's Arbeter Fraynd Group and Jewish labor movement before immigrating to Boston in 1906. There Tubiash became recording secretary of Independent Workmen's Circle until that organization reunified with the Workmen's Circle in 1931, and he subsequently joined Branch 928. In the 1940s and 1950s he was active in local efforts to support Histadrut. Obituary: *FAS*, May 5, 1944.

37. **Ben Swire** (Sveyer, 1892–1971) was a Russian-born Jewish coal hauler and anarchist. He immigrated to the United States around 1907 and was first drawn to the socialist territorialist movement, then "built the anarchist movement in Albany," where his home became an anarchist meeting place. Swire was also a member of national board of directors of the Workmen's Circle, secretary of that organization's Upstate District Committee, and a member of Albany's Branch 320. Obituary: *FAS*, April 1, 1971. **Max Rosenbaum** (Meks Rozenboym, 1888–1962) was a Russian-born Jewish tailor, storekeeper, and anarchist. Orphaned as a child in Warsaw, he joined the socialist movement and in 1908 immigrated to New York, where he became an anarchist. Rosenbaum then moved Wilmington, Delaware, where he cofounded a Workmen's Circle school. He returned to New York in 1928 and joined the Kropotkin Literary Society and Abba Gordin's Jewish Ethical Society. Obituary: *FAS*, October 1, 1962; see also *FAS*, July 15, 1958. **Paul T. Goodwin** (Gudvin, c. 1885–1946) was an Austrian-born Jewish clerk and anarchist. He lived in Pittsburgh from around 1909 to the early 1920s, then moved to the Bronx, then Memphis, and corresponded with the *FAS* from each location. Goodwin also lived for a time at the Sunrise Colony and in the 1940s became a supporter of Histadrut. Obituary: *FAS*, January 25, 1946. **L. Finkel** made financial donations to the *FAS* from 1920 to 1945. Census records suggest he may be Louis Finkel (1880–?), a Hungarian-born Jewish mattress maker who immigrated around 1900.

In Canada we always had a good, active group in Toronto, which nurtured in its ranks a number of intelligent comrades: Joseph Desser, Morris Langbord, Julius Seltzer, and others.[38] Their work found a certain resonance in the city among the Workmen's Circle and in cultural circles.

Winnipeg, the far-flung Siberianesque city, in those years excelled in its widespread cultural work centered around the I. L. Peretz School, which at the time seemed to be the largest and best-run Yiddish school on the North American continent. The influence of that circle of people, which united all the intellectual forces—anarchists, socialists, and Yiddishists—was evident everywhere I visited. Even their weekly bridge parties were conducted for a good cause (*mitzvah*): proceeds went to support the Peretz School.

The circle of our comrades there was intimate and incredibly friendly: the Prasoffs, Simkins, Rosens, Silversteins, and a dozen other families whose names I can't recall, all made my weeklong visit there extremely successful and satisfactory in all respects.[39]

---

38. **Joseph ("Joe") Desser** (Yosef Deser, 1885–1941) was a Russian-born Jewish tailor and anarchist. Orphaned as a young child, he immigrated to London in 1902 to join a brother and avoid service in the Polish army. There he became involved in the Jewish anarchist movement before moving to Toronto around 1908. Desser was a founder and secretary of the anarchist Fraye Gezelshaft Branch 339 of the Workmen's Circle, and his family's home became the center of the city's anarchist movement; Emma Goldman stayed there after moving to Toronto in 1934 until she found an apartment of her own. **Morris (Moshe) Langbord** (1880–1964) was a Russian-born Jewish anarchist who immigrated to Canada in 1906 and served as secretary of the Fraye Gezelshaft Branch 339. Obituary: *FAS*, February 1, 1964. **Julius Seltzer** (1881–1973) was a Russian-born Jewish clothing manufacturer and anarchist. After immigrating to New York from Bialystok in 1900, he became an anarchist under the influence of Johann Most and subsequently moved to Spokane, Schenectady, Ann Arbor, and finally, in 1912, Toronto, where he worked at a number of jobs before becoming a partner in a clothing factory. He was a member of the Fraye Gezelshaft Branch, and Emma Goldman called him "the only 'millionaire' in our ranks." Emma Goldman, *Living My Life*, vol. 2 (New York: Alfred A. Knopf, 1931), 990.

39. **Israel Prasoff** or Prasow (Prasov, 1884–1928) and **Samuel (Zalman) Prasoff** or Prasow (1887–1971) were Russian-born Jewish construction workers and anarchists. In Russia, Israel had been a Socialist-Revolutionary and Samuel belonged to the Bund, and they immigrated to Canada in 1904 following a pogrom in their city of Gomel. The brothers subsequently became prominent figures in Winnipeg's anarchist movement. In 1907 Samuel became the local agent for Emma Goldman's *Mother Earth*, and he hosted Goldman, Rudolf Rocker, and other anarchist speakers when they visited the city. Israel meanwhile was the first secretary of the anarchists' Fraye Gezelshaft Branch 564 of the Workmen's Circle, and both brothers wrote for the newspaper *Der keneder id* (The Canadian Israelite, 1910–12). Obituary for Israel: *FAS*, February 3, 1928. **Feivel ("Frank") Simkin** (1885–1983) was a

In smaller Canadian towns like London—home of the white-haired comrade Mayer Hornstein[40]—or Windsor and Victoria, there were also individual comrades who always generously helped put on lectures, raise funds for the newspaper, and spread our word among their circles.

Faraway Seattle, Tacoma, and Portland were not far behind. In each city there were a number of readers of the *Fraye arbeter shtime* who were happy to receive guests all the way from New York and to help however they could.

We also always received considerable assistance from many branches of the Workmen's Circle in cities and towns where there were no active comrades. These more remote branches played an important cultural role. Wherever they had their own schools for children, then a true cultural center was created with widespread activities. A city without a branch of the Workmen's Circle was a social wasteland occupying a vacant space on the earth.

Speaking of the outlying areas, it should be noted that with the exception of the very large cities, every year it became harder and harder to find a worker in Jewish radical circles. Former anarchists, socialists, Bundists, and plain revolutionists all ascended to better livelihoods than working in shops

Russian-born Jewish printer, publisher, and anarchist. He had been a member of the Bund and in 1906 immigrated to Winnipeg in order to avoid arrest. There Simkin founded a radical library and club and became an anarchist. He was a prominent member of the radical Branch 169 of the Workmen's Circle and in 1915 cofounded the anarchist Fraye Gezelshaft Branch after breaking with the Marxist members of Branch 169. Simkin also published Winnipeg's Yiddish newspaper, *Der keneder yid*, which later became *Der id* (The Israelite, 1912–1915) and then *Dos idishe vort* (The Israelite Press, 1915–1967). **William Rosen** (Rozen) and **Rebecca Rosen** (1886–1958) were Jewish anarchists who married in Winnipeg in 1907. Their daughter Sima Rosen later worked for the *FAS* in New York. **Jacob ("Jake") Silverstein** (Yakov Zilberstam or Zilbershtam, c. 1888–1963) was a Russian-born car mechanic and anarchist, and his wife **Dora Silverstein** (c. 1895–?) was a Russian-born Jewish doctor and anarchist. They both immigrated to Winnipeg around 1912 and subsequently joined the anarchist movement, helping to organize local lectures by Emma Goldman, Rudolf Rocker, Joseph Cohen, and others. Jacob wrote a memoir of the Jewish anarchist movement in Winnipeg that was serialized in the *FAS* (November 1, 1957, February 15, March 15, June 15, July 1, and July 15, 1958). Obituary for Jacob: *FAS*, June 15, 1963.

40. **Mayer Hornstein** (1867–1951) was a Russian-born anarchist peddler, farmer, and anarchist. In 1891 he immigrated to London, Ontario, with his wife, anarchist Shifra ("Sophia") Hornstein (1880–1949), née Rosenthal. They cofounded a Self-Education Club that in 1909 became a branch of the Workmen's Circle and also participated in anarchist activities across the border in Detroit. Mayer was remembered as a talented public speaker. Obituary: *FAS*, July 6, 1951.

and factories. Among them you could find every kind of intellectual and professional occupation other than industrial work. They still held onto their old traditions and spoke the same language—at celebrations, at least—but the real condition of their lives was quite different. Children were brought up to occupy higher positions and an elevated social life and were in general quite removed from radicalism. The little Yiddish they learned in the Jewish schools was quickly forgotten in the hectic life of colleges and their sports. Their parents, with very few exceptions, followed their children down the path of Americanization and usually worried very little about the past.

PART FOUR

The Great Depression and the Second World War

CHAPTER 51

Prosperity and Crisis

In the 1920s this country was enjoying the famous Coolidge prosperity. Fortunes were made overnight with no great effort, and one did not have to leave the house to earn a few thousand dollars willy-nilly. All you needed was to give a small amount of money to a broker—he took care of the rest. The broker bought stocks on margin with the money, held onto them for a few days—sometimes not even a few hours—and then sold them at a good profit. You could say that gambling on the stock market, on Wall Street, flourished and spread over the whole city, the whole country. Anyone with a few dollars to spare became a financier, a "rentier," a speculator, as God had commanded.

In time all the professionals—doctors, lawyers, engineers, pharmacists—who had set aside something for a rainy day, or for the education of their children, or for a long-needed vacation, were drawn in. It caught the imagination of every shopkeeper, who began to think that they were crazy for standing in a store all day, with customers and employees, when they could make a lot more money on Wall Street in a much easier way. In time it reached the waiters in restaurants, the shoeshine boys on the street—everyone was talking about Wall Street, stocks, bonds, profits, and easy money.

East Broadway too did not escape the gambling plague (*mageyfe*). Anarchists, socialists, community leaders, Jewish writers, union officials, and factory workers also believed this get-rich story. They gambled in stocks and in real estate, made easy money, and were living high.

Of course, not everyone gambled and made money. The most honorable people and the ordinary workers, the eternally unfortunate (*shlimazels*),

497

only heard about such things and never about their comrades. All they knew was that prices were rising, and workers had to struggle hard to get the smallest wage increase.

The economists, of course, invented a scientific term to describe such a phenomenon. They called it an "expanding economy"—an economy that continues to grow and benefit more people. In his 1928 campaign, Herbert Hoover's principal slogan was "a car in every garage" for every family. And, indeed, why shouldn't every farmer and worker have a car, with a comfortable garage, a chauffeur, and all the trimmings? What's the matter, can we in America not produce enough of all these things?

Hoover's luck, however, was not good. Under his administration, prosperity held out for no more than seven and a half months. On October 29, 1929, Wall Street suddenly collapsed. Millions of stocks were offered for sale in a single day. The more sellers, the fewer buyers, and the fewer buyers, the lower prices fell. The "margins" were wiped out before the market closed. During the night, thousands of telegrams were sent out to all "financiers" telling them to spend fresh cash to save their stocks, which were increasingly losing their value. The whole financial scam collapsed like a house of cards— it was nothing more than a soap bubble that sparkled brilliantly in the sun but burst without leaving a trace!

The panic was terrible. Hundreds of financiers and brokers committed suicide. The doctors, dentists, shopkeepers, and others continued their work for a while, repairing the damage and raising new money for better investments. Hardest hit, as always, were the innocent victims, the workers, who were thrown out of work. An army of unemployed began to grow, the likes of which had never been seen in the history of American economic crises. Soon a third of all workers became unemployed, many of them homeless and without food.

The process of an economic crisis is simple: as soon as part of the population loses the means to buy things, the turnover of supplies in the stores decreases. As a result, orders for goods to manufacturers are reduced, jobs in the factories are cut, and the number of people who can't buy anything increases. It's like a chain made up of links that begin to fall apart one after the other, until the whole chain disintegrates.

It is impossible to describe the misery and sufferings of the great masses in such a serious time. Beggars knocked on every door, stopped every passerby in the street. Apple peddlers by the thousands filled every city. "Hoovervilles" of beggars, villages slapped together from stray planks and cardboard, began to cover the land. Abandoned children wandered the roads and the railroad tracks, just as they had in Russia during the great famine in the first years after the revolution. The worst part was that no one knew what to do, how to climb out of the quagmire into which wild speculation had deluded the people. Hoover consoled the public, telling them that prosperity was "just around the corner" and would return soon. The economists and newspaper editorial writers complained, spoke in scientific terms that they themselves did not understand, and split hairs. Workers in many cases tried to help the needy by sharing their own food and spreading what little employment existed among more people, but how long could it last when there was no work at all?

The crisis reached its lowest point in 1932. In desperation, the people turned away from the Republicans, expelled them from the White House, and elected Franklin Delano Roosevelt along with his Democratic followers. That year's campaign showed no sign of a plan that would lead the country out of the crisis. Roosevelt talked about government finances, balancing the budget, and other such childish remedies. The people voted for him out of hatred for Hoover, the heartless moneybag who, through his Reconstruction Finance Corporation, had handed out millions to the rich and not a penny to the poor. His theory was that the rich would create jobs for the poor. Direct help to the unemployed is charity and humiliates those who take it. Better to starve than humiliate themselves! The people could also not forget the brutal attack on the war veterans in Washington, DC, when General MacArthur (who later became a war hero), at Hoover's command, made a pogrom (*pogromirt*) on the camp of twenty thousand veterans, burned their tents, and gave them a taste of poison gas.[1]

That winter, after the election, I made a lecture tour across the country and was shocked by the appalling conditions I found around me. All the factories stood idle. No smoke appeared from their tall chimneys. The trains

---

1. On July 8, 1932, members of the US Army cleared the encampment of the "Bonus Army," a group of World War I veterans who, in the face of the Great Depression, had marched on the Capitol to demand early redemption of service bonuses that were set to pay out in 1944. Cavalry, five light tanks, and infantry with fixed bayonets and teargas charged the protesters, injuring fifty-five; 135 were arrested.

were empty. The big train stations in Buffalo, Cleveland, St. Paul, and St. Louis—empty, deserted. On the farms, vegetables and fruits were plentiful in the fields, but it didn't pay to harvest and transport them to the cities where men, women, and children were starving. The long breadlines were frightful. I stood in a nasty cold rain for more than an hour to see what these thousands of people in line got for their waiting. They received too little milk to carry home to their children and the sick. The people were devastated and despairing. But there was no sign of revolt, not a spark of revolutionary upheaval, in any of the cities.

Some big cities began to show signs of finding a direct, voluntary way out. "Self-help" organizations began to organize for the exchange of services in a systematic way. In most of these, the perpetrators were anarchists, many of them followers of Benjamin Tucker, who proceeded along the lines that Pierre-Joseph Proudhon had marked out some seventy or eighty years before.[2] They organized the collection of food in exchange for the labor they supplied to the farmers. They acquired meeting places, some houses, and apartments in exchange for work on behalf of the property owners. In many cities they opened small factories to make clothes, shoes, and furniture for their own use. They opened bakeries and restaurants, which provided employment and food. But more than anything, however, they gave hope, uplifting people who saw an opportunity to do something, to help themselves.

This development encouraged me greatly. True, the beginnings were small, poor, and limited, but they were still a beginning in the right direction. "Self-help!"—a true American expression, organized and planned without the intervention of politicians and charities! Meager beginnings, in one crisis or another, will surely lead the people out of the swamp into which capitalism pushes them every few years.

---

2. **Benjamin Tucker** (1854–1939) was an American-born editor, translator, and individualist anarchist. As the editor of the newspaper *Liberty* from 1881 to 1908, he was America's foremost proponent of Pierre-Joseph Proudhon's mutualism and, later, Max Stirner's egoism. He expatriated to France in 1908. **Pierre-Joseph Proudhon** (1809–1865) was a French printer, philosopher, mutualist, and the first writer to declare himself an anarchist. He participated in the French uprising of 1848 and, although opposed to government, was subsequently elected to the Constituent Assembly before being jailed by Louis-Napoléon Bonaparte in 1849. An associate of both Karl Marx and Mikhail Bakunin, his ideas influenced both men, though each disagreed with him on different points.

Another phenomenon made itself visible: the farmers in the Midwest, the most conservative people in the country, began to mobilize, demonstrating resistance against the government officials and judges who tried to collect debts for the big corporations. Sheriffs were forcibly barred from holding auctions on foreclosed farm mortgages. Judges were deterred from issuing judgments by death threats. At public sales, all the neighbors would come and bid a minimal price, and purchase back a farm with all its supplies from the sheriff for a few pennies. None of them paid taxes. At the time of the milk strike, their armed pickets successfully resisted the police.[3] The signs of revival, or resistance, did not start in the cities, among the industrial workers, as stated in scripture [i.e., Marxist doctrine] but rather in the country among the farmers, the petite bourgeoisie, as we have designated them and abandoned to God's care.

---

3. In 1933 the Wisconsin Cooperative Milk Pool, a collective of dairy farms, launched a series of "milk strikes" by refusing to sell their milk below a set minimum price and blockading manufacturers to prevent dairies not participating in the strike from making deliveries.

CHAPTER 52

I Am Relieved of My Editorship

Due to my absence from New York, our 1932 annual convention was held later than usual. Immediately after the first session of the convention, I realized that there was an organized opposition to me and my handling of the *Fraye arbeter shtime*. There had been sharp criticisms and heated moments at every convention—this was a well-established tradition of our predecessors, from the very first days of Yanovsky's editorship and perhaps even earlier, from Roman Lewis and David Edelstadt's time. But criticism, no matter how sharp it may be, is one thing, and an organized opposition is, at our conventions at least, an entirely different matter. This kind of stuff occurred at union conventions but not among us, where it was really a question of working for an ideal and very often sacrificing ourselves, our families, and our jobs.

I hoped to avoid a fight. I never had large ambitions, and twelve years of work for the *Fraye arbeter shtime* was more than enough for me. So, at the first opportunity, I declared that I would no longer be a candidate for the position of editor. Instead of wasting our time criticizing the past, it would be better used to plan how to get the work done better from now on. The opposition, however, was not satisfied. Every session over the weekend was filled with criticism and attacks. The convention was able to complete its work only a week later by electing a committee to appoint a new editor for the newspaper. Saul Yanovsky, who was on a lecture tour at the time, sent a telegram from Chicago greeting the *Fraye arbeter shtime* and the changes that had been made, pledging his full support to the newly created editorial board. For the previous few years he had been very critical of the way I had run the paper and had often told me: "Let me help, and I will show you in one year's time how to have 50,000 readers for the *Fraye arbeter shtime!*"—so strongly did the man believe in his abilities, and so blind was he to the greatly changed circumstances among the Jewish working class.

When he came back from his tour, he became the de facto editor, with Abraham Frumkin as assistant editor, but he did not have a free hand as in the old days. It was not his newspaper. He had an editorial board to contend with, which for him was no easy task. On top of all this, Mark Mratchny was imported from Los Angeles, and he learned the trade and in due course was able to take over the editorship. At the convention later that year, Yanovsky demanded that he be released from the supervision of the board, which only interfered with his work. The convention did not grant his request. Instead, he was told to find a way to work with the other elected comrades. However, the convention did vote to celebrate Yanovsky's seventieth birthday with a special issue of the *Fraye arbeter shtime*, messages of greeting, events, and the like. This too was carried out.

During this time, the *Fraye arbeter shtime* became smaller and took on a tabloid format, meaning that the paper now had only four pages instead of the previous six, although the expenses were not reduced by doing this. The atmosphere in the editorial office remained far from congenial. At the second convention after I left the paper, I heard from afar that the fur was flying—Yanovsky attacked Mratchny, Michael A. Cohn attacked Yanovsky— and they almost came to blows. In those two years more bad blood had accumulated than anything seen in our movement previously.

At the next convention the editorship was handed over to Mark Mratchny. Yanovsky withdrew entirely, failing to realize his dream of fifty thousand readers. The new editor was, in our case, a stranger to the move- ment. In the few years that he had lived in America, in Detroit and Los Angeles, he had not been involved in the work of local groups, and he had very little knowledge of the history, traditions, and tendencies of our move- ment. Having previously been a teacher in a Yiddish school, he tended more in a Yiddishist direction than an anarchist one. Still, the annual conventions elected him editor one year after another, until he announced in 1939 that he would no longer accept the office. This coincided with the resignation of manager Sam Freedman, who for more than eight years had carried the heavy burden of caring for the newspaper's material existence. It became necessary to replace both positions at the same time, and under the circumstances of the moment this proved an impossible task. The *Fraye arbeter shtime* was in danger of extinction due to a lack of people who were willing to take on the task of publishing her.

The world stood at the edge of a yawning abyss. The Second World War had broken out in Europe. Many of us felt that in time we too would be drawn into the bloody whirlwind. Opinions in our ranks were divided and sharply opposed. Many comrades, myself included, felt that the Nazi barbarism necessitated that we take an active part in preparing public opinion in this country for entry into the war. But most of the comrades, it appeared to me at the time, took a principled stand against this war as against any other war. I could not bring myself to take over the editorship of the paper, which was offered to me at the time, and direct an anarchist newspaper in agitation for war against the conviction of most of the comrades. As an editor, I always felt strongly bound by the official decisions that expressed the views of the majority of comrades. But here, on a most important matter, our opinions were so different that I said: I can see no justification for accepting the office.

The situation was critical, but our movement showed much vitality, and the comrades were so devoted to the newspaper that the crisis was soon solved quite satisfactorily. Comrade Sol Linder agreed to take over the management, and Dr. Herman Frank took over the editorial side of the work. The paper continued, appearing every week, and had its fierce defenders as well as its sharp critics, as had always been the case. But because of the pressures during the war, no deliberations or conventions were held, and the movement's activities were largely neglected.

CHAPTER 53

The Sunrise Colony

It is not possible in this short chapter to give a clear idea of the great work that we undertook in founding and organizing the Sunrise Colony and the rich experiences we had there. Here we must be satisfied with a very brief overview of what occurred.[1]

The organization of the colony in the spring of 1933 was, in one sense, a result of the terrible crisis that gripped the entire country in the early thirties, but this was neither the only cause nor the principal one. The idea of cooperative and communist colonies, religious and secular (of which the former had a considerable following), is much older than our movement in America. Our Jewish immigrants had created a number upon their arrival. Chaim Weinberg, myself, and many other comrades had been talking about and planning such an undertaking for years. In the wake of the financial crisis, an organization was formed in New York City that convened meetings and took up the question seriously. Peretz Hirschbein and other important figures took part in these discussions.[2] Ely Greenblatt often visited from Detroit and took me to these meetings, trying to get me involved in such work.

On my way back from my lecture tour in early 1933, Greenblatt met me in Chicago at Sam Kagan's house and brought with him, as he put it, two

---

1. Cohen later wrote a detailed memoir of the Sunrise Colony that was published after his death: *In Quest of Heaven: The Story of the Sunrise Co-operative Farm Community* (New York: Sunrise History Pub. Committee, 1957).

2. **Peretz Hirschbein** (Perets Hirshbeyn, 1880–1948) was a Russian-born Jewish poet, playwright, and travel writer. He immigrated to the United States in 1911, was a contributor to the *FAS*, *Tsukunft*, and *Der tog*, and wrote several popular Yiddish plays.

candidates for a colony: comrades Israel Slakter and Warren.[3] I traveled with them to Detroit and spent a week there working out a plan for a colony of two hundred families and after many consultations called a public meeting for this purpose. The reaction was overwhelming. People were gripped by the idea as if it was their last hope of salvation in such a troubled time. An organization of comrades was immediately formed, with Abe Zubrin as secretary, and an appeal was published in the *Fraye arbeter shtime*.[4] The plan was simple and clear: bring together two hundred members, who would contribute up to $1,000 each. The capital would be used in three ways— one-third to purchase a suitable farm not far from a large city; one-third to build houses and provide tools for all kinds of occupations; and one-third for living expenses until its own production could bring in enough income. No mortgages or debts. The members needed to include all kinds of craftsmen, specialists, and professionals that are required in a society, to make it self-sufficient.

Everyone would live as one big family, on equal terms. Everyone would work for and safeguard the well-being of all. When a member withdrew, they would have to be satisfied with what the colony decided to return to them. The individual would have no property rights in the colony.

Because of the reactionary political nature that the "Left" had given to the term "communism," we described the projected colony as a "collectivist cooperative"; in reality, however, it was planned as a libertarian communist (*fray-komunistishn*) community, as the call made clear.

The plan would likely require a few years to complete. There were many volunteers willing to live in a communist colony during the Depression, but those with $1,000 in cash were limited among our ranks. In addition, we wanted to select our members as carefully as possible, choosing only people who, by their nature as well as their occupation, were properly adapted for such an undertaking. Two small events radically changed our plans: Ely Greenblatt found a farm near Detroit that was, it seemed, created by God

---

3. "Warren" may be Oscar Warren (Oskar Voren, 1886–1964), born Wernikowsky/ Vernikovsky, a Detroit storekeeper and anarchist who immigrated in 1906 and belonged to Branch 156 of the Workmen's Circle in Detroit. His wife, Rebecca Warren (Rebeka Voren, 1889–1980), was an active member of Detroit's Fraye Arbeter Shtime Group and secretary of the Froyen Grupe "Fraye Gezelshaft."

4. *FAS*, May 5, 1933. A translation appeared in *Freedom* (New York), June 1933.

for just such a purpose and a great bargain as well. The other event was my release from the *Fraye arbeter shtime*—I was in need of new activity. This was the synchronicity that was required. At the end of March, we had begun to think about the possibility, and two months later the whole thing was done. We were able to recruit more than a hundred members with capital of barely $40,000, and we bought the bargain for $158,000, with another $40,000 in back taxes that would need to be paid when necessary.

It was truly a great bargain: the farm had 10,000 acres of land—sixteen square miles—a third of which was good for cultivation. There were a number of very fine houses and about fifty derelict smaller houses that could be restored, a few thousand acres of land that were already sown; sixty good horses, a meager three thousand sheep, a few hundred pigs, enough feed for all of them, and a very large number of tools and machines for farming—in a word, it was a proper, well-established enterprise on a very large scale, and the price, you might say, was insignificant.

In order to purchase this bargain quickly, we were forced to change our plans: we had to rush to recruit members, lower the required deposit to $500, and take on debt, shouldering a burden of $5,000 a year in interest on the mortgage, somewhat more each year in taxes, and in a few years we would start paying down the principal. Professionals assured us that one successful year with a good harvest could bring in enough to pay off the entire debt. There was no reason to fear the debts we had assumed.

In June the first group settled on the farm, and before the summer was over we had about a hundred families living there. The demand to join was so great that we had difficulty regulating the influx and holding back candidates who would thrust their families upon us before we could screen them as planned. The members came from all the major cities in sixteen states. Most were from New York, Philadelphia, Detroit, and Chicago, but they also came from Boston, Los Angeles, Cleveland, and dozens of other cities.

Life on the farm was difficult for city dwellers that first summer, but their enthusiasm and satisfaction were so great that no one dwelled on the difficulties. Not only the colonists but also the dozens and hundreds of visitors were satisfied with our primitive conditions and helped with the labor in the fields and the repair of the old houses. The fields were filled with song, laughter, and anticipation. It was a true honeymoon period, which lasted far into the winter.

City Workers, Discouraged By Industry's Past Uncertainties Turn To Seek Security On Unique Farm

From city tenements to fragrant peppermint fields . . . this group of workers has gone to find security and happiness together . . . E. H. Greenblatt, above, right, their leader, and Joseph J. Cohen, secretary of the Sunrise Community, hold high hopes for the future.

Figure 29: The Sunrise Colony, 1933
Syndicated feature about the Sunrise Colony from the Newspaper Enterprise Association, including portraits of Ely Greenblatt and Joseph Cohen on the lower right

The members were, with very few exceptions, all radicals, mostly anarchists—the best that our movement possessed. Only one thing was missing: specialists in many occupations. We had too many housepainters and not enough carpenters; too many tailors and not enough farmers.

We were happy to have our own baker, a mason, a few butchers, and a number of dairy workers. In time we even managed to get a doctor, a nurse, a teacher, and a few young students who had taken a course at an agricultural school. However, we lacked a number of occupations. We were far from self-sufficient and had to employ hired labor.

We recruited more members in New York and Philadelphia, where the recruiting was done for us by committees: Dr. Benjamin Dubovsky, Dr. Charles Maley, and a number of our comrades in New York, and comrade Hyman Weinstock and others in Philadelphia.[5] The list of members soon numbered two hundred. Half of them planned to come a year or two later. Meanwhile, they had deposited up to $200.

That first summer we built a large new kitchen, which used two of the larger old houses as dining rooms for the whole colony; we built a dormitory for all the children with a school, a teacher, and learning materials; and we acquired enough cows for milk, built a steam laundry, and renovated most of the buildings. We were also forced to create a central sewer system for the whole colony—a huge undertaking that required difficult labor and considerable expenses. Everyone worked—men, women, and the older children. Most of them worked too hard, especially their first time. It was necessary to restrain some of the members in order to protect their health. Everyone was enthusiastic and highly satisfied.

Later, in the cold, damp days of autumn, enthusiasm began to wane. People began to prepare for elections, to work out rules and regulations, to think about going to town for a rest in the winter months, when there was much less work on the farm—a certain vagueness and pettiness entered into life. Differences of opinion, which are unavoidable among such a sizable number of people, became sharper. Sexual entanglements shook up several families. Some sort of big-shot financiers, former financial secretaries of Workmen's Circle branches, stated that on paper we were bankrupt and would soon have nothing to eat. After the election, the losing candidates— among them the first president, Ely Greenblatt—became very disappointed and embittered. Two camps formed: the administration, headed by me as general secretary and supported by a large number of anarchists, and an opposition, which included a majority in the executive committee, including a number of Yiddishists and simply disgruntled elements, with a few active anarchists as leaders. The results are not difficult to imagine.

The income from the farm that first summer was $50,000 in cash, in addition to food for the members and feed for the animals for the year. The

---

5. **Charles Maley** (Tsharls Mayly, 1881–1964) was a Russian-born Jewish dentist and anarchist. He immigrated to the United States in 1905 and became chief of the Prosthetic Division at Unity Hospital in Brooklyn.

overhead expenses were interest fees, salaries, gasoline, machines, and annu-
ities that ate up almost all the proceeds. It became clear that we would need
to greatly increase our income through the sale of more farm products and
other activities, so that our time and energy would not be wasted on foolishly rushing to meetings, which used to last well into the night and shattered
everyone's nerves.

The truth of the matter is that we had to carry out a coup d'état that winter—a political maneuver to cause the administration to resign and then to
elect another without the process of a campaign and voting. The board of
directors would instead be divided into several special committees that were
elected at a single meeting. There was a very large number of opposition
members. We felt that they would no longer be useful members of the colony. But we did not want to use coercive measures under any circumstances.
We had the crazy idea to allow anyone, throughout the month of April 1934,
to withdraw and receive half the money that they had paid immediately, and
the other half a year later.

The purpose was clear and perhaps even logical: to get rid of some of
the dissatisfied people, even though it might cost us a thousand or so dollars. But what happened was something entirely different. Eighteen people,
two-thirds of them good, active members, took advantage of the offer, causing a payout of $5,000, which we did not have at the time, and, worst of all,
the leaders of the opposition remained. They began attacking the colony, its
administration, and its prospects. The *Fraye arbeter shtime* opened its columns to them without any restraint. Dr. Michael A. Cohn and Saul Yanovsky
had opposed the plan of the colony from the beginning. New members were
poisoned with all kinds of horror stories by the time they reached the colony.
The foundations of our entire project were systematically undermined by a
few embittered people in our own ranks.

Of course, we had the power, and maybe even the social obligation, to
discipline or remove them, but we refused to do so under any conditions.
We had always before us the dreadful image of a dictatorship, to which an
administration—or a government, as in Soviet Russia—is driven by people
who are too self-absorbed and willing to sacrifice themselves and the whole
of society in order to assert their views and caprice. We sought libertarian
methods to heal the wounds and avoid catastrophe. Unfortunately we were
not able to discover such methods.

In the spring, a large number of new members arrived, as well as quite a few nonmember volunteers, young people with the knowledge and willingness to help build a colony. The population grew significantly more than during the first summer. We did not have to hire so many workers and pay so much in wages, but we were still forced to borrow money from a government agency for that purpose.

The New Deal had begun to build colonies in Hightstown and other places that year.[6] Two of its representatives, Udo Rall and Dr. W. E. Zeuch, visited us, spending several days, and became acquainted with all the possibilities and relationships among our members, and they recommended to Washington, DC, that our colony be given generous support.[7]

Government aid, however, is like an extremely poisonous drug—it is given with great assurances and much red tape, and is often too little, too late, more likely bringing death rather than health to the patient.

In Michigan, at that time, there were dozens of self-help organizations of the unemployed that carried out a range of activities, created their own currency (a kind of scrip), and created jobs and a means of existence for a few thousand families. The number of unemployed in the state was very large. The government handed out $2 million a week to help keep them alive. Jacob Baker, an individualist anarchist and an old acquaintance from New York, served in the Federal Emergency Relief Administration in Washington.[8]

---

6. The Jersey Homesteads in Hightstown, New Jersey, were a project of the New Deal's Resettlement Administration. Its nearly two hundred homes were intended for Jewish garment workers of New York City and Philadelphia, and the colony included a cooperative farm, clothing factory, and store. The settlement officially opened in 1936 but was a financial failure and closed in 1940.

7. **Udo Rall** (c. 1894–1980) was a German-born craftsman, an advocate of consumer and housing cooperatives, and a onetime anarchist. He immigrated to California as a teenager and in 1915–1916 taught arts and crafts at San Diego Normal School. During the First World War Rall was interned as an enemy alien and nearly deported due to his anarchism. In 1934 he moved to Washington, DC, to direct the Federal Emergency Relief Administration's Division of Self-Help Cooperatives and work for the Rural Electrification Administration. **William Edward Zeuch** (1892–1968) was an American-born economist, educator, and socialist. He was a former member of the New Llano Colony in Louisiana, where he cofounded Commonwealth College in 1923, and worked for the Subsistence Homesteads Division of the Department of the Interior. Zeuch later taught economics at Indiana University and then the University of Illinois.

8. **Jacob Baker** (1895–1967) was an American-born manager, industrial engineer, publisher, and anarchist. He contributed articles to the anarchist papers *The Mutualist* (1925–1928)

He was very interested in self-help endeavors and in our colony. With his encouragement, we incorporated under state supervision, with a dedicated staff and office in Lansing to ensure our well-being. However, the bureaucracy and red tape was so massive that a number of the state-sponsored organizations went under before aid arrived. After much trouble, we were able to obtain several hundred thousand dollars, tied to complicated regulations, to help our organization with significant loans. Over time, our colony raised $45,000 for that fund. I was chairman of our state-sanctioned organization and management fund. I spent much time visiting special bodies and negotiating with government representatives in Lansing and in Washington. The result of all this was that one fine day in the spring of 1936, the fourth year of the colony's existence, a government agent came and proposed a plan whereby we would turn the colony over to the government, which would pay for everything we possessed, making it possible to free ourselves of all the dissatisfied colonists, whose money we could return to them. Those who wanted to continue as colonists would be able to do so on the same farm, with government help and supervision.

I did not like the plan at all. But, on the other hand, the situation was as follows: most of my comrades had left for one reason or another. Over the previous three years, more than sixty anarchists had withdrawn from the organization. That spring there were seventy-five families in the colony, many of them dissatisfied. Besides, there was work in the cities again. Housepainters were making ten dollars a day in Detroit. We began to feel that the people would disappear. There were only a small number of genuine comrades left and quite a few who were good for nothing.

Regardless, at least I didn't go down without explaining myself first. The vast majority of members were enthusiastic and decided to negotiate and implement the plan. Naturally, things are sooner said than done when one is dealing with government. Its regulations change, as do conditions.

and *Freedom* (1933–1934) and founded the left-wing Vanguard Press (1926–1988), which published such books as *Kropotkin's Revolutionary Pamphlets* (1927), *The Letters of Sacco and Vanzetti* (1928), and Alexander Berkman's *Now and After*. Baker also sat on the executive committee of the League for Mutual Aid, and in 1933 his advocacy on behalf of the unemployed led to his appointment as assistant administrator of the Federal Emergency Recovery Act, the Civil Works Administration, and the Works Progress Administration. In this role he oversaw the WPA's guidebook series and helped get anarchist Henry Alsberg appointed director of the Federal Writers' Project. Obituary: *New York Times*, September 20, 1967.

After many twists and turns, the farm was bought by the government for $281,000—enough to pay off our mortgage, the back taxes, and our debt to the government, and still leave enough money to return our entire cash investment. In addition, we would keep all our belongings, machines, horses, sheep, cows, and that year's harvest. But there was no way for the colony to remain at the same location, as we were originally promised. Those of us who were determined to remain colonists were forced to look for a new place to continue our work.

As negotiations with the government began, we were embroiled in a lawsuit brought by several former members who, under the leadership of Ely Greenblatt and Charlie Sanders, sought to lay their hands on the vast assets the government was going to pay us.[9] They obtained, first, a federal court injunction prohibiting us from moving anything from the old farm to the new one; secondly, they demanded that the court appoint a receiver, who usually has very sticky fingers. Thirdly, they accused the administration of all kinds of crimes: forcing members to leave the colony, ruling over them with violence, not giving an account of income and expenses, and above all being lawless people, anarchists and communists, capable of any misdeed.

This was not a new thing. Communist colonies in America had previously had similar troubles and were accused of the exact same things. Our hearing took place in federal court before Judge Arthur J. Tuttle, a very strict but honest and intelligent man. For a week, from early morning until late in the evening, he listened to all who had something to say, and became acquainted with all the details and the many financial reports we had published and our account books, which had already been carefully examined by the government accountants twice before.

He dismissed all complaints, stating that we had acted even more generously than the law required toward those who hindered the work of the colony or withdrew. He praised our work to the heavens and told us to carry on as we saw fit. We were not obligated to do anything for those who had left the colony.

The lawsuit cost us several thousand dollars for lawyers in addition to the damage caused by the injunction. We decided that the former colonists

---

9. **Charles Sanders** (1890–1976) was a Russian-born Jewish shopkeeper and anarchist. He immigrated to Chicago in 1908, and after leaving the Sunrise Colony he settled in Salem, Missouri.

who had brought the suit—fifteen in number—should bear the cost, to be deducted from the sum of money to which they were entitled. All the former members received the sums they had paid for the upcoming year, 1937. Those who then returned received in additional seven dollars for each month that an adult family member lived and worked in the colony. Forty families withdrew. Most of them received twice as much money as they had paid in, and some received much more than that. This used up all the money the government had given us. We were left with about thirty families, and all the moveable property of the colony. We stayed there for a year, working on the land after selling it to the government, while at the same time looking for a new location for a colony.

But again, differences of opinions brought new troubles. Some wanted to resettle on a farm somewhere else in Michigan. Others had come to hate the entire region. They wanted a more favorable place with a better climate. We found and bought a neglected farm in a wonderful place in Virginia and began to transport the machines and livestock there. The number of members dwindled even further. There remained about twenty families, a collection of compatible, experienced people who had endured the ups and downs of the colony. Surely they would be able to live in peace and work harmoniously. That is what we all felt and believed.

But it turned out that the smaller the group, the greater the friction and dissatisfaction. We brought with us some of the stuff that had poisoned our existence in the old place. At the end of one year of living in the new location, I became convinced that it was hopeless and foolish to continue working under these circumstances. It seemed to some colonists that my long-standing leadership as general secretary was the cause of the colony's failure, and it would have better prospects if I resigned. We attempted this solution. In November 1938, I left the colony without receiving a cent and not knowing if I ever would. The remaining fifteen or sixteen families stayed for another year and then sold the place and returned each person's money. During the six years of the colony's existence, several hundred people had joined as members and paid large or small sums of money. No one lost a penny, other than the fifteen withdrawn members who had taken us to court. The colony did not owe anything to anyone, and I can say with a clear conscience that it did not harm anyone in any way. It was a wonderful experiment from which we learned much.

These are just some of the features that marked the beginning and the end of the enterprise, with many details omitted. I only want to, once again as briefly as possible, point out the bright and the dark sides of our great experiment:

1) Life in a libertarian communist society has a great impact on most people. To me it seems that there is a deep-rooted desire in the individual—almost an instinctive desire—to join a community and live among a wider circle. It is like a deep longing for a return to an older, long-gone form of coexistence. Cold, logical calculations, and the awareness that hundreds of experiments in this area in modern times have all ended in failure, have no effect on people who possess a desire for this kind of life. They feel, or convince themselves, that they will succeed in achieving this goal where others failed. Among the hundreds of people who visited the colony and spent some time with us, there was an insignificant number of skeptics who saw only the dark side of our lives. The vast majority were genuinely enthralled. David Pinski and Norman Thomas, to mention only two well-known personalities, could not find enough words of praise for our way of life.[10] Professor M. L. Wilson, undersecretary of agriculture under Henry A. Wallace, likened our experiment to the work of the first pioneers who came to this country, the scope of which is reflected in every school textbook.[11] He pointed out that to try to develop a communist way of life in a hostile capitalist environment, under the worst obstacles, is a huge undertaking that must be admired. Such an auspicious impression was made on most people. Dr. Jacob A. Maryson strongly

---

10. **David Pinski** (1872–1959) was a Russian-born Jewish writer, playwright, and Labor Zionist. He was involved in revolutionary circles in Warsaw and began writing groundbreaking dramas about urban working-class Jewish life and sexuality. In 1899 Pinksi immigrated to New York, where he worked on the *Abend blat* and coedited *Di arbeter tsaytung* and *Tsukunft*. He also became a leading Labor Zionist and editor of *Der idisher kemfer* and *Di tsayt*. In 1949 Pinski immigrated to Israel. **Norman Thomas** (1884–1968) was an American Presbyterian minister, pacifist, and socialist. He led the Socialist Party throughout the 1930s and was its six-time presidential candidate. According to Cohen, Thomas said of the Sunrise Colony: "Here we have a living and inspiring example of the coming Socialist order that will liberate mankind from its bondage!" (*In Quest of Heaven*, 72).

11. **Milburn Lincoln Wilson** (1885–1969) was an American-born agronomist. In 1933–1934 he served as director of the Subsistence Homesteads Division of the Department of the Interior, during which time he met with Cohen and other leaders of the Sunrise Colony and referred them to W. E. Zeuch for assistance.

encouraged us and advised us not to be too strict in our anarchist doctrines (*shulkhn-orekh*)—wisdom that we did not have the courage to follow.

2) In times of great economic crisis, cold calculation aligns with the instinctive desire to live in community and, albeit to a small extent, to dispel worries about one's own increasingly difficult survival. The individual in a communist colony does not have to worry about rent, grocery bills, doctors' fees, medicine, and all the other banal items that make life difficult during times of unemployment in the capitalist disorder. These worries fall on the community, on the managers and officers when they come together to conduct business. One of our members, a middle-aged worker, expressed the situation in a characteristic way. He kept a few coins on the table in his room, with which he would often chat like so: "So, you are cursed! I'm free of your evil reign (*memshole*)! I do not need to come to you anymore! Not to worry! I can move on quite comfortably without your mediation!" This attitude was shared by a large number of members. They found in it compensation for all the difficulties they faced.

3) The problem of labor is not a serious one in a communist colony. Those who don't want to work are relatively few in number. The problem is one of adapting the work to the people, so that they are interested and satisfied by what they do. In this regard, one can learn a lot from Charles Fourier's notes regarding the inclinations, feelings, and desires of individuals. In our colony, the work was not at all suited to people's habits, abilities, and age. This was one of the main problems.

4) The sex question (*geshlikht-frage*) in a colony is not more serious than in other environments, although women are given the same status as men and are no longer dependent on men's earnings. In six years of experience, we did not have a single serious incident in this area, or more incidents than anywhere else. Women are generally just as good colonists and communists as men. Life in the colony, terribly crowded and impoverished as it was, was nevertheless healthy, natural, and highly ethical. We had only one death out of a substantial population, and one case of a foolish, petty theft. No other group of people of this size has shown such a good record.

5) Communist coexistence and communal living are not as economical as living in a private household. We became firmly convinced of this after long, bitter experience. There are hundreds of tasks at which an individual housewife is more successful and more economical than the barracks-like

system of communal living. This is something to take seriously. The transition from family life to communal life is very difficult and must not be a sudden one.

6) Farming is in ordinary times not a profitable business and requires a large investment per family in land, buildings, machinery, and livestock. In a cooperative or communist colony, the investment can be much smaller—equipment can be used more often and with greater results. But our colony had too little money to start with. We were drowning in debt without any opportunity for further development. The standard of living was much lower than what the colonists were accustomed to—the biggest mistake that can be made in such an undertaking.

7) People's relationship to communal property and communal work is not satisfactory. That which belongs to everyone, is the concern of no one, in the sense of treating it with care, not leaving it in God's hands, and avoiding damage or loss through inattention and neglect. A good craftsman pays close attention to his tools. But an idealist (*luft-mentsh*), a former proletarian, does not know such things, and it is difficult to awaken such feelings in him. One has to continually remind people, scold them and subject them to strict rules. Our anarchist approach did not harmonize with such needs.

8) A communist colony has the tendency to diminish the importance of the individual, their self-esteem, and their reputation. In the capitalistic world, even the lowliest slave is master in his own home. In his family he is the authority, the breadwinner, the boss, and the thinker. His wife and children are dependent upon him. This elevates him in his own eyes, bestowing responsibility and dignity. In the colony he did not have any of these advantages. Women and children were put in a higher, more privileged position by the community than him. They no longer had to rely on him or bow to his whims. In the outside world, a man can distinguish himself with his clothing, his occupation, his generosity in making donations or contributions, and in dozens of other small ways. The colony takes away all these opportunities, as well. Clothing becomes uniform; work is determined by others and usually gives no satisfaction; donations are made by the community, not the individual. All other avenues are curtailed. The individual is lost, becoming an indistinguishable part of a larger whole. It is certainly possible to find solutions, but when one is drowning in debt and must care for everyone in the entire colony day and night, it is no easy task.

9) Dissatisfaction with things as they are is as prevalent in a colony as anywhere else. Differences of opinion are unavoidable. It does not matter what it is regarding. Here every little thing is transformed into a life-or-death question. After all, everyone depends on the well-being of the colony, which can be improved in many different ways or damaged by the slightest detail. Especially when people are distressed, embittered, or disappointed, there is no restraint, no balance, and no measure in people's words with each other. It becomes simply impossible to reach an understanding and to work harmoniously. When I now meet the fiercest leaders of the opposition, they ask me: "What were we really arguing about? What did we want?" No one can put their finger on the exact thing and say, "Here was the cause!" It was all petty things, foolishness, about which adults, good people (*mentshn*), intellectuals, did not have to argue. But at the time, in that difficult, serious environment, all the little things became very important and serious. They made life miserable and made it impossible to advance this tremendous undertaking the correct way.

CHAPTER 54

The New Deal

I have not the slightest doubt that Franklin D. Roosevelt, with his New Deal, sought to improve the situation of farmers and workers with only two purposes in mind—to save the country from catastrophe and to save capitalism from collapse. To these ends it was necessary to alleviate much of the plight of the poor, to stop mortgage foreclosures on homes and farms, to throw the workers a bone so that they would not revolt, and to secure the deposits of small businesses in the banks.

This was done. After more than 150 years of difficult struggles and countless martyrs, the workers now won legal recognition of their right to organize and to negotiate with employers collectively. The government, after all kinds of consultations and talk, came to the aid of the unions, making it possible for them to organize all workers. In those areas where officials and leaders understood the new message, feverish organizing activity soon began. The unions rose like yeast.

The friendly attitude of the government made this work easier, but the main burden fell on the workers. Even under the National Recovery Administration—"Labor's Magna Carta"—they had to fight hard and suffer much for the right to organize.[1] Employers showed strong resistance, bathing

---

1. The **National Recovery Administration** was a federal agency created by President Franklin D. Roosevelt in 1933 to combat the Great Depression. Its charter, the National Industrial Recovery Act, included Section 7(a), which guaranteed employees "the right to organize and bargain collectively through representatives of their own choosing . . . free from the interference, restraint, or coercion of employers." In 1935 the Supreme Court declared the act unconstitutional, but its protection of the right to unionize was reinstated by the National Labor Relations Act that same year.

in workers' blood in South Chicago and elsewhere.[2] They organized company unions to circumvent the requirements of the new laws, and they did everything they could to maintain their unrestricted power over the workers. The struggle was greatly complicated by the dirty work of the "Lefts," who sought to capitalize on the new fratricidal struggle that developed between the American Federation of Labor and the Congress of Industrial Organizations.[3] Rose Pesotta's book, *Bread upon the Waters*, gives a clear picture of the confused struggle in the ranks of labor at that time.

The most interesting development of that period was the new form of strike that the automobile workers used. Instead of walking out in order to strike, they remained in the big factories and barricaded the doors and gates, not allowing in any scabs and other unwanted guests.

At first the employers thought it was nothing more than a joke. They immediately obtained an injunction from a judge, who ordered the workers to leave the premises immediately. But wonder of wonders, the strikers were not intimidated by the injunction. They proclaimed to the world that the judge was a partner in a rich automobile company, owned a hundred shares in it, and if he had a spark of honesty and integrity in him, he would have known that he should never have heard such a case in which he was himself an interested party.

Luckily for the workers, the newly elected governor of Michigan was Frank Murphy, an honest and liberal man (though a devout Catholic) and later Supreme Court judge.[4] He had previously been mayor of Detroit, demonstrating his liberalism by allowing all radical groups in the city to hold demonstrations in front of City Hall without harassment. As governor, he immediately sent the state militia into the strike district, in Flint, with orders not to disturb the strikers in any way but to see to it that the employers and their helpers, the vigilante committees, did not engineer a bloodbath. His

---

2. Cohen refers here to the Memorial Day Massacre of 1937, in which Chicago police shot and killed ten unarmed protesters outside of the Republic Steel Mill.

3. The **Congress of Industrial Organizations (CIO)** was founded in 1935 by ten industrial unions, including the ILGWU and ACWA, that broke away from the AFL to focus on organizing unskilled workers in mass production. The CIO was more inclusive than the AFL, embraced more confrontational tactics such as the sit-down strike, and included a large left-wing contingent. In 1955 the CIO and AFL remerged to form the AFL-CIO.

4. **Frank Murphy** (1890–1949) was an American-born attorney and Democratic politician who served as governor of Michigan from 1937 to 1939.

action shook the whole state, the whole country, and the employers were helpless with the injunction they had received from the not-so-kosher judge.

The struggle lasted six weeks, and for six weeks the workers did not leave the factories. The strike committee supplied them with food and support. We at the Sunrise Colony, just thirty-five miles from Flint, sent as much food and whatever else we could to the strikers. At last the employers were forced to give in, recognize the union, sign a contract with it, and significantly improve the situation of the workers.

❋ ❋ ❋

The government's new direction under Roosevelt's administration looked to most of us anarchists at the time to be nothing more than an American brand of fascism. The government kept expanding its power and restricting the rights of its citizens. Administrative bureaucrats won the full support of everyone everywhere. The elected legislators, representatives of the people, increased the power of the president with their goodwill until it far exceeded the power of crowned rulers in other countries. The tendency of government in this country had shifted in the direction of centralization, concentration, the increase of government workers. A couple of million people now drew their livelihoods directly from the government as employees, in addition to the millions who were dependent on government pensions and were thus forced to act as officials demanded.

Such a situation seemed to us to be very dangerous to the freedoms of the people and to the prospects for the normal, free development of society. Such a system leads to the building of a powerful party machine that, even while maintaining the democratic procedure of free elections, can always impose its will and policies on the whole population—that is, it can establish a dictatorship under the cloak of democracy.

In our opposition to the government's New Deal policies, we gradually realized that our position coincided with that of the most reactionary forces in the country—the "rugged individualists"—who demanded freedom for themselves to be able to exploit others. The big capitalists, bankers, utility magnates, industrialists, the National Association of Manufacturers, and the Chamber of Commerce were all speaking the same language as us, demanding freedom, criticizing the steps taken by the government, and organizing the infamous "Liberty League," composed of the richest and most reactionary elements in the country.[5] Some of us began to suspect that something must be wrong with our worldview if we echoed the wishes and desires of the worst robbers of the people.

Theoretically, as anarchists, we had to be outspoken opponents of the New Deal as in all other practices that affirm the power of government, of the state. A small number of older comrades—many of them young in years and experience but old in their outlook—remained staunch opponents of everything the New Deal accomplished. I heard from close friends and acquaintances that Roosevelt was a greater danger to freedom than Hitler, because he was more driven and shrewder, but the number of such dogmatically unyielding people in our ranks was quite small. The majority of anarchists here in America, in our ranks, at least, over time began to look kindly on the New Deal and even went so far as to support Roosevelt in his later campaigns for a third and fourth term. This is a phenomenon that we need to take into account when we think seriously about our movement, its tasks, and its aspirations.

---

5. The **American Liberty League** was an elite conservative organization founded in 1934 by opponents of the New Deal. It framed its opposition in terms of "individual liberty" and protection of private property and allegedly plotted a coup to remove Roosevelt from power, known as "the Business Plot."

CHAPTER 55

Return to Stelton

In the fall of 1938 I left the Sunrise Colony following the conflicts arising from its relocation to Virginia. I settled not far from Boston and set out to record my recollections and experiences in connection with the colony. That autumn the comrades in Philadelphia greeted me with a beautiful and supremely friendly celebration of my sixtieth birthday, which they carried out as heartily as possible. But in a sense I felt that my years of practical activity in the movement were coming to an end. I had already served a double tour of duty in the movement—no less than forty-five years. How long worrying oneself and others with movement work is enough?

My comrades and close friends in Philadelphia and, in particular, Stelton were very worried about how I would make a living. They knew that I was too old to go back to work in a cigar factory, and I lacked the means to establish a chicken farm again. A couple of them—Joseph Bluestein, Israel Kaplan, Sol Vinick, and others—decided that I should come back to Stelton and resume the work that had been abandoned fifteen years before.[1] Through a letter and a personal visit to Boston, Bluestein and Kaplan persuaded me to agree and accept their offer that, with the help of my other close friends, they would provide me with a house, a piece of land, and the necessary equipment to raise chickens on a small scale, enough to feed and sustain my small family.

They fulfilled their obligations more than 100 percent. They built me a cozy and lovely house, practically with their own hands, in a nice spot in the colony and presented it to me as a gift that far exceeded my contributions to

---

1. **Solomon ("Sol") Vinick** (Vinik, 1889–1970) was a Russian-born Jewish mechanic, barber, and anarchist. He immigrated to the United States in 1905 and was a longtime resident of the Stelton Colony.

the movement. I do not know how much effort and money it took to accomplish such a costly undertaking. I do not know by whom and how the funds were collected to cover the expenses. I only know that they were, and the whole thing was handed over to me free of obligations. The practical side of this work in Stelton was done by the Bluesteins, the Kaplans, Sol Vinick, Abe Winokour, Sam Klonin, and Benny Moore.[2] They organized the committee. Other comrades in Philadelphia and New York apparently helped to raise the means. I take this opportunity to acknowledge this wonderful work of mutual solidarity and to express my heartfelt thanks to all those who had a hand in it.

❊ ❊ ❊

Thus, in the fall of 1939 I returned to Stelton and to my old job of raising chickens. The colony and school had changed much over the years. Physically, outwardly, these were changes for the better. The place that in 1915, when we first arrived, was rocky and bare, without a bit of shade, was now covered with an abundance of shade and fruit trees, which we had planted years earlier as scrawny saplings. The whole colony was still inhabited by over a hundred families, with most of the houses surrounded by flower gardens and green grass. Some of the comforts of city living—electric lighting and gas—were now provided here too. Outer appearances were not bad at all.

Internally, however, spiritually and socially, things had changed for the worse. The colonists were torn apart between the "Right" and the "Left," the school was in a precarious position, and social life had come to an almost complete standstill. A short time after I had originally left Stelton (for reasons already explained), the Ferms also departed the school and the colony. It became difficult to find teachers and chaperones. Abe Goldman, Dr.

---

2. **Abe Winokour** (Vinokur, 1894–1969) was a Russian-born Jewish paperhanger and anarchist. After immigrating to the United States around 1911 he was active in Philadelphia's Radical Library and New York's Ferrer Center. Winokour went to Mexico during First World War to avoid conscription, and in 1922 he moved to Stelton where his daughters attended the Modern School and he helped run the Kropotkin Library and the cooperative store. He married anarchist Anna Sosnovsky and was active in the Sacco-Vanzetti defense campaign and in the International Brotherhood of Painters, Decorators and Paperhangers of America. Winokour and his family moved to Mohegan around 1941, then to Los Angeles in 1948. Obituary: *FAS*, January 1, 1970.

Benjamin W. Barkas, John Scott, and others tried their luck but didn't stay long. A number of older youths, former students, were able to more or less successfully lead some of the activities and would have eventually been able to assume management of the entire school, including Will Pogrebysky, Zari Schwartz, and Rose Frumkin.[3] However, at this point the peace between the "Left" and "Right" completely collapsed. There were arguments and meetings that lasted all night as the "Left" attempted to seize control of the school board at the annual convention, just as they had done in other organizations. But here they did not succeed. The entire colony was too deeply rooted in the anarchist tradition and worldview for anyone to be able to change its course so radically. So they avoided any activity in connection with the school and withdrew the support they had previously given.

The school suffered greatly as a result.

Then came the Depression. Most of the colonists worked in the needle trades in New York and became unemployed. Our cooperative ventures collapsed under the pressure of credit, which is a poison for any cooperative. The entire colony was horribly impoverished, both materially and spiritually. There was only one accomplishment during this hard time that made sense and was beneficial: the workers organized a cooperative shop for making ladies' dresses and suits. This employed a few dozen people, union members, who saved the time, effort, and money they would otherwise spend traveling to the city to work.

----

3. **William ("Bill") Pogrebysky** (Vil Pogrebisky, c. 1906–1940s) was a Russian-born Jewish artist and teacher. In 1913 his family immigrated to the United States, where his mother Genya ("Anna" c. 1881–?) was a founding member of the Communist Party. Pogrebysky attended the Stelton Modern School, where he was a protégé of Hugo Gellert and took over teaching art classes after Gellert left in 1922, at just seventeen years of age. He married fellow former Stelton student Rose Frumkin and later taught art at Mohegan. In the 1930s he and Rose returned to Russia with their children, where he died fighting on the front in the Second World War. **Zachary ("Zack" or "Zari") Schwartz** (1907–1997), later known as Zachary Shaw, was an American-born Jewish teacher. The son of anarchist Anna Schwartz, he and his sister attended the Ferrer Modern School in New York, the Stelton Modern School, and the Stony Ford School. Schwartz then taught arts and crafts at Stelton and Mohegan, and later he and his wife Elizabeth ("Billie," later known as Lovet) Vasilio, another former Stelton student, taught at the Peninsula School of Creative Education in Menlo Park, California. Obituary: *New York Times,* January 6, 1998. **Rose Frumkin Pogrebysky** (c. 1909–1972) was an English-born Jewish anarchist. In 1912 she immigrated to the United States with her mother and father, anarchist David "Leibush" Frumkin, and attended the Stelton Modern School, where she met and married William Pogrebysky..

Sometime before I returned, the colonists had also managed to persuade the Ferms to come back and supervise the school again. Elizabeth was already in her eighties and could contribute little directly. But Alexis Ferm was fifteen years younger, energetic, and full of enough life to undertake this hard work. The Ferrer School's good reputation had already disappeared. Most children of the colonists—who had themselves changed greatly in composition—attended public school in a newly constructed, sturdy building near the colony. Children no longer came from the city in the same numbers as before. The school was a mere shadow of what it had been in its glory days. Alexis Ferm and two female teachers were employed at the school: Anna Schwartz, who had always been associated with the school and its activities, and Jo Ann Wheeler, a professional teacher with a good understanding of libertarian education.[4]

But fortune, it seemed, frowned upon Stelton. On top of all the other difficulties, the Second World War brought with it a huge army camp, where soldiers temporarily stayed before boarding ships to sail to the battlefield. The camp occupied the entire area between the colony and the railroad tracks miles away, and it overwhelmed the atmosphere of everything around it.[5] The naturalness, the freedom, the joyfulness of the place and surrounding area vanished. The whole environment there reflected the catastrophe that had befallen the world in those years. I did not stay long in my new home with my close friends. My wife's poor health forced me to leave Stelton for a second time, a year before her death. In the fall of 1943 we set out again to find a new home.

---

4. **Anna Schwartz** (1887–1978), née Druz, was a Russian-born Jewish teacher and anarchist. She joined the Jewish anarchist movement and was active in New York's Ferrer Center after immigrating in 1906. Schwartz then left her husband from an arranged marriage and in 1915 moved to Stelton with her two children, Mary and Zachary Schwartz. She taught at the Stelton Modern School and the Stony Ford School and was the final principal of Stelton's Modern School in 1948–1953. **Jo Ann Wheeler Burbank** (1905–2000) was an American-born teacher and anarchist. She graduated high school at age twelve, became a teacher at age seventeen, and was hired to teach at the Modern School in Mohegan in 1929. There Burbank met and became the companion of anarchist John G. Scott, and the couple taught at the Stelton Modern School in 1929–1930. In 1933–1934 she coedited the agrarian anarchist newspaper *Mother Earth* with Scott, but then the couple separated, and she returned to Stelton.

5. **Camp Kilmer**, which became the largest processing center for outgoing troops during the war, opened near Stelton in June 1942.

CHAPTER 56

The Dark Reaction

Events in Europe moved at an astonishing rate and all in the same direction: the direction of dictatorship, oppression, reaction, and a return to the Dark Ages. It looked as if the Russian Revolution, instead of leading the way forward, had reversed the direction of social development, toward the worst forms of government that mankind has experienced.

At the time, the reaction seemed to come from within, from the revolutionary workers themselves. The fragmentation of movements and parties into blocs after the Russian Revolution made it possible for the Bolsheviks to concentrate all power into the hands of a small group of party fanatics and impose their will on 150 million people. The divisions within the ranks of Italy's labor organizations made it possible for a former socialist, a demagogue with hardly any following, to impose his will on the people and drown all opposition in castor oil and blood. And everywhere there were socialists from one tendency or another, under one name or another, who led counterrevolutionary movements of reaction and a new kind of slavery. Benito Mussolini, Philipp Scheidemann, Gustav Noske, Józef Piłsudski, and Ramsay MacDonald ruled over the largest countries in Europe outside Soviet Russia—and the results were everywhere dire, worse than could have been imagined.[1]

---

1. **Philipp Scheidemann** (1865–1939) was a member of the Social Democratic Party of Germany, and for four months in 1919 he served as the first chancellor of Germany's Weimar Republic, during which his government dispatched troops and members of the far-Right paramilitary Freikorps to suppress strikes and left-wing uprisings. **Gustav Noske** (1868–1946) was a member of the Social Democratic Party of Germany and served as the Weimar

In Germany a new force arose, the National Socialists, who gained a strong hold on the masses at a time when the socialists and "communists" were fighting each other. The great strength of this new plague came from the boundless stream of hatred that poured from the Nazis' mouths and newspapers: hate, bitter, poisonous hate for everything and everyone, especially for the Jews, the defenseless victims (*korbones*), the scapegoat of every demagogue; Jews whose property could be confiscated, whose shops or jobs could be taken away, whose very lives could be extinguished (*hefker*) to satisfy one's sadistic instincts.

But the Jews were not the only ones the Nazis hated. They wanted to amplify the people's feelings of hate to encompass the whole outside world, all non-Germans, and even the non-Nazis among their own people. The Nazi Party's power and influence grew in proportion to the hate spread by Hitler, Goebbels, Rosenberg, and others. They awoke and nurtured feelings of jealousy, of every German's desire to rule over if not the whole world (fortunately, there could be only one Hitler), then at least over a Polish, Czechoslovak, or French city. There were enough cities, towns, and villages in the world for literally every Nazi to have a good chance of being the ruler of one of them. This, in my opinion, explains in a sense the power and influence of Nazism and fascism—it is the dark force of hatred and jealousy that is inherent in most people. Jesus's doctrine of love and humility has not weakened this poisonous instinct. As long as people believe in the necessity of rulership (*hershaft*), as long as the masses blindly follow leaders, obeying party orders, the instincts of hatred and jealousy will be exploited by all kinds of demagoguery, to the detriment of all humankind.

In any case, the factors that made Nazism possible, whatever they are, don't change the facts of what happened: Hitler came to power in 1933 and

---

Republic's first minister of defense, overseeing the brutal campaign of repression against the attempted German Revolution of 1919. **Józef Piłsudski** (1867–1935) was a former member of the Polish Socialist Party who served as chief of state of the newly independent Poland from 1918 to 1922, as its dictatorial prime minister from 1926 to 1928, and as the de facto head of its authoritarian Sanation regime until his death. **Ramsay MacDonald** (1866–1937) was a Scottish-born politician and socialist. He cofounded Britain's Labour Party in 1900 and served as the United Kingdom's prime minister in 1924 and again from 1929 to 1931. MacDonald's 1931 coalition with the Conservative and Liberal Parties to form a National Government that drastically cut social spending and adhered to a policy of appeasement toward Nazi Germany led to his expulsion from the Labour Party.

immediately began to show his hand. One by one, he rejected the conditions of the Treaty of Versailles, openly preparing for war and demanding more and more concessions.[2] In 1936 he had a good opportunity to try out the new weapons that his General Staff had secretly manufactured during the Weimar Republic. The counterrevolution in Spain allowed Hitler and Mussolini to show what they could do. Spanish towns and cities were bombed by German and Italian airplanes. Francisco Franco received generous help from these two friends. Men, money, and weapons from these two poverty-stricken countries—Germany and Italy—poured in without restraint. After a long, bitter struggle, the Spanish Loyalists were defeated by an enemy who had the resources of half of Europe behind him.

And the other half of Europe, in its hypocritical way, also helped the murderers of the Spanish people. Léon Blum, socialist prime Minister of France at the time, invented a new gimmick, "nonintervention," which he knew or should have known the dictators would never respect.[3] Our President Roosevelt, for whom the radicals could not find enough words of praise, heeding the pope and the millions of Catholic voters in this country, placed the rebel Franco on the same level as the legally elected government of Spain and allowed no weapons to be shipped there. The role that Soviet Russia played in helping the Loyalists also did not stand up to criticism from even its friends. The republic was doomed to fall.

We can't begrudge these governments—whether democratic or dictatorial—for helping Franco to defeat the Spanish people's movement for freedom. During their awakening, for the first time in history, an organized anarchist movement clearly materialized and sought to reorganize social life on a purely libertarian basis of anarchist-communist organization. Throughout Catalonia and many other Spanish provinces, libertarian communist enterprises sprang up—in the countryside as well as in the cities. The victory of the people in that struggle would have inevitably led to the

---

2. The **Treaty of Versailles**, signed between Germany and the Allied Powers at the end of the First World War, required Germany to demilitarize, concede territory, and pay massive reparations to Allied countries.

3. **Léon Blum** (1872–1950) was a French Jewish socialist politician who, as head of France's Popular Front government in 1936–1937, pursued a policy of neutrality toward the Spanish Civil War. The resulting Non-Intervention Agreement was signed by France, Britain, the Soviet Union, Italy, and Germany, but the latter three all quickly violated the pact.

establishment of anarchist centers in other parts of that country. The governments of the other countries, of course, could not allow this. They were frightened enough by the Bolshevik Revolution in Russia, which had abolished only one pillar of the old order—private property and the possibility of production for profit—leaving the second pillar, government (*hershaft*), not only untouched but also much stronger. They could easily imagine the global upheaval that would occur should the Spanish people succeed in taking their revolution a step further—and abolishing the twin evils (*tsores*) of capitalism and government together. In some parts of Spain this was close to being realized.

We organized meetings and raised large sums of money. Our small colony in Sunrise contributed $100 from the general treasury. The membership contributed twice as much. Younger comrades traveled to Spain to help in the struggle, undergoing great hardships to circumvent the "non-intervention" blockade—but to no effect: they could not change the outcome of the war. Preparations for the Second World War were in full swing. The heaving march of the well-disciplined German armies continued to be heard all across Europe. The Ruhr district, Austria, and Czechoslovakia fell under Hitler's heel without resistance, one after the other.

We remember the days of the Munich Agreement very well, when Neville Chamberlain, like a small-town negotiator, flew to Germany to beg Hitler for "peace in our time."[4] The policy of "appeasement" later took on a nasty aftertaste, and the word became a term of abuse. But were Chamberlain and the Cliveden Set really an exception in this regard?[5] Were they the only appeasers? We must be honest with ourselves and note that many people, especially radicals, were then opposed to war, no matter the price. An open letter appeared the *Fraye arbeter shtime* by its then-editor, Mark Mratchny, which appealed to Czechoslovak workers to not be deceived by patriotic provocateurs and, above all, to not get involved in a war with Germany.[6] His main argument was that for workers it makes no difference who ruled over

---

4. **Neville Chamberlain** (1869–1940) was a conservative British prime minister who, in hopes of avoiding war, infamously ceded part of Czechoslovakia to Nazi Germany by signing the Munich Agreement in 1938.

5. The **Cliveden Set** was a circle of prominent British conservatives widely viewed as sympathetic to Nazism.

6. *FAS*, September 23, 1938.

the country. They would be exploited by their own capitalists no less than by foreign ones. Their situation would be no worse.

For decades, this had been the attitude of all socialists and anarchists to the question of war: the worker has no fatherland, no reason to risk his life in a conflict that capitalists waged for their own predatory interests.

This argument sounds correct in theory, but it does not hold up in real life. It made a huge different to every human being whether the German militarists, with their savage pursuit of world domination and the extermination of entire peoples, were victorious or defeated. Unfortunately, very few people realized this at the time. Even Roosevelt, who had a much clearer view of the situation than most people in this country, then sent a conciliatory note to Hitler, attempting with kind words to urge him not to plunge the world into the flames of an all-consuming war. He didn't dare take a sharper tone, for fear that it would be interpreted as a provocation to war. In our circles, I and others like me were looked upon as crazy in 1938 when we dared to propose that war was inevitable, and that the more time to Hitler had to prepare his killing machine, the greater the catastrophe would be when it arrived. But few of us grasped the possibility that a situation might arise in which defending one's own life would coincide with defending a so-called fatherland. Chamberlain was not the only appeaser at that time. Nobody wanted war, neither the British, nor the French, who would be among the first victims of German militarism. "Give Hitler what he wants, as long as he leaves us in peace" was the attitude among a large part of the people in all countries.

But bloody events unfolded at breakneck speed. The more that was surrendered to Hitler, the more he demanded. Poland resisted for a while, but the Polish armies, which had been such a force to reckon with when it came to pulling the beards of the Jews and bullying defenseless people, did not display any excess of bravery when fighting against bigger barbarians than themselves. For almost a year, the French, as if hypnotized by the serpent-gaze of the German assassins, seemed powerless, lacking determination and a will to fight, sitting and waiting for the terrible catastrophe to arrive. I am no expert in military science, but it is my firm belief that this situation was not entirely the fault of the generals and warlords—the people themselves were indifferent to events. The "communists" openly agitated against the war. The antimilitarists, anarchists, syndicalists, and socialists had previously done their utmost to weaken the will of the people to go to war. The result was unavoidable.

The English people certainly had no reason to be overly enthusiastic for war, for risking their own lives for things happening far away from their home. Then Dunkirk shook them up and opened their eyes. The news came that three hundred thousand Englishmen were standing up to their necks in water, under German bombardment. The knowledge that the enemy was approaching their own home, and would soon bring destruction and devastation upon the peaceful island, galvanized the entire nation to heroic action, like an electrical current. Thousands of civilians in small boats, in yachts and canoes, braved the stormy waters of the Channel to rescue their countrymen. It was not the navy, not the government machine, that saved those desperate victims of Dunkirk, but the spontaneous, unorganized, heroic action of the entire English people, or at least the energetic elements of the people who saw the real possibility of a German invasion and their own barbaric subjugation. This was, in fact, the most critical moment of the war, the incident that determined the final outcome of the conflict. The awakening of the English people made the difference at that moment. Everything that happened after in that long-fought war was a result of that popular awakening.

Here in this country too there was a similar development. Opposition to war was very great. Not all opponents, or isolationists, as they were called, were bad people, fascists or Nazis. In our ranks there were many principled opponents for whom all militarism is the same (*ale Yunim hobn eyn ponem*) and all wars have the same root cause. I have more than once heard highly intelligent, good people, my close friends, say a kind of psalm: "We understand how you, as Jews, are for war; Hitler tortured and destroyed your people, but we cannot understand how you, as anarchists, can be for war!"

Even among Jewish anarchists, not everyone agreed on this question. People were afraid of the hysteria that war unleashes, of the reaction that must—in the opinion of many—inevitably sweep the land during wartime. The aftermath of the First World War was still too fresh in their memories for them to think clearly.

The Communist party line opposed the war until June 21, 1941. The Irish, large numbers of whom lived in the United States and had significant influence in political circles, had such strong feelings of hatred toward England that they would rather see the whole world burn if it meant defeat

Figure 30: "Our Country!" *Mother Earth*,
March 16, 1916
Cover illustration by Robert Minor

for England. There was certainly no shortage of staunch opponents of war among the people, who saw no danger in Hitlerism and consequently could not see why American youths should die or be maimed in the fields of Europe and other corners of the globe.

Japan's attack on Pearl Harbor and declarations of war by Germany and Italy brought an end to most people's hesitations, doubts, and qualms about principles. Life decided the answer to the question in its own way. Hitler, Mussolini, and Hirohito alone sealed their fate and the fates of their people, who followed them willingly on their slippery, bloody path.

One characteristic of the war that should be noted is that, outside of Germany, in no country did it evoke hysteria or ferocious patriotic enthusiasm. People took the fight seriously, with heavy hearts and determined wills, as a terrible tragedy forced upon them by an outside power. In this, we can find some comfort—an indication that war is losing its appeal and glamor.

People are beginning to discuss its severe and harmful effects on everyone. Through oceans of blood and tears, humanity will eventually arrive at the conviction that war is not a remedy to any problem.

This glorious moment has not yet come, despite the horrific causalities of the war and the much worse devastation that a Third World War will bring. All the diplomatic conferences in the world will not bring peace. Power politics, the race for wealth by individuals and nations, the will to rule and to plunder, inflated nationalism, and the destructive notion of unlimited sovereignty—all these things still play too large a role in the relations between peoples (*felker*) for us to hope for peaceful coexistence in the near future.

❋ ❋ ❋

In the aftermath of the Holocaust, which affected the Jews a thousand times more terribly than the pogroms of the past, the same story was being repeated in our ranks.

Most of the comrades had become confused, allowing themselves to be torn apart by the overwhelming pain and grasping at every burnt straw, as if this could bring salvation to the sufferings of the Jewish people. Former radicals like Hayim Lieberman, Jacob Glatstein, and others called the Jewish people back to the synagogue, to religion and Jewish piety, as if that were a guard against pogroms.[7] Others took refuge in Zion, where the Jews never knew happiness and peace, as if there—behind the desert of the Western Wall—protection and security would be found. They sought to rationalize all these reactionary, backward steps with beautiful, emotional speeches about how in Palestine a new and unique Jewish society was being created, with a labor movement, with communistic kibbutzim and the like, as if this had any bearing on pogroms and showed a practical solution to a barbaric

---

7. **Jacob Glatstein** (Yankev Glatshteyn, 1896–1971) was a Russian-born Jewish writer, poet, and Labor Zionist. He immigrated to the United States in 1914 and published his first short story in the *FAS* in October that year. Glatstein also published poetry in the anarchist paper under the pseudonym Klara Blum after editor Saul Yanovsky rejected poems he had submitted under his own name. He went on to become one of the most prolific and best-known Yiddish poets in America and was a founder of the Introspectivist *In zikh* poetry movement. He later wrote a weekly column for the Labor Zionist *Idisher kemfer* and sat on the national executive board of the Jewish National Workers Alliance.

attack like the one launched by Hitler. They forget all the lessons of history that have been written with rivers of blood over the last two thousand years. Religion never prevented barbarism among people and never prevented them from being attacked by barbarians—certainly not the Jews. Jews were murdered and tortured during the Crusades, in the Middle Ages, when people were pious to the point of madness. Jews were burned at the stake in Spain, slaughtered like sheep during Khmelnytsky's era in Ukraine, Poland, and other countries.[8] Neither piety of the victim nor that of the aggressor stopped the murderer's hand. It is neither from the synagogue nor from the church that one must seek salvation and a way out of these terrible troubles.

These same people forget that possessing one's own territory with one's own state, and all the paraphernalia that goes with it, is not a foolproof defense against torment, defeat, and annihilation. Greater nations than Palestine can and have been wiped out in barbaric conflicts that were to a great extent declared and encouraged by the dark sources of religion, nationalism, and patriotism. Buki ben Yogli wrote decades ago about the remarkable characteristics of those peoples bound to the earth by their navels—those who depend on their own piece of land for their entire livelihood—as they tear and bite at each other, seeking by any means to tear loose from the people who keep them bound to the land and make themselves the rulers of the territory in question.[9] In this description, he expressed all the fear and anxiety he felt for the fate of the Jewish people, should they also become tied by the navel to a piece of land and so be drawn into the bloody conflicts of the wild barbarians.

The desire to become "like the others" had, already in the time of the prophet Samuel, led the Jews on the path of monarchy, militarism, fragmentation, and destruction. But now these reactionary ideas were spread by progressive radicals, who should have had a better understanding of what was happening around them. It does not make sense for Jews to stand among

---

8. **Bohdan Khmelnytsky** (c. 1595–1657) was a Ukrainian military and political leader who led a successful Cossack uprising against the Polish-Lithuanian Commonwealth, during which Cossack troops and peasants massacred hundreds of thousands of Jews.

9. **Buki ben Yogli** (1846–1917) was the penname of Judah Leib Benjamin Katzenelson (Yehuda Leib-Binyamin Katsnelson), a Russian-born Jewish doctor, territorialist, and Hebrew writer. The story Cohen refers to is "Bein Adnei ha-Sadeh" (Among the People of the Field, 1901). Ironically, Katzenelson himself later became a Zionist after visiting Palestine in 1909.

and emulate those peoples and nations who today are ready to devour and strangle one another, in the ranks of ever-fighting armies—this was not the ideal and spirit that sustained the Jews as a people through the dark times of the Middle Ages. The Jewish perspective has always looked to the future, not the past. Jews knew instinctively that their liberation would come only when peoples would cease tearing at and biting each other—when the spirit of peace, freedom, and justice would spread throughout the world. By working toward this goal, in which we as a people are more deeply, bloodily invested than anyone else, we cannot, by imitating such ways, settle on a piece of land that is historically and geographically a powder keg and convince ourselves that there we can develop in peace and happiness. This is a deceptive mirage which will lead to no good results.

For example, it seems, on the surface, a perfectly natural thing that the Jewish labor unions' campaign for Palestine became an institution in the Jewish community.[10] Of course, Jewish workers in America should help their brethren in other countries to get back on their feet, organize, and better their lot. Even non-Jewish workers should be helped when possible or be called upon for help when needed. But if this help is tied to the ideal of a Holy Land, if you prioritize those there much more than millions of other Jews in Poland, Galicia, Romania, and other countries, then the whole affair takes on a different color. Then it is no longer a matter of helping workers, or Jews, but of helping the Zionists to establish themselves in Palestine regardless of cost or consequences. Such activity must fall outside the framework of the organized labor movement as such. Funds for Palestine should be collected by the Zionists—and they have every right to do so among their friends and sympathizers—but not by the unions, who have completely different obligations. The Zionist movement, with its grandiose dreams of a powerful Jewish state, its reactionary and dictatorial methods that it has used to impose the use of the holy language [i.e. Hebrew] upon everyone, and its periodic pogroms against Yiddish-speakers, leaves me—and apparently other Jews, as well—disgruntled. My father, a very pious Jew, a great

---

10. The General Organization of Workers in Israel, or **Histadrut**, was founded by Labor Zionists in Palestine in 1920 and is still the largest trade union body in Israel. US labor organizations, including the AFL, the ILGWU, and the ACWA, donated millions of dollars to the organization and its projects between 1920 and 1950. A number of Jewish anarchists and former anarchists also actively supported and raised funds for Histadrut.

Talmudist, went to the Holy Land *to die*.[11] This has been the great wish of devout Jews for many generations. This whole phenomenon seems artificial to me, inflated. I still remember the time when the first Zionists went there from Russia. Up until the Second World War, in those fifty or sixty years, some hundred thousand Jewish families had settled there. This cost the Jewish people—not counting the money of the people who went there on their own account—millions of dollars. It is no exaggeration to say that settling a family in Palestine cost $30,000–$40,000, and most families there are still in great poverty.

The same must be said about the organized labor movement there, the leaders of which are offended to hear Yiddish spoken. It costs the outside world a fortune to build and maintain their organization's apparatus. Under its own power and means, it could not exist.

The life of Jews there has many romantic features: the devotion of pious Jews who go there to die, destitute, lonely, far from their families; the boundless self-sacrifice of the *khalutsim* (pioneers), who face certain death in the malaria-infested swamps where they do backbreaking work without sufficient food; the successful communistic approach in the kibbutzim, where according to all reports there is a true communal spirit amid the terrible poverty with which they are still burdened—of course, there is beauty and romance in all of these and perhaps others as well. They are living proof that the mind and the will can elevate people above all material calculation and can overcome the most difficult, dangerous obstacles.

But this was not the aim and purpose of the Zionists, of the professional leaders and fantasy builders. They themselves live even there in another world, under different, much more comfortable conditions. To build the future for a people (*folk*) that, throughout its existence over thousands of years, almost never possessed its own territory, its own state, or pretentions of being the same as other peoples (*laytn*)—to build the future of such a people (*folk*) on the idea of a state and governmental rule seems to me a wasted effort, something for people who have nothing better to do in life.

After the bloody, catastrophic world war, a great number of Jewish refugees found a home in Palestine. This is, of course, a heartening phenomenon

---

11. Cohen's father, **Leib Kantorowitz** (1853–1941), came to the United States in 1912 with Cohen's mother Sarah (1852–1937) and immigrated to Jerusalem following Sarah's death.

of the utmost importance. But it has little to do with Zionism and the movement before the war. Neither the Zionists nor anybody else could have foreseen such a global catastrophe and prepared for it. It is easy to foresee the possibility of a time when the Zionists will themselves close the gates of the Holy Land and not allow any more Jews to enter, especially those who speak Yiddish. This is what they already would like to do, if they were not self-conscious about the outside world, to which they must come daily for additional aid.

In any case, at end of the 1920s we received news of bloody pogroms, as poverty-stricken Arabs, aroused by all kinds of charlatans and demagogues, fell upon the Jewish colonies and in places wrought no less havoc than the pogroms in tsarist Russia had.[12] The "Lefts," in their unbridled stupidity, defended these savage pogroms, claiming this bloody affair had been a revolutionary attack against British imperialism and its Zionist helpers. In the Jewish working-class community, the attitude of the "Left" made a very bad impression.

Within our ranks, we sadly and anxiously approached the task of entering a new bloodstained page into the history of the eternally suffering Jewish people. Still, the mood among the comrades was so strongly anti-Zionist and anti-nationalist, that when I wrote in a note in the *Fraye arbeter shtime* that those Jews who wish to settle in the land of their forefathers have a perfect right to do so, the orthodox anarchists could not forgive it. Over the twelve or fifteen years after that, we traveled a long way in the opposite direction. Our movement turned completely around!

The Arab attacks on Jews, however, were not the only pogroms that occurred in Palestine. More than once we have heard and read about pogroms in the Holy Land made by Jews against Jews. Chauvinistic students of the Jewish schools, the "Battalion of the Defenders of the Hebrew Language," Trumpeldor's people, and other hoodlums were from time to time allowed to make real pogroms against those who tried to use their mother tongue in their clubs, or against printers who published literary

---

12. During riots on August 23–29, 1929, also known as the Buraq Uprising, Palestinian Arabs killed 133 Jews and injured hundreds more, and 136 Arabs were in turn killed by British colonial police and Jewish retaliatory attacks. The immediate causes of the riots were conflicts over access to Jerusalem's Western Wall and rumors that Jews planned to seize the al-Aqsa Mosque.

works in Yiddish.[13] These pogroms were not much different from those made by the Arabs in anything but their scope, so there is a possibility that this violence may spread against the growing number of sinful heretics speaking the language of their childhood, the language that in the Diaspora is revered nearly as much by its own patriots.

❀ ❀ ❀

Sooner or later, humankind will have to come to the conviction that the state cannot solve the serious problems of society because the state is itself a contributor to social problems. The state is part of the conflict that must be solved. The state is a powerful opponent, privileged and armed. How can we expect the rulers to know the tribulations of those over whom they rule and exploit? The social question can only be solved in a social way through creation of voluntary organizations that engage in social concerns without force or exploitation, and without government.

---

13. Although a subject of much debate, most Zionists viewed Yiddish as a shameful vestige of diaspora and instead advocated the use of Hebrew, which became the official language of the State of Israel. The **Battalion of the Defenders of the Hebrew Language** was a youth organization founded in Tel Aviv in 1921 to enforce the use of Hebrew among Palestinian Jews, and it frequently assaulted meetings of Poale Zion and other organizations that were conducted in Yiddish. The group dissolved in 1933. **Joseph Trumpeldor** (1880–1920) was a Russian-born Jewish soldier, former anarchist, and Labor Zionist who promoted the use of Hebrew. He abandoned anarchism for Russian patriotism to fight in the Russo-Japanese War (1904–1905) and immigrated to Palestine in 1911. His death during a clash with Palestinian Muslims made him a Zionist martyr and inspired the formation of the Zionist Betar Movement, which collaborated with the Battalion of the Defenders of the Hebrew Language.

CHAPTER 57

Back to the Future

The path that the anarchist movement took over six decades was long, diffi-cult, and not always straight. It can be divided into definite stages, or periods, that are not sharply separated from one another. The first period, from the 1880s to the end of the nineteenth century, can be described as the roman-tic period—a time of boundless belief and a hopeful expectation that the social revolution would arrive tomorrow and put an end to all injustices in society. In that short period of time, daring deeds by individuals played a major role. The terrorist movement in France and individual acts of revenge in Germany, Spain, Italy, and other countries were the main expressions of the anarchist movement.

The second period, which overlapped with the first and took on its full expression in the first two decades of the twentieth century, can be described as the revisionist and constructive period. Comrades here and there shed the romanticism of their youth and asked serious questions about tactics and even foundational principles. Some did this *negatively*, criticizing and belittling the ideas and views of the past. Most articulate in this respect were Francesco Saverio Merlino, Dr. Jacob A. Maryson, and, in part, Saul Yanovsky. In 1892 Merlino wrote a series of articles that were later published as a pamphlet, called *The Necessity and Bases for an Accord*.[1] He strongly opposed the then-popular idea that anarchists did not need a

---

1. S. Merlino, *Nécessité et bases d'une entente* (Brussels: Alex. Longfils, 1892). The orig-inal articles were published in the Belgian journal *L'Homme libre* (The Free Man), begin-ning April 23, 1892. An English translation of the text can be found at the Marxists Internet Archive: https://www.marxists.org/subject/anarchism/merlino/accord.htm.

solid organization and could serve their ideal through individual expropriations and assassinations. He pointed out that this whole approach was as
mistake: we seek to reorganize the whole of society along certain lines, yet
we ourselves are not organized, and an attack on my neighbor's property
is by no means an attack on the institution of private property, just as an
attack on the person of a hated tyrant is not an attack on the institution of
authority.

This pamphlet, published in 1892 and reprinted in Johann Most's *Freiheit*
in a translation by Leon Moisseiff, was the beginning of a critical revision
that drew more and more serious attention over the years in the more serious anarchist publications.[2] The revisionists' critical approach provoked
a lot of antagonism among adherents of older views and seldom brought
the desired results, although Most himself agreed with the most important
points of Merlino's treatise.

Of much more value were the activities of other prominent comrades,
who conducted their worked *positively*, creatively, constructing new concepts and initiating new activities without wasting any time criticizing the
ideas and attitudes of the past. To this category belonged Peter Kropotkin,
Gustav Landauer, Francisco Ferrer, and the leaders and founders of the revolutionary syndicalist movement in different countries.

These two periods were, as has been noted, not sharply divided one from
the other. Kropotkin's constructive work began in the mid-1880s, when he
settled in England and began his scientific studies of mutual aid and the new
technical developments in industry and agriculture, which he covered in his
famous book *Fields, Factories, and Workshops*.[3] He did this work at a time
when most of the adherents of anarchism were still under the influence of
romantic expectations and enthusiasm. The effect of his new, constructive
turn began to be felt in the movement only years later, after the ideas of his
new work penetrated wider circles beyond his followers.

On the other hand, romantic sentiments did not cease to have an effect
in certain segments of the movement throughout this entire second period.
A number of energetic, capable comrades have, with some success, continued to inspire enthusiasm for the romantic period among the youth. Here

2. *Freiheit*, June 4–June 11, 1892.
3. Peter Kropotkin, *Fields, Factories, and Workshops, or, Industry Combined with Agriculture and Brain Work with Manual Work* (New York: G. P. Putnam's Sons, 1901).

in the United States, Emma Goldman, Alexander Berkman, and many lesser-known comrades excelled in this field.

Our generation, which came into the movement in the midst of these two periods, fell immediately under the influence of both tendencies. With youthful enthusiasm we embraced romanticism, while spiritually nourishing ourselves with the constructive ideas of the foremost positive thinkers of our movement. Romanticism, revisionism, and constructive anarchism all demanded our attention and loyalty at the same time. The reverberation of the romantic period reached us long after practical activity in that arena had ceased. Comrade Rudolf Rocker's inspiring account of that period in his book *Di geshikhte fun der teroristisher bevegung in Frankraykh* (The History of the Terrorist Movement in France) appeared when the French comrades were already on the road to public, constructive activity in syndicalism, when Sébastien Faure and Francisco Ferrer were already engaged in educational work rather than revolutionary agitation.[4] But, for us, Rocker's portrayal of the heroes of the past came as a revelation, which led many of us to follow the same path of self-sacrifice and courageous struggle.

The third period began in the 1920s, when it became more or less clear that the revolution in Russia had not brought liberation but instead new, terrible oppression. This period can be described as *defensive*—a time of struggling to maintain our existence as anarchists, to not be drowned in the mighty stream of blind, fanatical enthusiasm for making revolution for its own sake. During this period, many of our comrades began to doubt the effectiveness and desirability of revolution as a means of liberation. And once a person begins to raise doubts about what they previously and sincerely believed, they are, in sense, lost. Doubt is a slow-acting poison that kills all beliefs and destroys the force necessary for action. Our former discussions with revisionists were always about whether we could put *all* our hopes on the revolution to solve all our problems at once; now a large number of anarchists had begun to think that revolution is itself a dangerously harmful phenomenon, which inevitably leads to dictatorship and oppression. Such an attitude typically leads to opposition to revolution and any activity in that direction.

---

4. Rudolf Rocker, *Di geshikhte fun der teroristisher bevegung in Frankraykh* (London: Arbeter Fraynd, 1900).

Our movement crossed from one extreme to the other. Revolution and communism were, despite all revisionist efforts, considered by most to be the cornerstones of anarchism. The founders and builders of the constructive trend in our movement, through their zealous, positive activity, had expected to accelerate the coming of the revolution. They had changed only their tactics, their approach to activism: instead of relying on acts performed by individuals, as previously, they now emphasized the organized actions of masses of people in radical unions (*sindikatn*), educational institutions, and cooperative enterprises. The ultimate goal, however, remained the same: to lead developments toward a fundamental overturning of society, which would abolish the existing system and establish a new, anarchist order.

This can be seen clearly in the writings and, above all, in the actions of Kropotkin, Landauer, Ferrer, and the founders of revolutionary syndicalism. Their ideas constituted the general worldview of the majority of comrades in our movement. The extreme revisionists, for whom the critical, negative approach had over time become their main activity, were always a very small minority in our ranks, and they too had never really questioned the possibilities for revolution and communism in the ways that they were questioned after the Bolshevik experiment in Russia. However, in the 1920s the entire movement took a sharp turn in the opposite direction toward peaceful, gradual evolution within the framework of private property and profit, leaving anarchism without ground beneath its feet. Evolution through small improvements might lead to anarchism after thousands of years, but in the present it imposes no obligations on us and does not differentiate us in any way from liberals and other generally progressive people.

Anarchism is fundamentally a revolutionary worldview—an approach to social questions that calls for fundamental change and demands that this change be carried out by the people, through unwavering action. For us, it is no excuse to claim that conditions are not favorable or that the process of industrial and technical development is not sufficiently mature. We have no dialectic with which to cover up and explain our negligence when we have not done our duty. Either we are anarchists and believe in the possibility of free, peaceful communal life without any government or coercion, and do everything we can to bring such a social organization about; or we no longer wholeheartedly believe in such a possibility and do nothing practical for its realization other than spouting and repeating anarchist slogans (*posek*)—in which case we are no longer anarchists and must have the courage to say so. No middle ground is possible.

When one thinks seriously about the discussion and debate about revisionism that we conducted all those years, certain things become clear and stand out. First, it was concentrated on methods and tactics we can use to reach our goal and not about the goal itself. Those who did not have the same goal certainly should not have a place in our ranks. Second, different opinions about tactics were caused by recent events that put their stamp on the methods used by our movement. The conspiracies and personal *attentats* of the romantic period were not a special integral method of anarchism. Religious, political, and national movements have used these methods at one time or another when forced by circumstances. The *attentat* did not retain approval as a tactic. The more thoughtful comrades always abhorred it in practice, and it never had deep roots in the movement. Some of our comrades very early on saw it as a dangerous course and spoke out against it. Other comrades repudiated it later. But there is now unity of opinion regarding the question of terror, expropriation, and propaganda of the deed. This shows that the fundamental anarchist worldview is valid and healthy.

The question of organization, revolution, and participation in politics, much discussed for many years, has never been clearly defined. The problem of organization became very involved and mixed up during the romantic period because the conspiratorial methods employed did not allow for systematic organization. At the same time there were different opinions of principle on the question that had no connection with the tactics of that period.

Here in America, in the Jewish anarchist movement, the problem and question of organization disturbed many comrades for a long time. But we did not carry it to extremes. We tolerated a chairman at meetings and rules of order after a fashion. But of what kind of people is our movement composed? Who publishes our paper? For whom and to what purpose is the paper published? And from whom do we get contributions to carry on with the paper? From whom do we collect contributions to be sent to needy people? How shall we undertake larger projects? What books shall we publish? In sixty years, we have been unable to answer these questions with clarity. They were the cause of much misunderstanding, which did not add to the health and strength of our movement.

The question of parliamentary voting came up time and again in our movement, causing great distress and disturbance; we never resolved any clear-cut course of action on this problem. Of the anarchist theorists, we know that Proudhon did not keep from participating in the vote in parliament during the uprising of 1848–1849. Kropotkin, at the time of the Russian Revolution, spoke in favor of establishing a federated kind of government similar in form to that of the United States. Gustav Landauer, in the short-lived uprising in Bavaria, did not refuse to participate in government. In Spain, the comrades availed themselves of the vote in 1936 and made it possible to establish the so-called Loyalist government.[5] In other words, these examples show that our comrades had a flexible attitude toward practical solutions to the problems of life and were not bound by fanatical dogmatism. But the rank and file of our movement held to the negative, anti-parliamentary, anti-vote, anti-organization principles with a fanatical religious piety (*frumkeyt*). Our comrades get as emotionally disturbed as our great-grandfathers did when questions of eating pork or religious conversion came up. They want to be even more observant and pious (*frumer*) than the theorists who founded and developed the philosophy of our movement.

This is probably due to the fact that, in practice, parliamentarianism and politics are so closely bound to the immorality, lies, and self-interest of the people associated with them. We all know how very low the profession of politician has sunk in every country and how closely parliamentarianism is linked to the institutions of exploitation and oppression. But we must not ignore the fundamental fact that anarchism is, itself, a political theory, a doctrine that focuses not only on the relationships of individuals to each other but also of the individual to society. Not all anarchists recognize the economic side of our doctrine to be free communism. There have been, and still are, anarchist collectivists, anarchist individualists, and anarcho-syndicalists—each with a particular approach to the economic structure of the future society. What we all agree on is that there must be the greatest amount of freedom possible within society, not outside of it. This means that we will probably always have political questions to solve, even in the future society, and they will need to be resolved through a parliamentary

5. During the 1936 elections, the Spanish CNT-FAI suspended its longstanding "Do Not Vote" campaign, partially in hopes that a Popular Front government would release imprisoned anarchists.

method of consultation and decision making. The fact that in the present disorder politics and parliamentarianism have become synonyms for immorality and evil must not blind us to the very essence of things. Self-seeking people have always abused the best efforts of the people and used them for their own purposes. The question of whether anarchists can and should participate in politics is a practical question of tactics, not a theoretical matter of principle. It depends on the circumstances at the time and cannot be predetermined once and for all. It should not, in general, be transformed into a dogma that obscures every clear thought and makes people incapable of judging a particular situation correctly. Anarchism and dogma are two opposing concepts that cannot be harmonized.

Much more serious and important is our position on the question of revolution, which was much confused by our revisionism. It seems to me that belief in the revolution, even if it were scientifically proven that it is an impossible fantasy, can and must be understood as a *necessary fiction*— as Voltaire put it regarding God—in order to have a definite, clear goal for humankind and its instinctive pursuit for justice and humanity.[6] The goals and tasks that we set for the revolution serve us and all of humankind as a guide, a beacon that sets the course of our wanderings on this planet. Without such a compass, we are liable to wander in the desert, to throw ourselves this way and that, making no progress. As much as we wish to be useful and active in improving society, we must set a clear goal for ourselves. And it must be a great, inspiring goal, even if we must travel much further to reach it. That which is too near is often overlooked and forgotten. And this grand ideal must never be exchanged cheaply for unimportant improvements that become goals in themselves. Small goals cannot inspire the masses, cannot elevate people above the mundane.

This does not mean that we are opposed to immediate improvements or that we wish to revive the childish stupidity of yesteryear that held *the worse, the better!* Far from it. It only means that when collaborating with elements in society for immediate improvements we must keep in mind that we are participating in work that is *carried on by others in their own way.* Our participation should be such that it helps, not hinders, the work in question. But

---

6. In 1768 French Enlightenment philosopher Voltaire (1694–1778) wrote: "If God did not exist, it would be necessary to invent him."

Figure 31: "Onward!" *Fraye arbeter shtime*, July 3, 1891

The central figure in the image, standing astride a fallen log labeled "Social Democracy," carries a flag inscribed with the word "Anarchy" as an angel, holding a copy of the *Fraye arbeter shtime*, points toward the dawning sun surrounded by the words "Freedom," "Equality," and "Fraternity"; meanwhile, a capitalist, a priest, a king, and a policeman struggle to hold him back, as representatives of various political parties beckon and point in the opposite direction in our own movement, we as anarchists must not neglect working for our ultimate goal. We must carry on our agitation for the complete liberation of all humankind and the abolition of every possibility of domination and exploitation. In the name of anarchism, we cannot compete with reformers and liberals for immediate, small reforms—though we can help them in their work for these things. As anarchists, we have one task—to preach anarchism! We must keep our eyes on the future, on the great ideal that our movement set for itself so many years ago. We must look back to the future, with a clearer understanding of our task formed in light of our long years of experience.

Anarchist-Communist Manifesto

Approved by the First Annual Convention of the Jewish Anarchist
Federation of America and Canada

October 1–4, 1921, Philadelphia

The Crimes of the Capitalist System

The events of the last seven years, the terrible war that is continuing to this very day; the revolutions in Russia, Austria, Hungary, and Germany; the misery and despair that now reigns over the whole world—all this reinforces our conviction that the real salvation of humankind lies in the realization of our great ideal—anarchist communism.

The capitalist system, built on coercion, superstition, and private property, has plunged humankind into a deep swamp. It gave away the earth, all that is in it and on it, to a small group of people, leaving the great masses helpless, without the necessary means to be able to live freely and independently; it has divided people into rulers and subjects, and seeks, with the help of religion and patriotism, to maintain this division forever. The capitalist system, with the help of governments, plunged humanity into the horrific war that turned the whole world into one great bloodbath, and the people into wild animals. It has led the management of businesses to such a state that millions of people are left unemployed, homeless, and hungry.

The crimes of the capitalist system are greatly exacerbated by the fact that it has undermined the foundations of sociability between people. It has aroused and developed the lowest, most brutal instincts. Deceit, fraud, speculation, and mass murder have become the most respectable occupations.

The Jewish Anarchist Federation of America and Canada was initially named the Anarchist-Communist Groups of America. Joseph Cohen was instrumental in its formation and a member of the resolutions committee that wrote this manifesto, which was first published in the *FAS*, October 21, 1921.

Misery, poverty, and unemployment are the lifelong companions of the masses.

The Awakening

The devastating destruction caused by the world war, on the other hand, greatly disturbed the minds of the masses. The oppressed and exploited of all nations will inevitably perceive the injustices done against them, which cry to the heavens. They stir without awakening from their deep sleep. In some parts of the Old World, the storm of revolution has already broken out. Unfortunately, not one of the rebelling nations has yet achieved this goal. In Germany, the moderate socialists took control of the government but made no major changes for the better there. In Russia, the most extreme state socialists, the Bolsheviks, set out to establish "communism" and, in four years' time, over the bodies of thousands of revolutionaries, socialists, and anarchists, established state capitalism—including concessions, privileges, and private property. The martyrdom of all the victims (*korbones*) of the revolution failed to bring about the great ideal. And the reason for this is that they used the methods of the state—the instruments of enslavement and oppression—to try to build a free society. The Russian Jacobins formed a dictatorial government and sought to establish a communist society by force. The result is that they destroyed the initiative of the working masses, thereby endangering all the gains of the revolution.

A free society can be built only by free people, acting according to their conscience and feeling responsible for their actions. When one is subject to the will of another, there can be no responsibility. Where people cannot do what they want, there is no room for individual initiative, for enthusiasm, for love for work. There the wellsprings of creation are closed off and dry up. And that is why the Russian Revolution is fruitless.

We must learn to avoid the mistakes they have made and prepare ourselves and the entirety of the working people for activity on libertarian foundations.

Our Ideal

We recognize that the principal evils (*iblen*) of the present order are: a) the rule of one person over another; and b) private property. These two evils must be abolished and, in their place, we must introduce anarchist communism.

We are anarchist communists.

As anarchists, we strive for a social system without government or the state—in which all community affairs will be taken care of by voluntary organizations, without coercion.

As communists, we strive for the abolition of private property in all social riches and declare the right of every person to live and enjoy the gifts of nature and all socially created products, in accordance with the principles of justice.

This is our goal, the ideal toward which we strive, and the means by which we hope to achieve our goal must be in line with our ideal.

We are atheists. We recognize that religion, being built on dogmas and traditions, is a major obstacle to the evolution of humankind; that religious beliefs about right and wrong are aimed at upholding the institutions of property and slavery; that every religion, as a whole, seeks to perpetuate ignorance and superstition among the masses. We assume the obligation of combating the influence of religion by spreading scientific truths and working toward the establishment of moral relations between individuals and groups of people based on the rational principle of mutual aid.

We believe in people, in their healthy social instincts, in their ability to create and regulate their own lives. We strive for a truly free society, composed of free individuals and free communes, governed by mutual understanding, not by petrified written laws. We believe in evolution instead of crystallization, in the free development of the individual, and in the full responsibility of the free person.

We are revolutionists but not terrorists. We are working to bring about the social revolution, the complete overturn of the social order. However, we oppose any attempt to interpret our teachings as an incitement to violence and expropriation. Anarchism is a social doctrine based on freedom and full equality. Violence against tyrants has its historical justification, but it is not the result of anarchism. Expropriation, when practiced by individuals or small groups of people, is one of the most damaging acts for the revolutionary movement. The expropriation of natural and social resources must be carried out by the organized bodies, and in the interests, of the whole of society.

We are against any tendency to turn anarchism into a conspiratorial underground movement, which provides a breeding ground for all sorts of creatures who commonly infect revolutionary ranks. Only when all means of public activity have been exhausted should conspiratorial methods be used.

Justification

We consider the current arrangement as a temporary period in the development of society. We find that throughout human history there has been struggle between, on the one hand, the coercive institutions of the state, which have always hindered the free development of the individual and society, and on the other, voluntary organizations that have sought to facilitate, refine, and socialize human life. This struggle continues without ceasing.

Up to the present, the institutions of state oppression have prevailed, thanks to the ignorance of the masses who have been satisfied to be led and exploited. How could it be otherwise? For hundreds and thousands of generations, people have been taught that the world and the social order were created by an almighty, all-knowing God, who appointed some to rule and others to be ruled, that some should have plenty, and the masses too little. People have been taught to worship the wisdom of our fathers and to sanctify the institutions they have built, not to seek to change and not to criticize the power at the helm. Eventually, however, great changes came about in these ideas and teachings. People today do not want to blindly believe everything they are told. Increasingly they are raising their own heads and listening to their own consciences.

We Place Our Hopes on the Further Development of This Tendency

Working in this direction, we must make every effort to spread light and scientific truths among the masses, to awaken in them the desire and develop in them the ability to think and act independently, to take responsibility for their own actions and create through their own efforts.

Our Responsibilities in Peacetime

We are working to build as many libertarian organizations as possible, to cater to the needs of the people and bring a free, democratic spirit in all workers' and people's institutions.

We fight against any curtailment of freedom, no matter the source or against whom it is applied. Oppression and coercion are not humane means of determining what is good or bad in society. Only free discussion can lead to the creation of new concepts, and only free application of these new ideas can prove whether they are good for society or not.

We are campaigning for the abolition of privileges and private property, which drain the life force of the people, and for the socialization of all the riches of nature and the means of production.

We help to build and strengthen labor unions and instill in them a clear awareness that they will need to take possession of industry in their hands and become the managers of all social production.

We help to build the cooperative movement and prepare the people to provide for all their needs themselves, voluntarily, in a socialized manner, for the benefit of society in general, and not leave this responsibility to individuals who do it for profit, or to the state, which does it to assert its power.

We work to ensure that the education of the younger generation is conducted in a purely scientific and rational manner. The management of public schools should be removed from the hands of the politicians and turned over to the teachers and the parents in the lower grades, and to the students and teachers in the upper grades. All non-scientific and patriotic teachings should be removed from all textbooks.

In ordinary, so-called peaceful times, these enumerated means are the only ones that we, anarchists, can and need to use in order to achieve our goal: *to agitate, educate, and organize*; to bring the pursuit of freedom into people's hearts, and to see that our principles and methods are applied in the practical conduct of all voluntary organizations.

Our Responsibilities in Revolutionary Times

In extraordinary times, when large progressive sections of the people are shaken up and driven to rash actions, when the revolutionary current floods humanity and encourages people to make great, significant changes in society, we take our place in the first ranks of the fighting masses.

We regard periods of revolutionary struggle as natural phenomena, caused by the narrowness of the old order and its inability to allow free development and the realization of new concepts and forces in society. The rich and powerful will never relinquish their privileges voluntarily. It is necessary for the storm to remove the harmful institutions that stand in the way of the future. After all, we know that revolutionary periods are very conducive to the spread of new truths and the creation of new ways of life. Under the fire of revolution, humanity is able to build new worlds, *as long as the revolution is the expression of the people, of all of the progressive sectors of the people.*

Our task at such revolutionary times is to work with all our might to deepen and widen the upheaval, to involve more and more people in the revolutionary current and make clear to them the aspirations and goals of the revolution.

The true purpose of the social revolution is to abolish both the rule of one person over another, and private property. We must work hand in hand with all revolutionary groups that have the same goals, not allowing political parties to build a new state, and not allowing any group of people to reestablish a capitalist system of private property and exploitation.

Only in this way, building on the social instincts of the people and using libertarian means and methods before and during the revolution, can we hope to succeed in bringing about the introduction of a free social order. No other path will lead to this outcome. Dictatorships will not develop free individuals, and coercion will not create a new way of life.

Our Goal

This is our goal, and these are our means:

1. As anarchists, we see the state with its methods of coercion and oppression as an antisocial institution. We take up the task of

weakening its influence, of agitating that its activity should be limited, and, at a favorable opportunity, it should be completely dissolved.

2. As communists, we regard private property, with its methods of exploitation for profit, as a harmful, antisocial enterprise. We agitate for its abolition and reconstruction into a system of free communism, where all people will contribute according to their abilities and benefit according to their needs.

3. Our ideal is a free social order without coercion and without exploitation.

Our Methods

Our methods are:

a. Enlightenment through the spoken and written word

b. Awakening among the masses confidence in oneself and in one's own powers

c. Building new, voluntary institutions to provide people with what they need

d. Fighting the spirit of centralization in labor unions and establishing democratic people's management in all organizations

e. Fighting every attempt to restrict people's freedom, regardless of whom is targeted and who is responsible

f. Participating in all popular movements and revolutionary manifestations of the masses

g. Raising the banner of social revolution, striving for a society of freedom, equality, and fraternity.

We call on all those who value the ideal of equality and justice to join our ranks and combine forces to bring closer the great day of the liberating social revolution.

Index

Page numbers in *italic* refer to illustrations. "Passim" (literally "scattered") indicates intermittent discussion of a topic over a cluster of pages.

International Union of America, 449, 450n12

Bakunin, Mikhail, 45, 66n12, 214, 373; hundredth birthday celebration, 470

Baldwin, Roger Nash, 397

Balmashov, Stepan, 160

Bandes, Efim. *See* Miller, Louis E.

Baranov, M., 123–24n1

Barbour, Max, 115n, 185

Barkas, Benjamin W., 411, 527

Baroff, Abraham, 299

Baron, Aron, *289*, 404

Baron, Fanya, *289*

Baron, Leon, 132, 133n, 218, 317

Barondess, Joseph, 67, 76, 77, 84n7, 97

Battalion of the Defenders of the Hebrew Language, 541n13

Bauer, Henry, 140

Bayer (Baltimore comrade), 280, 481, 491

Bellamy, Edward: *Looking Backward*, 178; *Pennsylvania Nationalist*, 207

Bellows, George, 339n8, 353

Benequit, Isaac A., 204n7, 461, 463

Benno, Benjamin. *See* Greenstein, Benjamin

Bercovici, Konrad, 354–55n21

Bercovici, Révolte, 338n7, 355n21

Beresin, Morris, 34, 35, 311–12, 324–27 passim, 329n10, 331

Beresin, Rebecca G. (Gussie), 311n5, 329n10, 410

Berg, Charles, 350

Berger, Louise, 350

Berger, Victor, 318, 374

Berkman, Alexander, 20, 95, 222–23, 233, 357–58, 473; Anti-Militarist League, 351; arrest (1907), 146n16; arrest and trial (1917), 375–77; Becky Edelson and, 231n2; *Blast*, 91n1, 148n23, 360; deportation, 391–96; Ferrer Modern School, New York, 335, 337, 341; *Fraye arbeter shtime*, 452; Frick shooting, 91–99 passim, 107; Kronstadt rebellion, 388; legal appeal fund-raising, 110n4, 142; *Letters from Russian Prisons*, 475n10; Lexington Avenue explosion and, 348–49, 350; *Mother Earth*, 220; *Now and After*, 483, 514n; Philadelphia, 240, 321–223; Preparedness Day bombing and Mooney case, 136n, 360–61, 392; prison (Atlanta), 377, 391, 292; prison and escape attempt (Pennsylvania), 99, 140–43, 161, 225–27; *Prison Memoirs of an Anarchist*, 27, 315; Russian exit (1921), 403, 405; San Francisco, 357, 358, 360; World War I, 372n6, 373. *See also* Alexander Berkman Aid Fund

Berman, Barnett, 280

Bernard, Lazare Marcus Manassé. *See* Lazare, Bernard

Berner Street Club, London, 66n12, 123, 126, 127n9, 133n, 286n3, 480n16

Bernstein, Ethel, 473n7

Bernstein, Rose. *See* Mirsky, Rose

Bialostotzky, Benjamin Jacob, 453n3

Billings, Warren K., 359, 360, 487

Biluim, 43

Bimko, Fishel, 456n5